*Praise for*

# Virtual Machines
### Versatile Platforms for Systems and Processes

Virtual Machines *provides a unique, practical, and extensive guide through an area of computer science that has a rich history and an exciting future.*

—Jan Hoogerbrugge, Philips Research

*Viva versatile VMs!*
*Hardware is hard, inflexible, produced by gnomes with sub-micron tools. Virtual machines wrap a layer of software around this hardware, and suddenly computers become flexible, malleable, and start doing new tricks: running multiple operating systems, executing several instruction sets, allowing running programs to switch machines, or even rejecting unsafe code. Virtual machines are changing the way in which computer architects, operating system designers, programming language implementers, and security experts think about computers and computing. Smith and Nair's book is an up-to-date overview of virtual machines and their many uses.*

—Jim Larus, Microsoft Research

*Virtual machines are everywhere. Jim Smith and Ravi Nair make abundantly clear the deep impact of this technology on the design of modern computer architectures, programming languages, operating systems, and security techniques. I highly recommend this book for anyone interested in the future of computing systems.*

—Michael D. Smith, Harvard University

*Despite the widespread adoption of virtualization techniques in modern computer systems, no book covers the myriad of instantiations of this general implementation strategy. Smith and Nair have addressed this problem by providing a comprehensive description of virtual machines in a clear and in-depth manner, effectively using examples and case studies to illustrate essential concepts. This book is a must-read for students and practitioners working in language and system implementation.*

—Michael Hind, IBM Watson Research Center

*Look no further for your standard text book on virtual machines, a growing discipline of increasing importance to everybody involved in system software programming and deployment. Smith and Nair deliver a comprehensive classification of virtual machines, detailed descriptions of all major implementation techniques and elaborate discussions of relevant artifacts in the computing industry, with excellent coverage of recent innovations.*

—Bernd Mathiske, Sun Microsystems

# Virtual Machines
**Versatile Platforms for Systems and Processes**

## About the Authors

**James E. Smith**   is a Professor in the Department of Electrical and Computer Engineering at the University of Wisconsin-Madison. He first joined the University of Wisconsin in 1976, after receiving his PhD in Computer Science from the University of Illinois. From 1979 to 1981, he took a leave of absence to work for the Control Data Corporation in Arden Hills, MN, participating in the design of the CYBER 180/990. From 1984 to 1989, he participated in the development of the ACA ZS-1, a scientific computer employing a dynamically scheduled, superscalar processor architecture. In 1989, he joined Cray Research, Inc. in Chippewa Falls, WI. While at Cray Research, he headed a small research team that participated in the development and analysis of future supercomputer architectures.

In 1994, he re-joined the ECE Department at the University of Wisconsin. His recent research concerns the development of the virtual machine abstraction as a technique for providing high performance through co-design and tight coupling of virtual machine hardware and software. Prof. Smith was the recipient of the 1999 ACM/IEEE Eckert-Mauchly Award for his contributions to the field of computer architecture.

**Ravi Nair**   has been a Research Staff Member since 1978 at the IBM Thomas J. Watson Research Center, where he has helped in the architecture and design of a number of processors. He has worked in the areas of computer architecture, performance analysis, multiprocessor virtualization, design automation, and testing, and has several publications, patents, and IBM awards in these areas. Among the many design and analysis tools he has developed are binary rewriting tools for profiling, trace generation, and simulation. His current interests include processor microarchitecture, dynamic compilation, and virtual machine technology. Dr. Nair graduated with a B.Tech. degree in electronics and electrical communication from IIT, Kharagpur in 1974, and with a Ph.D. degree in Computer Science from the University of Illinois in 1978. He spent a sabbatical year at Princeton University and has also taught at Columbia University. Dr. Nair is a member of the IBM Academy of Technology and a Fellow of the IEEE.

# Virtual Machines
## Versatile Platforms for Systems and Processes

James E. Smith
*University of Wisconsin—Madison*

Ravi Nair
*IBM Thomas J. Watson Research Center*

ELSEVIER

AMSTERDAM · BOSTON · HEIDELBERG · LONDON
NEW YORK · OXFORD · PARIS · SAN DIEGO
SAN FRANCISCO · SINGAPORE · SYDNEY · TOKYO
MORGAN KAUFMANN PUBLISHERS IS AN IMPRINT OF ELSEVIER

MORGAN KAUFMANN PUBLISHERS

| | |
|---|---|
| Publisher | Denise E.M. Penrose |
| Publishing Services Manager | Simon Crump |
| Senior Project Manager | Angela Dooley |
| Editorial Assistant | Kimberlee Honjo |
| Cover Design | Hannus Design Associates |
| Text Design | Rebecca Evans |
| Composition | CEPHA Imaging Pvt. Ltd. |
| Technical Illustration | Dartmouth Publishing, Inc. |
| Copyeditor | Simon & Assocs. |
| Proofreader | Phyllis Coyne et. al. |
| Indexer | Northwind Editorial |
| Interior printer | The Maple-Vail Manufacturing Group |
| Cover printer | Phoenix Color, Inc. |

Morgan Kaufmann Publishers is an imprint of Elsevier.
500 Sansome Street, Suite 400, San Francisco, CA 94111

This book is printed on acid-free paper.

Cover Image: *Arc of Petals (Mobile)*, 1941 © Estate of Alexander Calder / Artists Rights Society (ARS), New York; The Solomon R. Guggenheim Foundation, New York, Peggy Guggenheim Collection, Venice, 1976.

**Library of Congress Cataloging-in-Publication Data**
Application Submitted

ISBN-13: 978-1-55860-910-5
ISBN-10: 1-55860-910-5

For information on all Morgan Kaufmann publications,
visit our Web site at www.mkp.com or www.books.elsevier.com

Printed and bound by CPI Group (UK) Ltd, Croydon, CR0 4YY

Transferred to Digital Print 2012

*To my mother,*

JES

*To my parents,*

RN

# Foreword

I've been a virtual machine addict for precisely as long as I've worked with computers. My first real job, which led to my first nontrival computer program, was to implement a virtual machine for a high-level programming language. There seemed to be something magical about the ability for a computer to imitate another computer, or my idea of what a computer *ought* to be.

Now almost 20 years later, less starry-eyed and more responsible, I am concerned that my work has utility, making it faster or easier to get something done than it would be otherwise. But lucky for me, virtual machines have proven ideally suited to the needs of the computing industry, where the appreciation of the virtual machine has expanded dramatically. It's no longer only an intellectual challenge to the researcher arguably on the "lunatic fringe" of programming language implementation, or the secret weapon of a small cadre of mainframe O/S engineers and pioneers of system virtualization. Several major trends have contributed to an explosion of interest in virtual machine technologies.

In particular the rise of the World Wide Web, by far the largest and most ubiquitous cross-platform computing environment to date, created enormous and visible opportunities for virtual machine-based computing. Initially targeting the WWW, VM technology hit the mainstream as a means of safely hosting cross-platform binary programs embedded in Web pages. From that beachhead it has expanded to become the prevalent approach to open platforms from Web and back office servers to cell phones and smart cards, where the equivalent benefits — cross platform applications that are not tied to the underlying hardware or operating system — invariably apply. Virtual machines form the basis of Sun's Java and Microsoft's .NET platforms, currently the most popular software environments on the planet. As new markets or applications are conceived, virtual machine technologies to support them are adapted from these stalwarts.

In other markets as well, virtual machine technology is seeing a renaissance. Companies such as VMware are finding virtual machine platforms to be an ideal way to provide greater resource control, scalability and performance across variations in host hardware or operating systems. Virtual machines are likely to be common at multiple levels of the data center or server farm.

When I was asked to review this book, it seemed an opportunity to read something I might not get to otherwise. I expected to focus on the chapter covering virtual machines for high-level languages. Little did I know that I would find myself excited by less familiar topics, for instance sending back surprised comments expressing admiration for the decades-old IBM AS/400 architecture, which I'd never understood before. It wasn't just the realization of how much those coming far before me had accomplished. Seeing virtual machine technology in a broader scope than my particular field made design decisions and deficiencies in my familiar Java virtual machine architecture clearer, and put in perspective why people trying to do certain things with the JVM have a hard time. Such perspective is valuable even to experienced practitioners of a particular VM art.

And I found myself once again thinking how cool it all is.

*Tim Lindholm*
*Distinguished Engineer, Sun Microsystems, Inc.*
*Palo Alto*
*February 28, 2005*

# Preface

Virtual machine (VM) technologies have been developed in a number of contexts — operating systems, programming languages and compilers, and computer architecture — to enable new capabilities and to solve a variety of problems in interfacing major computer system components. Virtual machines for supporting operating systems are receiving renewed interest after years of relatively little activity, because they allow effective resource sharing while maintaining a high degree of security. Virtualization is becoming popular for servers and other network applications especially where security is of crucial importance. In the area of programming languages, virtual machines provide platform independence, and they support transparent dynamic translation and optimization. In processor architectures, virtual machine technologies allow the introduction of new instruction sets, as well as dynamic optimization for power reduction and/or performance improvement.

Because of industry consolidation around a small number of standard interfaces, virtual machine technology will likely be an important enabling feature for innovations in all of the above fields. Any new instruction set, operating system, or programming language will almost certainly require some accompanying virtual machine technology if it is to become widely accepted. Not coincidentally, much of the impetuses for virtual machine technologies, and most of the more significant recent developments, have come from industry.

Historically, the various VM techniques have been spread across computer science and engineering disciplines. However, there are a number of underlying, cross-cutting technologies, and there is much to be gained by pulling them together so that VM implementations can be studied and engineered in a well-structured way. This book is an outgrowth of the idea that virtual machines should be studied as a unified discipline.

This book is also about computer architecture in its purist sense. As classically defined, an *architecture* is an *interface*. Virtual machines couple interfaces and extend the flexibility and functionality of the interfaces. Understanding architecture is key to understanding virtual machines, and this book is written from an architect's perspective, keeping interface issues clear and at the forefront. A goal is for the reader to come away with a much deeper understanding of the important computer system interfaces and the role these interfaces play when the major components interact.

The breadth of VM applications implies the audience for this book is fairly diverse. Although it is not currently recognized as a discipline with a targeted set of university courses, virtual machines makes an excellent topic for a graduate level course because it ties together the key disciplines of computer science and engineering: architecture, operating systems, and programming languages. Preliminary versions of this book have already been used, quite successfully, in graduate courses at four different universities. The book can also be used as a supplementary text for a compiler course on dynamic optimization or an operating system course covering classic system VMs. Virtual machine technologies are rapidly gaining broad acceptance in industry, and practicing professionals will find the book useful for self-education on this leading edge technology. The book can also serve as a useful reference as it collects material from a number of fields into one place.

The book begins by surveying the variety of VMs, putting them into perspective and building a framework for discussing VMs. The subsequent chapters describe the major types of VMs in an organized way, emphasizing the common, underlying technologies. Following is a rough outline summarizing each chapter.

In Chapter 1 we introduce the concept of abstraction and define the interfaces that are prevalent in today's computer systems. This is followed by a discussion of virtualization and its relationship to the interfaces. The notion of computer architecture is introduced next, followed by a survey of different types of virtual machines. VMs are shown to fall into two main categories, process virtual machines and system virtual machines. We end the chapter by refining this categorization further and suggesting a taxonomy for virtual machines.

In Chapter 2 we address issues related to the emulation of a source instruction set architecture (ISA) on a target ISA. We demonstrate the workings of a basic interpreter and show how threaded interpretation can help improve performance. The techniques developed are demonstrated using a CISC source ISA, the Intel IA-32, and a RISC target ISA, the IBM PowerPC. We then introduce the notion of binary translation, and discuss the problems of code discovery and code location. This is followed by a discussion of the handling of control transfers. Many ISAs have special features (in some cases, they might be called "quirks") that must be handled in special ways. These are discussed next. The chapter is rounded out with a case study of emulation in the Shade simulation system.

Chapter 3 discusses the implementation of process virtual machines. A process virtual machine supports an individual guest application program on a host platform consisting of an operating system and underlying hardware. We discuss the implications of VM compatibility and show how the state of a machine, consisting of the register state and the memory state, is mapped and maintained in a process virtual machine. We address the issues of self-modifying code and of protecting the region of memory used by the VM runtime software. VM emulation consists of two parts. First, the emulation of the instruction set is discussed, with reference to interpretation and binary translation discussed in Chapter 2. This leads to a discussion of code caching techniques. Next, the emulation of the interface to the host operating system is addressed. We end the chapter by describing the FX!32 system, which embodies many of the fundamental ideas discussed in the chapter.

Chapter 4 focuses on techniques for the optimization of translated code for better emulation performance. It discusses the framework needed to perform such optimizations and the profile information that must be gathered at program execution time in order to facilitate optimizations. Various profiling techniques are discussed. Because optimizations often work better on larger code blocks, the concepts of dynamic basic blocks, superblocks, traces, and tree groups are introduced. The chapter includes an extensive discussion on code re-ordering and its limitations. Various types of code optimizations, both local and inter-block, are presented. The chapter concludes with a case-study of Dynamo, a dynamic binary optimizer, which applies optimization techniques in a system where the source and target ISAs are identical.

Chapter 5 introduces high-level language virtual machines and traces the transition from the early Pascal P-code VMs to object-oriented VMs. The emphasis in this chapter is on the architecture of high-level language VMs, especially those features supporting object-oriented programming and security. The two important object-oriented VMs of today, namely the Java Virtual Machine and the Microsoft CLI, are described. The features of their bytecode, stack-oriented instruction sets are described. In both cases, the description of the instruction set is supplemented by a discussion of the overall platform that augments the virtual machines with a set of libraries and APIs.

Chapter 6 continues the discussion of high-level language VMs by focusing on their implementation. As in the preceding chapter, more attention is given to Java because of its widespread usage and the variety in its implementations. Two aspects given special consideration are security and memory management. The importance of garbage collection is discussed along with techniques for performing garbage collection. The interaction of Java objects with programs written natively outside the Java environment is discussed next. We then describe how the performance of Java can be enhanced through optimizations of code using techniques described in Chapter 4 as well as new techniques that are specific to the object-oriented paradigm. The concepts in the chapter are brought together using a case-study of the Jikes Research Virtual Machine.

In Chapter 7 we discuss co-designed virtual machines where a conventional ISA is implemented through a combination of an implementation-specific ISA and translation software that runs in concealed memory. We discuss techniques for mapping the state of the original ISA onto the implementation ISA and for maintaining the code cache containing translated code. Various sticky aspects, including the implementation of precise interrupts and page faults, are also discussed. We end the chapter with two case studies: the Transmeta Crusoe processor and the IBM AS/400 processor.

Chapter 8 deals with the classic system virtual machines. A system virtual machine supports a complete guest operating system and all its applications on a host platform. We provide a motivation for these virtual machines and outline the basic ways for implementing system virtual machines, including native and hosted VMs. We discuss techniques for the virtualization of the three main system resources: processors, memory, and I/O. The conditions for virtualizability of a processor, as first enunciated by Popek and Goldberg in the early '70s, are developed. Also discussed are techniques for virtualization when these conditions are not satisfied by an ISA. Memory virtualization is discussed with attention given both to systems with architected page tables and architected TLBs. Then virtualization is discussed for a variety of I/O devices. We next turn our attention to hardware assists to improve the performance of VM systems with the IBM z/VM as a running example. We end the chapter with two case studies, that of a hosted VM system developed by VMware, and that of the VT-x (Vanderpool) technology developed by Intel for their IA-32 architecture.

In Chapter 9 we shift our attention to the virtualization of multiprocessor systems. We introduce the notion of system partitioning and develop a taxonomy for different types of partitioning. We then discuss the principles behind physical partitioning and logical partitioning. The IBM LPAR feature is presented as a case study in logical partitioning. Following this is a discussion about logical partitioning using hypervisors. We then turn to a system VM-based approach to multiprocessor virtualization using a research system, Cellular Disco, as a case study. We end the chapter with a discussion of multiprocessor virtualization where the guest and host platforms have different ISAs, with special attention on bridging the differences in memory models between a host and a guest.

Chapter 10 is a discussion of emerging applications for virtual machine technology. We focus on three application areas which we feel will be important in the coming years. The first is security. We discuss the vulnerability to attacks of modern computer systems and outline the principles behind intrusion detection systems. The potential of VM technology in protecting and recovering from attacks is discussed. The role of binary rewriting technology in security is also discussed with reference to the RIO system. The second application we focus on is that of migrating computing environments from one machine to another. The techniques used in two systems, the Internet Suspend/Resume system and the Stanford Collective system, are described. The commercial application of this technology in VMware's VMotion is also discussed. Our third emerging application is computational grids. We outline the motivation behind the emergence of the grid as a computing infrastructure and compare it to the motivations behind other types of virtual machines. We end the chapter by showing how classic system virtual machines are proving to be an important enabler for emerging grid systems.

The Appendix is essentially a condensed course in computer systems, providing background material for the main chapters. It discusses the roles of the processor, memory, and I/O in a computer system. This is followed by a discussion of ISAs, including support for user applications as well as for the operating system. Page tables and TLBs are discussed next. We follow this with a discussion of the major components of an operating system and the system call interface between an application and the operating system. Finally we discuss multiprocessor architectures, including cluster architectures and shared-memory multiprocessor systems. Memory coherence and memory consistency issues in shared-memory systems are also addressed.

The book may be used in a course in a variety of ways. Overall, the book is structured for a course focused on virtual machines as a topic in itself (an approach we advocate). For an operating system oriented treatment of virtual machines, an instructor can go straight to Chapters 8 through 10 after introducing the taxonomy of virtual machines in Chapter 1. Chapters 2 through 5 can then be discussed to get an idea of implementation details. A more hardware oriented course can, however, go through Chapters 1 through 4 and then skip Chapters 5 and 6, before covering the remaining chapters. A language-oriented course can go straight to Chapter 5 from Chapter 1, and then backtrack to do Chapters 2 through 4, ending with Chapter 6 to put everything together. Chapter 10 should be of interest to virtually any course using the material in the book.

The specific interests of practitioners will largely determine the order in which they cover the material in the book. We have written the book in such a way that an interested reader can start at the beginning of any chapter of interest and follow the material in the complete chapter with only occasional excursions to sections in other chapters referred to in the text.

There are many people we would like to thank for having made this book possible. We would particularly like to thank the many reviewers. Michael Hind of IBM Research, Jan Hoogerbrugge of Philips Research, Jim Larus of Microsoft Research, Tim Lindholm of Sun Microsystems, Bernd Mathiske of Sun Microsystems, and Mike Smith of Harvard University patiently went through the text of the entire book and provided us with valuable feedback, sometimes critical, but always useful. We also thank a number of reviewers who went through specific chapters or sets of chapters and provided us with their valuable insights and comments. These reviewers include Erik Altman, Peter Capek, Evelyn Duesterwald, and Michael Gschwind, all of IBM Research, Renato Figueiredo of the Univ. of Florida, Michael Franz of UC Irvine, Wei Hsu of the Univ. of Minnesota, Toni Juan of UPC-Barcelona, Alain Kägi of Intel, Beng-Hong Lim of VMware, Eliot Moss of Univ. of Massachusetts, Amherst, Frank Soltis of IBM Rochester, Richard Uhlig of Intel, Romney White of IBM Endicott, Wayne Wolf of Princeton University, and Ben Zorn of Microsoft Research. We also appreciate the discussions with Vas Bala, Ek Ekanadham, Wolfram Sauer, and Charles Webb of IBM, on various aspects of virtualization.

The authors would also like to acknowledge Sriram Vajapeyam for his contributions during the early development of this material, and the students at the University of Wisconsin-Madison and Universitat Politècnica de Catalunya in Barcelona for their valuable feedback while participating in VM courses and conducting VM research. At the risk of omitting someone, the past and current students who have been particularly helpful are Nidhi Aggarwal, Todd Bezenek, Jason Cantin, Wooseok Chang, Ashutosh Dhodapkar, Timothy Heil, Shiliang Hu, Tejas Karkhanis, Ho-Seop Kim, Kyle Nesbit, and Subramanya Sastry.

This book owes a lot to the guidance, persistence, and encouragement provided by our publisher, Denise Penrose, and the support provided by her excellent staff at Morgan-Kaufmann Publishers, including Kimberlee Honjo, Angela Dooley, Alyson Day, and Summer Block.

First author: I would like to thank the people at IBM Research, and Dan Prener in particular, for their support during my 2000-2001 sabbatical – the time this book had its genesis. I am especially grateful to Erik Altman for being a sounding board throughout the writing of the book. I also thank my graduate students for their support and helpful suggestions. Finally, I am grateful to my children Barbara, Carolyn, and Jim, for their encouragement and patience during the writing of the book, and in general for putting up with a frequently distracted father.

Second author: I would like to thank Dan Prener, Eric Kronstadt, and Jaime Moreno for their encouragement and support in undertaking this project. Thanks also to Peter Capek, Dan Prener, Peter Oden, Dick Attanasio, and Mark Mergen for many interesting tea-time discussions. Finally, I would like to thank my wife, Indira, and my daughters, Rohini and Nandini, for their love and understanding at all times; they have given me more than I could have ever hoped for or imagined.

The authors are mutually grateful for the opportunity to renew a friendship that stretches back 30 years. We have had tremendous fun and have learnt a great deal in the process of writing this book. If you, the reader, experience just a fraction of what we have experienced, this book will have been worthwhile.

*James E. Smith*

*Ravi Nair*

# Contents

## Chapter Seven
# Codesigned Virtual Machines     329

## Chapter Eight
# System Virtual Machines     369

## Chapter Nine
# Multiprocessor Virtualization     445

# Chapter One

# Introduction to Virtual Machines

**M**odern computers are among the most advanced human-engineered structures, and they are possible only because of our ability to manage extreme complexity. Computer systems contain many silicon chips, each with hundreds of millions of transistors. These are interconnected and combined with high-speed input/output (I/O) devices and networking infrastructure to form the platforms upon which software can operate. Operating systems, application programs and libraries, and graphics and networking software all cooperate to provide a powerful environment for data management, education, communication, entertainment, and many other applications.

The key to managing complexity in computer systems is their division into *levels of abstraction* separated by *well-defined interfaces.* Levels of abstraction allow implementation details at lower levels of a design to be ignored or simplified, thereby simplifying the design of components at higher levels. The details of a hard disk, for example, that it is divided into sectors and tracks, are abstracted by the operating system (OS) so that the disk appears to application software as a set of variable-size files (see Figure 1.1). An application programmer can then create, write, and read files, without knowledge of the way the hard disk is constructed and organized.

The levels of abstraction are arranged in a hierarchy, with lower levels implemented in hardware and higher levels in software. In the hardware levels, all the components are physical, have real properties, and their interfaces are defined so that the various parts can be physically connected. In the software levels, components are logical, with fewer restrictions based on physical characteristics. In this book, we are most concerned with the abstraction levels that are at or near the hardware/software boundary. These are the levels where software is separated from the *machine* on which it runs.

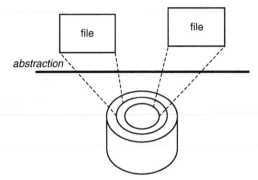

**Figure 1.1**     Files Are an Abstraction of a Disk. *A level of abstraction provides a simplified interface to underlying resources.*

Computer software is executed by a *machine* (a term that dates back to the beginning of computers; *platform* is the term more in vogue today). From the perspective of the operating system, a machine is largely composed of hardware, including one or more processors that run a specific instruction set, some real memory, and I/O devices. However, we do not restrict the use of the term *machine* to just the hardware components of a computer. From the perspective of application programs, for example, the machine is a combination of the operating system and those portions of the hardware accessible through user-level binary instructions.

Let us now turn to the other aspect of managing complexity: the use of *well-defined interfaces.* Well-defined interfaces allow computer design tasks to be decoupled so that teams of hardware and software designers can work more or less independently. The instruction set is one such interface. For example, designers at Intel and AMD develop microprocessors that implement the Intel IA-32[1] instruction set, while software engineers at Microsoft develop compilers that map high-level languages to the same instruction set. As long as both groups satisfy the instruction set specification, compiled software will execute correctly on a machine incorporating an IA-32 microprocessor. The operating system interface, defined as a set of function calls, is another important standardized interface in computer systems. As the Intel/Microsoft example suggests, well-defined interfaces permit development of interacting computer subsystems at different companies and at different times, sometimes years apart. Application software developers do not need to be aware of detailed changes inside the operating system, and hardware and software

---

1. Sometimes referred to informally as *x86.*

can be upgraded according to different schedules. Software can run on different platforms implementing the same instruction set.

Despite their many advantages, well-defined interfaces can also be confining. Subsystems and components designed to specifications for one interface will not work with those designed for another. There are processors with different instruction sets (e.g., Intel IA-32 and IBM PowerPC), and there are different operating systems (e.g., Windows and Linux). Application programs, when distributed as program binaries, are tied to a specific instruction set and operating system. An operating system is tied to a computer that implements specific memory system and I/O system interfaces. As a general principle, diversity in instruction sets, operating systems, and application programming languages encourages innovation and discourages stagnation. However, in practice, diversity also leads to reduced interoperability, which becomes restrictive, especially in a world of networked computers, where it is advantageous to move software as freely as data.

Beneath the hardware/software interface, hardware resource considerations can also limit the flexibility of software systems. Memory and I/O abstractions, both in high-level languages and in operating systems, have removed many hardware resource dependences; some still remain, however. Many operating systems are developed for a specific system architecture, e.g., for a uniprocessor or a shared-memory multiprocessor, and are designed to manage hardware resources directly. The implicit assumption is that the hardware resources of a system are managed by a single operating system. This binds all hardware resources into a single entity under a single management regime. And this, in turn, limits the flexibility of the system, not only in terms of available application software (as discussed earlier), but also in terms of security and failure isolation, especially when the system is shared by multiple users or groups of users.

*Virtualization* provides a way of relaxing the foregoing constraints and increasing flexibility. When a system (or subsystem), e.g., a processor, memory, or I/O device, is *virtualized*, its interface and all resources visible through the interface are mapped onto the interface and resources of a real system actually implementing it. Consequently, the real system is transformed so that it appears to be a different, virtual system or even a set of multiple virtual systems. Formally, virtualization involves the construction of an isomorphism that maps a virtual *guest* system to a real *host* (Popek and Goldberg 1974). This isomorphism, illustrated in Figure 1.2, maps the guest state to the host state (function $V$ in Figure 1.2), and for a sequence of operations, $e$, that modifies the state in the guest (the function $e$ modifies state $S_i$ to state $S_j$) there is a corresponding sequence of operations $e'$ in the host that performs an equivalent modification to the host's state (changes $S_i'$ to $S_j'$). Although such an

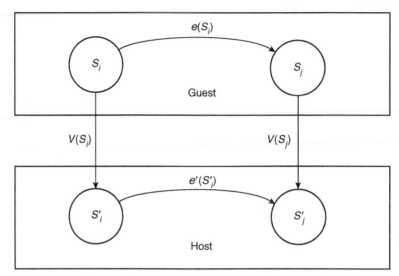

**Figure 1.2** Virtualization. *Formally, virtualization is the construction of an isomorphism between a guest system and a host; $e' \circ V(S_i) = V \circ e(S_i)$.*

isomorphism can be used to characterize abstraction as well as virtualization, we distinguish the two: Virtualization differs from abstraction in that virtualization does not necessarily hide details; the level of detail in a virtual system is often the same as that in the underlying real system.

Consider again the example of a hard disk. In some applications, it may be desirable to partition a single large hard disk into a number of smaller virtual disks. The virtual disks are mapped to a real disk by implementing each of the virtual disks as a single large file on the real disk (Figure 1.3). Virtualizing software provides a mapping between virtual disk contents and real disk contents (the function $V$ in the isomorphism), using the file abstraction as an intermediate step. Each of the virtual disks is given the appearance of having a number of logical tracks and sectors (although fewer than in the large disk). A write to a virtual disk (the function $e$ in the isomorphism) is mirrored by a file write and a corresponding real disk write, in the host system (the function $e'$ in the isomorphism). In this example, the level of detail provided at the virtual disk interface, i.e., sector/track addressing, remains the same as for a real disk; no abstraction takes place.

The concept of virtualization can be applied not only to subsystems such as disks, but to an entire machine. A *virtual machine* (VM) is implemented by adding a layer of software to a real machine to support the desired virtual machine's architecture. For example, virtualizing software installed on an Apple Macintosh can provide a Windows/IA-32 virtual machine capable of

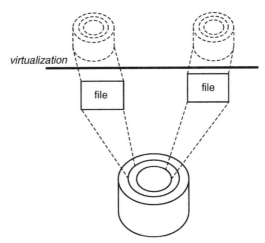

**Figure 1.3** Implementing Virtual Disks. *Virtualization provides a different interface and/or resources at the same level of abstraction.*

running PC application programs. In general, a virtual machine can circumvent real machine compatibility constraints and hardware resource constraints to enable a higher degree of software portability and flexibility.

A wide variety of virtual machines exist to provide an equally wide variety of benefits. Multiple, replicated virtual machines can be implemented on a single hardware platform to provide individuals or user groups with their own operating system environments. The different system environments (possibly with different operating systems) also provide isolation and enhanced security. A large multiprocessor server can be divided into smaller virtual servers, while retaining the ability to balance the use of hardware resources across the system.

Virtual machines can also employ emulation techniques to support cross-platform software compatibility. For example, a platform implementing the PowerPC instruction set can be converted into a virtual platform running the IA-32 instruction set. Consequently, software written for one platform will run on the other. This compatibility can be provided either at the system level (e.g., to run a Windows OS on a Macintosh) or at the program or process level (e.g., to run Excel on a Sun Solaris/SPARC platform). In addition to emulation, virtual machines can provide dynamic, on-the-fly optimization of program binaries. Finally, through emulation, virtual machines can enable new, proprietary instruction sets, e.g., incorporating very long instruction words (VLIWs), while supporting programs in an existing, standard instruction set.

The virtual machine examples just described are constructed to match the architectures of existing real machines. However, there are also virtual machines for which there are no corresponding real machines. It has become common for language developers to invent a virtual machine tailored to a new high-level language. Programs written in the high-level language are compiled to "binaries" targeted at the virtual machine. Then any real machine on which the virtual machine is implemented can run the compiled code. The power of this approach has been clearly demonstrated with the Java high-level language and the Java virtual machine, where a high degree of platform independence has been achieved, thereby enabling a very flexible network computing environment.

Virtual machines have been investigated and built by operating system developers, language designers, compiler developers, and hardware designers. Although each application of virtual machines has its unique characteristics, there also are underlying concepts and technologies that are common across the spectrum of virtual machines. Because the various virtual machine architectures and underlying technologies have been developed by different groups, it is especially important to unify this body of knowledge and understand the base technologies that cut across the various forms of virtual machines. The goals of this book are to describe the family of virtual machines in a unified way, to discuss the common underlying technologies that support them, and to demonstrate their versatility by exploring their many applications.

## 1.1 Computer Architecture

As will become evident, a discussion of virtual machines is also a discussion about computer architecture in a broad sense. Virtual machines often bridge architectural boundaries, and a major consideration in constructing a virtual machine is the fidelity with which a virtual machine implements architected interfaces. Therefore, it is useful to define and summarize *computer architecture.*

The architecture of a building describes its functionality and appearance to users of the building but not the details of its construction, such as the specifics of its plumbing system or the manufacturer of the bricks. Analogously, the term *architecture,* when applied to computers, refers to the functionality and appearance of a computer system or subsystem but not the details of its implementation. The architecture is often formally described through a specification of an interface and the logical behavior of resources manipulated via the interface. The term *implementation* will be used to describe the actual embodiment of an architecture. Any architecture can have several implementations, each one having distinct characteristics, e.g., a high-performance implementation or a low-power implementation.

The levels of abstraction in a computer system correspond to *implementation layers* in both hardware and software. There is an architecture for each of these implementation layers (although the term *architecture* is not always used). Figure 1.4 shows some of the important interfaces and implementation layers as found in a typical computer system. In software, for example, there is an interface between an application program and standard libraries (interface 2 in Figure 1.4). Another software interface is at the boundary of the operating system (interface 3). The interfaces in hardware include an I/O architecture that describes the signals that drive I/O device controllers (interface 11), a hardware memory architecture that describes the way addresses are translated (interface 9), an interface for the memory access signals that leave the processor (interface 12), and another for the signals that reach the DRAM chips in memory (interface 14). The OS communicates with I/O devices through a sequence of interfaces: 4, 8, 10, 11, and 13. Of these interfaces and architectures, we are most interested in those at or near the hardware/software boundary.

The *instruction set architecture* (ISA), which marks the division between hardware and software, is composed of interfaces 7 and 8 in Figure 1.4. The concept of an ISA was first clearly articulated when the IBM 360 family of

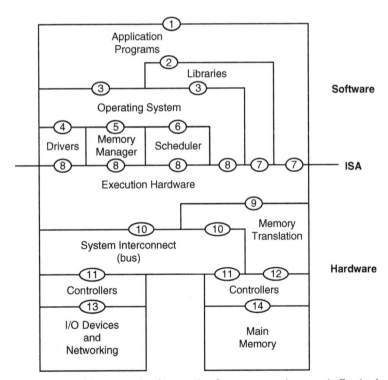

**Figure 1.4**  Computer System Architectures. *Implementation layers communicate vertically via the shown interfaces. This view of architecture is styled after one given by Glenford Myers (1982).*

mainframe computers was developed in the early 1960s (Amdahl, Blaauw, and Brooks 1964). With that project, the importance of software compatibility was fully recognized. The IBM 360 series had a number of models that could incorporate a wide range of hardware resources, thereby covering a broad spectrum of price and performance levels — yet they were designed to run the same software. To successfully accomplish this, the interface between the hardware and software had to be precisely defined and controlled, and the ISA serves this purpose.

There are two parts of an ISA that are important in the definition of virtual machines. The first part includes those aspects of the ISA that are visible to an application program. This will be referred to as the *user ISA*. The second part includes those aspects visible to supervisor software, such as the operating system, which is responsible for managing hardware resources. This is the *system ISA*. Of course, the supervisor software can also employ all the elements of the user ISA. In Figure 1.4, interface 7 consists of the user ISA only, and interface 8 consists of both the user ISA and the system ISA.

In this book we will also be concerned with interfaces besides the ISA. The application binary interface (ABI) consists of interfaces 3 and 7 in Figure 1.4. An important related interface is the application program interface (API), which consists of interfaces 2 and 7.

The *application binary interface*, which provides a program with access to the hardware resources and services available in a system, has two major components. The first is the set of all user instructions (interface 7 in Figure 1.4); system instructions are not included in the ABI. At the ABI level, all application programs interact with the shared hardware resources indirectly, by invoking the operating system via a *system call* interface (interface 3 in Figure 1.4), which is the second component of the ABI. System calls provide a specific set of operations that an operating system may perform on behalf of a user program (after checking to make sure the user program should be granted its request). The system call interface is typically implemented via an instruction that transfers control to the operating system in a manner similar to a procedure or subroutine call, except the call target address is restricted to a specific address in the operating system. Arguments for the system call are typically passed through registers and/or a stack held in memory, following specific conventions that are part of the system call interface. A program binary compiled to a specific ABI can run unchanged only on a system with the same ISA and operating system.

The *application programming interface* is usually defined with respect to a high-level language (HLL). A key element of an API is a standard library (or libraries) that an application calls to invoke various services available on the system, including those provided by the operating system. An API, typically defined at the source code level, enables applications written to the API to be ported easily (via recompilation) to any system that supports the same API. The API specifies an abstraction of the details of implementation of services, especially those that involve privileged hardware. For example, clib is a well-known library that supports the UNIX/C programming language. The clib API provides a memory model consisting of text (for code) and a heap and stack (for data). A routine belonging to an API typically contains one or more ABI-level operating system calls. Some API library routines are simply *wrappers*, i.e., code that translates directly from the HLL calling convention to the binary convention expected by the OS. Other API routines are more complex and may include several OS calls.

## 1.2 Virtual Machine Basics

To understand what a virtual machine is, we must first discuss what is meant by *machine*, and, as pointed out earlier, the meaning of "machine" is a matter of perspective. From the perspective of a *process* executing a user program, the machine consists of a logical memory address space that has been assigned to the process, along with user-level registers and instructions that allow the execution of code belonging to the process. The I/O part of the machine is visible only through the operating system, and the only way the process can interact with the I/O system is via operating system calls, often through libraries that execute as part of the process. Processes are usually transient in nature (although not always). They are created, execute for a period of time, perhaps spawn other processes along the way, and eventually terminate. To summarize, the machine, from the prospective of a process, is a combination of the operating system and the underlying user-level hardware. The ABI provides the interface between the process and the machine (Figure 1.5a).

From the perspective of the operating system, an entire *system* is supported by the underlying machine. A system is a full execution environment that can simultaneously support a number of processes potentially belonging to different users. All the processes share a file system and other I/O resources. The system environment persists over time (with occasional reboots) as processes come and go. The system allocates physical memory and I/O resources to the processes and allows the processes to interact with their resources via an OS that is part of the system. Hence, the machine, from the perspective of a system, is implemented by the underlying hardware alone, and the ISA provides the interface between the system and the machine (Figure 1.5b).

In practical terms, a virtual machine executes software (either an individual process or a full system, depending on the type of machine) in the same manner

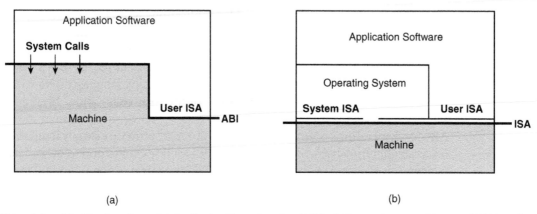

**Figure 1.5** Machine Interfaces. *(a) Application binary interface (ABI); (b) instruction set architecture (ISA) interface.*

as the machine for which the software was developed. The virtual machine is implemented as a combination of a real machine and virtualizing software. The virtual machine may have resources different from the real machine, either in quantity or in type. For example, a virtual machine may have more or fewer processors than the real machine, and the processors may execute a different instruction set than does the real machine. It is important to note that equivalent performance is usually not required as part of virtualization; often a virtual machine provides less performance than an equivalent real machine running the same software, i.e., software developed for the real machine.

As characterized by the isomorphism described earlier, the process of virtualization consists of two parts: (1) the mapping of virtual resources or state, e.g., registers, memory, or files, to real resources in the underlying machine and (2) the use of real machine instructions and/or system calls to carry out the actions specified by virtual machine instructions and/or system calls, e.g., emulation of the virtual machine ABI or ISA.

Just as there is a process perspective and a system perspective of machines, there are also process-level and system-level virtual machines. As the name suggests, a *process virtual machine* is capable of supporting an individual process. A process virtual machine is illustrated in Figure 1.6. In this figure and the figures that follow, compatible interfaces are illustrated graphically as "meshing" boundaries. In process VMs, the virtualizing software is placed at the ABI interface, on top of the OS/hardware combination. The virtualizing software emulates both user-level instructions and operating system calls.

With regard to terminology (see Figure 1.6), we usually refer to the underlying platform as the *host* and to the software that runs in the VM environment as the *guest*. The real platform that corresponds to a virtual machine, i.e., the

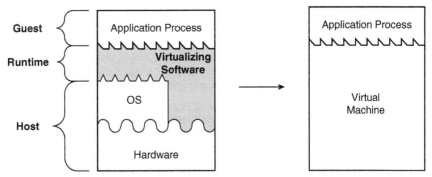

**Figure 1.6**  A Process Virtual Machine. *Virtualizing software translates a set of OS and user-level instructions composing one platform to another, forming a process virtual machine capable of executing programs developed for a different OS and a different ISA.*

real machine being emulated by the virtual machine, is referred to as the *native* machine. The name given to the virtualizing software depends on the type of virtual machine being implemented. In process VMs, virtualizing software is often referred to as the *runtime,* which is short for "runtime software."[2] The runtime is created to support a guest process and runs on top of an operating system. The VM supports the guest process as long as the guest process executes and terminates support when the guest process terminates.

In contrast, a *system virtual machine* provides a complete system environment. This environment can support an operating system along with its potentially many user processes. It provides a guest operating system with access to underlying hardware resources, including networking, I/O, and, on the desktop, a display and graphical user interface. The VM supports the operating system as long as the system environment is alive.

A system virtual machine is illustrated in Figure 1.7; virtualizing software is placed between the underlying hardware machine and conventional software. In this particular example, virtualizing software emulates the hardware ISA so that conventional software "sees" a different ISA than the one supported by hardware. In many system VMs the guest and host run the same ISA, however. In system VMs, the virtualizing software is often referred to as the *virtual machine monitor* (VMM), a term coined when the VM concept was first developed in the late 1960s.

---

**2.** Throughout this book, we will use the single-word form *runtime* as a noun to describe the virtualizing runtime software in a process VM; *run time* (two words) will be used in the more generic sense: the time during which a program is running.

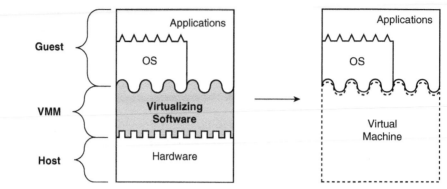

**Figure 1.7**  A System Virtual Machine. *Virtualizing software translates the ISA used by one hardware platform to another, forming a system virtual machine, capable of executing a system software environment developed for a different set of hardware.*

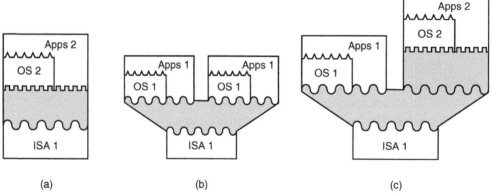

**Figure 1.8**  Examples of Virtual Machine Applications. *(a) Emulating one instruction set with another; (b) replicating a virtual machine so that multiple operating systems can be supported simultaneously; (c) composing virtual machine software to form a more complex, flexible system.*

Virtualizing software can be applied in several ways to connect and adapt the major computer subsystems (see Figure 1.8). *Emulation* adds considerable flexibility by permitting "mix and match" cross-platform software portability. In this example (Figure 1.8a), one ISA is emulated by another. Virtualizing software can enhance emulation with *optimization,* by taking implementation-specific information into consideration as it performs emulation. Virtualizing software can also provide resource *replication,* for example, by giving a single hardware platform the appearance of multiple platforms (Figure 1.8b), each capable of running a complete operating system and/or a set of applications. Finally, the virtual machine functions can be composed (Figure 1.8c) to form a wide variety of architectures, freed of many of the traditional compatibility and resource constraints.

We are now ready to describe some specific types of virtual machines. These span a fairly broad spectrum of applications, and we will discuss them according to the two main categories: process VMs and system VMs. Note that because the various virtual machines have been developed by different design communities, different terms are often used to describe similar concepts and features. In fact, it is sometimes the practice to use some term other than *virtual machine* to describe what is in reality a form of virtual machine.

## 1.3 Process Virtual Machines

Process-level VMs provide user applications with a virtual ABI environment. In their various implementations, process VMs can provide replication, emulation, and optimization. The following subsections describe each of these.

### 1.3.1 Multiprogramming

The first and most common virtual machine is so ubiquitous that we don't even think of it as being a virtual machine. The combination of the OS call interface and the user instruction set forms the machine that executes a user process. Most operating systems can simultaneously support multiple user processes through multiprogramming, where each user process is given the illusion of having a complete machine to itself. Each process is given its own address space and is given access to a file structure. The operating system time-shares the hardware and manages underlying resources to make this possible. In effect, the operating system provides a replicated process-level virtual machine for each of the concurrently executing applications.

### 1.3.2 Emulators and Dynamic Binary Translators

A more challenging problem for process-level virtual machines is to support program binaries compiled to a different instruction set than the one executed by the host's hardware, i.e., to *emulate* one instruction set on hardware designed for another. An example emulating process virtual machine is illustrated in Figure 1.9. Application programs are compiled for a *source ISA*, but

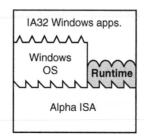

**Figure 1.9** A Process VM That Emulates Guest Applications. *The Digital FX!32 system allows Windows IA-32 applications to be run on an Alpha Windows platform.*

the hardware implements a different *target ISA.* As shown in the example, the operating system may be the same for both the guest process and the host platform, although in other cases the operating systems may differ as well. The example in Figure 1.9 illustrates the Digital FX!32 system (Hookway and Herdeg 1997). The FX!32 system can run Intel IA-32 application binaries compiled for Windows NT on an Alpha hardware platform also running Windows NT. More recent examples are the Aries system (Zheng and Thompson 2000) which supports PA-RISC programs on an IPF (Itanium) platform, and the Intel IA-32 EL (execution layer) which supports IA-32 programs on an IPF platform (Baraz et al. 2003).

The most straightforward emulation method is *interpretation.* An interpreter program executing the target ISA fetches, decodes, and emulates the execution of individual source instructions. This can be a relatively slow process, requiring tens of native target instructions for each source instruction interpreted.

For better performance, *binary translation* is typically used. With binary translation, blocks of source instructions are converted to target instructions that perform equivalent functions. There can be a relatively high overhead associated with the translation process, but once a block of instructions is translated, the translated instructions can be cached and repeatedly executed much faster than they can be interpreted. Because binary translation is the most important feature of this type of process virtual machine, they are sometimes called *dynamic binary translators.*

Interpretation and binary translation have different performance characteristics. Interpretation has relatively low startup overhead but consumes significant time whenever an instruction is emulated. On the other hand, binary translation has high initial overhead when performing the translations but is fast for each repeated execution. Consequently, some virtual machines use a staged emulation strategy combined with *profiling,* i.e., the collection of statistics regarding the program's behavior. Initially, a block of source instructions is interpreted, and profiling is used to determine which instruction sequences are frequently executed. Then a frequently executed block may be binary translated. Some systems perform additional code optimizations on the translated code if profiling shows that it has a very high execution frequency. In most emulating virtual machines the stages of interpretation and binary translation can both occur over the course of a single program's execution. In the case of FX!32, translation occurs incrementally between program runs.

### 1.3.3 Same-ISA Binary Optimizers

Most dynamic binary translators not only translate from source to target code but also perform some code optimizations. This leads naturally to virtual machines where the instruction sets used by the host and the guest are the same, and optimization of a program binary is the primary purpose of the virtual machine. Thus, *same-ISA dynamic binary optimizers* are implemented in a manner very similar to emulating virtual machines, including staged optimization and software caching of optimized code. Same-ISA dynamic binary optimizers are most effective for source binaries that are relatively unoptimized to begin with, a situation that is fairly common in practice. A dynamic binary optimizer can collect a profile and then use this profile information to optimize the binary code on the fly. An example of such a same-ISA dynamic binary optimizer is the Dynamo system, originally developed as a research project at Hewlett-Packard (Bala, Duesterwald, and Banerjia 2000).

### 1.3.4 High-Level Language Virtual Machines: Platform Independence

For the process VMs described earlier, cross-platform portability is clearly a very important objective. For example, the FX!32 system enabled portability of application software compiled for a popular platform (IA-32 PC) to a less popular platform (Alpha). However, this approach allows cross-platform compatibility only on a case-by-case basis and requires a great deal of programming effort. For example, if one wanted to run IA-32 binaries on a number of hardware platforms currently in use, e.g., SPARC, PowerPC, and MIPS, then an FX!32-like VM would have to be developed for each of them. The problem would be even more difficult if the host platforms run different operating systems than the one for which binaries were originally compiled.

Full cross-platform portability is more easily achieved by taking a step back and designing it into an overall software framework. One way of accomplishing this is to design a process-level VM at the same time as an application development environment is being defined. Here, the VM environment does not directly correspond to any real platform. Rather, it is designed for ease of portability and to match the features of a high-level language (HLL) used for application program development. These *high-level language VMs* (HLL VMs) are similar to the process VMs described earlier. However, they are focused on minimizing hardware-specific and OS-specific features because these would compromise platform independence.

High-level language VMs first became popular with the Pascal programming environment (Bowles 1980). In a conventional system, Figure 1.10a, the compiler consists of a frontend that performs lexical, syntax, and semantic analysis to generate simple intermediate code — similar to machine code but more abstract. Typically the intermediate code does not contain specific register assignments, for example. Then a code generator takes the intermediate code and generates a binary containing machine code for a specific ISA and OS. This binary file is distributed and executed on platforms that support the given ISA/OS combination. To execute the program on a different platform, however, it must be recompiled for that platform.

In HLL VMs, this model is changed (Figure 1.10b). The steps are similar to the conventional ones, but the point at which program distribution takes place is at a higher level. As shown in Figure 1.10b, a conventional compiler frontend generates abstract machine code, which is very similar to an intermediate form. In many HLL VMs, this is a rather generic stack-based ISA. This *virtual ISA*

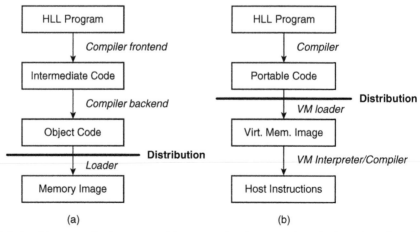

(a)                    (b)

**Figure 1.10**    High-Level Language Environments. *(a) A conventional system, where platform-dependent object code is distributed; (b) an HLL VM environment, where portable intermediate code is "executed" by a platform-dependent virtual machine.*

is in essence the machine code for a virtual machine. The portable virtual ISA code is distributed for execution on different platforms. For each platform, a VM capable of executing the virtual ISA is implemented. In its simplest form, the VM contains an interpreter that takes each instruction, decodes it, and then performs the required state transformations (e.g., involving memory and the stack). I/O functions are performed via a set of standard library calls that are defined as part of the VM. In more sophisticated, higher performance VMs, the abstract machine code may be compiled (binary translated) into host machine code for direct execution on the host platform.

An advantage of an HLL VM is that software is easily portable, once the VM is implemented on a target platform. While the VM implementation would take some effort, it is a much simpler task than developing a compiler for each platform and recompiling every application when it is ported. It is also simpler than developing a conventional emulating process VM for a typical real-world ISA.

The Sun Microsystems Java VM architecture (Lindholm and Yellin 1999) and the Microsoft common language infrastructure (CLI), which is the foundation of the .NET framework (Box 2002), are more recent, widely used examples of HLL VMs. Platform independence and high security are central to both the Java VM and CLI. The ISAs in both systems are based on *bytecodes;* that is, instructions are encoded as a sequence of bytes, where each byte is an opcode, a single-byte operand, or part of a multibyte operand. These byte-code instruction sets are stack based (to eliminate register requirements) and have an abstract data specification and memory model. In fact, the memory size is conceptually unbounded, with garbage collection as an assumed part of the implementation. Because all hardware platforms are potential targets for executing Java- or CLI-based programs, applications are not compiled for a specific OS. Rather, a set of standard libraries is provided as part of the overall execution environment.

## 1.4 System Virtual Machines

System virtual machines provide a complete system environment in which many processes, possibly belonging to multiple users, can coexist. These VMs were first developed during the 1960s and early 1970s, and they were the origin of the term *virtual machine*. By using system VMs, a single host hardware plat-form can support multiple guest OS environments simultaneously. At the time they were first developed, mainframe computer systems were very large and expensive, and computers were almost always shared among a large number of users. Different groups of users sometimes wanted different operating systems to be run on the shared hardware, and VMs allowed them to do so. Alternatively, a multiplicity of single-user operating systems allowed a convenient way of implementing time-sharing among many users. Over time, as hardware became much less expensive and much of it migrated to the desktop, interest in these classic system VMs faded.

Today, however, system VMs are enjoying renewed popularity. This is partly due to modern-day variations of the traditional motivations for system VMs. The large, expensive mainframe systems of the past are now servers or server farms, and these servers may be shared by a number of users or user groups. Perhaps the most important feature of today's system VMs is that they provide a secure way of partitioning major software systems that run concurrently on the same hardware platform. Software running on one guest system is isolated from software running on other guest systems. Furthermore, if security on one guest system is compromised or if the guest OS suffers a failure, the software running on other guest systems is not affected. The ability to support different operating systems simultaneously, e.g., Windows and Linux (as illustrated in Figure 1.11), is another reason for their appeal, although it is probably of secondary importance to most users.

In system VMs, platform replication is the major feature provided by a VMM. The central problem is that of dividing a single set of hardware resources among multiple guest operating system environments. The VMM has access to and manages all the hardware resources. A guest operating system and application programs compiled for that operating system are then managed under (hidden) control of the VMM. This is accomplished by constructing the system so that when a guest OS performs certain operations, such as a privileged instruction that directly involves the shared hardware resources, the operation is intercepted by the VMM, checked for correctness, and performed by the VMM on behalf of the guest. Guest software is unaware of the "behind-the-scenes" work performed by the VMM.

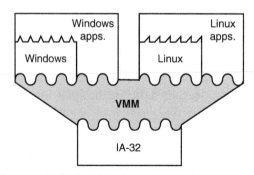

**Figure 1.11**   A System VM That Supports Multiple OS Environments on the Same Hardware.

### 1.4.1 Implementations of System Virtual Machines

From the user perspective, most system VMs provide more or less the same functionality. The thing that tends to differentiate them is the way in which they are implemented. As discussed earlier, in Section 1.2, there are a number of interfaces in a computer system, and this leads to a number of choices for locating the system VMM software. Summaries of two of the more important implementations follow.

Figure 1.11 illustrates the classic approach to system VM architecture (Popek and Goldberg 1974). The VMM is first placed on bare hardware, and virtual machines fit on top. The VMM runs in the most highly privileged mode, while all the guests systems run with lesser privileges. Then in a completely transparent way, the VMM can intercept and implement all the guest OS's actions that interact with hardware resources. In many respects, this system VM architecture is the most efficient, and it provides service to all the guest systems in a more or less equivalent way. One disadvantage of this type of system, at least for desktop users, is that installation requires wiping an existing system clean and starting from scratch, first installing the VMM and then installing guest operating systems on top. Another disadvantage is that I/O device drivers must be available for installation in the VMM, because it is the VMM that interacts directly with I/O devices.

An alternative system VMM implementation builds virtualizing software on top of an existing host operating system — resulting in what is called a *hosted VM*. With a hosted VM, the installation process is similar to installing a typical application program. Furthermore, virtualizing software can rely on the host OS to provide device drivers and other lower-level services; they don't have to be provided by the VMM. The disadvantage of this approach is that there can be some loss of efficiency because more layers of software become involved when OS service is required. The hosted VM approach is taken in the VMware implementation (VMware 2000), a modern system VM that runs on IA-32 hardware platforms.

### 1.4.2 Whole System VMs: Emulation

In the conventional system VMs described earlier, all the system software (both guest and host) and application software use the same ISA as the underlying hardware. In some important situations, however, the host and guest systems do not have a common ISA. For example, the Apple PowerPC-based systems and Windows PCs use different ISAs (and different operating systems), and they are the two most popular desktop systems today. As another example,

Sun Microsystems servers use a different OS and ISA than the Windows PCs that are commonly attached to them as clients. Because software systems are so closely tied to hardware systems, this may require purchase of multiple platform types, even when unnecessary for any other reason, which complicates software support and/or restricts the availability of useful software packages to users.

This situation motivates system VMs, where a complete software system, both OS and applications, is supported on a host system that runs a different ISA and OS. These are called *whole-system VMs* because they essentially virtualize all software. Because the ISAs are different, both application and OS code require emulation, e.g., via binary translation. For whole-system VMs, the most common implementation method is to place the VMM and guest software on top of a conventional host OS running on the hardware.

Figure 1.12 illustrates a whole-system VM built on top of a conventional system with its own OS and application programs. An example of this type of VM is Virtual PC (Traut 1997), which enables a Windows system to run on a Macintosh platform. The VM software executes as an application program supported by the host OS and uses no system ISA operations. It is as if the VM software, the guest OS, and guest application(s) are one very large application implemented on the host OS and hardware. Meanwhile the host OS can also continue to run applications compiled for the native ISA; this feature is illustrated in the right-hand section of the drawing.

To implement a system VM of this type, the VM software must emulate the entire hardware environment. It must control the emulation of all the

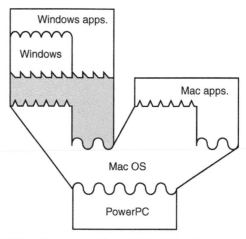

**Figure 1.12**   A Whole-System VM That Supports a Guest OS and Applications, in Addition to Host Applications.

instructions, and it must convert the guest system ISA operations to equivalent OS calls made to the host OS. Even if binary translation is used, it is tightly constrained because translated code often cannot take advantage of underlying system ISA features such as virtual memory management and trap handling. In addition, problems can arise if the properties of hardware resources are significantly different in the host and the guest. Solving these mismatches is the major challenge of implementing whole-system VMs.

### 1.4.3 Codesigned Virtual Machines: Hardware Optimization

In all the VM models discussed thus far, the goal has been functionality and portability — either to support multiple (possibly different) operating systems on the same host platform or to support different ISAs and operating systems on the same platform. In practice, these virtual machines are implemented on hardware already developed for some standard ISA and for which native (host) applications, libraries, and operating systems already exist. By and large, improved performance (i.e., going beyond native platform performance) has not been a goal — in fact minimizing performance losses is often the performance goal.

*Codesigned VMs* have a different objective and take a different approach. These VMs are designed to enable innovative ISAs and/or hardware implementations for improved performance, power efficiency, or both. The host's ISA may be completely new, or it may be based on an existing ISA with some new instructions added and/or some instructions deleted. In a codesigned VM, there are no native ISA applications. It is as if the VM software is, in fact, part of the hardware implementation.

In some respects, codesigned virtual machines are similar to a purely hardware virtualization approach used in many high-performance superscalar microprocessors. In these designs, hardware renames architected registers to a larger number of physical registers, and complex instructions are decomposed into simpler, RISC-like instructions (Hennessy and Patterson 2002). In this book, however, we focus on software-implemented codesigned virtual machines; binary translation is over a larger scope and can be more flexible because it is done in software.

Because the goal is to provide a VM platform that looks exactly like a native hardware platform, the software portion of a codesigned VM uses a region of memory that is not visible to any application or system software. This concealed memory is carved out of real memory at boot time and the conventional guest software is never informed of its existence. VMM code that resides in the concealed memory can take control of the hardware at practically any time and perform a number of different functions. In its more general form, the VM software includes a binary translator that converts guest instructions into native ISA instructions and caches the translated instructions in a region of concealed memory. Hence, the guest ISA never directly executes on the hardware. Of course, interpretation can also be used to supplement binary translation, depending on performance tradeoffs. To provide improved performance, translation is coupled with code optimization. Optimization of frequently executed code sequences is performed at translation time, and/or it is performed as an ongoing process while the program runs.

Perhaps the best-known example of a codesigned VM is the Transmeta Crusoe (Halfhill 2000). In this processor, the underlying hardware uses a native VLIW instruction set, and the guest ISA is the Intel IA-32. In their implementation, the Transmeta designers focused on the power-saving advantages of simpler VLIW hardware. An important computer system that relies on many codesigned VM techniques is the IBM AS/400 system (Soltis 1996). The AS/400 differs from the other codesigned VMs, because the primary design objective is support for an object-oriented instruction set that redefines the hardware/software interface in a novel fashion. The current AS/400 implementations are based on an extended PowerPC ISA, although earlier versions used a considerably different, proprietary CISC ISA.

## 1.5 A Taxonomy

We have just described a rather broad array of VMs, with different goals and implementations. To put them in perspective and organize the common implementation issues, we introduce a taxonomy illustrated in Figure 1.13. First, VMs are divided into the two major types: process VMs and system VMs. In the first type, the VM supports an ABI — user instructions plus system calls; in the second, the VM supports a complete ISA — both user and system instructions. Finer divisions in the taxonomy are based on whether the guest and host use the same ISA.

On the left-hand side of Figure 1.13 are process VMs. These include VMs where the host and guest instruction sets are the same. In the figure, we identify two examples. The first is multiprogrammed systems, as already supported on most of today's systems. The second is same-ISA dynamic binary optimizers, which transform guest instructions only by optimizing them and then execute them natively.

For process VMs where the guest and host ISAs are different, we also give two examples. These are dynamic translators and HLL VMs. HLL VMs are

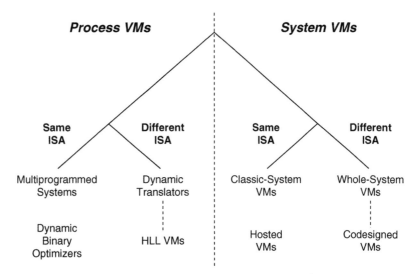

**Figure 1.13** A Taxonomy of Virtual Machines.

connected to the VM taxonomy via a "dotted line" because their process-level interface is at a different, higher level than the other process VMs.

On the right-hand side of the figure are system VMs. If the guest and host use the same ISA, examples include "classic" system VMs and hosted VMs. In these VMs, the objective is providing replicated, isolated system environments. The primary difference between classic and hosted VMs is the VMM implementation rather than the function provided to the user.

Examples of system VMs where the guest and host ISAs are different include whole-system VMs and codesigned VMs. With whole-system VMs, performance is often of secondary importance compared to accurate functionality, while with codesigned VMs, performance (and power efficiency) are often major goals. In the figure, codesigned VMs are connected using dotted lines because their interface is typically at a lower level than other system VMs.

## 1.6 Summary: The Versatility of Virtual Machines

A good way to summarize this chapter is with an example of a realistic system that could conceivably be in use today (Figure 1.14). The example clearly illustrates the versatility of virtual machine technologies. A computer user might have a Java application running on a laptop PC. This is nothing special; it is done via a Java virtual machine developed for IA-32/Linux. However, the

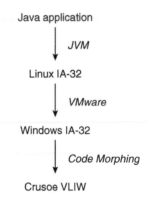

**Figure 1.14**  Three Levels of VMs. *A Java application running on a Java VM, running on a system VM, running on a codesigned VM.*

user happens to have Linux installed as an OS VM via VMware executing on a Windows PC. And, as it happens, the IA-32 hardware is in fact a Transmeta Crusoe, a codesigned VM implementing a VLIW ISA with binary translation (what Transmeta calls *code morphing*) to support the IA-32 ISA. By using the many VM technologies, a Java bytecode program is actually executing as native VLIW.

## 1.7  The Rest of the Book

The book can be divided into two major sections, along the lines of the VM taxonomy just described. Chapters 2 through 6 deal primarily with process virtual machines, and Chapters 7 through 9 deal primarily with system virtual machines.

It should now be evident that instruction set emulation is an important enabling technology for many virtual machine implementations. Because of its importance, we begin, in Chapter 2, with a detailed discussion of emulation. Emulation encompasses both interpretation, where guest instructions are emulated one by one in a simple fashion, and binary translation, where blocks of guest instructions are translated to the ISA of the host platform and saved for multiple executions. In many of the VM implementations, the need to use emulation is obvious (i.e., the guest and host ISAs are different), but, as we will see, the same techniques are important in other VMs, for nonobvious reasons (even in cases where the guest and host ISAs are the same). A case study is the Shade simulation system, which incorporates a number of emulation techniques.

Chapter 3 uses emulation as a starting point and describes the overall architecture and implementation of process VMs. Included are the management of cached binary translations and the handling of complicating issues such as precise traps and self-modifying code. The DEC/Compaq FX!32 system is used as a case study. The FX!32 system supports Windows/IA-32 guest binaries on a Windows/Alpha platform.

Performance is almost always an issue in VM implementations because performance is often lost during the emulation process. This loss can be mitigated by optimizing translated binaries, and Chapter 4 deals with ways of dynamically optimizing translated code. First, ways of increasing the size of translated code blocks are discussed, and then specific code optimizations are covered. Code optimizations include reordering instructions, to improve pipeline efficiency, for example, and a number of classical compiler optimizations, adapted to dynamically translated binary code. A special case occurs when the source ISA and target ISA are the same and optimization is the primary function provided by the VM. Consequently, Chapter 4 concludes with a discussion of special-case features of these same-ISA dynamic binary optimizers and includes the HP Dynamo system as a case study.

Chapters 5 and 6 discuss high-level language virtual machines. These virtual machines are designed to enable platform independence. To give some historical perspective, Chapter 5 begins with a description of Pascal P-code. Because modern HLL VMs are intended to support network-based computing and object-oriented programming, the features important for supporting these aspects are emphasized. The Java virtual machine architecture is described in some detail. Also included is a shorter discussion of the Microsoft common language infrastructure (CLI); where the goals and applications are somewhat broader than with Java, and the discussion is focused on those features that provide the added breadth. Chapter 6 describes the implementation of HLL VMs, beginning with basic implementation approaches and techniques. High-performance HLL VM implementations are then described, and the IBM Jikes research virtual machine is used as a case study.

Codesigned VMs, the first system-level virtual machines to be discussed, are the topic of Chapter 7. The codesigned VM paradigm includes special hardware support to enhance emulation performance. Consequently, much of the chapter focuses on hardware-based performance enhancements. The chapter includes case studies of the Transmeta Crusoe and IBM AS/400 system.

Chapter 8 covers conventional system VMs — that is, VMs that support multiple operating systems simultaneously, primarily relying on software techniques. Basic mechanisms for implementing system VMs and for enhancing their performance are discussed. Some ISAs are easier to virtualize than others, so features of instruction sets that make them more efficiently virtualized are discussed. The IBM 360–390+ series of VMs are described and used as a case study throughout the chapter. The more recently developed VMware hosted virtual machine, which is targeted at IA-32 platforms, is an important second case study.

Applying virtualization to multiprocessor systems is the topic of Chapter 9. Of major interest are techniques that allow the partitioning of resources in large shared-memory multiprocessors to form a number of smaller, virtual multiprocessors. These techniques can be implemented in a number of ways, ranging from those relying on microcode support to purely software solutions. Then ISA emulation in a multiprocessor context is discussed. Although most emulation techniques are the same as with uniprocessors, memory-ordering (consistency) constraints pose some new problems. In this chapter IBM logical partitioning (LPAR) and the Stanford Disco research VM are used as case studies.

Finally, Chapter 10, the concluding chapter, looks toward the future and considers a number of evolving VM applications that hold promise. These include support for system security, grid computing, and virtual system portability.

The book also includes an Appendix that reviews the important properties of real machines. The focus is on those aspects of architecture and implementation that are important when virtualization is performed. For some readers this will be familiar material, but other readers may benefit from browsing through the Appendix before proceeding with the book. The Appendix concludes with a brief overview of the IA-32 and PowerPC ISAs, on which many of the examples are based.

# Chapter Two
# Emulation: Interpretation and Binary Translation

**M**any virtual machine implementations are based on emulation. We define *emulation* as the process of implementing the interface and functionality of one system or subsystem on a system or subsystem having a different interface and functionality. For example, a VT100 terminal emulator running inside a window on a PC presents to the user an interface and functionality that is nearly identical to that of a real VT100 terminal. In fact, taken in this general sense, one could argue that virtualization itself is simply a form of emulation. In this chapter, however, we give emulation a narrower meaning by applying it specifically to instruction sets.

Instruction set emulation is a key aspect of many virtual machine implementations because the virtual machine must support a program binary compiled for an instruction set that is different from the one implemented by the host processor(s). For example, Intel IA-32 program binaries are more widely available than binaries for any other instruction set. Consequently, a user may wish to use a virtual machine to execute an IA-32 program binary on some other platform, for example, an Apple Macintosh, which incorporates a PowerPC processor. For high-level virtual machines, binary classes (using the Java terminology) incorporate a stack-based, bytecode instruction set that can be emulated on any of a number of different host platforms.

In terms of instruction sets, emulation allows a machine implementing one instruction set, the *target* instruction set, to reproduce the behavior of software compiled to another instruction set, the *source* instruction set. This is illustrated in Figure 2.1. Note that we use the terms *source* and *target* specifically

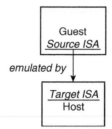

**Figure 2.1** Terms Describing the Emulation Process. *Emulation allows a guest to support a source instruction set while running on a host platform executing a target instruction set.*

for instruction set emulation, and we use the terms *guest* and *host* when referring to complete virtual machine environments and supporting platforms (which often involve more than just ISAs). The reader should also be aware that the literature often does not use consistent terminology when describing guest/host and source/target relationships.

For many virtual machine applications, it is important that the emulation of the instruction set be performed efficiently. The lower the overhead of emulation, the more attractive the virtual machine will be. This chapter will focus on techniques for emulation of conventional instruction sets that already have hardware implementations rather than those designed specifically for virtual machine implementation, such as the Java bytecode instruction set. The latter *virtual instruction sets* can be implemented with similar emulation techniques as conventional instruction sets, but they also have special properties and therefore can take advantage of other emulation techniques. High-level language VM-specific instruction sets will be discussed in Chapter 5.

A complete ISA consists of many parts, including the register set and memory architecture, the instructions, and the trap and interrupt architecture. A virtual machine implementation is usually concerned with all aspects of ISA emulation. In this chapter, however, we focus primarily on emulating the operation of user-level instructions in the absence of exceptions (traps and interrupts). The emulation of the memory addressing architecture, traps, interrupts, and other features are discussed in this chapter only as is necessary to understand instruction emulation. In Chapters 3 and 4, we extend the discussion to emulation of memory architecture, traps, and interrupts in the context of process virtual machines. In later chapters (primarily Chapters 7 and 8) we discuss emulation of system instructions and other ISA issues that are specific to system virtual machines.

To some degree, instruction emulation techniques can be applied to every type of VM we discuss in this book. Although we are interested primarily in the case where the source and target instruction sets are different, there are some virtual machine applications where the instruction sets are the same. In these situations, emulation may not be performed, strictly speaking, but the very same techniques are used for other purposes. One such application is same-ISA dynamic binary optimization, where a program binary is optimized at run time on the same platform for which it was originally compiled. Another example is in system VMs where the VMM must control and manage the execution of certain privileged guest OS instructions, and emulation-like techniques are used for this purpose.

Instruction set emulation can be carried out using a variety of methods that require different amounts of computing resources and offer different performance and portability characteristics. At one end of the spectrum is the straightforward technique of *interpretation*, while on the other is *binary translation*. Interpretation involves a cycle of fetching a source instruction, analyzing it, performing the required operation, and then fetching the next source instruction — all in software. Binary translation, on the other hand, attempts to amortize the fetch and analysis costs by translating a block of source instructions to a block of target instructions and saving the translated code for repeated use. In contrast to interpretation, binary translation has a bigger initial translation cost but a smaller execution cost. The choice of one or the other depends on the number of times a block of source code is expected to be executed by the guest software. Predictably, there are techniques that lie in between these extremes. For example, *threaded interpretation* eliminates the interpreter loop corresponding to the cycle mentioned earlier, and efficiency can be increased even further by predecoding the source instructions into a more efficiently interpretable intermediate form.

## 2.1 Basic Interpretation

Interpreters have a long and rich history. Some programming languages, e.g., the functional language LISP, rely on an interpreted implementation. Perl is a widely used language that is commonly implemented through interpretation. The FORTH language is probably better known for its "threaded code" interpretation model than for any other feature. A good reference is Debaere and Van Campenhout (1990). In this chapter, however, we are more interested in applying interpretation techniques to program binaries (machine code) rather than high-level languages.

In our narrower context, an interpreter program emulates and operates on the complete architected state of a machine implementing the source ISA, including all architected registers and main memory (Figure 2.2). The image

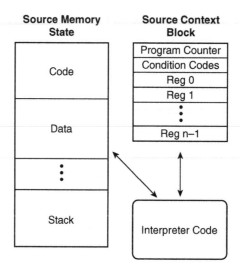

**Figure 2.2** Interpreter Overview. *An interpreter manages the complete architected state of a machine implementing the source ISA.*

of the guest memory, including both program code and program data, is kept in a region of memory maintained by the interpreter. The interpreter's memory also holds a table we call the *context block*, which contains the various components of the source's architected state, such as general-purpose registers, the program counter, condition codes, and miscellaneous control registers.

A simple interpreter operates by stepping through the source program, instruction by instruction, reading and modifying the source state according to the instruction. Such an interpreter is often referred to as a *decode-and-dispatch* interpreter, because it is structured around a central loop that *decodes* an instruction and then *dispatches* it to an interpretation routine based on the type of instruction. The structure of such an interpreter is shown in Figure 2.3 for the PowerPC source ISA.

The main interpreter loop is depicted at the top of Figure 2.3, and routines for interpreting the *Load Word and Zero* and *ALU* instructions are shown below the main loop. The *Load Word and Zero* instruction loads a 32-bit word into a 64-bit register and zeroes the upper 32-bits of the register; it is the basic PowerPC load word instruction. Note that in this example routine (and others to follow), for brevity we have omitted any checks for memory addressing errors; these would be included in most VMs. Sections 3.3 and 3.4 describe emulation of the memory-addressing architecture more completely. The *ALU* "instruction" is actually a stand-in for a number of PowerPC instructions that have the same primary opcode but are distinguished by different

```
while (!halt && !interrupt) {
    inst = code[PC];
    opcode = extract(inst,31,6);
    switch(opcode) {
        case LoadWordAndZero: LoadWordAndZero(inst);
        case ALU: ALU(inst);
        case Branch: Branch(inst);
        . . .}
}


Instruction function list

LoadWordAndZero(inst){
    RT = extract(inst,25,5);
    RA = extract(inst,20,5);
    displacement = extract(inst,15,16);
    if (RA == 0) source = 0;
    else source = regs[RA];
    address = source + displacement;
    regs[RT] = (data[address]<< 32) >> 32;
    PC = PC + 4;
}

ALU(inst){
    RT = extract(inst,25,5);
    RA = extract(inst,20,5);
    RB = extract(inst,15,5);
    source1 = regs[RA];
    source2 = regs[RB];
    extended_opcode = extract(inst,10,10);
    switch(extended_opcode) {
        case Add: Add(inst);
        case AddCarrying: AddCarrying(inst);
        case AddExtended: AddExtended(inst);
        . . .}
    PC = PC + 4;
}
```

**Figure 2.3**    Code for Interpreting the PowerPC Instruction Set Architecture. *A decode-and-dispatch loop uses a switch statement to call a number of routines that emulate individual instructions. The extract(inst, i, j) function extracts a bit field of length j from inst, beginning at bit i.*

extended opcodes. For instructions of this type, two levels of decoding (via switch statements) are used. The decode-and-dispatch loop is illustrated here in a high-level language, but it is easy to see how the same routines could be written in assembly language for higher performance.

In Figure 2.3, the architected source program counter is held in a variable called PC. This variable is used as an index into an array that holds the source binary image. The word addressed by this index is the source instruction that needs to be interpreted. The opcode field of the instruction, represented by the 6-bit field starting at bit 31,[1] is extracted using shift and mask operations contained in the extract function. The opcode field is used in a switch statement to determine a routine for interpreting the specific instruction. Register designator fields and immediate data in the instruction are decoded similarly using the extract function. The register designator fields are used as indices into the context block to determine the actual source operand values. The interpreter routine then emulates the operation specified by the source instruction. Unless the instruction itself modifies the program counter, as in a branch, the program counter must be explicitly incremented to point to the next sequential instruction before the routine returns back to the decode-dispatch loop of the interpreter.

The example of Figure 2.3 shows that, while the process of interpretation is quite straightforward, the performance cost of interpretation can be quite high. Even if the interpreter code were written directly in assembly language, interpreting a single instruction like the *Load Word and Zero* instruction could involve the execution of tens of instructions in the target ISA.

## 2.2 Threaded Interpretation

While simple to write and understand, a decode-and-dispatch interpreter can be quite slow. In this and subsequent sections, we will identify techniques to reduce or eliminate some of its inefficiencies. We begin by looking at *threaded interpretation* (Klint 1981).

The central dispatch loop of a decode-and-dispatch interpreter contains a number of branch instructions, both direct and indirect. Depending on the hardware implementation, these branches tend to reduce performance, particularly if they are difficult to predict (Ertl and Gregg 2001, 2003). Besides the test for a halt or an interrupt at the top of the loop, there is a register indirect branch for the switch statement, a branch to the interpreter routine, a second register indirect branch to return from the interpreter routine, and, finally, a branch that terminates the loop. By appending a portion of the dispatch code to the end of each of the instruction interpretation routines, as shown in Figure 2.4, it is possible to remove three of the branches just listed. A remaining branch is register indirect and replaces the switch statement branch found in the central dispatch loop. That is, in order to interpret the next instruction it is

---

**1.** PowerPC actually numbers the most significant bit (msb) 0; we use the convention that the msb is 31.

*Instruction function list*

```
LoadWordAndZero:
    RT = extract(inst,25,5);
    RA = extract(inst,20,5);
    displacement = extract(inst,15,16);
    if (RA == 0) source = 0;
    else source = regs[RA];
    address = source + displacement;
    regs[RT] = (data(address)<< 32) >> 32;
    PC = PC + 4;
    If (halt || interrupt) goto exit;
    inst = code[PC];
    opcode = extract(inst,31,6);
    extended_opcode = extract(inst,10,10);
    routine = dispatch[opcode,extended_opcode];
    goto *routine;

Add:
    RT = extract(inst,25,5);
    RA = extract(inst,20,5);
    RB = extract(inst,15,5);
    source1 = regs[RA];
    source2 = regs[RB];
    sum = source1 + source2;
    regs[RT] = sum;
    PC = PC + 4;
    If (halt || interrupt) goto exit;
    inst = code[PC];
    opcode = extract(inst,31,6);
    extended_opcode = extract(inst,10,10);
    routine = dispatch[opcode,extended_opcode];
    goto *routine;
```

**Figure 2.4**    Two Threaded Interpreter Routines for PowerPC Code. *With threaded interpretation, the central dispatch loop is no longer needed.*

necessary to load the opcode of the next instruction, look up the address of the relevant interpreter routine using the dispatch table, and jump to the routine.

Figure 2.5 illustrates the differences in data and control flow between the decode-and-dispatch method and the threaded interpreter technique just described. Figure 2.5a shows native execution on the source ISA, Figure 2.5b shows the decode-and-dispatch method, and Figure 2.5c illustrates threaded interpretation. The centralized nature of the dispatch loop is evident from Figure 2.5b. Control flow continually exits from, and returns to, the central dispatch loop. On the other hand, with threaded interpretation (Figure 2.5c) the actions of the dispatch loop in fetching and decoding the next instruction are replicated in each of the interpreter routines. The interpreter routines are not subroutines in the usual sense; they are simply pieces of code that are "threaded" together.

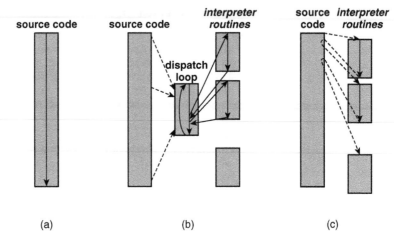

**Figure 2.5** Interpretation Methods. *Control flow is indicated via solid arrows and data accesses with dotted arrows. The data accesses are used by the interpreter to read individual source instructions. (a) Native execution; (b) decode-and-dispatch interpretation; (c) threaded interpretation.*

A key property of threaded interpretation, as just described, is that dispatch occurs indirectly through a table. Among the advantages of this indirection is that the interpretation routines can be modified and relocated independently. Because the jump through the dispatch table is indirect, this method is called *indirect* threaded interpretation (Dewar 1975).

## 2.3 Predecoding and Direct Threaded Interpretation

Although the centralized dispatch loop has been eliminated in the indirect threaded interpreter, there remains the overhead created by the centralized dispatch table. Looking up an interpreter routine in this table still requires a memory access and a register indirect branch. It would be desirable, for even better efficiency, to eliminate the access to the centralized table.

A further observation is that an interpreter routine is invoked every time an instruction is encountered. Thus, when the same source instruction is interpreted multiple times, the process of examining the instruction and extracting its various fields must be repeated for each dynamic instance of the instruction. For example, as shown in Figure 2.3, extracting instruction fields takes several interpreter instructions for a *Load Word and Zero* instruction. It would appear to be more efficient to perform these repeated operations just once, save away the extracted information in an intermediate form, and then reuse it each time the instruction is emulated. This process, called *predecoding*, is discussed in the following subsections. It will be shown that predecoding enables a more efficient threaded interpretation technique, *direct threaded interpretation* (Bell 1973; Kogge 1982).

### 2.3.1 Basic Predecoding

Predecoding involves parsing an instruction and putting it in a form that simplifies interpretation. In particular, predecoding extracts pieces of information and places them into easily accessible fields (Magnusson and Samuelsson 1994; Larus 1991). For example, in the PowerPC ISA, all the basic ALU instructions, such as and, or, add, and subtract, are specified using a combination of the opcode bits and extended opcode bits. They all have the same primary opcode (31) and are distinguished by the extended opcode bits that appear at the low-order end of the instruction word, far away from the opcode. Predecoding can combine this information into a single operation code. Also, register specifiers can be extracted from the source binary and placed into byte-aligned fields so that they may be accessed directly with byte load instructions.

Basic predecoding of the PowerPC ISA is illustrated in Figure 2.6. Figure 2.6a contains a small PowerPC code sequence. This sequence loads a data item from memory and adds it to a register, accumulating a sum. The sum is then stored

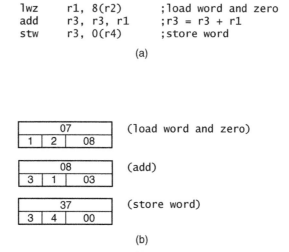

```
lwz     r1, 8(r2)      ;load word and zero
add     r3, r3, r1     ;r3 = r3 + r1
stw     r3, 0(r4)      ;store word
```
(a)

(b)

**Figure 2.6**   Predecoded PowerPC Instructions. *The extended opcode and opcode of the add instruction are merged into a single predecoded opcode. (a) PowerPC source code. (b) PowerPC program in predecoded intermediate form.*

back to memory. Figure 2.6b is the same code, in a predecoded intermediate form. This predecoded format uses a single word to encode the operation, found by combining the opcode and function codes as discussed earlier. Consequently, these codes need *not* be the same as the source ISA opcodes, and in the example given they are not. A second predecode word is used for holding the various instruction fields, in a sparse, byte-aligned format. When immediate or offset data are given, a 16-bit field is available. Overall, this yields an intermediate instruction format that is less densely encoded than the original source instructions but more easily accessed by an interpreter.

The *Load Word and Zero* interpreter routine operating on the predecoded intermediate code of Figure 2.6 is given in Figure 2.7. Here, we predecode into an array of instruction structs, which is adequate for the example instructions but would be more elaborate for the full PowerPC ISA. In this example, the interpreter routines for the predecoded intermediate form are slightly simpler than the corresponding routines given earlier in Figure 2.3, and the benefits of predecoding for the PowerPC ISA appear to be relatively small. However, for CISC ISAs, with their many varied formats, the benefits can be greater. In addition, predecoding enables an additional performance optimization, direct threading, to be described in the next subsection.

```
struct instruction {
        unsigned long op;
        unsigned char dest;
        unsigned char src1;
        unsigned int src2;
        } code [CODE_SIZE]

            .
            .
            .
Load Word and Zero:
        RT = code[TPC].dest;
        RA = code[TPC].src1;
        displacement = code[TPC].src2;
        if (RA == 0) source = 0;
        else source = regs[RA];
        address = source + displacement;
        regs[RT] = (data[address]<< 32) >> 32;
        SPC = SPC + 4;
        TPC = TPC + 1;
        If (halt || interrupt) goto exit;
        opcode = code[TPC].op;
        routine = dispatch[opcode];
        goto *routine;
```

**Figure 2.7**    Threaded Interpreter Code for PowerPC *Load Word And Zero* Instruction After Predecoding.

Because the intermediate code exists separately from the original source binary, a separate target program counter (TPC) is added for sequencing through the intermediate code. However, the source ISA program counter (SPC) is also maintained. The SPC keeps the correct architected source state, and the TPC is used for actually fetching the predecoded instructions. In general, with CISC variable-length instructions, the TPC and SPC values at any given time may bear no clear relationship, so it is necessary to maintain them both. With fixed-length RISC instructions, however, the relationship can be relatively easy to calculate, provided the intermediate form is also of fixed length.

### 2.3.2 Direct Threaded Interpretation

Although it has advantages for portability, the indirection caused by the dispatch table also has a performance cost: A memory lookup is required whenever the table is accessed. To get rid of the level of indirection caused by the dispatch table lookup, the instruction codes contained in the intermediate code can be replaced with the actual addresses of the interpreter routines (Bell 1973). This is illustrated in Figure 2.8.

Interpreter code for direct threading is given in Figure 2.9. This code is very similar to the indirect threaded code, except the dispatch table lookup is removed. The address of the interpreter routine is loaded from a field in the intermediate code, and a register indirect jump goes directly to the routine. Although fast, this causes the intermediate form to become dependent on the exact locations of the interpreter routines and consequently limits portability. If the interpreter code is ported to a different target machine, it must be regenerated for the target machine that executes it. However, there are programming techniques and compiler features that can mitigate this problem to some extent. For example, the gcc compiler has a unary operator (&&) that takes the address

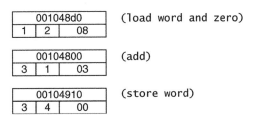

**Figure 2.8**    Intermediate Form for Direct Threaded Interpretation. *The opcode in the intermediate form is replaced with the address of the interpreter routine.*

```
Load Word and Zero:
    RT = code[TPC].dest;
    RA = code[TPC].src1;
    displacement = code[TPC].src2;
    if (RA == 0) source = 0;
    else source = regs[RA];
    address = source + displacement;
    regs[RT] = (data[address]<< 32) >> 32;
    SPC = SPC + 4;
    TPC = TPC + 1;
    If (halt || interrupt) goto exit;
    routine = code[TPC].op;
    goto *routine;
```

**Figure 2.9**   Example of Direct Threaded Interpreter Code.

of a label. This operator can then be used to generate portable direct threaded code by finding the addresses of the labels that begin each of the interpreter routines and placing them in the predecoded instructions. The interpreter can also be made relocatable by replacing the absolute routine addresses with relative addresses (with respect to some routine base address).

## 2.4   Interpreting a Complex Instruction Set

Thus far, when describing basic interpretation techniques, it has been useful to center the discussion on fairly simple instruction sets. A RISC ISA, the PowerPC, was used in our examples. Similarly, virtual instruction sets, such as Pascal P-code and Java bytecodes — to be discussed in Chapter 5 — are designed specifically for emulation and can be interpreted using the techniques described above in a straightforward manner. In practice, however, one of the most commonly emulated instructions sets is not a RISC or a simple virtual ISA; rather it is a CISC — the Intel IA-32. In this section we consider the additional aspects (and complexities) of interpretation that are brought about by a CISC ISA, using the IA-32 as the example.

One of the hallmarks of a modern RISC ISA such as the PowerPC is the regular instruction formats. That is, all instructions have the same length, typically 32 bits, and the instruction formats are fairly regular, for example, the register specifiers usually appear in the same bit positions across instruction formats. It is this regularity that makes many of the steps of interpretation straightforward. For example, the interpreter can extract the opcode and then immediately dispatch to the indicated instruction interpreter routine. Similarly, each of the instruction interpretation routines can extract operands and complete the emulation process simply.

Many CISC instruction sets, on the other hand, have a wide variety of formats, variable instruction lengths, and even variable field lengths. In some ISAs the variability in instruction formats was intended to increase code density and "orthogonality" of the instruction set. The VAX ISA is a good example (Brunner 1991); in the VAX, every operand can be specified with any of the many addressing modes. In other ISAs, the variability reflects the evolution of the instruction set over time, where a number of extensions and new features have been added, while maintaining compatibility with older versions. The IA-32 is a good example of this evolutionary process. The IA-32 started as an instruction set for 16-bit microcontroller chips with physical addressing and dense instruction encodings and eventually evolved into a high-performance, 32-bit general-purpose processor supporting virtual memory. This evolutionary process continues, and it has recently been further extended to 64 bits.

### 2.4.1 Interpretation of the IA-32 ISA

Figure 2.10 illustrates the general form of an IA-32 instruction. It begins with from zero to four prefix bytes. These indicate if there is repetition for string instructions and/or if there are overrides for addressing segments, address sizes, and operand sizes. Then after the prefix byte(s) (if any), there is an opcode byte, which may be followed by a second opcode byte, depending on the value of the first. Next comes an optional addressing-form specifier ModR/M. The specifier is optional, in the sense that it is present only for certain opcodes and generally indicates an addressing mode and register. The SIB byte is present for only certain ModR/M encodings, and it indicates a base register, an index register, and a scale factor for indexing. The optional, variable-length displacement field is present for certain memory-addressing modes. The last field is a variable-length immediate operand, if required by the opcode.

Because of all the variations and the presence or absence of some fields, depending on the values in others, a straightforward approach to interpreting a CISC ISA, and the IA-32 ISA in particular, is to divide instruction interpretation into two major phases, as illustrated in Figure 2.11. The first phase scans and decodes the various instruction fields. As it does so, it fills in fields of a

| Prefixes | Opcode | Opcode | ModR/M | SIB | Displacement | Immediate |
|----------|--------|--------|--------|-----|--------------|-----------|
| 0 to 4 | | optional | optional | optional | 0,1,2,4 bytes | 0,1,2,4 bytes |

**Figure 2.10**　General Format for IA-32 Instructions.

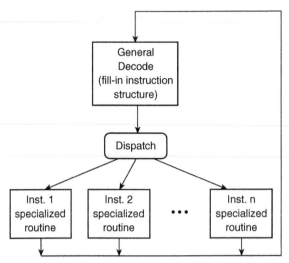

**Figure 2.11**    Program Flow for a Basic CISC ISA Interpreter.

general instruction template. This template, in essence, contains a superset of the possible instruction options. Then there is a dispatch step that jumps to routines specialized for each instruction type. These routines emulate the specified instruction, reading values from the relevant instruction template fields as needed.

Figure 2.12 is a three-page figure that contains pseudo C code for such an interpreter, styled after the approach used in the Bochs free software IA-32 interpreter (Lawton). Not all procedures used in the example are given, but where their code is not present, they are given mnemonic names that summarize their function. Interpretation is focused on an instruction template, the structure IA-32instr, which is defined at the top of Figure 2.12a. The major CPU interpreter loop is at the bottom of Figure 2.12b. This loop begins interpreting an instruction by filling in the instruction template. Included in the instruction template is a pointer to an instruction interpreter routine. After the template is built, the CPU loop uses the pointer to jump to the indicated routine. Some instructions can be repeated (based on a prefix byte), and this is determined by the "need_to_repeat" test.

The IA-32instr structure consists of the opcode (up to two bytes), a mask that collects the prefixes (up to a total of 12 possible prefixes), a value that contains the instruction length and a pointer to the instruction interpretation routine. Then there are a number of substructures used for collecting operand information. As is the case with the structure as a whole, these are defined to contain a superset of the operand information for all the instructions. The total size of the structure is on the order of 6 words.

The code that fills in the template structure is given at the top of Figure 2.12b. This code scans an instruction from left to right, first looking for prefix bytes and filling in the prefix mask. It then determines whether the opcode is one or two bytes, and uses the opcode to do a table lookup to find a decode action and a pointer to the routine that will eventually be used to interpret the instruction. The lookup table is the second of the major data structures used for interpretation, shown at the bottom of Figure 2.12a. The lookup table returns a pair: <DecodeAction, InterpreterFunctionPointer>. DecodeAction contains addressing mode information, the presence or absence

```
struct IA-32instr {
  unsigned short opcode;
  unsigned short prefixmask;
  char ilen; // instruction length.

  InterpreterFunctionPointer execute; // semantic routine for this instr.

  struct {
    // general address computation: [Rbase + (Rindex << shmt) + displacement]
    char mode;       // operand addressing mode, including register operand.
    char Rbase;      // base address register
    char Rindex;     // index register
    char shmt;       // index scale factor
    long displacement;
  } operandRM;

  struct {
    char mode;       // either register or immediate.
    char regname;    // register number
    long immediate;// immediate value
  } operandRI;
} instr;



//
// BIG fetch_decode table indexed by the opcode
//
IA-32OpcodeInfo_t IA-32_fetch_decode_table[] =
{
  { DecodeAction, InterpreterFunctionPointer},
  { DecodeAction, InterpreterFunctionPointer},
  { DecodeAction, InterpreterFunctionPointer},
  .................

};
```

**Figure 2.12a**   Major Data Structures for an IA-32 Interpreter. *Instruction template and decode table.*

```
IA-32instr
IA-32_FetchDecode(PC){
    fetch_ptr = PC;

    // 1. parse prefixes
    byte = code[++fetch_ptr];
    while (is_IA-32_prefix(byte)) {
        add_prefix_attribute(byte, instr);
        byte = code[++fetch_ptr];
    }

    // 2. parse opcode
    instr.opcode = byte;        // its code[fetch_ptr];
    if (instr.opcode == 0x0f){
        instr.opcode = 0x100 | code[++fetch_ptr]; // 2 Byte opcode.
    }

    // 3. Table Look up based on opcode to find action and function pointer.
    decode_action = IA-32_fetch_decode_table[instr.opcode].DecodeAction;
    instr.execute =
            IA-
32_fetch_decode_table[instr.opcode].InterpreterFunctionPointer;
    // Semantic routines for IA-32 instrs, e.g., ADD_RX_32b(IA-32instr i);

    // 4. Operand Resolution -- setup the operandRI and operandRM fields above.
    if (need_Mod_RM(decode_action)) {
        parse_Mod_RM_byte(instr);
        if (need_SIB_byte(instr->operandRM.mode)) fetch_SIB_byte(instr);
        if (need_displacement(instr->operandRM.mode)) fetch_displacement(instr);
    }
    if (need_immediate(decode_action)) fetch_immediate(instr);

    // 5. bookkeeping and return.
    instr.ilen = bytes_fetched_for_this_instr;
    return instr;
}

void cpu_loop()
{
    while (!halt) {
        instr = IA-32_FetchDecode(PC);
        if (!IA-32_string_instruction) {
            instr.execute();
        }
        else {
            while(need_to_repeat(instr.prefixmask))
                instr.execute();
                handle_asyn_event();    // i.e. an interrupt
            }
        }
        PC = PC + instr.ilen;
        handle_asyn_event();
    }
}
```

**Figure 2.12b**   Template-Filling Routine and Major Emulation Loop for IA-32 Interpreter.

*Instruction function list*

```
// ADD: register + Reg/Mem --> register
void
ADD_RX_32b(IA-32instr instr)        // X means: either Reg or Mem{
    unsigned op1_32, op2_32, sum_32;
    op1_32 = IA-32_GPR[instr.operandRI.regname];
    if (mem_operand(instr.operandRM.mode)) {
        unsigned mem_addr = resolve_mem_address(instr);
        op2_32 = virtual_mem[mem_addr];
}
    else {
        op2_32 = IA-32_GPR[instr.operandRM.Rbase];
    }
    sum_32 = op1_32 + op2_32;
    IA-32_GPR[instr.operandRI.regname] = sum_32;
    SET_IA-32_CC_FLAGS(op1_32, op2_32, sum_32, IA-32_INSTR_ADD32);
}


void
ADD_XR_32b(IA-32instr instr)
{


}


void
ADD_RI_32b(IA-32instr instr)
{


}
```

**Figure 2.12c**   Instruction Interpretation Routines for an IA-32 Decode-and-Dispatch Interpreter.

of immediate values, etc., and the `InstructionFunctionPointer` is a pointer to a specific interpreter routine. Finally, the operand specifiers are decoded and displacement and immediate values are filled in.

Figure 2.12c illustrates the instruction function list, with one (of the many) instructions, a 32-bit add instruction, being given in detail. This interpreter routine uses information from the `IA-32instr` template as it executes. After interpretation is complete, the CPU loop increments the program counter and proceeds to the next instruction.

A basic decode-and-dispatch interpreter as just described is well structured and relatively easy to understand, but it will be quite slow. One reason for this slowness is its generality. That is, it does all the sequential decoding first, covering all possible cases, before it proceeds to an instruction interpretation

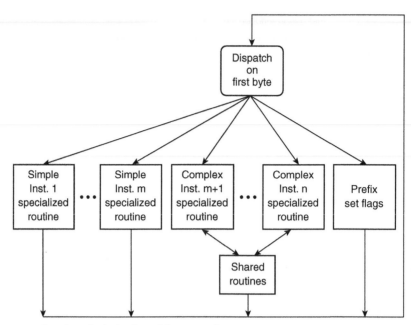

**Figure 2.13**    Interpreter Based on Optimization of Common Cases.

routine. A more efficient interpreter can be built around the principle: "make the common case fast." For the IA-32 ISA, the common case is: (1) no prefix bytes, (2) a single-byte opcode, (3) simple operand specifiers, often just registers. Based on these observations, an interpreter can be structured along the lines illustrated in Figure 2.13. This interpreter first dispatches to a routine based on the first instruction byte (alternatively, two bytes could be used, with a much larger dispatch table). Then these simpler, common instructions are interpreted immediately via specialized routines that decode the remainder of the instruction bytes. For the less common cases, there are more complex interpretation routines that may share routines for the more involved operations. If the first byte should happen to be a prefix, then its value can be recorded, with control returning to the dispatch code. With this implementation, a sequence of simple IA-32 instructions will be emulated relatively quickly, very much like an equivalent sequence of RISC instructions.

### 2.4.2 Threaded Interpretation

Recall that with threaded interpretation, decode-and-dispatch code is appended to the end of every instruction interpretation routine. For a RISC, as we saw earlier, this is a relatively small amount of code and results in the removal of several branch instructions. However, if the complex decode routine for the IA-32 ISA, illustrated in Figure 2.12b, were to be appended to every instruction interpretation routine, the interpreter would become very large, and any performance improvement would be relatively small. Consequently, to implement a threaded interpreter for a CISC ISA, one should append a simple decode-and-dispatch routine, optimized for the common cases, to each instruction interpretation routine and use a centralized decode-and-dispatch routine for the more complex cases. This is illustrated in Figure 2.14, where simple instructions are threaded from one to the next but where, when a complex case is encountered, a centralized decode routine is executed, followed by a dispatch to an instruction interpretation routine. In effect this is a hybrid of the decode-and-dispatch and threaded methods.

If predecoding and direct threaded interpretation are to be used for a CISC ISA, there are two significant problems. The first is that a general, fixed-length predecoded instruction format would probably look very similar to the instruction template IA-32instr used in the decode-and-dispatch interpreter. This would lead to a very large predecoded program. In this case, each

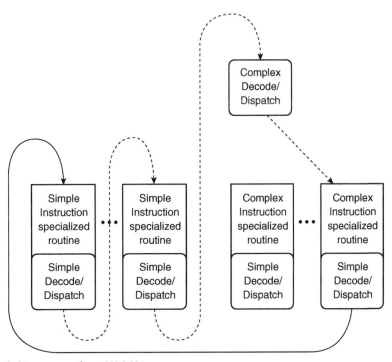

**Figure 2.14**   Threaded Interpreter for a CISC ISA.

instruction consumes about six words. An alternative is to use a small number of intermediate predecoded forms with some specialization for instruction types. Or one can predecode a single CISC instruction into multiple, simple, predecoded instruction forms. This is very similar to binary translation to a RISC ISA (binary translation is covered in the next section).

The second significant problem that occurs with predecoding most CISC ISAs is the need to perform *code discovery*. Ordinarily, the predecoding step operates on a program binary *before* instructions are interpreted. With variable-length instructions, however, it is not always practical, (or may be even possible) to scan a binary and correctly identify all instruction boundaries or, in some cases, to separate data from instructions. The code-discovery problem also occurs with binary translation and is described in more detail in Section 2.6. Because of the code-discovery problem, predecoding a conventional CISC ISA becomes an iterative, two-stage process, with simple decode-and-dispatch interpretation first being used to discover instructions, followed by predecoding into an intermediate form and direct threaded interpretation. Overall, this is very similar to the staged emulation methods incorporating binary translation, to be discussed later in this chapter.

Based on the foregoing, one could conclude that predecoding a CISC ISA is so similar to binary translation that one should simply perform binary translation and be done with it. However, predecoding, as opposed to binary translation, has one major advantage: better portability. With binary translation, there must be a code generator specialized for every target ISA, although retargetable binary translators have been developed (Cifuentes, Lewis, and Ung 2002; Scott et al. 2003). With predecoding, the intermediate form remains largely platform independent, and the interpreter routines can be written in a portable high-level language. Hence, one can combine a simple RISC-like intermediate form with fast direct threaded interpreter routines and a staged interpretation strategy, to arrive at a high-performance yet portable interpreter for a CISC ISA.

### 2.4.3 A High-Performance IA-32 Interpreter

We conclude this section on CISC interpretation with an example that illustrates features of an IA-32 decode-and-dispatch interpreter optimized for speed. The example is based roughly on a description of an IA-32 interpreter used as part of the DEC/Compaq FX!32 system (Chernoff et al. 1998; Hookway and Herdeg 1997). In the FX!32 system, the 32-bit IA-32 architecture is emulated on a 64-bit Alpha platform. This particular interpreter is written in assembly language, which makes it nonportable but allows very highly optimized code. In this example, we use assembly code similar to that described for the FX!32; however, it is written using 64-bit PowerPC code rather than Alpha code. The interpreter uses a decode-and-dispatch style that is specialized for the common cases.

The main loop uses the technique of *software pipelining* (Lam 1988) to interleave different phases of program interpretation in the same inner loop in order to reduce execution time. The following are the key registers used in the dispatch loop, along with a brief description of their usage.

*r1* and *r2* hold a byte stream of prefetched IA-32 instructions; a minimum of 8 bytes of prefetched instructions are kept.

*r3* holds the instruction buffer length; this register is used not in the main dispatch loop but in the buffer maintenance routine.

*r4,* at the top of the loop, holds the length of the current instruction (in bits).

*r5* is loaded with the upper two bytes of the next instruction; these two bytes contain sufficient information to determine both the opcode and the length of the next instruction.

*r6* holds a pointer to the interpretation routine for the current instruction.

*r7* is loaded with a pointer to the interpretation routine for the next instruction.

*r8* points to the dispatch table of interpreter routines; each entry is 8 bytes.

*r9* points to a table of IA-32 instruction lengths; each entry is 1 byte.

*r10* holds an instruction pointer that is used for prefetching from the IA-32 code stream.

*r11* is loaded with 8 bytes of prefetched IA-32 instructions; these prefetched instructions are used by buffer maintenance code (not shown).

The decoding of instructions is layered, with the common cases being handled more efficiently. Most instructions in the IA-32 instruction set have 6 bytes or fewer. Hence the dispatch loop is optimized for this case. Figure 2.15 shows the central dispatch loop. The first two instructions in the routine perform a check on the instruction length; if the length is greater than 6, then it requires special handling and there is a branch to routine long_inst (not shown). The next three instructions of the routine extract the first 2 bytes of the *next* IA-32 instruction to be interpreted and convert it to a double-word (8 bytes) offset placed in r5. As mentioned earlier, the first 2 bytes of an IA-32 instruction contain information about the length of an instruction as well as its opcode.

```
loop:
        cmpwi   cr0,r4,48           ;compare length (in r4) with 48 (bits)
        bgt     cr0, long_inst      ;branch to long_inst if length > 48
        sld     r5,r1,r4            ;shift instruction I+1 into r5
        extrdi  r4,r5,16,0          ;extract upper 2 bytes of I+1 from "buffer"
        sldi    r5,r4,3             ;multiply by 8: convert to double word offset
        lbzx    r4,r4,r9            ;look up instruction length for I+1
        ldx     r7,r5,r8            ;look up interpreter routine for I+1
        ld      r11,0(r10)          ;prefetch next 8 bytes
        mtctr   r6                  ;move I's interpreter routine pointer into ctr
        bctrl                       ;dispatch I; branch to ctr and link
        mr      r6,r7               ;move register; to maintain software pipeline
        b       loop                ;continue loop
```

**Figure 2.15**   Main Dispatch Loop for High-Performance IA-32 Interpreter Code Written in 64-Bit PowerPC Assembly Language.

The next three instructions perform a series of memory loads. The first two are table lookups to find the length of the next source instruction and a pointer to its interpreter routine. In both cases the tables contain 64K entries because they are indexed with the upper 2 IA-32 instruction bytes. This approach leads to some redundancy in the table because 2 bytes are not always required to determine the operation type and instruction length, but a direct table lookup reduces the number of instructions required significantly. The third load instruction prefetches the next 8 instruction bytes, using the instruction prefetch pointer held in r10. This is part of the instruction buffer mechanism described later. After the three loads are issued, the current instruction is dispatched for interpretation via a branch and link instruction. Finally, r7 is copied into r6 to maintain the software pipeline as the "next" instruction becomes the "current" instruction.

The key point in organizing the dispatch loop in a software-pipelined fashion is to overlap the three loads related to future source instructions with the interpretation of the current instruction. If any of these three loads misses in the data cache, then the miss delay will be overlapped with the current instruction interpretation that follows. Perhaps this feature is most critical for prefetching instruction bytes (load of r11), because this particular load has a higher probability of missing in the cache. Note that IA-32 instructions are actually *data* as far as the interpreter code is concerned, and they contend for the data cache along with the actual IA-32 data.

In addition to the dispatch code, there must also be code (not shown) to manage the instruction prefetch buffer, held in registers r1 and r2. This buffer-maintenance code is executed as part of each interpreter routine. For instructions that cause a transfer of control (e.g., a branch or jump), the register buffer is filled with instructions from the target of the control transfer, and the various registers are updated appropriately. For all other instructions the buffer-maintenance code shifts the instruction buffer "up" by the length of the instruction just completed. For any given instruction, this is a length that is known by the interpretation routine. The buffer shift involves shifting the upper buffer r1 and filling it in from below with instruction bytes from r2. The buffer length (held in r3) is decremented and checked to see if the number of buffered bytes has fallen below 8. If it has, the prefetched instruction word (in r11 from the dispatch loop) is copied into the lower buffer r2, and the buffers are adjusted. Register r10 is maintained as a pointer to the next block of instructions to be prefetched.

With respect to performance, the FX!32 developers report that their hand-optimized decode-and-dispatch interpreter takes an average of 45 Alpha instructions to emulate a single IA-32 instruction (Chernoff et al. 1998). Because IA-32 instructions are more complex than the Alpha RISC instructions, they further estimate that it takes about 30 Alpha instructions per IA-32 Pentium Pro micro-operation (the rough equivalent of a RISC instruction).

## 2.5  Binary Translation

With predecoding, all source instructions of the same type are executed with the same interpretation routine. For example, all *load word and zero* instructions, irrespective of the actual registers used, are executed with the code given in Figure 2.9. Performance can be significantly enhanced by mapping each individual source binary instruction to its own customized target code. This process of converting the source binary program into a target binary program is referred to as *binary translation* (May 1987; Sites et al. 1993). Figure 2.16 shows an example of binary translation from a small IA-32 program sequence to the PowerPC ISA. Note that in this and following examples, the emulation of IA-32 condition codes is omitted for simplicity. Emulation of condition codes is discussed separately in Section 2.8.2.

The architected register values of the IA-32 source instructions are maintained in a register context block held in memory and are fetched into the registers of the target PowerPC ISA. Some of the target registers are permanently assigned to either contain or point to certain important and frequently used source resources. For example, r1 points to the register context block, r2 points to the memory image of the source machine, and the program counter is held in r3. The process of mapping source registers to target registers, as in the case of the program counter, is a very clear example of the guest-to-host

```
addl    %edx,4(%eax)
movl    4(%eax),%edx
add     %eax,4
```

(a)

```
r1 points to IA-32 register context block
r2 points to IA-32 memory image
r3 contains IA-32 ISA PC value

lwz     r4,0(r1)        ;load %eax from register block
addi    r5,r4,4         ;add 4 to %eax
lwzx    r5,r2,r5        ;load operand from memory
lwz     r4,12(r1)       ;load %edx from register block
add     r5,r4,r5        ;perform add
stw     r5,12(r1)       ;put result into %edx
addi    r3,r3,3         ;update PC (3 bytes)

lwz     r4,0(r1)        ;load %eax from register block
addi    r5,r4,4         ;add 4 to %eax
lwz     r4,12(r1)       ;load %edx from register block
stwx    r4,r2,r5        ;store %edx value into memory
addi    r3,r3,3         ;update PC (3 bytes)

lwz     r4,0(r1)        ;load %eax from register block
addi    r4,r4,4         ;add immediate
stw     r4,0(r1)        ;place result back into %eax
addi    r3,r3,3         ;update PC (3 bytes)
```

(b)

**Figure 2.16**  Binary Translation from an IA-32 Binary to a PowerPC Binary. *(a) Intel IA-32 source binary sequence. (b) PowerPC target binary.*

*state mapping* that is a basic part of the virtualization process, as discussed at the beginning of Chapter 1.

Figure 2.17 compares predecoding (with threaded interpretation) and binary translation. In both cases, the original source code is converted to another form. But in the case of predecoding, interpreter routines are still needed, while in binary translation the converted code is directly executed.

As shown in Figure 2.16, binary translated code may keep the target registers in a register context block held in memory, just as with interpretation. However, because each instruction translation is customized, state mapping can be used to map the registers in the source ISA directly to target ISA registers. By enabling the direct access of registers in the target code, memory accesses

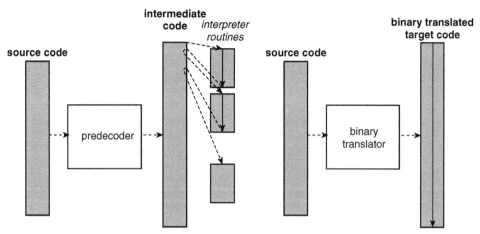

**Figure 2.17** Threaded Interpretation, Using Intermediate Code, and Binary Translation.

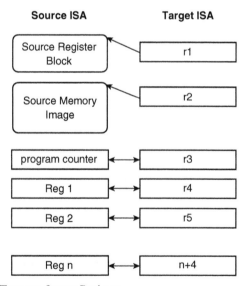

**Figure 2.18** State Mapping from Target to Source Registers.

to the context block is eliminated. Such state mapping, especially of general-purpose registers, is generally not employed in interpreters, except perhaps for special registers that are implied by the opcode, such as the program counter or a condition code register.

Figure 2.18 illustrates state mapping. Here, some of the target ISA registers point to the memory image and register block of the source ISA (as before).

```
            r1 points to IA-32 register context block
            r2 points to IA-32 memory image
            r3 contains IA-32 ISA PC value
            r4 holds IA-32 register %eax
            r7 holds IA-32 register %edx


            addi    r16,r4,4        ;add 4 to %eax
            lwzx    r17,r2,r16      ;load operand from memory
            add     r7,r17,r7       ;perform add of %edx
            addi    r16,r4,4        ;add 4 to %eax
            stwx    r7,r2,r16       ;store %edx value into memory
            addi    r4,r4,4         ;increment %eax
            addi    r3,r3,9         ;update PC (9 bytes)
```

**Figure 2.19**  Binary Translation with State Mapping Maintained over Translation Block Boundaries.

In addition, some of the target registers are mapped directly to some of the source registers; that is, source values are maintained in target registers. Other portions of the source state, such as the program counter and the stack pointer, may also be held in target registers. After mapping is performed, some target registers should be left over for use by the emulator code. Further discussion of register state mapping is in Section 2.8.1.

Binary translation with register state mapping is illustrated in Figure 2.19, where the three IA-32 instructions in Figure 2.16 are translated to seven PowerPC instructions, only one of which is involved in updating the source program counter. The speed of execution of the translated code now starts becoming comparable to the original source code. Furthermore, this sequence can be reduced even more through optimization (as will be described in Chapter 4); for example, the second instance of the common subexpression "addi  r16,r4,4" can be eliminated.

## 2.6  Code Discovery and Dynamic Translation

### 2.6.1  The Code-Discovery Problem

From the preceding discussion one might infer that it is possible to predecode or binary translate a program in its entirety before beginning emulation. This is referred to as *static predecoding* or *static translation* because only static (pre-execution) program information is used. There are many situations, however, where such a static approach is difficult, if not impossible, to implement (Horspool and Marovac 1980).

Consider the following scenario. A sequence of instructions is being translated and an indirect jump instruction is encountered. The target of such a jump is held in a register. With static predecoding or static translation, it is difficult (or practically impossible) to determine the register contents (and the target of the jump instruction) because the register isn't assigned a value until run time. Furthermore, if an attempt is made to proceed with predecoding or translating the instructions immediately following the jump, there is no guarantee that the locations immediately following the jump contain valid instructions. In some cases, further analysis of other code may allow one to conclude that the location following the jump is a valid instruction, but the results of such an analysis are not always available.

It would appear reasonable to assume that the compiler and linker keep instructions contiguous to one another and separate from all data items. However, this is sometimes not the case. Some compilers (and assembly language programmers) intersperse data with code. For example, some compilers may provide a (read-only) mask that specifies which registers have been saved by a procedure caller at the time of the call. This mask may be placed immediately after the jump-and-link instruction that implements the call. Also, a compiler may "pad" the instruction stream with unused bytes in order to align branch or jump targets on word or cache line boundaries for performance reasons. Whatever the reason for interspersing data in code sections, it poses difficulties in statically identifying the starting points of all instruction sequences in a given region of memory.

Despite the foregoing observations, static predecoding and binary translation may still seem fairly straightforward from the simple examples given in the previous subsections because, in those examples, we were considering RISC instructions with fixed-length encodings. Instructions are of variable-length in CISC ISAs such as the IA-32. Hence, sequences of IA-32 instructions can begin at any byte boundary rather than on a word boundary as in common RISC ISAs. Even if it is known that a certain location in memory is part of a section of code, it is usually difficult in a CISC ISA to determine whether or not an arbitrary byte is at the start of a new instruction sequence. In Figure 2.20, for example, it is not obvious whether the byte beginning with 8b marks the

```
                              mov %ch,0  ??
          31 c0 8b b5 00 00 03 08 8b bd 00 00 03 00
                              movl %esi, 0x08030000(%ebp)??
```

**Figure 2.20**   Finding IA-32 Instruction Boundaries in an Instruction Stream.

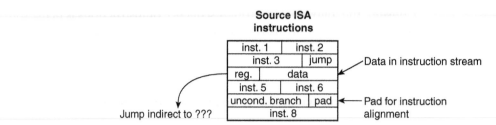

**Figure 2.21**    Causes of the Instruction Discovery Problem.

start of a sequence beginning with a mov1 instruction, or ends some previous instruction, with the next byte, b5, starting a mov instruction.

To summarize, in real code using conventional ISAs, especially CISC ISAs, code discovery can be a problem because of variable-length instructions, register indirect jumps, data interspersed with the instructions, and pads to align instructions; see Figure 2.21.

### 2.6.2    The Code-Location Problem

As discussed earlier, translated code is accessed with a target program counter (TPC), which is different from the architected source program counter (SPC). This creates a problem when there is an indirect control transfer (branch or jump) in the source code. The destination address of the control transfer is held in a register and is a source code address, even though it occurs in the translated code. During emulation, then, there must be some way to map an SPC address to a TPC address. The code shown in Figure 2.22 will not work

```
mov1    %eax, 4(%esp)       ;load jump address from memory
jmp     %eax                ;jump indirect through %eax

                 (a)
```

```
addi    r16,r11,4           ;compute IA-32 address
lwzx    r4,r2,r16           ;get IA-32 jump address from IA-32 memory image
mtctr   r4                  ;move to count register (ctr)
bctr                        ;jump indirect through ctr

                 (b)
```

**Figure 2.22**    Translation of an Indirect Jump Code Sequence. *The value in the jump register is a source code address in both cases; consequently, this code translation will not work correctly. (a) IA-32 source code; (b) PowerPC target code.*

properly because the target code cannot jump to a source code location. This problem is referred to as the *code-location problem.*

In general, the code-discovery and code-location problems require sophisticated solutions that will be discussed in the next section. However, there are special situations where the solutions are simpler. One of these we have already seen: instruction sets with fixed-length (typically 32-bit) instructions that are always aligned on fixed boundaries, as is typical in RISC ISAs. Another special situation occurs with source instruction sets that are explicitly designed to be emulated, such as Java bytecodes. These virtual instruction sets do not allow data to be interspersed with code (other than immediate values associated with instructions), and they have restricted control flow instructions (branches and jumps) that enable easy code discovery.

### 2.6.3 Incremental Predecoding and Translation

For an arbitrary ISA, code discovery is a problem both for predecoding and for binary translation. In both cases, a general solution is to translate the binary while the program is operating on actual input data, i.e., *dynamically,* and to predecode or translate new sections of code *incrementally* as the program reaches them. Because the overall process is more or less the same for both predecoding and binary translation, we will simply refer to both as *translation.*

The overall process is illustrated in Figure 2.23. High-level control is provided by an *emulation manager* (EM), which is part of the runtime support. Other major components include an interpreter and the binary translator. The interpreter may be either a decode-and-dispatch interpreter or a simple threaded interpreter as described in Section 2.2. The important point is that the interpreter operates on the original source binary code.

As blocks of code are translated (or predecoded), they are placed into a region of memory reserved for them. As more and more code is translated, this memory region could become quite large, however, which is potentially wasteful for code that is rarely used. Therefore, to reduce the memory space that holds translated code, it is typically organized as a *code cache* (Deutsch and Schiffman 1984). The objective of the code cache is to hold the more recently used blocks of translated code. We defer details of code caching and code cache management to Chapter 3. For the remainder of this chapter, the reader can simply assume that the code cache is always large enough to hold the translated code.

Finally, a *map table* associates the SPC for a block of source code with the TPC for the corresponding block of translated code. The map table essentially provides a way of indexing into the code cache, and it is typically implemented

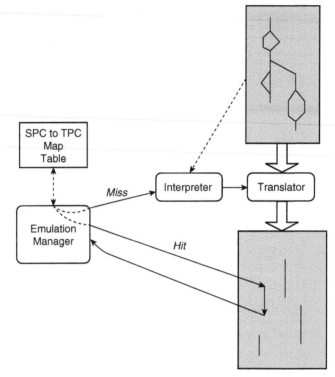

**Figure 2.23** Overview of Dynamic Translation System. *Dotted lines indicate data accesses; solid lines indicate flow of control.*

as a hash table. The SPC comes from the interpreted or translated program, and the TPC points to the beginning of the translated block in the code cache. If the EM wants to find a block of translated code (or determine if it has yet been translated), the SPC is applied to the map table. The corresponding TPC value (pointing into the code cache) is produced if the code block has been translated (i.e., if there is a *hit* in the code cache). Otherwise the map table indicates that there is a code cache *miss*, and additional translation is required.

The system translates one block of source code at a time. In a simple translation scheme, the natural unit for translation is the *dynamic basic block*. A dynamic basic block is slightly different from a conventional basic block, determined by the static structure of a program (see Figure 2.24a). A *static basic block* of instructions contains a sequence with a single entry point and a single exit point. In essence, static basic blocks begin and end at all branch/jump instructions and branch/jump targets.

|                | Static<br>Basic Blocks |          |                | Dynamic<br>Basic Blocks |         |
|----------------|------------------------|----------|----------------|-------------------------|---------|
|                | add...<br>load...<br>store .... | block 1 |        | add...<br>load...<br>store ... |       |
| loop:          | load ...<br>add ....<br>store<br>brcond skip | block 2 | loop: | load ...<br>add ....<br>store<br>brcond skip | block 1 |
|                | load...<br>sub... | block 3 |              | load...<br>sub... | block 2 |
| skip:          | add...<br>store<br>brcond loop | block 4 | skip: | add...<br>store<br>brcond loop |       |
|                | add...<br>load...<br>store...<br>jump indirect | block 5 | loop: | load ...<br>add ....<br>store<br>brcond skip | block 3 |
|                | ...<br>... |          | skip:          | add...<br>store<br>brcond loop | block 4 |
|                | (a) |          |                | ...<br>... |         |
|                |                        |          |                | (b)                     |         |

**Figure 2.24**  Static Versus Dynamic Basic Blocks. *(a) Static basic blocks are code sequences with one entry point and one exit point. They begin and end with control transfer instructions or targets of control transfer instructions. (b) Dynamic basic blocks are often larger than static basic blocks and are determined by the actual flow of control at run time.*

A dynamic basic block is determined by the actual flow of a program as it is executed. A dynamic basic block always begins at the instruction executed immediately after a branch or jump, follows the sequential instruction stream, and ends with the next branch or jump. In Figure 2.24b, when the static loop shown is first entered from the top, the instruction at loop happens to be the target of a branch, yet it does not terminate the dynamic basic block. The dynamic basic block continues until the first conditional branch is encountered. Dynamic basic blocks tend to be larger than static basic blocks. Note that the same static instruction may belong to more than one dynamic basic block. For example, the add instruction at label skip belongs to dynamic basic block 2 as well as the shorter dynamic basic block 4. In the remainder of this book the term *basic block* will mean "dynamic basic block" unless stated otherwise. Translation methods in this chapter will operate on one dynamic basic block at a time. A translation unit larger than a single dynamic basic block can often be beneficial, however. Such larger translation units are discussed in Chapter 4.

A simple, incremental translation process works as follows. After the source binary is loaded into memory, the EM begins interpreting the binary using a simple decode-and-dispatch or indirect threaded method. As it proceeds, the interpreter dynamically generates the intermediate code or translated target binary. This translated code is placed in the code cache, and the corresponding SPC-to-TPC mapping is placed into the map table. When a branch or jump is encountered, the interpreter has completed translation of a dynamic basic block.

The EM then follows the path of the source program's control flow (using the map table) and either directly executes the next block if it is already translated (there is a hit in the table) or begins translating the next dynamic basic block if it hasn't been previously translated (a miss in the table). Incrementally, more of the program is discovered and translated, until eventually only translated code is being executed (except for the emulation manager code that connects the control flow from one translated block to the next — Figure 2.25). The entire process is summarized in the flowchart given in Figure 2.26.

An apparent complication to the translation process occurs when a branch goes into the middle of a block that is already translated. The destination translation block could be divided into two pieces at that point. However, in order to discover such a situation, it would be necessary to maintain an

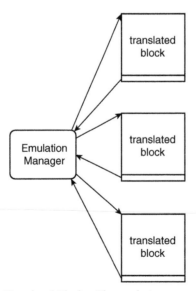

**Figure 2.25**  Flow of Control Involving Translated Blocks. *The emulation manager handles control transfers from one translated block to the next.*

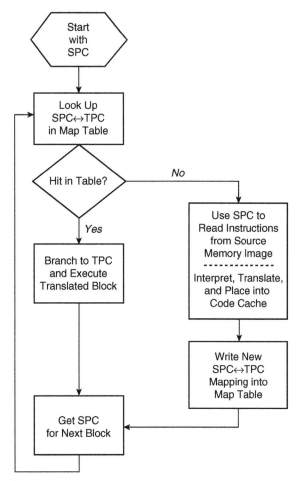

**Figure 2.26**   Dynamic Translation Flowchart.

additional data structure to keep track of address ranges of translated code blocks and then to search the structure whenever a miss occurs in the map table. This apparent complication does not occur when dynamic basic blocks are used (a major reason for using dynamic basic blocks). A new translation is always started when there is a miss in the map table, even if it leads to replicated sections of translated code.

### Tracking the Source Program Code

It is important that the translation system keep track of the SPC value at all times while emulation is taking place. In the translation system, control is

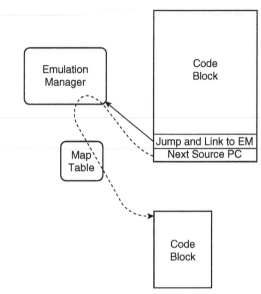

**Figure 2.27**    Linking Translated Blocks via a Stub.

shifted as needed between the interpreter, the EM, and translated blocks in the code cache, and each of these components must have a way of tracking the SPC. First, the interpreter uses the SPC directly as it fetches source instructions. When the interpreter transfers control to the EM at the end of a basic block, it passes the next SPC to the EM. Similarly, when a block of translated code finishes executing, the value of the next SPC must be made available to the EM. One way of doing this is to map the SPC to a register on the host platform, with the register being updated either at each translated instruction or at the end of each translated block (as in Figure 2.19). Another possibility is shown in Figure 2.27. Here the value of the next SPC is placed in a "stub" at the end of the translated block. When the translated block finishes, control is transferred back to the EM using a jump-and-link (JAL) instruction. The link register can then be used by the EM to access the SPC from the end of the translated code block (Cmelik and Keppel 1994).

### Example

Figure 2.28 is an extended example that illustrates all the parts of Figure 2.27. In this example two basic blocks of IA-32 code have been binary translated to blocks of PowerPC code. The following sequence takes place as one translated

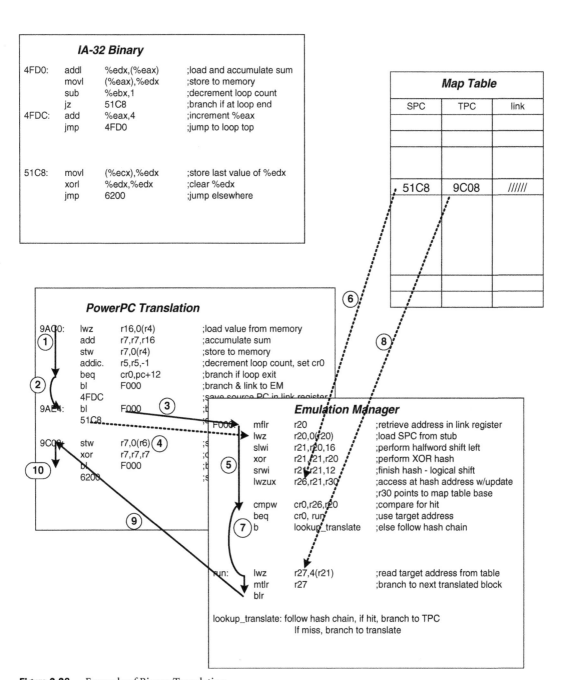

**Figure 2.28**   Example of Binary Translation.

block finishes and control is transferred to the next translated block, via the emulation manager.

1. Translated basic block is executed.
2. Branch is taken to stub code.
3. Stub does branch and link to emulation manager entry point.
4. EM loads SPC from stub code, using link register.
5. EM hashes SPC to 16 bits and does lookup in map table.
6. EM loads SPC value from map table; comparison with stub SPC succeeds.
7. Branch to code that will transfer code back to translation.
8. Load TPC from map table.
9. Jump indirect to next translated basic block.
10. Continue execution.

### Other issues

There are other issues related to instruction set emulation and dynamic translation that will be covered in Chapters 3 and 4. Here are the more important of these.

*Self-modifying code* — Although in many applications it is uncommon, programs occasionally perform stores into the code area; i.e., the code is self-modifying. When this happens, translated code held in the code cache may no longer correspond to the modified source code. Consequently, mechanisms must be in place to invoke retranslation. The handling of self-modifying code is covered in Section 3.4.2.

*Self-referencing code* — Here, the program performs loads from the code area. When this happens, the data that is read must correspond to the original source code, not the translated version. Handling of self-referencing code is also covered in Section 3.4.2.

*Precise traps* — If the translated code should experience an exception condition (an interrupt or trap), the correct state corresponding to the original source code, including the SPC of the trapping instruction, must be produced. Providing precise state at the time of a trap or interrupt is an important recurring topic throughout both Chapters 3 and 4.

### 2.6.4 Same-ISA Emulation

Although it may seem like an odd idea at first, there are important VM applications where the source and target ISAs are the same and where the emulation techniques described in this chapter are used. Of course, there is no logical reason why an instruction set can't be used for emulating itself. For example, using interpretation techniques, instructions from a source binary can be discovered, parsed, and emulated regardless of whether the target and source ISAs are the same or different. And, naturally, "binary translation" is greatly simplified when the source and target ISAs are identical.

The important, useful aspect of same-ISA emulation is that the emulation manager is always in control of the software being emulated. Emulation software discovers and inspects each source instruction and, in the process, can identify details concerning operations to be performed by that specific instruction. Furthermore, it can monitor the execution of the source program at any desired level of detail. This monitoring, or *code management*, capability is the key to several applications of same-ISA emulation. One application is simulation, where dynamic program characteristics are collected during the simulation process. Simulation is the primary application of the Shade System, discussed as a case study in Section 2.9. A second application is operating system call emulation in virtual machines where the ISAs are the same but the host operating system differs from the guest operating system. By using emulation techniques, all operating system calls in a guest's source binary can be detected and can be translated to host operating system calls. A third application is the discovery and management of certain privileged operations that require special handling in some system VMs; these will be discussed in Chapter 8. A fourth application, discussed in Chapter 10, is "program shepherding" where the targets of control transfer and other instructions are monitored to ensure that they do not exploit security holes. Finally, there is the application to same-ISA dynamic binary optimization where runtime information is used to help optimize a program binary as it executes, even though no ISA translation is performed. This final application can be used as an end in itself, but, perhaps more importantly, it allows the other applications to be implemented while mitigating any resulting performance losses.

Same-ISA interpretation requires no special discussion; the techniques are exactly as described earlier. For binary "translation"[2] (without optimization), the simplest technique is just to copy the code, using exactly the same code in the

---

**2.** Because the source and the target use the same ISA, we put translation in quotes; however we are using the same process as is used when true translation is done.

target as in the source (except where there are operating system calls or instructions requiring special handling). Same-ISA dynamic binary optimization is discussed in Section 4.7.

## 2.7 Control Transfer Optimizations

Using the simple translation method described thus far, every time a translation block finishes execution, the EM must be reentered and an SPC-to-TPC lookup must occur. There are a number of optimizations that reduce this overhead by eliminating the need to go through the EM between every pair of translation blocks. These optimizations are described in the following subsections.

### 2.7.1 Translation Chaining

Chaining in binary translators is the counterpart of threading in interpreters. Instead of branching to the emulation manager at the end of every translated block, the blocks can be linked directly to each other. This is illustrated in Figure 2.29.

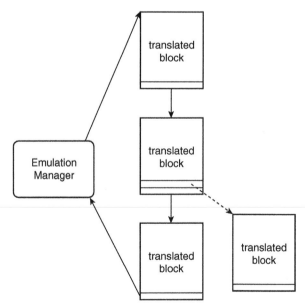

**Figure 2.29**     Chaining of Translation Blocks Avoids Indirect Transfers Through the Emulation Manager.

In this scheme, blocks are translated one at a time, but they are linked together into chains as they are constructed. Linking is accomplished by replacing what was initially a jump and link (or branch and link, *bl*, in PowerPC) back to the EM, as shown in Figure 2.27, with a direct branch to the successor translation block. The address of the successor block is determined by using the SPC value to access the map table and find the corresponding TPC (if the corresponding basic block has been translated).

If the successor block has not yet been translated, then the normal stub code is inserted. At some time later, after the successor has been translated and the predecessor block exits to the EM, the EM will access the map table, find the entry in the table, and retrieve the TPC for the successor block. At that point, the EM can set up a link to the successor block by overwriting the jump-and-link (branch-and-link in PowerPC parlance) in the predecessor with a direct jump to the successor. The steps in this process are illustrated in Figure 2.30. The code example from Figure 2.28, with chaining added, is given in Figure 2.31.

Chaining works in those situations where the SPC can be placed in a stub at the end of a translation block, as in Figure 2.27. These are situations where the destination of a branch or jump never changes. However, for register indirect jumps, especially procedure returns, the target may change from one execution of the jump to the next. Because a single SPC cannot be associated with the translation block terminated by the register indirect jump, chaining is not convenient in these cases. The easiest way to handle indirect jumps, therefore, is always to go through the EM and to let the EM look up the correct TPC via the map table. Faster methods for handling indirect jumps are described in the next two subsections.

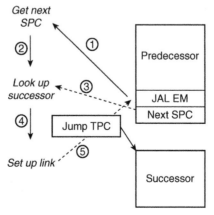

**Figure 2.30** Creating a Link from a Translated Predecessor Block to a Successor Block.

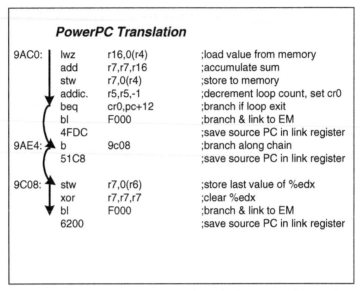

**Figure 2.31**  Translated PowerPC Code from an Earlier Example, with Chaining Implemented.

### 2.7.2 Software Indirect Jump Prediction

As pointed out earlier, implementing indirect jumps by map table lookup is expensive in execution time. It requires several instructions to hash the SPC to form an index into the map table, then at least one load and a compare to find a matching table entry, and finally a load and an indirect jump to the TPC address. In many cases, however, the jump target never or very seldom changes. In these cases, a form of software jump prediction can be employed to reduce the overhead of indirect jumps. This is essentially an implementation of *inline caching*, developed for fast Smalltalk emulation (Deutsch and Schiffman 1984). Figure 2.32 illustrates the technique. In the example, Rx symbolizes a register holding the indirect jump target PC value. In a series of *if* statements, the most frequent SPC addresses, with their matching TPC addresses, are encoded into the translated binary code (given here in high-level form for clarity). Then the register value for an indirect jump can be compared with the SPC value; if there is a match, then a branch to the destination (possibly translated as a PC relative

```
if(Rx == addr_1) goto target_1;
else if (Rx == addr_2) goto target_2;
else if (Rx == addr_3) goto target_3;
else table_lookup(Rx);          do it the slow way
```

**Figure 2.32**  Software Indirect Jump Prediction via Inline Caching. *Source PC values are given as immediate values* addr_i; *corresponding target PC values are given as* target_i.

branch) takes place. Typically, the comparisons are ordered, with the most frequent SPC destination address being given first. Of course, in the worst case, if all the prediction(s) are wrong, then the map table lookup must be performed anyway, so that additional performance is lost. Hence, this technique should be coupled with *profiling* that provides accurate information regarding indirect jump targets (Section 4.2.4).

When using this method, the EM maintains a side table that keeps track of the successor translated blocks that can be reached via such software predictions. In the event that the successor translated block is removed from the code cache, the software prediction code in the predecessor block must also be modified or removed (and is replaced with a map table lookup).

### 2.7.3 Shadow Stack

When a translated code block contains a procedure call via an indirect jump to a target binary routine, the SPC value must be saved by emulation code as part of the source architected state, either in a register or in a memory stack (depending on the source ISA). Then when the called procedure is finished, it can restore this SPC value, access the map table, and jump to the translated block of code at the return address. As pointed out earlier, this map table lookup adds overhead to the emulation process. The overhead can be avoided if the target return PC value can be made available directly, i.e., as a link address.

To perform this optimization, the return (link) value of the target code is pushed onto a *shadow stack* maintained by the emulation manager (Chernoff et al. 1998). Note that this return value is not necessarily the memory address immediately following the procedure jump; if the jump is at a translation block boundary, for example, then the target return value may be linked to the beginning of the next translated block. In any case, when it is time to return, this translation code address is popped from the shadow stack and a map table lookup can be avoided. There is one problem, however. The source code could have changed the contents of its stack between the call and the eventual return. Consequently, before the shadow stack can be used to provide a target return address, the value on the top of the stack must be checked against the corresponding source return address. Hence, the shadow stack frame is expanded to include not only the return address of the target translated code but the return address of the source binary. The return address of the source is compared with the source field in the shadow stack return address. If there is a match, then the target return address from the shadow stack can be used. If there is a mismatch, then the source return address is used to access the map table in the conventional manner.

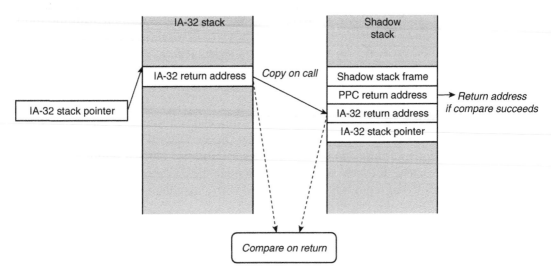

**Figure 2.33**   Shadow Stack Implementation to Expedite Returns to Translated Code.

The shadow stack mechanism where the source ISA is IA-32 and the target ISA is PowerPC is illustrated in Figure 2.33. The IA-32 uses an architected stack. When the code performs a procedure call, the PowerPC return address is pushed on the shadow stack; along with the IA-32 return address. Then when it is time to return, the IA-32 return address is loaded from the emulated IA-32 stack. This address is compared with the IA-32 return address saved on the shadow stack. If these match, then the shadow stack PowerPC return value is consistent with the source code return value, and the PowerPC return value can be used to jump to the return translation block. Otherwise, the IA-32 return value retrieved from the IA-32 stack is used to hash into the PC map table for the return address.

Note that the IA-32 stack pointer is also saved on the shadow stack. If the guest program should happen to cut back the IA-32 stack by discarding a number of stack frames, this can be detected by comparing the pointer on the shadow stack with the emulated IA-32 stack pointer. If there is a mismatch, the emulated IA-32 stack pointer can then be used for cutting back the shadow stack so that it is consistent with the emulated source stack.

## 2.8   Instruction Set Issues

Thus far, we have provided several examples of instruction set emulation. There are many more details to be taken care of in translating and interpreting a complete instruction set. Some of these details will be discussed in this section; some are specific to certain instructions sets, and others apply more generally.

### 2.8.1 Register Architectures

Virtually every ISA uses registers of some kind. Registers are at the very top of the storage hierarchy and are critical to performance. Hence, the way registers are handled is a key issue during emulation. The general-purpose registers of the target ISA are used for a number of functions, including (1) holding general-purpose registers of the source ISA, (2) holding special-purpose registers of the source ISA, (3) pointing to the source register context block and to the memory image, and (4) holding intermediate values used by the emulator.

If the number of target registers is significantly larger than the number of source registers, then all the foregoing uses for target registers may be satisfied simultaneously. For example, in emulating an IA-32 on a 32-register RISC such as the PowerPC, all the IA-32 general-purpose registers and some of the special registers, such as the program counter, can be mapped to target registers, and there are registers left over to point to the register context block, to the source memory image, and scratch registers for use by emulation code.

In other cases, there may not be enough target registers to perform all the foregoing functions, especially when the source and target ISAs have approximately the same number of general-purpose registers. In these cases, the usage of the target general-purpose registers must be carefully managed. Two registers are needed to point to the register context block and to the source memory image; these pointers are used very frequently during the emulation process. Similarly, a target register should be assigned to the program counter. Such an assignment of registers is used in Figure 2.18, for example. If interpretation is being used, a target register should also be designated to hold the SPC. If binary translation or predecoding is used, an additional register may hold the TPC. If the source ISA has a stack pointer, condition codes, or other frequently used special registers, target registers should be assigned to these as well. In total, this could consume from three to ten target registers. Thus, between three and ten general-purpose target registers may be needed for holding the state of source ISA resources, beyond those needed for mapping source general-purpose registers.

After assigning target registers to the most common or performance-critical source resources, the emulation manager must allocate the target's remaining general-purpose registers. If interpretation is used, the remaining registers may be used as scratch registers by the interpreter. If translation is used, then source registers can be mapped to target registers on a translation block basis.

All registers read in the translated code are copied from the context block into target registers when the translation block is entered. Any modified registers are copied back to the context block when the translation block is exited. If the translation block is especially large, then source registers may be spilled to the context block. In some of the binary translation examples given earlier, e.g., Figure 2.19, these intermediate spills to the context block are not shown, though they would be used in practice.

## 2.8.2 Condition Codes

Condition codes are special architected bits that characterize instruction results (zero, negative, etc.) and are tested by conditional branch instructions. However, across ISAs there is little uniformity in the way condition codes are used or whether they are used at all. The Intel IA-32 ISA sets condition codes implicitly as a side effect of executing most instructions; consequently, the condition codes are updated nearly as often as general-purpose registers. The SPARC ISA contains explicitly set codes, which update condition codes only when it is anticipated that they will actually be used. The PowerPC ISA has a number of condition code registers that are also explicitly set. Adding to the complication, some ISAs do not use any condition codes; the MIPS ISA is an example.

Emulation complexity varies significantly, depending on whether the source ISA, the target ISA, both, or neither uses condition codes. The easiest situation is if neither ISA uses condition codes. Almost as easy is the case where the source ISA does not use condition codes but the target ISA does. Here, some additional target instructions may be required to generate condition code values, but there is no need to maintain any source condition code state. The emulation of MIPS on a PowerPC is illustrated in Figure 2.34. Here, a conditional branch in the MIPS ISA is translated to two instructions in the PowerPC ISA — one that sets a condition register (cr1 in the figure) and a second that performs the conditional branch by testing cr1.

```
beq    r1,r2,offset
```
(a)

```
cmpw   cr1,r1,r2
beq    cr1,offset
```
(b)

**Figure 2.34**    Binary Translation of a Conditional Branch from the MIPS ISA to the PowerPC ISA. *(a) MIPS branch equal; (b) PowerPC translation to a compare instruction followed by a branch.*

If a target ISA has no condition codes, then the source condition codes must be emulated, and this emulation can be time consuming. The most difficult problems usually occur when the source ISA has implicitly set condition codes and the target ISA has no condition codes. It is because of these difficulties that we have been ignoring the emulation of IA-32 condition codes in examples up to now.

Recall that implicitly set condition codes are modified as a side effect of many instructions. In the Intel IA-32, the condition codes are a set of "flags" held in the EFLAGS register. The IA-32 integer add instruction always sets six of these condition codes (flags) whenever it is executed. The condition codes set by the add are:

*OF:* indicates whether integer overflow occurred

*SF:* indicates the sign of the result

*ZF:* indicates a zero result

*AF:* indicates a carry or borrow out of bit 3 of the result (used for BCD arithmetic)

*CF:* indicates a carry or borrow out of the most significant bit of the result

*PF:* indicates parity of the least significant byte of the result.

In a straightforward emulation, every time an IA-32 add is emulated, each of the condition codes is evaluated by the emulation code. Evaluation of most of the condition codes is straightforward. For example, the sign of the result can be determined using a simple shift. In other cases, as in the evaluation of AF or PF, generating condition code values is more complex. In general, computing all the condition codes for a given source instruction takes many target instructions, often more than emulating the rest of the instruction, and it can slow emulation considerably.

It turns out, however, that although the condition code values are set frequently, they are seldom used. To make condition code emulation more efficient, a common technique is to perform *lazy evaluation*, where the operands and operation that set the condition code, rather than the condition code settings themselves, are saved (Hohensee, Myszewski, and Reese 1996; Hookway and Herdeg 1997). This allows the generation of condition codes only when needed and at the time they are needed. For example, one can maintain a lazy condition code table that has an entry for each condition code bit. The entry contains the opcode of the most recent instruction to modify the condition code bit, its operands, and its result. However, the condition code itself is not generated. Then if a later instruction, e.g., a conditional branch, needs to use one or more condition code bits, the condition code table is accessed and the needed condition code(s) are generated.

For example, the IA-32 add instruction modifies all the condition code bits. If an add operates on two registers containing the values 2 and 3, all entries in the table will contain: add : 2 : 3 : 5 after the instruction completes. Then if a later instruction needs to test the SF (sign), the SF entry of the table is consulted, and the result field (5) is used to generate the sign (0). Because many instructions modify all condition code bits or because some subset of the bits are always modified together, there are various tricks that can be used to reduce the number of condition code table entries and table updates to optimize for the common case.

During binary translation, the translator can analyze sequences of instructions to determine whether implicitly set condition codes will actually be used. For example, in Figure 2.35 there are two consecutive add instructions followed by a jmp. In this example, the condition codes set by the first add instruction are not used and do not have to be generated. This dataflow analysis can be performed as part of an overall optimization process (Section 4.4). There still may be cases where it is not known whether condition codes will be needed, and in these cases lazy evaluation can be used as described earlier. Also, to support efficient lazy evaluation, it may be advantageous to reserve target registers for holding condition code information, at least for the common situations.

Returning to the example in Figure 2.35, at the time the jmp is translated, it may not be known whether the condition codes set by the second add instruction will be needed. For example, the jmp instruction and its destination (at label1) may be translated separately and are in two different translation blocks. Here, registers (r25–r27) are used for lazy condition code evaluation, and operand values and opcode information are saved in the registers. In this example, the code at the jmp destination address does, in fact, test the condition codes. Consequently, there is a branch to the condition code emulation routine, genZF, in order to set the ZF condition code flag. The genZF routine performs a multiway jump based on the opcode (add) and then evaluates the ZF condition code.

There are still problems, however, because it is possible for a trap to occur during emulation, and the precise (source) state, including all the condition codes, must be materialized at that point. In the foregoing example, the first add instruction could cause a memory protection fault when it loads its operand from memory. If this occurs, the condition codes (or the lazy equivalent) must be available. In general, there must be some way to produce the condition codes for any potentially trapping instruction at the time a trap occurs, although in this situation performance is usually not an issue. Methods for materializing the correct condition code state when a trap occurs are discussed in Section 4.5.2,

```
        addl    %ebx,0(%eax)
        add     %ecx,%ebx
        jmp     label1
                .
                .
label1:
        jz      target

            (a)
```

```
    r4 ↔ %eax       IA-32 to
    r5 ↔ %ebx          PowerPC
    r6 ↔ %ecx              register mappings
            .
            .
    r16 ↔  scratch register used by emulation code
    r25 ↔  condition code operand 1      ;registers
    r26 ↔  condition code operand 2      ; used for
    r27 ↔  condition code operation      ;   lazy condition code emulation
    r28 ↔  jump table base address

    lwz     r16,0(r4)           ;perform memory load for addl
    mr      r25,r16     ;save operands
    mr      r26,r5              ;   and opcode for
    li      r27,"addl"          ;       lazy condition code emulation
    add     r5,r5,r16           ;finish addl
    mr      r25,r6              ;save operands
    mr      r26,r5              ;   and opcode for
    li      r27,"add"           ;       lazy condition code emulation
    add     r6,r6,r5            ;translation of add
    b       label1
            .
            .
label1:
    bl      genZF               ;branch and link to evaluate genZF code
    beq     cr0,target          ;branch on condition flag
            .
            .
genZF
    add     r29,r28,r27         ;add "opcode" to jump table base address
    mtctr   r29                 ;copy to counter register
    bctr                        ;branch via jump table
            .
            .
"sub":
            .
            .
"add":
    add.    r24,r25,r26         ;perform PowerPC add, set cr0
    blr                         ;return

                    (b)
```

**Figure 2.35**  Lazy Evaluation of IA-32 Condition Codes with Binary Translation. *(a) Intel IA-32 code sequence; (b) PowerPC translation using lazy condition code evaluation.*

where the general problem of trap and interrupt emulation is described in the context of optimized code.

Finally, even if the target ISA uses condition codes, they may not be entirely compatible with the source ISA condition codes (May 1987). For example, the SPARC ISA has conditions codes N, C, Z, V, which are equivalent to the IA-32 SF, CF, ZF, OF, but it does not have codes corresponding to AF and PF. Consequently, emulation is simplified for some of the condition codes (provided the condition code register of the target can be easily read/written), but more expensive emulation is still needed for the other condition codes.

### 2.8.3 Data Formats and Arithmetic

Emulating most of the instructions that transform data (e.g., adds, logicals, shifts) is fairly straightforward. The problem is simplified because data formats and arithmetic have become more or less standardized over the years. For integers, the two's complement representation has found universal acceptance; for floating-point, the IEEE standard is commonly implemented.

If both the source and the target ISAs implement two's complement arithmetic, the emulation of arithmetic operations is easily done, especially when identical data widths are supported in both ISAs. Most ISAs offer a basic set of shift and logical instructions that can be used to compose different variations of shift and logical instructions in a source ISA.

Although the IEEE floating-point *format* is commonly used, there are some differences in the way floating-point *arithmetic* is performed on different implementations. For example, the IA-32 uses 80-bit intermediate results, unlike most other ISAs. This means that the precision of IA-32 intermediate results will differ from an ISA that uses 64-bit intermediate results. It is possible, but quite cumbersome, for a non-IA-32 target ISA to perform IA-32 emulation and obtain identical results. As another example of arithmetic differences, the PowerPC ISA provides combined multiply-add instructions, which cannot always be emulated exactly by using the obvious simple sequence consisting of a multiply instruction followed by an add instruction because the intermediate precision of the multiply add may be higher than that required by the IEEE standard. Once again, emulation is possible though cumbersome.

There are often cases where the source ISA requires a functional capability not available in the target ISA. For example, some instruction sets provide integer divide instructions, while others provide more primitive shift/subtract "divide step" instructions or instructions to convert and use the floating-point divider. As another example, some ISAs implement a large variety of addressing modes, while others have a smaller set of simple addressing modes. Invariably the simpler ISA has sufficient primitives to implement the more complex instructions in the other ISA. For example, an auto-incrementing load can be done with a combination of an add instruction and a load.

Finally, immediate data can cause slight emulation difficulties because different ISAs often have different immediate lengths. Mapping shorter immediate values to longer ones is obviously easier than mapping long immediate values to shorter immediate fields. However, all ISAs have some way of building full-length constants using a small number of instructions, so all immediate values can be handled, regardless of length.

### 2.8.4  Memory Address Resolution

In general, different ISAs can access data items of different sizes. For example, one ISA may support loading and storing of bytes, halfwords (16 bits), and full words, while another may only support bytes and words. Multiple instructions in the less powerful ISA can invariably be used to emulate a single memory access instruction in the more powerful ISA.

Most ISAs today address memory to the granularity of individual bytes. However, if a target ISA does not, then emulating a byte-resolution ISA on a machine with word resolution requires shifting out (and saving) the low-order byte address bits when performing memory access and then using the saved byte offset bits to select the specific bytes (or halfwords) being accessed. Performing a store of a data item less than a full word in size requires first performing a word load, inserting the data item into the word (via shifts and mask operations), and then performing a word store. The opposite problem of emulating a word-addressed ISA on a byte-addressed target is very straightforward; it is a case of emulating a less powerful ISA on a more powerful one.

### 2.8.5  Memory Data Alignment

Some ISAs align memory data on "natural" boundaries and some do not. That is, a word access must be performed with the two low-order address bits being 00, and a halfword access must have a 0 for the lowest-order bit. If an ISA does not require addresses to be on natural addresses, then it is said to support "unaligned" data. A conservative approach is to break up word or halfword accesses into byte accesses. Usually if an ISA does not support unaligned data directly, however, it has supplementary instructions to simplify the process, and these can be used. Typically, as a safety net, the ISA also specifies a trap if an instruction does attempt an access with an unaligned address.

Run-time analysis of the target code may help in reducing code expansion by substituting word accesses for aligned cases. In some situations it may be effective to use run-time profiling information to reduce the dynamic cost of emulating such accesses. This will be discussed further in Section 4.6.4.

### 2.8.6 Byte Order

Some ISAs order bytes within a word so that the most significant byte is byte 0 (and in a 32-bit word, the least significant is byte 3). This is referred to as the *big-endian* byte order (Cohen 1981). Other ISAs order bytes in the *little-endian* byte order, which addresses the least significant byte as 0 and the most significant as byte 3. For example, the character string "JOHN" is stored as JOHN in a big-endian machine and as NHOJ in a little-endian machine. In either case, if the bytes are accessed in the sequence 0, 1, 2, 3, then the string is accessed in order J, O, H, N.

It is common to maintain the guest data image in the same byte order as assumed by the source ISA. Consequently, to emulate a big-endian source ISA on a little-endian target ISA (or vice versa), the emulation code can modify addresses when bytes (or halfwords) are accessed from the guest memory region. For example, consider a load byte instruction. To get the correct data, the low-order two-address bits can be complemented (i.e., to convert byte address 00 to 11, 01 to 10, etc.). As a more complicated example, if an unaligned word address is used, then the bytes can be individually loaded from addresses found by sequencing through individual byte addresses and complementing the addresses before accessing memory. That is, if the source ISA specifies address xxx01001, then the bytes to be loaded are at locations xxx01010, xxx01001, xxx01000, xxx01111. Or, alternatively, a pair of load words combined with shifts and logical instructions can be used to assemble the correct data in the register of the target. In any case, it is an awkward, time-consuming process that is hard to avoid, in general. Some ISAs support both endian orders (via a mode bit), and a target ISA with this feature would clearly simplify the emulation process.

Finally, note that byte-order issues extend into the host operating system calls. That is, guest data accessed by the host operating system also has to be converted to the proper byte order. This can be done in the "jacket" or "wrapper" code that supports OS call emulation (see Section 3.7).

### 2.8.7  Addressing Architecture

The memory addressing architecture is a very important part of an ISA, and it poses a number of difficult problems when emulating full applications. The address space sizes of the source and target ISAs may be different, and/or their page sizes may be different or their privilege levels different. These address space issues are fairly complex, and often the virtual machine architecture as a whole must be considered in order to provide a good solution; that is, it is not a matter of instruction emulation alone. Because the virtual machine as a whole provides a proper address space environment, this problem is deferred to Chapter 3, which discusses specific virtual machine implementations.

## 2.9  Case Study: Shade and the Role of Emulation During Simulation

Simulation is a key part of computer system design. Simulators are used for studying the performance of memory hierarchies and the internal behavior of superscalar microarchitectures. They are also useful for developing compiler optimizations and debugging. Simulators typically operate on benchmark programs or kernels and emulate these programs as a part of the simulation process. That is, a simulator includes emulation, but it does more. In simulation, the objective is to study the *process* of performing computation, not the computation itself; that is, one is seldom interested in the actual output produced by a simulated program (especially when the program is being simulated for the 100th time with exactly the same input data!). In addition to emulating a program, a simulator may model the internal workings of a processor or memory system. It may directly track the operation of hardware features, or it may generate instruction or memory address traces for further evaluation by other simulation tools. Often performance is sacrificed in order to collect process-related information, such as branch misprediction accuracy or numbers of instructions issued on particular cycles.

Shade is a simulation tool developed for high-performance simulation (Cmelik and Keppel 1994, 1996); consequently, it contains a sophisticated emulator that forms a basis for flexible and extensible simulation. It does this by providing a set of functions that can be linked into the emulator. Some of the functions are provided as part of the Shade toolset, or the user can write additional functions.

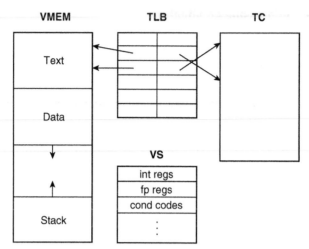

**Figure 2.36** Primary Data Structures in Shade. *The source memory image (VMEM), the source register state (VS), the cache for holding translated instructions (TC), and the table mapping source to target PCs (TLB).*

Shade first translates the ISA being simulated (what we have been referring to as the source ISA[3]) into sequences of target instructions. In general, basic block-size units are translated. The translated code not only performs emulation but also generates simulation trace data via function calls embedded in the translated code. Because we are interested primarily in emulation, we skip the details of trace generation, but the reader can refer to the excellent articles describing Shade cited earlier.

Figure 2.36 gives the important elements of Shade. The source ISA memory image is kept in a large array VMEM. The register state, including the condition codes, and control registers are held in the table VS. A trace cache (TC) is the code cache mechanism that holds translated blocks of target instructions. Finally, the mapping between source PC values and target PC values is maintained in the *translation lookaside buffer*, or TLB.[4]

To speed up emulation, the source program counter (VPC) and the base of the source memory image (VMEM) are permanently mapped to target registers. A pointer to the base of the TLB is also permanently mapped to a target register.

---

**3.** What we refer to as the *source* and the *target* are called the *target* and the *host* in Shade documentation.

**4.** This TLB should not be confused with the translation lookaside buffer used in many processors for caching virtual address translation information.

While executing a block of translated code, source register values (held in the VS) used in the block are temporarily copied into target registers. As they are computed, result register values are copied back into the VS.

Translated blocks in the TC may be chained together to avoid TLB lookups. The translation cache is managed in a simple way: Translations fill the TC linearly as they are produced. When the TC becomes full, it is simply flushed, and translation begins filling it again. This method is clearly simple — it avoids having to "unlink" translation blocks, and the TC is generally large enough that it does not reduce performance significantly.

The structure of the Shade TLB is shown in Figure 2.37. It is structured as a two-dimensional array, where a source PC hashes into a row, and each row contains $n$ <source, target> pairs. The lookup algorithm linearly scans the row until it has a match (and finds the target PC) or until it hits the end of the array. If it hits the end, it assumes there is no translation and forms one. The inner loop of the emulation code checks the first translation in the list. If there is a hit, it proceeds; otherwise, it calls a routine that does the linear search. This search routine then places a matching entry in the first position, so the most recently used is always the first one checked. If all $n$ entries are full, then a new entry pushes the rightmost entry off the end and it is lost. This means there may be some "orphan" translations in the TC, and a redundant retranslation may later be added to the TC. However, the occasional flushes of the TC clear out the orphans. Finally, a further optimization is to align each of the TLB rows to a cache line boundary so that if there is a miss during the initial lookup, the remaining entries will be brought into the cache when the initial miss is serviced.

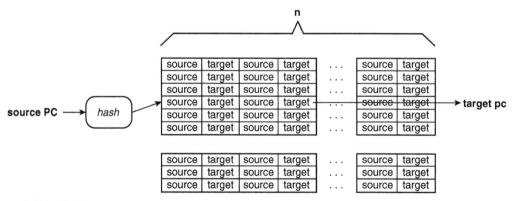

**Figure 2.37** Shade TLB Structure.

## 2.10 Summary: Performance Tradeoffs

Figure 2.38 summarizes all the emulation methods we have discussed, and we now compare their characteristics. As criteria for comparison, we consider start-up time, memory requirements, steady-state performance, and code portability. We provide qualitative performance characteristics; a more quantitative evaluation of interpreter performance was done by Romer et al. (1996).

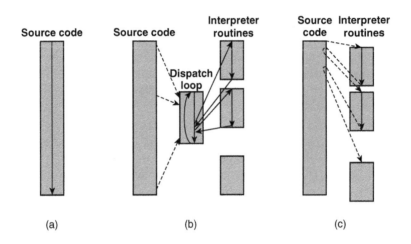

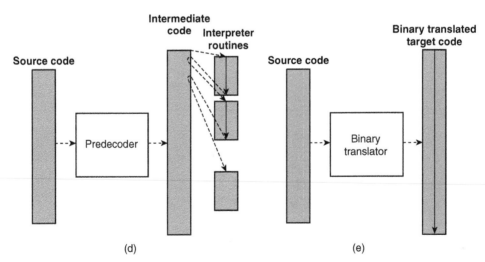

**Figure 2.38** Summary of emulation Methods. *(a) No emulation; (b) decode-and-dispatch interpretation; (c) indirect threaded interpretation; (d) predecoding and direct threaded interpretation; (e) binary translation.*

The relative importance of the criteria depends on the VM being implemented. For example, memory requirements may be important in a VM in an embedded application but not in a server application. Portability may be important in HLL VMs but not in codesigned VMs.

### Decode-and-Dispatch Interpretation

*Memory requirements: low* — There is one interpreter routine for each instruction *type* in the target ISA.

*Start-up performance: fast* — There is essentially zero start-up time because no preprocessing or translation of the source binary is required.

*Steady-state performance: slow* — A source instruction must be parsed each time it is emulated. Furthermore, the source code must be fetched through the data cache, which puts a lot of pressure on the cache (and leads to a potential performance loss). Finally, this method results in a high number of control transfers (branches).

*Code portability: good* — If the interpreter is written in an HLL, it is very portable.

### Indirect Threaded Interpreter

*Memory requirements: low* — More memory is required than with decode-and-dispatch interpretation because the dispatch code sequence must be included in every interpreter routine. The amount of extra memory depends on the complexity of decoding; for a RISC ISA it would be relatively low, and for a CISC it could be much higher. The memory cost can be mitigated via hybrid implementations.

*Start-up performance: fast* — As with decode-and-dispatch interpreters, there is essentially zero start-up time; no preprocessing is required.

*Steady-state performance: slow* — This is slightly better than decode-and-dispatch because several branch instructions are eliminated. There is high data cache usage, as in decode-and-dispatch interpreters.

*Code portability: good* — The interpreter code is as portable as with decode-and-dispatch interpretation.

### Direct Threaded Interpreter with Predecoding

*Memory requirements: high* — The size of predecoded memory image is proportional to the original source memory image (and is probably larger).

Memory requirements can be somewhat reduced if the intermediate form is cached and blocks of seldom-used predecoded instructions are removed from the cache.

*Start-up performance: slow* — The source memory image must first be interpreted in order to discover the control flow. Also, generating the decoded intermediate form can be time consuming.

*Steady-state performance: medium* — This is better than indirect threading because the individual instructions do not have to be parsed (and decoded) every time they are executed. If the predecoded form contains target addresses of interpretation routines, then the dispatch table lookup is eliminated. There is high data cache usage because the predecoded instructions are still treated as data by the interpreter code.

*Code portability: medium* — If the predecoded version contains specific locations for interpreter routines, then the interpreter becomes implementation dependent. Compilers that support finding the address of a label may mitigate this disadvantage.

### Binary Translation

*Memory requirements: high* — The size of predecoded memory image is proportional to the original source memory image. As with predecoding, memory requirements can be reduced if blocks of translated code are cached.

*Start-up performance: very slow* — The source memory image must first be interpreted in order to discover the control flow; then translated binary code must be generated.

*Steady-state performance: fast* — The translated binaries execute directly on hardware. Performance is improved even more if translated blocks are linked directly together. Furthermore, pressure on the data cache is reduced because translated code is fetched through the instruction cache.

*Code portability: poor* — Code is translated for a specific target ISA. A new translator (or at least the code-generation part) must be written for each target ISA.

# Chapter Three
# Process Virtual Machines

A typical computer user works with a large number of programs that coexist in a system environment consisting of one or more processors, memory, a file system, and a number of peripheral devices. The user invokes and interacts with the programs by employing the interface supported by libraries and the operating system. An important restriction, however, is that the user can run only programs that have been compiled for the user's operating system and the processor's instruction set. One of the important applications of virtual machines is to circumvent this restriction and allow the user to run programs compiled for other systems. As we shall see, a number of VM architectures can provide this capability, but the simplest VM approach from the user's perspective, and the one described in this chapter, is to provide a virtual environment at the program, or *process, level*. By using a process VM, a guest program developed for a computer other than the user's host system can be installed and used in the same way as all other programs on the host system; the user as well as the other programs interact with the guest program in the same way as they interact with native host programs.

Computer programs are compiled, distributed, and stored as executable binaries that conform to a specific *application binary interface,* or ABI, which includes features of both the hardware instruction set and the operating system. For example, a very widely used ABI is the one designed to execute on a processor supporting the Intel IA-32 ISA and the Microsoft Windows operating system. A few years ago, Intel developed a new, 64-bit ISA, now called IPF, which is implemented in the Itanium family of processors. Existing IA-32 application programs will not run directly on Itanium platforms, even though the Windows operating system has been ported to Itanium platforms. So to allow users to run the large number of existing IA-32/Windows applications

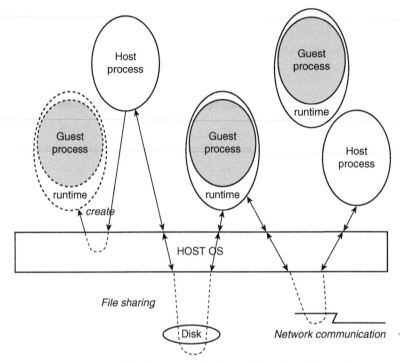

**Figure 3.1**   A Guest Process, with Process VM Support in the Form of Runtime Software, Interacting with Host Processes.

on Itanium platforms, the people at Intel developed a *virtual* IA-32/Windows environment. The resulting process VM, the IA-32 EL (execution layer), allows IA-32 programs to appear to an Itanium user exactly as they would on a native IA-32 platform (Baraz et al. 2003). Another version of the IA-32 EL process VM with a different OS interface supports IA-32/Linux applications.

Figure 3.1 illustrates a typical process virtual machine environment. As shown in the figure, *runtime* software essentially encapsulates an individual guest process, giving it the same outward appearance as a native host process. From the perspective of the guest process, all the other processes appear to conform to its worldview. Consequently, the guest process can interact with the native host processes in the same way the host processes interact with each other. Furthermore, the guest process can interact with other guest processes as though they were running on a real machine.

In this chapter, we discuss process VM implementations in a more or less top-down fashion. In the next section, we discuss the overall structure of a process VM. Then there is a section discussing compatibility issues, followed by sections on each of the major aspects of a process VM. These include the mapping of guest state to host state and emulation of the memory-addressing architecture, instructions, exceptions, and operating system calls. Also related to process VM implementation is a section discussing code cache management techniques. Then there is a section on the integration of a process VM into a host environment; this includes process VM loading and initialization. The chapter concludes with a case study of the Digital FX!32 system, a VM that supports the IA-32/Windows ABI.

## 3.1 Virtual Machine Implementation

The major computation blocks and data structures of a process VM are shown in Figure 3.2. The major blocks perform the following functions.

- The *loader* writes the guest code and data into a region of memory holding the *guest's memory image* and loads the runtime code. Although the memory image contains the guest's application code as well as data, it is all data as far as the runtime is concerned because source code is not directly executed. Rather, the source code is used as input "data" to interpretation and/or binary translation routines.

- The loader then turns control over to the *initialization* block, which allocates memory space for the code cache and other tables used during the emulation process. The initialization process also invokes the host OS to establish signal handlers for all the trap conditions that can occur (at least those for which signals are supported by the host OS). After initialization, the emulation process can begin, typically using a range of emulation techniques in a staged manner.

- The *emulation engine* uses interpretation and/or binary translation to emulate the guest instructions using the basic methods in Chapter 2. If binary translation is used as an emulation method, translated target code is held in a *code cache*. The code cache, which is written by the translator, is an executable code area while emulation is in progress. If emulation is performed via interpretation with a predecoded intermediate form, the predecoded instructions are stored in a similar cache structure.

- Because of the limited size of the code cache, the *code cache manager* is responsible for deciding which translations should be flushed out of the cache to make room for new translations as they are generated.

- A *profile database* contains dynamically collected program information that is used to guide optimization during the translation process. The uses

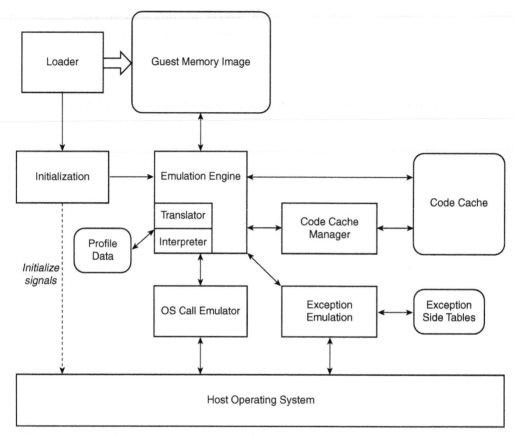

**Figure 3.2**   Implementation of a Process Virtual Machine.

of profile data, as well as optimization methods, are described in more detail in Chapter 4.

■ As emulation proceeds and the guest program performs a system call, the *OS call emulator* translates the OS call into an appropriate call (or calls) to the host OS and then handles any associated information returned as a result of the call.

■ The runtime must also handle traps that may occur as a result of executing either an interpreter instruction or a translated instruction, and it must handle any interrupts that are directed at the guest process. The runtime does this with the *exception emulator*. In some cases, the exception emulator takes over when an emulation-triggered trap causes an OS signal to be delivered to the runtime; in other cases, emulation routines discover an exception condition and jump to the exception emulator. An important aspect of runtime exception handling is generating the correct, precise guest state (including program counter, register values, and trap conditions) when an exception condition occurs.

■ *Side tables,* i.e., data structures generated as part of the translation process, are used by the runtime as part of the overall emulation process. One important use of side tables is in implementing a precise exception model with respect to the source ISA. Other uses of side tables will be described as they are introduced.

The design of all the major blocks will be described in more detail in the following sections; first, however, we define a framework for discussing and reasoning about compatibility in process VMs.

## 3.2 Compatibility

In any virtual machine implementation, a critical issue is *compatibility,* that is, the accuracy with which a guest's behavior is emulated on the host platform, as compared with its behavior on its native platform. Ideally, the behavior should be identical, although, as will become apparent, there are many practical situations where complete compatibility is not necessary for a process virtual machine to be useful.

When we define compatibility, we include all types of behaviors, with one important exception: We exclude differences that are purely performance related. That is, compatibility is a matter of correct functioning, not how fast the function is performed. Although performance is not part of the *definition* of compatibility, it is certainly an important *consideration* when implementing many VMs. In fact, the level of compatibility achieved sometimes depends very much on the degree of performance degradation that one is willing to accept.

In this section, we focus on VM compatibility in general and process-level (ABI) compatibility in particular. Because of the focus on process compatibility, most of our discussion and many of the examples are in terms of process compatibility and program emulation.

### 3.2.1 Levels of Compatibility

One could take a purist's view and argue that compatibility requires 100% accuracy for all programs all of the time. For some system VMs, e.g., codesigned VMs, strict ISA compatibility is usually a requirement. However, such a strict definition of compatibility would exclude many useful process virtual machine implementations. Consequently, we further refine the notion of compatibility to allow for qualified forms of compatibility.

We refer to the strict form of compatibility as *intrinsic compatibility*. Another term sometimes applied to a VM with intrinsic compatibility is *complete transparency* (Bruening 2004). Satisfying intrinsic compatibility is based entirely on properties of the virtual machine. Intrinsic compatibility holds for all guest software and for all possible input data. This includes assembly language programs, written by a devious programmer with the intent of "breaking" compatibility. When using an intrinsically compatible virtual machine, the user is assured that any software will behave the same way as on its native platform, with no further verification being required; that is, the verification is done at the time the VM is constructed. This is typically the standard used by hardware designers for ISA compatibility in microprocessors. However, it is a very strict requirement for a process VM; in many cases it is more strict than is really necessary or than can be achieved.

Probably more useful for process VMs is what we call *extrinsic compatibility*. This form of compatibility relies not only on the VM implementation but also on externally provided assurances or certification regarding properties of the guest software. Extrinsic compatibility may hold for some programs run on a virtual machine but not for others. For example, all programs compiled with a certain compiler and that use a certain set of libraries may define a level of extrinsic compatibility. Alternatively, a program may be compatible as long as it has limited resource requirements; e.g., its architected memory space requirements are less than the maximum that can be supported on a native platform. Or a software developer may take a particular program and, through debugging and other verification techniques, declare or certify that the program will give compatible behavior when run on a given process VM. For example, the Digital FX!32 system was developed with the goal of providing transparent operation; however, Digital maintained a list of Windows applications that were certified to be compatible. With extrinsic compatibility comes the requirement of clearly stating the external properties that must hold in order for compatibility to be achieved, e.g., the compiler that should be used or the logical resources needed.

### 3.2.2 A Compatibility Framework

As a practical matter, proving that compatibility holds, whether intrinsic or extrinsic, is an extremely difficult problem. In systems as complex as virtual machines, compatibility is usually ensured via test suites along with the logical reasoning of people intimately familiar with the system at hand. Because compatibility is too difficult to prove in any rigorous way, we would at least like some framework within which we can reason about compatibility and discuss compatibility issues.

Rather than consider the system as a whole, including the guest software, virtual machine software, operating system, and hardware platform, we first decompose the system and structure it in a way that is consistent with the way process VMs are usually constructed. Then we can reason about the parts.

To build a framework for discussing compatibility, we consider the isomorphism described in Chapter 1 (Figure 1.2). That is, we focus on (1) the mapping of state (or "resources" that contain the state) between the guest and the host, and (2) the operations that transform the state in the guest and the host. An application program performs operations on state in two ways: by executing instructions belonging to the user ISA and through operating system calls (made either explicitly or via traps and interrupts). Consequently, we divide the state into *user-managed state* and *OS-managed state*. The user-managed state is operated on by the user-level ISA and consists primarily of architected main memory and registers. The OS-managed state includes the contents of disk files and other storage devices as well as the state associated with resources such as graphics displays and networks.

### State Mapping

With regard to the user-managed state, we generally assume straightforward mappings between guest and host states. The resource holding the state does not necessarily have to be of the same type, however. For example, guest registers may be mapped to host main memory. The key point is that for a given resource holding guest state, e.g., specific register or memory location, the associated resource in the host is readily identified, and it can be easily determined whether the associated guest and host states are equivalent. The operating system–managed state is a little more difficult to deal with because it can be held in many forms, and operations on the state are often expressed in terms of OS abstractions; however, the state-mapping concept is the same.

### Operations

As a program runs on a native platform, it executes user-level instructions, occasionally transferring control to the operating system (through system calls, traps, or interrupts). When the operating system is finished servicing a call, trap, or interrupt, it transfers control back to the user-level instructions.

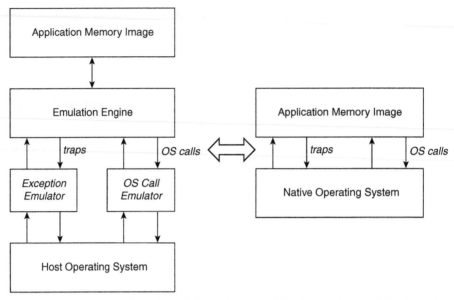

**Figure 3.3**   Correspondence Between Transfers of Control Between User Instructions and the Operating System in a Process Virtual Machine (left) and a Native Platform (right).

The user-level instructions modify the user-managed state, and the operating system performs operations that modify the OS-managed state and/or the user-managed state. The points where control is transferred between the user code and the OS (i.e., traps and OS calls) are a key element of our compatibility framework.

In a process VM, there are sets of operations and control transfers that correspond with those on the native platform. The emulation engine uses interpretation and/or binary translation to emulate user instructions, and the OS and exception emulators perform the operating system functions. To do this, the runtime's emulation routines may or may not call the underlying host OS, depending on the operation being emulated. In any case, for each transfer of control between user code and the OS on a native platform, we identify a corresponding point where control is transferred in the virtual machine (Figure 3.3). Establishing a one-to-one mapping between these control transfer points is a portion of the structure we impose on process VMs as part of our framework. In most implemented process VMs such a mapping can be established, so this requirement is not practically limiting. Given this mapping, we can then focus on equivalence of mapped states at the points where control is transferred between user instructions and the OS (and vice versa).

### Sufficient Compatibility Conditions

Given that corresponding control transfer points have been identified, we give the following conditions for compatibility.

1.  At the point of control transfer from emulating user instructions to the OS, the guest state is equivalent to the host state, under the given state mapping. An important consequence of this condition is that equivalent user-managed state does *not* have to be maintained at an instruction granularity; it must only be maintained at the granularity of OS control transfers. These are the only points where the state may be made visible to the "outside world." This allows for substantial flexibility in the way that instruction emulation can be done. In particular, translated target code can be reorganized and optimized substantially — as long as the user-managed state is the same when control is transferred to the OS or exception emulator.

    On the other hand, we make the conservative assumption that *all* the user-managed state may be exposed to the outside world when the OS takes over, so at that point in time all guest and corresponding host states are required to be equivalent. For example, a system call that performs a file read or write may only modify a specific portion of the guest process's memory state, not all of it. Yet we require that all the state be equivalent. To make less conservative assumptions would require deep analysis of the underlying host OS to determine the portion of the user-managed state that may be read or written by each of the host OS system call or trap handlers. This may be straightforward in some cases, such as file I/O, but in others it may not be. To avoid analysis of the host OS, we make the conservative assumption that all the user-managed state may potentially be accessed and must therefore be equivalent at the time of control transfers.

2.  At the point of control transfer back to user instructions, the guest state (both user managed and OS managed) is equivalent to host state, under the given mapping. The combined runtime and host OS actions, which emulate the guest's native OS actions, should produce system behavior, as well as modifications to the guest state (file contents, for example), that are equivalent to that for the guest's native platform. Here, an additional consideration is that for some OS behavior, e.g., driving a graphics terminal or a network interface, the ordering of operations must also be equivalent as well as the overall state changes observed at the control transfer point.

Figure 3.4, based on the VM isomorphism of Figure 1.2, illustrates guest operation on its native platform and the corresponding operation on the host platform. On its native platform, the guest software transitions back and

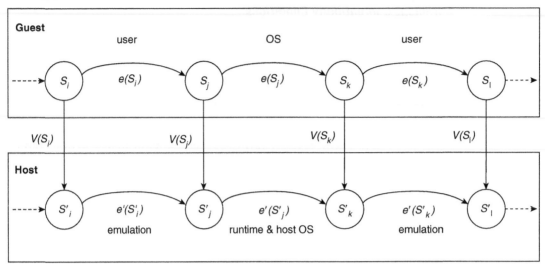

**Figure 3.4** Compatibility, Illustrated in Terms of the Isomorphism Between Guest and Host States in a Process VM. *At points where control is transferred between the OS and user instructions, the states must be equivalent.*

forth between user instructions and OS operations. At each of these transition points, a similar transition point in the host platform can be identified. At these points, the states mapped by *V* must be equivalent.

### Discussion

The compatibility framework just outlined assumes that process VMs are structured in a certain way, and the sufficient conditions for compatibility are stated relatively informally. However, the conditions are formal enough for us to discuss compatibility issues in this and later chapters in a concise manner. It should also be evident that a process VM does not have to be structured the way we assume (along the general lines of Figure 3.2), and it does not have to satisfy the foregoing conditions to be compatible. Rather, we assume a structure that is common to most realistic process VMs, and the sufficient conditions that we consider are reasonably good for compatibility, given the commonly used VM structure. The important thing is that by having such a compatibility framework, one can more easily identify compatibility issues when they arise and then evaluate their significance.

As we have defined it, to achieve intrinsic compatibility the conditions just stated must hold for all programs and data. In contrast, for extrinsic compatibility, conditions are imposed on a subset of guest software. These conditions may be described in terms of any of the features of the compatibility framework. We now give a number of examples.

With respect to state mapping, the memory address space available to a guest program may be less than the maximum size on a native platform; consequently, a proper state mapping can only be provided for programs whose memory space requirements do not exceed a certain VM-imposed limit. Hence, extrinsic compatibility is achieved only for processes that do not exceed a certain size.

With respect to mapping of control transfers, there may be situations where some control transfers to the OS are potentially eliminated during binary translation. This can occur if certain potentially trapping instructions are removed during the target code-optimization process (as we will see in Chapter 4). Here extrinsic compatibility can be achieved for those programs where the trap conditions are known not to occur (possibly depending on the input data).

With respect to user-level instructions, there may be cases where guest floating-point arithmetic is not done exactly as on its native platform (see Section 2.8.3). For these VMs, extrinsic compatibility can only be achieved for programs where the floating-point accuracy is sufficient to satisfy the user's needs.

With respect to OS operations, there may be cases where the host OS does not support exactly the same functions as the guest's native OS. The guest may avoid these OS features as a way of achieving extrinsic compatibility.

Compatibility issues in process VMs receive an enlightening and thorough discussion in Breunig's thesis (Bruening 2004). In that work, some compatibility issues are refined further than we do here. For example, memory state equivalence of the heap and stack are considered separately.

### 3.2.3 Implementation Dependences

The division between architecture and implementation is central to the design of computer systems (Section 1.2). This division, as exemplified by the ISA, separates the functional features of a design from implementation features. Nevertheless, there are situations where implementation features do become visible in the architecture and cause functional differences. These often-subtle effects can sometimes make completely accurate emulation difficult at best.

Probably the most common examples involve caches. One example such occurs in processors that have separate instruction and data caches, as is commonly done today. If the program writes into its own instruction space (i.e., self-modifying code), some processor implementations do not automatically update the instruction cache contents (or flush the instruction cache, which would have the same effect). Rather, the old version of the modified instructions remains in the cache until it is replaced. This can lead to nondeterminism because the results of a program may then depend on external events such as context switches, which affect the instruction cache contents. To avoid this problem it is up to the programmer (or compiler) to flush the instruction cache after self-modifying code is executed. This can be done either explicitly, via instructions provided for this purpose, or implicitly, through a carefully constructed code sequence that causes the modified cache locations to be replaced. The net effect, however, is that the instruction cache becomes visible to the architecture — its presence can affect the function of software.

This might seem like a small problem. In fact, during emulation, it is sometimes easiest to make self-modifying code execute the "logical" way, i.e., by always using the most recent version of code. This can be done, for example, by using the techniques to be described in Section 3.4.2. However, there have been cases where clever programmers use the interactions between instruction caches and self-modifying code as a way of identifying exactly which processor implementation is executing their software and then using this information to select, at run time, a version of a procedure that is optimal for the given implementation. What if code of this type finds a "nonexistent" hardware implementation, as might be caused by emulation?

An even more troublesome scenario can arise if real implementations of an ISA provide a stricter implementation than is required by the specification. Consider the instruction cache example again. An ISA specification may state that self-modifying code is only guaranteed to take effect if the cache is explicitly flushed by executing a certain instruction; otherwise, the results are undefined (there are real ISAs specified this way). However, it may be that all existing implementations actually implement self-modifying code in the "logical" way, even when the instruction cache flush instruction is not executed. Consequently, there may be self-modifying code that does not flush the instruction cache properly yet still "works" on real implementations. Now, a developer of a VM may depend on the instruction cache flush instruction to trigger the flushing of binary translated code residing in a code cache. This not only means that self-modifying code without the explicit instruction cache flush may behave differently on the virtual machine implementation, but it may cause some guest code to "break," from the perspective of the user. In fact, the VM implements the specification and is correct, strictly speaking, but this would be of small consolation to the user whose code no longer works.

There is often no good solution to implementation "leaks" of the type just described, but it is a problem that a VM developer should be keenly aware of. Great care should be taken in reading the fine print of architecture specifications and hardware manuals that describe implementation dependences. Significant effort should be given to imagining complex scenarios where implementation dependences can become observable and may even be exploited. The bottom line is that vigilance is probably the only answer to such implementation dependences.

## 3.3 State Mapping

We are now ready to construct process VMs. We begin with the mapping of user-managed state, primarily state held in registers and memory. Then in later sections we discuss various aspects of emulation, i.e., the operations that transform the state.

When we describe state mapping, we often do it in terms of resource mapping, because it is the resources (registers and memory) that actually contain the state. For example, if we say that a guest memory location maps to a host memory location, we are implying that the state held in the two memory locations is the same. Figure 3.5 illustrates a typical state mapping. In this example, the guest data and code map into the host's user address space and share the user address space with the runtime code and data.

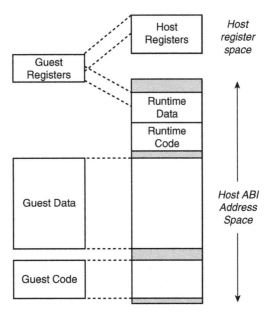

**Figure 3.5** Mapping of Guest State to Host State.

Because a process VM views memory as a logical address space supported by the host machine, when we speak of *memory* in this context, we are referring to a logical address space, not the implemented real memory. This view is reflected in Figure 3.5, where regions of the guest memory address space map onto regions of the host memory address space.

The guest register state is mapped into host registers and/or is maintained in the runtime data region of memory. This latter mapping illustrates an important point — that the guest state does not have to be maintained in the same type of resource as on a native platform. Similarly, in some situations it may be convenient to map guest memory onto file system storage rather than the host's main memory. However, the way that these state mappings are done has a significant bearing on the emulation techniques used and on the resulting performance that is achieved.

### 3.3.1 Register Mapping

Register space mapping is fairly straightforward and was discussed in Sections 2.5 and 2.8.1; we summarize here. If the number of guest ISA registers is less than the number of host ISA registers, it may be possible to map all guest registers into host registers for the duration of emulation. In addition, there is usually a register context block maintained in memory by the runtime. The runtime loads and unloads register contents from/to this block as the emulator is entered and exited. That is, the runtime may use all or most of the registers when it performs tasks other than emulation and then turns the registers over to the guest whenever emulation is in progress.

If the number of registers in the guest and host are the same, or nearly so, it may be theoretically possible to map all host registers to guest registers, but this could pose a problem if the emulation process requires registers for its own use (as is the case with interpretation) or if the runtime performs dynamic optimization of frequently executed code. In some ISAs, loading and unloading registers from the context block can be a problem because in order to perform a store to the register context block, a register is needed to hold the address of the context block. If all the registers are used by the emulation process, then this additional register is simply not available.

If the number of guest registers is larger than the number of host registers, then some of the guest registers must be mapped to a register context block in the host's memory. The runtime, usually through the translator, is then responsible for managing the host register space by moving guest registers into and out of the host registers as emulation proceeds.

### 3.3.2  Memory Address Space Mapping

The guest and host instruction sets each have their specific memory architectures, and it is the job of the runtime emulation process to map the guest's address space to the host's address space and to maintain protection requirements. Specifically, when a guest program performs a load, a store, or an instruction fetch, it is to some address $A$ within the guest's address space defined by the guest ISA. However, after state mapping, the data or code at guest address $A$ may actually be placed at some other address, $A'$, within the host's address space, and the runtime emulation software must be able to perform the required address space mapping. Just as with instruction emulation, there is a range of possibilities for performing address space mapping spanning different performance levels, determined by the relative amount of emulation performed by software compared to the amount performed directly on the host hardware.

#### *Runtime Software–Supported Translation Tables*

Figure 3.6 illustrates the most flexible method for memory architecture emulation. As with instruction interpretation, described in the previous chapter, the more flexible methods also tend to be more software intensive. Figure 3.6 shows a software translation table maintained by the runtime, similar

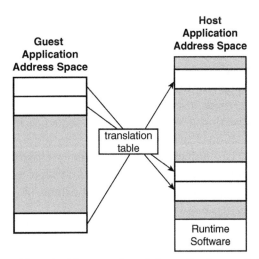

**Figure 3.6**  Emulating Memory Address Architecture via a Software-Implemented Address Translation Table.

```
Initially, r1 holds source address
             r30 holds base address of translation table

    srwi  r29,r1,16        ;shift r1 right by an immediate 16
    slwi  r29,r29,2        ;convert to a byte address in table
    lwzx  r29,r29,r30      ;load block location in host memory
    slwi  r28,r1,16        ;shift left/right to zero out
    srwi  r28,r28,16       ;  source block number
    slwi  r29,r29,16       ;shift up target block number
    or    r29,r28,r29      ;form address
    lwz   r2,0(r29)        ;do load
```

**Figure 3.7**    Code Sequence for Performing a Load Instruction with Software-Mapping Method.

to a conventional page table. The guest addresses do not have to be contiguously mapped in the host address space. The guest address space can be divided into blocks, each of which, in practice, would be some whole multiple of the host page size. Then a guest address is translated to a host address by performing a table lookup to find the offset within the host space where the guest block begins.

Figure 3.7 contains an example of code that emulates a load instruction using a software-implemented translation table. In this example, it is assumed that the mapped memory blocks are each 64KB. The translation table itself is maintained as part of the runtime, and its base address is held in host register r30. To perform the load, the source address is shifted by 16 bits to get the 64KB block number. This number is converted to an offset added to the table base, and the sum is used to access the proper table entry. This entry contains a pointer to the address block in the host address space. The block address replaces the block address in the original guest address and can then be used for performing the requested load. Actually, the PowerPC has two instructions designed for these types of operations: the rlwimi (rotate left word immediate then mask insert) and rlwinm (rotate left word immediate and with mask) instructions. We use a longer sequence here in order to make the overall operation clearer.

The similarity to the address translation used in conventional virtual address systems for converting virtual to real addresses should be apparent. Figure 3.8 depicts a method that extends this similarity further. Here, the runtime opens a disk file for holding data belonging to any portions of the guest address space that are not resident in the host address space. Although similar to a conventional virtual memory, the guest virtual address space is actually mapped to a region of the host virtual address space rather than to real memory.

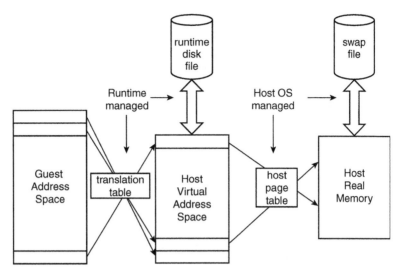

**Figure 3.8**  Mapping a Guest Address Space into a Region of the Host Space. *The runtime software manages the region of host address space in much the same way as the host OS manages its real memory.*

The host virtual addresses space, in turn, is mapped to the host real memory by the underlying host system.

At any point in time, a given guest memory block may or may not be present in the host memory. Hence the translation table is enhanced with a "valid" bit to indicate whether or not the accessed guest block is present in the host address space. The runtime software accesses the translation table, not only to perform the address lookup but also to test the valid bit and branch to memory management software in the runtime when an accessed block is not present. The runtime memory manager then decides which block to replace, performs the necessary disk I/O, modifies the translation table, and then returns to emulation.

This step-by-step software-intensive mapping method is conceptually similar to the simple decode/dispatch interpretation for instructions. However, its use need not be restricted to interpretation; it can serve with any emulation scheme, including binary translation. The relative overhead of the scheme would be considerable in a binary translation environment but may be unavoidable if there is a semantic mismatch between the guest and host ABIs. A prime example is the case where the host application address space is not large enough to hold a typical guest application, e.g., if a 64-bit guest is being emulated by a 32-bit host platform. The key point is that *if all else fails*, this software-intensive method can be used.

### Direct Translation Methods

We next consider address space mapping methods that rely more on the underlying hardware and less on VM software. As such, they are somewhat analogous to the binary translation methods for instruction emulation. There are two direct translation methods, as illustrated in Figure 3.9, one being a special case of the other.

Figure 3.9a shows a mapping where the guest address space has been displaced by a fixed offset but is still contiguous within the host space. In this case, the offset value can be held in a host register that is added to each guest address during emulation. In the example shown in the figure, the runtime is placed at the beginning of the host address space, and the guest program is placed on top, each location in the guest address space offset by a fixed amount to determine its location in the guest address space. This fixed offset mapping is used in the emulation code given in Figure 2.16.

Figure 3.9b shows the important special case where the fixed offset is 0, meaning that the guest addresses have the same locations in the host virtual address space. The runtime software now needs to be located in a region beyond

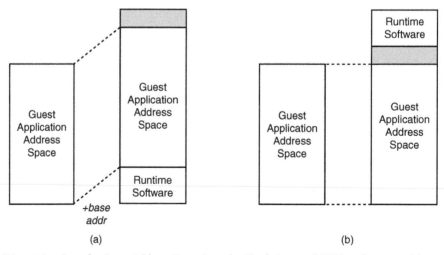

**Figure 3.9**   Direct Mapping of a Guest Address Space into the Host's Space. *(a) When the guest addresses are offset by some constant in the host's space; (b) when the guest addresses are placed at the same locations within the host's space.*

the portion of the address space allocated for the guest, as shown in the figure. This results in a very simple mapping of guest addresses to host addresses during emulation. In this case, source memory load and store instructions can often be translated one-to-one to target loads and stores, with no need for any additional address translation instructions.

### Compatibility Issues

Depending on the performance and compatibility level desired, the relative sizes of the guest and host address spaces have significant implications when selecting the memory mapping and translation method to use. An important consideration is that the runtime software (both code and data) share the same address space with the guest application.

If one wants intrinsic compatibility and a high-performance VM implementation, then it is probably necessary for the host address space to be larger than the guest address space so that both the maximum-size guest process and the runtime software can fit into the host address space at the same time. Then a direct mapping method can be used, as in Figure 3.9b. This is often the case, as when the IA-32 ISA is emulated on a platform containing a 64-bit ISA (Baraz et al. 2003; Hookway and Herdeg 1997).

If the host address space is not larger than the combination of the runtime and the maximum guest process, then either performance or intrinsic compatibility must be sacrificed. Using a software translation method as in Figure 3.8 will yield intrinsic compatibility at the cost of several target instructions per source load or store instruction.

On the other hand, the memory actually used by a guest application is not necessarily the maximum size permitted by the host ABI; in most cases, in fact, a guest application does not reach its maximum size. Furthermore, in many situations users compile programs using standard libraries (of unknown size to the typical user), and most user programs do not rely on a specific memory size or on specific memory addresses. In these situations a form of extrinsic compatibility is quite sufficient. In particular, compatibility is achieved as long as the virtual memory requirements of the guest do not exceed what is left over after the runtime is placed in memory. Furthermore, if the runtime is strategically placed with respect to the guest process, then efficient direct translation can be used. By *strategic placement*, we mean placement in a region that is not being used by the guest process. This might mean that the runtime is implemented in position-independent manner so that it can operate correctly regardless of where it is placed in memory. This allows the runtime to place itself in a region of memory that does not conflict with the locations in use by the application. Depending on loader conventions, some applications may be placed in upper memory, others in lower memory, and still others in a number of noncontiguous memory regions. In addition, the runtime can potentially be moved during the course of emulation as the application allocates or deletes blocks of memory.

## 3.4 Memory Architecture Emulation

Given an address space mapping and implementation method, there are several aspects of memory architecture that must be emulated in a process VM. Specifically, there are three important features of ABI memory architecture, i.e., memory as seen by a user application, that must be taken into consideration:

- **The overall structure of the address space**, e.g., whether it is divided into segments or is a flat, linear address space. For most of our discussion, we assume a flat, linear address space because most current ABIs use a linear address space (although it may be further subdivided into a heap and stack, for example). Techniques for virtualizing segmented memory can be built upon these linear space techniques.

- **The access privilege types that are supported**. Some ABIs support read, write, execute (R, W, E) privileges, while others restrict their support to only R and W.

- **The protection/allocation granularity**, i.e., the size of the smallest block of memory that is allocated by the operating system and the granularity at which protection privileges are maintained. In most systems the granularity of memory allocation is the same as that for protection, even though, strictly speaking, they need not be the same.

Most common ABIs define a specific size and range of addresses that are available to a user. Figure 3.10 illustrates the address space defined for the Win32 ABI. Two 64KB blocks (at the top and bottom of the 31 bit address space) are reserved by the system. All other locations in the 31-bit address space are available to a user process. The user may reserve blocks of memory for later use. A user may also commit a region of memory, which means that the user is given access and that disk space is allocated for paging. A key point is that a user process is granted access to all addresses within the non-reserved range. As pointed out earlier, this may have important implications

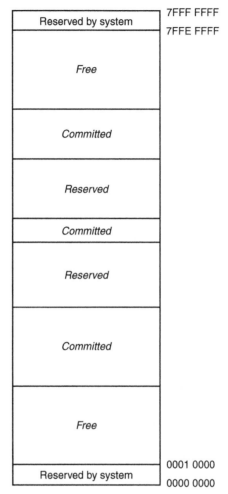

**Figure 3.10**    Win32 ABI Memory Architecture. *The system reserves regions at the upper and lower ends of memory. The user can reserve a specific range of addresses and later commit it to use or leave it free.*

because the runtime must share the address space with a user process in a transparent way.

### 3.4.1  Memory Protection

An important aspect of memory architecture is memory protection. Most ISAs allow access restrictions to be placed on different regions of the memory space.

These restrictions are usually specified as some combination of read, write, and execute (or none).

If a software translation table is used (Figure 3.6), then emulation of protection checking is straightforward. Protection information can be kept in the translation table, and checking can be completely emulated as part of the translation process. This is essentially a software version of the way it is done in a conventional virtual memory system. As pointed out earlier, this method is functionally correct but slow.

With direct or offset addressing (Figure 3.9), however, there is no software translation table for maintaining privilege information. Clearly, a software table can be added for the special purpose of protection checking, though this method suffers in efficiency. Depending on the support provided by the host OS, a more efficient method that relies on the underlying host hardware for protection checking can be implemented. This requires that the runtime has some means of directing the host OS to implement page protection matching the guest emulation requirements. The nature of the host support and its use in implementing efficient protection checking are described in the next subsection.

### Host-Supported Memory Protection

Memory protection can be emulated by a host platform using two commonly found host OS features:

1. A system call invoked by the application (via the runtime in this case) specifying a page and the access privileges (read, write, execute, none) for the page.
2. A signal for a memory access fault that can be delivered to the runtime whenever a memory access violates the privilege specified for the containing page.

Some host operating systems support these features directly. In Linux, for example, the mprotect() system call and the SIGSEGV signal provide these functions. The mprotect system call has arguments that are (1) a virtual address aligned to a page boundary, (2) a size, and (3) a protection specification that is the bitwise OR of none, read, write, execute. The SIGSEGV signal is delivered if a page is accessed with the wrong privileges.

In addition to the direct methods supported by the OS as described earlier, there are indirect ways of emulating protection features. For example, the mmap() Linux system call can be used for mapping a region of the address space for which the runtime wants access control. The region is mapped to a file that

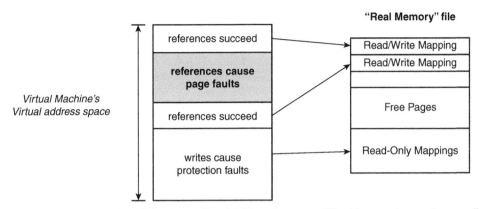

**Figure 3.11**    Mapping a Portion of the Guest Virtual Address Space to a File. *The mapping can be controlled via mapping, unmapping, and read-only mappings.*

has the required access privileges, as shown in Figure 3.11. If the application software attempts a disallowed access, a SIGSEGV signal is delivered (Bovet and Cesati 2001).

In the absence of any of these convenient ways to provide the runtime with the ability to control access to the guest software through host-implemented features, the runtime can always fall back to the less efficient software mapping method of accessing memory.

### Page Size Issues

We now consider the case where the host and guest pages are of different sizes; obviously, this difference must be considered when allocating and protecting memory. As far as assigning specific access privileges to the guest pages, the method described in the preceding section is fairly simple when the guest page size is a multiple of the host page size. In this case all the host pages that correspond to the single guest page are given the same protections. However, when the guest page size is smaller than that of the host, two or more different guest pages may be included in the same host page. This causes a problem if the protections are different for guest pages that share the same host page. Figure 3.12 illustrates a case where a guest code page and data page share the same host page. The guest pages should have different access privileges, but in the host system they must be given the same protections. As always, the software-based mapping method can be used to solve this problem, but with significant overhead.

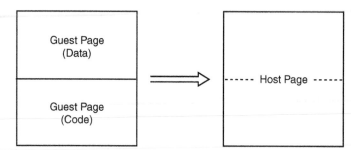

**Figure 3.12**    Guest Page Smaller Than Host Page. *If the guest page size is smaller than the host page size, then some host pages may be divided between code and data. This causes difficulties when emulating memory protection.*

Aligning the code and data regions on host page boundaries would seem to fix the problem, but this essentially relocates regions of the guest address space, and the ISA emulation software must correct for this realignment by adding constant offsets to guest addresses within relocated regions. This may not only affect the efficiency of emulation but may also reduce the portability of emulation code by adding a host platform dependency.

An alternative is to maintain protection checking through the host platform as described earlier, but to take a conservative approach, giving the entire host page the lesser privilege of the different guest pages that share it. The runtime must then handle any "extra" traps generated either through signal handler software or by reverting to software mapping (and privilege checking).

Another issue with matching guest and host memory architectures is that the types of protections defined in the two ISAs may not match. If the host supports a superset of guest protections, the guest can be granted the correct protections. However, if the host supports only a proper subset of the guest protections, then the VM software must use conservative protection assignments or rely on software checks, as described earlier.

An important case is where the host supports only RW privileges while the guest uses RWE. This is the most common case of a mismatch that occurs in practice. With emulation via interpretation, the interpreter code can easily check execute protection as part of its normal operation with relatively little slowdown, i.e., through a software translation table. With binary translation, execute protection for the guest code has to be checked only at the time the runtime reads the guest code and performs translation. In addition, the runtime must be able to detect the situations where the application changes the protection, but this can be done easily as part of the OS call translation process (Section 3.7). When this occurs, any affected translated code must be discarded.

### 3.4.2 Self-Referencing and Self-Modifying Code

Occasionally, an application program either refers to itself (i.e., it reads from its code region) or attempts to modify itself by writing into the code region. This poses potential problems when binary translation is used, because the code actually executing is translated code, not the original source code. If the original source code would have read or written itself, then the translated version must produce exactly the same results. Such instances of self-referencing and self-modifying code must be accurately emulated by the runtime.

#### *Basic Method*

The basis for the solution is the same for both problems. In particular, an accurate memory image of the guest program code is maintained at all times. All load and store addresses in the translated version are mapped into the source memory region, regardless of whether code or data is being addressed. Consequently, the self-referencing case (Figure 3.13a) is automatically implemented correctly.

For self-modifying code (Figure 3.13b), the original source code region is write-protected by the runtime. That is, the page-level write access privilege is turned off for all pages containing translated source code. This can be done via a system call made by the runtime (e.g., via Linux `mprotect()`). Consequently, any attempt to write a page containing translated code results in a protection trap and the delivery of a signal to the runtime. At that point, the runtime can flush either the entire code cache or just the translations corresponding to the modified page (by using a side table that keeps track of the page(s) from which translated code blocks originated). Then the runtime should temporarily enable writes to the code region, enter interpretation mode, and interpret forward, at least until it gets through the code block that triggered the fault. This interpretation step guarantees forward progress when a translated code block modifies itself. Then the runtime can reenable write-protection and proceed with normal operation, which will eventually result in retranslation of code in the modified page.

#### *Pseudo-Self-Modifying Code*

The method just described is a high-overhead way of dealing with self-modifying code, but in most situations it does not hurt performance significantly because in many programs self-modifying code tends to be rather uncommon (or nonexistent). Nevertheless, there are certain programs or types of programs where self-modifying code or pseudo-self-modifying code

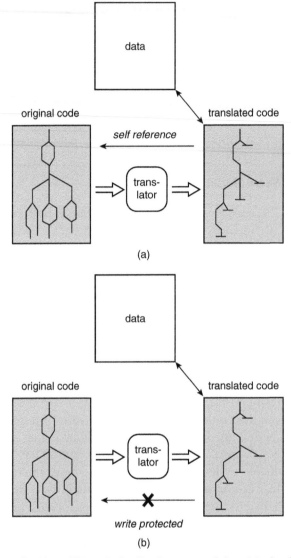

**Figure 3.13** Self-Referencing and Self-Modifying Code. *Keeping a copy of the original code can be used for solving the problem of (a) self-referencing code and (b) self-modifying code.*

does occur frequently enough to cause a large performance loss. *Pseudo-self-modifying* code describes the situation where writeable data areas are intermixed with code. That is, a write into a "code" page does not literally modify code, but will trigger a write-protection fault. This code sometimes appears in assembly language routines, such as device drivers, some performance-critical game kernels, and embedded code.

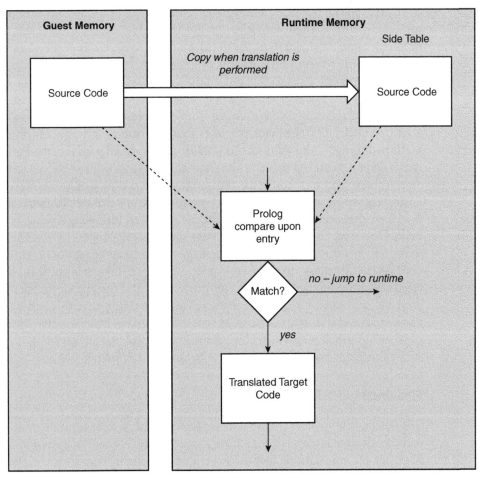

**Figure 3.14** Handling Pseudo-Self-Modifying Code via Dynamic Checks.

To deal with frequently occurring pseudo-self-modifying code, one approach is to check dynamically whether the source binary code has been modified before the corresponding translated target code is executed (Dehnert et al. 2003). That is, if write-protection faults to the same code region repeatedly occur, the runtime can retranslate the code in the page being written to and, for each translation block, save the original source code in a side table (see Figure 3.14). Then as a prolog to each of the translation blocks, the translator inserts check code that compares the current version of the source code with the original side table version of the source code. Write-protection for the page in question can then be turned off. As long as the prolog check code finds the source code unchanged (and it will in the case of pseudo-self-modifying code), then execution of the translated code can proceed. This method results in slowdowns (by at least a factor of 2, because the code comparison is time consuming), but it is still much faster than repeated protection faults, interpretations, and retranslations.

A potentially faster alternative is to make the prolog code a separate code block that can be linked and unlinked from its corresponding translation block (Dehnert et al. 2003). Immediately after a write-protect fault, the runtime links in the prolog code, and write-protection for the modified page is turned off. The check code is executed the next time the potentially modified code is entered, and, if the source is found to be unmodified, the prolog can be unlinked and write-protection reenabled. With this method, the check is performed only the first time that potentially modified code is executed following a write-protect fault. However, there is problem in making forward progress when the code that performs the write is in the same page that is being modified. That is, the code repeatedly traps, disables write-protection, later finds that the source code region is unmodified, reenables write-protection, and then modifies the source code region, resulting in another trap. The probability that this will happen can be reduced if source code can be write-protected at finer granularity than a page, as described in the next subsection. In any case, the slower method given in the foregoing paragraph can always be used as a fall-back.

### Fine-Grain Write-Protection

The basic write-protect method, as we have been considering it thus far, protects the source code region at a page granularity; if there is a write into the page, all the translations formed from instructions in that source code page are flushed from the code cache. An improvement on this approach uses software to keep track of source code blocks at a finer granularity (Dehnert et al. 2003). For each page that contains translated source instructions, the runtime can maintain a finer-granularity protection table, containing a write-protect bit mask per page. Each bit in a page's mask corresponds to a small region of the page, e.g., 128 bytes. Then as code is translated, the translator sets bits in the mask as it translates source instructions. If a particular page contains a combination of code and data, then any data-only regions (at the 128-byte granularity) will not have their fine-grain write-protect bits set. When a write into a source code page results in a trap to the runtime, the runtime can retrieve the fine-grain write-protect mask for the given page and compare the faulting address with the bits in the bit mask. If, for example, the faulting write was to a data-only region, then the write-protect bit for that region will not be set, and translated instructions do not have to be flushed. The finer-granularity bit mask can also be used to reduce the flushed translations when a fine-grain code region is written to (through the use of side tables that track the translation blocks corresponding to instructions in each of the fine-grain regions).

### True Self-Modifying Code

For cases where true self-modifying code frequently occurs, an approach for avoiding write-protect faults for the binary translator is to remove the self-modifying code via idiom recognition. That is, the translator code recognizes the common scenarios where self-modifying code occurs and invokes special translations. For example, self-modifying code may be used for writing the immediate field of an instruction contained in an inner loop and then executing the loop. This is illustrated in Figure 3.15a, where the immediate field of an IA-32 add immediate instruction is frequently modified. This case can be handled by converting it into equivalent data region read/write operations. In Figure 3.15b, the add immediate instruction is translated to a load that retrieves the immediate field from the source code (which is a data region from the perspective of the translated code) followed by an add instruction that uses the register value rather than an immediate.

In other situations, a given region of source code may be modified in only a small number of different ways. This occurs in some device-independent drivers, where the driver itself writes an implementation-dependent piece of code and then executes it. In these situations, the runtime can save the various source code versions along with the corresponding translated code. Then when code modification is detected, the runtime can compare the modified source code against the saved source code versions. If it finds a match, the corresponding saved translation can be retrieved and used. This method still incurs significant overhead, but at least it avoids repeated retranslations.

```
label:   add %eax, 0x123456         ;add immediate
```

(a)

```
lwz r29, label+1(r2)         ;r2 points to the IA32 memory image
add r4,r4,r29                ;r4 contains %eax
```

(b)

**Figure 3.15**   Translating an Instruction Containing a Frequently Modified Immediate Field. *(a) An IA-32 add immediate instruction; (b) a PowerPC translation, where the immediate value is loaded from the original source code memory image.*

### Protecting Runtime Memory

Because the runtime software (including both its code and data) shares an address space with guest application software, the runtime must be protected from the guest application. For example, if an emulated program should, through a bug or by intent, attempt to access a region in the address space where the runtime resides, then this should be reported as a memory fault with respect to the emulated application. To maintain compatibility and give correct results, the guest program should not be allowed to read from or write into the runtime's memory area and continue on its way.

If a software translation table with protection checking is implemented (Figure 3.6), then such an access violation can easily be detected as part of the translation process. The runtime maintains access privileges in the memory map, so the runtime itself is protected. Although effective, this method would be quite slow.

A higher-performance solution is used in the Omniware VM (Lucco, Sharp, and Wahbe 1995; Wahbe et al. 1993). In this system, underlying host hardware is used for address translation (as in Figure 3.9), but protection checking is done in software. To streamline software protection checking, guest data and code are divided into power-of-2–sized segments. By relying on such segments, checking can be done fairly efficiently via a single shift (to extract the segment address bits) and a comparison. If only one data segment is active at any given time, then the address bits of the currently accessible segment can be held in a host register, making the comparison process even faster. Furthermore, by analyzing program control flow, optimizations similar to the ones used in HLL VMs for reducing null pointer and array range checks (Section 6.6.2) can be applied. This reduces the overhead even more, resulting in a reported total overhead of about 10% (sometimes less). Although this technique protects the runtime from out-of-bounds accesses made by the guest, forcing power-of-2 segments may compromise intrinsic compatibility by putting restrictions on the memory address space that are not present on a native platform.

A method that uses underlying hardware for both address translation and protection checking is found in the Dynamo system (Bala, Duesterwald, and Banerjia 2000). With this method, the runtime is responsible for calling appropriate host OS routines to set the memory protections. Execution is divided into two modes. In *emulation mode* translated guest code is executing; at all other times, including when the binary translator is generating code, the VM is in *runtime mode*. It is only when the VM is in emulation mode that the runtime code and data must be protected from the translated code. Consequently, the memory protections should be different when in emulation mode and runtime mode.

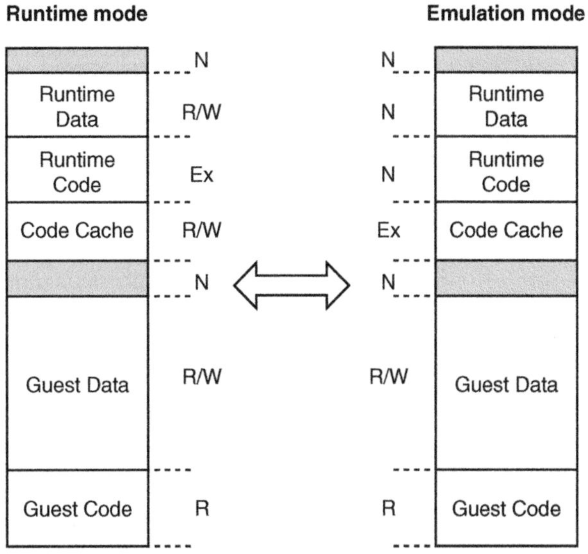

**Runtime mode**                          **Emulation mode**

| Runtime Data | R/W |
| Runtime Code | Ex |
| Code Cache | R/W |
|  | N |
| Guest Data | R/W |
| Guest Code | R |

N at top; correspondingly emulation side: N, N, N, Ex (Code Cache), N, R/W (Guest Data), R (Guest Code)

**Figure 3.16**  Memory Protection Settings Using Cached Translated Code. *The protections for runtime mode are on the left and for emulation mode they are shown on the right.*

Figure 3.16 illustrates memory protections during the time spent in runtime mode and during emulation mode. In runtime mode, the runtime code is executable; the runtime data structures are all accessible with read and/or write permissions. The code cache is read/writeable because it must be accessed and modified during the translation process. In emulation mode, all the runtime data structures become inaccessible and the code cache is execute-only; the only data that can be accessed is in the guest's memory image.

To change the protections based on the mode, the runtime uses a system call, e.g., Linux mprotect(), to change the privilege of the runtime data and code to no-access and the code cache to execute-only, just prior to switching from runtime mode to emulation mode. When control is returned to the runtime, it can reestablish read/write privileges. This leaves the problem of the emulation software attempting to jump or branch into the runtime region. This is checked as part of the interpretation and/or binary translation process. During interpretation, branch and jump destinations can be explicitly checked by the interpreter. For translated code, all branches and jumps within a translated code block are to direct addresses within the block itself. All indirect jumps or branches that may leave a translated code block are done through either the map table or link pointers in the translation block. Both of these are written by the runtime, and it can check the addresses at the time they are written.

This method is effective, but it suffers from a relatively high overhead whenever there is a mode switch. However, if code caching is effective (and it usually is), this overhead is rarely suffered after the guest's instruction working set has been translated.

If guest registers are mapped into the host memory space, another protection problem remains, however. Ordinarily, registers are naturally protected from memory load and store instructions because they are in their own separate, small address space and can only be accessed directly via register designators. If the guest register context block is mapped into the host memory space, however, a rogue load or store in translated guest code can conceivably access the memory-mapped registers. If this were to happen, behavior would differ from the native guest program, and results would likely be corrupted. A memory-mapped register region is not shown in Figure 3.16, but it would be a read/write area that exists outside the guest's normal memory image.

Mapping guest registers to memory is often hard to avoid. It is practically mandatory if the number of source registers is more than the number of target registers. It is also an important feature of same-ISA optimization (Section 4.7), where some optimizations may increase register "pressure," leading to spills of register contents to memory.

This is a place where it is important to distinguish between intrinsic and extrinsic compatibility. For intrinsic compatibility, there must be some way to protect the memory-mapped registers no matter what guest software tries to do, and a solution is to rely on software protection checking of loads and stores (as discussed earlier in this section). For extrinsic compatibility, a solution is to certify that a given program has no bugs that cause loads or stores to make accesses outside declared program data structures. One would ordinarily hope that programs satisfy this property, but nevertheless its requirement for correct operation means that intrinsic compatibility is not achieved.

## 3.5 Instruction Emulation

Emulation is at the heart of a process-level VM, and the emulation engine can have a relatively sophisticated architecture of its own. Instruction emulation was the topic of Chapter 2. Both interpretation and binary translation were discussed at length. In this section, we discuss the integration of instruction emulation into an overall VM. We focus on high-performance emulation engines; lower-performance versions are relatively straightforward subsets.

For optimal performance, the emulation engine typically combines multiple emulation methods, for example, interpretation and binary translation. After initialization, the emulation engine begins interpreting the source binary and may later switch over to translation or even to optimized translation. The next section describes the important performance tradeoff involved, and the subsequent section describes the overall structure of a high-performance emulation engine.

### 3.5.1 Performance Tradeoff

To understand the basic framework that is typically used for high-performance emulation, it is important first to consider a key performance tradeoff among the emulation methods. This tradeoff was suggested at the end of the last chapter and involves start-up time versus steady-state performance for a specific emulation technique (e.g., translation or interpretation).

The *start-up time* is a one-time cost for converting code in one form to code in a different form prior to emulation. Examples include converting an original binary into an intermediate interpreted form, and full binary translation to the target ISA. In same-ISA dynamic optimizers the conversion may consist of code optimization without converting to a different ISA, but there is a start-up time cost for doing so. On the other hand, simple decode/dispatch interpretation requires no initial conversion and therefore effectively has a zero start-up time.

*Steady-state performance* can best be expressed as the average rate at which instructions are emulated, e.g., the time required per emulated instruction, whether emulation is being done via interpretation or via translation.

The overall time for emulating an instruction $N$ times is expressed as $S + NT$, where $S$ is the one-time start-up overhead for the given instruction and $T$ is the time required per emulation in steady state. The critical performance tradeoff is illustrated with an example shown in Figure 3.17. The start-up time for binary translation is 1000 cycles and $T$ is two cycles per instruction. For interpretation, start-up time is zero cycles and $T$ is 20 cycles per interpreted instruction. The total emulation time for binary translation starts at 1000 and slopes upward very slowly. On the other hand, interpretation time is initially much lower than translation and climbs steadily, until it eventually surpasses translation time. That is, there is a performance crossover point. If $N$ is small, then interpretation requires fewer cycles. If $N$ is large, then binary translation is better overall. In the example, the tradeoff point occurs when $N$ is approximately 55; that is, if $N$ is less than 55, interpretation gives better overall performance; if $N$ is larger than 55, then it is worthwhile to perform binary translation.

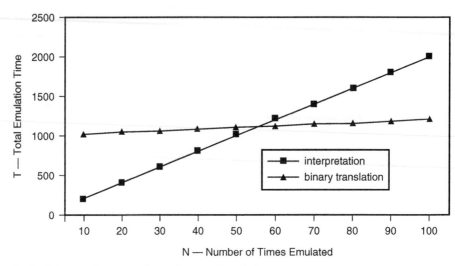

**Figure 3.17** Tradeoff Between Interpretation and Binary Translation.

### 3.5.2 Staged Emulation

Based on the performance tradeoff just described, a typical high-performance emulation framework implements multiple emulation methods and applies them in stages (Hansen 1974; Hölzle and Ungar 1996). Figure 3.18 illustrates a staged emulation framework containing both an interpreter and a binary translator. These are controlled by the runtime's emulation manager.

When a specific program is to be emulated, it is difficult to predict in advance how many times instructions in the program will be emulated, so it is difficult to know which emulation method will be optimal. Consequently, the process begins by emulating code blocks with a low start-up overhead method, such as interpretation, as shown in Figure 3.18. As interpretation proceeds, *profile data* is collected. (Profiling will be described in greater detail in Chapter 4.) Among other things, this data indicates the number of times a particular instruction or block of instructions has been emulated. After this number reaches some threshold level (e.g., 50 times), the emulation manager essentially predicts that this block of instructions is likely to be emulated frequently in the future, and it invokes the binary translator to perform a full binary translation. Thereafter, the block of code is emulated via the translated code. One can take the earlier scenario even further. If a translated block is used very frequently, then it may be selected for additional optimizations, which may be more time consuming upfront, but where the higher steady-state performance more than pays for the additional optimization time.

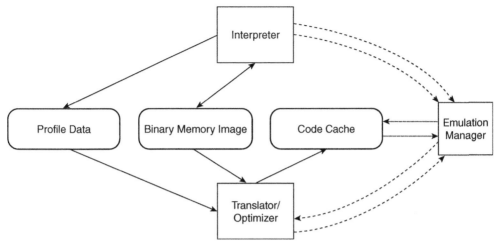

**Figure 3.18**   An Emulation Framework That Switches Between Interpretation and Binary Translation, Depending on the Performance Tradeoff. *Solid lines show data transfers; dashed lines show the flow of control within the emulation engine.*

Figure 3.19 shows the emulation process in more detail. The interpreter is used until a branch or jump is reached, and at that point the source-to-target PC map table is accessed (see Figure 2.28). If the PC hits in the table, then the next code block has been translated, and control is transferred to the code cache. Consequently, execution remains in the code cache, possibly following many linked translated blocks until a block without a forward link is reached. At that point control is transferred back out to the emulation engine. When a PC misses in the map table, the profile database is checked to see if the next dynamic basic block is "hot," i.e., whether it has been executed a number of times more than the preset threshold. If not, the profile data is updated and control passes back to the interpreter. Otherwise, the next dynamic block is translated and placed into the code cache. If the cache is full, the cache manager is invoked to free up space. Before a newly translated block is placed into the cache, the map table is updated, and links with existing blocks in the code cache are established (see Section 2.6.3).

If either the interpreter or the translated code reaches a system call instruction, control is transferred back to runtime and the OS emulator may be invoked. When control eventually returns to the emulation engine, it does a PC map table lookup and proceeds with emulation. If the translated code generates an exception condition, a host OS signal is delivered to the runtime and control is transferred to the exception emulator. Similarly, if the interpreter encounters an exception condition, control is transferred to the exception emulator.

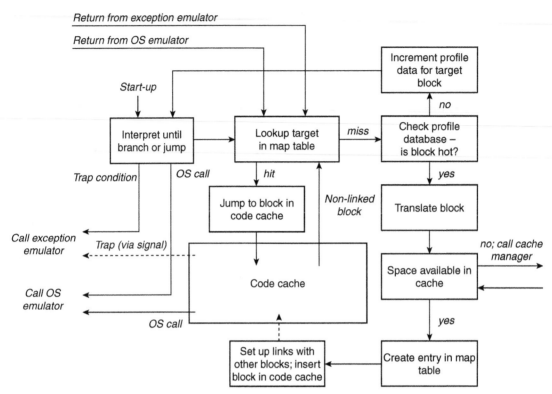

**Figure 3.19** Execution Flow of an Emulation Engine.

The staged emulation strategy just described begins with interpretation and moves to binary translation of basic blocks, as described in the previous chapter. A common additional optimization is to combine basic blocks into larger units for translation and optimization. A frequently used translation unit of this type is the *superblock*, a block of code with a single entry point but possibly several exit points. Superblocks and superblock optimization are discussed in Section 4.3. The techniques discussed in this chapter work with basic blocks as well as with larger translation units, such as superblocks. The three levels of emulation — interpretation, binary translation of basic blocks, and binary translation with optimization (on superblocks) — allow a number of staged interpretation strategies. For example, here are two commonly used strategies.

■ Interpret with simple profiling. Then when a threshold is reached, generate and optimize superblocks that are held in the code cache. This method is used in the FX!32 system (Hookway and Herdeg 1997), the Aries System

(Zheng and Thompson 2000) and the HP Dynamo same-ISA optimizer (Bala, Duesterwald, and Banerjia 2000).

- Skip the interpretation stage and immediately perform simple binary translation on dynamic basic blocks; the translation includes code for gathering profiling data on the basic blocks. As translated basic blocks become hot, form superblocks and optimize the superblocks. This method is used in the Sun Wabi system (Hohensee, Myszewski, and Reese 1996), the IA-32-EL system (Baraz et al. 2003), and the Mojo same-ISA optimizer (W.-K. Chen et al. 2000).

## 3.6 Exception Emulation

Exception conditions can occur at virtually any time during instruction execution, often unpredictably. The correct handling of exceptions poses some of the more difficult challenges for compatible emulation. We use the term *exception* to denote any trap or interrupt. A *trap* is the direct result of program execution and is produced by a specific instruction. An *interrupt* is an external event, for example, caused by the I/O system, and is not associated with a particular instruction.

We use the conventional definition of exception preciseness — i.e., an exception is *precise* if (1) all instructions prior to the faulting instruction have been executed, (2) none of the instructions following the faulting instruction have been executed, and (3) without loss of generality, the faulting instruction has not been executed. (If the ISA semantics say that it should be executed, then this adjustment can easily be made.) We assume that all exceptions in both the source and target ISAs are defined to be precise. In the case of an external interrupt, we define preciseness with respect to some instruction being executed at approximately the same time as when the interrupt occurs.

For a process VM implementation, we further divide exceptions into the following two additional categories.

> *ABI visible* — These are exceptions that are visible at the ABI level. They include all exceptions that are returned to the application via an OS signal; i.e., they are a function of the source operating system as well as of the user-level ISA. For example, if the guest OS allows a signal for a memory protection fault, then the trap becomes ABI visible. This category also includes those exceptions that cause the application to terminate (as defined by the guest OS) because at the point of termination a precise application state may be required.

***ABI invisible*** — There is no signal and the application does not terminate when the exception occurs because the ABI is essentially unaware of its existence. An example of an invisible exception is a timer interrupt that the OS uses for scheduling. Depending on the signals supported by the host OS, page faults may also fall in the category of ABI-invisible exceptions.

### 3.6.1 Exception Detection

Traps, caused as a by-product of instruction execution, are the more difficult type of exception to deal with, and we discuss them first. During instruction emulation, traps can be detected in one of two ways. First, a trap condition can be explicitly checked as part of an instruction's interpretation routine. For example, overflow caused by an add instruction can be detected by explicitly comparing the input operands and the final sum. We refer to this as *interpretive trap detection*. If the interpreter routine finds a trap condition, it jumps to a runtime trap handler. Second, a trap condition can be detected by host platform hardware when an instruction in the emulation code is executed. That is, a target instruction traps because the corresponding source instruction being emulated would also have trapped. If there is a signal supported by the host OS that matches the trap condition, then the signal can be delivered to the runtime trap handler. Clearly, ignoring efficiency issues, the first method, checking via interpretation, can always be done. On the other hand, the more efficient second method is dependent on the semantic match between source and target ISAs, details of the emulation process, and support from the host OS.

In order for the host platform to support detection of exceptions as a by-product of emulation, a key element is the host OS signal mechanism. To implement this method, the runtime should register all exceptions for which the host OS supports signals at the time the runtime is initialized. However, as emulation proceeds, if the guest application happens to register a signal by performing a system call, the runtime OS emulation code intercepts the system call and records it as a "guest-registered" signal in a table.

During emulation, when an exception occurs that causes a trap to the host OS, the host OS delivers the appropriate signal to the runtime. At that time, the runtime checks the guest's signal table to see if the guest had registered the signal. If so, the runtime adjusts the guest state so that it appears that the guest's OS is signaling, and it transfers code to the guest's signal-handling code. Otherwise, the runtime handles the trap condition indicated by the signal.

There are three cases to be considered, depending on the nature of the trapping condition.

1. The trapping condition is also ABI visible on the host platform. In this case, the runtime signal handler will be invoked, and it can take the proper action as just described.

2. The trapping condition is not ABI visible in the host platform. In this case, the earlier approach will not work and explicit checks for the trapping condition will have to be placed in the emulation code along with a jump to the runtime if the trap condition holds; i.e., interpretive trap detection must be used.

3. A trapping condition is visible in the host ABI but not in the guest ABI. In this case, there may be extraneous traps. Here, the runtime trap handler will have to determine whether the trap condition would have been visible to the source instruction.

In some cases, multiple guest trap types may map to one host trap type. For example, the host may have a single exception condition that covers both integer and floating-point overflow, whereas the guest may have separate exceptions for the two types of overflow. In this case, the runtime must inspect the trapping instruction to determine the exception to be reported to the guest.

## 3.6.2 Interrupt Handling

Some interrupts may be ABI visible; that is, the application may register a signal handler for certain interrupt conditions. When interrupts occur, they do not necessarily have to be handled immediately because they are not associated with any particular instruction. In general, there is an acceptable response latency during which the emulated application may be put into a precise state before control is transferred to the interrupt handler. Typically, at least several tens or hundreds of instructions can be emulated within the acceptable response latency.

Because the runtime has registered all signals, if an interrupt does occur, the signal will first be delivered to the runtime. If interpretation is being performed, the current interpretation routine can be completed before the runtime passes control to the guest interrupt handler. A realistic interrupt response latency is usually long enough to accommodate the completion of an interpreter routine.

If binary translation is being used for emulation, however, the situation is more complicated. When an interrupt occurs and a signal is delivered to the runtime, execution within a block of translated code may not be at an interruptible point. Generally, when code is translated, side tables are maintained so that if a source instruction traps, it is possible for the runtime to provide a correct precise state for the trapping instruction (these mechanisms are described later). This is not the case with interrupts, because essentially every instruction is interruptible and the constraints for precise state recovery at arbitrary points in the translated code would be too restrictive.

A further complication of binary translation is that when the runtime passes control to chained translation blocks, it may be an arbitrarily long time before control gets passed back to the runtime. If, for example, execution is within a loop of several translation blocks chained together, a very long time may elapse before the loop is exited. This means that special steps may have to be taken to provide an acceptable interrupt response time. To summarize the problem, when an interrupt signal is delivered to the runtime, the translated code may not be in an interruptible state. Yet if the runtime passes control back to the translated code and "waits" until the code returns to the runtime (at which time it is in an interruptible state), the runtime may not reassume control within a required interrupt response time window.

To solve the interrupt response problem, the following steps can be followed. (1) When the interrupt occurs, a signal is sent to the runtime and control is transferred from the currently executing translated code block to the runtime. (2) After receiving the signal, the runtime eliminates the possibility of a chained loop within the translated code blocks by locating the currently executing translated block and unlinking it from subsequent translation blocks, e.g., by overwriting the link at the end of the current translated code block so that it jumps back to the runtime when it is finished. (3) The runtime returns control to the translated code at the point where the interrupt signal was received. (4) The current translation block finishes and then jumps back to the runtime. (5) The runtime handles the interrupt. Note that this method assumes translation blocks have two properties: (a) There are no loops internal to a single translation block; (b) at the end of each translation block, the target code is at a precise interruptible state. Both of these assumptions are typically provided in binary translation systems, and neither unduly burdens the translator or inhibits performance.

### 3.6.3 Determining Precise Guest State

After an exception condition has been discovered, the runtime must be able to provide the proper precise state for the emulated guest process. If interpretation is being used, this is fairly straightforward; but if binary translation is used, the process of determining the precise state may be much more complex, especially if the translated binary instructions have been reordered or otherwise optimized. The following subsections discuss precise state restoration during both interpretation and simple binary translation; the difficulties brought about by code reordering and optimization are discussed in the next chapter.

### *Interpretation*

With interpretation, instructions are typically emulated one at a time in the original program sequence. Consequently, the source PC is updated as interpretation proceeds. Furthermore, the correct source state (both memory and registers) is updated at each instruction boundary. For example, consider the Add interpreter code given earlier in Figure 2.4 repeated here in Figure 3.20). If the add overflows, it may be detected via a trap when the sum = source1 + source2 statement is executed. At this point in the interpreter routine, the source PC has not yet been updated and still points to the (overflowing) add integer instruction. The result register RT has not been updated (it can be updated via the runtime signal handler if specified by trap semantics).

The signal handler in the runtime will be provided with a *target* PC that points to the sum statement in the interpreter routine. However, the runtime signal handler should use the *source* PC (maintained during interpretation) to go back into the original source code to find the source instruction that was being emulated at the time the trap occurred. Note that using the source PC maintains portability of the interpreter code; i.e., its behavior is not tied to specific locations of interpreter code.

```
Add:
        RT = extract(inst,25,5);
        RA = extract(inst,20,5);
        RB = extract(inst,15,5);
        source1 = regs[RA];
        source2 = regs[RB];
        sum = source1 + source2;
        regs[RT] = sum;
        PC = PC + 4;
        If (halt || interrupt) goto exit;
        inst = code[PC];
        opcode = extract(inst,31,6);
        extended_opcode = extract(inst,10,10);
        routine = dispatch[opcode, extended_opcode];
        goto *routine;
```

**Figure 3.20**  Add Interpreter Routine. *Overflow during the add operation may trap and cause a signal to be delivered to VM software. The source PC will point to the trapping source instruction.*

### Binary Translation: Locating the Program Counter

With binary translation, the restoration of state following an exception begins by determining the source PC of the faulting instruction. Then given the PC, the rest of the precise application state is recovered. In this subsection we focus on determining the source PC of the trapping instruction.

One difficulty in determining the PC of the trapping source instruction is that at the time the trap occurs, the runtime is provided with the PC of the translated target code rather than the source PC. Unlike interpretation, however, binary translation typically does not keep a continuously updated version of the source PC. This means that there must be some indirect mechanism for finding the source PC of a faulting instruction, given the translated target PC. In order to track down the corresponding source instruction, it is useful to keep PC-related information in a side table.

For recovering the precise source PC, a *reverse translation* side table may be used (see Figure 3.21). The most straightforward implementation of a reverse translation table contains <target PC, source PC> pairs, indicating for each target PC (i.e., an address in the translated binary) the corresponding

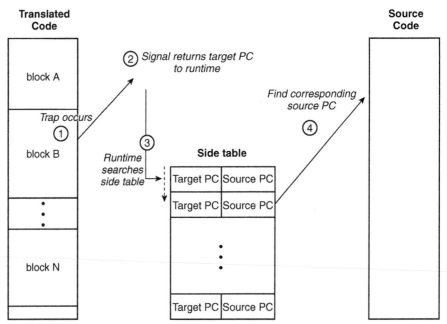

**Figure 3.21**  Finding the Trapping Source PC, Given the Target PC. *(1) The trap occurs and (2) the signal handler returns the target PC to the runtime software. The runtime (3) does a search of the side table (4) to find the corresponding source PC that caused the trap.*

source PC from which it was translated. Then given the PC of a trapping target instruction, the runtime can scan the table for the trapping instruction's PC; when it finds a match, the corresponding source PC, the second half of the pair, becomes available.

The table, in the form just described, has a couple of inefficiencies. First, the target PC lookup may require a linear scan of the table. Second, the table will be fairly large; because it holds a pair of address pointers for each translated instruction, the table could easily be larger than the translated code. The linear scan can be replaced with a binary search if the target PCs are in sequential numerical order. For some code cache management algorithms, e.g., those using FIFO replacement, this will be the case naturally. And, as we will see in Section 3.8.2, FIFO replacement is one of the better strategies for code caches.

The table size can be reduced by taking advantage of locality in target and source PC values. For example, one could hold a subset of the PCs to their full length, with others being expressed as deltas from the full-length versions. The PCs at the beginning of each translation block can be kept in full, while PCs within the translation block are deltas from the initial PCs. A further simplification can be made if the target ISA has fixed-length instructions. In this case, the side table needs to contain only an array of source PCs that can be accessed directly via the target PC values.

An additional complication occurs if a given target instruction corresponds to more than one source instruction (so the target PC corresponds to more than one source PC). This can happen, for example, when a RISC ISA is mapped to a CISC ISA. Two RISC instructions, a load instruction and an ALU instruction, may be translated to a single CISC instruction that both loads from memory and performs an ALU operation. In this case, when a trap occurs, it may be difficult to identify which source instruction is the one with the exception (although in the example just given this is not the case). A related complication occurs when the translated code is rearranged or optimized so that the target instructions are executed in a different program order than are the corresponding source instructions. Both of these issues will be discussed in greater detail in Chapter 4; generally speaking, the solution is to identify the beginning of the translated block that contains the trapping source instruction and then to return control to the runtime, which can analyze and/or interpret the original source code to sort out the correct source state and PC value.

To support the required runtime analysis (and to reduce side table space requirements), the side table can be organized according to translation blocks, with an entry for each block. This entry holds the beginning target PC along with enough information to allow reconstruction of the complete translated code block. Refer to Figure 3.22. If the translation block is contiguous, this information would be no more than a count of the number of translated

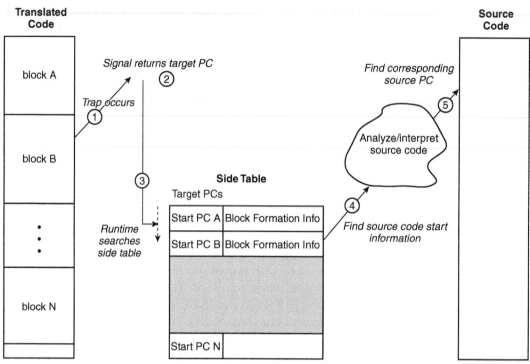

**Figure 3.22** Using an Optimized Side Table to Find the Trapping Source PC. *(1) The trap occurs and (2) a signal delivers the target PC to the runtime. (3) The runtime then performs a search to find the trapping translation block. (4) The table entry contains enough information to allow analysis and/or interpretation of the source code blocks. (5) To find the source PC corresponding to the trapping target PC.*

source instructions. If the block is noncontiguous, then a sequence of start source PCs and counts would suffice or, even simpler, the initial source PC and control flow information used when forming the initial translation, e.g., the taken branches and/or jump targets. Given this information, the runtime interprets the source code to identify the trapping source instruction. To optimize the process, a hybrid side table structure can be used. For example, if the same target instruction frequently traps, then its corresponding source PC can be cached in a side table to avoid repeated analysis and interpretation.

### Binary Translation: Register State

When an exception occurs during execution of translated code, the correct, precise register state must be restored, just as it would be in the original source code. In this subsection, we consider methods that can be used when the optimization level of a translated binary is relatively low. In particular, it is assumed that no code reordering is done and no register state updating instructions have been removed due to optimizations. Other, more complex register restoration methods are often closely tied to the specific optimization techniques used, and the discussion of these methods is deferred until Chapter 4, where binary optimization is covered in depth.

The simplest case occurs when the emulator uses a consistent source to target register mapping and register state is updated in the same order in both source and translated code sequences. By a *consistent* register mapping, we mean that the mapped location of a specific source register (either in a target register or in memory) remains the same throughout emulation. In this case, the source register state can be recovered from the target register state at any point.

A slightly more complex case occurs if the source-to-target register mapping varies between or even within the translation blocks, but the order of register updates is the same in both source and target code. In this case, a side table for the translated code blocks can be used to indicate how the register mapping should be restored. Alternatively, as in the case of trap PC identification, the source code can be analyzed again from the beginning of a translation block, the current register assignments regenerated, and the resulting information used to restore the correct source register state.

### Binary Translation: Memory State

Memory state is changed by store instructions. As long as the source program store instructions are all emulated in the original program order, it is fairly straightforward to maintain precise memory state. If, in addition, all potentially trapping source instructions are emulated in the same order with respect to the store instructions, then the memory state at the time of a trap can be guaranteed to be consistent with the source PC that is recovered.

If code is reordered, then, as we shall see in Chapter 4, the presence of memory stores constrains the reordering that may be done. In particular, a potentially trapping instruction cannot be moved below a store that follows it in the original source code. Otherwise, because memory has been overwritten, the memory state will not be recoverable if the moved instruction does trap. Of course, there are optimizations (or hardware) that can buffer memory stores, but we defer discussion of these techniques to later chapters.

On the other hand, if a trapping instruction is moved ahead of a store, then it may be possible for the runtime trap-handling code to emulate (typically via interpretation) the store instruction to complete the store update. Again, because it is tied in with code-optimization methods, details of this technique are deferred to Chapter 4.

## 3.7 Operating System Emulation

The operating system interface is a key part of the ABI specification, just as the user-level instructions are. However, because a process-level VM is required only to maintain compatibility at the ABI level, it does not emulate the individual instructions in the guest's OS code; rather it emulates the function or semantics of the guest's OS calls, typically by converting them to host OS operations. There are two important cases to be considered, one of which is easier to implement than the other (although neither is easy!). In the first case, the guest and host operating systems are the same; e.g., they are both Linux or Windows. The other, more difficult case occurs when the operating systems are different. In this section, we discuss both cases, beginning with the simpler, "same OS" case.

### 3.7.1 Same-Operating-System Emulation

A runtime emulates a guest's OS by a combination of host OS calls and operations performed by the runtime itself. The basic emulation techniques are discussed briefly in the following subsections.

#### Operating System Call Translation

When the guest and host operating systems are the same, the problem of OS call emulation is primarily one of matching the OS interface syntax. The OS functions required by the guest are available in the host, but it may be necessary to move and format arguments and return values, possibly forming some data conversions in the process. For example, an OS running on a platform with relatively few registers, such as the IA-32, may pass arguments in a memory resident stack, while the same OS running on a RISC-based platform with many registers may pass arguments in registers. In this case, arguments must be copied from the stack to registers, or vice versa, when emulating a system call. This wrapper code is illustrated in Figure 3.23, where source code is translated to target code. The system call in the source code is converted to a jump (or procedure call) into the runtime. The runtime then executes wrapper code that copies and/or converts arguments from the guest to the host and then

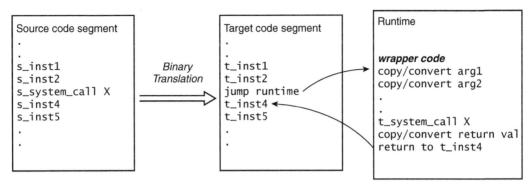

**Figure 3.23** System Call Conversion When Guest and Host Operating Systems Are the Same.

makes the appropriate system call on the host platform. An alternative, faster implementation would inline the wrapper code and guest system call.

### Runtime-Implemented Operating System Functions

Not all guest OS operations need to be translated and passed on to the host OS. Depending on the runtime implementation and emulation method, some calls may be handled directly by the runtime. One such case is a guest OS call to establish a signal on behalf of the emulated guest application. Recall that the runtime, at the beginning of program emulation, establishes signal handlers for all signals supported by the host OS. Any exception conditions get reported to the runtime first so that it may provide the correct state to the guest process and to ensure that the runtime always retains control of the emulation process. If the application tries to establish a signal handler via a system call, the runtime handles this call directly by recording the application's signal in a side table and then returning to the guest process. Subsequently, if the guest application should trigger the signal, it first passes through the runtime before it is actually delivered to the application.

Another important area where the runtime handles guest OS calls directly is memory management. Because it essentially controls the process VM on which a guest application is running, it is the runtime that is responsible for the overall memory management. So, for example, if the guest application asks for more memory via the Linux brk() system call, then, depending on the runtime's memory management implementation, the call may be handled directly by the runtime and does not have to be passed to the host OS. The HP Dynamo technical report (Bala, Duesterwald, and Banerjia 1999) and

Bruening's doctoral dissertation (Bruening 2004) contain fairly thorough discussions of the memory management functions performed by the runtime. As another example, if runtime emulation routines check memory protection via a software table (see Section 3.4.1) and the guest application makes a system call to change memory access privileges, then the privilege change should be emulated at the level of the runtime by modifying the software mapping table.

### Nasty Realities

The discussion of OS emulation just given leaves the impression that it is a fairly straightforward process. It is not. One thing that simplifies our discussion is that we tend to focus on the Linux operating system for examples (although other versions of the UNIX OS are similar). Linux OS communication is primarily through OS calls contained in the ABI and through the signal mechanism. Even so, the foregoing discussion has been simplified.

The Windows OS is much more complex, both in the number of ways a user application and the OS communicate with each other and in the communication mechanisms themselves. Probably the most thorough discussion of the problems and their solutions are contained in Bruening's doctoral dissertation (Bruening 2004) and in a related DynamoRIO paper (Bruening, Duesterwald, and Amarasinghe 2001). The major issues are briefly summarized next. A further complication when dealing with Windows is that documentation is at the API level (i.e., at the level of the user libraries that call the OS) rather than the ABI level, where the calls actually occur.

Three important "abnormal" user/kernel communication mechanisms in Windows are callbacks, asynchronous procedure calls, and exceptions. As described by Bruening, all three can be emulated in similar ways, so we focus on callbacks (Figure 3.24). Windows is essentially an event-driven OS; for example, a mouse click is an event that may cause input to be delivered to a user program. Events are passed to a user process (or a user thread, to be more precise) through message queues; at certain points in its execution, the OS checks a thread's message queues. If it finds an event, it calls a user routine (a callback handler) that has been registered for handling the event. This involves saving the context of the user thread and initiating a new context to run the callback handler. After setting up the callback handler, the Windows OS returns to user mode through a special dispatch routine. Then when the callback handler is finished, it normally reenters the OS kernel, where a check for further pending messages is made before returning to the original user program.

A challenge in implementing callbacks in a process VM is to maintain the runtime's overall control of the VM and to manage the execution of the

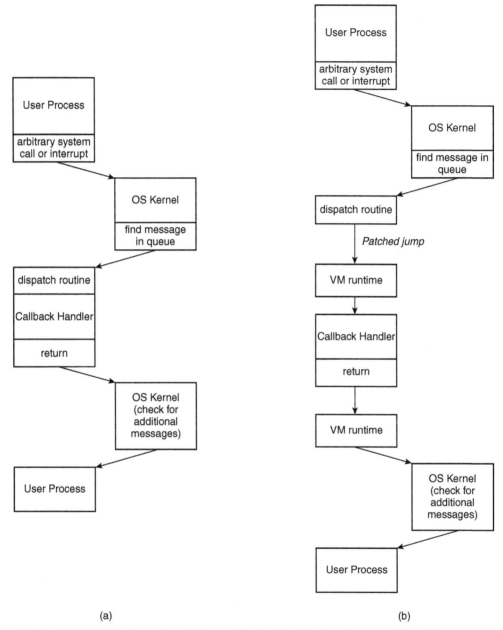

(a)                                          (b)

**Figure 3.24**   Method for Implementing Windows Callbacks. *(a) Typical Windows control flow when a message queue contains a message that invokes a callback handler. (b) To emulate and maintain control during callbacks, the runtime intercepts the transfer both to and from the callback handler.*

callback routine. First, the runtime has to gain control before the callback handler is entered. This is done by modifying the dispatch routine by placing a jump to the runtime at the beginning of the routine. At that point, the runtime can save any of its state that is not saved by the OS during the switch to the handler (as is the case in the DynamoRIO system). Then to detect a return from the callback, the runtime looks for a particular OS call (or a call to an API routine, which returns control to the OS); at that point, it can restore any saved runtime state prior to the switch back to the original user context.

### 3.7.2 Different-Operating-System Emulation

Although it may bear some superficial similarity to instruction set emulation, emulating an OS interface is fundamentally different than emulating instruction execution. An ISA reads data from memory, executes instructions that transform the data, and writes data values back to memory. Instruction sets are *logically complete,* in the sense that any function can be performed on input operands to produce a result, given enough time. Furthermore, most ISAs perform the same basic functions: memory load/stores, arithmetic/logical operations, and branches/jumps. Hence, with ISA emulation it is not a matter of *whether* emulation can be done, just how *efficiently* it can be done and how long it will take.

In contrast, the OS deals with the outside world and with real I/O devices. Furthermore, an operating system implements and manipulates fairly complex entities (e.g., processes, threads, files, message buffers) with a well-defined set of operations. In this environment it is quite possible that the host OS simply cannot provide a function required by a guest OS, no matter how much time or human ingenuity is available. A simple example is a system call that returns the time of day. If the host OS does not maintain a time-of-day clock and the guest OS does, then no matter how much effort is put into it, the guest OS will not be able to coerce the host OS into providing the correct time of day. Similarly, the guest OS may have calls that support certain disk file operations that are simply not supported by the host. There are also semantic mismatch problems, where no combination of host operations can exactly emulate a guest operation; i.e., if a number of operations are combined, there may be additional side effects.

It is difficult to come up with a set of overall rules or strategies for different-OS emulation because of the wide variety of cases that must be handled. Consequently, OS emulation is very much an *ad hoc* process that must be implemented on a case-by-case basis and that requires considerable knowledge of both the guest and host operating systems. The process is somewhat similar to porting code from one OS to another — but in some respects it is more difficult, because with porting, one can examine the original code as a whole and then make modifications using an overall strategy. With emulation, however, the conversion must be done dynamically, with relatively little context within which a particular system call can be analyzed.

In general, a guest OS call is supported by a runtime wrapper routine, as described earlier. A single guest call may require multiple host OS calls for emulation, or the runtime itself may perform some or all of the emulation rather than passing it to the host OS.

### Example: Enforcing File Limits

To a large extent, both Linux and Win32 provide similar functionality with respect to file I/O. There are other cases, however, where they differ, for example, in setting file limits. When a Linux process is created it can be given an upper limit on the size of files that it can write, RLIMIT_FSIZE. There is no corresponding limit in Win32. Consequently, an interesting emulation problem occurs when a Linux guest process is run on a Win32 host. In this case, it is up to the runtime to maintain the Linux RLIMIT_FSIZE. It can do this by holding a table of file limits, with a table entry for each of the guest's open files. Then as part of the wrapper for disk write functions, the runtime can maintain the file limit table (and enforce the required limits). In addition, the Linux calls `getrlimit()` and `setrlimit()`, which read and write the limit, should be implemented directly by the runtime without calls to the Win32 host.

Practically speaking, if the guest and host operating systems are different, then there is relatively little likelihood that a completely compatible OS emulation can be performed; some compromises and approximations will be required. A compromise often used is to restrict the set of applications that can be emulated (and in the process to restrict the system calls that must be emulated). An example is the Wabi system (Hohensee, Myszewski, and Reese 1996) developed by Sun Microsystems to emulate only certain widely popular Windows applications, such as Word and Excel, on Solaris platforms.

## 3.8  Code Cache Management

The code cache is a central part of a binary translation system, and managing the code cache is one of the important emulation-related functions performed by the runtime. Although it is similar to a conventional hardware cache in some respects, the code cache differs from a conventional cache memory in at least three significant ways.

1. The cached blocks do not have a fixed size. The size of a code cache block depends on the size of the translated target block, and this can vary from a few instructions to many tens of instructions.

2. The presence and locations of the blocks are dependent on one another because of chaining. If a translated block is removed from the code cache, then any link pointers directed toward the removed block must be modified.

3. There is no copy of the cache contents in a "backing store." After a block is removed from the code cache, it must be regenerated from the source binary image before it can be placed back into the cache.

All three of the foregoing have a significant effect on the code cache management algorithms that are used.

### 3.8.1 Code Cache Implementations

The code cache itself contains blocks of target code, formed by translating source code. In addition to the actual code cache, supporting side tables must be provided. Thus far in our discussion, we have identified two key operations involving the code cache that must be performed during the overall emulation process.

■ Given a source PC at the beginning of a block, find the corresponding target PC in the code cache, if the translation exists. This is done whenever emulation control is to be transferred to the code cache via a source PC, e.g., when passing from interpretation to translated code.

■ Given a target PC in the code cache, find the corresponding source PC. This is done to find the precise source PC when an exception occurs.

These two operations are performed by the map table (Figure 2.28) and the reverse translation side table (Figure 3.22), respectively.

### 3.8.2 Replacement Algorithms

In a practical implementation the size of the code cache is limited, and, depending on the working set size of the emulated application, it may eventually fill up with translated blocks. When this happens, some code cache management is required to make room for new translations by removing one or more of the translated blocks from the cache. Just as with conventional caches, there are a number of possible replacement algorithms. However, the differences between code caches and conventional caches cited earlier have a significant impact on the choice of replacement algorithms. We discuss a number of possible replacement strategies in the following subsections.

### Least Recently Used

A least recently used (LRU) algorithm replaces a cache block that has gone unused for the longest period of time. Because of temporal locality, this is often a good strategy for conventional caches. Unfortunately, because of the specific properties of the code cache, an LRU cache replacement algorithm is relatively difficult to implement. First of all, there is an overhead in keeping track of the least recently used translation blocks; this would probably require a couple of extra memory accesses per block to update LRU information each time a block is entered. Second, when an arbitrary block is removed, any blocks that are linked to it must have their link pointers updated (to direct them back to the VM rather than to the removed block).

To implement delinking of blocks, *backpointers* can be added to the overall code cache structure. These backpointers can be maintained as part of the PC map table (or in a separate side table). In Figure 3.25 an implementation is given where they are part of the map table. For each table entry (i.e., for each translation block) the backpointers, structured as a linked list, point to translation blocks that chain to the given block. When a block is replaced, the list can be followed to find and modify all the chain pointers pointing to the block.

A third problem with LRU replacement is that it may select a translated block from an arbitrary location in the middle of the translation cache, and the new block replacing it may not be exactly the same size as the block (or blocks) that it replaces. Clearly this will lead to cache fragmentation and will require mechanisms both to keep track of the sizes and locations of unused space and to perform occasional compaction of the cache (which will bring along additional complications, such as adjusting links connecting code blocks).

Finally, a somewhat lesser problem is that maintenance of the reverse-translation side table (shown in Figure 3.22) becomes more complicated. If this table is arranged in order of increasing target PCs, it permits a binary search (rather than a linear search) for performing a lookup in the reverse translation table. If LRU replacement is used, however, such an order cannot be guaranteed for the target PCs.

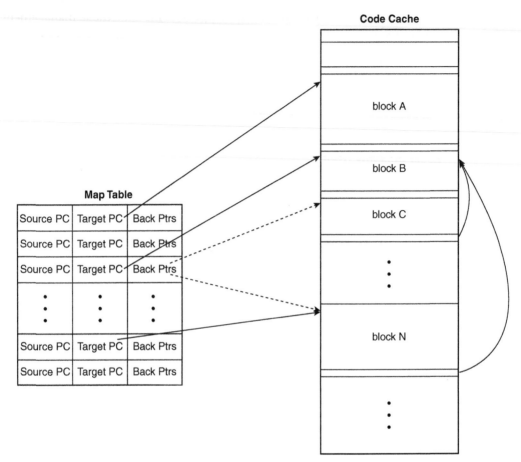

**Figure 3.25**  Code Cache and PC Map Table. *In this example, blocks C and N both link to block B; consequently, the map table entry for block B has backpointers to both blocks C and N.*

Because all these difficulties arise in practice, LRU, and LRU-like algorithms are not typically used for code caches. Rather, replacement algorithms that reduce (or eliminate) backpointer and fragmentation problems are preferred. The following subsections describe a number of such code cache replacement algorithms, beginning with the simplest and going to the more complex.

### Flush When Full

Perhaps the most basic algorithm is simply to let the code cache fill and then to flush it completely and start over with an empty cache (Cmelik and

Keppel 1994). Although this is a brute-force approach, it has some advantages. First, larger translation blocks, such as superblocks, are based on frequently followed control flow paths, i.e., the directions that conditional branches commonly take. Over time, however, the frequently followed paths may change. Flushing provides an opportunity to eliminate control paths that have become stale and no longer reflect the common paths through the code. The new translation blocks formed after flushing are more likely to be representative of the paths currently followed by the code. Second, in systems like Shade, where the translation map table is not chained but has a fixed number of entries in each row for colliding source PCs (Figure 2.37), a translated block will occasionally be "orphaned" when its map table pointer is removed to make room for another. Flushing removes these orphans and reclaims their code cache space.

On the other hand, the big disadvantage of the flush-when-full approach is that all the blocks being actively used (i.e., the members of the current working set) have to be retranslated from scratch, leading to a high-performance overhead immediately after the flush.

### Preemptive Flush

A more sophisticated scheme is based on the observation that many programs operate in phases. A phase change is usually associated with an instruction working set change. Consequently when there is a program phase change, a new region of source code is being entered and a larger percentage of the time is spent in block translations, as illustrated in Figure 3.26. By monitoring the rate at which new translations are being performed, the code cache can be preemptively flushed to make room for the translations of new working set members (Bala, Duesterwald, and Banerjia 2000). The number of translations

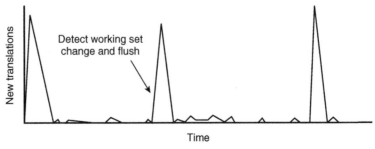

**Figure 3.26**  Code Cache Flushing When the Instruction Working Set Changes. *When an increase in new translations is detected, the entire code cache is flushed to make room for a new working set.*

after the flush will be lower than what would be needed if the cache becomes full in the middle of a phase, because retranslations of the working set are avoided.

### Fine-Grained FIFO

FIFO replacement is a nonfragmenting algorithm that exploits temporal locality to some extent and is not a brute-force approach, as is complete flushing. With FIFO replacement, the code cache can be managed as a circular buffer, with the oldest block(s) being removed to make room for the newest. If the new block being inserted into the cache is of size $n$, then the set of oldest blocks whose aggregate size is at least $n$ is replaced. The reverse-translation side table can be managed in a corresponding FIFO manner. A "head" pointer keeps track of the oldest translation block in the cache, and this is the point where replacements will begin.

This scheme overcomes a number of the disadvantages of LRU (albeit at a slightly reduced hit rate). However, it still needs to keep track of chaining via backpointers because individual translation blocks are replaced.

### Coarse-Grained FIFO

This scheme partitions the code cache into very large blocks; for example, the blocks may be a fourth or an eighth of the entire cache. These large blocks are managed on a FIFO basis. With this scheme, the backpointer problem can be simplified or eliminated.

The backpointer problem can be simplified by maintaining the pointers only on a FIFO block basis. For example, if a translation block contained in FIFO block A links to a translation block contained in FIFO block B, then the backpointer list for FIFO block B is updated with a pointer to the translation block in A. However, if a translation block links to another block contained in the same FIFO block, then no backpointer is needed. See Figure 3.27. When a FIFO block is replaced, all the backpointers associated with it are followed to remove links from translation blocks coming from other FIFO blocks. Due to temporal locality in programs, the number of intra-FIFO block links, which do not have backpointers, is likely to be considerably larger than the number of inter-FIFO block backpointers, which need to be dealt with when a FIFO block is replaced.

A coarse-grained FIFO approach was proposed in Mojo (W.-K. Chen et al. 2000), where only two major blocks were used, with no backpointers between blocks. Also, note that, in a sense, complete flushing is a degenerate special case of coarse-grained FIFO (i.e., it uses only one block).

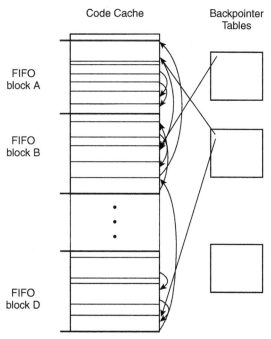

**Figure 3.27** Code Cache Managed with a Coarse-Grained FIFO. *Backpointers are needed only for chain pointers that cross FIFO replacement block boundaries.*

### Performance

A study of code cache replacement algorithms (Hazelwood and Smith 2004), based on the Dynamo/RIO dynamic optimization system (Bruening, Garnett, and Amarasinghe 2003), determined that a coarse-granularity FIFO scheme, e.g., dividing the cache into eight large blocks, tends to have lower overhead than either fine-grained FIFO or flush when full. The graph in Figure 3.28 shows

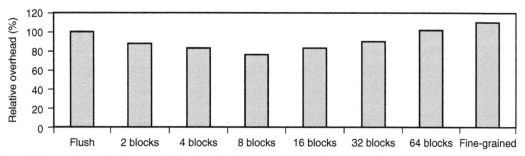

**Figure 3.28** Relative Overhead of FIFO Code Cache Management Schemes. *Overheads are relative to a flush-when-full method (Flush).*

overhead (relative to flush when full) averaged over a number of benchmark programs, including SPEC benchmarks and some Windows programs. The code cache size was artificially restricted for each benchmark to determine performance effects when the code cache is stressed (when it is not stressed, then the replacement algorithm makes little difference).

## 3.9 System Environment

As the last step in our development of process VMs, we consider the integration of guest processes into the host system environment. In a system that supports process VMs, it is desirable to make the installation and execution of guest applications as transparent as possible, i.e., without the users' having to take any extraordinary actions. The goal is to give the user seamless, transparent access to both host and guest applications.

The major issue in supporting an integrated environment is the encapsulation of all guest code in an emulation environment at the time it is loaded. In general, guest code may be loaded at the time of process creation, or it may be dynamically linked later. The type of environment that is to be supported is illustrated in Figure 3.29. Here we see that a guest process may create either another guest process or a host process; similarly, a host process may create either a host process or a guest process. And as a guest process executes, it can call a dynamically linked library (DLL) routine that may be a guest routine (and hence emulated), or it may call a natively coded host routine. In general, a host process will not call a guest DLL, so we do not consider this case.

The environment just described achieves a fairly high level of interoperability between guest and host processes. In some cases, especially if the guest and host operating systems are different, the level of interoperability may be less. For example, the ability for a guest process to invoke a host DLL may be impaired.

In order to implement the system illustrated in Figure 3.29, there must be two different loaders: one for host binaries and the other for guest binaries. There are several approaches for invoking the correct loader when a process is created. There are three possibilities (Hookway and Herdeg 1997) that are summarized here.

1. Modify the host's kernel loader routine (and any user space loaders that may be used on the host system), first to identify the type of binary being loaded (host or guest) and then to call the proper loader routine. This approach is conceptually straightforward but requires modification

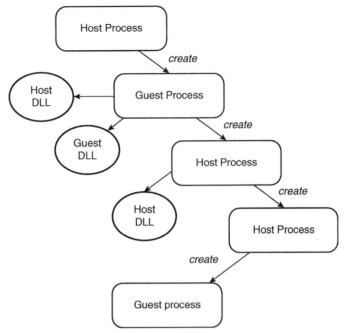

**Figure 3.29**   The Integration of Host and Guest Processes in a Process VM. *In a process virtual machine, host and guest processes can be created in arbitrary sequences. A host process will call only host DLLs, while a guest may call either a host DLL or a guest DLL.*

of kernel loader code. If the process VM system is to be implemented without kernel modifications, then this approach cannot be used.

2.  When a guest program binary is installed, it is converted into a host-executable file by appending some host-executable code and including the guest binary image as a large data structure. The host-executable portion of the program invokes a guest loader that loads the guest binary data structure and begins emulation. This method requires the user to identify guest binaries when they are installed so that the installer can attach the host-executable code that calls the loader frontend. In a sense, this method encapsulates a guest process at the time it is installed. This could lead to problems if guest executables are loaded from remote systems, however. That is, they must be installed within the "domain" of the process VM system.

3.  Host processes are modified so that special loader code can be "hooked" on to system calls that load user processes, e.g., the CreateProcess call in Win32 or the exec() call in Linux. This method is used in FX!32 (described in more detail later), where it is called *enabling*. After a process has been

enabled and it wishes to call `CreateProcess`, a library call is first made to a special preloader (*transparency agent* in FX!32 terminology). The preloader checks to see if a guest process is being created. If so, it calls the guest process loader; if not, it creates the host process, as requested, and then enables it, before allowing it to start running. Consequently, any later processes that the newly enabled host process attempts to create will also perform the guest/host preloader check. To get this bootstrap method started in the first place, any "root" user processes, for example, the log-in shell, must be explicitly enabled.

As noted, the first method requires kernel modification, the second requires executable modification at install time, and the third modifies processes dynamically as they run. For the third method to work, it must be possible to enable an arbitrary host process. For example, in FX!32, all the calls to `CreateProcess` go through a single API routine that the preloader (transparency agent) is able to locate. However, if a call to create a process can occur at an arbitrary point in a host process, then enabling it would be much more difficult. One possibility is to perform the equivalent of emulation on all host processes as well as user processes. This would allow the runtime to locate all system calls that are made. Slowdown could be kept very low because "binary translation" would amount to little more than identifying and caching superblocks, with no actual translation taking place. This technique will be explained in more detail in Chapter 8, in the context of system virtual machines.

With respect to DLLs, we assume that host DLLs can be invoked only by host processes. Consequently it is not necessary to locate those points in a host process where a DLL may be invoked. Because guest processes are always emulated, calls to the dynamic linker can be intercepted by the runtime. The runtime can then locate the DLL being called. This can either be from a library of guest code, in which case the DLL also comes under runtime control for emulation, or it may be a DLL written in the host ISA (for faster guest process execution).

## 3.10 Case Study: FX!32

FX!32 was developed by Digital Equipment Corporation to enable the transparent execution of IA-32 applications on Alpha platforms running the Windows operating system (Hookway and Herdeg 1997; Chernoff et al. 1998). FX!32 provided a process virtual machine model, as described in this chapter (although it is not called a *virtual machine* in FX!32 documentation and articles). FX!32 performs staged emulation, using both interpretation and translation. But unlike other systems, it does not dynamically translate code. Rather, the developers of FX!32 decided to perform translation and optimization *between* program runs, not *during* a program run. This approach is based on the performance tradeoff between run time and translation/optimization time. By not translating and optimizing dynamically, virtually all of a program's run time can be devoted to emulation. Furthermore, because translation and optimization are done between program runs, much more time can be dedicated to these tasks, and a more highly optimized binary can be produced.

During the initial run of a program in the FX!32 system, it is interpreted only. During interpretation, execution profile information is collected in a hash table. The profile information contains, among other things, the targets of indirect jump instructions. Then between program runs, the translator can use the profile information to discover code regions starting with jump targets and then translate and optimize the resulting code. This optimized code is stored in a database on the disk.

During subsequent runs of the program, the translated and optimized code is loaded from disk and executed. If the translated code attempts to jump to a region of code that has not been translated, then the interpreter takes over with the original version of guest code. Additional execution profile information is collected, as before, so that after the program finishes, more code can be translated and optimized. Eventually, all parts of the guest code that are executed will be translated, optimized, and stored on disk.

Conceptually, this method is similar to staged emulation with interpretation and dynamic translation. In particular, an interpreter and translator are alternately invoked, with the code being translated in an incremental fashion as it is discovered. The difference is that translated code is cached on the disk between runs, rather than being translated and held in a code cache every time it is executed. Furthermore, all discovered code is translated; it does not depend on how often the code is emulated, as in a conventional staged emulation strategy.

Using this approach increases the importance of fast interpretation, because the interpreter is used for the entire first program run and for newly discovered sections of code during successive runs. The fast interpreter is similar in structure to the one described in Section 2.4.3. The binary translation process is similar to that described in Chapter 2, so we will not discuss it further here. Rather, we will focus on the overall FX!32 system environment.

The main FX!32 components are illustrated in Figure 3.30. The interpreter (called an *emulator* in FX!32) and the translator are the main parts of the emulation engine, and these have already been discussed. The other five components are the transparency agent, the runtime, the database, the server, and the manager.

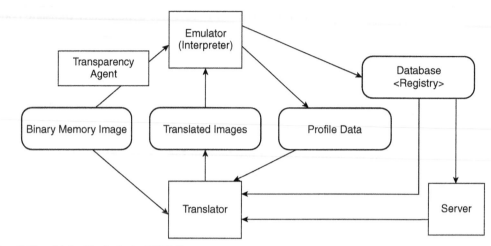

**Figure 3.30** Major Blocks in the FX!32 System.

The transparency agent is responsible for providing seamless (transparent) integration of host and user processes by performing the preloading function described earlier, in Section 3.9. The transparency agent is a DLL that is inserted into the address space of a host user process and that hooks calls on the Win32 `CreateProcess` system call as well as other calls related to process creation and management. This enabling process consists of a series of Win32 system calls that first allocate a small region of memory in the host process being enabled and then copy in the agent DLL code. A small number of root processes must be explicitly enabled as part of the FX!32 installation process. These are the login shell (`explorer.exe`), the service control manager, and the remote procedure call server. After these are enabled, all subsequent host processes created are also enabled by the transparency agent, in a recursive manner.

The runtime, as indicated in the previous paragraph, acts as a loader for guest IA-32 processes, initializes the guest environment, and manages the overall emulation process as a guest program runs. It invokes translated code, finds the source PC values for untranslated code, and invokes the interpreter when needed. The runtime also locates all the Win32 API calls and provides jacket routines that copy arguments from the IA-32 stack into Alpha registers (and performs any data conversion that may be required). Consequently, many of the API calls are performed with the host's optimized Alpha code.

The FX!32 database contains information regarding the installed IA-32 applications. This information includes, among other things, profile data for the application as well as any translated/optimized code. When the runtime first encounters an IA-32 program, it registers the image in the database and generates a unique image identifier by hashing the image's header. Then when

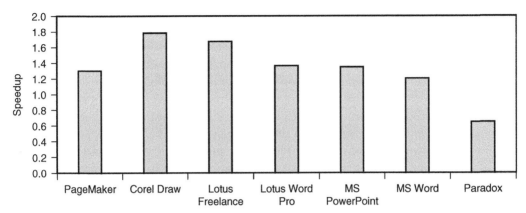

**Figure 3.31** FX!32 Performance on Windows Benchmark Programs. *Performance on an Alpha 21164A is compared with a contemporary Pentium processor (Chernoff et al. 1998).*

the runtime loads an IA-32 application, it searches the database using the image identifier. If the runtime finds a translated image, it loads the translated code along with the IA-32 image.

The server is started whenever the system is booted. Its main responsibility is to automatically run the translator and optimizer between program runs. Finally, the manager provides the user some control over FX!32 resource usage. Through the manager, the user can control the amount of disk space consumed by the database, the information that should be kept in the database, and the conditions under which the translator should be run.

Performance of the FX!32 system was quite good. Figure 3.31 shows performance for some Windows benchmark programs (Chernoff et al. 1998). This data compares a 500-MHz Alpha 21164A processor with a 200-MHz Pentium Pro processor. These two processors were of roughly equivalent technology generations. Alpha performance is for binaries that have been optimized (i.e., for a second run using the same input data as the first). Performance is given as speedup with respect to the Pentium Pro, so any number larger than 1 is an improvement. The Alpha is significantly faster, with one only exception, where performance is roughly 0.65 of the Pentium Pro. The 21164A executes 4.4 Alpha instructions per IA-32 instruction, or 2.1 Alpha instructions per Pentium Pro micro-operation. The much higher 21164 clock frequency yields an overall performance improvement.

## 3.11 Summary

In this chapter, we considered a number of process VM implementation options. For example, instruction emulation can be done via (1) interpretation,

(2) binary translation, or (3) a staged combination. Address mapping and memory protection can be done (1) via a runtime-managed table or (2) using direct mapping. The options most suitable for a given implementation depend on performance, complexity, and compatibility tradeoffs.

The most general method for implementing emulation is to use instruction interpretation with software memory mapping and protection checking. This method accommodates intrinsic compatibility, but it would likely be the slowest emulation method. On the other hand, if (1) the register state of the guest fits within the host register file, (2) the guest memory space fits within the host space, (3) the guest page size is a multiple of the host page size, and (4) the guest privilege types are a subset of the host privilege levels, then, in general, binary translation with hardware address mapping and checking is likely to be the fastest emulation method, and it also is likely that intrinsic compatibility can be achieved.

The foregoing conditions may at first appear to be rather restrictive; however, some important practical cases do satisfy these constraints. One of the important practical cases is the virtualization of the IA-32 ABI on a RISC platform (or an Intel IPF/Itanium platform). In this case, for example, the IA-32 register file usually fits comfortably inside the host's register file, and the 32-bit IA-32 address space fits into a typical 64-bit address space.

In many other situations, process VMs can be constructed to satisfy extrinsic compatibility constraints. That is, they only provide compatibility for some, but not all, guest binaries. The most important compromise that has to be made occurs when the host and the guest support different operating systems. In this case, emulation of the guest's OS is likely to be incomplete. This would restrict the applications to those that depend on a subset of system calls or a subset of OS features. Whether compatibility is satisfied would have to be verified on a per program basis, in all likelihood.

Although the topic of this chapter was process-level virtual machines, much of the discussion was focused on emulation frameworks, including staged emulation, code caching, and memory and exception emulation. These emulation frameworks and techniques have much broader application than process VMs. What sets the process VMs apart from the others is the point at which OS calls are intercepted and emulation is performed — for a process VM this point is at the user interface to the OS. Subsequent chapters will focus on other points of emulation, specifically including emulation of the system ISA. Furthermore, a similar emulation framework is used in same-ISA dynamic binary optimizer systems (described as part of the next chapter). And many of the same techniques are employed in high-level language virtual machines, such as the Java VM, to be discussed in Chapters 5 and 6.

# Chapter Four
# Dynamic Binary Optimization

A fter compatibility, performance is often the most important consideration in virtual machine implementations. This chapter picks up where
the previous chapter left off and focuses on improving performance of the
emulation process. When compared with interpretation, merely performing
simple binary translation yields a large (order of magnitude) performance
gain. However, applying optimizations on translated code provides additional
improvements over basic translation.

In many VMs, simple optimizations are performed just to smooth some
of the "rough edges" left over from an initial binary translation. For example,
a simple instruction-at-a-time translation of the first two IA-32 instructions
in Figure 2.19 (repeated here as Figure 4.1a) yields five PowerPC instructions. A straightforward optimization, *common subexpression elimination*, looks
across the original IA-32 instruction boundaries, discovers that two different PowerPC instructions compute r4+4, so the second can be eliminated
(Figure 4.1b).

In some VMs, more aggressive optimizations can help close the gap between
a guest's emulated performance and native platform performance, although it
is very difficult to close the gap completely. Nevertheless, there are a few VM
applications where optimization is one of the primary reasons for building
the VM in the first place. One example is codesigned VMs, to be covered in
Chapter 7. Another example is same-ISA dynamic binary optimizers, where
the goal is to improve performance on the native platform; these are discussed
in Section 4.7 of this chapter.

Optimizations include simple techniques, such as translation block chaining, covered in the previous chapter. More advanced optimizations form
large translation blocks, each containing multiple basic blocks, and employ

**147**

```
addl    %edx,4(%eax)
movl    4(%eax),%edx

addi    r16,r4,4      ;add 4 to %eax
lwzx    r17,r2,r16    ;load operand from memory
add     r7,r17,r7     ;perform add of %edx
addi    r16,r4,4      ;add 4 to %eax
stwx    r7,r2,r16     ;store %edx value into memory
```

(a)

```
addi    r16,r4,4      ;add 4 to %eax
lwzx    r17,r2,r16    ;load operand from memory
add     r7,r17,r7     ;perform add of %edx
stwx    r7,r2,r16     ;store %edx value into memory
```

(b)

**Figure 4.1**    Optimization Enhances Binary Translation. *(a) A simple translation from IA-32 to PowerPC. (b) The second* addi *can be eliminated.*

optimization techniques that span the original basic block boundaries. Some optimizations involve reordering translated instructions to improve pipeline performance. Other optimizations apply techniques from conventional compilers (as is done in Figure 4.1). Finally, some optimizations exploit knowledge of program-specific execution patterns, collected as part of the ongoing emulation process. These statistics regarding a program's behavior, or its *profile*, serve as a guide for making optimization decisions.

Program profiling is often used to initiate shifts between emulation stages, e.g., between interpretation and binary translation, and it is also important for implementing some specific optimizations of translated code. Profile information can be collected with software by inserting instructions into an interpreter or translated code; it can also be collected by hardware or through some combination of hardware and software. Once collected, profile data is used for optimizing the performance of an emulated program. Two of the most important pieces of profiling information are (1) the instructions (or basic blocks) that are more heavily executed, i.e., where the program spends most of its time, and (2) the sequence in which basic blocks are most commonly executed. In addition to these two principal types of profile information, specific optimizations may depend on the behavior of particular data variables or addresses, and this additional information may be collected via profiling as needed.

An advantage of run-time translation and optimization is that program profile data can provide information that may not have been available when a program was originally compiled. For example, consider the code shown in Figure 4.2a. Assume this represents target ISA code translated from source

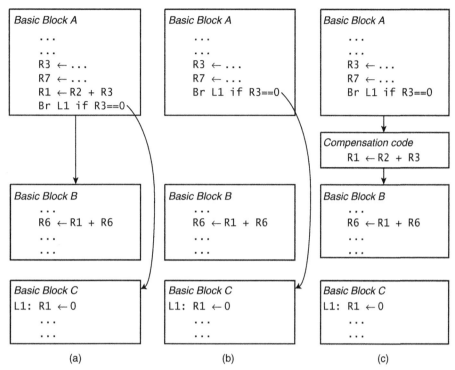

**Figure 4.2** An Optimization Based on Profile Information. *(a) BEQ to basic block C is predominantly taken. (b) Optimization removes assignment of R1 from basic block A. (c) Compensation code assigning R1 is added to handle the rare branch fall-through case.*

ISA binary code (not shown). As with other examples in this chapter, we use a register transfer notation rather than a conventional assembly language in order to make the example more easily understood. Three basic blocks (A, B, and C) have been translated; the basic block A is followed by one of the two other blocks, depending on the outcome of the conditional branch at the end of block A. Inside block A, register R1 is set to a new value that is later used in block B. If the conditional branch is decided so that block C follows the first block, then register R1 is immediately reassigned before it is used. Now let's say that profiling this piece of code indicates that the branch is predominantly decided in the direction of block C. Then the code that assigns a value to R1 in block A is useless most of the time. Consequently, an interblock optimization might remove the initial assignment to R1 from block A, as shown in Figure 4.2b. The resulting code will then provide improved performance because the assignment of a value to R1 is eliminated for most emulations of the original code sequence. On rare occasions, however, the branch may be decided the other way, i.e., toward block B. To deal with such an event, the optimizer must insert *compensation code* before block B is entered. In the example, the compensation code provides the proper assignment to register R1 (Figure 4.2c).

As just shown, a common optimization strategy is to use profiling to determine the paths that are predominantly followed by the program's control flow (as determined by conditional branch and jump outcomes) and then to optimize code on that basis. In some cases, these optimizations move instructions from one block to another, as was done in the example. Furthermore, some host processor implementations may rely heavily on compilers to perform code reordering in order to achieve good performance. For example, the processor may have a simple pipeline that issues instructions in order, and/or it may implement a VLIW instruction set that depends on software to combine independent instructions into a single VLIW (see Appendix Section A.1.1). For these situations, the source program binary may not be optimally ordered for the target processor, so the optimizer performs code reordering, often with the help of profile information.

As a complement to interblock optimizations such as the one just described, the basic blocks themselves may be rearranged in memory so that the most commonly followed execution path has instructions in consecutive memory locations. This is likely to improve performance by improving the efficiency of instruction fetch. If necessary, basic block rearrangement may involve the reversing of conditional branch predicates. For example, in Figure 4.3, the code given earlier in Figure 4.2 is shown with the common execution path restructured as a straight-line code sequence. This straight-line sequence is an example of a *superblock* — a sequence of code with one entry point (at the top) and potentially multiple side exit points (Hwu et al. 1993). And, as in this example, exit points that come out of the middle of the superblock often feed into blocks of compensation code.

Most inter-basic block code optimizations do not actually require rearranging the locations of basic blocks; for example, the optimization in Figure 4.2 does not require that a superblock be formed. However, the two types of optimizations do seem to go together naturally. The superblocks nicely localize the regions of optimization, and the localized code also provides additional performance benefits when fetching instructions, as will be discussed later in the chapter.

Optimization is tightly integrated with emulation and is usually part of an overall framework that supports staged emulation, introduced in the preceding chapter. An emulation framework contains software that coordinates multiple emulation methods and shifts among the emulation methods based on a guest program's run-time behavior.

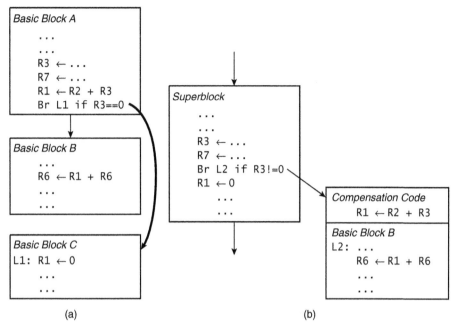

**Figure 4.3**  Superblock formation. *Code is rearranged so that the most frequently occurring blocks are contiguous. To accomplish this, the branch in (a) is reversed from equal to not equal. After rearrangement (b), a superblock having one entry point and two exit points is formed.*

Staged emulation, briefly described in Section 3.5.2, is based on the tradeoff between start-up time and steady-state performance. Some emulation methods have fast start-up performance with low steady-state performance, while other methods have slower start-up with high steady-state performance. A relatively sophisticated example of staged emulation, containing three stages, is shown in Figure 4.4. In this example, emulation is initially performed via interpretation (using the source ISA binary memory image). Profile information is collected concurrently with interpretation. The profile information helps identify frequently used code regions. Then these frequently executed code regions are binary translated as dynamic basic blocks and placed in a basic block cache for reuse. With the benefit of additional profile data, the frequently used basic blocks are combined into larger translation blocks, i.e., superblocks, which are then optimized and placed in the code cache. And, as emulation progresses, the optimizer may be invoked additional times to further optimize the blocks in the code cache.

To encompass the spectrum of staged emulation strategies, we can identify at least four potential emulation stages: interpretation, basic block translation (possibly with chaining), optimized translation (with larger blocks such as

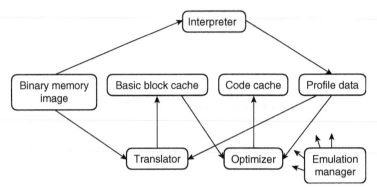

**Figure 4.4**    A Staged Optimization System. *Stages progress from simple interpretation to binary translation to highly optimized translation blocks.*

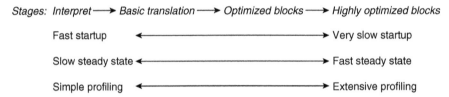

**Figure 4.5**    Spectrum of Emulation Techniques and Performance Tradeoffs.

superblocks), and highly optimized translation, which uses profile information collected over a relatively long period of time.

Figure 4.5 shows the spectrum of emulation methods and corresponding performance characteristics. The tradeoff between start-up time and steady-state performance has already been discussed (Section 3.5.1). In addition to emulation, profiling methodologies fit across the same spectrum. For the higher levels of emulation, more extensive profiling is needed, both in types of profile data collected and the number of profile data points required. Of course, more extensive profiling may add overhead, especially if done entirely in software.

There are a number of staged emulation strategies that, depending on the source and target ISAs, the type of VM being implemented, and the design objectives. The original HP Dynamo system (Bala, Duesterwald, and Banerjia 2000) and the Digital FX!32 system (Hookway and Herdeg 1997) first interpret and then generate optimized, translated code. The DynamoRIO system (Bruening, Garnett, and Amarasinghe 2003) and IA-32-EL (Baraz et al. 2003) omit the initial interpretation stage in favor of simple binary translation followed later by optimization. Other emulation frameworks omit extensive optimizations, because in some applications the overhead and/or support involved may not be justified; the optimization itself takes time, and the level of profiling required may be time consuming. The Shade simulation system (Cmelik and Keppel 1994) contains only interpretation and simple translation; in that application, optimization is not called for.

In the remainder of this chapter, the foregoing ideas are expanded upon. Profiling techniques, both software and hardware, are first described. Then we discuss optimization methods that use profile information to form large translation/optimization blocks. Next we consider optimizations that reorder the instructions within the enlarged translation blocks; for some processors, this may increase the degree of parallelism available for the underlying hardware to exploit. Then we consider other optimizations that are simple versions of classic compiler optimizations. Some of these optimizations can also take advantage of profile data collected at run time.

The optimization framework and techniques given in this chapter are targeted primarily at emulation of conventional ISAs (e.g., IA-32 and PowerPC). However, dynamic optimization is also an important part of high-performance HLL VMs (e.g., for Java), as covered in Chapter 6, and many of the techniques in this chapter can be extended to HLL VMs. The codesigned VMs covered in Chapter 7 also rely heavily on dynamic optimization. In that chapter, we focus on optimization methods that can take advantage of special hardware support provided as part of a codesign strategy.

## 4.1 Dynamic Program Behavior

At the time a virtual machine begins emulating a program, nothing is known about the structure of the code being emulated, yet to improve performance the emulation software may need to apply optimizations that depend very much on both the program's structure and dynamic behavior. The optimization system can use profiling to learn about the program's structure as it is being emulated. It can then combine this profile information with typical program behavior to guide the optimization of translated code. In this section we discuss some of the important characteristics of program behavior that researchers and designers have discovered over the years. These properties underlie many of the optimization heuristics implemented in virtual machines.

One important property of programs is that dynamic control flow is highly predictable. As the program counter sequences through the program, any given conditional branch instruction is very often decided the same way (taken or not taken) a large fraction of the time. For example, consider the small piece of code in Figure 4.6, which searches a linear array of 100 elements for a particular value (−1).

```
                        R3 ← 100
                   loop:R1 ← mem(R2)              ; load from memory
                        Br found if R1 == -1      ; look for -1
                        R2 ← R2 + 4
                        R3 ← R3 -1
                        Br loop if R3 != 0        ; loop closing branch
                          .
                          .
                          .
                   found:
```

**Figure 4.6**  Simple Loop That Searches for the Value −1.

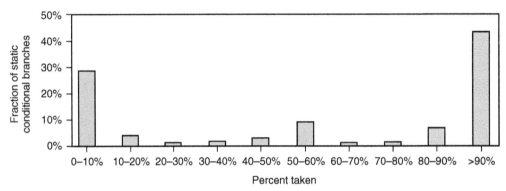

**Figure 4.7**  Distribution of Taken Conditional Branches. *Conditional branches are predominantly decided in one direction (taken or not taken).*

If the value of −1 appears only infrequently, then the conditional branch that closes the loop is predominantly taken. On the other hand, the branch that detects the occurrence of −1 is predominantly not taken. This bimodal branch behavior is typical in real programs. Figure 4.7 contains average statistics for conditional branch instructions in a set of integer SPEC benchmark programs (SPEC). For these programs, 70% of the static branches are predominantly (at least 90% of the time) decided one way; 42% of the branch instructions are predominantly taken and 28% are predominantly not taken.

Furthermore, a high percentage of branches are decided the same way as on their most recent previous execution. This is illustrated in Figure 4.8, where 63% to 98% of branches are decided in the same direction as on their last execution, depending on the benchmark program.

Another important property of conditional branch instructions is that backward branches, i.e., branches to lower addresses, are typically taken, because they are often a part of a loop. On the other hand, forward branches are often not taken, for example, if they test for errors or other special loop exit conditions, as is the case in the example of Figure 4.6.

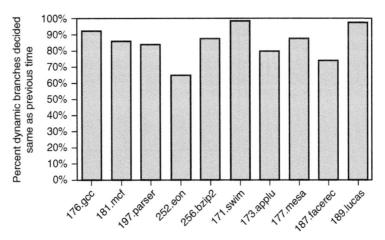

**Figure 4.8** Consistency of Conditional Branches. *A high percentage of branches are decided the same way as on their immediately preceding execution.*

The predictability of indirect jumps is also important for dynamic translation and optimization. With indirect jumps, the issue is determining the destination address of the jump. Because the jump destination is in a register and the register contents may be computed at run time, the jump destination may change over the course of program execution. Some jump destination addresses seldom change and are highly predictable, while others change often and are very difficult to predict. Jump instructions that implement switch statements may sometimes be difficult because the selected case may change frequently. Indirect jumps that implement the returns from procedures are sometimes difficult to predict because a procedure may be called from many different locations. Figure 4.9 shows that for a set of SPEC benchmark programs slightly more than 20% of indirect jumps have a single destination throughout program execution, while almost 60% have three or more different destinations.

The final program characteristic in which we are interested is data value predictability. The data values used by a program are often predictable, and in many cases they change relatively little over the course of a program's execution. Figure 4.10 shows the fractions of instructions that compute the same value every time they are executed. The leftmost bars show, for all instructions and by instruction type, the number of static instructions that always compute the same value. The rightmost bars are the fractions of dynamic instructions that execute the static instructions in the left bars. About 20% of all instructions that produce values are associated with a static instruction that always produces the same value.

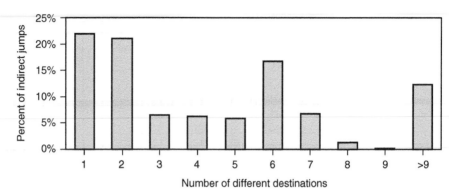

**Figure 4.9** The Number of Destinations for Indirect Jumps. *Slightly more than 20% of indirect jumps have a single destination; others have a number of destinations.*

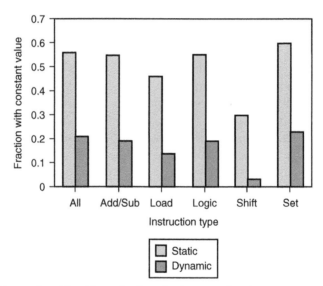

**Figure 4.10** Fractions of Instructions That Always Produce the Same Result Value.

## 4.2 Profiling

Profiling is the process of collecting instruction and data statistics for an executing program. This statistical profile data can be used as input to the code-optimization process. In general, optimizations based on profiling work because of the predictability of programs just described. That is, program characteristics measured for past behavior will often continue to hold for future behavior and can therefore be used for guiding optimizations.

### 4.2.1 The Role of Profiling

Traditionally, code profiling has been used as a way of providing feedback to the compilation process under control of a software developer; refer to Figure 4.11a. Here, the compiler first decomposes the source program into a *control flow graph*, then analyzes the graph as well other aspects of the program and inserts *probes* to collect profile information. A probe is a short code sequence that records execution information into a *profile log* held in memory. For example, profiling probes may be placed at the sites of branch instructions to record branch outcomes. The compiler generates code with these probes inserted. Next, the program is run with a typical data input set, and the probes generate profile data for the complete program. The profile log is then analyzed offline and results are fed back into the compiler. The compiler uses this information to generate optimized code. The optimizer may work from the original HLL program or, more likely, from an intermediate form generated by the compiler (Chang, Mahlke, and Hwu 1991) or the original compiled binary (Cohn et al. 1997). In some cases, hardware may support profile collection through either counters or timer interrupts that permit collection of statistical samples via software.

When used in this conventional setting, the program can be fully analyzed and profile probes can be optimally placed, based on the program's structure. It is not necessary to place a probe on every branch path to collect information for constructing a complete profile of branch paths. Also, a profile can be collected for an entire run of a program to gain fairly complete profile information. For improved profile coverage, multiple profiling runs with different input data sets can be used.

In contrast to the static optimization case just described, with dynamic optimization (e.g., as in the process VM shown in Figure 4.11b), the program structure is not known when a program begins. The runtime's emulation engine is simply given a guest binary image in memory, and both instruction blocks and overall program structure must be discovered in an incremental way, as discussed earlier in Section 2.6. Without an overall view of program structure, it is difficult, if not impossible, to insert profiling probes in a manner that is globally optimal. Furthermore, profiling must be more predictive; i.e., determination of program characteristics should be made as early as possible to achieve maximum benefit. This means that optimization decisions must be made on the basis of statistics from a partial execution of the program.

There is an important performance tradeoff involving profiling overhead and the steady-state performance benefits that accrue from profiling. The profiling overhead consists of the time required for initial analysis of the program structure in order to place profiling probes, followed by the actual collection

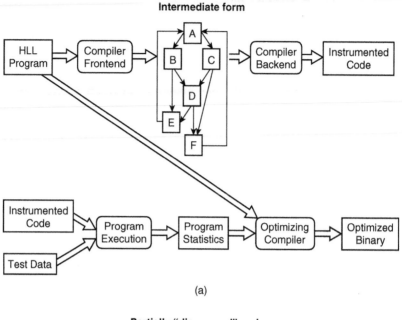

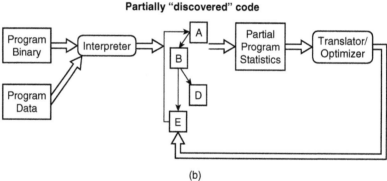

**Figure 4.11** Using Program Profiling. *(a) Traditional profiling applied across multiple program runs; (b) on-the-fly profiling in a dynamic optimizing VM.*

of profile data. The benefit is execution time reduction due to better optimized code. With the conventional offline profile-based optimization method, these costs are paid once, typically during later stages of program development as code is being optimized prior to release for production use. Therefore, any cost in performance overhead is experienced by the program developer in terms of longer "turnaround" time between successive profile/recompile phases. After the optimized program has been deployed to the field, however, there is no additional performance overhead, and benefits are realized every time the optimized code is run.

When dynamic optimization is being used, there are overhead costs every time a guest program is run. These costs are in the form of program analysis in order to place profiling probes as well as the cost of collecting the profile data after the probes have been placed. And of course, in a dynamic optimization environment, the overhead of optimization must be outweighed by the benefits of executing the optimized code. An interesting compromise solution is used in the FX!32 system (described in Section 3.10), where all code translation and optimization is done between program runs and optimized code is saved on disk between runs.

Because of the tradeoffs involved, different VM applications, and the variety of optimizations that may be performed, there are a number of possible profiling techniques that are of interest when performing dynamic optimization in a VM environment. In this section we will overview the spectrum of profiling techniques. Some of these will be useful for supporting dynamic optimizing process VMs, described later in this chapter. Others will be more useful with HLL VM implementations, discussed in Chapter 6.

### 4.2.2 Types of Profiles

There are several types of profile data that can be used in a dynamically optimizing VM. The first type simply indicates how frequently different code regions are being executed. This information can be used to decide the level of optimization that should be performed for a given region. The heavily used code regions, or *hotspots*, should be optimized more, and lightly used code can be optimized less (or not at all) because the optimization process itself is time consuming and potentially performance degrading. For example, in the framework of Figure 4.4, a code sequence may be interpreted until it is determined to be "hot" and then binary translated to speed up future emulation.

A second important type of profile data is based on control flow (branch and jump) predictability, where the profiler collects control flow statistics that can be used for determining aspects of a program's dynamic execution behavior. This information may be used as the basis for gathering and rearranging basic blocks into larger units of frequently executed code, such as the superblocks of Figure 4.3. These larger code units provide opportunities for optimizations over a scope larger than single basic blocks and may also lead to better performance due to instruction cache locality effects.

Other types of profile data may be used to guide specific optimizations. This profile data may focus on data or address values. For example, if an optimization depends on whether load and store addresses are aligned on natural boundaries (see Section 4.6.4), then profiling of load and store addresses

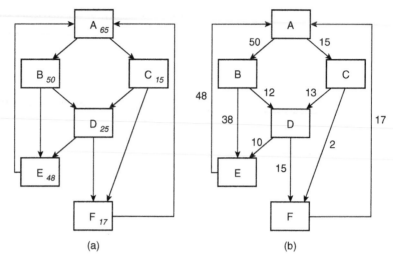

**Figure 4.12** Profiling Applied to a Control Flow Graph. *Boxes (nodes) represent basic blocks, and arrows (edges) indicate control transfers. (a) A basic block profile (or node profile); (b) an edge profile.*

can determine whether this condition holds (at least most of the time) and the optimization should be applied. Or if a program variable is found to hold the same value most (or all) of the time, then program code can be streamlined (or "specialized") for the very common case. These more specific types of profile data will not be discussed further in this section but will be described when required by a particular optimization technique.

The first two types of profile information described earlier are almost universally used by dynamic translation/optimization systems and deserve additional explanation. Figure 4.12 shows a program's control flow graph. The control flow graph contains *nodes*, which correspond to the program's basic blocks (as defined in Section 2.6), and *edges*, which connect the basic blocks and represent flow of control (due to branches and jumps). In the figure, basic block A ends with a conditional branch; one path of the branch, i.e., the fall-through path, goes to basic block B, while the taken path of the branch goes to basic block C.

To determine the hot regions of code, one should profile each basic block and count the number of times each is executed during some time interval; the blocks most frequently executed are the hot ones. A *basic block profile* (or *node profile* in graph terminology) is illustrated in Figure 4.12a. In this example, the numbers contained in the nodes are the counts of the number of times the corresponding basic block has been executed. The blocks A, B, and E are the hottest blocks.

Alternatively, the *edge profile* is shown in Figure 4.12b. The edge profile contains counts of the number of times each control flow edge is followed. In the figure, the edge profile is shown by labeling each of the edges with the number of times it is followed.

In general, there are more edges than nodes, so it may appear slightly more expensive to profile all the edges. However, algorithms have been developed for significantly reducing the number of edges that must be probed in order to compute a complete edge profile (Ball and Larus 1994). Furthermore, the edge profile data provides a more precise view of program execution than the basic block profile; i.e., the basic block profile can be derived from the edge profile by summing the number of incoming edges to each block (or by summing outgoing edge counts). We see in Figure 4.12b, for example, that the basic block D must be executed 25 times — found by adding the profile counts on the incoming edges to basic block D (12 plus 13). Note that the converse property is not necessarily true; i.e., the edge profile cannot always be derived from a basic block (node) profile.

Another type of profile based on control flow is the *path profile* (Ball and Larus 1996). A path profile subsumes an edge profile by counting paths containing multiple edges rather than individual edges. For some optimizations, such as superblock formation, the path profile (at least in theory) is the most appropriate type of profile because the basic blocks arranged to form a superblock should be contained in a commonly followed path. Although it has been shown that collecting path profile data is not necessarily more complex than gathering edge profile data, more up-front program analysis is required in order to decide where to place the profile probes. This up-front analysis probably makes it impractical for most dynamic optimization systems because not enough of the program's structure is known *a priori*. A heuristic for finding frequent paths is simply to follow the sequence of the frequent edges. Although this heuristic does not always find the most frequent paths, significant counterexamples are relatively rare (Ball, Mataga, and Sagiv 1998), and most optimization algorithms approximate the path profile by using a heuristic based on the edge profile.

### 4.2.3 Collecting Profiles

There are two ways of collecting a profile: with instrumentation and with sampling. *Instrumentation-based profiling* typically targets specific program-related events and counts all instances of the events being profiled, for example, the number of times a basic block is entered or the number of times a conditional branch is taken versus not taken. Generally speaking many different events can be monitored simultaneously. Monitoring can be implemented by inserting

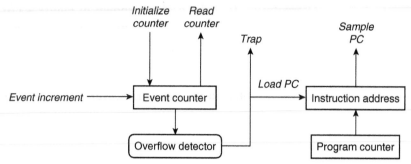

**Figure 4.13** Hardware Used for Sampling. *An event counter triggers a trap; the PC captured at the time of the trap produces the sample.*

probe instructions into the code being profiled or by using underlying profiling hardware to collect data. Using software instrumentation slows down the program being profiled considerably but can be performed on any hardware platform. Hardware instrumentation adds much less overhead but is not very well supported by current hardware platforms. The Intel Itanium platforms are a notable exception (Choi et al. 2002). Furthermore, hardware instrumentation generally does not have the flexibility of software instrumentation; the types of program events to be profiled are built into the hardware.

With *sampling-based profiling*, the program runs in its unmodified form, and, at either fixed or random intervals, the program is interrupted and an instance of a program-related event is captured (see Figure 4.13). For example, program counter values at taken branches may be sampled. After a number of such samples have been taken, a statistical picture of the program emerges; for example, where the program hotspots or hot edges lie.

An important tradeoff between the two profiling methods is that instrumentation can collect a given number of profile data points over a much shorter period of time, but commonly used software instrumentation slows down the program during the time the profile is being taken. Sampling slows down a program much less, at least as perceived by the user, but requires a longer time interval for collecting the same amount of profile information. Of course, the slowdown depends on the sampling interval (typical sampling intervals may be many thousands of instructions).

On a per data point basis, sampling generally has a higher absolute overhead than instrumentation because it causes traps to the profile collecting software. But this overhead is spread out over a much longer total time interval, so the perceived slowdown during the profiling process is less. In addition, multiple samples can be collected and buffered before signaling the user-level profiling software (Dean et al. 1997). With instrumentation, a profile is quickly taken, optimizations are performed, and instrumentation software is either completely or partially removed.

The preferred profiling technique depends on where in the emulation spectrum (Figure 4.5) the optimization process is taking place. For interpretation, software instrumentation is about the only choice, and even there the options are rather limited, as we shall see. For optimizing translated code that may benefit from further optimization, or in dynamic optimization systems where no initial translation is required, there is a much wider variety of options. In general, dynamic optimization systems use instrumentation because it allows the overall optimization process to move much more quickly from slower, less optimized code to highly optimized versions. Sampling is more useful when a longer-running program is already well optimized but further higher-level optimizations may be beneficial. In the following subsections, we will overview profiling methods for both interpreted and translated code.

### 4.2.4 Profiling During Interpretation

There are two key points to consider when profiling during interpretation: The source instructions are actually accessed as data, and the interpreter routines are the code that is being executed. Consequently, any profiling code must be added to the interpreter routines. This implies that profiling is most easily done if it is applied to specific instruction *types* (e.g., opcodes) rather than specific source instructions. It can also be applied for certain classes of instructions that are easily identified during the interpretation process, for example, the destinations of backward branches — as we will see, these are often used as the starting points for forming large translation blocks.

To perform basic block profiling while interpreting, profile code should be added to all control transfer (branch and jump) instructions (after the PC has been updated) because the instructions immediately following these instructions, by definition, begin new basic blocks. Counting the number of times each of these destination instructions is executed constitutes a basic block profile. For edge profiling, the same control transfer instructions can be profiled, but both the PC of the control transfer instruction and the target are used to define a specific edge.

The profile data is kept in a table that is accessed via source PC values of control transfer destinations (basic block profiling) or the PC values that define an edge. This table is similar to the PC map table used during emulation (described in Section 2.6), in that it can be hashed into by the source PC. The entries contain the basic block or edge counts. For conditional branches, counts can be maintained for cases both taken and not taken. Figures 4.14 and 4.15 illustrate

*Instruction function list*

```
branch_conditional(inst) {
      BO = extract(inst,25,5);
      BI = extract(inst,20,5);
      displacement = extract(inst,15,14) * 4;
      .
      .
      // code to compute whether branch should be taken
      .
      .
      profile_addr = lookup(PC);
      if (branch_taken)
            profile_cnt(profile_addr, taken);
            PC = PC + displacement;
      Else
            profile_cnt(profile_addr, nottaken);
            PC = PC + 4;
}
```

**Figure 4.14**    PowerPC Branch Conditional Interpreter Routine with Profiling Code Added (in italics).

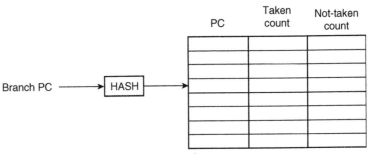

**Figure 4.15**    Profile Table for Collecting an Edge Profile During Interpretation. *A branch PC accesses the table via hashing; a taken or not-taken counter is incremented, depending on the branch outcome.*

the interpreter-based profiling method for conditional branches. Figure 4.14 is the interpreter routine for a PowerPC conditional branch instruction. A data structure for collecting edge profiles is given in Figure 4.15.

In the branch interpreter routine, the PC of the branch instruction is used for performing a profile table lookup via a hash function. Then entries in the profile table are updated appropriately. If the branch is taken, the taken count is incremented; otherwise the not-taken count is incremented. Alternatively, for basic block profiling, the source PC at the end of the branch interpreter routine can be used as the key to the profile table, and only one count per PC is maintained.

### Profile Counter Decaying

As just described, the profile counts held in the profile table increment indefinitely. In practice this leads to an obvious problem — a count may eventually overflow the size of its count field. An immediate solution is to use *saturating* counts; i.e., when a counter reaches its maximum value, it stays there. An additional enhancement lies in the observation that many optimization methods focus on relative frequency of events, e.g., which basic blocks are more heavily used, not the absolute counts. Furthermore, when it comes to making dynamic optimization decisions, recent program event history is probably more valuable than history in the distant past.

This leads to a counter "decay" process. To implement counter decay, the profile management software periodically divides all the profile counts by 2 (using a right shift). After decay, the counts maintain their relative values, and, as the program phase changes and a profiled event becomes inactive, counts carried over from the previous phase will eventually decay to zero. Consequently, at any given time the profile counts reflect the relative activity over a relatively recent period of time.

### Profiling Jump Instructions

Up to this point, when profiling control flow, e.g., edge profiles, we have been concerned primarily with conditional branch instructions. Profiling indirect jumps is slightly complicated because there may be a number of target addresses, and in some cases they may change frequently. This is the case, for example, in return jumps from procedures that have many call sites. This means that a complete profile mechanism that tracks all the targets would consume both more space and more time than conditional branch edge profiling. The process can be simplified, however, by noting that profile-driven optimizations of indirect jumps tend to be focused on those jumps that very frequently have the same target (or a small number of targets). Consequently, it is only necessary to maintain a table with a small number of target addresses (say one or two) and track only the more recently used targets. If the target changes frequently among a large number of addresses, then these counts will always be low, and optimizations based on frequent jump targets will likely provide little benefit anyway.

### 4.2.5 Profiling Translated Code

When profiling translated code, each individual instruction can have its own custom profiling code. Among other things, instrumenting individual

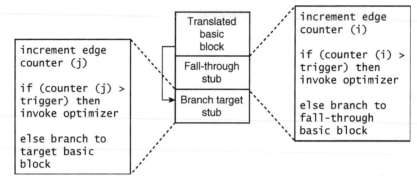

**Figure 4.16** Edge Profiling Code Inserted into Stubs of a Binary Translated Basic Block.

instructions means that profiling can be selectively applied. It also means that profile counters can be assigned to each static instruction at the time the instrumentation is inserted so that profile counters are directly addressed and no hashing is needed. Profile counters can be held in a simple array, with an index into the array hardcoded into the profile code for a specific instruction.

Figure 4.16 illustrates the insertion of instrumentation for edge profiling into translated basic blocks (as in Section 2.6). Here, instrumentation is placed into stub code at the end of each translated basic block. In this example, the optimization algorithm is invoked if a profile value exceeds a specified threshold value, or *trigger*. An advantage of placing profile code in the stub region is that profile code can be easily inserted and removed as needed.

### 4.2.6 Profiling Overhead

Software profiling adds instructions to the overall emulation process. For example, in Figure 4.15, instructions must be added to (1) access the hash table (this will require the hash function plus at least one load and compare) and (2) increment the proper count (two more memory accesses plus an add instruction). For profiling during interpretation, this may add an additional overhead of 10–20% because interpretation already requires executing a number of target instructions per interpreted source instruction. For profiling translated code, fewer instructions may be needed if the profile table lookup is replaced with directly addressable counters, but the *relative* overhead is still significantly higher than with interpretation because translated code itself is much more efficient than interpreted code. In addition to performance overhead, profiling leads to memory overhead for maintaining tables. For example, a profile table such as in Figure 4.15 would require perhaps four words of data for each instruction being profiled.

Profiling overheads can be reduced in a number of ways. One way is to reduce the number of instrumentation points by selecting a smaller set of key points, perhaps using heuristics, and to use the collected data at these points to calculate the profile counts at the others. Another method, based on code duplication, is especially attractive for same-ISA optimization and is described in Section 4.7.

## 4.3 Optimizing Translation Blocks

As was pointed out in the introduction to this chapter, there is often a two-part strategy for optimizing translated code blocks. The first part of the strategy is to use knowledge of dominant control flow for enhancing memory locality by placing frequently followed sequences of basic blocks into contiguous memory locations. In practice these are usually superblocks. In the second part of the strategy, the enlarged translation blocks are optimized, with emphasis on optimizations that are skewed to favor the commonly followed sequence. That is, the optimization increases performance if the common sequence is followed, with a possible loss of performance in the uncommon case. Although the two parts of the strategy are actually relatively independent, both are useful and are often applied in the same system. A common approach is first to form a localized block and then to optimize it as a unit. In the following discussion we will follow the same order.

### 4.3.1 Improving Locality

There are two kinds of memory localities. The first is *spatial locality*, where an access to a memory location is soon followed by a memory access to an adjacent memory location. The second is *temporal locality*, where an accessed memory location is accessed again in the near future. Instruction fetches naturally have a high degree of both types of localities, and instruction-fetch hardware tends to perform better when locality is greater. By rearranging the way code is placed in memory, moreover, both types of localities can be further enhanced.

The methods and benefits of improving code locality are best explained via an example. Figure 4.17a shows a region of code as originally placed in memory. Basic blocks are labeled with uppercase letters, and branch instructions are shown. Other instructions are represented with horizontal lines. Figure 4.17b is the control flow graph for the same code sequence, with edge

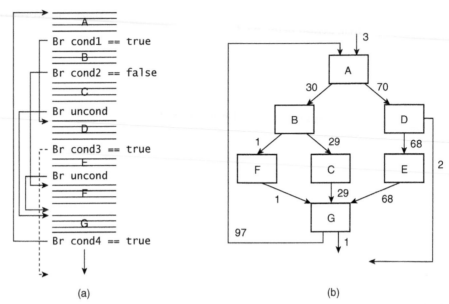

**Figure 4.17** Example Code Sequence. *(a) Basic blocks as initially arranged in memory; (b) edge profile for example code.*

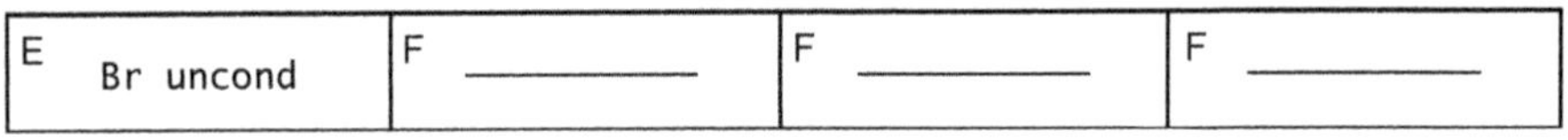

| E | | F | F | F |
|---|---|---|---|---|
| Br uncond | | ——— | ——— | ——— |

**Figure 4.18** Cache Line Containing Instructions from Basic Blocks E and F.

profile information given. The most common path through the code is A, D, E, G. Block F is rarely executed.

First consider how the example code will map onto cache lines; this reveals two ways in which performance may be lost in a typical high-performance processor. Figure 4.18 shows a cache line that contains a total of four instructions at the boundary between basic blocks E and F. Because block F is rarely used, there is relatively little useful locality (spatial or temporal) within this line; nevertheless, the whole line is placed in the cache just to hold the single instruction from block E. It would be better to use the cache space consumed by instructions from block F for other instructions that are more frequently used. Also, when the line is fetched from the cache, only one of the four instructions is useful. Performance may be lost because of relatively low instruction-fetch bandwidth.

To improve performance, profile information can be used to rearrange the layout of the blocks in memory (Pettis and Hansen 1990). A rearranged

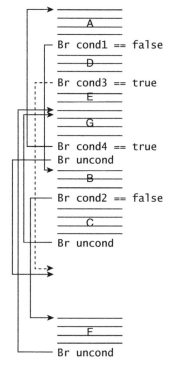

**Figure 4.19**    Example Code After Relayout to Improve Locality.

layout is shown in Figure 4.19. To accomplish the new layout, some of the
conditional branch tests are reversed. For example, the test at the end of block
A is changed from true to false. Furthermore, some unconditional branches
may be removed altogether, for example, the branch that ends block E. Also,
as part of the relayout process, block F, which is rarely used, can be placed
in a region of memory reserved for such seldom-used blocks. These blocks
will generally not consume instruction cache space. Finally, instruction-fetch
efficiency is improved, for example, when executing the code sequence in
blocks E and G, which are always executed in sequence.

Another method for improving spatial locality (and to provide other optimization opportunities) is to perform *procedure inlining* (Scheifler 1977). With
conventional procedure inlining, the body of a procedure is duplicated and
placed at its call/return site. Procedure inlining is illustrated in Figure 4.20,
where procedure xyz is called from two locations (Figure 4.20a). After inlining
has been performed, the code belonging to procedure xyz is duplicated and
placed at the two call sites, as shown in Figure 4.20b. The call and return instructions for procedure xyz are removed. It may also be possible to remove some

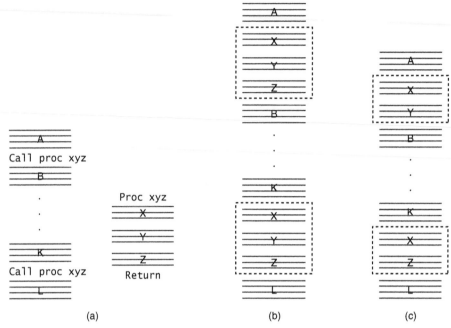

**Figure 4.20** Procedure Inlining. *(a) A code sequence calling a procedure from two call sites. (b) With conventional procedure inlining, procedure B is duplicated and placed at the original call sites. (c) With partial procedure inlining, only a specific control flow path is inlined at each call site.*

register save/restores that surround the call and return in the original code. Hence, inlining not only increases spatial locality in the instruction stream but also eliminates much of the overhead of calls and returns.

In dynamic optimization systems, procedure inlining is often implemented in a dynamic form, based on commonly followed paths discovered at runtime. The leads to dynamic or *partial procedure inlining,* which is based on similar concepts as dynamic basic blocks, discussed in Section 2.6.3. The important point is that because code is discovered incrementally at runtime, it is often not practical to discover and inline a full procedure containing multiple control flow paths. For example, in Figure 4.20a, when procedure xyz is called from the first call site, the path of execution may flow through blocks X and Y; when it is called from the second call site, the path of execution may flow through blocks X and Z. When partial procedure inlining is applied, as shown in Figure 4.20c, only the specific dynamic paths are inlined at the call sites.

Unlike simple code relayout, as described earlier, inlining may increase the total code size when the same procedure is called from several different sites. This may have a negative effect on instruction cache performance. It also may increase register "pressure," i.e., the demand for registers within the region of the inlined code. Consequently, partial procedure inlining is typically used only for those procedures that are very frequently called and that are relatively small — many library routines fit these criteria. Profile information can be used to identify procedures that are good candidates for inlining (Chang et al. 1992; Ayers, Schooler, and Gottlieb 1997).

Specific algorithms for implementing both code relayout and inlining have been used in conventional optimizing compilers. Rather than describe these conventional methods in detail, however, we will consider only the methods useful during dynamic translation and optimization.

We now describe three ways of rearranging basic blocks according to control flow. The first way, *trace* formation, follows naturally from the discussion just given. However, the second way, *superblock* formation, is more widely used in virtual machine implementations, because superblocks are more amenable to interbasic block optimizations, as we shall see. The third way of arranging code is to use *tree groups*, a generalization of superblocks, which are useful when control flow is difficult to predict, and provides a wider scope for optimization. In the following subsections, we discuss traces, superblocks, and tree groups and then turn to optimization methods based on traces and superblocks.

### 4.3.2 Traces

This code-relayout optimization essentially divides the program into chunks of contiguous instructions containing multiple basic blocks (Fisher 1981; Lowney et al. 1993). In the example of Figure 4.17, the sequence ADEG is the most commonly executed path and is placed in memory as a single contiguous block of code. This sequence forms a *trace* [1] — a contiguous sequence of basic blocks. A second, lesser used trace in the example is BC. Block F alone forms a rarely used trace containing only one basic block.

It should be clear that edge profile data can be useful for determining the frequently followed paths. Classically, with an offline profile method (see Figure 4.11a) traces are formed via the following steps.

**1.** A profile is collected during one or more executions of the program using test data.

---

[1]. Sometimes the term *trace* is also applied to superblocks; for example, the *traces* held in a trace cache (Rotenberg, Bennett, and Smith 1996) can be more precisely described as superblocks (all superblocks are traces, but not all traces are superblocks).

2. Using the profile data, begin with the most frequently executed basic block that is not already part of a trace; this is a trace *start point*.

3. Using edge or path profile data, begin at the start point and follow the most common control path, collecting basic blocks along the path until a *stopping condition* is met. One stopping condition is that a block already belonging to another trace is reached. Another example stopping condition is the arrival at a procedure call/return boundary (if the procedure is not being inlined). A more complete set of stopping conditions is given in Section 4.3.4.

4. Collect the basic blocks into a trace, reversing branch tests and removing/adding unconditional branches as needed.

5. If all instructions have been included as part of some trace, stop; otherwise go to step 2.

If we follow this algorithm with the example in Figure 4.17, then we start with block A and follow it to D and E and stop at G. In this case, we use loop-closing branches as a stopping condition (as is often done). Then the next trace starts at B and stops at C. Finally, F is left as the last trace. Figure 4.21 illustrates the traces with respect to the control flow graph; when these traces are laid out in memory, they will appear as in Figure 4.19.

In a dynamic environment (as in Figure 4.11b), the foregoing process of trace formation can be modified appropriately and would build up traces in an incremental manner as hot regions of code are discovered. In practice, however,

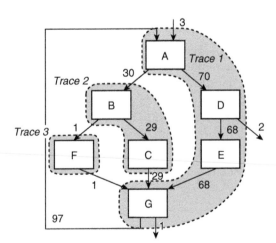

**Figure 4.21** Using Edge Profiles or Collect Basic Blocks into Traces.

traces as just described are not commonly used as translation blocks in today's dynamic translation/optimization systems; superblocks and tree groups are more commonly used, so we defer discussion of dynamic trace formation to the next section.

### 4.3.3 Superblocks

A widely used alternative to the trace is the superblock (Hwu et al. 1993); by construction, superblocks have only one entrance at the top and no side entrances. In contrast, a trace may have both side entrances and side exits. For example, in Figure 4.21, the trace ADEG contains a side exit from block D and two side entrances into block G. As we shall see in Section 4.5.3, disallowing side entrances simplifies later code optimizations.

It might first appear that if superblocks are formed using a method like the one described for traces, the result is relatively small superblocks; for example, in Figure 4.22a ADE, BC, F, and G form a complete set of superblocks. These blocks are smaller than the traces and in some cases may be too small to provide many opportunities for optimizations. However, larger superblocks can be formed by allowing some basic blocks to appear more than once. This is illustrated in Figure 4.22b, where larger superblocks have been formed. Here, the superblock ADEG contains the most common sequence of basic blocks (according to the profile information given in Figure 4.12). Now, because block G in superblock ADEG can only be reached via a side entrance, block G is replicated for the superblocks that contain BCG and FG. The process of replicating code that appears at the end of a superblock in order to form other superblocks is referred to as *tail duplication*.

### 4.3.4 Dynamic Superblock Formation

Superblocks can be formed via a profile-driven static algorithm just as traces are; i.e., by first using test input data to collect a profile and then as part of a static compilation step forming all the superblocks. However, because superblocks are a common choice for virtual machine implementations and are formed at run time, we will consider only their *dynamic* formation in detail. The key point is that they are formed incrementally as the source code is being emulated.

A complication that comes from using superblocks is that basic block replication leads to more choices, especially the choice of when to terminate a superblock, so a number of heuristics are followed. There are three key questions regarding dynamic superblock formation: (1) At what point in the code

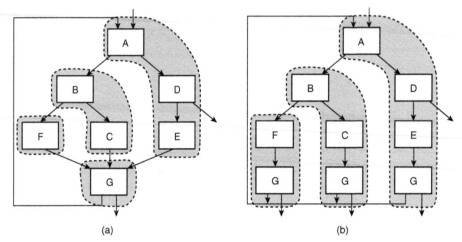

**Figure 4.22** Superblocks. *Superblocks are regions of code with only one entry point and one or more exit points. (a) Superblocks containing no replicated code; (b) superblocks with replicated code (e.g., block G) are larger and provide more optimization opportunities.*

should a superblock be started? (2) As a superblock is being built, what should the next basic block be? (3) At what point should a superblock be terminated? We will discuss each of these in turn, focusing on heuristics that appear to work well in practice.

### Starting Points

In general, a superblock should start at a heavily used basic block. Consequently, as code is initially being emulated, either through interpretation or simple basic block translation, profile information is collected in order to determine those heavily used basic blocks where superblock formation should be started. For this purpose, there are two methods for determining profile points. One is simply to profile all basic blocks. Another is to use heuristics based on program structure to select a narrower set of good candidate start points and then to profile only at those points. One such heuristic is to use the targets of backward branches as candidate start points. Heavily used code will very likely be part of a loop, and the top of every loop is the target of a backward branch. A second heuristic is to use an exit arc from an existing superblock. These arcs are good candidates because, by definition, the existing superblocks are known to be hot, and some exit points will also be hot (although perhaps somewhat less so than the original basic block). In addition, exit points are often not the targets of backward branches and would otherwise be overlooked by the first heuristic. Using heuristics for determining candidate start points reduces the initial number of points to be profiled significantly, and it reduces those that must be monitored for "hotness" as the incremental formation process proceeds.

Regardless of how candidate start points are selected for profiling, most superblock formation methods define a *start threshold* value. When a profiled basic block's execution frequency reaches this threshold, a new superblock is started. In IA-32 EL (Baraz et al. 2003), profiling continues until a certain number of hot basic blocks have reached the threshold (or until one reaches twice the threshold); at that point, superblock formation is started. The value of the start threshold depends on the staged emulation tradeoff involving interpretation versus translation overhead, as discussed earlier; a threshold of a few tens to hundreds of executions is typical.

### Continuation

After a superblock is begun at an initial basic block, the next consideration is which subsequent blocks should be collected and added as the superblock is grown. This can be done using either node or edge information. There are two basic heuristics for using this information: One is *most frequently used* and the other is *most recently used.*

In an example of the most-frequently-used approach (Cifuentes and Emmerik 2000), node profile information is used to identify the most likely successor basic block(s). For this purpose, a second threshold, a *continuation threshold,* is set to determine the possible candidates. This continuation threshold will typically be lower than the start point threshold; for example, a typical continuation threshold might be half the start threshold. Because blocks other than start points must be profiled, a relatively complete set of profile data must be collected for all basic blocks.

At the time the start threshold is reached and superblock formation is to begin, the set of all basic blocks that have reached the continuation threshold is collected. This is the *continuation set.* Then the superblock formation algorithm starts with the hottest basic block and builds a superblock, following control flow edges and including only blocks that are in the continuation set. When a superblock is complete (stopping points are discussed shortly), the emulation process can resume with profiling until another basic block achieves the start threshold. An alternative, however, is to go ahead and form additional superblocks using the members of the continuation set. That is, of the blocks remaining in the continuation set, take the hottest as a new start point and build a second superblock, removing blocks from the continuation set as they are used. This process continues until all the blocks in the continuation set have been exhausted. This method of building multiple superblocks at once has the advantage of amortizing some of the superblock formation overhead over multiple superblocks.

A most-recently-used method (Duesterwald and Bala 2000) relies on edge-based information. The superblock formation algorithm simply follows the actual dynamic control flow path one edge at a time, beginning at the time the start point is triggered. That is, it is assumed that the very next sequence of blocks following a start point is also likely to be a common path — a reasonably good assumption, given the observations on program behavior in Section 4.1. With this method, only candidate start points need to be profiled — there is no need to use profiling for continuation blocks. Hence, one benefit of this approach is that the profile overhead can be substantially reduced versus a most-frequently-used algorithm. A similar approach has been advocated for procedure layout (Chen and Leupen 1997).

Finally, an alternative and more sophisticated approach combines edge profiling and the most-frequently-used heuristic (Berndl and Hendren 2003). This approach relies on correlating sequences of conditional branches (edges in an edge profile) to detect the most likely paths that connect basic blocks into superblocks.

### Stopping Points

At some point the superblock formation process must stop. Again, heuristics are typically used, and the following are possible choices. Any given system may use some or all of these heuristics (or possibly others).

1. **The start point of the same superblock is reached**. This indicates the closing of a loop that was started with this superblock. In some systems, superblock formation can continue even after a loop is closed, which in effect leads to dynamic loop unrolling.

2. **A start point of some other superblock is reached.** When this occurs, superblock formation stops and the two superblocks can be linked together (Section 2.7).

3. **A superblock has reached some maximum length.** This maximum length may vary from a few tens to hundreds of instructions. A reason for having a maximum length is that it will keep code expansion in check. Because a basic block can be used in more than one superblock, there may be multiple copies of a given basic block. The longer superblocks grow, the more basic block replication there will be.

4. When using the most-frequently-used heuristic, **there are no more candidate basic blocks that have reached the candidate threshold.**

5. **An indirect jump is reached, or there is a procedure call.** The use of this stopping heuristic depends on whether partial procedure inlining is enabled, and, if enabled, whether the procedure satisfies criteria for inlining. Tradeoffs involving inlining are discussed further in the context of HLL VMs (see Section 6.6.2).

### *Example*

As an example, we first use the most-frequently-executed method for superblock formation (Cifuentes and Emmerik 2000). Consider the control flow graph shown in Figure 4.17. Say the start point threshold is set at 100 and the continuation threshold at 50. Then, as shown in the figure, basic block A has just reached the start point threshold. Blocks D, E, and G have reached the continuation threshold. Because A has reached the start threshold, superblock formation begins, and superblock ADEG is formed. In this example, formation stops because of the branch from G back to A. At this point, the superblock can be optimized as a unit, with any needed compensation code being added at the exit points. Then, as execution proceeds, block B may next reach the threshold and superblock BCG will most likely be formed. Again, superblock formation stops because G leads to the start point of existing superblock ADEG. Finally, block F might eventually reach the threshold, causing superblock FG to be formed. If F never reaches the threshold, then it is never placed in a superblock. Figure 4.23 shows the final code layout for the example superblocks. Each superblock is a contiguous-code region, and basic block G is replicated three times.

If the most recently executed method is used (Duesterwald and Bala 2000), then only block A is profiled, because it is the only target of a backward branch in this example. When the profile count for block A reaches a threshold value, say, 100, then superblock formation immediately begins and follows the execution flow as it happens. This will most likely lead to superblock ADEG (if the branches are decided in their most probable direction). Then block B is initialized for profiling, because it is now the destination of a superblock exit. After the profile count of B reaches 100, then another superblock will be formed, again following the "natural" flow as it occurs. In this case, it will most likely be BCG. Hence, both the most-frequently-executed and most-recently-executed methods seem to have the same result. However, note that at the time A reaches the threshold, there is about a 30% chance that the branch exiting A will go to B rather than D, and superblock ABCG will be formed rather than ADEG.

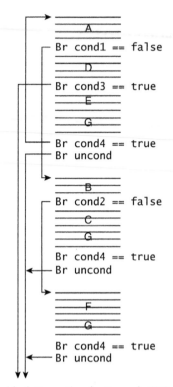

**Figure 4.23**    Code Layout Following Superblock Formation for Example CFG.

A subsequent superblock would then be DEG. This illustrates that there are cases where a most-recently-executed method may not select superblocks quite as well as a most-frequently-executed method. Tree groups, described in the next subsection, are aimed at just those situations.

### 4.3.5  Tree Groups

Although traces and superblocks (as well as dynamic basic blocks) are the most commonly used units for translation and optimization, there are other possibilities. Traces and superblocks are based on the principle that conditional branches are predominantly decided one way (Figure 4.7). However, there are some branches for which this is not the case. For example, in Figure 4.7, almost 20% of the branches range between 30–70 and 70–30, taken versus not-taken. Almost 10% of the branches are about 50–50. For branches that tend to split their decisions, a superblock or trace side exit is frequently taken. When this happens, there is often overhead involved in compensation code (Figure 4.2).

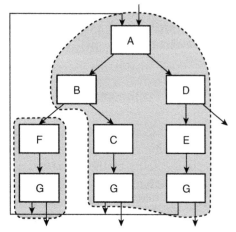

**Figure 4.24** Tree Group. *A tree group encompasses multiple commonly followed control flow paths.*

Furthermore, optimizations are typically not done along the side exit path, thereby losing performance opportunities.

For those situations where conditional branch outcomes are more evenly balanced, it may be better to use *tree regions* or *tree groups* rather than superblocks (Banerjia, Havanki, and Conte 1997). Tree groups are essentially a generalization of superblocks, and they offer more optimization opportunities. They have one entrance at the top and may have multiple exits, but they can incorporate multiple flows of control rather than a single flow of control as with a superblock. That is, as the name suggests, they form trees of connected basic blocks. A tree group for the code illustrated in Figure 4.17 is given in Figure 4.24. A tree group is formed by using tail duplication, as is done with superblocks. The branch at the end of block A in Figure 4.17 is a 30–70 branch, so we include both exit paths in the tree group. On the other hand, the edge from F to G is rarely taken, so it is not included in the major tree region. However, it may later be used as part of a smaller tree region, as shown in the figure.

Just as with traces and superblocks, tree groups can be constructed using collected profile information. For example, a variation of the most-frequently-executed heuristic might set a start threshold at 100 and a continuation threshold at 25 (the continuation threshold is lower than with superblocks, to "encourage" the formation of larger trees). Then for our example code, an initial tree group would consist of blocks ADEGBCG, as show in Figure 4.24; a later tree region might be the smaller FG. Tree groups can also be constructed incrementally. For example, in Figure 4.24 one might first form the tree group ADEG (actually a superblock). Then after additional program emulation and profiling, the path BCG can be added to form the final tree group. The problem with forming tree groups incrementally, however, is that reoptimization may be needed each time a new path is added to the tree group.

## 4.4 Optimization Framework

In the following sections, we begin with traces and superblocks and consider ways of optimizing code within these large translation blocks. In this section, we first discuss some of the overarching issues that are common to all the optimization methods.

In general, dynamic optimization, as discussed in this chapter, differs from static compiler-based optimization in that the optimizer operates only over well-delineated, "straight-line" code regions, e.g., traces or superblocks. Another difference is that high-level semantic information from the original program is not available; information must be extracted from the executable binary. For example, data structure declarations are unavailable. The overall philosophy is that fast, low-overhead optimizations should be used to gather the "low-hanging fruit." In contrast, dynamic optimization for HLL virtual machines (Chapter 6) is much less restricted. In HLL VMs, there is more semantic information available to the optimizer, and the scope of optimization may be much larger than with the optimizations discussed in this chapter.

Dynamic optimizations are performed in addition to any optimizations the original compiler may have done. Because optimization is being performed at run time, however, there are new optimization opportunities that may not have been available to the static compiler. In general, these new opportunities involve optimizations along frequently followed paths that cross basic block boundaries. For example, when consecutive blocks are considered, redundant instructions may be found and removed, or instructions may be reordered across basic block boundaries.

### 4.4.1 Approach

Figure 4.25 illustrates the overall approach to optimization. Based on profile information, basic blocks are first collected to produce a straight-line code sequence that forms a trace or superblock. These instructions are converted into an intermediate form and placed in a scheduling/optimization buffer by the translation software. The intermediate form contains essential dependence information but would typically use a single assignment format (Cytron et al. 1991) so that nonessential dependences do not appear. In order to simplify

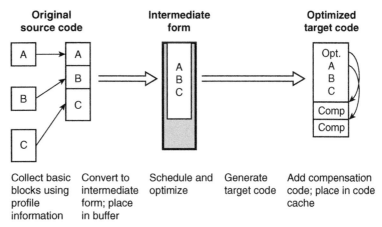

**Figure 4.25** Major Steps in the Scheduling/Optimization Process.

eventual target code generation, the intermediate form is similar to the one that a compiler might use for the target instruction set. Then code scheduling and optimization take place, followed by register assignment. As the code is optimized, side table information is also generated. For example, a side table may be used for tracking the relationships between source register values and target register values in order to implement precise state recovery in the event of a trap or interrupt; this is explained later. In some cases, compensation code is added at the intermediate entry and exit points of the scheduled, optimized trace (Figure 4.26). In practice, these entries and exits will be infrequently used, but, as we shall see, the compensation code is still required for correctness in the event they are used.

An example of an interbasic block optimization that uses dynamic information was given at the beginning of this chapter (Figure 4.2), where the knowledge that the most common control path went from block A to block C allowed formation of a superblock containing basic blocks A and C. Then as an optimization, the assignment to R1 in block A was removed. This resulted in compensation code being added at the exit to block B.

### 4.4.2 Optimization and Compatibility

An important consideration during the optimization process is maintaining compatibility. In Section 3.2 we discussed compatibility issues in general. To reiterate, for practical process VMs, we maintain an isomorphic relationship between the guest VM and the native platform (Figure 3.4). As part of this relationship, we first assume that all control transfer points (a system call,

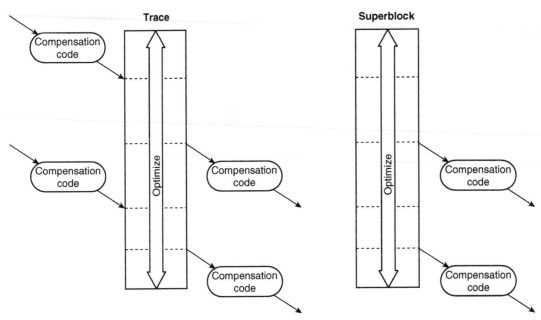

**Figure 4.26** Optimization of Traces and Superblocks. *A trace (left) and a superblock (right) are collections of basic blocks (shown with dotted lines) that are combined using commonly executed program paths. Optimizations can be performed across the entire trace or superblock, with compensation code being added for the uncommon intermediate entrances and exits.*

return, trap, or interrupt) between the guest process and the OS on its native platform will map to a corresponding transfer of control between the guest process and the virtual machine runtime. Furthermore, at the time of one of these transfers to the runtime, it should be possible to reconstruct the entire guest process's state, both registers and memory. With respect to optimizations, it is the traps that we are most concerned with, both the control transfer aspect and the state reconstruction aspect, i.e., forming the precise state. We address both of these in the following paragraphs.

We define a process VM implementation to be *trap compatible* if any trap (except a page fault) that would occur during the native execution of a source instruction is also observed during the emulation of the corresponding translated target instruction(s). And the converse is also true: Any trap that is *observed* during execution of a target instruction should also occur in the corresponding source instruction. We exclude page faults because they are the result not of an action of the running process but of the allocation of resources by the host OS. Page fault compatibility is treated in Chapter 7 in the context of codesigned VMs that are system VMs.

```
         Source                              Target
         . . .                               . . .
       r4 ← r6 + 1                        R4 ← R6 + 1      Remove
       r1 ← r2 + r3  ──────▶ trap?        R1 ← R4 + R5      dead
       r1 ← r4 + r5                        R6 ← R1 * R7    assignment
       r6 ← r1 * r7                        ...
       ...
```

**Figure 4.27**  A Code Optimization That Removes an Apparently Redundant Instruction. *If the removed instruction would have trapped due to overflow, however, no trap will occur in optimized version.*

Consider the example on the left side of Figure 4.27. In this example, the first instruction of the source code (on the left) computes r1, which turns out to be a "dead" assignment, because the next instruction does not read r1 but overwrites it. This apparent redundancy may have occurred as a by-product of forming dynamic translation blocks. An obvious optimization would be to remove the instruction making the redundant assignment (r1 ← r2 + r3). However, this could violate trap compatibility as we have defined it because the removed instruction may trap due to overflow. That is, if the instruction is removed, an overflowing instruction in the original source code is skipped, and the program's execution after optimization is not exactly the same as before the optimization.

With respect to the converse condition for trap compatibility given earlier, it may sometimes be the case that a trap will occur due to the execution of a target instruction that would not have occurred during execution of the source program. However, if the runtime is able to detect these traps and not make them visible to the guest program, then the converse condition still holds. That is, the trap is not "observed" by the guest program because the runtime filters out any spurious traps.

At the time of a trap, the memory and register state corresponding to a particular point in the guest program's execution (as identified by the trap/interrupt PC) becomes visible. *Memory* and *register state compatibility* are maintained if the runtime can reconstruct them to the same values they would have had on a native platform. The requirement of supporting state compatibility can have a significant effect on the optimizations that can be performed. For example, in Figure 4.28 (on the left), it might be beneficial to reorder the instruction that computes r6 to a point higher in the code sequence to allow its execution to be overlapped with independent instructions (because multiplications typically take several cycles to execute). In this example, the multiply instruction can be overlapped with the add instruction that writes to r9. The rescheduled code is shown in the middle of the figure. However, if the add that produces R9 should overflow and trap, then the value in R6, as seen by the trap handler, will not be the same as in the original code sequence.

|  | Source |  | Target |  | Target with saved reg. state |
|---|---|---|---|---|---|
|  | . . . |  | . . . |  | . . . |
|  | r1 ← r2 + r3 |  | R1 ← R2 + R3 |  | R1 ← R2 + R3 |
|  | r9 ← r1 + r5 | reschedule | ➤R6 ← R1 * R7 |  | S1 ← R6 * R7 |
|  | r6 ← r1 * r7 |  | ⌐R9 ← R1 + R5 —→ trap? | | R9 ← R1 + R5 |
|  | r3 ← r6 + 1 |  | R3 ← R6 + 1 |  | R6 ← S1 |
|  | . . . |  | . . . |  | R3 ← S1 + 1 |
|  |  |  |  |  | . . . |

**Figure 4.28**  Code That Is Reordered to Overlap Execution of a Multiplication with an Independent Instruction. *If the multiplication overflows, the state observed by trap handler is changed.*

Register compatibility is easier to maintain than memory state compatibility because register values can be backed up (or checkpointed) more easily. This is illustrated in the rightmost code sequence of Figure 4.28. Here, the code is reordered, but the result of the multiplication is initially placed into a scratch register, S1. The value in S1 is then copied into register R6 at the same place R6 would have been updated in the original code. If an overflow trap should occur, the runtime can recover the original state from S2, using techniques to be described in Section 4.5.

In the case where *intrinsic compatibility* (see Section 3.2.1) is required, then optimizations should be restricted to those that make all register and memory state recoverable at the time any potentially trapping instruction is emulated. However, if the developer of the VM software can make some assumptions about the producer of a binary — for example, that certain types of bugs are not present, that a particular compiler will used for the source binary, that only certain trap handlers will be used, or that some traps will never be enabled — then additional optimizations can be performed while still providing *extrinsic compatibility* under the given assumptions. We will return to the topic of compatibility in Section 4.6.2, after specific optimizations have been described.

### 4.4.3  Consistent Register Mapping

Initially, we assume there are always sufficient target registers available to map source register values to target registers and to accommodate any optimizations that may be performed. This may require that there be more available target registers than original source registers. This is not an unreasonable assumption, however, because the IA-32 is a commonly used source ISA, and the target ISA is often a RISC ISA, with many more registers than an IA-32. The relative numbers of source and target registers are an important consideration, however, and this issue was discussed in Section 3.3.1.

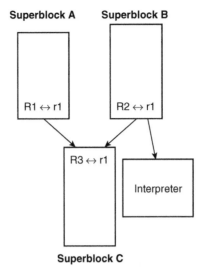

**Figure 4.29**  An Inconsistent Register Mapping. *When one superblock branches to another, the source-to-target register mapping must be correctly managed. Furthermore, when jumping to the interpreter, the interpreter must know the specific mapping being used so that it can correctly update its register context block in memory.*

Given a sufficient number of target registers, we assume that individual source registers can be permanently mapped to target registers. Although in theory a less permanent mapping could be done on a per-translation-block basis, such a flexible mapping method leads to complications when a transition is made from one translation block to another or from a translation block to the interpreter. This is illustrated in the following example.

Figure 4.29 shows a situation where two different translated superblocks (A and B) branch to the same translated superblock, C. If superblocks A and B use different register mappings (e.g., one uses R1 for source register r1 while the other uses R2), then one (or possibly both) of them may be inconsistent with the mapping in the common destination superblock, C. Consequently, extra register copy instructions must be inserted at the end of superblocks A and B to make their mappings consistent with the destination superblock, C. A similar situation occurs if superblock B jumps to the interpreter because the conditional branch at its end is not taken. When interpreter is entered, then the runtime must copy target register values into the register context block the interpreter keeps in memory. If the register mapping is not consistent among translation blocks, then a side table must be provided to assist the runtime with the copying. The table would indicate the specific mapping used by each translated superblock.

To simplify the process, often a fixed source-to-target register mapping is maintained at all translation block boundaries, with the mapping being more flexible within the superblock boundaries. In some cases, this may cause additional register copy instructions at the time a translation block is exited. It must be noted, however, that such a fixed mapping is not necessary — through careful bookkeeping at the time translation is performed, the translator (with the assistance of side tables) can make sure that source and destination mappings always match when a transition is made; this process will be explored in Section 4.6.3.

## 4.5 Code Reordering

An important optimization performed in a number of virtual machine applications is code reordering. In many microarchitectures, performance is affected by the order in which instructions are issued and executed. The most significant examples are simple pipelined microarchitectures that execute instructions strictly in program order. This was done in many of the early RISC processors and is still done in a number of embedded processors. Another example is VLIW processors that expect the compiler to reorder instructions so that several independent instructions can be packed together within the same long instruction word. The Intel IPF (formerly IA-64) implementations (i.e., Itanium) are modern high-performance processors that take this approach. Finally, in many cases, performance of dynamic out-of-order superscalar processors can benefit from code reordering because of variations in functional unit latencies, especially cache memory latencies.

Because of its importance, we will consider code reordering before looking at other optimizations. Code reordering is a fairly easy optimization to understand, and several important issues can first be discussed with respect to reordering and later extended to other types of optimizations.

### 4.5.1 Primitive Instruction Reordering

The key issues related to code reordering are easier to understand if we first consider reordering pairs of instructions. This will enable us to see the steps that are required for implementing precise traps or for adding compensation code at side entry and exit points to ensure correctness. This pairwise-reordering approach may seem a little pedestrian, but it is conceptually useful for understanding the important issues. By considering reordering in this manner, we are reducing the problem to "primitives" from which more complex algorithms are built.

The types of reordering allowed and any required compensation code, i.e., the rules for reordering, depend on the types of instructions involved. We therefore divide instructions into four categories.

*Register updates, denoted as "reg"* — instructions that produce a register result, i.e., that change the register portion of the architected state. This category typically includes load instructions as well as ALU/shift-type operations that write to registers. These instructions have the property that their state modification(s) can be "undone," e.g., by saving about-to-be-overwritten values in other target registers or spilling them to a region of memory. The saved state may be required in the event that a reordered instruction traps and the runtime needs to recover the precise source ISA state.

*Memory update instructions, "mem"* — instructions that place a value in memory; i.e., that change the portion of architected state residing in main memory. In most instruction sets, only memory store instructions are in this category. A key property is that the updating of the memory state cannot be easily undone. In general, any instruction whose modification to the process state cannot be undone should be put in this category. This includes memory accesses to volatile locations (described below).

*Branch instructions, "br"* — a branch instruction that determines control flow but does not produce any register or memory result. Branches cannot trap.

*Join points, "join"* — the points where a jump or branch target enters the code sequence (i.e., the trace). Although these are not instructions strictly speaking, they can affect scheduling when instructions are moved above or beyond join points.

As an example, the instructions in Figure 4.30 have been designated with the category to which they belong. In this and other examples, we use a register transfer notation to make the various instruction dependences easier to see.

*Accesses to volatile memory locations* — A *volatile* memory location is one that may be accessed by an entity other than the process at hand, for example, by another process or thread in a multiprocessing system or by the I/O system if memory-mapped I/O is being used. Very often, there are severe constraints on optimizations when volatile memory locations are involved. For example, instructions accessing volatile locations cannot be removed,

```
...
R1 ← mem(R6)              reg
R2 ← mem(R6 +4)          reg
R3 ← R1 + 1              reg
R4 ← R1 << 2             reg
Br exit if R7 == 0       br
R7 ← R7 + 1              reg
mem (r6) ← R3            mem
```

**Figure 4.30**   Code Sequence with Instructions Denoted According to Scheduling Category.

and in many cases they may not be reordered. More discussion of memory reordering in multiprocessor VMs is in Chapter 9. For our analysis of code reordering, it is best to categorize volatile memory accesses as "mem" — even if they are not stores. For example, in Figure 4.30 if the first two load instructions are to volatile memory locations, then they should each be categorized as "mem" rather than "reg." A final comment is that in some VM applications, the emulation system does not know *a priori* whether memory locations are volatile and must then make very conservative assumptions about optimizations involving any memory operations.

We now consider scheduling situations in terms of the foregoing instruction categories. There are 16 different cases; i.e., both instructions in a pair are one of the four types. A few of the 16 cases are degenerate, however; e.g., reordering two join points has no real effect. The focus of this discussion will be the requirements of maintaining a consistent register assignment and implementation of precise traps (to be discussed in greater detail in Section 4.5.2).

To provide some overall organization, we consider first code movement involving branches, then code movement around join points, and finally code movement in straight-line code.

The first two cases we consider are illustrated in Figure 4.31a. These involve moving instructions from above to below a branch exit point. Instructions that change the architected state, whether writing to a register or to memory, can be moved below a conditional branch that exits a trace or superblock. When this is done, compensation code is added at the exit point to duplicate the update performed by the instruction being moved. This ensures that if an early exit is taken, the state is the same as in the original code sequence. For example, in Figure 4.31b, a shift instruction is moved after a conditional branch. In the event that the branch is taken, a duplicate of the reordered instruction is placed on the target path as compensation code.

The cases where instructions are moved above a conditional branch are illustrated in Figure 4.32a. A register update instruction can be moved ahead of a conditional branch as shown, but special provisions must be made for

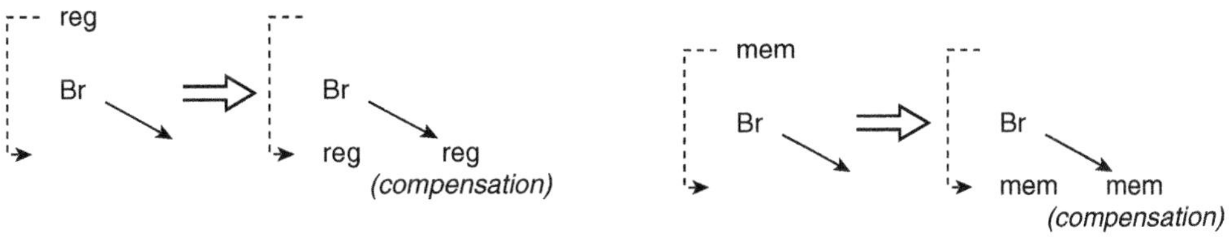

(a)

```
...                          ...
R1 ← mem(R6)                 R1 ← mem(R6)
R2 ← mem(R6 +4)              R2 ← mem(R6 +4)
R3 ← R1 + 1                  R3 ← R1 + 1
R4 ← R1 << 2                 Br exit if R7 == 0
Br exit if R7 == 0           R4 ← R1 << 2
R7 ← R7 + 1                  R7 ← R7 + 1              R4 ← R1 << 2
mem (R6) ← R3                mem (R6) ← R3
```

(b)

**Figure 4.31**    Moving Instructions Around a Conditional Branch Instruction. *(a) Two cases are shown: moving a register update instruction below a branch and moving a store below a branch. In both cases, compensation code is required. (b) An example of a register update instruction (R4 ← R1 ≪ 2) being moved below a conditional branch; a duplicate is used as compensation code on the taken branch path.*

supporting precise traps. If a register instruction writes to register R in the original sequence, the old value in R must be maintained, at least until the flow of execution reaches the original position of the register update instruction (i.e., after the branch). One way to do this is to place the new value into a temporary register, T (thus saving the old value of R) and then later copying the new value into R. This is illustrated in the first two code sequences of Figure 4.32b. Here, a multiply instruction is moved above the branch. The result of the multiply instruction is held in register T1, and then later (after the branch) it is copied into the original destination register, R6. In many cases, the explicit copy instruction may not be needed. For example, in the rightmost column of Figure 4.32b, the explicit copy is removed. Temporary register T1 is still needed to prevent overwriting the value in R6 in the event that the branch is taken. The key point is that at every instruction in the sequence (including at the branch exit), the correct value of R6 is available, either in R6 itself or in some other register. In other words, in the target code, the *live range* of the original value in register R6 is extended at least to the point where it would have been overwritten in the original code sequence.

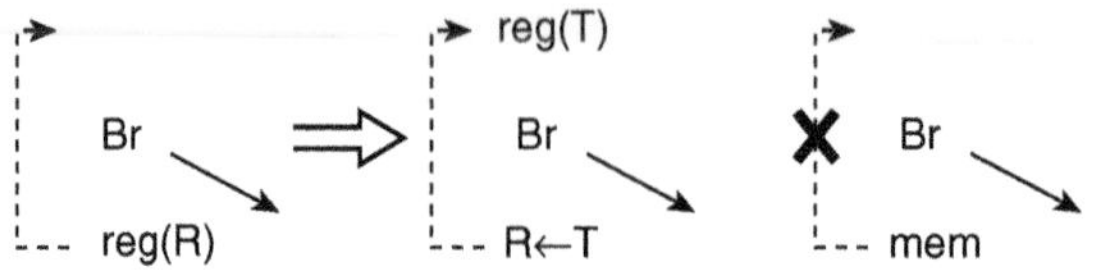


(a)

```
...
R2 ← R1 << 2
Br exit  if R8 == 0
R6 ← R7 * R2
mem (r6) ← R3
R6 ← R2 + 2
```

```
...
R2 ← R1 << 2
T1 ← R7 * R2
Br exit if R8 == 0
R6 ← T1
mem (T1) ← R3
R6 ← R2 + 2
```

```
...
R2 ← R1 << 2
T1 ← R7 * R2
Br exit if R8 == 0
mem (T1) ← R3
R6 ← R2 + 2
```

(b)

**Figure 4.32** Moving Instructions from Below a Conditional Branch to Above. *(a) A register update instruction can be moved above a branch instruction as long as the old value remains available until after the branch. This may require the update value to be placed in a temporary register in case the branch exit is taken. A mem update (store) instruction cannot be moved above a branch. (b) An example where a multiply instruction (R6 ← R7 * R2) is moved above a conditional branch.*

Also, as illustrated in the rightmost code sequence of Figure 4.32a, a mem instruction cannot be moved ahead of the branch because we are assuming that once a mem instruction writes to memory, the previous memory value is unrecoverable. Hence, it would not be possible to back up the old value as was done with the register instruction.

We now turn to cases where an instruction is moved up past a join point (found in traces but not superblocks; there are no entry points in superblocks except at the top). This is the "dual" situation to the foregoing cases, where an instruction was moved past a branch exit point.

As shown in Figure 4.33a, both types of state-updating instructions, reg and mem instructions, can be moved above a join point. The compensation code is a duplicate of the moved instruction. The compensation guarantees that the state is correctly updated, regardless of the way the block is entered. Also, note that the moved instruction is actually the one at the join point, and the join point essentially moves down one instruction. Consequently, no actual code movement takes place; only the target of the join point is changed. This scheduling operation is useful only if additional upward code movements can be made. Figure 4.33b is an example where a load instruction at a join point is moved above the join point. The case where a mem (store) instruction is moved above a join point is similar.

Moving state-updating instructions (register updates or stores) below a join point will cause the state to be updated regardless of the entry path. In all but a

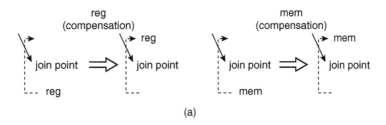

(a)

```
      ...
 ↘  R1 ← R1 + 1        R7 ← mem (R6)      ...
    R7 ← mem (R6)                       R1 ← R1 + 1
    R7 ← R7 + 1                      ↘  R7 ← mem (R6)
      ...                              R7 ← R7 + 1
                                        ...
```

(b)

**Figure 4.33**   An Instruction Is Moved Above a Join Point. *(a) A register update or a mem instruction (a store) can be moved above a join point; if so, compensation is added by performing a duplicate instruction on the join path. (b) An example where a load instruction is moved above a join point.*

few very special situations, this will result in an incorrect state update if the join path is used. Consequently, we will not consider rescheduling that involves this type of code motion.

Now we turn to code movement in straight-line regions of code. First consider instructions that update registers as shown in Figure 4.34a. This case is similar to moving a register instruction above a branch point. When the instruction is moved, it initially updates a temporary register, T. Then later, at the point where it would have updated the register in the original sequence, the temporary register can be copied into the architected register. Of course, as was the case earlier, if the value is overwritten before the block of translated instructions ends, then the copy instruction is not needed. An example is in Figure 4.34b. If a memory-update instruction should cause a trap, then the state can be restored to that prior to the mem instruction in the original sequence, and interpretation can then be used to emulate execution in the original program order. In this case the trap will occur again and the state will be correct.

Other types of straight-line code reordering lead to problems, most notably moving a store above any other instruction that modifies the state. As noted earlier, the store cannot be "undone," so if there is a trap caused by the instruction that precedes it in the original schedule (but follows in the final schedule), the precise state cannot be restored.

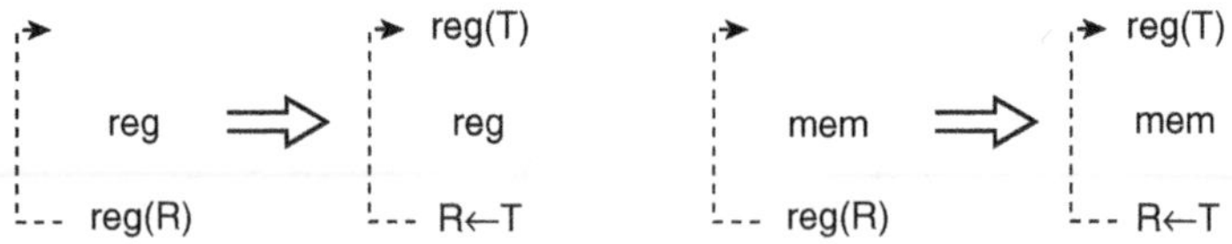

(a)

```
    ...                      ...
R1 ← R1 * 3              R1 ← R1 * 3
mem(R6) ← R1             T1 ← R7 << 3
R7 ← R7 << 3            mem(R6) ← R1
R9 ← R7 + R2            R7 ← T1
    ...                 R9 ← T1 + R2
                            ...
```

(b)

**Figure 4.34**    Code Movement in Straight-Line Code Sequences. *Register updating instructions can be moved above potentially trapping instructions, but the computed value is held in a temporary register, in case a trap does occur.*

### Summary

The various types of code reordering are given in Table 4.1. The columns of the table are the instruction types that are the first instruction of a pair to be reordered and the rows are the second. The table entries indicate the action that can be taken: whether reordering is allowed, and, if so, the action to be taken when reordering is performed. These actions permit precise state recovery when traps occur. We observe that reordering is always possible if a register instruction is the second of the pair; i.e., a register instruction can be moved "up" in a schedule arbitrarily (as long as data dependences are not violated). Other allowed code motions involve the movement of reg or store instructions from above to below branches, and the movement of a store from below to above a join point (with proper compensation).

### 4.5.2   Implementing a Scheduling Algorithm

Now that we have discussed scheduling primitives, we consider a complete code-scheduling algorithm. The algorithm is based on one given by Bich Le (1998) and schedules code that has been organized into superblocks.

**Table 4.1**   Instruction Reordering by Type

| Second | First | | | |
|---|---|---|---|---|
| | reg | mem | br | join |
| reg | Extend live range of reg instruction | Extend live range of reg instruction | Extend live range of reg instruction | Add compensation code at entrance |
| mem | Not allowed | Not allowed | Not allowed | Add compensation code at entrance |
| br | Add compensation code at branch exit | Add compensation code at branch exit | Not allowed (changes control flow) | Not allowed (changes control flow) |
| join | Not allowed (can only be done in rare cases) | Not allowed (can only be done in rare cases) | Not allowed (changes control flow) | No effect |

For handling precise traps, register assignments are performed to maintain extended live ranges so that if a trap occurs, the register state can always be backed up to some point prior to the trapping instruction. Then interpretation of the original source code can establish whether the trap is in fact real and will provide the correct state if it is. The example given here translates from an IA-32 instruction sequence to a PowerPC sequence. In the example, maintaining IA-32 condition codes is initially ignored; then at the end of this section is a discussion of condition code handling.

### Step 1: Translate to Single-Assignment Form

The instructions belonging to the superblock are translated to the target ISA and placed in a rescheduling buffer. As the instructions are placed in the instruction buffer, they are put in single-assignment form (a register is assigned a new value only once). To help with maintaining the consistent register mapping, incoming register values are mapped to their consistent target registers. Any new values generated in the superblock are placed in temporary "registers," labeled ti, in order to maintain the single-assignment discipline.

```
Original Source Code        Translated in Scheduling Buffer
add    %eax,%ebx            t5  ← r1 + r2, set CR0
bz     L1                   bz      CR0, L1
mov    %ebx,4(%eax)         t6  ← mem(t5 + 4)
mul    %ebx,10              t7  ← t6 * 10
add    %ebx,1               t8  ← t7 + 1
add    %ecx,1               t9  ← r3 + 1, set CR0
bz     L2                   bz      CR0, L2
add    %ebx,%eax            t10 ← t8 + t5
br     L3                   b       L3
```

### Step 2: Form Register Map

A register map (RMAP) is generated to track the values as assigned in the original source code. For each of the IA-32 source registers, eax, ebx, etc., the RMAP keeps track of the single-assignment register that holds the corresponding value at any given point in the code sequence.

| Original Source Code | | Single Assignment Form | Register Map (RMAP) | | | |
|---|---|---|---|---|---|---|
| | | | eax | ebx | ecx | edx |
| add | %eax,%ebx | t5 ← r1 + r2, set CR0 | t5 | r2 | r3 | r4 |
| bz | L1 | bz    CR0, L1 | t5 | r2 | r3 | r4 |
| mov | %ebx,4(%eax) | t6 ← mem(t5 + 4) | t5 | t6 | r3 | r4 |
| mul | %ebx,10 | t7 ← t6 * 10 | t5 | t7 | r3 | r4 |
| add | %ebx,1 | t8 ← t7 + 1 | t5 | t8 | r3 | r4 |
| add | %ecx,1 | t9 ← r3 + 1, set CR0 | t5 | t8 | t9 | r4 |
| bz | L2 | bz    CR0, L2 | t5 | t8 | t9 | r4 |
| add | %ebx,%eax | t10← t8 + t5 | t5 | t10 | t9 | r4 |
| br | L3 | b      L3 | t5 | t10 | t9 | r4 |

### Step 3: Reorder Code

The instructions in the intermediate form are reordered. As the code is reordered, the rows of the RMAP are reordered along with the corresponding instructions. Here, the instructions are denoted with labels a:, b:, c:, etc. to make their identification in the rescheduled code easier. In this example, the load instruction, c, is moved up above branch b to give the load a longer time to complete before its output value is needed. Similarly, the add instruction, e, which depends on the multiply, d, is moved downward, below the branch that follows it. As explained earlier, the movement of the add instruction below the branch requires compensation code to be added at exit label L2.

| Before Scheduling | | After Scheduling | | Register Map (RMAP) | | | |
|---|---|---|---|---|---|---|---|
| | | | | eax | ebx | ecx | edx |
| a: t5 | ← t0 + t1,set CR0 | a: t5 | ← r1 + r2,set CR0 | t5 | r2 | r3 | r4 |
| b: bz | CR0, L1 | c: t6 | ← mem(t5 + 4) | t5 | t6 | r3 | r4 |
| c: t6 | ← mem(t5 + 4) | b: bz | CR0, L1 | t5 | r2 | r3 | r4 |
| d: t7 | ← t6 * 10 | d: t7 | ← t6 * 10 | t5 | t7 | r3 | r4 |
| e: t8 | ← t7 + 1 | f: t9 | ← r3 + 1,set CR0 | t5 | t8 | t9 | r4 |
| f: t9 | ← t3 + 1,set CR0 | g: bz | CR0, L2 | t5 | t8 | t9 | r4 |
| g: bz | CR0, L2 | e: t8 | ← t7 + 1 | t5 | t8 | r3 | r4 |
| h: t10 | ← t8 + t5 | h: t10 | ← t8 + t5 | t5 | t10 | t9 | r4 |
| i: b | L3 | i: b | L3 | t5 | t10 | t9 | r4 |

```
Compensation:
L2: t8  ← t7 + 1
```

### Step 4: Determine Checkpoints

Instruction checkpoints are determined. These are used when an instruction traps or there is an early exit branch from the superblock. When a trap occurs, it must be possible to back up to some earlier point where a precise state can be recovered so that interpretation can proceed forward. These *checkpoints* are places where *all* instructions in the original sequence have been completed up to that point. To find these points, we consider an instruction to be "committed" if all preceding instructions in the original sequence have been completed. The points at which instructions commit are listed here. Then, for each instruction, the checkpoint (in other words, the backup point if it traps) is the closest instruction that has been committed. These are shown in the checkpoint column in the example. When the superblock is entered, the initial register mapping is the checkpoint, denoted as @.

| | | Register Map (RMAP) | | | | Commit | Checkpoint |
|---|---|---|---|---|---|---|---|
| *After Scheduling* | | *eax* | *ebx* | *ecx* | *edx* | | |
| a: | t5 ← r1 + r2,set CR0 | t5 | r2 | r3 | r4 | a | @ |
| c: | t6 ← mem(t5 + 4) | t5 | t6 | r3 | r4 | | a |
| b: | bz  CR0, L1 | t5 | r2 | r3 | r4 | b,c | a |
| d: | t7 ← t6 * 10 | t5 | t7 | r3 | r4 | d | c |
| f: | t9 ← r3 + 1,set CR0 | t5 | t8 | t9 | r4 | | d |
| g: | bz  CR0, L2 | t5 | t8 | t9 | r4 | | d |
| e: | t8 ← t7 + 1 | t5 | t8 | r3 | r4 | e,f,g | d |
| h: | t10← t8 + t5 | t5 | t10 | t9 | r4 | h | g |
| i: | b  L3 | t5 | t10 | t9 | r4 | i | h |

## Step 5: Assign Registers

Registers are assigned in a more or less conventional way, except for the way live ranges are determined. For determining live ranges, we need to consider the normal live ranges in the rescheduled instruction sequence and extended live ranges that are necessary for precise state recovery if there is a trap. The extended live ranges are based on the checkpoints. For each instruction that is a checkpoint, the live ranges of registers in its register mapping must be extended to the last point where it is used as a checkpoint. For example, instruction *d* serves as a checkpoint until instruction *e* appears in the reordered sequence. Registers t5, t7, r3, and r4 are in the register map for instruction *d*. Consequently, these registers must be kept live until instruction *e* appears in the reordered sequence. This means that if instruction *e* should trap, say, due to an overflow, then the register values at instruction *d* will be available and can be restored.

Actually, live range extension can be relaxed somewhat. We need to maintain checkpoints only for instructions that can trap or branch out of the superblock, because these are the only points where it is necessary that correct source state be available. In our example, the places where live ranges have been extended are marked with an "x."

| Register Live Ranges | After Assignment | Register Map (RMAP) |
| --- | --- | --- |

```
          Register Live Ranges                    After Assignment                      Register Map (RMAP)
   r1 r2 r3 r4 t5 t6 t7 t8 t9 t10                                              eax     ebx     ecx     edx
    |  |  |  |  |                         a: r1 ← r1+r2,set CR0                 r1      r2      r3      r4
       x  |  |  |  |                      c: r5 ← mem(r1 + 4)                   r1      r5      r3      r4
       x  |  |  |  |                      b: bz        CR0, L1                  r1      r2      r3      r4
          |  |  |  |  |                   d: r2 ← r5 * 10                       r1      r2      r3      r4
          |  |  |     |     |             f: r5 ← r3+1,set CR0                  r1      r2      r5      r4
       x  |  |     |     |                g: bz        CR0, L2                  r1      r2      r5      r4
       x  |  |     |  |  |                e: r2 ← r2 + 1                        r1      r2      r3      r4
          |  |     |  |  |                h: r2 ← r2 + r1                       r1      r2      r5      r4
          |  |        |  |  |             i: b         L3                       r1      r2      r5      r4
```

After live ranges are determined, then registers are assigned as shown. Because the PowerPC has many more registers than the IA-32, there are plenty of registers available for the assignment. During assignment, it should be an objective for the consistent register mapping to be in place when the trace or superblock is exited. Thus, the RMAP of the last instruction should, as much as possible, reflect the consistent register mapping. Copy instructions, if needed, are then added to force the consistent mapping. Similarly, if a side exit should be taken, it may be necessary to add compensation code in order to restore the RMAP.

### Step 6: Add Compensation Code

Compensation code is added. In the example, compensation code is needed because instruction *e* was moved below branch *g*. Consequently, the same operation (r2 ← r2 + 1) must be added at the target of branch *g*. In addition, register r5 must be copied to register r3 in order to restore the consistent register mapping. The final translated and reordered PowerPC code is shown here on the right.

```
After Assignment               Compensation Code Added          PowerPC Code
a: r1 ← r1+r2,set CR0          a: r1 ← r1+r2,set CR0           a:     add.   r1,r1,r2
c: r5 ← mem(r1 + 4)           c: r5 ← mem(r1 + 4)            c:     lwz    r5, 4(r1)
b: bz        CR0, L1          b: bz        CR0, L1           b:     beq    CR0, L1
d: r2 ← r5 * 10              d: r2 ← r5 * 10               d:     muli   r2,r5,10
f: r5 ← r3+1,set CR0          f: r5 ← r3+1,set CR0           f:     addic. r5,r3,1
g: bz        CR0, L2          g: bz        CR0, L2'          g:     beq    CR0, L2'
e: r2 ← r2 + 1              e: r2 ← r2 + 1               e:     addi   r2,r2,1
h: r2 ← r2 + r1             h: r2 ← r2 + r1              h:     add    r2,r2,r1
i: b         L3              i: b         L3               i:     b      L3
                                r3 ← r5                           mr     r3,r5

                             L2':r3 ← r5                    L2':mr     r3,r5
                                 r2 ← r2 + 1                      addi   r2,r2,1
```

### Precise State Recovery

Continuing with our example, when a trap occurs, the runtime first finds the trapping superblock and corresponding source basic blocks (possibly with the aid of side tables). It then reconstructs the RMAP at the checkpoint for the trapping instruction. It does this by retranslating the original source basic blocks and then performing rescheduling and register assignment. At that point, the runtime can use the reconstructed RMAP to reset the register values corresponding to the trapping instruction's checkpoint. The checkpoint algorithm guarantees that this can be done. Then the runtime can begin interpreting the original source code at the checkpoint.

For example, say that instruction $d$ traps. Then the runtime needs to back up to a precise state with respect to the original source sequence. Hence, it backs up to instruction $d$'s checkpoint. In this case the checkpoint is instruction $c$. When the RMAP entry for $c$ is reconstructed, the registers eax, ebx, ecx, and edx map to r1, r5, r3, r4, respectively. Therefore, the runtime restores these values to the mapped IA-32 registers and begins interpreting forward, beginning with instruction $c$. The trap will recur when instruction $d$ is interpreted, and the state at that time will be correct.

As another example, assume that instruction $c$ traps but the branch at $b$ will be taken (and will exit the superblock prior to $c$ in the original code). In the translated target code, instruction $c$ executes and traps. The checkpoint for $c$ is instruction $a$. The registers r1, r2, r3, and r4 hold the register state at instruction $a$. Consequently, if interpretation starts at instruction $a$ with these values, the branch will be taken, and the trap does not occur. Eventually, as interpretation proceeds, a source PC will map to a translated superblock in the code cache, and the emulation will jump back into the code cache.

As an alternative to interpretation, one can also maintain a simple (not reordered or optimized) binary translation off to the side. Then rather than interpreting after the state has been restored, the runtime software can branch into the simple, in-order translation. This faster method for handling traps requires more memory and can be applied to those specific cases where a given instruction traps repeatedly.

Finally, a complementary method for precise state reconstruction is to add *repair code* (Gschwind and Altman 2000), executed by the runtime after a trap occurs. Repair code is similar to the compensation code placed at the side exits of a superblock. However, in the case of precise trap implementations, the "side exit" is actually a trap. The concept is illustrated in Figure 4.35, which is taken from the example in Figure 4.28. Here, the code sequence is reordered, with repair code (the instruction R9 ← R1 + R5 in this example) being recorded in a side table. Then if the multiply instruction should trap, the repair code is executed by the runtime trap emulator to generate the correct precise value for register R9.

```
        Source                    Target
        . . .                     . . .
    r1 ← r2 + r3              R1 ← R1 + 3
    r9 ← r1 + r5              R6 ← R1 * R7      trap
    r6 ← r1 * r7   reschedule  R9 ← R1 + R5            Repair code
    r3 ← r6 + 1              R3 ← R6 + 1            R9 ← R1 + R5
        . . .                     . . .
```

**Figure 4.35**  Using Repair Code to Reconstruct Precise State After a Trap. *The instruction sequence is reordered, with repair code being generated at a potential trap (exit) point. If the multiply instruction should happen to trap, repair code executed by the runtime trap handler recovers the precise value for register R9.*

### Condition Code Handling

For handling condition codes, an efficient method is to use lazy evaluation, as described in Section 2.8.2. With lazy evaluation, condition codes are only evaluated when needed. For the purposes of conditional branch evaluation, data flow analysis can be performed within a translation block to determine which condition codes will actually be needed by the executing code. In the extended reordering example, only two instructions set condition codes that are potentially used within the translation block (instructions *a* and *f*), so these are the only instructions where condition codes are actually evaluated; but note that even then, the target ISA (PowerPC) versions of the condition codes are generated, not the source ISA (IA-32) versions.

A more difficult problem occurs when an interrupt or trap is triggered and condition codes must be materialized in order to provide the precise source ISA state. The basic method is similar to the one used for providing precise register state. More specifically, lazy evaluation can be implemented by extending the live ranges of the input operands to condition code-setting instructions. If needed, these operands are used by the runtime's trap/interrupt routine to materialize the condition codes.

In the foregoing code-reordering algorithm, "condition code checkpoints," similar to the regular checkpoints, are maintained. The only difference is that these checkpoints are restricted to the committed *condition code–setting* instructions. Then the condition code checkpoints extend the live ranges of the operands that feed into a condition code–setting instruction. In the example, instructions *a, d, f, e,* and *h* correspond to IA-32 source code operations that set condition codes. In the example, the condition code checkpoints are similar to the regular checkpoints, except the condition code checkpoint for instruction *d* is *a* (not *c*, because *c* does not change condition codes). Consequently, the live ranges of the mapped registers at instruction *a* must be extended through instruction *d* in the reordered code. Taking this into account, the initial value of r1 must have its live range extended (denoted with a "y" in the following table). This further affects the register assignment because the original value in register r1 must be kept beyond instruction *a*, in case instruction *d* should trap and condition codes (generated by instruction *a*) must be materialized. In this example, the PowerPC versions of the condition codes happen to be generated by instruction *a*. However, these are not adequate for generating all the needed IA-32 condition codes. Extending the live range of register r1 means that register r6 must be used for holding the result of instruction *a*. This will eventually result in an additional register copy (r1 ← r6) when the translation block is exited, in order to maintain the consistent register mapping.

### *Step 5a: Assign Register with Condition Codes*

| Register Live Ranges | After Assignment | Register Map (RMAP) |
|---|---|---|

```
       Register Live Ranges              After Assignment                    Register Map (RMAP)
r1 r2 r3 r4 t5 t6 t7 t8 t9 t10                                        eax    ebx    ecx    edx
 |  |  |  |  |  |  |  |  |                a: r6 ← r1+r2,set CR0        r6     r2     r3     r4
 y  x  |  |  |  |  |  |                   c: r5 ← mem(r6 + 4)          r6     r5     r3     r4
 y  x  |  |  |  |  |  |                   b: bz      CR0, L1           r6     r2     r3     r4
       |  |  |  |  |  |  |                d: r2 ← r5 * 10              r6     r2     r3     r4
       |  |  |  |  |  |  |                f: r5 ← r3+1,set CR0         r6     r2     r5     r4
       x  |  |  |  |  |  |                g: bz      CR0, L2           r6     r2     r5     r4
       x  |  |  |  |  |  |  |             e: r2 ← r2 + 1               r6     r2     r3     r4
          |  |  |  |  |  |  |             h: r2 ← r2 + r6              r6     r2     r5     r4
          |  |  |  |  |  |             i: b      L3                  r6     r2     r5     r4
```

Now, if instruction *d* happens to trap, the register state can be backed up to instruction *c* (as before), and the operands that produce the condition codes (registers r1 and r2 at the time the translation block is entered) can also be restored for condition code evaluation. Interpretation is then used for materializing the correct register state and condition code state at instruction *d*.

## 4.5.3 Superblocks Versus Traces

As mentioned earlier, most dynamic translation systems use superblocks rather than the more general traces. To understand why, we need to examine a number of issues. First, we consider instruction cache and branch prediction performance, and then we consider issues that come into play when dynamic superblock/trace formation and optimization are implemented.

An obvious consideration with respect to instruction caching is that a superblock may add replicated code due to tail duplication, which can increase the working set size and decrease instruction cache efficiency. Mitigating this effect is that only heavily used regions of code are converted to superblocks. Also, superblocks lead to more straight-line code fetches, which will enhance the cache-fetch efficiency. If code expansion due to tail duplication becomes excessive (and the runtime can keep track of this as it forms superblocks), then additional constraints can be put on superblock formation, such as restricting their length.

With respect to branch predictors, as with instruction caches, there is a working set size disadvantage; e.g., in Figure 4.22b block G is triplicated so the branch at its end will have three different entries in a branch predictor table. On the other hand, superblocks may also be beneficial because, in effect, a superblock encodes some global branch history information. For example, the three branches corresponding to the end of G belong to three different paths. Hence, superblocks essentially embed path correlation information and perhaps a simpler branch predictor can be used, or a given predictor may work better.

As far as optimizations are concerned, both side exit and join points may inhibit interbasic block optimizations involving code motion because it may not always be possible to add compensation code (see Table 4.1). For example, code often cannot be moved below a join point. Getting rid of join points, therefore, removes some code reordering constraints.

Another advantage of removing join points becomes evident by considering the trace/superblock formation and optimization process. It is important to keep in mind that the basic blocks that are observed during trace/superblock formation are dynamic basic blocks, not static basic blocks. Consequently, determining whether a code region join point is already part of an existing trace adds complexity and bookkeeping to the formation algorithm. In particular, because only dynamic basic blocks are observed, it is not known *a priori* that a point in the middle of the block may later be discovered to be a join point. Hence, during the code-discovery process, checking to see if a branch target has already been translated requires not only looking at known branch targets, but also keeping track of, and searching, address ranges within already-translated basic blocks.

A related problem occurs because a preexisting translated trace has presumably been optimized, and this optimization may have been done without knowledge that a join point would later be discovered and added. Consequently, the optimization may no longer be safe after a join is discovered and added, so the optimization may have to be undone or at least revised, adding further complication.

It is perhaps worth noting that trace scheduling was originally implemented in a static compilation environment (Fisher 1981) where the complete control flow graph could be analyzed when forming traces and where there were fewer compatibility constraints that would inhibit optimizations—that is, only compatibility with the high-level language program had to be maintained, not compatibility with an existing binary.

From a different perspective, one thing that makes superblocks simple is that they require compensation code only at exit points, which is relatively straightforward. Furthermore, the only entry point is at the top, where the initial conditions (i.e., register state) are more easily maintained. In effect, the tail duplication required by superblocks is like adding superset compensation code at all join points and skipping all the analysis; i.e., the compensation code is "pre-added." Because it performs exactly the same state updates in the same order, it does not have to be segregated as special compensation code but remains main-line code.

## 4.6 Code Optimizations

There are a number of optimizations that can be applied within translation blocks to reduce execution time. Even if the original source binary code was optimized when it was produced, additional optimization opportunities are often present in the dynamic environment. For example, superblock formation removes control flow join points, creating a locally different control flow than in the original code. Partial procedure inlining converts what would originally be interprocedural analysis into intrablock analysis.

In general, many code optimizations have been proposed and used in practice (Aho, Sethi, and Ullman 1986; Cooper and Torczon 2003), and we will focus on ones that are more likely to be present during dynamic optimization. We begin by describing a set of common optimizations through examples. It is often the case that performing an optimization of one type enables additional optimizations. The examples are structured to illustrate this point.

### 4.6.1 Basic Optimizations

Figure 4.36 illustrates a combination of common optimizations. The first is *constant propagation*. Here, the constant value 6 is assigned to R1; then R1 is used in the following instruction, so the constant 6 is propagated into the next instruction (which would effectively become R5 ← 6 + 2). Then an optimization known as *constant folding* is performed. The constants 2 and 6 are combined into the constant 8, and the add instruction is replaced with the assignment of the constant 8 to register R5. Following constant propagation and folding, the multiplication in the third instruction is converted via *strength reduction* into a shift by 3.

The foregoing example may at first appear to be far-fetched. What compiler would have generated such nonoptimal code in the first place? Actually, this

```
R1 ← 6            R1 ← 6            R1 ← 6
R5 ← R1 + 2       R5 ← 8            R5 ← 8
R6 ← R7 * R5      R6 ← R7 * R5      R6 ← R7 << 3

    (a)               (b)               (c)
```

**Figure 4.36**    Constant Propagation and Folding (a) to (b) Followed by Strength Reduction (b) to (c).

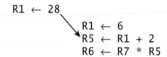

```
R1 ← 28
           R1 ← 6
           R5 ← R1 + 2
           R6 ← R7 * R5
```

**Figure 4.37**    A Control Flow Join Point That Inhibits Code Optimization.

example illustrates a point made earlier. Consider Figure 4.37, which illustrates the original source code. It is the same as in Figure 4.36a, except we see that the assignment to R5 was at a control flow join point in the original code. Hence, in the original sequence, the compiler could not perform constant propagation. It is only because superblock formation removed the join point that the constant propagation (followed by other optimizations) was enabled.

Another example where superblock formation leads to a potential optimization is shown in Figure 4.38. Often the assignment of a value may be partially dead. That is, it is dead on one control flow path but not on others. This is illustrated in Figure 4.38a. Here, the assignment to R3 above the BNE is dead if the branch is not taken, but it is not dead if the branch (to L1) is taken. This suggests an optimization known as *code sinking*. If the first assignment to R3 is moved below the branch, with a compensating copy being placed at destination L1 (Figure 4.38b), then the partially dead assignment leads to a fully dead assignment on the not-taken path. Consequently, the assignment to R3 on the not-taken path can be removed (Figure 4.38c). This optimization is most beneficial if the not-taken path is the most common one. In terms of superblock optimization, the sequence of instructions on the not-taken path might be part of the superblock. Then code sinking is simply a reordering, with compensation code being added at a superblock exit.

Figure 4.39 illustrates another pair of common optimizations. In the original code sequence, there is a copy from register R1 into R4. *Copy propagation* causes register R1 to be substituted for R4 in the multiply instruction. This does not reduce the number of instructions, but in a superscalar processor it will increase parallelism because the copy and the multiplication can be performed in parallel after copy propagation. Finally, after copy propagation, the value held in register R4 is dead; i.e., it is not read by any following instructions before it is overwritten. As a second optimization, therefore, *dead-assignment elimination* removes the copy to R4.

```
R1 ← 1                                      R1 ← 1
R3 ← R3 + R2                                Br L1 if R7!=0
Br L1 if R7!=0                              R3 ← R3 + R2
R3 ← R7 + 1      L1: R3 ← R3 + 1            R3 ← R7 + 1          L1: R3 ← R3 + R2
                                                                    R3 ← R3 + 1

              (a)                                              (b)
```

```
                R1 ← 1
                Br L1 if R7!=0
                R3 ← R7 + 1   L1: R3 ← R3 + R2
                                  R3 ← R3 + 1
                          (c)
```

**Figure 4.38**  Example of code sinking. *(a) The assignment to R3 is partially dead; (b) after code sinking, the assignment on the not-taken branch path is fully dead; (c) the dead assignment to R3 can then be removed.*

```
R1 ← R2 + R3          R1 ← R2 + R3          R1 ← R2 + R3
R4 ← R1               R4 ← R1
R5 ← R5 * R4          R5 ← R5 * R1          R5 ← R5 * R1
     .                     .                     .
     .                     .                     .
     .                     .                     .
R4 ← R7 + R8          R4 ← R7 + R8          R4 ← R7 + R8
     (a)                   (b)                   (c)
```

**Figure 4.39**  Copy Propagation (a) to (b) Followed by Dead-Assignment Elimination (b) to (c).

```
R1 ← R2 + R3          R1 ← R2 + R3          R1 ← R2 + R3
R5 ← R2               R5 ← R2               R5 ← R2
R6 ← R5 + R3          R6 ← R2 + R3          R6 ← R1
     (a)                   (b)                   (c)
```

**Figure 4.40**  Copy Propagation (a) to (b) Followed by Common-Subexpression Elimination (b) to (c).

Another example of an optimization enabled by copy propagation is in Figure 4.40. Here, the copy from R2 to R5 is propagated to the second add. Then R2 + R3 becomes a common subexpression that can be eliminated from the second add. At this point, the copy to R5 may become a dead assignment and can be removed (not shown in the figure).

The final example optimization is the *hoisting of an invariant expression out of a loop*, Figure 4.41. Here, if neither R2 nor R3 is modified in the loop, then the add to register R1 is invariant throughout the loop's execution. Hence, it needs to be done only once, before the loop is entered.

```
L1:   R1 ← R2 + R3              R1 ← R2 + R3
      mem (R4) ← R1      L1:    mem (R4) ← R1
      R4 ← R4 + 4               R4 ← R4 + 4
           .                         .
           .                         .
           .                         .
      Br L1 if R7!=0           Br L1 if R7!=0

          (a)                      (b)
```

**Figure 4.41**    Hoisting a Loop Invariant Expression Out of a Loop. *(a) The computation of R1 done repeatedly inside the loop is (b) moved outside the loop and done only once.*

This completes our survey of common optimizations: redundant branch removal, constant propagation, copy propagation, constant folding, code sinking, strength reduction, dead-assignment elimination, and hoisting of invariant expressions. Although any of these optimizations, as well as others, can be applied, the different optimizations have different effects on compatibility, and this is often a critical factor in deciding whether they should be applied.

### 4.6.2  Compatibility Issues

An optimization is *safe* with respect to traps if, after the optimization is performed, every trap in the original source ISA code is detected in the translated target code and either traps to a handler in the runtime or branches directly to the runtime. Furthermore, the precise architected state at that point must be recoverable. There are no hard-and-fast rules for determining exactly which optimizations are safe, but optimizations that do not remove trapping operations tend typically to be safe. For example, copy-propagation, constant-propagation, and constant-folding optimizations are usually safe. There may be some end cases where compatibility becomes an issue, for example, if constant folding happens to result in overflow. This case can be determined at optimization time and can be disabled in those rare cases where it occurs.

On the other hand, a number of optimizations may not always be safe. Dead-assignment elimination, if it removes a potentially trapping instruction, is not safe because it may break trap compatibility — e.g., the original source code might trap if an instruction performing a dead assignment is executed. If the dead-assignment elimination removes a nontrapping instruction then it is likely to be safe. However, if such nontrapping dead-assignment code is removed, then it may still be necessary to extend the live ranges of its input values, just in case some other instruction traps and the values are needed for precise state construction.

Similarly, hoisting instructions out of loops may not be safe because trap compatibility may be violated. For example, in Figure 4.41 a potentially trapping instruction is hoisted. In a static sense the instruction has not been removed, but in a dynamic sense instructions have been removed — in the original code, the hoisted add was executed every time through the loop.

Strength reduction may be safe in some cases but not in others. For example, the reduction of a multiplication to a shift in Figure 4.36 is likely to be unsafe, because an overflow during the multiplication will not occur when the substituted shift is performed. On the other hand, reducing a multiplication by an addition (e.g., replacing R1*2 with R1 + R1) would likely be safe — an overflow will be detected.

### 4.6.3 Inter-superblock Optimizations

All the optimizations discussed thus far have a scope that is restricted to a single superblock. During the optimization process only a single superblock is buffered and analyzed. The register state at the time the superblock is entered and exited is precisely consistent with the register state at the same points in the source code. Even though superblocks are relatively large and provide good optimization opportunities, there may be room for additional optimizations that span superblock boundaries. One solution is to use tree groups, as described in Section 4.3.5. Another solution is to optimize across superblocks incrementally.

At the time two superblocks are linked together, they can both be reexamined and reoptimized, based on the new knowledge of control flow and a more complete context. In theory, this could be a complete reoptimization and reformulation of both superblocks that are being linked. However, this would lead to additional optimization overhead and could affect the recovery of precise state (i.e., superblock exits may no longer be precise exception points with a consistent register mapping). Furthermore, the original superblocks are optimized to take into account the most common control flow path, and modifying some of these optimizations to account for early exit paths may be counterproductive. Consequently, it is probably a better approach to stick with the original superblock optimizations and optimize across superblocks only at the "seams."

An example is given in Figure 4.42. Here, register r2 is dead within the first superblock but may be live on exit path L1. If, however, the destination superblock of the early exit branch is examined when the superblocks are linked, it is apparent that the assignment to r2 is in fact dead within the original superblock and may be removed (subject to safeness requirements discussed earlier).

This optimization can be implemented via two side tables (Bala, Duesterwald, and Banerjia 1999). An *epilog* side table keeps a mask indicating

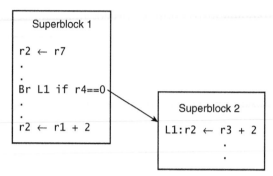

**Figure 4.42** Two Superblocks to Be Linked. *After linking, the first assignment to r2 can be determined to be dead.*

the registers that are potentially dead at the time a superblock is exited, along with a pointer to the last instruction to assign the register a value (this is the potentially dead register). A *prolog* side table keeps a mask indicating the registers that are written before being read when a superblock is entered. Figure 4.43 illustrates the tables for the example given earlier in Figure 4.42. When two superblocks are to be linked, the bit masks of the exited and entered superblocks are ANDed. Any bits that remain set indicate dead register values. The pointer in the epilog can then be used for finding them.

Another possible optimization is to remove some of the register copies at exit points that are intended to maintain a consistent register state mapping. In the final code for the extended example given in Section 4.5.2, the copies of r5 to r3 (both at the bottom of the superblock and at the early exit) are present only to provide a consistent mapping of register ecx to r3. Here, if the mapping could be changed (so that ecx is mapped to r5) when the subsequent superblock is entered, then the copy instructions are no longer needed. To implement this optimization, there should be a side table for each superblock entry point, indicating the register mapping when it is entered (or indicating those mappings that differ from the standard consistent mapping). This table is also be consulted when there is a trap or interrupt to ensure that the correct precise state is restored.

### 4.6.4 Instruction-Set-Specific Optimizations

Each instruction set has its own features and quirks that could lead to special optimizations that are instruction-set specific. We now show two examples that illustrate the principles involved.

The first example is unaligned load optimization. Some ISAs, primarily RISC ISAs, are designed so that load and store instructions provide better

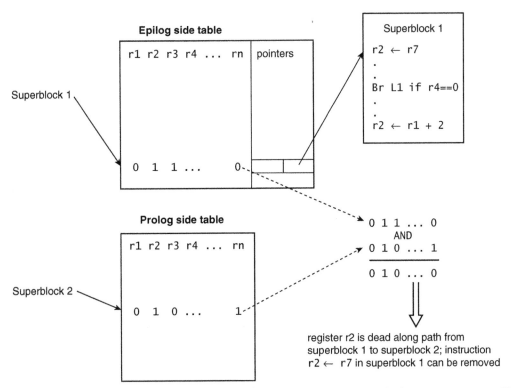

**Figure 4.43** Epilog and Prolog Side Tables. *Epilog and Prolog side tables detect dead registers across superblock boundaries.*

performance if their addresses are aligned to "natural" boundaries; e.g., a word address has its two low-order bits as 00 (see Section 2.8.5). If a load or store instruction should access data that is not naturally aligned, i.e., is "unaligned," then it will trap. The trap handler can then perform the unaligned access using multiple instructions. Because it relies on a trap, this method is extremely slow, so an alternative is to use the normal aligned load or store for those accesses that have very high probability of being aligned and using an inlined multi-instruction sequence for those cases that have some significant probability of being unaligned. Of course, the static compiler for such an instruction set strives to align data as much as possible. The compiler also knows when data may be unaligned and inserts the multi-instruction sequences. However, when a source ISA that features unaligned accesses is emulated by a target ISA that does not, handling unaligned accesses leads to a dynamic optimization opportunity.

If the source ISA allows unaligned accesses, then as part of dynamic profiling, the load and store instructions with unaligned addresses can be identified. That is, at the early emulation stage when profiling is enabled, all loads and stores with unaligned addresses are recorded in a table. Then the binary translator consults this table of profile data. If a load or store has never had an unaligned address, then the translator assumes this will always be the case, and the normal (aligned) target load/store instruction is used. If, on the other hand, unaligned accesses did occur for a given load or store, then the binary translator inserts the appropriate multi-instruction sequences. Of course, there must still be a trap handler to cover those cases where the profile information does not correctly identify a memory access instruction that later uses an unaligned address.

The second example of an instruction-set-specific optimization is known as *if conversion* (Mahlke et al. 1992). Some instruction sets implement special features to allow removal of certain conditional branch instructions. These special features include predication (Hsu and Davidson 1986), nullification (Kane 1996), and conditional move instructions. An example of code that might benefit from this optimization is shown in Figure 4.44a. In this example, there is a small if-then-else piece of code that leads to a small "hammock" region (Figure 4.44b). An assembly language version of this code is in Figure 4.44c. To execute the example code, a conditional branch and possibly an unconditional branch are required. Although branch prediction can often mitigate the performance-degrading effects of conditional branches, performance losses can be large when the prediction is incorrect.

For the purpose of this example we have "enhanced" the PowerPC instruction set by adding an integer conditional move instruction (the PowerPC instruction set has conditional move instructions for floating-point data but not integer data). This conditional move instruction (cmovgt in the example) moves the first source register into the destination register if the specified condition register indicates "greater than." With the conditional move instruction, the hammock region can be implemented as shown in Figure 4.44d. Here, both r5+1 and r5−1 are computed. Then the conditional move essentially selects the correct one. The result is a code sequence free of conditional branches (or any other branch, for that matter).

## 4.7 Same-ISA Optimization Systems: Special-Case Process Virtual Machines

Some process virtual machines perform dynamic optimization *without* performing binary translation. That is, these dynamic optimizers have the same source and target ISAs. Although not usually referred to as virtual machines, they do provide a process with a performance-enhanced execution

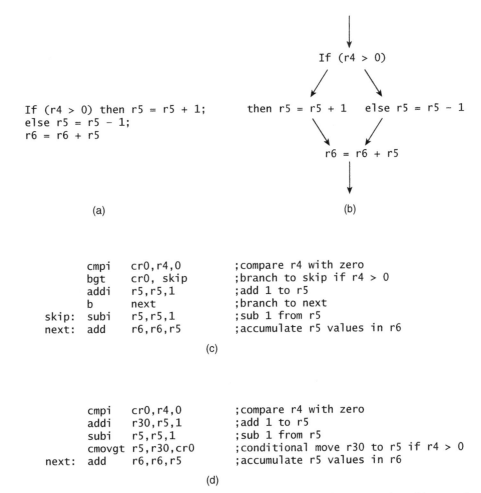

```
If (r4 > 0) then r5 = r5 + 1;
else r5 = r5 - 1;
r6 = r6 + r5
```

(a)

(b)

```
        cmpi    cr0,r4,0        ;compare r4 with zero
        bgt     cr0, skip       ;branch to skip if r4 > 0
        addi    r5,r5,1         ;add 1 to r5
        b       next            ;branch to next
skip:   subi    r5,r5,1         ;sub 1 from r5
next:   add     r6,r6,r5        ;accumulate r5 values in r6
```

(c)

```
        cmpi    cr0,r4,0        ;compare r4 with zero
        addi    r30,r5,1        ;add 1 to r5
        subi    r5,r5,1         ;sub 1 from r5
        cmovgt  r5,r30,cr0      ;conditional move r30 to r5 if r4 > 0
next:   add     r6,r6,r5        ;accumulate r5 values in r6
```

(d)

**Figure 4.44**　Example of If-Conversion. *(a) Original code; (b) illustration of "hammock" formed by control flow; (c) assembly code with branches; (d) assembly code after if-conversion.*

environment, and they use many of the same techniques as in binary-translating process VMs. Unlike other process VMs, however, the objective of same-ISA dynamic binary optimizers is not compatibility. For example, the objective might be performance, as in the Mojo system (Chen et al. 2000), the Wiggins/ Redstone system (Deaver, Gorton, and Rubin 1999) and the original HP Dynamo system (Bala, Duesterwald, and Banerjia 2000), or it might be increased security, as in the later DynamoRIO project (Bruening, Garnett, and Amarasinghe 2003). Although it does not provide the same level of transparency as the systems just mentioned, Kistler and Franz (2001) also developed an advanced dynamic optimization framework that employs many features of the process VMs discussed in this section.

Because of their similarities, many techniques proposed for translating process VMs are also used in same-ISA dynamic binary optimizers, albeit in a simpler form. On the other hand, because the source and target ISAs are exactly the same, these dynamic optimizers also have some special opportunities and advantages for overall performance improvement.

- ▪ It is easier to perform fast initial "emulation" of the nonoptimized source binary because the source binary can be copied directly into a basic block cache, with profiling code being added. Then as hot code sections are found, they can be placed in an optimized superblock cache. This approach is illustrated in Figure 4.45, and it is used in the Mojo system as well as the

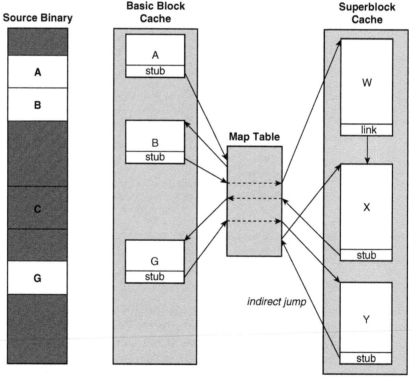

**Figure 4.45** Dynamic Binary Optimization Using a Basic Block Cache. *Source basic blocks are copied into a code cache for initial emulation. Hot blocks are later collected into optimized superblocks. In this example, there is no chaining in the basic block cache because these blocks are executed infrequently or only during start-up. Also, in this example it is assumed that the basic block cache and superblock cache share a PC map table, but an implementation could also use separate tables.*

IA-32-based DynamoRIO. Note that the original HP Dynamo system uses interpretation during start-up, not basic block caching. An argument for using interpretation is that it avoids saving and restoring a large number of registers (as in the PA-RISC ISA) every time there is a switch between the cached "translated" code and the runtime. On the other hand, in the IA-32 ISA, there are only a few registers, so the method of using a basic block cache has more reasonable overhead. Carrying this concept still further, a technique known as *patching* (described in more detail in the next subsection) can be used to avoid interpretation and/or basic block caching of unoptimized code altogether. Patching, in effect, uses the original source code (not a cached copy) for initial emulation prior to optimization. Consequently, patching can be used only because the source and target ISAs are the same.

■ When the same ISA is being used, dynamic optimization is not a necessity. In particular, if dynamic optimization is found to provide no performance benefit (or even a loss), then the dynamic optimizer can "bail out" and simply run the original code. For example, if the instruction working set is quite large and there is thrashing in the code cache due to repeated retranslations, then a bailout may be triggered.

■ Sample-based profiling may be more attractive, because running the original code does not result in any apparent performance loss to the user. Hence, the original binary can be sampled over a relatively long period of time before optimization begins.

■ For software-instrumented profiling, an interesting technique that has been used successfully is to duplicate the code to be profiled, with one copy being fully instrumented and the other (original) copy containing branches into the instrumented version (Ronsse and De Bosschere 2000; Arnold and Ryder 2001). When profile information is to be collected (this can be controlled via the branches in the original copy), the original code copy branches into the instrumented version. After profile information is collected, the instrumented version branches back into the original copy.

■ There are no instruction semantic mismatch problems. For example, both the source and the target have exactly the same condition code semantics and hence eliminate the overhead of emulating special cases in software.

Problems with same-ISA optimization can occur, however, because the source and target memory spaces and register files are of the same size. This places tight constraints on the emulation process, especially with respect to compatibility. Because the register files of the source and the target are the same size, there are no scratch registers for use by the optimizer, and this may limit the types of optimizations that can be performed. It also may lead to problems when the runtime saves and restores the guest's registers, because it may be necessary already to have a free register in order to load/store registers to memory (Bala, Duesterwald, and Banerjia 2000). Also, for intrinsic compatibility, there must be provision for large binaries that consume most, or all, of the address space, as discussed in Section 3.3.2 — of course, if the address space requirements of the guest become too large, the runtime can bail out, release its address space, and revert to normal execution.

### 4.7.1 Code Patching

Code patching is a time-honored technique (Gill 1951) that is widely used in debuggers and other code profiling and analysis applications (Larus and Schnarr 1995; Tamches and Miller 1999; Hunt and Brubacher 1999). As noted earlier, code patching can also be applied to same-ISA dynamic binary optimizers. With patching, code is scanned when it is first encountered, but it is not copied into a code cache; rather it is left in place, with certain instructions being replaced with other instructions, i.e., "patches" (usually branch instructions that exit the source code). These patches typically pass control to an emulation manager and/or profiling code. The original code at the point of a patch is maintained in a *patch table* by the emulation manager so that patches can be later removed, if necessary. For example, if a superblock in the code cache is flushed, then the patch redirecting the flow of control to the superblock should be removed.

Figure 4.46 illustrates the same example as given in Figure 4.45, with patching used instead of basic block caching. Note that in this example, map table lookups have been eliminated. Control can be passed to optimized superblocks via patches made at the time superblocks are formed. A particularly interesting situation is illustrated at the bottom of the figure, where there is an indirect jump exiting superblock Y. In conventional emulation systems, this would typically result in a map table lookup (unless software jump prediction is used and is successful — see Section 2.7.2). However, with patching, the indirect jump at the end of superblock Y can use the source PC to transfer control directly back into the source code. If the destination source code has already been optimized, a patch in the source binary immediately redirects control back into the superblock cache. The branch at this patch point would likely be a highly predictable branch, so the map table lookup is avoided, and the performance loss is negligible.

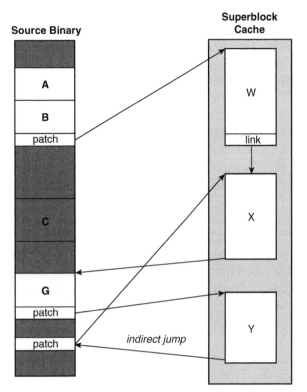

**Figure 4.46** Example from Figure 4.45 with Code Patching. *Map table lookups are no longer needed, because control can be transferred directly into the original source binary.*

Besides this performance advantage, another, more obvious advantage is that there is less replicated code; there doesn't have to be a source code copy in the basic block cache. Patching also has some disadvantages; the most significant is that it makes the handling of self-referencing code about as difficult as self-modifying code. With conventional code caching, the source binary is left intact, so self-referencing code automatically reads the correct data (see Section 3.4.2). With code patching, this will not be the case. Consequently, the source code has to be protected by making it execute-only. Then an attempt to read the source code as data will result in a trap, which can be handled by the runtime. The runtime can use its patch table to construct the correct data to be returned to the reading instruction.

The ADORE system (Lu et al. 2004) is an example of a system that supports dynamic binary optimization via code patching. The ADORE system targets the Intel IPF instruction set binaries and uses hardware-profiling information to support optimizations, including insertion of data-prefetch operations (Lu et al. 2003).

### 4.7.2 Case Study: HP Dynamo

The Dynamo system started as a research project at HP Labs (Bala, Duesterwald, and Banerjia 1999). Originally developed for a platform running UNIX and the HP PA8000 ISA, the Dynamo infrastructure has been retargeted toward the IA-32 ISA with both Windows and Linux operating systems (Bruening, Duesterwald, and Amarasinghe 2001). Subsequently the project was transferred to the RIO research project at MIT as the DynamoRIO system. The DynamoRIO system has been extensively studied and is a valuable resource for both its innovations in process VM implementation and its well-documented performance features. Many of the techniques described in this chapter are Dynamo innovations or are at least used in the Dynamo system.

The basic design of Dynamo is very much along the lines of Figure 4.4. It starts out interpreting, and then after an execution threshold is reached it optimizes superblocks. As pointed out in the previous section, in the original HP PA8000 implementation, interpretation is chosen over basic block caching because of the large number of registers that would have to be saved and restored when a cached basic block is entered and exited (from the runtime). In the later DynamoRIO IA-32 implementation, basic block caching is used.

For superblock formation, Dynamo profiles backward branches and exit points from existing superblocks. When the threshold is reached (i.e., a hotspot is found), it uses a most-recently-executed heuristic (*most recently executed tail* in Dynamo terminology) to build superblocks. Figure 4.47 shows data from the Dynamo Technical Report illustrating the relationship between the hotspot threshold and overall speedup for a set of benchmark programs (note that for programs where performance is lost, Dynamo "bails out," so little performance is actually lost). Overall, a threshold of 50 was deemed the best choice.

Dynamo uses many of the optimization techniques described earlier, but it tends not to reorder code (it is intended to be run on an out-of-order superscalar processor). The Dynamo study found that of the safe optimizations (i.e., those where trap compatibility can be maintained), strength reduction was the most commonly applicable, and redundant branch removal was second. Of the more aggressive, potentially unsafe optimizations, redundant loads and dead-assignment elimination were the most common, with code sinking also providing a significant number of optimization opportunities. A load instruction is redundant if there is a preceding load (or store) instruction to the same address and the value previously loaded or stored remains in a register. The redundant load is then replaced with a register copy. Of course, if there is any possibility that the load or store is to a volatile memory location, then it cannot be considered redundant.

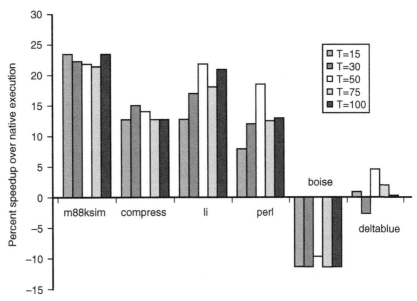

**Figure 4.47**   Relative Speedup as a Function of the Threshold Value for Superblock Formation. *The Y-axis gives percent speedup over native execution. The T values are the "hot" thresholds for initiating superblock formation.*

For code cache management, Dynamo uses the preemptive flush method. That is, it monitors the rate at which new superblocks are formed. If the rate begins to increase substantially, it assumes a new program phase is being entered and flushes the code cache at that point. Repeated flushing, however, indicates an instruction working set too large to fit in the code cache, so Dynamo bails out and executes the original code without optimizing it.

As noted earlier, Dynamo researchers were faced with the lack of scratch registers when performing same-ISA optimization. Because the source and target ISAs necessarily have the same number of registers, there is none left over for other operations. For example, software jump prediction, as in Section 2.7.2, requires an extra register for comparisons against an indirect jump's source register. Also, most operations that involve code motion result in extended register live ranges, and, consequently, the need to hold more register values at the same time. Finally, when there is a switch from the code cache to the runtime software, at least some registers must be saved so that the runtime can use them for its execution.

In conventional systems, the solution is to spill registers to a save area. However, in the HP ISA (and many other ISAs), a register pointer (to the register save area) is required in order to save the registers (in other words, a register must be freed in order to free registers); this leads to a quandary. The Dynamo solution is to perform a second register allocation pass after an optimized superblock has been formed. During this second pass, it looks for registers containing dead values within a superblock and uses one of them for the register save area pointer. If such a dead register cannot be found, then it temporarily spills a live register to memory in order to maintain the save area pointer. This general approach raises a couple of questions that are not directly addressed in the Dynamo report. The first is the matter of strict register state compatibility following a trap; i.e., reusing an apparently dead register destroys its contents, which might lead to register state incompatibility in a trap handler. The second is the issue of protecting the register save area (Section 3.4.3). A "rogue" load or store that happens to access the register save area could lead to incompatible, erroneous results. These problems indicate that it is difficult to achieve intrinsic compatibility in a dynamic optimizer. If there is some (external) assurance that applications being optimized are free of these problems (and many debugged applications would not exhibit these problems), then the dead-register approach would work well.

In order to integrate the Dynamo process VM into the host platform, it is assumed that the kernel loader is used for loading the guest application. The kernel loader links the execution start-up code, crt0, into the guest application. When the loader is finished, it transfers execution to crt0 to initialize the process. In Dynamo, a custom version of crt0 is used. This new version of crt0 maps the Dynamo code as a linked library and calls Dynamo's entry point. Then the Dynamo runtime takes control of execution of the guest process.

Dynamo performance is shown in Figure 4.48. Dynamo is applied to source binaries that have been optimized originally at different levels by the HP compiler. The figure shows performance for three increasing levels of optimization (from +O2 to +O4). The O4 level is also enhanced with conventional code profiling that is fed back into the compilation process (Figure 4.11a). Performance is given as total run time (execution time), so a lower number is better. We see that Dynamo improves overall performance for all three optimization levels when applied alone, but it does not improve performance for +O4+profiling.

The reasons are illustrated in Figure 4.49, which breaks down improvements for Dynamo with O2 optimization. This figure shows that the biggest part of the gain occurs before any of the optimizations is performed. In other words, most of the performance gain comes from partial procedure inlining and superblock formation. This is the same gain that can be provided by feedback profiling (in +O4+profiling). That is, the profile information is used for relaying out the code to enhance locality. We also see from Figure 4.49 that the "conservative" (safe) and "aggressive" optimizations provide similar benefits (although on different benchmarks). This indicates that a significant amount

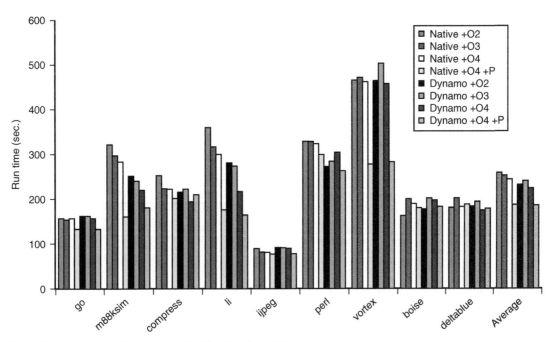

**Figure 4.48**  Dynamo Performance for Nine Benchmark Programs.

of the overall performance gain remains if the aggressive unsafe optimizations are not performed. Finally, note that the cases where performance is lost with Dynamo (e.g., benchmarks go, jpeg, vortex, and boise), there will be a bailout, so that performance losses no longer occur.

### 4.7.3  Discussion

When compared with traditional off-line feedback-directed optimization (see Section 4.2.1), as is done with +O4+profiling in Figure 4.48, it appears that dynamic binary optimization holds few or no performance advantages. To a large extent, off-line optimization uses similar profile-based information to perform similar optimizations, although one significant difference is that with dynamic optimization, the optimizations applied to a code region can change if program behavior changes over the course of its execution. Also, in practice many binaries have not received an intensive optimization effort; i.e., for various reasons, binaries are sometimes "shipped" with little optimization. In these cases dynamic binary optimization may provide performance advantages by allowing optimization to occur in the field.

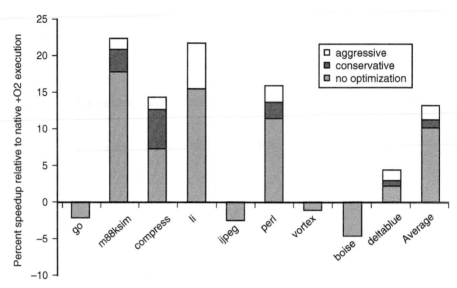

**Figure 4.49** HP Dynamo Performance Improvements for Superblock Formation Only (No Optimization), Aggressive Optimization, and Conservative Optimization.

An additional matter to consider is that the underlying HP hardware platform used in the initial Dynamo study does not predict indirect jumps; rather, instruction fetching temporarily stalls when an indirect jump is encountered. Consequently, replacing indirect jumps with inline branches and partial procedure inlining, which eliminates some indirect jumps, results in significant performance gains on the HP hardware. When using hardware with indirect jump prediction (as in most current microprocessors), the performance advantages of dynamic optimization are significantly reduced. In the IA-32 version, DynamoRIO (Bruening, Duesterwald, and Amarasinghe 2001), indirect-jump handling is cited as a significant cause of overall performance losses. Much of the performance loss caused by indirect jumps results from the map table lookup that occurs in order to find the target PC value in the code cache. As we have pointed out, however, the code-patching method avoids these hash table lookups; in fact, this feature alone may be sufficient reason to favor code patching over complete code caching in dynamic binary optimizers.

## 4.8 Summary

Although optimization is not necessary for functionally correct VM implementations, it is important for many practical VM implementations. Because virtualization adds performance overhead, it is important to minimize performance losses, and optimization techniques can mitigate performance losses.

The most common structure for a VM implementation is to use staged emulation with interpretation or simple translation, followed by optimized binary translation. Profiling is typically enabled during the earlier stages, and sometimes for optimized code, in order to guide the optimization process. Overall, the largest performance gains usually come from the formation of translation blocks with good locality characteristics, e.g., inlined procedures and superblocks. After translated superblocks are linked together, performance can often approach native host execution.

The largest complication to the overall optimization process is the need to recover the correct state at the time of a trap or interrupt. How strict this requirement is depends on the type of VM being implemented and on the user's requirements (and applications). If very strict requirements must be met, e.g., if intrinsic compatibility is required, then in most VMs optimization is probably limited to code relayout and simple optimizations that do not remove instructions.

Another complicating factor is the relative sizes of the guest and host register and memory spaces. If the host has larger register files and memory space, then optimization is simplified and is often straightforward. On the other hand, if the host has no more registers and address space (or, worse yet, less), then optimization becomes more complex, and in some cases there can be significant slowdowns.

Finally, we often think of dynamic optimization as being applied to process VMs, either in conjunction with ISA translation or purely for optimization. However, these techniques are not restricted to process VMs. For example, optimization is a very important part of codesigned VMs (Chapter 7). Furthermore, as we shall see in Section 8.2.3, code caching and/or code patching are important parts of some conventional system VM implementations.

# Chapter Five

# High-Level Language Virtual Machine Architecture

A computer system implements a particular ISA and runs a specific OS only as a means to an end. It is the real work done by application programs that is important. Nevertheless, in a conventional computing environment, a compiled application is firmly tied to a particular OS and ISA. To move an application program to a platform with a different OS and/or ISA, it must be *ported*, which involves recompilation at the least but may also involve rewriting libraries and/or translation of OS calls. Furthermore, porting must be done on a per-program basis, and, after porting is done, any later upgrades or bug fixes must be applied to all the ported versions, followed by recompilation.

The process VMs described in Chapter 3 are an approach for making applications portable in a more transparent and general way. In a process VM, a virtual execution environment is provided to a guest process. The process VM has to be developed once, and then, at least in theory, any application program that is developed for the VM's source ISA and OS will run without any additional effort. This is done by emulating the application's ISA and the OS calls. However, as discussed in Chapter 3, the OS interface is difficult to emulate (or may be impossible to emulate exactly if the host and guest operating systems are different). Furthermore, because conventional ISAs all have their quirks, writing a high-performance, accurate emulator to map from one conventional ISA to another is a painstaking task.

Thus, a conventional process virtual machine is a pragmatic "after-the-fact" solution to the application portability problem. It is after the fact in the sense that neither the guest program nor the host platform were designed with the thought that the guest program would be run on the host platform. In contrast, by taking a step back, one can *design* a special guest-ISA/system interface, with VM-based portability to a variety of host platforms as a primary goal. Therefore, to a large extent, the new ISA is designed to be free of quirks and requirements for implementation-specific computational resources. Also, the system interface supported by the VM is raised to a higher level of abstraction than that found in a typical OS interface by consolidating common OS features and defining an abstract interface (a set of libraries) that can be supported by all conventional operating systems.

Just as important as portability, the guest ISA can be designed so that it reflects important features of a specific high-level language (HLL) or a class of HLLs (e.g., object-oriented languages). This leads to efficient implementations of the targeted HLL(s), and it simplifies the compilation process by separating machine-independent and machine-dependent portions of the compiler. Because efficient support for specific HLLs is one of the goals of these VMs, we refer to them as *high-level language virtual machines* (HLL VMs).

An HLL VM is similar to a conventional process VM, but the ISA is usually defined for user-mode programs only and is generally not designed for a real hardware processor — it will only be executed on a virtual processor.[1] Consequently, we refer to it as a *virtual ISA*, or V-ISA. The system interface is a set of standardized libraries (called "APIs") that can access files, perform network operations, and perform graphics operations, for example. The HLL VM is designed to be supported on a number of operating systems and hardware platforms (ideally, all of them — but at least the commonly used ones).

Here it is important to interject that a virtual instruction set architecture usually contains much more than just instructions. In a modern V-ISA, the data aspects are at least as important as the instructions. Consequently, the specification for a modern V-ISA includes lengthy definitions of *metadata,* and it is the metadata that often dominates the overall specification. In contrast, the instruction definitions are quite simple, by design. In fact, one could reasonably argue that the term *data set architecture* would be more fitting than *instruction set architecture.* In any event, we will use the acronym V-ISA because it is the counterpart of the ISA in a conventional computer system.

---

1. However, Sun (McGahn and O'Connor 1998) and ARM (ARM 2002) have developed processors that support the Java ISA.

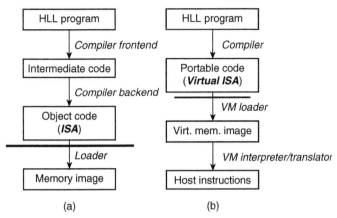

**Figure 5.1** Relationship Between (a) a Conventional Compiler and Loader and (b) a Compiler and Loader in an HLL VM.

One can view HLL VMs from a languages/compiler perspective; see Figure 5.1. The conventional steps in getting from a high-level language program to a binary executing on hardware is shown in Figure 5.1a. The compiler frontend first parses the program and converts it to an intermediate form. Then a compiler backend takes the intermediate form, perhaps performs optimizations on it, and generates object code. The object code is in an ISA-like format, except for some symbolic information that must be resolved at load time. Finally, a loader converts the object code into a memory image that is executed by the underlying hardware processor. The program is generally distributed in the object code ("binary") form, and, because this code is specific to an ISA and OS, it can be run only on compatible platforms. With an HLL VM (Figure 5.1b), the compiler frontend parses and converts the program into a virtual ISA form, which is in some respects similar to a conventional intermediate form. Then the program is distributed in this form. At the time it is ready for execution on an HLL VM, a VM loader is invoked and converts the program into a form that is dependent on the virtual machine implementation. Additional optimizations may be performed as part of the emulation process. Emulation involves interpretation and/or binary translation from the guest V-ISA to the host ISA. The VM loader and interpreter/translator are major components of the HLL VM implementation.

Over the years, language designers have developed a number of HLL VMs targeted at specific HLLs or families of HLLs. An HLL VM that popularized the approach shown in Figure 5.1b was implemented for the Pascal programming language, using a V-ISA known as *P-code*. The best-known current example of an HLL VM was designed to support the Java programming language

(Gosling, Joy, and Steele 1996), although other languages have been successfully compiled to it. Java programs are first compiled to Java *binary classes*,[2] which contain both a rich collection of metadata and low-level instructions encoded as "bytecode" sequences. The Java virtual machine (JVM) then loads the binary classes and executes them. A more recent HLL VM, the common language infrastructure (CLI), is part of the Microsoft .NET framework. The CLI is designed to be a target for a relatively broad class of commonly used HLLs, with object-oriented languages being of primary interest; however, non-object-oriented languages are supported as well.

Because of the importance of the Java and CLI VMs and because these two VMs have many similarities, the next two chapters will be structured somewhat differently than the other chapters. Rather than describing a variety of general features and then concluding with relatively brief case studies, we instead develop much of the discussion around Java and the JVM. The Java virtual machine is widely used and has been the focus of a large amount of well-documented study. The Microsoft CLI is also discussed, primarily to highlight the differences with the JVM as well as the features that are more clearly delineated in the CLI than in the JVM.

This chapter concentrates on HLL VM architecture, i.e., the functional specification and a description of important properties. The next chapter concentrates on HLL VM implementation; i.e., the ways that one actually constructs an HLL VM, including techniques for enhancing performance of HLL implementations. In some cases, this division is rather arbitrary — it is difficult to discuss pure architecture without delving into some aspects of implementation. In these two chapters, we heavily emphasize HLL VM support for object-oriented languages. However, it is not practical for us to discuss object-oriented programming languages and concepts in any significant detail. We provide only a brief overview of the more important Java language features in this chapter. Consequently, for a good understanding of this material, it is essential that the reader have some familiarity with an object-oriented language such as Java or C#. There are a number of good books that can be consulted for learning or reviewing this material; for example, the Java and C# "in a nutshell" books (Flanagan 1999; Drayton, Albahari, and Neward 2002) contain fairly concise descriptions.

Before describing the important object-oriented HLL VMs, we first describe an important historical HLL VM — which will also provide an opportunity to illustrate important platform-independence properties of many HLL VMs.

---

**2.** Binary classes are often referred to as *class files*, but they do not, strictly speaking, have to be stored as files; hence, the more generic term *binary classes*.

As we shall see, however, platform independence is only the tip of the iceberg when it comes to the features of modern component-based, network-oriented HLL VMs.

## 5.1 The Pascal P-Code Virtual Machine

The Pascal P-code virtual machine (Nori et al. 1975) was one of the keys to the widespread popularity of the Pascal high-level programming language because it greatly simplified the porting of a Pascal compiler. Because of its historical importance and its simplicity, a brief case study of the P-code virtual machine is a good way to introduce some of the important HLL VM concepts. Figure 5.1 illustrates the basic idea. A compiler frontend parses a Pascal program and generates a P-code program. P-code is a simple, stack-oriented instruction set, summarized shortly. The combination of the Pascal compiler and the P-code virtual machine yields a complete Pascal compiler and execution system for the given host platform. Only one compiler has to be developed (distributed as P-code), and porting Pascal to a new host platform is reduced to implementing the virtual machine, which is much easier than writing a complete Pascal compiler from scratch.

There are actually two major parts of a P-code virtual machine; one is the P-code emulator (often an interpreter), and the other is a set of standard library routines that interface with the host operating system to implement I/O. For example, the library routines `readln()` and `writeln()` read a line of input and write a line of output. These routines can be called via P-code but may themselves be written in (or compiled to) the host platform's native assembly code. Writing these standard library routines in native code is part of the VM development process, along with writing an interpreter.

### 5.1.1 Memory Architecture

The P-code V-ISA uses a memory model that consists of a program memory area and a constant area, a stack, and a memory heap for data. A program counter (PC) fetches instructions from the program area; otherwise, program memory cannot be read or written. Figure 5.2 illustrates the data areas of memory. All the data areas are divided into *cells*, and each cell can hold a single value. The actual size of a cell is implementation dependent but clearly must be large enough to hold the largest value that can be specified in P-code. The compiler generates values held in the constant area; these are typically immediate operands used by the program. A single stack acts as both a procedure

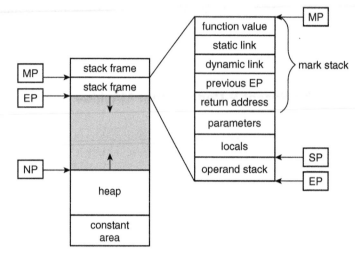

**Figure 5.2** P-Code Memory Architecture.

stack, e.g., for holding procedure linkage information, parameters, and local variables, and as an operand (or evaluation) stack for instruction execution. At any given time, the mark pointer (MP) points to the beginning of the stack frame for the currently active procedure, and the extreme pointer (EP) points to the maximum extent the current frame can reach (in a valid Pascal program, this extreme extent can be determined at compile time).

The heap space sits on top of the constant area and is for dynamically allocated data structures. At any given time the new pointer (NP) delineates the maximum extent of the heap. In Pascal, the user code is responsible for releasing heap-allocated data structures when they are no longer needed, and the virtual machine software is responsible for overall management of the heap area. Conceptually, the stack grows down from the top and the heap (sitting on top of the constant area) grows up from the bottom. Before the NP is adjusted upward, it is checked against the EP to make sure there is enough memory remaining; otherwise there is an exception.

When a procedure is called, it is given a new stack frame. The stack is divided into several sections as shown on the right side of Figure 5.2. The return function value, static link, dynamic link, previous EP, and return address are a fixed-size region at the beginning of the stack frame, collectively called the *mark stack*. The MP points to the base of the mark stack (as well as the base of the entire frame).

The *function value* returns a result value from the function (if there is any); the *static link* is used for linking together statically nested procedures and for accessing local variables within the scope of the active procedure. The Pascal language supports nested procedures, with the scope of local variables determined by the static procedure nesting. That is, the local variables declared within a given source code procedure can be accessed by any procedures nested within that procedure. The *dynamic link* is the MP value for the previous frame, and it allows the stack to be popped back to the previous frame. The *previous EP* is similarly used to establish the EP value when the active procedure returns. The *return address* is the PC value to which the active procedure should return.

Following the mark stack on a stack frame are parameters passed to the procedure and the local variable declared within the given procedure. Finally, the operand stack is used for holding operands and intermediate values when stack instructions are executed. The stack pointer, SP, points to the current top of the operand stack and moves up and down as computation proceeds (unlike the EP, which marks the farthest extent of SP).

### 5.1.2 Instruction Set

The basic instruction set includes instructions that push or pop stack values from/to memory areas as well as arithmetic, logical, and shift instructions that operate on the stack. The instructions are typed; so, for example, there are both add integer (adi), and add real (adr) instructions. There are also Boolean, character, set, and pointer types. Most load and store instructions (that push and pop the stack) contain an opcode and an offset indicating the relative location of an operand. The arithmetic, logical, and shift instructions consist of only an opcode; they pop operands from the stack, perform the operation, and push the result back onto the stack. Following is an example of code that adds 1 to a local variable. The variable happens to be three cells above the mark stack. Because the variable is local to the procedure containing this code, it is at nesting level 0 with respect to this procedure.

```
lodi  0  3    // load variable from current frame (nest 0 depth),
              // offset 3 from top of mark stack.
ldci  1       // push constant 1
addi          // add
stri  0  3    // store variable back to location 3 of current frame
```

### 5.1.3 P-Code Summary

Overall the P-code V-ISA is quite simple, consisting of a small instruction set with elementary operations and a virtual machine implementation that is straightforward. In many respects, P-code set the standard for later HLL virtual machines, including the Java virtual machine; it shares the following features with the more recent HLL VMs.

■ It uses a stack instruction set that requires a host platform to provide only a minimum amount of register support, making it easily translated to virtually any host ISA. Using a stack ISA for P-code also leads to small "binaries," an especially important feature when many desktop computers had small hard drives (or none at all) and supported only 64KB of main memory.

■ Its memory is divided into cells, whose implementation details, e.g., number of bits per cell, are hidden from the ISA.

■ Main memory is partitioned into a stack and a heap, whose extents are not an architecture feature. Furthermore, instructions are never concerned with absolute memory addresses. This allows memory size to be an implementation feature of the host platform.

■ The interface to the OS is through standard libraries. This, at least in theory, insulates programs from the underlying host OS. In the case of P-code, however, achieving OS independence tended to reduce its standard libraries to the least common denominator, which resulted in relatively weak I/O capabilities. Maintaining platform-independent, standard libraries remains a very important consideration/problem in modern HLL VMs. Not only is there the least-common-denominator problem, but there is also a temptation to add library "extensions," which compromise platform independence.

The major differences between the P-code virtual machine and modern HLL VMs are largely caused by the need to support a networked computing environment and the object-oriented programming paradigm. These differences are highlighted in the next section.

## 5.2 Object-Oriented High-Level Language Virtual Machines

The P-code virtual machine was developed to be part of a stand-alone environment where users could compile and run programs on their own local machines. The use of P-code greatly simplifies the porting of a Pascal compiler to a given host platform. After a P-code emulator is developed, programs can be compiled and run on the host platform, with the compiler being trusted to provide good code. This approach has proven to be an effective one, and a number of high-level language compilers have been developed with underlying virtual machine support.

In the modern network computing environment the situation is much more complex. In this environment, there are a number of interconnected platforms, incorporating a variety of processor architectures, operating systems, memory sizes, I/O devices, etc. In this environment, it would be very difficult to compile, distribute, and maintain software for all the possible combinations (or even the more popular ones). The application of HLL VM technology can greatly simplify the task. A HLL VM is developed for each platform in the network, and any programs compiled to meet the specification of the VM can be sent across the network for execution on any of the various platform types. In this application environment, the HLL VM is not intended primarily for easing the porting of compilers, as was the case with P-code; rather, it enables the platform-independent distribution of application software.

The degree of platform independence in a modern HLL VM also goes beyond that provided by P-code, by encompassing data as well as instructions. P-code focused on the instruction set aspects of platform independence; the data representations are fairly basic, with layout of data structures implicitly encoded in the P-code programs themselves. In contrast, the popular HLL VMs use V-ISAs that refer to data in a more abstract manner (via metadata). Consequently, data structures and other resource-related information are encoded in a platform-independent fashion, just as the instructions are. This is illustrated in Figure 5.3. A program file consists of platform-independent code and platform-independent metadata. The metadata describes the data structures (typically objects), their attributes, and their relationships. As shown in the figure, the VM software consists of an emulation engine that can either interpret the code or translate it into native code. The VM infrastructure also consists of a loader that can convert the metadata into internal

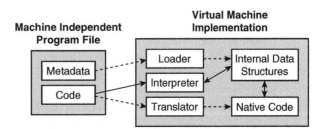

**Figure 5.3** Transformation of a Machine-Independent Program File to Machine-Dependent Code and Data. *Dotted lines indicate transformation of code and data; solid lines indicate movement of code and data during emulation.*

machine-dependent data structures, taking the host platform's word size and addressing features into account.

Currently, there are two major HLL VMs being used and promoted for platform-independent network computing — the Sun Microsystems Java virtual machine (JVM) and the Microsoft common language infrastructure (CLI). Both JVM and CLI include the same basic techniques for HLL VM implementation, some of which are similar to P-code and to the process VMs of Chapter 3. The modern HLL VMs also include a number of other interesting and rather sophisticated features. Besides support for platform-independent software, key features of network-oriented HLL VMs include the following.

*Security and Protection* — It must be possible to load programs from untrusted sources (including one of the least trustworthy of sources, the Internet) yet execute them locally as part of a user process without compromising the security of the local system. A user's files and other local hardware resources must be secure from any program downloaded over a network. Also, as an element of a secure implementation, the VM implementation software must be protected from the application software, yet both application and VM software typically are part of the same process running on a host platform. The metaphor is that each guest program is executed within it own *sandbox*, i.e., an environment where it is confined to operate. The program can do what it wants within the sandbox but cannot disturb any resources outside the sandbox, unless given explicit permission. In .NET terminology, a sandboxed guest program is referred to as *managed code* because its execution is performed under the management of the VM runtime. This management includes not only security checking but other functions, such as automatic garbage collection. Because it is helpful and descriptive, we will use the term *managed* code, to distinguish it from *unmanaged* code that runs outside the sandbox. As will become apparent, the ability to load an untrusted application and run it in a managed, secure fashion is a much bigger challenge than mere platform independence.

*Robustness* — The advantages of robust software are not restricted to the network computing environment, of course, but robust software becomes critical when dealing with the complexities of a platform-independent network environment. For developing large-scale software systems, the object-oriented programming model has a number of advantages and is widely used. Furthermore, the object model fits very well with distributed computing and dynamic linking. It also fits well with component-based programming, which can enhance programmer productivity considerably. Consequently, the object-oriented paradigm has become the model of choice for modern HLL VMs. Both Java and the CLI are designed to support object-oriented software. Other features that contribute significantly to robustness are VM support for strong type-checking and garbage collection.

*Networking* — In some environments, available networking hardware may only provide limited bandwidth. This limitation favors software that uses network bandwidth sparingly and efficiently. Consequently, application software should be loaded incrementally, on demand, via dynamic linking. This can save bandwidth by loading only software that is used, by spreading bandwidth usage over time, and by improving program start-up time because execution can begin as soon as the first software routines are loaded. There are also advantages to using dense instruction set encodings, both to reduce the bandwidth required for moving a program across a network and to reduce memory requirements on the local platform (which may also be limited in some applications).

*Performance* — While offering all the features just listed, it is also desirable to provide good performance. In general, one might be willing to sacrifice some performance — nothing comes for free after all — but a good HLL VM should be part of an overall framework that provides the user with good performance. To achieve this, many of the techniques described in Chapters 2 through 4 for conventional process VMs can be applied. In addition, there are techniques that are specific to (or more advantageous when applied in) the object-oriented, networked environment.

When all of the foregoing features are wound together into a single HLL VM, it is difficult to unravel the specific VM properties and associate them with specific features. The HLL V-ISAs and supporting VM implementations have become quite complex; many papers and thick books have been written on both the JVM and CLI architectures and implementations. We cannot begin to provide this level of detail; rather, our goal is to understand and illustrate the important principles and techniques.

In the following subsections, we discuss the basic techniques for supporting the four primary features just listed. In subsequent sections, we describe the Java virtual machine in some depth because it is conceptually simpler than the more recent Microsoft CLI. The JVM discussion will be followed by a discussion of the CLI, with its differences with JVM being highlighted.

Before proceeding, we pause briefly to discuss architecture/implementation terms again. First, there is some ambiguity when discussing Java virtual machine architecture and implementation; there is no widely used distinction between the two. That is, the term *Java virtual machine* may be used for the functional specification, e.g., the class file format, V-ISA, etc., and the same term is often applied to a specific implementation. Usually, the difference can be determined from the context. When there is any possibility of confusion, we will add *architecture* or *implementation* to *Java virtual machine*. The Microsoft common language infrastructure is an architecture, or functional specification. The Microsoft common language runtime (CLR) is a specific implementation of the CLI developed by Microsoft. The Microsoft *shared-source CLI*, despite the name, is another example of a CLI implementation (*shared-source CLR* would be more appropriate). Sometimes, it is useful to discuss only the instruction set portion of a VM architecture. In the case of Java, it is generally referred to as *Java bytecodes* because, as we shall see, the instructions can be viewed as a stream of bytes. The instruction part of the CLI is known variously as the *Microsoft intermediate language* (MSIL), the *common intermediate language* (CIL), or simply the IL. The combination of a JVM implementation and a set of standard Java libraries (APIs) is called a *Java platform*. Finally, a CLI implementation, along with a set of standard libraries, implements the Microsoft .NET framework.

### 5.2.1 Security and Protection

A given application running on a local platform should have access to certain specified files (program and data) on both its local system and on remote systems. Meanwhile, there must be the ability to prevent the guest application from accessing other files on both the remote and local systems. In addition, the VM implementation software that is running the application should be protected from the application itself, even though both are running on the host platform as part of the same process. Therefore, the type of protection that must be provided is different from that supported by a conventional operating system, where users are protected from one another, but a given user's programs have access to all of that user's resources. In the HLL environment, untrusted programs are invited into the user's domain but must have strictly limited access within that domain. That is, a guest program is treated as managed code that can only operate within its protection sandbox. In modern HLL VMs such as Java, the VM implementation provides much of this additional protection "above" the operating system. As we shall see, a fundamental aspect of the popular HLL VMs is that the high-level languages (e.g., Java or C#) are strongly typed and legal programs must strictly define the scope of both data accesses (to objects) and control flow. This information is then conveyed to the VM through the V-ISA.

There are three main aspects to the overall security/protection sandbox. The first is gaining access to public data, e.g., stored in files that are on remote systems, while being prevented from accessing any other data on the remote system. Here, we include locating public files as part of the overall process. The second aspect is that similar properties must hold for local files. And the third aspect is that the managed application must be prevented from accessing memory or executing code that is outside the sandbox, even though it shares the process memory space with the VM runtime software. To simplify explanation of the basic principles, the following discussion is based on the original Java sandbox model. The original sandbox is relatively inflexible and was primarily targeted at *applets* — small application programs accessed via the Internet; it remains the default security model. The more recent security model (used in Java 2) provides greater flexibility, including finer-grained access control and significantly less reliance on trusted code. This model will receive more discussion in Section 6.2.

Remote files are found via agreed-upon naming conventions. A specific convention is not part of a standard *per se*, but most current operating systems, including Linux and Windows, use hierarchical file systems based on directories. Consequently, naming conventions typically rely on this hierarchical structure. Furthermore, the Internet connects these systems and also uses a hierarchical naming system. Hence, as part of an overall framework — whether a Java platform or the .NET framework — there is normally a naming convention based on a combination of Internet addresses and local file structure addresses. For example, in the Java platform a particular method might be denoted as

```
edu.wisc.ece.jes.testpackage.shape.area
```

which is formed as a concatenation of an Internet address (in reverse order) — `ece.wisc.edu` — and a pathname — `~jes/testpackage/shape/area`. The critical thing is that a local system, given a name that follows the convention, must be able to find the stored representation of the requested item.

Protection of resources within the remote system's domain is not really a responsibility of the HLL VM running on the local system, even though data on the remote system may be part of an overall network computing framework. It is up to the user(s) of the remote system to determine which data files and/or directories should be made accessible over the network and which permissions (read or write) should be granted. Hence, even if the local system gives a correct path, if the file is not publicly accessible, then an attempt to access it will be denied permission. As noted earlier, this simple protection method is only the Java default. By using security, authentication, and cryptography APIs, a much more flexible security infrastructure can be built and supported by HLL VM platforms; for example, the Java 2 Standard Edition platform

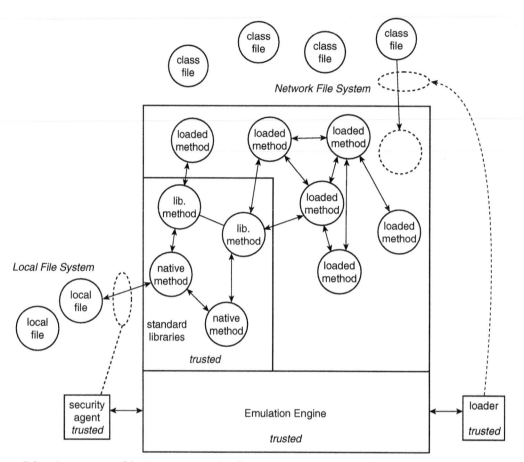

**Figure 5.4**    Components of the Java Protection Sandbox.

contains a number of APIs to support network-based security (Gong, Ellison, and Dageforde 2003). However, such VM platform security involves a number of higher-level issues that are well beyond our scope, although there is some additional discussion in the next chapter.

As shown in Figure 5.4, a Java program consists of a number of binary classes (or *modules* in .NET terminology), in a standard format, consisting of both platform-independent code and metadata. These binary classes may be held in a local file system, or they may be accessible via a network. The VM implementation includes a loader (or set of loaders) able to take a binary class, verify that it is correct, and then translate it into an implementation-dependent format that is loaded into the VM's memory region. The verification process will be described in more detail later. A loader is *trusted* software; that is, the local user trusts it to work correctly and to be secure. The trusted loader may be supplied by the user or, more likely, by a software developer trusted by the user. The binary classes define the loaded methods and object types, which are operated on by the methods.

There are both user methods and system methods, some of which may be native methods. The application program contains user methods. System methods belong to standard libraries (APIs) that are part of the local VM implementation and are often handled as trusted software.[3]

Native methods are maintained as native binary code, as the name suggests. Native methods can be compiled from any of a number of high-level languages, including C, or assembly language. They are useful for interfacing with legacy code and features of the underlying host platform, such as OS calls. They can also be used by programs written in other languages to draw on the rich set of APIs implemented in Java. The HLL methods and native methods can interact by following established conventions at their respective interfaces; the Java/native interface (JNI) defines a convention for Java. Native methods are often incorporated as parts of trusted libraries, but a user may also write and install native methods (at his or her own risk because they are not subject to the same security checks as conventional methods).

The emulation engine, another trusted component, emulates the V-ISA code embodied in methods using techniques similar to those described in Chapters 2 through 4. That is, it may use interpretation or may execute code that has been translated (compiled) to native instructions. If a managed application program needs to access a local file or any other local resource, it can only do so through a security manager within which the user has either directly or indirectly provided permissions (Section 6.2). Whenever the managed application requests access to a local file, for example, the request is made through a method belonging to a standard library. The standard library method consults the security manager to see if permissions should be granted. If so, the file access proceeds.

The managed application code includes software in the form of actual binary classes and methods they contain. This untrusted application software and the VM software share the same address space and run at the same privilege level within the host system; consequently, the VM software must be protected from the application as it executes. For example, arbitrary access to the VM tables via application program load and store instructions must be prohibited.

---

**3.** However, system methods written in Java do not have to be trusted, strictly speaking; they can be verified just as any other method. Doing so would tend to increase system integrity, but it would also slow down the JVM start-up time, so it is not commonly done.

Similarly, the application code should not be allowed to jump to arbitrary locations in the VM code.

A combination of static and run-time checks implement address space protection. As the emulation engine executes a managed guest application, it can perform a memory bounds check on every load, store, or jump instruction that static (load-time) code analysis cannot guarantee to be safe. These checks ensure that the guest only accesses its portion of the address space; i.e., it stays within the sandbox. Today's more popular HLL VMs, including both the JVM and CLI, are targeted at strongly typed HLLs and rely to a high degree on static (load-time) checking for protection, with minimal run-time checking. Because the strongly typed HLL approach is widely used, it is the one we focus on. In contrast, with conventional binaries, as would be generated by C or C++, static binary code analysis is rather limited, and many loads, stores, and jumps would require dynamic run-time checking. An especially efficient implementation of this full dynamic-checking approach simply forces all accesses to be within predefined, easily checked guest memory segments (Wahbe et al. 1993). This technique allows virtually any HLL to be used for generating guest programs. Such an approach is taken in the Omniware system (Lucco, Sharp, and Wahbe 1995).

We provide more detail in the next chapter when discussing Java virtual machine implementation, but the basic approach to checking is first to restrict the virtual ISA so that all the data structures are defined as part of the metadata and all memory accesses are to fixed fields within typed structures. The metadata, of course, reflects the object structure defined in the high-level language program. Similarly, all branch instructions are to fixed offsets within the code region. The only indirection allowed for control transfers is through explicit call and return instructions. As part of the loading process, the load and store instructions in the machine-independent code are checked for consistency with respect to the metadata specifications. The loader also checks all control flow (branch and jump) instructions for consistency. These load-time static checks provide most of the protection against out-of-bounds loads, stores, and control transfers. Exceptions are for those accesses that use a computed index value into a data structure, e.g., arrays. These accesses are checked dynamically at run time, along with checks for accesses using null pointers (actually *references*, in Java terminology).

In summary, we see that the sandbox around a managed execution environment consists of a number of interacting components. The files and other resources on a remote system are protected by the remote system itself, based on its conventional protection mechanisms. The files and other resources on the local machine are protected by trusted libraries and a security manager. Finally, the VM runtime software is protected from untrusted application software by a combination of static checking performed by a trusted loader and dynamic checks performed by a trusted emulation engine.

### 5.2.2 Robustness — Object-Oriented Programming

As noted earlier, the two most widely used HLL VMs are both based on an object-oriented model. We can't possibly cover all the aspects of object-oriented programming here. Rather, we provide a quick overview to introduce terminology and to make the following discussion of HLL VM implementations easier to understand.

In an object-oriented programming environment, the data-carrying entities are *objects*. The data contained in each object can only be accessed and manipulated via *methods*, or procedures, that are defined for that type of object. A *class* defines a type of object and its associated methods. At run time, objects may be created as *instances* of the class. In essence, the objects are a complex programmer-defined data type, and the methods are specific to the particular type for which they are defined. Objects can only be accessed via managed pointers, or *references*, that are generated at the time the object is created. In Java and CLI, *arrays* are defined as part of the language and are essentially an intrinsic form of object.

The data portion of an object consists of a number of fields. These fields may be individual data elements, or they may be references to other objects and arrays. The data portion of an object can be either *static* or *dynamic*. If it is static, then only one copy of the associated data is created, and it is shared by all objects of the given type. If data is dynamic, then a new copy of the data is generated for each object that is created.

Through *inheritance*, new classes can be defined by extending an existing class. A derived class has the same members (e.g., fields) as the base class from which it is inheriting. When a class is *extended*, the function of an existing method for the base class can be overridden, by defining a new method having the same name and *signature*. A method's signature is an ordered list of its argument and return types. The new, overriding method is the one applied to the subclass. Furthermore, a subclass can have other members and methods that do not exist in the base class.

Inheritance, as just described, is a way of achieving *polymorphism* among subclasses. With inheritance and polymorphism, the exact code executed when a method is called depends on the specific type of the object given as an argument. Finally, an *interface* is similar to a class but has no associated object; it only contains method signatures. However, if a class (which does have an associated object) implements an interface, then the methods identified by the interface's signatures operate on the class's object. A subclass can only extend one class, but it can implement multiple interfaces.

Invoking a method that operates on an object is often likened to "sending a message" to the object, where the message indicates what should be done and may return a response value. The actual details of the object's implementation, for example, the way it is laid out in memory, are hidden and can therefore be implementation dependent. What is important is that methods always produce the same results regardless of the implementation.

There are also ways of restricting the scope over which an object can be accessed by other parts of a program. In Java, for example, a class may be declared to be *public, private,* or *protected.* These designations indicate the visibility (and ability to use) an object outside of a given library of objects. The public and private designations are more or less self-explanatory: If a class is public, it can be used by code outside the library; if it is private, it can only be used by other classes inside the same library. Protected classes are similar to private ones, except any inheriting class is given access.

### Example

Figure 5.5 is a Java program that defines a Rectangle class via two methods, one that finds the area and one that finds the perimeter of the Rectangle. The program also extends the Rectangle class with a Square class. The Square class has a somewhat simplified perimeter method that will override the Rectangle's perimeter method. The main program reads pairs of integers from the command line. These integers represent a rectangle's length and width. If the sides are the same, a Square object is instantiated; otherwise, a Rectangle is instantiated. Then the area and perimeter methods are called, with a reference to the Square or Rectangle as the argument. The particular perimeter method used depends on the type of object to which the reference points. That is, the specific perimeter method is *dynamically dispatched* at run time. This program is admittedly contrived — the sides array is somewhat superfluous — but it allows us to illustrate a number of JVM features in a small example.

### Garbage Collection

One of the nice features of the object-oriented model is that, from the programmer's perspective, memory is a large, virtually unbounded space populated with objects. These objects essentially "float" in the memory space, with references tethering them to executing programs. Objects can be created dynamically, used for a while, and then abandoned by overwriting or deleting all references to the object. For example, in the code given in Figure 5.5, when the reference a

```java
public class Shapes {
    public static void main (String args []) {
        Rectangle a;
        int length, width;

        for ( int i = 0; i < 4 ; i++) {
            length = Integer.parseInt (args [2*i]);
            width = Integer.parseInt (args [2*i+1]);
            if (length==width)
              a = new Square (length);
            else
              a = new Rectangle (length, width);
            System.out.println(a.area());
            System.out.println(a.perimeter());
        }
    }
}

class Rectangle {
    protected int sides [];
    public Rectangle (int length, int width) {
        sides = new int [2] ;
        sides [0]  = length;
        sides [1] = width;
    }

    public int perimeter ( ) {
        return 2*(sides[0] +sides [1]);
    }

    public int area ( ) {
        return (sides [0]*sides[1]);
    }
}

class Square extends Rectangle {
    public Square (int length) {
        super (length, length);
    }
    public int perimeter ( ) {
        return 4*sides [0];
    }
}
```

**Figure 5.5**    A Java Program That Computes the Area and Perimeter of a Sequence of Squares and Rectangles.

is reassigned to a new Rectangle or Square, the previous Rectangle/Square object is no longer referenced and becomes *garbage*.

While this model of an unbounded memory space is nice from the programmer's perspective, in a real implementation the memory cannot be unbounded, of course. Consequently, there must be some way of recycling the memory resources used by objects that are no longer needed. In some object-oriented languages, C++, for example, it is expected that the programmer will explicitly release an unneeded object so that memory management software can reuse its memory. This places a burden on the programmer, however, and if object memory is not properly released, a "memory leak" can develop where unused objects grow in number until the processor's memory resources are exhausted. On the other hand, if a program bug allows the same memory to be freed twice (a *double-free*), then a security hole may be created.

To avoid memory leaks and double-free bugs as well as to enhance program robustness, the modern HLL VMs relieve the programmer of the burden of keeping track of unneeded, garbage objects. In particular, the VMs automatically collect garbage in a manner that is hidden from the application program. The VM implementation is able to find objects for which references no longer exist and to collect these objects on behalf of the user. The programmer is not burdened with explicitly returning unused objects to memory management software, and the possibility of programmer memory management bugs is eliminated.

### 5.2.3 Networking

In the network computing environment, network bandwidth is sometimes a limited resource. In an HLL VM there are at least two ways that network bandwidth usage can be reduced. The first is by reducing the size of a program (or dynamically linked library routines) that must be moved over the network. This leads to program encodings (i.e., instruction sets) that can specify a program in a dense manner. A key point is that with a VM performing emulation, the information transported over the network is a *specification* of the program to be executed, not necessarily the actual instructions that will eventually be executed. Translation converts the specification into real native instructions — interpretation does the same, for that matter, albeit much less efficiently.

Using a stack-oriented instruction set with variable-length instructions leads to a fairly compact program specification, especially when compared with the relatively sparse encoding found in a typical RISC ISA, which uses lots of registers and fixed-length instructions. With an operand stack, it is not uncommon for an instruction to require only one byte, i.e., to specify the opcode; the operands are implied by their positions on the stack.

Although the stack instruction sets used in most modern HLL VMs may save some network bandwidth, the addition of metadata adds to network bandwidth requirements. Overall, it is probably a wash, with modest savings of network bandwidth (at best). However, as described earlier, the presence of the metadata brings some additional advantages that a conventional program binary does not offer. The bigger win with respect to network bandwidth savings comes from dynamic loading of program (class) files. That is, a VM implementation generally loads only binary classes that it anticipates it will need, thereby not wasting network bandwidth on binary classes that are never used.

### 5.2.4 Performance

An object-oriented language provides a number of significant advantages when compared with a language such as C, which is really only a step above assembly language. However, the object-oriented model also makes it significantly more difficult to achieve high performance on conventional hardware. Hence, for many (but not all) applications there is heavy emphasis on improving HLL VM performance. Most of the emulation techniques described in Chapters 2–4 can be used for enhancing HLL VM performance. The execution engine of an HLL VM implementation can use interpretation, binary translation to native code, or some combination.

The Java instruction set is designed for straightforward interpretation. On the other hand, the Microsoft intermediate language is not intended to be interpreted (however, it could be, albeit very slowly). Both the Java instruction set and MSIL use rather constrained, well-specified control flow instructions (branches and method calls), so the code-discovery problem is very simple. As soon as a method is entered, all the code belonging to the method can be immediately discovered. This leads to just-in-time (JIT) compilation, where a method, when first entered, is compiled[4] in its entirety. Often, JIT compilation generates nonoptimized or lightly optimized code. Beyond the two basic methods of interpretation and JIT compilation lies a range of more advanced staged emulation strategies. For example, an implementation can begin interpreting, with profiling added. Then hot methods can be compiled (or sections of hot methods). Finally, the compiled methods that are very frequently used can be much more highly optimized. Section 6.6 contains further discussion of higher-performance HLL VM implementation techniques.

## 5.3 The Java Virtual Machine Architecture

To look at HLL VMs in more detail, we focus on the Java virtual machine (JVM) (Lindholm and Yellin 1999). The JVM came before the Microsoft CLI and is

---

**4.** In the context of HLL VMs, translation is usually referred to as *compilation.*

in some sense a purer form of HLL VM. The CLI, on the other hand, is part of the more general .NET framework, where both managed and unmanaged applications can easily interoperate, if the user wishes. Following the discussion of the Java VM in this section, we overview the CLI in the next section.

### 5.3.1 Data Types

Java consists of primitive data types and references, along with objects, which are composed of the primitive types and references.

#### Primitive Data Types

The Java HLL VM supports a number of primitive data types from which objects are composed. The types are `int` (integer), `char`, `byte`, `short`, `float`, `double`, and `returnAddress`. A `boolean` value is implemented in the JVM as a primitive type `int` or `byte`. It is important to note that the primitive types are defined according to the values they can take, not the number of bits of storage they will consume in the implementation; for example, an integer data type is defined to represent any integer in the range $-2^{31}$ to $+2^{31} - 1$. Nor are the actual bit patterns explicitly specified. This allows the primitive types to be held in an implementation-dependent fashion on any given host platform. Of course, many implementations will represent integers with 32-bit words and a two's complement representation, but other implementations could use more storage bits and/or other representations. The `returnAddress` type, by the way, is a rather obscure type not present in the Java HLL but present in the Java ISA. It is used by "miniature subroutines" implemented with `jsr` and `ret` instructions (these are typically used in implementing the Java HLL `finally` clauses, and we don't discuss them any further).

#### References

In addition to the foregoing primitive types, the JVM includes a `reference` type, which can hold reference values. A reference value points to an object stored in memory (discussed next). A reference can also have a `null` (undefined) value if it has not been assigned. As is the case with primitive types, a reference has an implementation-dependent internal representation; the number of bits necessary for holding a reference is not defined as part of the Java ISA.

### Objects and Arrays

As described earlier, objects carry data held in logical structures declared by the programmer. As such, objects are composed of primitive data types and references that may point to other objects. An `array` object is a special, intrinsic type of object, with explicit instruction set support. Each array is defined, at the time it is declared, to have a fixed number of elements that do not change during the program's execution. The elements of an array must all be of the same primitive type or must all be references. If they are references, then they must all point to objects of the same type. In their basic form, arrays have a single dimension, but multidimensional arrays can be built using arrays of references.

## 5.3.2 Data Storage

In the JVM, there are three general types of data storage — global, local, and operand. *Global* storage is main memory, where globally declared variables reside. *Local* storage is temporary storage for variables that are local to a method. *Operand* storage holds variables while they are being operated on by the functional instructions (arithmetic, logical, shifts). All storage is divided into *cells* or *slots*, where a cell or slot can usually hold a single data item (the exceptions are double-precision floating-point numbers and long integers, which consume two slots). The actual amount of space required by a cell or slot is implementation dependent, but all addressing is in terms of the logical memory cells.

### The Stack

Local and operand storage are allocated on the stack, and procedure arguments are passed on the stack as well. Instructions can never place arrays and objects on the stack; only references and individual array elements can be placed on the stack. As each method is called, a stack frame is allocated (Figure 5.6), with arguments, local storage, and operand storage being allocated in that order. Local storage for a given method is of fixed size; the proper amount of stack space required for local storage can be determined at compile time. As noted earlier, the stack holds data in slots. In many conventional ISAs, operand storage is a register file; but just as in P-code, both Java bytecodes and MSIL use the stack for operands. Depending on the actual instruction sequence, a stack often has advantages with the respect to instruction set encoding density (no instruction fields are needed for specifying registers), and a stack is amenable

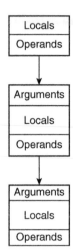

**Figure 5.6**    Java Stack Structure.

to platform independence (the host platform can have any number of registers in its ISA).

### Global Memory

The logical main memory architecture in Java contains a method area for holding code and a global storage area for holding arrays and objects. The global memory area is managed as a heap of unspecified size with respect to the JVM architecture; i.e., its total size is an implementation-dependent feature. The heap can hold both static and dynamic objects, including arrays; these objects are created on the heap at run time. When an object is dynamically created on the heap, a reference is generated to point to it at that time. Objects in the heap can only be accessed via a reference having a type that matches the type of the object. For example, in Figure 5.5 the reference a is declared to be of type Rectangle, and it can only be used for pointing to objects of type Rectangle (or a subclass of Rectangle).

### Constant Pool

Instructions often use constant values, as integer operands or as addresses in local memory, for example. The ISA allows some constant values to be placed in the instruction stream as immediate operands. But in general the constants have a range of lengths, and some of them are used by a number of different instructions. So to make the Java ISA a little more compact and uniform, constant data associated with a program is placed in a block known as the *constant pool.* Any instructions that need constant values can then index into the constant pool to retrieve them. Note that although the exact representations of integers and references when held in global memory or the stack are not defined part of the ISA, their representations when held in the constant pool are defined as part of the ISA. For example, an integer in the constant pool is represented as a 32-bit two's complement number. It is important to keep in mind that the constant pool is a part of a program's specification, just as much as the actual instructions are, and it does not change as a program executes.

### Memory Hierarchy

Figure 5.7 illustrates the memory hierarchy in Java. In the figure, an array has been allocated on the heap, and a reference to the array is included as part of another object. Also note that in the lower left corner is an object with no references pointing to it. This is an object ready to be garbage collected. A specific field within a referenced object is accessed via an offset contained in the

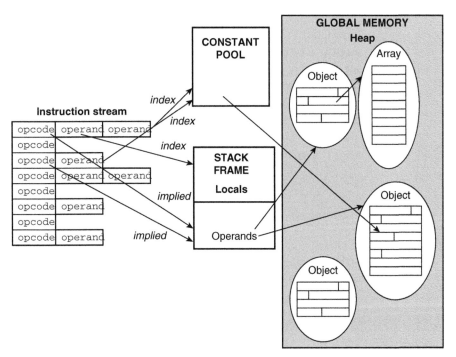

**Figure 5.7**  Memory Hierarchy Used by a Java Program.

constant pool. That is, there is no indirection when identifying a field (other than the indirection provided by the reference itself).

### 5.3.3   Java Instruction Set

The Java ISA is stack based, and, at least superficially, it is similar to the one used in P-code.

#### Instruction Formats

All instructions contain an opcode byte and zero or more subsequent bytes, depending on the opcode. Figure 5.8 shows the common instruction formats. Each instruction field consists of exactly one byte, although two or more such byte fields may be concatenated to form a single operand. Many instructions are a single byte, i.e., just the opcode, as shown in Figure 5.8a. Some instructions consist of an opcode and an index byte (or bytes). Two examples are in Figure 5.8b and c. The index bytes are used as indices into the constant pool or into local storage locations. Another class of instruction formats consists of an opcode and one or more data bytes (Figure 5.8d and e). The data bytes may be immediate data or offsets for PC-relative branch instructions. Because the instructions appear as a stream of bytes — either opcodes, indices, or data — an instruction set of this type is commonly referred to as a *bytecode* instruction set or simply as *bytecodes*. Using a single opcode byte implies there are 256 or fewer total opcodes; but a special wide opcode, when appended to a regular opcode, essentially creates a new instruction that performs the same operation as the regular opcode but with additional index bytes. And a bytecode

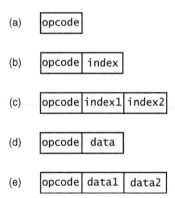

**Figure 5.8**   Typical Bytecode Instruction Formats.

instruction set can always be expanded by adding "escape code" bytes similar to the ones used for extending conventional instruction sets when all opcodes have been used up.

A basic property of the Java instruction set is that each of the primitive types has specific bytecode instructions that can operate on them. For example, the iadd opcode (integer add) is defined to operate only on integer operands on the stack. In a legal Java bytecode program, the operand types must match those required by the opcode. In the following instruction descriptions, we will typically use the integer forms of instructions as examples; the ISA defines similar instructions for the other primitive types.

The following subsections will overview the various types of instructions. A complete list of instructions can be found in a book focused on the Java virtual machine (e.g., Lindholm and Yellin 1999; Venners 1998). Instruction descriptions include the instruction format (opcode first), followed by operand byte(s), if any. All operand bytes are shown separately, even if they only have meaning when concatenated. For example, a 16-bit data item is represented as two bytes: data1 and data2.

### Data-Movement Instructions

Figure 5.9 illustrates the basic flow of data movement. All loads and stores from global or local memory must be to the operand stack, and all functional instructions operate on operands held on the stack.

One set of data-movement instructions push constant values onto the stack. There is some redundancy in these stack instructions; i.e., some constants can

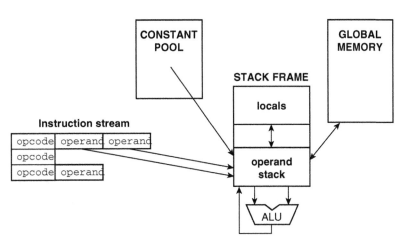

**Figure 5.9**   Data Movement Supported by the Java ISA.

be pushed onto the stack via more than one type of instruction. For example, any of five different instructions can push the constant 1 onto the stack. The advantage of having this redundancy is that it can improve code density and/or interpretation speed. The most common constants (e.g., small integers) are each given their own opcode, so a one-byte instruction is sufficient. For example, iconst1 is a single-byte instruction that pushes the integer constant 1 onto the stack. Other short constants can be pushed via the bipush data or sipush data1 data2 instructions — these require two or three instruction bytes, respectively. Any arbitrary constant can be pushed via the ldc index instruction (two bytes total), provided it is in one of the first 256 slots in the constant pool. (Of course, the constant pool entry itself contains additional data bytes.) Finally, the ldc_w index1 index2 instruction uses three bytes and can load a constant from any of 16K slots in the constant pool. The main difference between the ldc instructions and the push instructions is that the former requires a level of indirection when being interpreted. If translated (compiled) code is used, there is no practical difference between the two types of instructions.

A second set of data-movement instructions manipulate the stack entries. For example, the pop instruction pops the top element from the stack and discards it. The swap instruction swaps the positions of the top two stack elements, and dup duplicates the top stack element to form the top two stack elements.

The third set of data-movement instructions moves values between the local storage area of the current stack frame and the operand stack. These instructions specify the local storage address via a constant — either directly in the instruction or via an index to the constant pool. Also, the type of the data being moved is explicitly given in the opcode. This information is used for type checking when the program is initially loaded (to be discussed later). For example, the iload_1 instruction takes the integer from local storage slot 1 and pushes it onto the stack. The iload index instruction specifies the local storage slot number via a constant pool entry pointed to by the index. Similarly, istore_1 and istore index instructions move data from the stack to local storage in the current stack frame.

The final set of data-movement instructions deal with global memory data, either objects or arrays. An object is created via the new index1 index2 instruction that concatenates two bytes to form an index into the constant pool. The constant pool entry essentially specifies the object, and a new instance of the object is created on the heap and initialized. A reference to the object is pushed onto the stack. Similarly, the newarray type instruction creates an array containing elements of a specified primitive type.

For accessing data held in objects, the primary data-movement instructions are the getfield index1 index2 and putfield index1 index2 instructions, which point to a constant field entry containing information regarding the field, e.g., its type, size, and offset into the object that contains it. As with all data-movement instructions, these move data between the addressed data item and the operand stack. The getstatic and putstatic instructions are similar, except they deal with static rather than dynamic objects. There are similar instructions that move data to and from arrays.

In addition to instructions that create and access objects and arrays, there are instructions that can perform run-time checks to see what type of object is being pointed to by a reference. For example, the checkcast index1 index2 instruction indexes into the constant pool to find the specification for a specific class or interface. Then the object pointed to by a reference on the top of the stack is checked to see if it is an instance of the type specified by the constant pool entry. If not, a CheckCastException is thrown. This instruction is used for checking whether a run-time cast (conversion of an object reference) is safe (e.g., the reference being cast is to a member of the same class or a subclass of the object to which it currently points). This instruction allows a program to test for a potentially unsafe cast and to handle it in a graceful way via the exception mechanism (described later).

### Type Conversion

Some instructions convert one type of data item on the stack to another. An example conversion instruction is i2f, which pops an integer from the stack, converts it to a float, and pushes the float back onto the stack. Not every possible pair of primitive types is supported directly by a conversion instruction, however. In some cases a combined pair of instructions performs a conversion.

### Functional Instructions: Arithmetic, Logicals, Shifts

There are a number of instructions that take input operands, perform operations on them, and produce a result. For the most part, these instructions consist of a single byte. Operands are always taken from the stack and results are placed on the stack. Three examples follow. The iadd instruction pops two integers from the stack, adds them, and pushes the sum onto the stack. The iand instruction pops two integers from the stack, performs a logical AND on them, and pushes the result onto the stack. The ishfl instruction pops two integers from the stack, shifts the top element left by an amount specified by the second element, and pushes the result onto the stack.

Because the internal representations are implementation dependent, what the shift and logical instruction do, strictly speaking, is to convert the integer value to a standard two's complement form before performing the operation and then convert it back to the internal representation before pushing it on the stack; i.e., the logicals and shifts operate *as if* the values are stored as 32-bit two's complement numbers, regardless of whether they are actually stored that way or not.

### Control Flow Instructions

The control flow instructions (e.g., branches and jumps) are designed to expose all control flow paths within a method. This feature enables both complete discovery of all code within a method at the time it is first entered and load-time tracking of all variable types held in local storage (as explained shortly).

One set of conditional branches compares the top stack element with zero. For example, the ifeq data1 data2 instruction pops an integer from the stack and compares it with zero. If it is equal to zero, then there is a PC relative branch to an offset found by concatenating the two data bytes. Other conditional branch instructions compare two data items with each other. For example, the if_icmpeq data1 data2 instruction pops two integer values from the stack and compares the first with the second. If they are equal, then there is a PC relative branch to an offset found by concatenating the two data bytes. Finally, there are conditional branches to check for null/nonnull references. For example, ifnull data1 data2 pops a reference from the stack and checks it for null.

There are also more complex control flow instructions. The lookupswitch instruction, given here, is typically used to implement a switch statement:

```
lookupswitch default1 default2 default3 default4
npairs1 npairs2 npairs3 npairs4
match1_1 match1_2 match1_3 match1_4
      offset1_1 offset1_2 offset1_3 offset1_4
match2_1 match2_2 match2_3 match2_4
      offset2_1 offset2_2 offset2_3 offset2_4
additional n-2 match/offset pairs
```

This is all one instruction, laid out in a way to make it more readable. In this instruction, the four default bytes are concatenated to yield a PC relative branch offset if none of the cases match. The four npairs bytes indicate the number of match/offset pairs included in the switch statement. The integer at the top of the stack is popped and is compared with each of the match values (four bytes each). If a match is found, then there is a PC relative branch to the corresponding `offset` value (four bytes). If there is no match, the branch is to the `default` location.

Methods are called via one of the `invoke` instructions, which take a statically defined set of arguments. The return instructions are defined to return either no value or a single value. There are four types of invoke instructions. One of the more commonly used is `invokevirtual index1 index2`, which begins by indexing into a constant pool location that contains a description of the called method. This description includes the address of the method, the number and types of arguments it takes, the number of locals it uses, and its maximum operand stack depth. Arguments on the stack are checked to make sure they match the specified argument types. If they do, a stack frame of the appropriate size is allocated, and the arguments are pushed as locals onto the stack. Then there is a jump to the called method. The return PC is saved on a stack, but the return PC value is not accessible, other than indirectly through a return instruction.

The other types of invoke instructions are: `invokeinterface`, which is used for invoking an interface method; `invokespecial`, which provides special operations for certain types of methods, initialization methods, for example; and `invokestatic`, which is used for static methods.

A typical return instruction is `ireturn`, which begins by popping an integer from the current stack frame before removing the current stack frame. The integer is then pushed back onto the stack (for use by the calling method). Finally, there is a return jump to the calling method. The simple `return` instruction is used when there is a void return value.

As pointed out earlier, we see that an important property of control flow instructions is that all control paths can be easily tracked. All branches (including the switches) are to fixed, compile-time PC offsets, so they are known at load time. Furthermore, the method calls and returns can be tracked as well, because they jump directly to a method (via a fixed index into the constant pool), not indirectly through a pointer.

### *Operand Stack Tracking*

Besides the individual instruction specifications, the Java bytecode ISA also defines some overall properties that must hold in order for a sequence of instructions to be part of a valid program. These overall properties represent an important difference between HL V-ISAs and conventional ISAs. One such property is that at any given point in the program, the operand stack must have the same number and types of operands, and in the same order, regardless of the path that was followed to get to that point. This allows the loader to analyze the program prior to execution in order to check the types that are being moved to or from memory (either global or local). That is, the types of the values on the operand stack can be tracked through *static* program analysis; it is not necessary to look at the actual types dynamically as the program is executed in order to make sure the proper types are being used. This property also means that the maximum depth of the operand stack can be determined for each method at the time it is compiled.

Figure 5.10 presents three examples to illustrate the static stack-tracking property. All three examples have control flow paths that diverge (due to conditional branches) and then reconverge. Hence, there are multiple paths

```
          iload    A        //push int. A from local mem.
          iload    B        //push int. B from local mem.
          If_cmpne 0 else1   //branch if B ne 0
          iload    C        //push int. C from local mem.
          goto     endelse1
else1     iload    F        //push F
endelse1  add               //add from stack; result to stack
          istore   D        //pop sum to D
```

(a)

```
          iload    B        //push int. B from local mem.
          If_cmpne 0 skip1   //branch if B ne 0
          iload    C        //push int. C from local mem.
skip1     iload    D        //push D
          iload    E        //push E
          if_cmpne 0 skip2   //branch if E ne 0
          add               //add stack; result to stack
skip2     istore   F        //pop to F
```

(b)

```
          iload    A        //push int. A from local mem.
          If_cmpne 0 else1   //branch if A ne 0
          aload    B        //push reference B from local mem.
          goto     endelse1
else1     iload    C        //push integer C from local mem.
endelse1  iload    D        //push int. D from local mem.
          If_cmpne 0 else2
          astore   E        //pop reference to local mem.
          goto     endelse2
else2     istore   F        //pop integer to local mem.
endelse2  …
```

(c)

**Figure 5.10**   Examples of Code Sequences with Reconverging Control Flow. *(a) A valid sequence; (b) an invalid sequence where converging paths have different numbers of operands depending on the path followed; (c) an invalid sequence where reconverging paths have different types of operands depending on the path followed.*

that will lead to the reconvergence point. Figure 5.10a is a legal code sequence. It first pushes an integer A onto the stack. Then it tests B; if B is equal to zero, it pushes a second integer, C, onto the stack. Otherwise, it pushes the integer F onto the stack. At that point the two control paths reconverge and the top two stack elements are added and then stored to D. The key point is that when the two control paths reconverge, the operand stack has two integers regardless of the path taken.

The second code sequence (Figure 5.10b) is not a legal one. If B is equal to zero, the integer C is pushed onto the operand stack; then integer D is pushed onto the stack regardless of the value of B. Next, the code sequence tests E. If E is zero, the top two stack elements are added; otherwise nothing is done. Finally, the top of the stack is stored to local memory location F. This code has the property that if B is equal to zero, then the stack has two elements when the branch on the value of E is performed; otherwise the stack has only one element at the same point in the code. Now, it may be the case that E is zero whenever B is zero, and vice versa. However, it may not be possible to determine this fact by static analysis of the code, so the exact stack contents at the end of this code sequence are unknown.

The third code example (Figure 5.10c) is also illegal. It pushes a reference onto the stack if A is zero; otherwise it pushes an integer. Then it pops a reference if D is zero; otherwise it pops an integer. Here, the stack contents are different, depending on the path taken to reach the compare with D. If it happens that D is zero whenever A is zero, and vice versa, then the data types will "work out" at run time. However, as in the earlier case, it may not be possible to determine this through static analysis.

Because of the way the V-ISA specifies control flow (branches and procedure call/returns), a relatively simple analysis can determine if the proper stack discipline is followed. Because all branches are to constant locations within the same method, all paths in the method can be determined statically. At a method invocation, it is known that anything on the operand stack will not be touched by the invoked method, so the operand stack will have the same values when the method returns (with the possible addition of a return value whose type is given by the invoke opcode). Hence, the analysis algorithm simply traces all the static control flow paths and simulates a stack symbolically. If the symbolic stack contents ever differ at a control flow convergence point, then the program is not valid.

### Example Program

Figure 5.11 is a bytecode compilation of the Java Rectangle perimeter method given in Figure 5.5. The numbers in the leftmost column are the PC values

```
public int perimeter () ;

 0:  iconst_2
 1:  aload_0
 2:  getfield#2; //Field:  sides reference
 5:  iconst_0
 6:  iaload
 7:  aload_0
 8:  getfield#2; //Field:  sides reference
11:  iconst_1
12:  iaload
13:  iadd
14:  imul
15:  ireturn
```

**Figure 5.11**    Java Bytecodes for the perimeter Method Defined for the Rectangle Class (in Figure 5.5).

(as byte addresses) corresponding to the given instructions. The first instruction pushes a constant 2 onto the operands stack, and the second instruction pushes local variable 0 onto the stack (by convention, local variable 0 is the argument being passed to perimeter(); in this case it is a reference to the rectangle object). The getfield instruction then gets the reference to the sides array from the Rectangle object. The object reference is on the stack, and constant pool entry 2 contains a description of the field that is being accessed, i.e., that it is a reference. The getfield instruction pushes the reference to the sides array on the stack. Then the next two instructions (iconst_0 and iaload) push index number 0 onto the stack (on top of the reference to array sides) and load element 0 from the array sides (via the reference and index number taken from the stack). The next four instructions are similar to the preceding four, and they load the value of sides[1] onto the stack. At that point, the bottom of the stack is a constant 2, the next stack value is sides[0], and the top of the stack is sides[1]. Then the iadd, imul sequence forms 2*(sides[0] + sides[1]). Finally, the last instruction returns, with the integer result on top of the stack.

### 5.3.4  Exceptions and Errors

In the Java architecture, some exceptions (or errors) are defined as part of the ISA and may be thrown as a result of program execution. Other exceptions can be user defined and are explicitly thrown by executing a throw instruction (described later).

A key property of the JVM is that all exceptions must be handled *somewhere*. That is, there is no global way to turn them off, as is the case with most conventional ISAs, where there is usually a mask bit corresponding to each trap condition. The rationale for dealing with exceptions this way is not really specific to high-level VMs; rather, it is an overall program robustness consideration. If an exception is not handled by the method that throws the exception, then the current stack frame is popped and the calling method takes over responsibility; if the calling method doesn't have a handler, then another stack frame is popped, etc., until eventually the main program is reached. At that point if there is no handler, a standard handler takes over (and likely terminates the program). In a way, this approach forces the programmer to think about all exceptions in order to deal with them actively rather than just turning them off and forgetting about them.

In Java there is a distinction made between errors and exceptions. *Errors* are not necessarily caused by behavior that is inherent to the application program; rather, they may be caused by limitations of the VM implementation or VM bugs. *Exceptions,* on the other hand, are caused by program behavior that occurs dynamically — as the program executes. Static checking catches many programming mistakes and oversights, but some types of behavior cannot be caught until run time. An example of an error is `StackOverflowError`, which indicates that the available stack space is exhausted. There is no architected stack size in the V-ISA, and some VM implementations may run out of stack space before others. Hence, when this error occurs, it is not necessarily due to a program bug; it may just be an indication that the host platform does not have enough memory for the application's needs. On the other hand, it could also result from a program bug, such as runaway recursion. As another example, the `InternalError` indicates that the VM has encountered some type of internal bug. Just as with any well-designed program, the VM implementation software itself should contain internal error checking. If the VM should catch such an internal bug, it throws this error.

The Java ISA defines a number of exceptions. These are the program exceptions that must be checked for dynamically. Two common exceptions are the `NullPointerException` and the `ArrayIndexOutOfBoundsException`, which are clearly described by their names. All references ("pointers") must be checked to make sure they are not null at the time they are used (although some explicit checks may be removed by optimizations). Also, all array indices must be checked. Array indices are the only way of indirectly accessing a Java data structure. There are a number of exceptions related to type checking and object accesses. For example, an `IncompatibleClassChangeError` occurs when a `getfield` instruction is applied to a static field; even though the name indicates an "error," it is in fact an exception.

In the Java ISA, it is possible to specify an exception handler, depending on where an exception occurs. To accomplish this, the JVM associates a table with each method, the *exception table*. Here is an example entry in an exception table:

| From | To | Target | Type |
|------|-----|--------|------|
| 8 | 12 | 96 | Arithmetic Exception |

This table entry indicates that if an arithmetic exception occurs anywhere between instructions at locations 8 and 12, then there should be a jump to a handler at location 96. The table is built from information encoded in the high-level language program, for example, with Java try and catch regions. If a From/To region encloses a method call, then unless the method has a handler of its own, the handler in the calling method is used.

At the time an exception is thrown, the operand stack is immediately flushed. The JVM then looks up the exception type in the exception table. If the exception type and the PC at the time of an exception match a table entry From/To range, then there is a jump to the target PC specified in the table. Otherwise, the current stack frame is removed, the PC at the time of the call is reinstated, and the table is checked again. This continues until either there is a table match or the outermost procedure (main) is reached.

Besides the exception table, JVM support for exceptions includes the instruction `athrow index1 index2`. This instruction explicitly throws an exception. The values `index1` and `index2` form an index into the constant pool. The constant pool location contains a description of the exception being thrown.

### 5.3.5 Binary Classes

When an HLL VM program is distributed, not only is the code included, but so is a detailed specification of the data structures and their relationships, i.e., the *metadata*. In Java terminology, the combination of code plus metadata is a *binary class* that is typically included in a *class file* (in the Microsoft CLI it is called a *module*). The format of the binary class is, in effect, the "official" interface supported by the underlying virtual machine — the binary class format plays the same specification role as in a conventional ISA. Thus far, we have described the components of a binary class in a general way. In the remainder of this section we describe the overall structure of a Java binary class.

All the Java binary classes that form a complete program do not have to be loaded when a program is started (although they could be). Rather, the binary classes can be loaded on demand, at the time they are needed by the program. Among other things, this saves bandwidth for loading binary classes that are never used, and it allows a Java program to start up quickly, using only some initial binary classes. For efficiency, the first time a binary class is used, it is parsed and placed into *method memory*, a part of the VM implementation. Then on subsequent calls, it is much more efficient to consult the preprocessed method information in the method memory.

Either each component of a binary class is of a fixed size or the size is explicitly given immediately before the component contents. In this manner, the loader can parse the entire binary class from beginning to end, with each of the components being easily recognized and delineated. Within each component, the same principle is used.

Figure 5.12 gives the layout of a binary class. It consists first of some header information, beginning with a *magic number* that identifies this block of data as a binary class. The magic number is simply a character sequence that is the

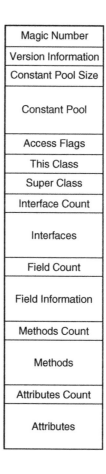

**Figure 5.12**    Format of a Java Binary Class.

same for all Java binary classes. When presented with a file purported to contain a binary class the loader can use the magic number as a quick, initial check to gain some assurance that it does in fact contain a binary class. The header also contains version information for the binary class. Over time, it is expected that there will be extensions to the Java VM, and the version number can be used by the loader to restrict its checks and operations to the correct version.

Following the header information is a sequence of large structures, each preceded by a size indication or the number of contained elements. The major structures are the Constant Pool, a table describing method Interfaces, a table describing object Fields, a table containing the Methods, and a table of Attributes that contains much of the detailed information for the other tables. The following subsections describe each of these major structures as well as some of the minor ones.

### Constant Pool

The constant pool essentially holds all the constant values and references used by the methods that are to follow. Each of the constants is appended with type information so that type checking can be performed when the constant is used. Many of the constants are in symbolic form, i.e., the names of classes, interfaces, methods, and fields.

### Access Flags

As the name suggests, these flags provide access information, for example, whether this particular type (class) is public, whether it is an interface rather than a class, whether it is final (i.e., it can never be dynamically overridden).

### This_Class and Super_Class

This region contains the names of this class and the superclass of this class. Both are given as indexes into the constant pool. The names themselves are in the constant pool. All classes except for the Object class (see Section 5.4.2) have a super_class. For the Object class, the super_class is zero.

### Interfaces

This region contains a number of references to the superinterfaces of this class, i.e., the interfaces through which this class can be directly accessed. These are given as indices into the constant pool. The constant pool entries are references to the interfaces.

### *Fields*

This component contains the specification of the fields declared for this class. This information is included in a small table for each field; the table includes access information (public, private, protected), a name index (an offset into a constant pool entry that contains the name of this field), a descriptor index (which contains an index into the constant pool where the descriptor for this field can be found), and attributes information.

### *Methods*

This component contains information regarding each method, e.g., the name and descriptor, as well as the method itself, encoded as a bytecode instruction stream. Each method can also have attribute tables, for example, giving the maximum operand stack depth for the method and the number of locals. The code itself appears as part of an attribute table. Also included is the exception table, described earlier, which give types of exceptions to be checked and the PC ranges over which they should be checked.

### *Attributes*

The attributes region contains the detailed information regarding the other components listed earlier. In general, an HLL VM would have a fairly large number of attribute types.

### 5.3.6 The Java Native Interface

The Java native interface (JNI) allows java code and native compiled code to interoperate. For example, it allows Java code to call a routine compiled from C, and vice versa, although we will emphasize the former situation in this discussion. By using the JNI, a C program can even invoke a Java virtual machine.

An overview of the JNI and its operation is given in Figure 5.13. On the left-hand side of the figure, the "Java side," we see the Java architecture as described in the preceding sections. Code (and data) compiled to the native platform ISA resides on the right-hand side of the figure, i.e., the "native side." It is important to note, however, that the Java side can be compiled from any language where there is a compiler that can produce standard binary classes; for example, C# could be used. The native side can be compiled from C or from any other language for which JNI support exists, including assembly language. Each side of Figure 5.13 compiles to its own binary format. On the Java side,

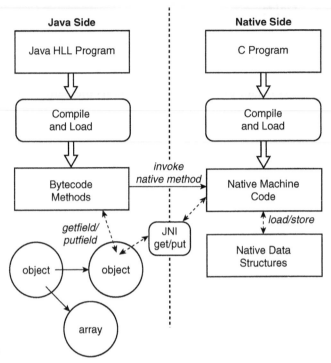

**Figure 5.13**   Java Native Interface. *The Java native interface allows Java software and native compiled software to interoperate.*

these are standard binary classes; on the native side, they are program binaries in the native platform's machine code. Data on the Java side exists as objects and arrays on the heap and variables on the stack. On the native side, data is organized in whatever way the compiler happens to lay it out; i.e., it is compiler dependent.

The JNI provides an interface for a Java method to call a native method (as shown in the figure). To do this, the native method must be declared as `native` by the calling Java class. After compiling the Java class that declares the native method call, it can be given to a program `javah`, which will produce a header file for the native method. Then the header and native method code can be compiled to form the callable native method.

The JNI specification allows control to be transferred back and forth between Java code and native methods; arguments can be passed and values can be returned. Furthermore, exceptions can be caught and thrown in the native code for handling in the Java application. In order for code on the native side to access data from the Java side (or for that matter to create objects on the Java side), the JNI provides a number of native methods — for example, `GetArrayLength` will obtain the length of a Java array, and `GetIntArrayElements` allows the native code to obtain a pointer to a Java array's elements. Similarly, code on the native side can get and put object field data through JNI methods.

## 5.4 Completing the Platform: APIs

In Section 5.2 we stated that a Java platform is a combination of a JVM and a set of standard libraries, or APIs. The JVM is at the core of the platform, but it is the APIs that provide most of the features that are visible to users and software developers. These include support for secure network computing and component-based software, as well as many traditional functions, such as support for graphical user interfaces (GUIs). Similarly, the .NET framework is built around the CLI, but it is also includes a very large number of APIs that implement its rich set of features. Although the focus of this book is on the virtual machine, not the APIs, we would be remiss in not discussing some of the capabilities they provide. Furthermore, some of the APIs directly interact with the virtual machine and objects at a low level; these are of particular interest to us and will be discussed further.

### 5.4.1 Java Platforms

A number of computer companies provide Java platforms. To support inter-operable application software, these platforms must conform to a standard specification and contain the same APIs. The current Java specification is for the Java 2 platform (Shannon et al. 2000). Also specified are *editions*, which are targeted more at general categories of applications and users. Each of the editions is distinguished from the others by the packages of APIs it incorporates.

> *J2SE — Standard Edition:* As the name suggests, this edition is targeted at probably the largest number of Java users and developers. The standard edition platform supports typical PC users and client-side applications within an enterprise computing environment. It also incorporates APIs to support reusable component-based software development based on JavaBeans (discussed briefly later).

> *J2EE — Enterprise Edition:* This edition is directed at development of large enterprise software infrastructure, including server-side applications. It includes the Enterprise JavaBeans API, which supports component-based development of distributed server applications.

*J2ME — Micro Edition:* This edition defines a lighter-weight platform for consumer-based embedded systems, which are often resource limited. Consequently, it contains a smaller set of targeted APIs. Examples of embedded systems that may be based on the Micro Edition range from set-top boxes to pagers and smart cards.

### 5.4.2 Java APIs

There is a long list of Java APIs, too many to present and discuss here. Rather, we give some of the more important "core" API packages that exemplify the variety available, and then we single out some specific, particularly important low-level functions for additional discussion in subsequent subsections.

### *java.lang*

This is the core Java programming language API package; it contains classes that are at the heart of the Java programming language. These begin with the Object class — the superclass of all the Java classes. It also contains "wrapper" classes that contain primitive data types, such as Character and Integer when stored in the heap as individual items. In addition, java.lang contains low-level runtime and system static methods as well as floating-point math support. Other selected members of java.lang that are of special interest to us follow.

The Class class maintains descriptions of Java classes. Each class that is loaded has a Class object associated with it. Among other things, a class's Class object allows a program to extract information regarding the classes it is using, via a process known as *reflection*, described in the next subsection.

The Process object serves as a platform-independent interface to native processes external to the JVM, and the Thread class supports multithreading within the JVM. Use of the Thread class is discussed further in Section 5.4.4.

The SecurityManager is the class that defines the methods that implement a security policy. These methods are called in order to determine if a requested operation (e.g., to read or write a file) should be permitted. The security manager's overall role is described briefly in Section 5.2.1, and it is discussed further in Section 6.2.2.

### *java.util*

This package contains a number of classes that perform fundamental data structure operations as well as maintaining date and time facilities. For example, the Vector class supports arrays of objects that may grow as objects are added; the Enumeration interface is very commonly used for looping through the elements of a data structure. The Hashtable class supports associative arrays (typically implemented as hash tables). java.util.zip contains classes with methods for compressing and decompressing zip files, and java.util.jar contains classes for file archiving.

### *java.awt*

The java.awt (abstract windowing toolkit) contains classes for constructing GUIs from components and graphics shapes. Layout manager classes control graphics components held in container objects.

### *java.io and java.net*

The java.io API package contains classes for performing input/output operations. These classes manage data streams and file system I/O, and they are the counterparts of the I/O libraries supported by conventional high-level languages and operating systems. The java.net API package contains classes for networking support. For example, the socket class allows a program to connect to a port and read and write data through the port.

We now consider two general functions where the core API part of the Java platform interacts very closely with the lower-level operation of the JVM. These are by no means the only situations where such close interaction is required, however; they are singled out because they are fundamental to many applications that run on Java platforms.

### 5.4.3 Serializability and Reflection

One of the basic concepts of object-oriented programming is concealing internal features of an object. However, there are situations where it is important to discover features of objects. Serializability and reflection involve exposing the features of an object to programs operating on the object and to the world outside a given VM. For example, one may want to communicate an object from one Java program to another; perhaps the two programs are running on different platforms connected by a network. This is commonly done as part of remote method invocation (RMI), where, for example, a client may want to invoke a method on a remote server and an object may be passed as an argument or return value. Each of the platforms may have a different way of storing objects in memory, so simply copying the internal data structures

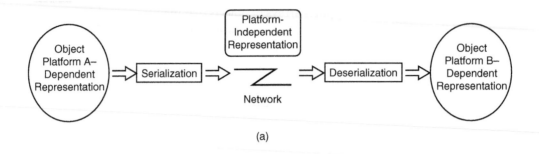

(a)

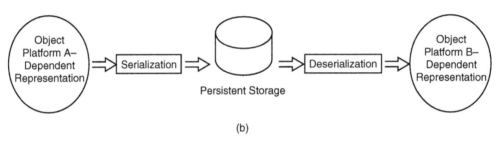

(b)

**Figure 5.14**  Serialization. *Serialization converts an object into an implementation-independent form that can be (a) passed over to a network to a different platform or (b) stored persistently for later use.*

that implement an object will not work. Instead, an object to be communicated must be converted into an implementation-independent form. Then the receiving program can convert the implementation-independent form into its own internal implementation-dependent form (see Figure 5.14a).

As another example, objects created by a program only live as long as the program exists; when the program terminates, the objects go away. However, there are many situations where it is desirable for objects to *persist* between program executions, stored on a disk, for example. Here, again, the solution is to convert objects into an implementation-independent form for storage and later retrieval (see Figure 5.14b). These two situations are similar: In the network example an object is passed from one program to another through space, and in the other it is passed through time.

The process of converting an object into an implementation-independent form is called *serialization*. In order to serialize an object it must be declared to be serializable, which means that it implements the `Serializable` interface. This interface then allows an object to be written as a byte stream in a canonical form. Serialization serializes not only a given object but all the objects for which the original object contains references, all the objects for which those objects contain references, etc. The serialization process involves *reflection*, that is, the ability to look inside an object to find all of its members. Then once found, they can be organized as a standardized byte stream.

Besides serialization, a number of other interesting applications require reflection in order to determine class information at run time. In a typical program development environment, the compiler can access information regarding classes used by a program at compile time, so the compiler can incorporate this class information as it generates new binary classes. However, there are situations where class information is not known at compile time, that is, where a running program may be given a reference to an object whose type is unknown. In these situations, information concerning the object must be retrieved at run time. This is done through reflection. In Java, the java.lang.reflect API is an interface to a class's Class object, which exists for every class used by a program and contains a description of the class. The Class objects are constructed by the JVM when an object type is loaded.

Reflection is a key enabler for component-based programming. In Java, basic program components are called *JavaBeans*. To facilitate component-based program design, JavaBeans must conform to a set of specified *design patterns* or coding conventions. For example, all readable properties of a JavaBean must have an accessory method of the form getproperty_name. Then if a program invokes an accessory method on an object, with, for example, the getFields() method, it will be given an array containing Field objects reflecting all the accessible public fields of the class or interface represented by this Class object.

A visual component-based program design tool allows a programmer to work at a high level by manipulating JavaBeans. Under programmer direction, the tool can load a JavaBean and analyze the bean's interface using the Reflection API and the JavaBean design patterns. With the information collected via the Reflection API, the developer's tool presents a graphical representation of the JavaBean that the developer can then use to modify the properties of the bean and enable communication between components by connecting an event source in one bean to an event listener in another.

### 5.4.4 Java Threads

In a typical JVM implementation, much of the multithreading support is provided by Java libraries that are part of the java.lang. This makes sense, because support for multiple threads must ultimately be provided through the OS on the underlying platform, and the way to communicate with the underlying OS is through libraries.

As noted earlier, the java.lang API includes a Thread class. Threads can be defined by extending this class (and inheriting its methods). Methods defined for the Threads class, include: run(), which starts a thread, stop(), which stops a thread, and suspend() and resume(), which, as their names imply, allow the suspension and resumption of a thread. Calling run() for an object of type Class will initiate a new thread. The JVM gives each Java thread its own stack, and the threads synchronize through mechanisms called *monitors*.

Monitors are supported at the lowest level by architected locks and two Java bytecode instructions. There is a lock associated with each object and each class (the Class object for a given class contains its lock). Only one thread at a time can own a particular lock. A lock actually operates as a counter rather than as a single bit flag (as one might expect). The bytecode instruction monitorenter acquires the lock for the object pointed to by the reference on the top of the operand stack. If the lock is already held by another thread, then the requesting thread simply blocks and waits. If the lock is not held by another thread, then the lock is incremented and the requesting thread continues execution. Note that the acquiring thread may already hold the lock, in which case it does the increment and goes on. The monitorexit instruction decrements the lock for the object pointed to by the reference on top of the operand stack. If the lock becomes zero as a result of the decrement, then it is released and can be acquired by a waiting thread (if there is one).

The basic lock mechanism can be used for implementing monitors that guard critical sections or for locking individual objects. A *critical section* is a code region that only one thread can execute at a given time. Critical sections typically manipulate shared data structures that require exclusive access, usually when they are updated. The synchronize keyword in the high-level Java language compiles down to monitorenter and monitorexit instructions.

Besides the bytecode instructions, the class Object declares a number of methods that support additional synchronization.

wait() — releases the lock and enters the *wait set* for the given lock. It remains there until it is *notified* (see later). The wait set is essentially a VM-supported pool of threads waiting for a notification regarding the lock.

wait(long timeout, int nanos) — releases the lock and enters the "wait set" for the given lock. It remains there either until it is notified or until timeout milliseconds plus nanos nanoseconds have elapsed.

notify() — wakes up one thread in the lock's wait set.

notifyAll() — wakes up all threads in the lock's wait set.

The wait and notify mechanisms are typically used for supporting monitors that manage cooperation among threads typified by producer–consumer interaction, where, for example, one thread might produce data items and place them in a shared buffer to be consumed by a different thread. The producer thread notifies the consuming thread when data is in the buffer. The consuming thread, after emptying the buffer, waits until it is again notified.

## 5.5 The Microsoft Common Language Infrastructure: A Flexible High-Level Language Virtual Machine

The common language infrastructure (CLI) is a virtual machine architecture that is part of Microsoft's .NET framework (Box 2002). The common language runtime (CLR) is Microsoft's implementation of the CLI. Although it supports object-oriented network-based computation, just as Java does, the CLI objectives are ostensibly broader than those for Java.

### 5.5.1 The Common Language Interface

The aspect of the CLI that is most similar to the Java environment is that it can support object-oriented programs within a managed runtime environment that includes features such as built-in protection checking and garbage collection. Although a number of high-level languages (some with extensions) can be compiled to Java binary classes, the JVM was designed specifically to support the Java HLL. In contrast, the CLI is designed to support multiple, interoperating high-level languages, and it also can support programs that do not have to be (or cannot be) verified by a loader. Hence, an essential feature that separates the CLI from the Java virtual machine is that the CLI strives for HLL independence as well as platform independence. This is illustrated in Figure 5.15.

The common language runtime (CLR) is an implementation of the CLI, and is part of the overall .NET framework. The modules are of a standard format and contain both metadata and code in the Microsoft intermediate language (MSIL). In the figure, modules (the analog of Java binary classes) can be generated from a number of languages, including, but not restricted to, C# (an object-oriented version of C that provides a garbage-collected heap), Java, Visual Basic .NET, and Managed C++. Managed C++ programs can run in the managed runtime environment provided by the CLR, but not all Managed C++ modules must be verifiable.

In the CLI, a code module can be verified for type safety in a manner similar to Java binary classes, and verifiability is a desirable property to have.

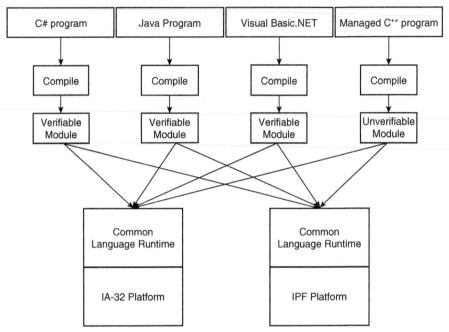

**Figure 5.15**  The Common Language Interface Supports Language Interoperability. *The CLI allows both platform independence and a high degree of high-level language independence.*

The managed C++ compiler has a flag that forces all code to be verifiable (and generates errors when the C++ programmer uses unsafe constructs). Verification helps establish a run-time protection domain that allows untrusted code to execute safely. Nevertheless, unverifiable (unsafe) programs are allowed as part of the managed program environment. A programmer may choose to generate unverifiable code that can still interoperate with verifiable code. In order to use unverifiable code, however, the user must permit it through a security manager.

Regardless of whether they are verifiable, all programs must be valid. Some programs may be constructed in an illogical manner; for example, a program may have a stack underflow that is detectable by inspecting the code at load time. A program such as this is invalid (as well as being unverifiable) and should not be allowed to run. Hence, there are three categories of application programs: those that are verifiable and valid, those that are unverifiable and valid, and those that are invalid. This is in contrast to Java, which only allows two types (verifiable and unverifiable). Furthermore, verifiable and unverifiable programs may be mixed (at the programmer's discretion), so, for example, a verified program can call an unverifiable library routine. Because multiple

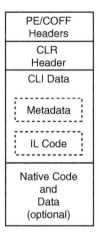

**Figure 5.16**  Overall Structure of a CLI Module.

languages and both verifiable and unverifiable programs are supported in an integrated way, the CLI provides a more complete, all-purpose application program environment than the JVM. This feature may be more significant in the short term as unsafe legacy code is mixed with newly developed verifiable code. In the long term, one would expect that unsafe legacy code will eventually be replaced with safe, verifiable code.

CLI modules are organized into assemblies, just as Java binary classes are organized into packages. Figure 5.16 shows an overview of a typical CLI module. It is contained in a standard Microsoft Portable Executable and Common Object File Format (PE/COFF), further highlighting interoperability; the OS handles it just like any other executable file. The module contains header information and CLI metadata and code, and it may also contain native code and data. The metadata consists of a number of regions that contain, among other things, object definitions and constants (called *streams* in the CLI). In general the concepts are similar to those in a Java binary class.

It is interesting to compare language interoperability in the CLI with that provided in Java (as illustrated earlier in Figure 5.13). An analogous figure for the CLI is given in Figure 5.17. Here, all programs compile onto the MSIL byte-codes, including C programs, for example. The data structures are all in the common metadata format. However, as described in the next section, the metadata format includes blocks of data and unmanaged pointers, which an MSIL program can manipulate in any manner (as in C). This code is unverifiable, but it can still execute within the managed environment.

Hence, in the CLI, interoperability is not implemented at the method call level (as in Java), but interoperability is supported in a more integrated way

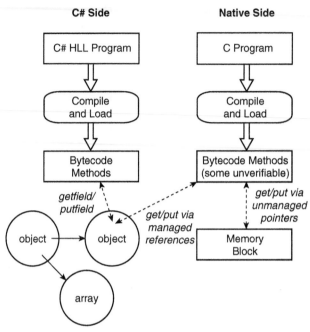

**Figure 5.17** Verfiable and Unverifiable Code Interoperate in the CLI. *MSIL bytecode programs interoperate via common metadata, including memory block data, that may be accessed via unmanaged pointers.*

that also extends to data: a type defined in one language can be used across languages. This more highly integrated approach does not come without a cost, however. It may require significant changes to existing language implementations (as was the case with Visual Basic, whose object model had to be changed to the C# model). Achieving interoperability may also require standardization in programming conventions. For example, if one language has case-sensitive variable names and the other does not, then for interoperability they should probably stick to a common denominator and not rely on case sensitivity. The Common Language Specification (CLS) contains a set of standard rules intended to ensure interoperability among high-level languages.

## 5.5.2 Attributes

The CLI supports attributes to allow the programmer to pass information at run time via compiled metadata that is part of a package. This information may be directed at the runtime software or the executing program. Some attributes are built in; i.e., they are intrinsic to the CLI. Custom attributes are also supported as a way of enabling user-defined extensions. The programmer can assign an attribute to virtually any item held in a module, including fields, classes, methods, or parameters. Then a running program can access the attribute via reflection, implemented with the `GetCustomAttribute` method. Based on the attribute, the program can then take some action. For example, consider a situation where a number of different companies are working together on a large international engineering design product. Some of the engineers may be working in units of inches and others in centimeters, and each is writing software based on one unit or the other. Traditionally, this type information is conveyed by comments placed in the code or via other external documentation, including word of mouth. However, this places the burden on the user to carefully check for such documentation to avoid mistakes. By assigning an attribute of either `[inches]` or `[centimeters]` to an object's data field, the unit being used is automatically conveyed to other programs as part of the metadata. A method accessing a data field can use reflection to check the unit attribute and convert the value in the field, if necessary.

Attributes can also pass information to the runtime software — for example, that an object has to have its fields laid out in a specific way (so that it can be accessed via native code, perhaps). A built-in attribute `[serializable]` is passed to the runtime to indicate than an object may be serialized and should therefore be implemented in a particular way.

### 5.5.3  Microsoft Intermediate Language

The instructions contained in the intermediate language MSIL (Lidin 2002) are similar in concept to Java bytecodes. The MSIL is stack oriented, with all operations taking place via an operand (or evaluation) stack. Rather than provide the same level of detail as we did for Java bytecodes, we instead focus on the significant ways in which the MSIL differs from Java bytecodes.

Figure 5.18 illustrates the MSIL memory architecture. For a given method, a local data area and an argument area are defined, but they are not defined as part of a stack frame as in Java. In an implementation they would probably be held on an implementation-specific stack, but there are no instructions in the MSIL that assume they are part of the same stack. That is, they are simply regions of memory accessible when a method is executing. Rather than having a constant pool, MSIL supports a number of metadata tables, referred to as *streams*, which contain information similar to that held in the Java constant pool. Furthermore, instructions can push constant values, either long (four bytes) or short (one byte), onto the operand stack. The metadata tables are accessed via *tokens* that are supported by the MSIL. A token contains four

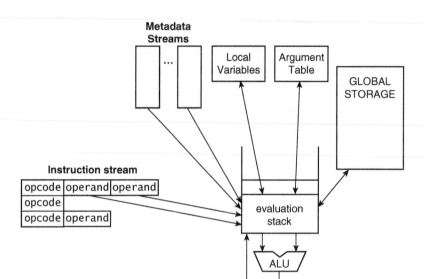

**Figure 5.18** MSIL Memory Architecture.

bytes: One byte is a metadata table (stream) identifier, and the other three bytes point to a particular entry in the table. One of the constant streams holds program-referenced character strings, and there is a special MSIL instruction that can retrieve a string.

The instruction set depends on the same stack-tracking feature as Java to enable static type checking. Also, as with Java bytecodes, all verifiable control flow instructions either have constant PC relative offsets or are method call/returns. Both arrays and vectors are intrinsic data types, but there are explicit MSIL instructions only for vectors, which are similar to the one-dimensional Java arrays. The multidimensional MSIL arrays are accessed via standard API routines. It is also possible to create a managed pointer to a particular array element, to avoid repeated address arithmetic and range checking.

A small example of MSIL code, and its Java counterpart, are given in Figure 5.19. In this example, the instructions match one to one. One ISA difference is that MSIL has more flexibility in specifying data widths; for example, the .i4 indicates an integer of four bytes. Other possibilities (depending on the instruction) are i1, i2, and i8 (integers) and u1, u2, u4, and u8 (unsigned). Another evident difference is that when performing arithmetic, the Java bytecodes explicitly specify the type of operation to be performed. For example, in Java there are separate add-integer and add-float instructions. In contrast, in MSIL there is a single generic add instruction, and the particular

```
0:  iconst_2           0:  ldc.i4.2
1:  aload_0            1:  ldarg.0
2:  getfield  #2       2:  ldobj      <token>
5:  iconst_0           5:  ldc.i4.0
6:  iaload             6:  ldelem.i4
7:  aload_0            7:  ldarg.0
8:  getfield  #2       8:  ldobj      <token>
11: iconst_1           11: ldc.i4.1
12: iaload             12: ldelem.i4
13: iadd               13: add
14: imul               14: mul
15: ireturn            15: ret

        (a)                    (b)
```

**Figure 5.19**    Example of (a) Java Code and (b) Corresponding MSIL Code.

type can be inferred from the types of operands at the top of the stack. In a sense, putting the type of operation in the opcode as in Java is redundant, because stack tracking permits the inference of the type of operation required. However, implementing this inference as part of an interpreter would slow down interpretation. It is apparently the intention (although not an absolute requirement) that MSIL will not be interpreted but will always be compiled before being executed, e.g., by a JIT compiler. Finally, in Java, items such as field descriptors are all in the constant pool, whereas MSIL uses metadata tokens, and the tokens point to items in one of the several streams contained in a program module.

If they are not specifically designed to do so, conventional programming languages such as C and C++ do not run as verified code in CLI. In C and C++ programs, memory can be allocated and accessed without the restrictions of Java or C# programs. Blocks of memory of unspecified type can be allocated, and pointers can be manipulated as data; i.e., arbitrary arithmetic, logical, and shift instructions can be performed on pointers, and they can be freely copied. To support C-like memory operations (and control flow), MSIL contains a number of unverifiable instructions.

Unmanaged pointers are simply represented as 32-bit integers on the native platform. With unverifiable code, it is possible to allocate and access C-style blocks of memory. The local block-allocate instruction (localloc) creates a block of untyped memory; a copy-block instruction (cpblk) copies a block of memory from a location indicated by one unmanaged pointer to an area indicated by a second unmanaged pointer. The initialize-block (initblk) instruction initializes all the elements of a memory block to a specified value. Because the pointers to the blocks of memory are unmanaged, they can be used in much the same way as in C.

With regard to control flow, the managed code branch instructions are adequate for both verifiable and unverifiable code. For procedures calls, there is a call-indirect (`calli`) instruction that uses an unmanaged pointer for identifying the called procedure.

### 5.5.4 Isolation and AppDomains

A final feature of the CLI of interest is its support for isolated, independent applications running on the same VM. This feature is probably most useful for increasing overall system efficiency when multiple application programs are running at the same time; this would be the common mode of operation in a server, for example. As a matter of security, these application programs should be isolated from each other, because they typically perform functions for a number of different users. A straightforward way of implementing isolation is to give each program its own virtual machine, which, in turn is supported as a user-level process by the host platform's operating system. This method is illustrated in Figure 5.20a. It is a rather heavy-weight resource-intensive approach, however, with lots of unneeded replication at both the VM level and the host process level.

A possible solution in Java is to implement isolation via the class loader system, by giving each application a different namespace (see Section 6.1). However, class loaders, as it turns out, do not provide absolute separation, and this has resulted in security holes (McGraw and Felten 1999).

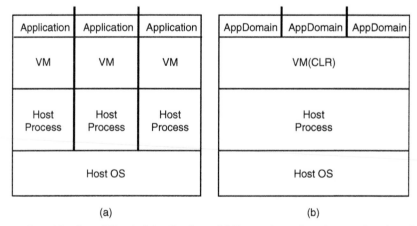

**Figure 5.20**   Supporting a Number of Identical Applications. *(a) By running each on its own virtual machine; (b) by using AppDomains.*

To solve the isolation problem in an efficient way, the CLI supports AppDomains (application domains), which provide the desired lightweight isolation. A number of independent processes can share the same virtual machine, with complete isolation (see Figure 5.20b). Hence, only one VM and one host platform are required, thereby maximizing the system resources available to the programs doing the work. Note that each of the processes may contain multiple threads, as is always the case with CLI processes.

## 5.6 Summary: Virtual ISA Features

Process VMs targeted at conventional ISAs are in a sense backward looking, in that they are attempting to provide compatibility with platforms developed years (often decades) in the past. In contrast, The HLL virtual ISAs (e.g., Java bytecodes and the Microsoft CIL) are forward looking; they are developed with support for evolving and future applications as the goal. When coupled with libraries, the VM platform provides flexible support for the object-oriented programming paradigm, secure network computing, and component-based program development.

To summarize this chapter, we compare the features of the virtual ISAs with those of conventional ISAs. This summary is centered on a number of issues identified in the preceding chapters, where process VMs are constructed and conventional ISAs are virtualized. This comparison provides additional insight regarding the features of existing virtual ISAs and may provide direction for developing future ones.

### 5.6.1 Metadata

A conventional ISA does not have metadata. The compiler uses information regarding declared data structures at the time it generates binary code and then throws it away; all data-structure information becomes implicit in the binary code. In a V-ISA, data-structure information is maintained along with the program's binary code. Then at load time and at run time, this metadata information enables type-safe code verification, which is a key part of enforcing security. And in the case of the CLI, it enables close interoperability of code generated from different programming languages. The metadata information also has potential for improving emulation performance by providing the underlying emulation engine with data-related information that would be very difficult to discover from binary code alone.

## 5.6.2 Memory Architecture

In a conventional ISA, logical memory is a fixed size, with addresses that are a feature of the ISA (and can be made known to a running program). The address space may be flat and linear, or it may be segmented; but if it is segmented, the segments are often of fixed size. This feature can lead to a "fit" problem when emulating a guest ISA on a host platform that has a smaller logical memory size. There can also be fit problems even if the memory sizes are the same because in most process VMs, the VM software must share an address space with a guest application process.

Furthermore, in a conventional memory architecture, the ISA makes specific addresses visible to the user program. For example, if a sbrk() system call is performed in a UNIX system (to get more memory), a specific user-readable address pointer is returned. Furthermore, a user process can change the protections on the basis of specific memory addresses, at page-size granularity, for example, with the mmap() system call. This page-size granularity leads to process VM implementation problems, for example, if the guest page size is smaller than the host page size.

These problems do not occur in the common virtual ISAs because memory architecture is more abstract and is of indefinite size. The basic approach is to allocate memory regions (e.g., objects or stack frames) based on a process's logical requirements and to provide a reference to the base of the memory region when it is allocated. The stack and heap are of undefined size, and the actual contents of the stack pointer or an object reference are not made available to a user process because the V-ISA has no provisions for doing so. Memory accesses can be made relative to the stack pointer and object references, but the actual values they contain cannot be explicitly read or written. This restricts the V-ISA-level process to having only a logical view of memory, and real memory locations are irrelevant.

Although the architected memory space (for stack or heap) is of indefinite size, the actual implementation resources must be finite. Consequently, it is possible for a process to ask for more memory space resources than are available. When this happens, there is an exception that informs the user process this has occurred, and the process can, perhaps, take corrective action. This is not a large limitation, however, because many modern high-level programming languages that work with stacks and heap objects have this limitation anyway. What is being done here is that the idea of a memory space of indefinite size is being moved down to the V-ISA level; e.g., even a V-ISA "assembly language" programmer must deal with an indefinite memory space.

### 5.6.3 Memory Address Formation

In a conventional ISA, address computation is essentially unrestricted. That is, addresses can be generated using any of the available instructions, so arbitrary addresses to any part of memory can be generated for use by virtually any load or store. This leads to a number of problems with respect to process VM implementations. One problem is that the regions of memory used by the VM software (the runtime) are difficult to protect from the emulated guest program (see Section 3.4.3). This becomes especially problematic if guest registers are memory mapped.

The solution used in the common V-ISAs is to prevent arbitrary address arithmetic for loads and stores. The first part of this solution is to force all addressing to take place via explicit memory pointers (references). In addition, performing arbitrary arithmetic on references is prohibited. This is done by having a special reference type and by restricting the operations that can be performed on a reference. Finally, if a reference is known to access only a given structure (an object), then the declared structure and properties of the object can be used to validate an address. Depending on the availability of information, the check can be performed statically at compile (translation) time or at run time.

### 5.6.4 Precise Exceptions

With a conventional ISA, the entire process state at the time of a trap or interrupt must be precise, and many instructions may trap. Furthermore, it is often the case that global mask bits can enable or disable traps and interrupts, and these mask bits potentially can change over the course of a program's execution. As we saw in Chapters 3 and 4, the requirement for precise traps can lead to complications and/or performance loss when a VM is implemented.

In the case of V-ISAs, there are typically fewer instructions that can cause exceptions, and the requirement to test for exceptions is encoded into the program and cannot be changed via mask bits. Hence, the decision about whether an exception must be checked can be based on locally available information; it does not depend on global mask bits. Furthermore, the requirements for precise exceptions are somewhat relaxed. For example, in Java the state of the operand stack does not have to be precise (in fact the operand stack is discarded when an exception is thrown). Furthermore, if an exception handler is not local to a method, then none of the local variables held in the frame must be precise after an exception is thrown and the method's frame is discarded.

### 5.6.5 Instruction Set Features

With regard to conventional ISA features that can facilitate (or complicate) emulation, the two major ones are the register set and condition codes. It is awkward to emulate a guest register set having more registers than the host register set. To binary translate such a guest instruction set, a register context area has to be defined in the host memory, and register load/stores have to be performed to move data between the host registers and the register context area. Besides the data-movement overhead involved, protecting the register context area becomes a problem, as noted earlier.

Of course, the smallest possible register set has no registers at all; local values and operands can be maintained on a stack rather then being held in registers. It is for this reason (as well as code density) that most of the common V-ISAs are stack oriented. With respect to condition codes, the bigger problems occur when emulating an ISA with condition codes on a host platform that does not support condition codes. Hence, it is preferable to avoid condition codes in ISAs, as in current V-ISAs.

### 5.6.6 Instruction Discovery

With arbitrary ISAs, code discovery is problematic (see Section 2.6). The root cause is indirect jumps to potentially arbitrary locations. When combined with variable-length instructions and embedded data, it is hard (or impossible) to discover code that goes beyond an indirect jump. Clearly, the solution is to restrict indirect jumps. In particular, in V-ISAs they are restricted to be explicit procedure (or method) calls and returns where the return addresses are protected from modifications. Then, because all conditional branches are to PC-relative addresses where the offset is a constant, control flow is statically discoverable. V-ISAs also separate data from code, although they do permit variable-length instructions. However, because all control flow is exposed and explicit and there is no embedded data, variable-length instructions by themselves do not pose a problem. The net result is that the virtual ISAs are explicitly designed so that at the time a method is first invoked, all the code contained in the method can be discovered immediately.

### 5.6.7 Self-Modifying and Self-Referencing Code

For most user applications, self-modifying and self-referencing code are not essential; in fact they are typically discouraged. Consequently, self-modifying and self-referencing code are most easily dealt with by simply making them impossible to do; such operations are not embodied in the commonly used V-ISAs. Interestingly, and somewhat ironically, the emulation engine running on the host platform may rely heavily on self-modifying code in order to give good performance. For example, writing translated (or JIT-compiled) code into a code cache is a form of self-modifying code.

### 5.6.8 Operating System Dependences

As discussed in earlier chapters, when performing process emulation, it is guest operating system dependencies that are probably more difficult to deal with than instruction set dependencies. All instruction sets contain some elemental instructions that make them functionally complete — any function can be performed; it's just a matter of how efficiently it will be done. With operating systems, however, this may not be the case. Different systems may perform process management, file I/O, networking, graphics, etc. differently.

Hence, in HLL VMs, the preferred way to deal with OS dependencies is to arrive at some kind of least common denominator set of functions and to implement them with standard libraries. These standard libraries must be ported to all desired host platforms. This approach is more easily said than done, however, and on some platforms the fit may not be perfect. However, the library interface is usually at a higher level than a conventional OS interface, so the library writer has more flexibility in achieving at least an acceptable level of compatibility.

# Chapter Six

# High-Level Language Virtual Machine Implementation

T he collection of binary classes or modules that make up a program specify its operation in terms of the HLL VM *architecture*. It is up to the HLL VM *implementation* to carry out the specified operations. This chapter discusses HLL VM implementations, primarily by describing the Java VM, the best known of the HLL VMs. A CLI implementation is similar in many respects. We describe the major implementation components and then look at ways of improving performance in HLL VM implementations. We complete the chapter with a case study of a specific high-performance JVM, the Jikes research VM.

The organization of a typical JVM implementation (Venners 1998) is shown in Figure 6.1. The three major components are the class loader subsystem, the memory system, including a garbage-collected heap, and the emulation engine (sometimes referred to as the *execution engine*). These major components are, in turn, implemented with lower-level components. We first describe the major components briefly and then provide greater detail.

### Memory and State Registers

The memory consists of an area for program code, a global memory area, and stacks for both the architected Java code and for native library code. The program area is implicitly defined for the most part; common sense tells

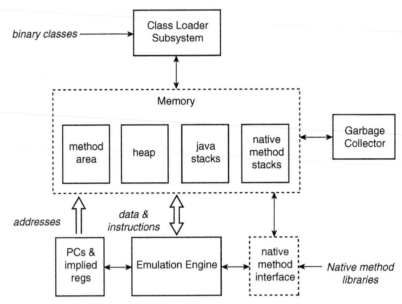

**Figure 6.1**    A Java Virtual Machine Implementation.

us there must be some region for holding the program. However, program memory can only be accessed via the program counter; it is never explicitly accessed with load and store instructions. Furthermore, the program counter contents can never be directly inspected.

The Java stack area was described in Section 5.3.2 and needs no further explanation. The native stack and its interaction with the Java stack are described subsequently as part of the native method interface. Associated with the stack is an implied register, the stack pointer. Just as with the program counter, the stack pointer is used by instructions for accessing memory, but it is not explicitly accessible; i.e., there is no way for a program to inspect the contents of the stack pointer. The exact size of the stack is not architected; that is, it is implementation dependent. If its size is ever exceeded by a running program, the StackOverflowError exception is thrown.

The global memory is a dynamically allocated heap. When a new object instance is created, its memory is allocated from the heap. As with the stack, the heap is of unspecified size. If the heap runs out of space, an OutOfMemoryError is thrown. To reduce the likelihood that this will happen, a garbage collector can be used to reclaim heap memory no longer needed by a running program.

### Garbage Collector

Many Java objects are created, used, and then are no longer needed by the program. This occurs when the last (or only) reference to an object is destroyed or is overwritten. At that point, the object becomes *garbage*, because it is no longer useful to the running program. Because any real JVM implementation will have a limited amount of memory, it is advantageous to reclaim, or collect, the memory space used by the garbage objects so that the physical memory resources can be reused. Consequently, most JVM implementations have a garbage collector, which is responsible for finding those objects no longer needed in order to make room for other, new objects.

### Emulation Engine

The emulation engine, supported by the native method interface and implied registers (i.e., the program counter and the stack pointer), is responsible for emulating the Java bytecode instructions. It can be a simple interpreter, or it can perform a full or partial translation (compilation) to native host instructions. Higher-performance implementations may use profiling and staged emulation techniques to first detect hotspots and then translate to native instructions held in a code cache, as discussed in earlier chapters. Even if a simple interpreter is used, some pretranslation of the program file is performed. For example, some of the indirection in the program file (such as the use of the constant pool) would likely be removed, with immediate values being embedded directly in instructions.

### Native Method Interface

To access operating system–managed functions, the JVM uses a set of standard libraries. These libraries can perform file I/O and graphics operations, for example. Many of the libraries are written in Java, and their associated binary classes are loaded and emulated in essentially the same way as the application-specific methods. However, in practice, at least some of the library code is written in the host's native code in order to bridge the gap between the platform-independent and platform-dependent parts of the overall system. Many calls to the host OS are made through native methods, for example. Providing these native methods (along with other standard library methods) is part of the overall JVM implementation process.

### Class Loader Subsystem

The class loader subsystem performs a number of vital functions for supporting a networked computing environment. Of course, it converts the class file containing metadata and instructions into an implementation-dependent memory image. It is also responsible for finding the binary classes in the first place, often dynamically and on demand, either from the system or from other systems in a network. The loader subsystem is responsible for verifying correctness and consistency of binary classes and is an integral part of maintaining overall security within the network environment. We discuss class loading in more detail in the next section.

## 6.1 Dynamic Class Loading

When a method is called for the first time by a program, the class loader locates the requested binary class; typically it is held in a file. Then it checks the integrity of the binary class and performs any translation of code and metadata in order to make the requested method ready to run.

An important aspect of the network environment is that it must be possible to identify (name) variables, methods, and other data items in a standard, universal way. All variables and methods must be declared as part of a class (which must have a name). Each compiled class is stored as a separate entity, e.g., in a separate file, and one or more classes can be combined into a logical entity known as a *package*. Thus every method or variable has what is called a *fully qualified name*, which consists of the package name, the class name, and the method or variable name, separated by periods, for example, `testpackage.block.mass`. For accessing packages across the Internet, there is a naming convention that is based on Internet domain names. For example, a package might be given the following fully qualified name:

`edu.wisc.ece.jes.testpackage.shape.area`

Here, the Internet domain name ece.wisc.edu (in reverse order, by convention) is prefixed to an internal path name, `jes.testpackage`, to provide a full package name. The access rights to packages, classes, and fields are defined in the following way.

■ A package is accessible according to the access rights on the local system, for example, if the read or execute permission allows public access when it is being accessed by an external (nonlocal) user.

- Classes within a package are accessible to all other classes within the same package (this scoping property is one of the reasons for having packages in the first place).

- A class that is declared as public is accessible from other packages; a nonpublic class is only accessible from within its own package.

- All fields of a class are accessible from within its own class. Fields are accessible from a different class in the same package if they are not private.

The class loader system implements dynamic loading and is a critical part of the security system. A Java VM implementation must contain a *primordial class loader*, whose operation is defined as part of the JVM specification. In addition, users may also define class loaders as part of a class loader subsystem. The primordial class loader can be relied upon to do the right thing with respect to security; i.e., it is a trusted JVM component.

As just noted, there can be multiple user-defined class loaders, but each one defines a separate *namespace*. A loaded class is "tagged" with the name of the loader that loaded it, so if two classes loaded by different loaders happen to have the same name, they are in different namespaces and can be kept separate. Classes loaded into one namespace cannot interact with classes in other namespaces; indeed they cannot even become aware of the presence of the other namespaces. Hence, in effect, there is a barrier between the different namespaces. Different class loaders are typically used to load classes from different origins; hence, the namespace becomes identified with the origin.

Unlike the primordial class loader, which must be designed to be trustworthy, the user-supplied class loaders are only as trusted as the user who supplies them. This issue can be simplified somewhat because a user-supplied loader can be designed so that it relies on the primordial class loader for assistance in loading binary classes, for example, as a means for ensuring security.

After it locates a binary class, the loader parses it and translates it into internal data structures for emulation by the execution engine. This involves converting the metadata contained in the binary class into an implementation-dependent form that is more amenable to emulation. As part of this process the loader performs some consistency checks. It first checks the magic number at the beginning of the binary class to make sure the given data is at least claimed to be a binary class (this check will mostly turn up simple errors where the VM is being invoked for a "wrong" file). More importantly, the loader checks to make sure all the components are of the sizes indicated in the binary class and that proper formats are used in the various metadata structures. It can also check to make sure the numbers and types of arguments match between calling and called methods. Within the binary class, fully qualified references are resolved. This is often done on demand. The fully qualified references are symbolic. After being resolved, the fully qualified (symbolic) reference is replaced with a direct reference.

Another important function of the loader is to verify the integrity of the bytecode program. That is, it checks to make sure the stack values can be tracked statically, as required of all well-formed programs. Then it performs all the static type checking to make sure there are no program errors and that the protection boundaries will be respected by the program. This process is described in more detail in the next subsection. The loader checks to make sure all references in the constant pool are within the bounds of the programs, and it checks to make sure all branch instructions are to addresses within the procedure where they reside. Finally, after the program is verified as being properly formed, memory is initialized and control passed to the emulation engine.

## 6.2 Implementing Security

The basic protection sandbox was described in general terms in Section 5.2.1. This is the default security model used in Java, although the model has been greatly enhanced in the Java 2 specification. In this section we first elaborate on the basic security model and then describe the Java 2 enhancements.

In the sandbox model, the overall objective is to form a barrier around the Java execution environment so that a user application is confined to operate within the bounds of the sandbox and cannot affect any other system or network resources, whether unintentionally or maliciously. As discussed in Section 5.2.1, there are three main parts to the sandbox.

First, remote files must be protected. As pointed out earlier, the protection of remote files is within the province of the remote system. Any files on the remote system are given access privileges by the owner of the file, and, ultimately, these are maintained by the remote OS, whether Windows, Linux, or any other OS. These are the same privileges as for any type of remote access, whether inside or outside the Java execution framework.

Second, local files must be protected from a running Java program. That is, the owner of the local files, typically the user running the Java program, must control access to the files. This part of the protection sandbox is implemented via the security manager, described in more detail in Section 6.2.2.

Third, the JVM code and data must be protected from the running Java program. That is, the Java program should not be allowed to read or write data associated with the Java VM side tables, for example. Furthermore, the program should not be allowed to branch or jump to arbitrary locations in the JVM. This third part of the protection sandbox is implemented via a combination of static and dynamic checking, with static checking performed by the loader playing a key role in this process. The next subsection discusses this intraprocess protection part of the sandbox, and this is followed by the discussion of the security manager.

### 6.2.1 Intraprocess Protection

One of the more challenging aspects of building a modern network-oriented HLL VM is the ability to take untrusted program code from the network, combine it with trusted VM code to form a single host-supported user process, and then execute the untrusted program efficiently. A basic objective is to make sure the application code only accesses its own memory locations and can interact with the JVM (and the rest of the host platform) only via method calls to libraries containing locally trusted code.

It is the ability to construct a protection sandbox that most clearly separates the modern HLL VMs from the earlier P-code-like VMs. To understand this, consider the typical P-code environment. Here, the compiler is a trusted element; i.e., it is assumed by the user to be correctly implemented. The Pascal language is designed so that the compiler can check data-type information at compile time, based on the data declarations made by the programmer. After this checking is complete, the P-code is generated. Then the static data-type information is no longer needed; rather, it is built into the code that accesses the data, and the user can be assured that the P-code will only access data in the correct way. The P-code alone can be passed to other users to run on their computer systems, thereby achieving platform independence. It is up to the individual users to trust the provider of the P-code program.

The earlier scenario would be fine if other users were always willing to trust the source of their programs, but of course this level of trust is often not present in the networked computing environment. Yet a user would like to be able to execute programs that are made widely available for network-based computing. A solution to the problem of untrusted code is to transmit not only the application code but also a checkable description of the data structures on which the code will operate, i.e., the metadata. Then when the program is loaded by the end user, the (trusted) loader will perform static checks of the program with the declared metadata information. If the program code is consistent with the metadata, then the user can be assured that the program will only access its data in a proper (protected) way. Furthermore, the loader can check the control flow information of the program to make sure it branches only to locations within the program itself or performs procedure calls using proper protocols. This is the reason that HLL ISAs stress static type checking and statically traceable control flow information. And, of course, the ability to perform this high degree of static checking derives from the strong typing features incorporated in the high-level language in which the program was written in the first place (e.g., Java or C#).

Now we will illustrate in more detail the features of the Java ISA that allows intraprocess protection. There are two main elements of intraprocess protection. First, it must be guaranteed that the program only accesses its own memory; i.e., it can never make data accesses outside the bounds of its declared memory region. Second, it must be guaranteed that the program will not branch outside its own code region. It can only leave the code region via a library call, and the libraries are trusted code.

We first give an informal inductive argument for the protection of data accesses. Just as data flow is centered on the stack (see Figure 5.9), our argument will revolve around the stack (Figure 6.2). Before any memory accesses have been performed, and with an empty operand stack, the only way to put

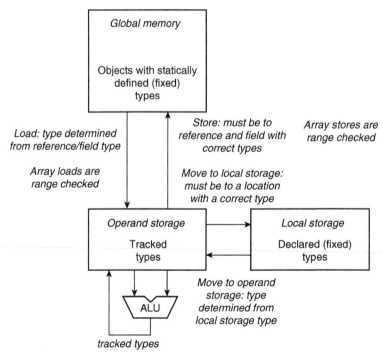

**Figure 6.2**   Data Flow and Intraprocess Protection Checking.

a reference onto the operand stack is from the constant pool or from local memory. The constant-pool entries are statically checked by the loader, as noted earlier, so they can be guaranteed to be valid references (or are null). All local memory locations holding reference types are initialized to null references. Furthermore, all movement between the stack and local memory uses absolute addresses for the local memory locations. Hence, the loader can check the local memory types with the data-movement opcodes to make sure that only reference types are placed into local memory reference locations.

Once on the stack, the types of all elements can be statically tracked (as described near the end of Section 5.3.3). In particular, recall that for any valid program, the number and types of elements on the stack can always be determined from the static code itself. The loader verifies this is the case at the time the program is loaded. Among other things, this means that any data movement of references from the stack to local memory can be checked for the correct types statically.

Pulling all the foregoing together, starting from initial conditions, before any global memory accesses have been made, any reference values on the operand stack either are null or are verified reference values taken from the constant pool (either directly or indirectly through local memory). Furthermore, the types of these references are statically known.

Next, consider accesses to global memory. The first access to global memory is to a location specified by a reference on the operand stack. Because of the ability to track reference types on the stack and in local memory, this reference type is known statically. Hence, if an object is accessed, the field information for the access can also be checked statically (there is an exception for arrays, given in the next paragraph). If the access is a load, the data type being loaded is known statically; if it is a reference type, then the type is also known and can be tracked statically while it is on the stack or in local memory. Similarly, if a value (data or reference) is stored to an object field memory, it can also be checked prior to being stored because of static tracking in local storage and static field definitions; hence the value stored to memory will be consistent with the static field information. By a similar argument, and to complete the induction step, if all data types can be determined from static information prior to a memory access $i$, then the next memory access, $i + 1$, must also yield statically trackable type information.

An important exception to the argument just given involves array accesses. All loads or stores to arrays must use an array reference; these can also be statically checked for type information. However, arrays differ from other objects in that the exact element being accessed may be computed at run time. This means that the actual index into an array must be checked dynamically to make sure it is within the bounds of the array. Furthermore, all references, whether for an array or for a general object, must be checked for null values, in the event that they have not been assigned to an object when they are first used.

Another important place where dynamic checking is required occurs with dynamic casting or conversion of an object reference to a different type. Allowing arbitrary casting of references can break that part of the protection sandbox enabled by static checking, because static checking depends on knowledge of object types. However, casting can be done in situations where the reference is being cast to a superclass (*upcasting*) or a subclass (*downcasting*). The safety of upcasting can be checked at compile time; however, downcasting requires a run-time check to make sure the reference being cast is to a subclass (or the same class) as the object type to which it currently refers.

To summarize, a program, even if it is from an untrusted source, can be checked to make sure it makes no unallowed memory accesses. This is done by a combination of static (load-time) and dynamic (run-time) checks. In Java, much of the checking is done statically. By relying on static type checking, dynamic checking is mostly confined to null pointer checking, bounds checking for array accesses, and dynamic casts to make sure they are being properly done within the class hierarchy. In the high-performance Java discussion to be presented later, we will include analysis methods and optimizations that are able to remove some of these dynamic checks.

Finally, consider the protection provided for control transfers, i.e., the constraint that there never be a branch or jump that leaves the program's valid code region. Control transfers are only through branches, switch statements, and method calls. All the branches and switch statements are to PC relative constant values. Therefore, all the branches and jumps can be statically checked to make sure they branch to instructions only within the given procedure. The only way to exit a method is through a method call/return (or when the program terminates). Therefore, if all methods are internally checked, the overall program is checked.

## 6.2.2 Security Enforcement

In a Java implementation, the security manager is a class belonging to the java.lang API that contains a number of methods for checking to make sure potentially unsafe operations cannot be performed. These operations include reading a specified file, writing a specified file, opening a socket connection to a specified host and port number, and creating a new process, among many others. Such operations are made available to untrusted user programs via methods in (trusted) Java libraries, e.g., the java.io API, that interact directly with the host OS. Before performing a requested action involving an OS call, the trusted library methods first check with the security manager, via the appropriate method call, to make sure it should be allowed.

A security manager check method simply checks the requested operation to see if it is permitted and either throws a security exception if it is not permitted or returns if it is. The security manager is attached when a Java application is initiated and cannot be changed, deleted, or replaced with another thereafter. Hence, an individual user can specify the checks made via the security manager, i.e., which files should be accessed and how, which network ports can be used, etc. Then whenever a Java application is started, these checks will be in effect as long as the application runs.

If the user chooses to use no security manager, then the application has unrestricted access to the user's resources. Of course, the Java application cannot exceed the privileges of the user, because the JVM runs as a user process. Any attempt to go outside the user's resources will be caught by the underlying OS on the host platform.

The security manager cannot protect against everything, overallocating memory or spawning too many threads, for example. In situations like this, it is difficult or impossible to discern the difference between an erroneous or malicious program and one that has large resource requirements. For example, how could one determine the difference between runaway recursion and recursion that is simply very deep? In effect, detecting the difference would be equivalent to solving the classic Turing Machine halting problem. Consequently, some denial of-service attacks are possible, despite the presence of a security manager.

The security manager can be written to implement relatively complex policies. The loaders and security manager may be customized by a software developer or user. For example, the security manager can check to see if a request is made from a locally provided method or from one loaded over the network and can allow different resource accesses depending on which is the case.

## 6.2.3  Enhanced Security Model

The basic security sandbox was extended by adding signing in JDK 1.1 and then enhanced with access control in Java 2 (McGraw and Felten 1999). Adding the notion of identity and signing gets away from the all-or-nothing sandbox approach and allows more flexible, finer-grained security policies, where code from different sources may be granted different access privileges to user resources.

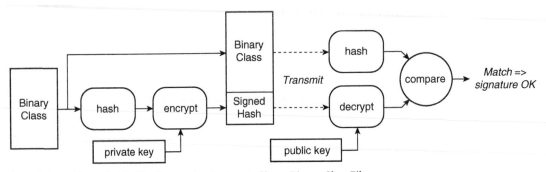

**Figure 6.3**    Using a Public Key Encryption System to Sign a Binary Class File.

If particular outside program sources can be securely identified, then a wide variety of security policies can be implemented, each one depending on the specific source of a given application program. A technology that supports secure identification of sources is *signing*. The basic idea of signing is simple: if a piece of code brought in from the outside can be signed in a nonforgeable way, then the local security system can inspect the signature and provide access privileges appropriate for the given (signed) piece of code.

Signing is based on public key encryption systems (Diffie and Hellman 1976). In a public key encryption system there is public key/private key pair. A message is encrypted with the public key and is decrypted with the private key. The critical feature of the system is that the private key cannot be determined from the public key in any practical way. Consequently, only the owner of the private key can decrypt a message.

The application of public key encryption technology to signing application code (and other types of data) is illustrated in Figure 6.3. The source of application code (a binary class) first hashes the code down to a smaller size (for reasons of overall efficiency) and then encrypts the hashed version with the private key. The hashed, encrypted version is a signature appended to the binary class and is sent across a network to someone who wishes to execute it. At the receiving end, the received binary class is again hashed (with the same hash function as before), and the signature is decrypted. The two versions of the hashed code are then compared. If they are the same, then the user is assured that the owner (sender) of the binary class is as claimed. The security manager can then grant access to local resources in accordance with a policy established by the local user.

Because the identity of a program's source can be securely identified, the application of the all-or-nothing sandbox for all program sources is no longer necessary. Fine-grained, configurable security policies can be implemented.

For example, programs from one outside source may be allowed to open network connections, while others cannot. One program may be given access only to file A, while another may be given access only to file B.

This flexible approach does pose some potential problems when binary classes from different sources are allowed to interoperate as part of the same program. For example, what if a method belonging to a binary class from a source not having access privileges to a given file calls a method from a source that does have access privileges to the file and then performs a file access indirectly through the called method? The security manager can solve this problem by inspecting the method call stack to check on access privileges not only of a method making a request but of all earlier methods in the call sequence (Wallach and Felten 1998).

Stack inspection is illustrated in Figure 6.4. Each stack frame is appended with *principal* information indicating whether the method came from a trusted system source or an untrusted source. Also, there is information regarding the access privileges that reside with the source of the method. After a sequence of method calls, the resulting stack frames are shown in the figure. Untrusted method 2 had permissions to write file A but is restricted from accessing other files. On the other hand, method 4 does have permission to write to file B.

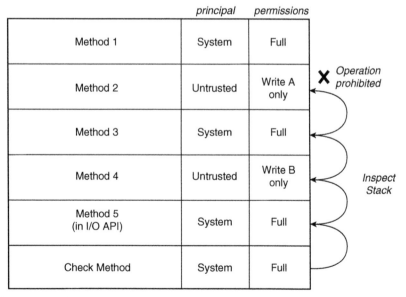

**Figure 6.4**  Method Call Stack Extended with Resource Access Permissions. *The security manager inspects the stack to enforce protection.*

Now, when method 4 attempts a write to file B, it will do so via the I/O API method 5 that first calls a security manager check method. The security manager walks the stack in reverse order, checking access permissions of all the methods that it finds on the stack. When it comes to method 2, it finds that permission to write file B should not be granted and throws an exception.

## 6.3 Garbage Collection

In an object-oriented programming environment, objects can be freely created, used, and later discarded when they are no longer needed. The programmer is given the illusion of an unbounded memory space and does not have to worry about explicitly allocating and managing a fixed-size memory. Of course, in reality, memory resources are not unbounded, and eventually a program can run out of memory resources (which would result in an OutOfMemory exception being thrown). To prevent this from happening (or at least forestall it), objects that are no longer accessible (i.e., "garbage") can be collected and then reused for new objects.

In our simple example in Figure 5.5, when the reference a is assigned to a new Rectangle object, the prior Rectangle object it pointed to becomes inaccessible. This is the typical way that an object becomes garbage — the last (or only) reference to it is overwritten with a reference to a different object of the same type. In other cases, the last reference may simply be discarded, e.g., by popping it from the stack.

A garbage collector is part of essentially every JVM implementation, although it is not strictly required as part of the JVM specification. When the JVM is running low on memory resources or at periodic intervals, the garbage collector is invoked to find the inaccessible garbage objects and collect their memory resources for later use. A typical situation is illustrated in Figure 6.5. Here, a *root set* of references point to objects held in the global memory heap. Some of these objects, in turn, contain references that point to other objects, and so on. Also, there are some objects that cannot be reached through a sequence of references beginning with the root set; these are the garbage objects.

To begin a garbage collection operation, it is first necessary to identify the root pointers. By referring back to Figure 5.7 (and considering the Java instruction set) we can see that the root set must contain references somewhere on the stack, including both local storage and the operand stack, or in the constant pool. The root set must also include references contained in static objects. Any access to global memory, i.e., through a getfield or

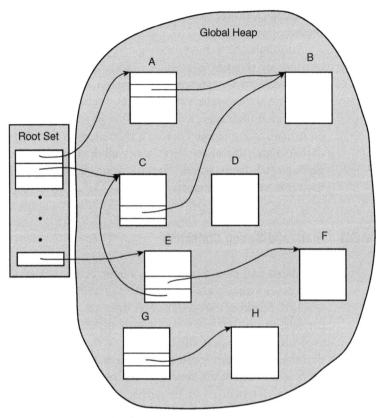

**Figure 6.5** A Garbage-Collected Heap. *The objects G, D, and H are garbage.*

putfield instruction, must get its reference from one of these places, and any object that cannot be accessed via a series of references beginning with some member of the root set simply cannot be reached. Hence, garbage collection finds all the objects that can be accessed, beginning with the root set of references; any objects not found during this process are garbage that can be collected. There are a number of approaches for performing these operations (Jones 1996; Wilson 1992; Appel 1991), and in the following subsections we summarize some of the major classes of garbage-collection techniques.

During the discussion, a number of tradeoffs are considered. Time spent collecting garbage is time not spent computing, so the overhead of garbage collection is an important overall implementation consideration. Moreover, different methods organize the heap differently, collect the garbage into free space differently, and may implement object references differently. Consequently, the important tradeoffs to be considered involve garbage-collection time, object-allocation time, object-access time, and the efficiency with which the heap space is used.

Although there have been garbage collectors that keep a count of the number of references to each object on the heap and consider as garbage any object whose reference count goes to zero (Collins 1960), such reference counting collectors are relatively uncommon in JVMs. Most JVMs use the general method suggested earlier, that is, to start with a set of root references and then *trace* through chains of references in the heap to find all the objects that are reachable or are "live." Then all the unreachable objects are considered garbage and are recycled. The following discussion of garbage collectors will focus on tracing collectors.

### 6.3.1 Mark-and-Sweep Collectors

The mark-and-sweep collector is a basic collector that starts with the root references and traces through all the reachable objects, *mark*ing each one as it is reached. Marking may consist of setting a flag bit contained as part of the object implementation or in a separate bitmap, where each entry in the map is associated with an object. If an already-marked object is reached, then tracing down that particular path stops. After all live objects have been found and marked, there is a *sweep* stage, where all the objects are inspected and the unmarked ones are determined to be garbage and can be reused. As garbage objects are found during the sweep stage, they can be combined into a linked list of free objects.

Overall, this is a relatively fast way of identifying and collecting garbage. However, the free objects are of varying size and are scattered around the heap space, interspersed with the live objects. Simply linking together free objects leads to a memory fragmentation problem that in turn leads to a significant inefficiency when a new object is created and a suitably sized free space must be found for it. Specifically, the allocation algorithm must search the linked list to find an appropriately sized block of contiguous free memory). Eventually fragmentation becomes so great that compaction is required.

Inefficiencies can be reduced, however, by using segregated free lists. That is, by dividing the heap into a set of fixed-size chunks having a range of sizes, e.g., from 16 bytes to 2KB, and maintaining the free space as multiple linked lists, one for each chunk size (Comfort 1964). Then the object allocator can simply go to a free list and get a chunk of the appropriate size (i.e., the smallest one that is large enough to hold the object being allocated). Provisions must be made for occasionally rebalancing the space in each size category, but overall allocation efficiency is significantly improved. In general, dynamic memory allocation is very closely associated with garbage collection. An excellent survey of memory allocation techniques, including segregated free lists, is Wilson et al. (1995).

A conceptually straightforward approach to improving allocation efficiency is to consolidate all the garbage space into a large contiguous region from which new objects can be created. There are two ways of consolidating the garbage space: by compacting and by copying. These are described in the next two subsections.

### 6.3.2 Compacting Collectors

A compacting collector, as its name suggests, essentially "slides" the live objects to the bottom (or top) of the heap memory area so that all live objects are adjacent. What is left is a contiguous region of free space. For example, Figure 6.6 shows the contents of memory with live objects (shaded in dark gray) and garbage objects (shaded in light gray). During compaction, the live objects are moved to a contiguous region of the heap (at the bottom in this example), and the unused space also becomes a contiguous region, from which new objects can be allocated.

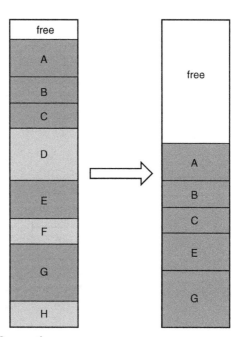

**Figure 6.6**   Example of Garbage Compaction.

Although conceptually simple, a compacting collector is relatively slow, in that it makes multiple passes through the heap. One pass does the marking, and then subsequent passes compute the new locations for the live objects, move the objects, and update all references to point to the new locations. Other methods, to be summarized shortly, improve efficiency by reducing the number of passes and/or analyzing only a subset of the heap during each collection step.

Compacting collection also highlights an issue that occurs with any of the schemes that move objects in memory as a part of garbage collection. That is, the references to the objects must be changed when objects are moved, and this complicates (and slows) the overall process. However, to reduce the number of reference updates, some systems have used a *handle pool* for consolidating pointers to each of the individual objects. Then a reference to an object points to the associated pointer in the handle pool. This is illustrated in Figure 6.7. With the handle pool, it is not necessary to find and update all the references to an object when the object is moved; rather, only the pointer in the handle pool has to be changed, and all references are then automatically modified in the process. The big disadvantage of this approach is that every object access includes an additional level of indirection.

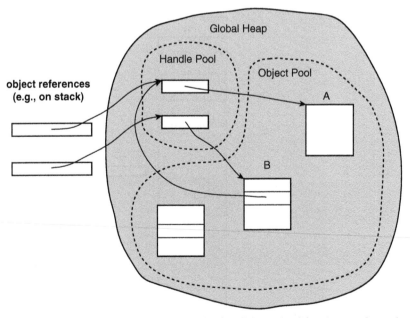

**Figure 6.7**    Handle Pool. *Using a level of indirection (through a handle) can simplify pointer updates when an object is moved during garbage collection.*

### 6.3.3 Copying Collectors

To reduce the number of passes through the heap during collection, a copying collector trades memory space for collection time. It does this by dividing the heap into two halves. At any point in time, one half is unused while the other contains the active heap. When the active half fills up, the collector makes a pass through the heap just as it does during a mark phase; however, it combines the sweep with the mark phase. When it finds a live object, it immediately moves it into the unused half of the heap and continues the pass through the heap. When the pass through the heap is complete, the live objects are in contiguous locations in what was formerly the unused half of the heap, the remainder of the second half is free, and the first half of the heap (which was formerly active) becomes unused. A copying collector is illustrated in Figure 6.8. A copying collector is faster than a compacting collector, but it also has higher memory requirements because half of the heap space, by definition, is unused at any given time.

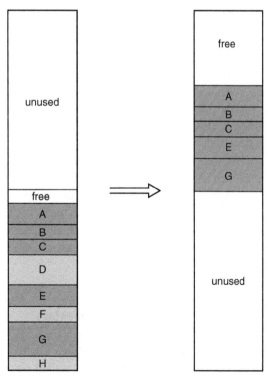

**Figure 6.8**    Example of Garbage Collection via Copying.

### 6.3.4 Generational Collectors

Both compacting and copying collectors move a very large fraction of dynamic objects every time collection is performed. A long-lived object may be moved many times during its lifetime; this rather wasteful movement can be avoided by observing that object lifetimes have a bimodal distribution. First, many objects have very short lifetimes; this is often a by-product of good object-oriented programming practice. Second, objects that do not have short lifetimes tend to have very long lifetimes. Consequently, generational garbage collectors attempt to group objects according to their age in order to avoid repeated copying of the long-lived objects.

In a basic generational collector, the heap is divided into subheaps. For simplicity, we describe the implementation with two subheaps, but generalization to more than two subheaps is straightforward. Of the two subheaps, one is intended to hold the older, or *tenured*, objects. Meanwhile, the other subheap serves as a *nursery* for newly created objects. The nursery is garbage-collected much more frequently than the tenured subheap. If an object survives a certain (usually small) number of collections in the nursery, it is moved to the tenured subheap. Consequently, the longer-lived objects eventually are placed in the tenured section of the heap, where the garbage collections are infrequent, thus avoiding unnecessary object movement.

Not only is the total overhead for collecting reduced, but a smaller portion of the heap is collected each time the collector is invoked. This means that if the running process is stopped while collection takes place, the "pause" time is much reduced. With a large heap and a conventional compacting or copying collector, the time that a program is stopped for collection can be noticeable to the user.

The two subheaps of a generational collector do not necessarily have to be managed the same way. In fact, they can be managed differently to take advantage of performance tradeoffs. A specific hybrid algorithm studied as part of the Jikes JVM project (Attanasio et al. 2001) uses a copying collector for the nursery, which yields fast allocation of new objects, and a mark-and-sweep collector for the tenured objects, which reduces collection time by eliminating pointer updates.

### 6.3.5 Incremental and Concurrent Collectors

All of the basic collectors described earlier stop program execution while they perform collection and then return control to the program. Collection can be time consuming (even if generational collection is used), so program

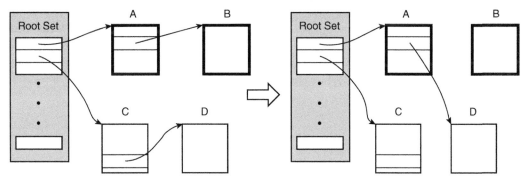

**Figure 6.9**   A Problem with Concurrent Garbage Collection. *A reference in an object may be modified after the object has been marked.*

execution may pause for a significant time period while the collector is working. Collection time may be spread out if collection is done incrementally as the program runs rather than all at once. Furthermore, in real-time applications, the garbage-collection time may be limited to provide adequate response latencies. If multiple processors are available, it may be advantageous to collect garbage concurrently with one thread while normal program execution proceeds using other threads. In both cases, a partially collected heap may be in a state of flux while the program is running. This implies there must be some synchronization between the running program and the garbage collector, so the program does not attempt to reference an object at the time it is being moved; i.e., at a time when pointers may be temporarily inconsistent. Or the program may be changing references at the time the collector is tracing a reference path, leading to similar synchronization problems.

Many of the conventional stop-and-collect methods can be converted to incremental versions. A basic problem with concurrent or incremental collections is that at any given time, an object may have been scanned and marked. Then while collection is still in progress, a reference in the already-scanned object may be changed to point to an object that has not yet been marked. An example is in Figure 6.9. In this example, the objects A and B have been marked (as indicated by the bold boxes). The other objects have not yet been marked. Then before they can be marked, the pointer to object B is replaced with a pointer to object D. If this is the only pointer to D, then D may never be marked and will be incorrectly discarded as garbage. The object B may also be incorrectly retained, but this is not a problem; it will be collected on the next garbage-collection pass.

There are a number of solutions to this problem; they all provide some form of synchronization between the running application (which may change the contents of the heap) and the collector. One of the common solutions is to provide *write barriers* for references to objects that have already been marked. These write barriers basically check for the case where a pointer in an already-marked object is overwritten. When this occurs, the object pointed to is marked (and put on the queue of objects whose pointers should be followed as marking proceeds).

### 6.3.6 Discovering the Root Set

As stated at the beginning of this section, before beginning garbage collection it is necessary to identify the root pointers. The root set for Java programs (and similarly for CLI) consists of references held in the stack, the constant pool, and contained in static objects. However, this is what one might call the "architected" root set. In a particular VM implementation, the actual pointers may reside in registers and various implementation-specific runtime memory locations. For example, the architected stack elements may be assigned to registers by the dynamic compiler, and some of these could be spilled to memory.

Therefore, at the time garbage collection is invoked, it is necessary to construct the architected root set from the implementation storage locations that may potentially hold root set pointers. The basic solution for finding the root set is for the compilation/optimization system to keep side tables, or maps, that indicate where the architected root set elements may be found, if needed for garbage collection. This solution requires that the VM runtime and compilers keep track of the architected root values as dynamic compilation and optimization are performed (Stichnoth, Lueh, and Cuerniak 1999).

The foregoing approach is referred to as *type accurate* or *exact* because it uses the exact root set as a starting point. A less conservative solution is to take all the implementation registers and memory locations that can *possibly* hold root pointers and assume they *do* hold root pointers (Boehm and Weiser 1988). These will form a superset of the true root set. Some of these may be eliminated from consideration (e.g., if they hold small integer values that are clearly not memory addresses). Then the garbage collector begins with this root superset. This approach frees the compilation/optimization system from keeping track of root set references and saves runtime side table space for keeping track of the mappings at all potential garbage-collection points. A problem with this superset approach, however, is that a garbage collector that moves objects, e.g., a compacting collector, cannot be used, because a region of memory may be identified as an object of a given type when it is not really an object. Then if such an apparent "object" is moved, it will damage any real objects that contain the apparent object as part of their memory region.

### 6.3.7 Garbage-Collection Summary

No one collector works best across all programs because programs vary in working set size, object sizes, heap sizes, and the rate at which objects are created (and freed). Hence, we cannot arrive at hard-and-fast conclusions regarding the "best" collector (as the hundreds of papers on the topic attest). We can summarize the important performance tradeoffs in general terms, however. Table 6.1 qualitatively compares the major collector categories in terms of (1) collection time, (2) object allocation time, (3) object access time, and (4) memory efficiency (i.e., the relative total heap space that can maintain a working set of a given size). In addition to these criteria, all the "moving" collectors, i.e., the compacting and copying collectors, require an exact root set, as noted earlier.

The use of a generational collector is a somewhat orthogonal consideration because a generational collector can be used with any of the basic approaches (or as a hybrid). The advantage of a generational collector is that it reduces collection time by focusing only on those objects where garbage is most likely to be found (the nursery). Today, generational collection is usually considered to be a winning strategy. A study of garbage collection in the Jikes JVM (Attanasio et al. 2001) describes the performance tradeoffs with respect to specific benchmark programs.

**Table 6.1**    Comparison of Basic Garbage Collectors

| Collector | Collection Time | Object Allocation Time | Access Time | Memory Efficiency | Comments |
|---|---|---|---|---|---|
| Mark and sweep | Good | Poor | Good | Medium | Allocation requires search for proper-size free memory block |
| Mark and sweep (multisizes) | Good | Medium | Good | Medium | Multisizes help allocation time more than it benefits memory efficiency |
| Compacting | Poor | Good | Good | Good | Collection requires multiple passes |
| Copying (with handles) | Medium | Good | Poor | Poor | Memory efficiency poor due to unused space |
| Copying (without handles) | Medium to poor | Good | Good | Poor | Pointers must be found and updated for all moved objects |

## 6.4 Java Native Interface

The Java native interface (JNI), as described in Section 5.3.6, is a way of allowing Java programs and native compiled programs to interoperate. An important consideration when implementing the JNI is the accessing of Java data structures in a safe way, i.e., in a way that maintains the integrity of Java objects and the stack.

From the perspective of a Java program, a call to a native method is in some respects similar to executing a single (very complex) instruction. There are arguments and a return value, but the Java stack is not used by the called method; rather, the native methods use their own platform-dependent stack. The management of this native stack must be done by trusted JVM code. The JVM implementation supports both a Java stack and a native stack, with one native stack per Java thread (see Figure 6.10). When there is a call to a native method, it is intercepted by the JVM, which then sets up the native stack frame, transfers arguments, and then transfers control to the called method. Similarly, on a return, it places a result onto the Java stack frame and returns control to emulation. In the JNI, a native method may "call back" a Java method; when this happens, a Java stack frame is placed on the stack frame of the calling native method.

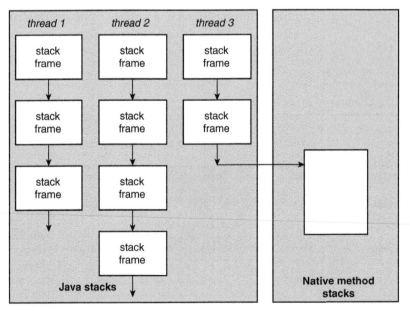

**Figure 6.10** Java and Native Stacks. *In a VM implementation, the native library stack is managed separately from the architected VM stack.*

A native method can be given access to objects and arrays via the JNI. However, once the native method has an array or object reference, the array or object must be protected from garbage collection. That is, the native method assumes the object to be at a particular memory location, and an object-moving garbage collector would violate this assumption. Even with a nonmoving collector, if the native method should happen to have the only reference at some point, then the garbage collector may attempt to collect it (because the reference will not be in the garbage collector's normal root set). To prevent this from happening, the JNI method that passes the native method a reference also "pins" the referenced object so that it will not be moved or collected. With a non-moving collector, the JVM could also add the reference to the root set.

## 6.5 Basic Emulation

The emulation engine in a JVM can be implemented in a number of ways, with different complexities and performance levels. The simplest method uses straightforward interpretation of bytecode instructions. In general, this is no different than interpretation of a conventional ISA as described in detail in Chapter 2. A more advanced, and commonly used, emulation method performs just-in-time (JIT) compilation (Tabatabai et al. 1998; Aycock 2003). With a JIT compiler, methods are compiled at the time they are first invoked, i.e., "just in time" for execution. This compilation essentially performs a translation from the bytecode instructions to native host instructions. Method-at-a-time JIT compilation is enabled because, in contrast to a conventional ISA, the Java ISA is designed so that all the instructions in a method can easily be discovered at the time the method is first entered.

A JIT compiler bears a very close relationship to the binary translators discussed earlier in this book and could just as easily be called a JIT "translator." In fact, it seems that the reason one is called a "compiler" and the other is a "translator" is that two different groups of people came up with the names. A JIT compiler differs from a conventional compiler in that it doesn't have a frontend that parses a high-level language program and performs syntax checking before converting it to an intermediate form. The bytecode program, having passed through the loader, is assumed to be syntactically correct. The bytecode instructions are essentially an intermediate representation themselves, although most JIT compilers will transform the bytecode instructions into a different intermediate form before performing optimizations.

A dynamic, run-time compiler can perform most (if not all) of the optimizations performed by a classical static compiler as well as others that are more specific to Java programs. Many optimizations are time consuming, however, and this adds to the run-time overhead of executing a Java program. Consequently, a JIT compiler may include multiple optimization levels, with more sophisticated optimizations being applied to methods that are more frequently executed. This leads to a form of staged optimization applied at the method level. An even more efficient strategy is to apply optimizations selectively only to code regions that are heavily used rather than to the entire method that may contain such a region.

A typical high-performance emulation engine begins with interpretation, supplemented with profiling to locate frequently used methods. Then when a usage threshold is reached for a given method, the method is compiled with minimal optimization. Later, depending on the level of use, selected code sections within hot methods may be further optimized. The Sun HotSpot (Meloan 1999; Paleczny, Vick, and Click 2001) and the IBM DK (Suganuma et al. 2000) follow this overall strategy. Some systems skip the initial interpretation step in favor of a simple compilation; this approach is taken in the Jikes RVM (to be described in more detail later), for example. A more complete discussion of dynamic optimization in HLL VMs is given in the next section.

## 6.6 High-Performance Emulation

As with most other virtual machine applications, performance is an important consideration in HLL VMs. There are two challenges when dealing with HLL VMs. The first is the same as in other dynamic optimizing VMs: to offset the run-time optimization overhead with the program execution-time improvement. The second challenge is to make an object-oriented program go fast. Object-oriented programs typically include frequent use of addressing indirection for both data and code, as well as frequent use of small methods (which suffer the relatively high overhead of method invocation). In this section we will discuss optimization techniques for HLL VMs. These will be discussed in the context of Java, using Java examples, but similar techniques are equally applicable to the CLR, running C# programs, for example.

We begin with a brief discussion of the overall framework of a high-performance HLL emulation engine. Then we describe optimizations that can be performed by a run-time compiler and the virtual machine run-time system. A comprehensive survey of adaptive optimization, including an extensive bibliography, can be found in Arnold et al. (2005).

### 6.6.1 Optimization Framework

The general flow of a dynamic optimization framework is given in Figure 6.11. This flow should look familiar — it is similar to the one used for dynamic binary optimization in process virtual machines discussed in Chapter 4. Many of the same principles hold, so we will not discuss them in detail here. The framework supports a progression from simple interpretation to successively higher levels of compilation, depending on the frequency at which sections of code (i.e., methods) are executed. In some schemes, the interpretation stage is skipped, and the number of optimization levels also varies depending on the particular implementation.

Profiling is an important part of the overall optimization strategy. Profile data can be collected by the interpreter, or it can be provided by compiled code as it executes. A spectrum of instrumentation and sampling techniques can be used, as described in Section 4.3. Often, profiling is done at the method level rather than the basic block level as in Chapter 4. One can construct a call graph, similar to a control flow graph, which has methods as nodes and arcs connecting caller and callee nodes. An example is given later as part of Figure 6.12.

At a minimum, the profile data should track method usage, e.g., node counts in the call graph. When a method usage threshold is reached (or some more complex cost–benefit analysis indicates that it is called for), the next level of optimization is applied to the "hot" method. Other profile information can

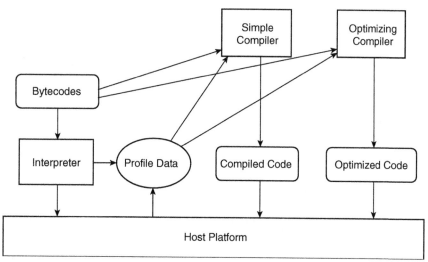

**Figure 6.11**    A Typical Dynamic Optimization Framework.

track edge counts in the call graph to guide method inlining, or conventional edge profiling can be used for code layout optimizations. Finally, dynamic data and pointer information may be profiled in order to generate specially optimized code that takes advantage of the values and/or data types that occur very frequently within a code region.

The compilers can provide a range of optimizations, some of which are applied at a relatively low level, e.g., involving redundant-subexpression elimination or strength reduction. Other optimizations restructure and specialize code. Some optimizations are rather specific to the object-oriented paradigm, and others are more general. Finally, some optimizations are performed directly via the compiler acting on the bytecode program as input. Other optimizations are performed dynamically by the runtime system, apart from the compiler. These latter optimizations may support garbage collection or enhance data locality by reorganizing heap objects, for example. In the next section we discuss a number of the more important optimization techniques, including both compiler-based optimizations and runtime-based optimizations.

### 6.6.2 Optimizations

#### Code Relayout

Just as with dynamic binary optimization discussed in Chapter 4, code relayout is a simple and very effective optimization when applied in the context of HLL VMs. Figure 4.19 illustrates code relayout. Most code relayout algorithms "straighten" the code so that basic blocks along the most commonly followed control flow paths are in contiguous locations in memory (Pettis and Hansen 1990). The benefits are more efficient instruction fetching, due to both improved temporal and spatial locality, and improved conditional branch predictability. Code relayout often provides one of the larger performance benefits among all the optimizations.

#### Method Inlining

Method inlining is referred to as *procedure inlining* in Section 4.3.1. With inlining, a method call is replaced with the actual code contained in the method; i.e., the method code is placed "inline" with the calling code (Suganuma, Yasue, and Nakatani 2002). The overheads of passing parameters, managing a stack frame, and the actual control transfers (e.g., a jump and return) are saved, at the possible expense of a larger binary program image.

Object-oriented programming tends to encourage many small methods, so performance can often be improved significantly by avoiding all the overhead code, i.e., the *calling sequence* that is associated with a method call. Another significant benefit of inlining is that it increases the scope over which later code analysis and optimizations can take place; e.g., analysis can make less conservative assumptions regarding potential data accesses outside the method being optimized. Inlining very small methods, where the code size of the method is less than the code size of the method's calling sequence, is almost always a win. When inlined, such a small method will not only execute faster, but it will also consume less instruction space than the original (noninlined) code, resulting in improved instruction cache behavior (or at least no degradation).

With larger methods, the benefits of inlining are reduced because the calling sequence takes a smaller percentage of the overall execution time and because there is an increase in total code size (and instruction cache requirements). If not applied selectively, the inlining of larger methods, especially those called from a number of different sites, can lead to *code explosion*, resulting in poor cache behavior and performance losses. Therefore, to apply inlining on medium-to-large methods, some kind of cost–benefit analysis is required, and the cost–benefit relationship can be rather complex. The cost in terms of code expansion can be estimated relatively easily, but how this translates to performance cost is more complex and would typically be a programmed-in function derived from off-line experimentation. The benefit is primarily a function of the size of the method and the frequency with which a method is called; that is, the most frequently called methods will lead to the greatest benefit and are the primary candidates for inlining.

To determine the frequency of method calls, a common technique is to instrument the method call sites with counters to collect profiles of caller–callee pairs. At certain intervals (perhaps fixed time intervals or when some profile counter exceeds a threshold), the optimizing system can construct a *call graph*, with edges annotated with call (method invocation) frequencies. An example call graph is given in Figure 6.12a. In the figure, the main method calls methods A and X; method A calls methods B and C, and method X calls methods C and Y. The edges of the call graph are annotated with the number of calls during the sampling interval. For example, in Figure 6.12, method C has been called 1500 times by method A and 25 times by method X. After constructing and maintaining such an annotated graph, the dynamic optimization system can analyze the graph to determine which methods should be inlined.

Then, for example, one might define a "start" threshold for triggering inlining analysis as 1500; that is, when an edge in the call graph is traversed for the 1500th time, the dynamic optimization system is invoked. During the analysis, other methods besides the one that triggers the analysis may be

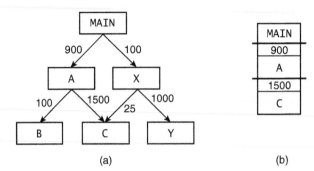

**Figure 6.12** Tracking Method Calls. *(a) With a call graph; (b) via stack frames.*

inlined, depending on the cost–benefit analysis; e.g., a small method is more likely to be inlined than a larger one, even if they both have the same invocation counts in the call graph. In this example, it may be decided that method C should be inlined in A and that A should then be inlined in main, so main, A, and C are all merged together. Also, it may be decided that method Y should be inlined in X.

This overall approach to inlining is a good one, but it requires construction of the call graph and typically involves some kind of overall analysis of the call graph. A simpler technique that avoids constructing the call graph and the overall analysis is to wait until a profiling counter reaches the start threshold and then to "walk" backwards through the stack to view what is effectively the currently active portion of the call graph (Hölzle and Ungar 1996). In our example, at the time the start threshold of 1500 is reached, the stack is as shown in Figure 6.12b. The profile counts are included in their associated stack frames, although they can also be held in a table off to the side. In any event, a walk up the stack may decide to inline B and A, as before. Although this technique uses a very narrow view of the call graph, it is nevertheless effective. In the example, method Y is not inlined as before, but if the X-to-Y call count later reaches the start threshold, it may be inlined at that time.

### Optimizing Virtual Method Calls

In general, inlining can easily be applied to static methods and methods declared by the programmer to be final methods. When one of these methods is invoked from a given call site (e.g., via the invokestatic instruction), the method code called never changes. Hence, once inlining is performed on one of these methods, the inlined code will always be the correct code.

```
                      If (a.isInstanceof(Square)) {
                            inlined code for perimeter of a square
Invokevirtual <perimeter> ⟹                      ·
                                                 ·
                                                 ·
                      }
                      Else invokevirtual <perimeter>
```

**Figure 6.13**   An Inlined Method Call Protected by a Guard.

In an object-oriented language, however, many methods are not static or final; i.e., the methods are associated with dynamic classes. Because of class hierarchies and resulting polymorphism, the actual code to be executed by a virtual method invocation can change, depending on the particular subclass of the object being referenced. Returning to the example given in the previous chapter (Figure 5.5), if the perimeter method is applied to a Rectangle object, the Rectangle version of the perimeter method code is invoked; in the case of a Square, a different perimeter method is invoked. The determination of which code to use is determined at run time via a dynamic method table lookup. Because a virtual method's code can change dynamically, depending on the type of object it is given, method inlining would appear to be inhibited for any method called via the invokevirtual instruction. However, in many cases a virtual method is invoked with the same type of object the vast majority of the time (or all of the time). For example, say the earlier example has a much larger loop (reading input from a file instead of a command line), the Square shape is much more common than the Rectangle shape; or, in the extreme case, the Square may be the only shape that actually occurs for a given execution of the program. Such a situation can be determined by profiling the types of references for which a given virtual method is invoked.

If one particular method is invoked the vast majority of the time, then the method code for the most common subclass can be inlined, with *guard* instructions placed above the inlined code. The guard simply tests the type of reference on which the following method is to be invoked. If it is of the expected (common) type, then the guard will let control pass to the inlined version of the method. On the other hand, in the rare case when the reference is for a subclass different from the expected one, the guard can branch to a noninlined invokevirtual instruction. For our earlier example, such a guarded inlined method is given in Figure 6.13. The If statement checks the type of the object reference on which the perimeter method is being invoked (via the isInstanceof method) and then performs the inlined code version if it is a Square.

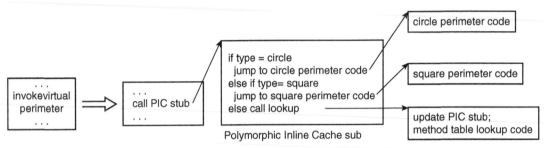

**Figure 6.14** Example of Polymorphic Inline Caching.

If the method call is truly polymorphic so that full inlining is not useful, then at least the overhead of a dynamic method table lookup can be avoided using a technique similar to that for software jump prediction during binary translation (Section 2.7). This technique is referred to as *polymorphic inline caching* (PIC) (Hölzle, Chambers, and Ungar 1991) and is illustrated in Figure 6.14. In this example, it is assumed there is a much wider variety of shapes than in our rectangle/square example. With a PIC, the runtime system is responsible for maintaining the stub code, placing the most frequently used jumps at the top of the sequence.

### Multiversioning and Specialization

The foregoing approach to inlining of virtual method calls is essentially a form of *multiversioning* (Artigas et al. 2000; Gupta, Choi, and Hind 2000). With multiversioning there are two (or more) versions of code, and one version is selected, depending on run-time information, for example, data values or type information. With method inlining one version is inlined method code, the other version is an `invokevirtual` instruction, and the guard selects one of the versions. This same general approach can be applied to other types of code, not just virtual method calls.

For example, in Figure 6.15, profiling data values may determine that the elements of the array A are almost always zero. A guard (shown in italics in the figure) checks to see if A[i] is zero; if so, it uses a version of code that skips the rest of the instructions and simply sets B[i] to zero.

An important aspect of multiversioning is *specialization* (Grant et al. 1999; Suganuma et al. 2001). If some variables or references are always assigned data values or types known to be constant (or from a limited range), then simplified, specialized code can sometimes be used in place of more complex, general code. This is the case in Figure 6.15, where the specialized case occurs when A[i] is zero. Specialization can be used in conjunction with multiversioning,

```
                                        for (int i = 0; i < 1000; i++) {

for (int i = 0; i < 1000; i++) {            if (A[i] == 0)

  if (A[i] < 0) B[i] = -A[i]*C[i]; ⟹
  else B[i] = A[i]*C[i];
                                         ┌ ─ ─ ─ ─ ─ ─ ┐  ┌──────────────────────────────┐
}                                        ┆ B[i]= 0;    ┆  │ if (A[i] < 0) B[i] = -A[i]*C[i]; │
                                         └ ─ ─ ─ ─ ─ ─ ┘  │ else B[i] = A[i]*C[i];          │
                                                          └──────────────────────────────┘

                                        }
```

**Figure 6.15**     Multiversion Code. *For the common case where C[i]=0, there can be a simpler, specialized code version.*

as shown in Figure 6.15, or it can be enabled via code analysis that indicates that only a single, specialized version is ever needed.

An alternative to constructing multiple versions is to compile only a single code version (or a small number of versions) and to *defer* compilation of the general, more complex case (Chambers and Ungar 1991; Whaley 2001). For example, profiling may find that only one value has occurred up to some point in a program's execution, so an optimizing compiler may skip the general case code. In effect, it is speculating that only the special case ever occurs. However, there should be a guard to check for the general case; if it occurs, the general code can be compiled at that time. Deferred compilation is illustrated in Figure 6.16. This is the same code as in Figure 6.15, except that if A[i] is nonzero, the code jumps to the dynamic compilation system so that it can produce the required code to allow execution to proceed.

### On-Stack Replacement

The stack is at the center of instruction execution in most HLL VMs, including both Java and the Microsoft CLI. Consequently, the stack is also an important

```
                                        for (int i = 0; i < 1000; i++) {

for (int i = 0; i < 1000; i++) {            if (A[i] == 0)

  if (A[i] < 0) B[i] = -A[i]*C[i]; ⟹
  else B[i] = A[i]*C[i];
                                         ┌ ─ ─ ─ ─ ─ ─ ┐  ┌──────────────────────────────┐
}                                        ┆ B[i]= 0;    ┆  │ Jump to dynamic              │
                                         └ ─ ─ ─ ─ ─ ─ ┘  │ compiler for deferred        │
                                                          │ compilation                  │
                                                          └──────────────────────────────┘

                                        }
```

**Figure 6.16**     Deferred Compilation. *With deferred compilation, code is not generated for the uncommon case until it actually occurs.*

consideration when optimizations are performed. To understand the relationship between the stack and program optimizations, a distinction should be drawn between the *architected* stack, i.e., the stack as specified by a Java or MSIL program, and the *implementation* stack, which is actually used during program execution (after compilation and/or optimization). For example, after method inlining, the actual implementation stack will not contain frames for inlined methods; the frame for the calling and the inlined method are merged. Furthermore, the implementation stack contents may differ from the architected stack contents after some types of optimizations, such as specialization. That the implemented stack differs from the architected stack makes no difference as long as the results are correct. The architected stack is a means for specifying the function to be performed by a program; it does not necessarily reflect the exact manner in which the function is implemented.

An important corollary to the foregoing is that at a given point in a program's execution, the implementation stack contents (including both the number of frames and the number of elements in each frame) may depend on the optimizations that have been performed on the program. Furthermore, there are situations where dynamic optimization may require that the contents of the implementation stack be modified on the fly. This process of modifying the stack in response to a dynamically changing optimization level is referred to as *on-stack replacement,* or OSR (Hölzle, Chambers, and Ungar 1992; Fink and Qian 2003). Some of the situations where OSR may be used to support optimization include the following.

1. When inlining (or any other optimization) is performed, the cleanest way to insert the newly optimized code into the program flow is to wait until the method containing the optimized code is called the *next* time. However, this approach obviously does not provide benefits until the method is next called, and it may be a long time before a long-running method is called again. The extreme case occurs when a program is dominated by a single loop containing the optimized code and the loop is executed many millions (or billions) of times. In this case, the optimized method may never be called again, and therefore the optimized code must be inserted earlier if any benefits are to accrue.[1]

---

1. It is not clear, however, that this type of behavior happens often enough in real programs to make such a technique worthwhile. This type of behavior is sometimes observed in kernel benchmarks (also known as *microbenchmarks*), and this may in fact be the prime motivation for considering such an optimization method in the competitive benchmark-oriented environment in which high-performance VMs are often developed.

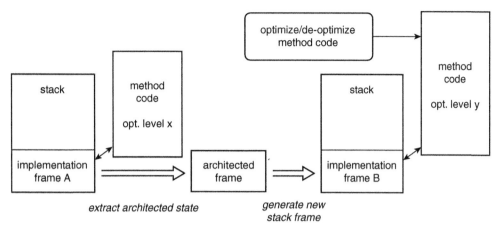

**Figure 6.17** On-Stack Replacement. *With on-stack replacement, one version of a stack frame is replaced by another. This typically occurs when the optimization level of the code accessing the stack frame changed dynamically.*

2. When deferred compilation is implemented, new code may be generated while a method is in midexecution. That is, if the guard indicates that an uncommon path is to be followed, new code has to be generated, and the current implementation stack frame may have to modified to account for the newly compiled (and possibly much larger) code region.

3. When a debugger is implemented as part of an overall VM framework, the user would expect to observe the architected instruction sequence and stack contents rather than the results of optimized code and the implementation stack contents. In this situation, it may be necessary to deoptimize a method. This is the opposite of the two earlier situations; here, OSR may be called upon to modify the implementation stack into a form that is less optimized and more nearly approximates the architected version.

On-stack replacement is illustrated in Figure 6.17. Here, the optimization level of code accessing the stack is being modified on the fly, so the structure and/or contents of the implementation stack frame change. The basic steps of OSR are: (1) Extract the architected frame state from the current implementation frame (and any other implementation data that may be maintained for this purpose); (2) generate a new implementation frame that is consistent with the new code version; (3) replace the current implementation stack frame with the new one.

An important application for OSR is illustrated in Figure 6.18. Here, multiple stack frames are being replaced by a single frame (or vice versa).

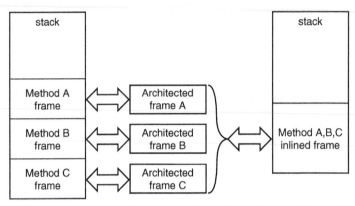

**Figure 6.18** On-Stack Replacement. *On-stack replacement can be used to replace multiple stack frames with a single frame (or vice versa).*

This may happen if method inlining is being performed (or is being removed for debugging).

In general, OSR is a relatively complex operation, both in constructing the architected stack state and in building a new implementation stack frame. If the initial stack frame is being maintained by an interpreter or a nonoptimizing compiler, then extracting the architected stack state is straightforward. If the stack frame is for optimized code, however, there must often be some special provision for OSR. For example, the compiler may define a set of program points where OSR can potentially occur and then ensure that the architected values are live at that point in the execution. This is reminiscent of checkpoints and live range extension that are used by some binary optimizers when rescheduling code (see Section 4.5.2).

In many cases, the steady-state performance benefits enabled by OSR are relatively small. However, OSR allows the implementation of debuggers that work in the context of optimizing compilation systems. In addition, when used with deferred compilation, start-up times can be reduced by avoiding compilation/optimization of unused code sections, and the instruction "footprint" is smaller, which can improve cache performance.

### Optimization of Heap-Allocated Objects

By its very nature, good object-oriented programming freely creates a large number of heap-allocated objects. However, there are a number of overheads associated with objects. Creating objects and garbage collection have relatively high costs. Furthermore, because accessing fields held in an object often

```
class square {
int side;
int area;
}
void calculate() {
    a = new square();
    a.side = 3;
    a.area = a.side * a.side
    System.out.println(a.area);
}
```

```
void calculate() {
    int t1 = 3;
    int t2 = t1 * t1;
    System.out.println(t2);
}
```

**Figure 6.19**    Scalar Replacement. *With scalar replacement, an object field is replaced by a scalar variable so that access delays are reduced.*

involves levels of address indirection, individual object field accesses suffer small overheads that add up. To deal with creation overhead, if profiling indicates a particular type of object is frequently allocated, then the code for the heap allocation and object initialization can be inlined.

Scalar replacement (Carr and Kennedy 1994) is an optimization that can be very effective in some situations for reducing object access delays. This optimization replaces an object field with a scalar value. An example is shown in Figure 6.19. Here, on the left, a small object a is created, its two integer fields are assigned values, and one of the fields is printed. If it can be determined that object a is only used by this piece of code before being discarded, the object creation (and later garbage collection), along with the field references, can be replaced by simple scalar references, as shown on the right in Figure 6.19. Scalar replacement when applied to objects requires reference *escape analysis* (Choi et al. 1999), that is, an analysis to make sure all references to the object are within the region of code containing the optimization. In this example, no references to a escape from the optimized code region.

The physical placement of data fields within an object is an implementation-dependent feature. Consequently, improved data cache performance can be achieved by ordering object fields according to usage patterns (Chilimbi, Davidson, and Larus 1999; Kistler and Franz 2000). Furthermore, some field references can be removed entirely by using conventional compiler optimizations. For example, redundant `getfield` and `putfield` operations can be found and removed. This is illustrated in Figure 6.20. Here, the same field is accessed twice (as a.side and as c.side). Based on dataflow analysis, the redundant access can be found, and the corresponding field value is held in (and copied from) a temporary location, t1 (possibly a register), avoiding the second getfield (to c.side).

```
a = new square;              a = new square;
b = new square;              b = new square;
c = a;                       c = a;
...                          ...
a.side = 5;      =======>    t1 = 5;
                             a.side = t1;
b.side = 10;                 b.side = 10;
z = c.side;                  z = t1;
```

**Figure 6.20**    Example of Redundant `getfield` (load) Removal.

### Low-Level Optimizations

Besides the optimizations given earlier, which tend to be especially effective when applied to object-oriented programs, many conventional optimizations, discussed earlier, in Chapter 4, can also be applied. These include dead-code removal, branch optimization, copy and constant propagation, strength reduction, and code rescheduling, among others. Because they have already been covered we will not go into further detail here. However, we do cover some extensions and other considerations that are more specific to the object-oriented context.

One potentially significant overhead found in object-oriented HLL VMs is the need to perform array range and null reference checking. In theory, every time an array is accessed or a reference is used, these checks must be performed; perhaps just as important, an exception may be thrown. This means there are two potential causes of performance loss. One is the need to perform range/null check itself, and the other is the inhibition of other optimizations because of a potential thrown exception if the check should fail. In the latter case, the architected process state must be precise at the time of an exception, and, just as with binary optimizers, some optimizations may be inhibited if a precise state must potentially be materialized.

The overhead of null pointer checking can be largely eliminated by using an "illegal" out-of-range address to represent the null pointer value, i.e., a memory address for which the Java process does not have read or write privileges. Then an attempt to use a null pointer will result in a trap, which, via an OS-supported signal mechanism, can be reported back to the JVM runtime system. However, the *potential* for an exception (and the need to restore a precise state) remains, so some code optimizations, for example, involving code motion, may still be inhibited.

A common way to deal with range/null check operations is to treat them as if they are regular instructions and then to perform the analogous optimizations. For example, just as a redundant instruction can be removed or an

```
p = new Z                                    p = new Z
q = new Z                                    q = new Z
r = p                                        r = p
...                                          ...
p.x = ...   <null check p>   ===========>   p.x = ...   <null check p>
... = p.x   <null check p>                   ... = p.x
...                                          ...
q.x = ...   <null check q>                   r.x = ...
...                                          q.x = ...   <null check q>
r.x = ...   <null check r(p)>
```

**Figure 6.21**   Removing Redundant Null Checks. *After redundant null checks are identified and removed, optimizations involving code motion are enabled.*

```
                                        If (j < A.length)
                                        then for (int i = 0; i < j; i++) {
for (int i = 0; i < j; i++) {              sum += A[i];
    sum += A[i];   <range check A>  ===>  }
}                                       else for (int i = 0; i < j; i++) {
                                           sum += A[i];   <range check A>
                                        }
```

**Figure 6.22**   Hoisting an Invariant Check. *An array range check is hoisted outside a loop. Then in the common case, no inner loop range check is required.*

invariant instruction hoisted out of a loop, so, too, a redundant or invariant check can be removed or hoisted. A simple example is in Figure 6.21. Here, the same object reference (held in p and r) is used for a series of getfield and putfield operations. If the first putfield (p.x = ...) passes the null check, then the getfield using the same reference will as well. The null check property can also be propagated to reference r. Thus, only the first null check for p is needed, and the later checks for p and r become redundant. After the redundant null checks are removed (right-hand side of the figure), then the putfield to q.x can be rescheduled after the putfield to r.x.

An example of hoisting an invariant check is in Figure 6.22. In the code on the left, an array range check is performed every loop iteration. However, the check can be hoisted outside the loop (right-hand side of the figure) and only needs to be performed once. After the check has been hoisted outside of the loop, it takes the form of a guard for two versions of the code, one that does not perform the check and the other that does.

As a final example, a technique known as *loop peeling* can be performed to avoid null pointer problems. In Figure 6.23 the loop body contains an object reference with a null check. Hence, code motion around the reference is inhibited. However, the first loop iteration can be peeled (right-hand side

```
for (int i = 0; i < 100; i++) {
        r = A[i];
        B[i] = r*2;
        p.x += A[i] ;   <null check p>
}
```

⟹

```
r = A[0];
B[0] = r*2;
p.x = A[0];   <null check p>
for (int i = 1; i < 100; i++) {
        r =A[i]
        p.x += A[i] ;
        B[i] = r*2;
}
```

**Figure 6.23**    Loop Peeling. *By peeling the first loop iteration, the null checks in the remaining loop iterations can be removed.*

of the figure); if this first iteration does not cause a null pointer exception, none of the other iterations will. Hence, the null check is not needed for the remaining loop iterations, and other code optimizations can be enabled.

### Optimizing Garbage Collection

Garbage collection is a key part of a high-performance VM implementation, and there are a number of ways the compiler can provide assistance to the Java runtime to enhance garbage-collection efficiency. First, there may be times when the heap state is temporarily inconsistent, for example, when object references are being modified. At these points, to avoid errors, garbage collection should not be initiated. Consequently, the compiler can provide the garbage collector with "yield point" at regular intervals in the code. At these points a thread can guarantee a consistent heap state so that control can be yielded to the garbage collector. Also, the compiler can help with specific garbage-collection algorithms. For example, if a generational collector is used, then write barriers must be provided by the compiler.

## 6.7  Case Study: The Jikes Research Virtual Machine

The Jikes research virtual machine (RVM) was developed at IBM Research and has been made available to the general VM research community (Arnold et al. 2000). Jikes is based on an earlier research effort, Jalapeno, and was initially described in research papers using that name. The discussion here is based on descriptions of both the Jalapeno and the Jikes systems.

The overall optimization strategy is to compile only; there is no interpretation step. First, there is a baseline compiler that translates bytecodes directly into native code. This compiler performs no register allocation *per se*; rather, the generated code simply emulates the Java stack. Then for optimization, there

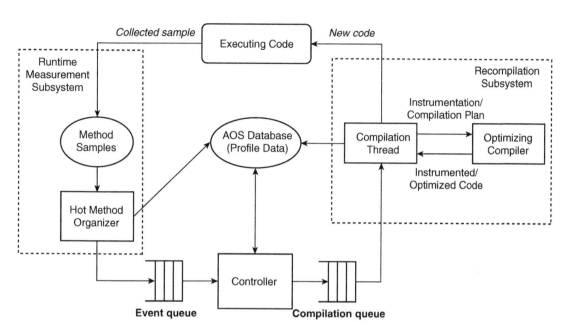

**Figure 6.24** The Jikes Adaptive Optimization System (AOS).

is a dynamic compiler that supports three levels of optimization, invoked in stages, depending on an estimate of cost–benefit.

Jikes is a multithreaded implementation, with threads responsible for optimization running concurrently with executing program threads. Jikes multiplexes Java application and runtime threads onto threads supported by the underlying host platform, e.g., AIX pthreads. To allow preemptive thread scheduling, the compiler places yield points, typically at method prologs, epilogs, and loop back edges. At a yield point, the code tests a control bit; if the thread scheduler wants to preempt a thread, it will set the thread's control bit. At the next yield point, the thread will call the thread scheduler.

The overall architecture of the Jikes adaptive optimization system (AOS) is shown in Figure 6.24. The major subsystems are the runtime measurement system, the recompilation system, and the controller. These subsystems all interact with the AOS database, which contains profiling data and a history of optimization decisions.

The runtime measurement subsystem gathers raw performance data by sampling at yield points. That is, when a thread switches, a back-edge yield point increments an activity count for the method containing the edge. If it is at a method prolog, the activity count for the calling method is incremented; if it is at a method epilog, the activity count for the called method is incremented.[2] The system can also support other types of compiler-inserted instrumentation to perform edge profiles, basic block profiles, or value profiles, depending on the optimizations that are under consideration. Performance data is initially kept in raw form. Periodically, the raw method samples are analyzed by a separate thread, the hot method organizer, which summarizes and puts the profile data in a form more easily used by the rest of the optimization system.

The controller is responsible for coordinating the activities of the runtime measurement and the recompilation subsystems. It instructs the measurement subsystem to initiate, continue, or change profiling activities. When a method is sampled, that is, found to be active during a thread switch, the hot method organizer places it on the event queue for the controller to consider for recompilation. The controller then makes decisions regarding the recompilation, e.g., whether recompilation of the method should be performed and, if so, at what optimization level.

An important part of the controller's function is to determine whether a method should be recompiled at a higher optimization level. To do this, Jikes uses an analytical cost–benefit model. Say that a given method $m$ is currently compiled at optimization level $i < N$, where level $N$ is the highest optimization level. Then the controller estimates (1) $Ti$, the expected time the program will spend executing method $m$ if it is not recompiled; (2) $Cj$, the cost (time required) of recompiling method $m$ at level $j \geq i$; (3) $Tj$, the expected execution time the program will spend in $m$ after recompilation. Note that a recompilation at the same level, $i$, is considered because there may be more profiling data available than what was available the previous time $m$ was compiled at level $i$; this additional profiling data may change the particular optimizations performed at level $i$. Then the controller determines the optimal level $j$, where $Cj + Tj$ is minimized. Recompilation is performed at level $j$, unless, of course, $Cj + Tj \geq Ti$ and no recompilation is done.

Although this cost–benefit analysis seems very straightforward, the real difficulty comes in estimating the $C$ and $T$ values. Consequently Jikes uses a combination of heuristics and experimentally derived parameters. To arrive at an estimate of the $T$ values, the controller assumes that at its current optimization level, the method will consume as much execution time in the future as it already consumed; i.e., that $Ti = Tcurrent$. The $Tj$ values are determined by first estimating the speedups of the different optimization levels using off-line benchmarks. The speedup of optimization level $k$ versus level 0

---

2. These yield points and profiling heuristics reflect the current Jikes implementation, not the one in the paper describing Jikes (Jalapeno) (Arnold et al. 2000).

is *Sk*. Then *Tj* = *Ti* \* *Si/Sj*. Finally, the recompilation cost *Cj* is estimated to be a linear function of the size of the method to be recompiled. The multiplying constant is again determined by off-line benchmarking. If the controller decides that recompilation should be done, it places the pertinent information into the recompilation queue, to be serviced by one of the compilation threads.

The recompilation subsystem consists of a number of threads that remove compilation plans from the compilation queue. Because they run as separate threads, they can execute concurrently with the Java application threads. A compilation plan consists of the optimizations that should be performed, profile data that will be used by the optimizer, and an instrumentation plan, i.e., the profiling instrumentation the compiler should put in the code it generates (for potential future optimizations).

The AOS database contains a history of profile data and the compilation plans, status, and history of recompiled methods. The controller and recompilation subsystem can query this database to guide further recompilation decisions and optimizations.

The Jikes compiler has three levels of optimization. A brief summary of the optimizations performed at each level is given next.

*Level 0:* Includes many of the conventional compiler optimizations, such as copy and constant propagation, common subexpression elimination, dead-code elimination, branch optimizations, and several others. So-called *trivial* methods are inlined — these are methods where the code in the method is smaller than the method's calling sequence. In addition, some simple code relayout is performed, and register allocation follows a simple linear scan algorithm.

*Level 1:* Because many of the classical optimizations are done in level 0, the additional optimizations deal with higher-level code restructuring — there is more aggressive inlining, based on profile information, and there is more aggressive code relayout.

*Level 2:* Uses a static single assignment (SSA) intermediate form, where each register variable is assigned a value only once (Cytron et al. 1991; Cooper and Torczon 2003). Using this form allows a number of global optimizations (or more effective versions of conventional optimizations, such as common-subexpression elimination). It also includes some optimizations that can lead to significant code expansion unless judiciously applied (with the benefit of profile data). For example, loop unrolling replicates the body of a loop, thereby increasing opportunities for other optimizations and eliminating a number of loop-closing branches.

The developers of Jikes have published a number of benchmark results. We give some of the results for the SPECjvm98 benchmark suite. There are seven programs with class files ranging from 10KB to nearly 1.4MB. Performance results are given to measure "start-up" performance and "steady-state" performance. There are two differences between start-up and steady state. First, the steady-state data sets are approximately an order of magnitude larger than the start-up data sets. Second, each steady-state benchmark is run for five iterations by the same JVM instance and the best iteration performance is reported. The start-up behavior will be influenced much more heavily by initialization of data structures, class file loading, and compilation overheads. The steady-state performance is closer to what one might expect in a more realistic production environment, where the start-up overheads have more time to be amortized.

For comparison, a number of compilation scenarios are benchmarked and compared with the simple baseline compilation. In one set of scenarios, the compiler with each of the three optimization levels is run as a JIT compiler. That is, the first time a method is invoked, it is immediately compiled at the given optimization level and remains there throughout the program's execution. The AOS implementation uses all optimization levels in a staged manner, and optimization is performed on a per-method basis. With AOS + FDO (Feedback Directed Optimization), more complete profiling information is maintained, so better inlining decisions can be made and optimizations can be better targeted within methods.

Performance is evaluated as speedup over the simple nonoptimizing baseline compiler. Figure 6.25 shows start-up results for each of the benchmarks and the harmonic mean speedup for all seven. For the JIT compilers, the lower the optimization level, the better the performance (compress is the only notable counterexample where JIT 1 outperforms JIT 0). For the start-up benchmarks, the extra time required for optimizations cannot be amortized, due to the relatively short run times (with the exception of compress, where code quality is more important than in the other benchmarks). All the JIT compilers are below the baseline, because they provide at least level-0 optimization for all methods, even those executed only once. The AOS and AOS + FDO dynamic compilation methods perform best, giving a speedup of about 1.75, because they only take the time to perform compilation beyond baseline, possibly followed by additional optimizations, where there is good likelihood of performance benefit.

Figure 6.26 shows results for the steady-state benchmarks. Here, the results are quite different than for the start-up case. Now, the higher the optimization level for the JIT compilers, the better the performance. Using level 0 as a JIT gives a speedup of 1.9 over the baseline, and going up to level 2 yields a speedup of about 2.25. Interestingly, using the AOS staged optimization typically falls

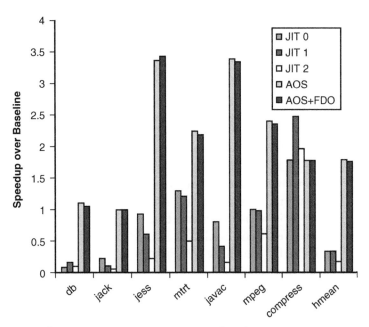

**Figure 6.25**  Jikes Start-up Performance on Seven SPECjvm98 Benchmarks.

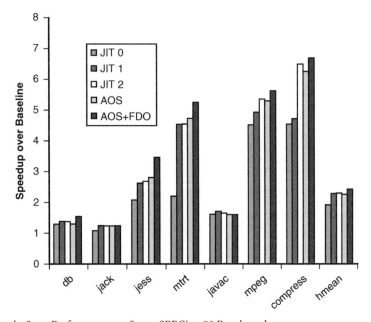

**Figure 6.26**  Jikes Steady-State Performance on Seven SPECjvm98 Benchmarks.

slightly short of the level-2 JIT. Because the same code is executed during each iteration, the JIT performance runs can complete compilation during the first iteration and then execute four iterations with no profiling or compilation overhead. On the other hand, the AOS performance runs profile and recompile through all five iterations. For two benchmarks, AOS without FDO actually beats JIT2, however, because AOS sometimes recompiles a method at a later time (in program execution) than JIT2 does. This later compilation allows more class loading to take place, eliminating some unresolved references, and thus the code generated by AOS is more highly optimized. Finally, because the AOS + FDO is able to perform additional profile-guided optimizations, for some benchmarks it provides significant speedup over the method-granularity optimizations used by the AOS implementation.

It is also interesting to see where an advanced JVM spends its time. An execution profile for Jikes is given in Figure 6.27. This particular profile is for the entire SPECjvm98 benchmark suite, with each being executed for one iteration. Across different applications, the execution profile may vary significantly from this average performance, especially in time spent in

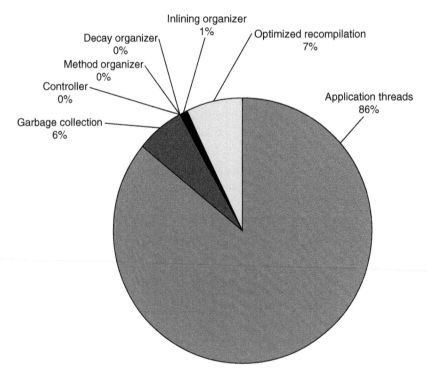

**Figure 6.27**    Where the Jikes System Spends Its Time.

garbage collection. Over the entire benchmark suite, performing optimized recompilation consumes only 7% of the total time, and all the other tasks related to adaptive optimization, i.e., the various control and bookkeeping functions, consume negligible time. We see that 86% of the time is spent in execution application threads and 6% is spent in the garbage collector. This tends to highlight the importance of garbage collection in a JVM; about as much time is spent in garbage collection as in performing optimizations on the code.

## 6.8 Summary

The conventional belief is that programs running on an HLL VM are relatively slow. This is a misleading notion. Some of the early Java VMs *were* slow. A heavy reliance on interpretation is naturally slow during steady-state emulation, and dynamic optimizing methods that are not selective, i.e., simple JIT compilation, will have high start-up times. However, modern HLL VM implementations rely on compiled code and are much more selective regarding when to apply optimizations and where. This leads not only to less overhead but to better optimizations in the steady state. Furthermore, slowdown due to the dynamic VM paradigm should not be confused with slowdown due to support for object-oriented programming. Object-oriented programming leads to more robust programs and a high level of code reusability (among other advantages), but sometimes there is a performance cost for these important software engineering advantages. Inherent in object-oriented code are additional levels of indirection that may not be found in conventional C-type code, for example. But this is usually caused by the object-oriented nature of the software, not the fact that it is running on a VM.

With the development of the Java platform and the more recent Microsoft .NET framework, HLL VMs already have achieved a "critical mass." At some point in the (not-too-distant) future, virtually all application programs are likely to be developed for a platform-independent HLL VM. This will change common programming practice (programming in C will be viewed in much the same way as programming in assembly language is viewed today), and it will likely change the way that hardware platforms are implemented. If all software is developed for a platform-independent HLL VM, the level of standardization is raised and the underlying hardware ISA becomes much less relevant.

# Chapter Seven
# Codesigned Virtual Machines

**B**oth hardware and software have undergone radical changes since the first commercially available computers appeared in the early 1950s. In contrast, the basic character of the interface between hardware and software has been virtually unchanged during that time. Consequently, the instruction set architectures (ISAs) currently in use reflect a perspective and a division of labor between hardware and software that is decades old. At a time when hardware resources were very expensive and hardware was relatively simple, it made sense for the ISA to be a direct reflection of the specific hardware implementation. If the hardware had an accumulator, then the ISA had an accumulator. Over the years, however, hardware resources have become plentiful and inexpensive. Today, hundreds of millions of transistors are available on a single chip. As a consequence, underlying processor hardware has grown to be quite different from the image presented by the commonly used ISAs. For example, consider the Intel IA-32, one of the older microprocessor ISAs in use today. The IA-32 uses a CISC ISA, originally conceived for sequential in-order execution with relatively few general-purpose registers and stack-based floating instructions. A modern IA-32 implementation, however, converts the CISC ISA into what is essentially a RISC ISA running on a dynamic superscalar microarchitecture having lots of registers and register-based floating-point instructions (Hinton et al. 2001; Keltcher et al. 2003). This CISC-to-RISC conversion is done entirely in hardware (see Figure 7.1).

The reason behind hardware-intensive dynamic translation of legacy ISAs is the need to maintain their role as the interface between hardware and software. Today's ISAs are valuable interfaces, ones in which huge software and infrastructure investments have been made. Compatibility has also become the largest obstacle to implementing new ISAs that are better suited

**329**

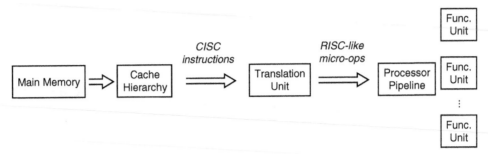

**Figure 7.1**    CISC-to-RISC Conversion. *Conventional high-performance microarchitectures for a CISC instruction set use hardware to translate CISC instructions into RISC-like micro-ops.*

to today's technology. Fortunately, virtual machine technologies permit new ISAs by enabling a different approach to general-purpose processor design. Virtual machine technologies can turn processor development into a *codesign* effort, where the host architecture (the target ISA in particular) is designed concurrently with the VM software that runs on it. Because the host hardware is developed as an integral part of the VM, it is not necessary to use an existing host platform or target ISA. Taken together, however, the codesigned hardware and software support a conventional source ISA (and all the software developed for it).

These *codesigned virtual machines* open new avenues for architectural innovation. Because software becomes part of the "hardware" platform, the interface between hardware and conventional software is shifted upward, and there are new opportunities for dividing the implementation between hardware and software in an optimal way. Because codesigned VMs support an entire system, OS plus applications, they are a form of system virtual machine. However, unlike most other system virtual machines, codesigned VMs are not intended to virtualize hardware resources other than the processor, nor are they intended to support multiple VM environments. Rather, the goals include performance, power efficiency, and design simplicity.

Perhaps the first codesigned VM was the IBM System/38 (Bertsis 1980), later known as the AS/400 (Soltis 1996) and currently the iSeries. The System/38 was designed to support a guest ISA with higher-level semantics than could be directly supported by hardware. This reduces the "semantic gap" between a conventional ISA and higher-level software (Myers 1982). A second objective was to separate the source ISA from the target ISA so that successive hardware platforms could be redesigned while maintaining software compatibility. The success of this approach was demonstrated as the AS/400 family evolved, changing its host platform ISA from the original proprietary CISC ISA to an

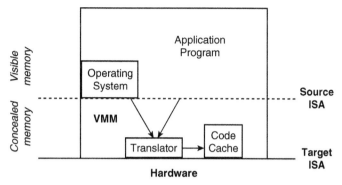

**Figure 7.2** Virtual Machine Monitor. *A codesigned virtual machine architecture supports a conventional source ISA via a combination of hardware and software running in concealed memory.*

extended PowerPC ISA. This migration took place in a completely transparent way from the users' perspective.

Another commercially available codesigned VM, developed by Transmeta (Halfhill 2000; Klaiber 2000) implements a target instruction set where a number of independent instructions placed in a very long instruction word (VLIW). The codesigned software is responsible for finding independent instructions in a conventional source ISA (the IA-32) and packing them into the target VLIW ISA. Because they are independent, the instructions in a VLIW can be issued for execution in parallel without complicated hardware support. Therefore, the advantage of this codesigned VM implementation is that it does not require the complexity (and power consumption) of an out-of-order issue unit as used in most superscalar processors.

An overview of a codesigned VM is shown in Figure 7.2. It is a system VM, as noted earlier, and all the VM software resides in a region of memory that is completely concealed from all conventional software. In keeping with the naming convention used for system VMs, we refer to the virtual machine software as a virtual machine monitor (VMM).

The primary function of the VMM is to emulate the source ISA; in this respect there are many similarities to process VMs. For example, emulation is often done in stages, with the focus on dynamic translation into a code cache. There are differences with respect to process VMs, however, the two most significant being the following.

1.  There must be intrinsic compatibility (Section 3.2) at the ISA level rather than the ABI level. Because the interface at which virtualization takes place is the ISA, not only must the user-level instruction set be emulated, but the entire system-level ISA must be emulated. This includes the memory

architecture, for example, so page fault compatibility must be maintained. It also means that I/O can be dealt with at the hardware level, not the abstracted OS call level as in process VMs.

2. The reason for using a virtual machine implementation is improved performance, power efficiency, design simplicity, or some combination of these. Compatibility is a requirement but is not the motivation for constructing a codesigned VM.

Codesigned VMs also bear some similarity to conventional superscalar processor designs (Figure 7.1): Both perform translation from a source ISA to a target ISA implemented in hardware. The difference is that one does the translation in software while the other does it in hardware. We should note, however, there have been a number of proposals for innovative processor implementations that are similar to codesigned VMs, typically relying on microcode or special-purpose coprocessors, rather than VM software to perform translation or to assist with interpretation (Debaere and Van Campenhout 1990; Nair and Hopkins 1997; Chou and Shen 2000; Patel and Lumetta 2001). Nevertheless, in a conventional superscalar design of a CISC ISA, hardware (in one form or another) must carry the burden of performing the complex decomposition from CISC instructions to the RISC micro-ops that are directly executed. This is no doubt a contributor to the high cost of hardware design verification — a design cast into silicon is hard to debug and expensive to change.

Relying on hardware-based translation also limits the extent of the ISA translation that can be done. For example, inter-instruction optimization is difficult, and in a conventional superscalar implementation there is none. This is illustrated in Figure 7.3. With conventional hardware translation, Figure 7.3a, each source instruction is translated to micro-ops independent of the other source instructions, i.e., in a context-free manner. On the other hand, with software translation and optimization, as in Figure 7.3b, blocks of source instructions can be translated and optimized as a group, leading to more optimization opportunities (May 1987). Moreover, with the conventional hardware method, power consumption tends to be higher, due to the large amount of hardware for transforming source instructions into an executable form and scheduling them for execution.

Codesigned VMs are not as widely used as other types of VMs; there are few examples that are commercially available, and they remain the subject of research. They are of interest primarily because of their potential for supporting significant innovations in processor design. Furthermore, many of the hardware-based techniques developed for codesigned VMs can potentially

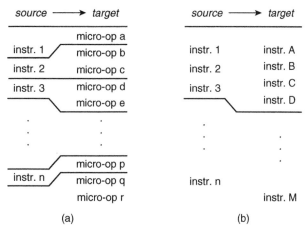

**Figure 7.3**   Code Translation Methods. *(a) Context-free translation, where each individual source instruction is translated to target instruction(s) (micro-ops); (b) context-sensitive translation, where blocks of source instructions are translated to blocks of source instructions.*

be incorporated as extensions to existing ISAs so that other types of VMs, e.g., process VMs and HLL VMs, can be implemented more efficiently on standard platforms.

In the remainder of this chapter, we describe the implementation of codesigned VMs. This includes features that make the emulation process in codesigned VMs more efficient as well as specific performance and/or efficiency features that are enabled by the codesigned VM paradigm. The bulk of the chapter focuses on codesigned VMs intended to implement conventional ISAs; e.g., the Transmeta Crusoe implements the IA-32 ISA. It is this type of codesigned VM that has received the most attention in recent years, especially from researchers. Consequently, many of the techniques described in this chapter are centered on fast emulation of conventional ISAs. The IBM AS/400, in contrast, uses a source ISA that is at a higher level than most conventional ISAs and therefore relies more on innovative software than innovative hardware techniques to achieve its goals. The techniques used in the AS/400 are discussed primarily as part of the case study in Section 7.8.

## 7.1   Memory and Register State Mapping

State mapping is easier with a codesigned VM than with many conventional VMs. Because the target ISA is designed specifically for the source ISA, the host register file(s) can be made large enough to accommodate the guest's

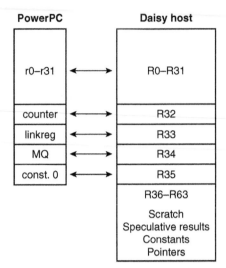

**Figure 7.4** Mapping of Guest PowerPC Integer Registers to the Host Platform Register Set, as Done in the IBM Daisy System.

requirements, with extra scratch registers left over to enhance performance and/or simplify the translation process. An example of PowerPC state mapping for integer registers, as used in the IBM Daisy processor (Ebcioglu et al. 2001), is illustrated in Figure 7.4. Here, the PowerPC integer registers r0–r31 are mapped directly to host registers R0–R31. Then the branch unit counter and link register are mapped to registers R32 and R33. The PowerPC MQ register was originally used for multiplication and division but is now obsolete; in the original Daisy system it was mapped to host register R34. The constant value of 0 is placed in R35 to allow fast emulation of those cases where r0 is defined to be 0 in the PowerPC ISA. Finally, host registers R36–R63 are scratch registers to be used by the VMM emulator for such things as holding speculative values produced during code optimization, for constants, and for pointers to VMM tables.

For memory state mapping, the key element of a codesigned system VM is the *concealed memory*. Concealed memory is a reserved region of the memory space where the VMM, code cache, and other emulation software and tables reside. There can be both concealed logical (virtual) memory and concealed real memory. The concealed memory is never made visible to any of the conventional guest software.

Because the VMM takes control immediately after system reset, it essentially has control of the system from the beginning, including the boot process, so it can make sure the conventional software never sees the concealed memory. When the guest OS boots (under VMM control) and checks to see how much

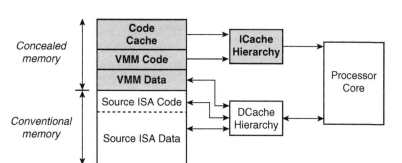

**Figure 7.5** Memory System in a Codesigned Virtual Machine. *The shaded areas are those where host instructions and VMM data reside.*

real memory is available, e.g., by reading a control register, the VMM intercepts the read and does not inform it of the existence of the concealed real memory. And any attempt to access concealed memory by conventional software results in exactly the same behavior as if the memory were not present (typically a trap).

Figure 7.5 illustrates an implementation of real memory in a codesigned VM. The shaded area of main memory is concealed, accessible only via the VMM. The shaded blocks hold target ISA instructions and VMM tables. The concealed memory region is of fixed size and does not change after system initialization. Instructions either are always translated and fetched from the code cache or are VMM code; consequently the instruction cache hierarchy holds only target ISA instructions, and their presence in the instruction cache is concealed from the guest software.

With respect to logical addressing of memory, it is simplest to allow the guest OS to manage the conventional (nonconcealed) part of real memory as it normally would and to map guest virtual addresses using the guest ISA's address translation architecture. For mapping and addressing of concealed memory, there are a number of options, some of which are illustrated in Figure 7.6.

In the first option, concealed logical memory shares an address space with the guest (Figure 7.6a). The conventional memory addressing and address translation are maintained as in the guest system, so the host address space must be enlarged, with the guest space fitting inside. Because the guest space is likely to be consistent with one of the "standard" sizes (e.g., 32 or 64 bits), the host space is either the next-larger "standard" size (e.g., 64 or 128 bits) or a nonstandard size (e.g., 33 or 65 bits). This approach is straightforward, but the expansion of the logical address space size may make the host ISA awkward or expensive to implement (which defeats the purpose of a codesigned VM).

A second option is to have two separate logical address spaces, one for concealed memory and one for conventional memory (Figure 7.6b). All the

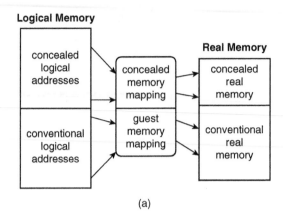

(a)

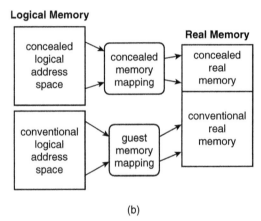

(b)

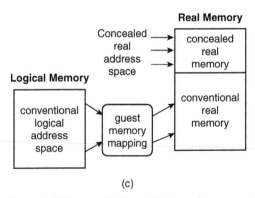

(c)

**Figure 7.6** Methods for Mapping Concealed Memory. *(a) Extend the host address space; (b) provide a separate address map; (c) use real addresses.*

VMM software, code cache, associated tables, etc. are placed in the concealed address space, which maps to concealed real memory. This approach implies that load and store instructions must select one of the two mapping tables (e.g., by using different opcodes to select the mapping table or by using a mode bit). Note that all instruction fetches are to concealed memory addresses. Because the VMM controls all instructions that are executed (either through interpretation or because VMM-translated code is executing), the VMM can always ensure that the proper load and store instructions are used.

A third option is to use real addressing for concealed memory, i.e., to bypass address translation when accessing concealed memory (Figure 7.6c). In a sense, this is a special-case form of option 2. One way of implementing this is to provide separate sets of load/store instructions for accessing memory, one with real addresses and the other via the guest mapping table(s). Also note that the VMM has the option of bypassing address translation even when accessing conventional real memory. In effect, the VMM always operates within the real address space and uses logical addressing only when emulating the guest software. With this approach, a mode bit can then be used for selecting the type of memory addressing to be used, rather than using opcode-based selection.

A key issue regarding concealed memory is how far into the memory hierarchy the concealed memory reaches. It is easiest to keep the concealed portion of memory in RAM and not allow it to extend to secondary storage (disks). If the concealed memory extends to the disk, then the disk (and any bus addresses it uses) must also be concealed from the guest OS. Furthermore, the VMM becomes responsible for managing the concealed secondary memory, including any paging that it might support. Because VMM and the code cache can be kept relatively small (on the order of a few tens of megabytes) and because it simplifies the system design, most of the proposed and implemented codesigned VMs use the diskless option, with VMM software being stored in ROM. The extension of concealed memory to secondary storage is discussed in Section 7.5.

## 7.2 Self-Modifying and Self-Referencing Code

In a codesigned VM, self-modifying and self-referencing code are generally handled using the techniques described in Section 3.4.2. As pointed out in the previous section, it is easiest to keep the original guest OS's virtual-to-real page mapping intact. Then, because the source code is held in the guest's memory in its original form, any load or store accesses to an instruction page will naturally proceed correctly.

For self-modifying code, any attempt to write into the guest code region must be caught, and this is most easily done by write-protecting the source code region, so that any attempt to write it will cause a trap that can be directed to the VMM. The VMM can then flush the code cache of translations derived from the modified page and allow the page to be written.

In a typical process VM (as in Chapter 3), the VMM can write-protect a page via a system call to the host OS in order to change the page table protections. In a codesigned VM, however, the solution is a little more complicated because it is the guest OS that manages its own page tables, not the VMM. This includes the pages that contain the page tables themselves, so changing the page protections in a guest page table would violate the principle of keeping all of the guest memory state intact. The most straightforward solution is to use the TLB to enforce write-protection of guest code pages. If the TLB is managed by the VMM, as it normally would be, then the TLB entries are enhanced with a special "write-protect" bit, for use only by the VMM for detecting self-modifying code. Whenever an entry for a code page is loaded into the TLB, the VMM sets the write-protect bit. In order to keep track of the source code pages, the VMM maintains a table of all the guest virtual pages from which it has translated (or interpreted) code. This is done at the time code is translated or interpreted.

To reduce performance losses due to self-modifying code (both real and pseudo-self-modifying), the software-based methods described in Section 3.4.2 can be applied. In addition, because of the codesigned paradigm, special hardware support can be provided to further reduce performance losses caused by pseudo-self-modifying code. In the Transmeta Crusoe, a special hardware structure is added to speedup fine-grained write-protection checking (Dehnert et al. 2003; Banning et al. 2002). The special hardware structure is managed by the VMM and is similar to a small software-managed TLB. This *write-protect table* can hold the fine-grained write-protect masks (Section 3.4.2) for a few source code pages, along with hardware for comparing a potentially faulting store address with the bits in the bit mask (see Figure 7.7). After an address translation is performed with the normal TLB, the real address is presented to the write-protect table. If the normal TLB detects a write-protect fault, the smaller write-protect table can automatically filter out those cases where the write is not to a translated code region. As noted earlier, the TLB write-protect bit is a special bit used solely for protecting code pages. The VMM loads the write-protect table with the bit masks for a set of source code pages that are actively being written; this is usually a small number, if there are any at all.

A final issue involves I/O writes to guest code memory. If an I/O device writes to a guest code page, then these writes must also be caught. Again, the

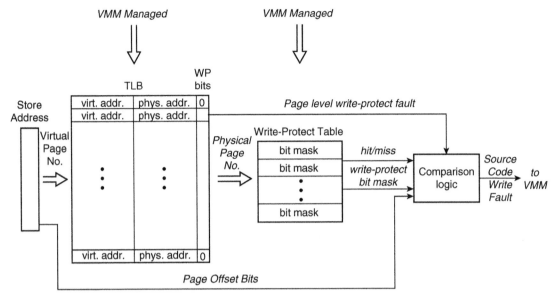

**Figure 7.7**    Fine-Grained Write-Protection Method for Source Code Regions. *A fault is triggered to the VMM if the TLB indicates a write-protect fault and there is a miss in the write-protect table or the comparison logic indicates the write address is to a write-protected fine-grained code region.*

VMM helps enforce this by keeping track of all the real guest pages for which active translations exist in the code cache. To do this, the VMM has to maintain a hardware table for I/O writes, most easily held in the memory controller. The VMM makes entries in this table for all the real pages that hold guest code pages. A store to any of these pages results in an interrupt to the VMM, which can then flush the translations that are derived from the guest code page.

## 7.3  Support for Code Caching

A central element of a codesigned VM implementation, as with other emulating VMs, is the code cache. Because performance and efficiency are key factors in a codesigned VM, code cache performance is of utmost importance. It is useful to consider the issues that may lead to performance losses when using a code cache. Because the blocks of translated code held in a code cache are of unequal size, accessing the code cache becomes more complex than accessing a conventional cache, where blocks are of equal size. A code cache access begins by hashing the source PC (SPC) value to an entry in a map table, reading a corresponding SPC value (or tag) from the map table, and performing a comparison to determine if there is a hit (Figure 2.28). If so, the target PC (TPC) at the map table entry can be used for accessing the code cache. If the first probe of the map table mismatches, then additional probes of the table may be required in order to handle potential hash collisions.

The access delay for the code cache can be quite long, due to the multiple memory accesses and indirect jumps required. A single dispatch table lookup can take on the order of 10–15 instructions, leading to significant performance losses. In a simple code cache implementation, all control-transfer instructions (branches and jumps) perform a map table lookup. However, to improve performance for direct jumps and branches, superblock chaining (Figure 2.29) is an effective solution. With this method, the map table lookup for direct jumps and branches is eliminated entirely. For indirect control transfers the problem is more difficult, however, because register-indirect jumps have their destination addresses stored in a register, and destination addresses can change during the program's execution. Furthermore, the register address is the SPC value, not the TPC value. This means that the source jump address held in a register must be translated from SPC to TPC every time the translated indirect-jump instruction is executed. A straightforward approach is to consult the map table for every indirect jump; but, as noted earlier, this is slow and hence indirect jumps will add a significant performance cost.

To save table lookup overhead for each and every indirect jump, many dynamic optimizers/translators implement a form of software-based jump target prediction (see Section 2.7.2, illustrated again in Figure 7.8). Here, a sequence of instructions compares the indirect SPC address held in a register against an embedded translation-time SPC address. A match indicates a correct "prediction," and the inlined direct branch instruction to a TPC is executed; if there is no match, then the code jumps to the slow map table code.

The software prediction method is of somewhat limited value, however. First, if the software prediction is incorrect, then time is wasted by first testing the possibilities when the dispatch table lookup has to be performed anyway. Second, there are a number of indirect jumps that are very difficult to predict using this method, for example, returns for procedures that have a number of call sites and therefore a number of constantly changing destination addresses. The indirect-jump problem is probably the greatest source of performance loss in a software-only code cache system.

```
if ((Rx) == #addr_1) goto #target_1
else if ((Rx) == #addr_2) goto #target_2
else map_lookup (Rx)          ; do it the slow way
```

**Figure 7.8**    Example of Software Indirect Jump Prediction.

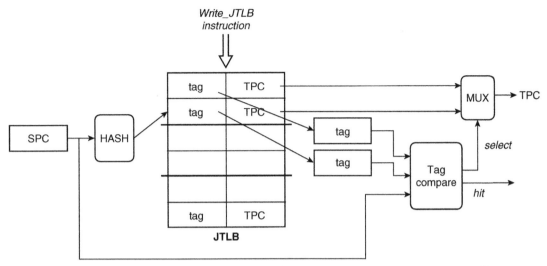

**Figure 7.9**   Jump Translation Lookaside Buffer (JTLB). *This example uses a two-way set associative table.*

### 7.3.1  Jump Translation Lookaside Buffers

In a codesigned VM, the high-overhead software map table can be replaced with a specially designed hardware cache of map table entries (Gschwind 1998a; Kim and Smith 2003). We refer to such a table as a *jump translation lookaside buffer* (JTLB), because it is similar in concept to the software-managed address TLBs used in virtual memory systems. A JTLB is illustrated in Figure 7.9. Each entry in the JTLB contains a tag and a TPC value. The JTLB can be fully associative, set associative, or direct mapped. This example is a two-way associative table. Entries are written into the JTLB by the VMM and always contain correct translations (this can be ensured, for example, by requiring that if a translated block is removed from the code cache, then the VMM must remove any associated entries from the JTLB). The JTLB is accessed by hashing the SPC value (this can consist of taking upper address bits as in a conventional TLB or cache, or it can be a more complex hash function). After the hash, the tag value is compared with the full or partial SPC, depending on the hash function used. If there is a JTLB hit, then the TPC value stored in the entry that hits is the desired jump address in the code cache.

A JTLB can be integrated into a codesigned ISA in a couple of ways. The first is a JTLB_Lookup instruction that accesses the JTLB with an SPC address held in a register and then reads out a TPC and places it in a second register. A third register (or condition code) indicates a hit or miss in the JTLB.

```
JTLB_Lookup Ri, Rj, Rk     ; TPC to Ri, hit/miss to Rj
Jump Ri, Rj==0             ; conditional indirect jump
Jump map_lookup            ; do it the slow way
```

**Figure 7.10**    An Instruction Sequence That Accesses the JTLB.

An example is in Figure 7.10. Here, the JTLB_Lookup instruction takes an SPC value in Rk, puts the associated TPC value in Ri (if there is a hit), and places the hit/miss outcome in Rj. This instruction is followed by a conditional jump on the value in Rj; if there is a miss, control transfers to the map_lookup routine. This routine will place the correct code cache mapping in the JTLB (if the code has been translated); otherwise, the VMM will begin interpretation or will translate the accessed code. A second, simpler way to integrate the JTLB into the ISA is to combine the lookup with the conditional jump, i.e., a Lookup_Jump Rk instruction that performs the jump to the TPC if there is a hit, otherwise it falls through.

This method still requires that when a jump is encountered, instruction fetching must stall until the JTLB is accessed and the jump is executed. An additional enhancement is to predict the TPC value immediately after a Lookup_Jump instruction is fetched, using a more or less conventional branch target buffer (BTB) (see Figure 7.11). Then the predicted instruction stream is accessed from the code cache immediately. Meanwhile, the Lookup_Jump proceeds up the pipeline (along with the predicted TPC). When the Lookup_Jump instruction issues and accesses the JTLB, the prediction is checked. A misprediction causes a pipeline flush, with fetching being redirected to the correct TPC. A miss in the JTLB causes a flush and a fall-through in the original code sequence (which would then jump to the map_lookup routine).

### 7.3.2   Dual-Address Return Address Stack

Either the software prediction approach or the JTLB approach, when supplemented with a BTB prediction, can be very effective, as long as the BTB prediction is correct a high percentage of the time. For many indirect jumps this will be the case, but for procedure return jumps it is often not the case. The problem is that a procedure may be called from a number of places, so a return jump can have a number of different targets that frequently change.

To deal with this problem in a conventional microarchitecture, most modern processors employ a hardware return address stack (RAS) mechanism that can predict a return instruction's target address very accurately (Kaeli and Emma 1991). It basically mimics the software procedure stack by pushing the fall-through PC onto a hardware prediction stack whenever there

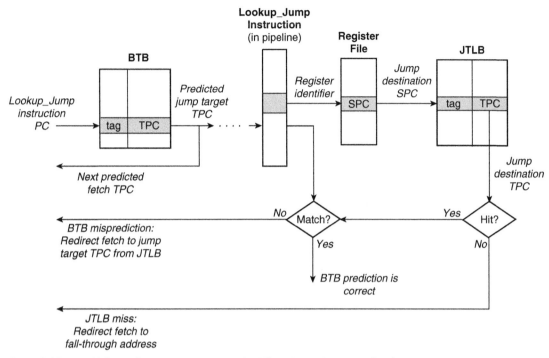

**Figure 7.11** An Enhanced Lookup_Jump Instruction That Uses a BTB to Predict the TPC.

is a procedure-call (jump) instruction. However, in a codesigned VM, this approach cannot be used in its conventional form because the saved return destination address would be an SPC, whereas the corresponding TPC is actually needed for a return destination address prediction. Furthermore, if the procedure jump is at the end of a translated superblock, as it often would be, then the address of the instruction following the jump is not the correct return address anyway (the correct address is at the beginning of a different superblock).

In a codesigned VM, a specialized dual-address RAS mechanism can be used for return address prediction (Gschwind 1998b; Kim and Smith 2003). Each entry in the dual-address RAS (DRAS) contains an address pair, consisting of a return address SPC and its corresponding TPC, as shown in Figure 7.12. The DRAS can be thought of as a hardware implementation of the shadow stack mechanism used in the FX!32 (see Section 2.7.3).

In order to push an address pair onto the DRAS, a special push-DRAS instruction pushes both return addresses. Finding the return destination SPC at superblock construction time is straightforward. Finding the TPC value

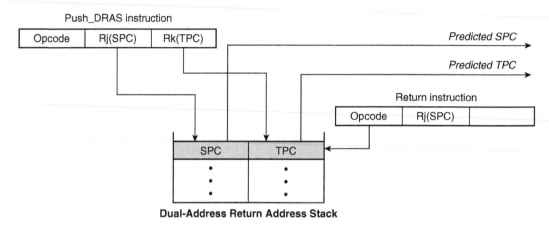

**Figure 7.12**    Dual-Address Return Address Stack. *The Push_DRAS instruction pushes both SPC and TPC. The return instruction uses TPC as a prediction.*

is similar to setting up superblock linking. If the corresponding TPC is not known at superblock construction time, an invalid address is written in the TPC field of the push-DRAS instruction. Later when the return target superblock is constructed, the invalid address is replaced with a valid TPC. Alternatively, if a JTLB is present, it is accessed at the time of a procedure call, and the TPC value is pushed onto the prediction RAS. In either case, the prediction RAS should be pushed/popped for all procedure calls and returns — sometimes even with an invalid TPC to maintain correct stack ordering.

When a return instruction is fetched, the next fetch address is predicted with the popped TPC. The SPC part of the pair flows down the pipeline with the return instruction and is compared to the register value when the return instruction is issued. If the two values do not match, a RAS misprediction is detected, and fetch needs to be redirected. Fetch redirection is accomplished by a jump to the dispatch table code. This is done by having the return jump instruction "fall-through" to the next instruction if there is a misprediction. The next instruction is a jump to the dispatch table code. Note that if a JTLB is also used, a simplification is to replace the *dual* RAS with a *single* RAS, where only the TPC is pushed. The JTLB can be relied upon to provide the correct TPC.

## 7.4  Implementing Precise Traps

Just as in other VMs, implementing precise traps is an important problem in codesigned VMs. In general, one can use techniques similar to those described in Chapters 3 and 4. That is, during the translation process, the optimizing software maintains software checkpoints. If code motion is involved, register live ranges are extended to ensure that checkpoint values can be restored when there is a trap. Then interpretation beginning at a checkpoint prior to a trapping instruction establishes the correct, precise state. In codesigned VMs this approach is facilitated because the host ISA can be designed to have enough registers so that live ranges can be extended without excessive register pressure. Nevertheless, this software-based approach does limit the types of code motion that can be performed (see Section 4.5.1). For example, many instructions cannot be moved below store instructions. By adding hardware support for checkpoints, this restriction on code motion can be removed, thereby relaxing the requirements for register live range extension.

### 7.4.1 Hardware Support for Checkpoints

In codesigned VMs, the designer has the option of providing hardware support for precise traps in translated code. The basis for the approach is to use hardware to set a checkpoint at the time each translation block is entered (Figure 7.13a). Then if there is a trap anywhere in the translation block, the

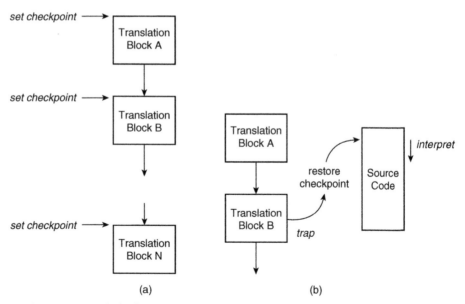

**Figure 7.13**   Hardware-Supported Checkpointing. *(a) Checkpoints are set at every translation block entry point. (b) When there is a trap, the checkpoint is restored, and interpretation begins at the beginning of the source code that formed the trapping translation block.*

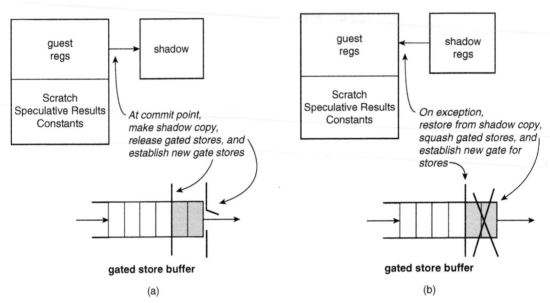

**Figure 7.14** Checkpoint Hardware Operation. *(a) When a checkpoint is committed (and a new one is established), the gated store buffer is released and a new checkpoint is established. (b) If a trap is detected, the contents of the store buffer are flushed and the shadow copy is written back into the register file.*

state at the beginning of the block can be restored via the hardware. At that point, interpretation is used to provide the precise exception state, just as with the software method. The basic sequence is illustrated in Figure 7.13b.

The mechanism for supporting checkpoints is illustrated in Figure 7.14 (Klaiber 2000). When a new translation block is entered, the state from the previous block is committed, and a new checkpoint is set (Figure 7.14a). Setting register checkpoints is fairly easy. The host hardware can support a shadow copy of the guest registers (Smith, Lam, and Horowitz 1990), and registers are checkpointed by copying them *en masse* into the shadow registers. With proper hardware design (and circuit layout) this copying can be done in a very small number of cycles (as few as one). An alternative approach uses shadow registers at a finer granularity (Nystrom et al. 2001) and avoids discarding all the computation done in a code block when an exception is detected.

Checkpointing memory in a similar manner would be much harder because keeping a shadow copy of main memory would be very expensive, in both time and space. Hence, an alternative is to keep all memory store operations buffered in the processor until a translation block is exited (and its state changes can be committed) (Klaiber 2000). Refer to Figure 7.14a. At the time a checkpoint is committed and another is set, a gate is closed at the tail of the store buffer so that any instructions following the gate are inhibited from completing. Meanwhile, the gate at the head of the store buffer (established at the previous checkpoint) is opened so that stores can complete by writing to memory. These writes can occur in the background as computation proceeds. Note that all load instructions must check the store buffer as well as the data cache, in case a load is to an address that is in the buffer. This includes preceding, uncommitted stores in the same translation block and any residual, committed stores from a preceding block.

If an exception should occur during execution of the translation block (Figure 7.14b), then the buffered stores are flushed and the registers are restored from the shadow copy. At that point the state is the same as it was when the block was first entered. Then interpretation of the source code can take over to finish the job of locating the trapping instruction and providing a precise state.

An advantage of the hardware-supported checkpoint method is that the code inside a translation block can be reordered by software in any fashion (subject to true data dependences, of course), even when the block includes store instructions. Hence, the restrictions on code motion given in Section 4.5.1 are relaxed. The only limitation is the fixed size of the store buffer, and this can constrain the translation block size in some cases (the number of stores in the block cannot exceed the store buffer size).

On the other hand, software reordering of loads and stores can lead to violation of memory ordering compatibility. In a shared-memory multiprocessor there are hazards associated with reordering loads and stores as observed by other processors (see Appendix Section A.7.3), which means that reordering may be limited in shared-memory multiprocessor implementations. The reason is that after the software reorders the instructions, the original order is lost; yet correct operation in parallel programs may depend on the original ordering. A method for dealing with multiprocessor memory ordering is described in a patent by members of the IBM Daisy project (Altman et al. 2002). This method is based on acquiring exclusive access to cache lines as stores enter the store buffer and then flushing the buffer and restarting if a different processor should attempt access to the line before the stores in the buffer are released.

### 7.4.2 Page Fault Compatibility

Thus far, we have not considered the recovery of the precise guest state when page faults occur. In most process VMs, page faults are not an issue because they are manifestations of OS policies, are handled by the OS, and are hidden from the process. A codesigned VM is a system VM, not a process VM, which means that the guest OS must observe exactly the same page faults as it would if it were running on a native platform. If the guest OS has mapped a logical page to a conventional real page, then it must not trigger a page fault; similarly, if the guest OS has not mapped a page and it is accessed, then it must page fault. Implementing page fault compatibility is relatively simple for the data region of the guest's memory. If the host implements the same memory mapping as the guest (Figure 7.6) and lets the guest OS manage conventional memory, then page faults to the data region will be detected naturally by the host system. These faults will return control first to the VMM, which can use techniques as described in Section 4.5.2 to determine if the fault is spurious (due to optimizations and/or code reordering) and to produce the correct, precise state before control is handed over to the guest OS.

Likewise, when interpreting instructions, the interpreter loads instructions from the conventional region of memory, so page faults for instruction fetches will occur naturally. For executing translated instructions from the code cache, however, the problem is more difficult because the guest instructions are not actually fetched; rather, translated instructions are fetched from concealed memory. The codesigned VM must therefore implement some mechanism that will trigger a page fault when a translated instruction is fetched from the code cache and the corresponding guest instruction *would have* caused a page fault had it been fetched on a native source platform. There are a number of possible approaches to solving this problem. One approach is *active*, another is *lazy*. Both approaches are discussed in the following paragraphs. Note that in this discussion we assume an architected page table and page faults. Special considerations for an architected TLB and TLB faults will be discussed in a separate subsection.

### Active Page Fault Detection

The active approach to instruction page fault detection is to monitor potential page replacements by the guest operating system. When a source instruction page is replaced by the OS, all the translation blocks based on the replaced source page should be flushed from the code cache.

To determine when an instruction page is potentially being replaced by the guest OS, the VMM monitors the guest OS's modifications to the architected page table. This can be done by marking memory that holds the page table as "write-protected." Assuming the page table is architected, the region of memory that holds the page table can be identified by the VMM. Write-protecting pages is most easily done if VMM software manages the TLB. Then the write-protection information is added to the implementation of the TLB and does not require any changes to the architected page table in main memory. The VMM should also monitor any other operations that may change a virtual to real page mapping, e.g., changes to the page table pointer.

In addition, the VMM keeps a table of virtual page numbers for each page containing source instructions. At the time a block of source instructions is translated, an entry is made in the table (if it is not already in the table). Then whenever the page table mapping is modified, there is a trap (or jump) to the VMM, and the VMM determines if the page table entry for a source instruction page is being modified. If so, the VMM flushes all the translations in the code cache derived from that page. This requires a pair of side tables. One side table tracks all the translation blocks derived from each page; these are the translation blocks that must be flushed. The second table (or an extension to the first), keeps track of any link backpointers (see Section 3.8.2). The link pointers are changed so that they point into the VMM emulation manager. After this is done, an attempt to transfer control into the removed page will instead jump to the emulation manager. Subsequently, the emulation process will detect the instruction page fault when it attempts to emulate an instruction from the code page and it misses in the page table. Finally, if hardware structures containing SPC-to-TPC address translations are implemented, such as the JTLB and DRAS (Section 7.3), then these structures should be flushed of any entries corresponding to flushed translations.

### Lazy Page Fault Detection

With the lazy solution, when a source code page is replaced by the guest OS, the code cache is not immediately flushed of corresponding translations. Rather, it waits until there is an attempt to actually use the translated code. To accomplish this, every time the translated code crosses a source page boundary, the page table is probed to see if the mapping is the same as on the original translation (Ebcioglu et al. 2001).

The method is illustrated in Figure 7.15. First, it must be possible to determine when translated code crosses a source page boundary. This is most easily done if all the code in a translation block is derived from the same source page. If this is the case, then source pages boundaries are crossed only when there are link jumps, e.g., when block HIJ jumps to block KL in Figure 7.15. Otherwise, if translated code can come from different source pages, then the crossing points within the translated code should be distinct, at least with respect to precise state updates (the transition from E to F in Figure 7.15). In either case, at the time a source page boundary is crossed, the first instruction is a Verify_Translation instruction, inserted by the translator. This instruction probes the page table to see if the page mapping has changed. The Verify_Translation instruction provides the virtual address of the newly entered source page along with the

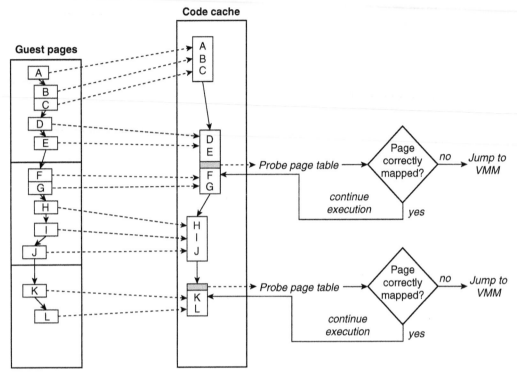

**Figure 7.15**    Detecting Instruction Page Faults via Instructions That Probe the Page Table.

real address at the time the block was translated. The instruction attempts to translate the virtual page number to a real page number and, if successful, compares it with the real address provided by the instruction. If the virtual page is mapped to real memory and the two real addresses match, then execution of the translated code proceeds. Otherwise, the VMM takes over and generates a page fault and/or translates the source code page that has just been entered.

### Architected Translation Lookaside Buffers

With architected TLBs, both the active and lazy methods can be adapted in a straightforward way. But, because of performance issues, the active approach is somewhat problematic. If the active approach is used, then translations are flushed every time a TLB entry for a source code page is overwritten. Then the code must be retranslated if the TLB entry is later restored. If there is a fairly large number of source instruction pages and a lot of TLB activity for instruction pages, this approach could lead to a very high overhead. With the lazy approach, `Verify_Translation` instructions can be used, as before. The only difference is that they generate an architected TLB fault rather than a page fault when the translation is not present.

## 7.5 Input/Output

For the most part, implementing I/O in a codesigned VM is straightforward. If the VMM does not use any I/O devices itself, then all the guest device drivers can be run as is (although instructions in the driver code are emulated, just as all other guest instructions are). Any I/O instructions or memory-mapped I/O is simply "passed through" by the VMM so that the I/O system sees the same signals that it would if the guest were running on a native platform.

As noted in Section 4.5.1, memory-mapped I/O results in volatile memory locations, and the presence of volatile memory locations should inhibit optimizations involving removal and/or reordering of memory loads and stores to those locations. To identify code regions that access volatile memory, an access-protect bit, similar to the write-protect bit of Section 7.2 can be added to the TLB. Then if a memory-mapped I/O routine performs loads or stores to an access-protected memory page, there is a trap to the VMM, which can then deoptimize translations containing the accesses to volatile memory in order to ensure that they all occur in the correct sequence (Kelly, Cmelik, and Wing 1998). As an additional enhancement, the implementation ISA can be extended to include special volatile versions of load and store instructions, which do not trap when the access-protect bit is set; if these are used in deoptimized I/O code, then their execution will proceed without trapping.

If a VMM uses no I/O devices, then it is restricted to reside entirely in concealed memory. This means, for example, that code translations cannot be cached to disk and reused as is done in the FX!32 system described in Section 3.10. All translations must be done from scratch each time a program is run; and when translated code is removed from the code cache, it is discarded and must be retranslated before it can be used again.

If the requirement of complete transparency can be relaxed somewhat, then concealed memory can be extended to secondary storage (disk). In order for this to be accomplished, there must be a portion of a disk (or possibly an entire disk) reserved for use by the VMM as concealed secondary storage. The most straightforward way to do this is to provide a special disk driver that is VMM-aware (Figure 7.16). It is the loading of this special disk driver that breaks complete VMM transparency. This limits the use of the codesigned processor to those operating systems for which the special disk driver has been developed and deployed. The disk driver code can restrict the OS to that portion of

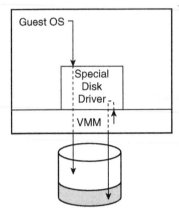

**Figure 7.16** Concealed Secondary Storage. *By adding a special disk driver, concealed secondary storage (shaded) can be implemented. Both the guest OS and VMM software can call the driver, but only the VMM can access the concealed region of the disk.*

the disk that is visible (actually, the guest OS is only informed of the nonconcealed region). Meanwhile, the VMM uses the disk driver to access its concealed region of disk.

To avoid relaxing transparency even more, the VMM is entirely responsible for managing the concealed secondary memory. This implies that it is not backed up or archived, for example, so this restricts its use to caching code translations (or for paging VMM software). This large, persistent code cache would be useful for reducing initial start-up time for big programs (including the OS when it is booted). However, checks have to incorporated to make sure that any source code with cached translations has not changed since the time of the translation, possibly by keeping a copy of the original source code and performing an instruction-by-instruction check (Conte, Sathaye, and Banerjia 1996). Furthermore, the concealed secondary storage would only be useful for large blocks of translated codes — for small blocks it would probably be faster to translate from scratch than to make disk accesses. An interesting (and less transparent) disk-based code caching approach was proposed for dynamic rescheduling of VLIW binaries based on page-sized code blocks (Conte and Sathaye 1995).

## 7.6 Applying Codesigned Virtual Machines

Thus far, we have described a number of mechanisms that allow a codesigned VM to emulate full ISAs and execute instructions efficiently from a code cache. These mechanisms are only enablers; however, to be useful these mechanisms must be applied in codesigned VMs that provide real advantages, such as improved performance, power efficiency, and software flexibility. Advantages can be achieved at two levels, in effect at a macro level and at a micro level.

At the macro level, entirely new ISAs can be implemented. Some of the proposed and implemented target ISAs for codesigned VMs have been aimed at exposing instruction-level parallelism to hardware in a more efficient manner than with conventional instruction sets. Most conventional instruction sets still reflect the sequential model of execution prevalent decades ago. Consequently, hardware is burdened with discovering parallelism in the instruction stream at run time; this is the essence of modern superscalar processors.

Two of the better-known codesigned VMs, the Transmeta Crusoe (Klaiber 2000; Halfhill 2000) and the IBM Daisy/BOA (Ebcioglu et al. 2001; Sathaye et al. 1999), implement VLIW instruction sets as their target ISA. The codesigned software is responsible for finding independent instructions in the source binary and packing them together in the VLIWs. The advantage of a VLIW implementation is that it does not require the complexity (and power consumption) of an out-of-order issue unit as in most superscalar processors.

A proposal for a different style of codesigned VM has a similar goal — to simplify instruction issue logic — but it does this by exposing chains of dependent instructions to the hardware (rather than independent ones as with a VLIW) (Kim and Smith 2003). Then multiple in-order instruction issue units can be given the dependent chains of instructions. Each issue unit processes instructions in order, which simplifies hardware, but the multiple issue units can issue instructions out of order with respect to each other. A research project at the University of Illinois (Merten et al. 2001) provides a number of interesting codesigned hardware components targeted primarily at profiling and optimization, rather than ISA innovation.

The goal of the IBM AS/400 implementation (Soltis 1996) is to provide a high-level object-oriented source ISA. Besides being well suited for efficient support of object-oriented system and application software, this approach allows many of the hardware resource management mechanisms, e.g., page management, to be placed in the implementation-dependent VMM. Another advantage of the codesigned approach was demonstrated by the AS/400 designers when they successfully replaced the original host ISA (a proprietary CISC) with an extended PowerPC ISA and migrated users in a completely transparent way.

At the micro level, codesigned VMs permit the implementation of specific performance enhancements (which may be related to the selected host ISA). For example, in a VLIW platform, all code scheduling is performed by the software translation system, so the ability to reorder instructions is crucial to the success of a VLIW-based computer. Consequently, in the codesigned VMs that use VLIW target ISAs, there is special support to enable reordering of instructions, especially load and store instructions, because dependences among load and store instructions are difficult to determine statically (i.e., to *disambiguate* them).

Finally, an important feature of codesigned VMs is that implementation-dependent profiling hardware can be built in for use by dynamic translating/optimizing software (Conte, Menezes, and Hirsch 1996; Heil and Smith 2000; Merten et al. 2000). This profiling hardware can be matched to optimizations used by the codesigned software translation code as well as features in the microarchitecture.

To make the foregoing advantages more concrete, the next two sections give case studies of two of the more important codesigned VMs, the Transmeta Crusoe and the IBM AS/400.

## 7.7 Case Study: Transmeta Crusoe

Although some elements of the codesigned VM paradigm had been used previously, for example, to provide code portability, the Transmeta Crusoe broke new ground in using a codesigned VM for achieving power efficiency and design simplicity. The TM5000 series was introduced in early 2000; these processors are described here. The follow-on Efficeon (TM8000) series was introduced in 2003, it incorporates larger caches than the TM5000 series, and its VLIW instructions are twice as wide.

The Crusoe implements the Intel IA-32 ISA with an underlying proprietary VLIW instruction set that uses dynamic code translation and optimization, centered on a code cache. The microarchitecture of the TM5800 processor is illustrated in Figure 7.17. The VLIW (or a *molecule*, in Transmeta parlance) consists of four instructions (*atoms*). It is a classic VLIW in the sense that the individual instruction fields in the VLIW are dedicated to specific functions. These instruction fields feed a branch unit, a floating-point unit, an integer unit, and a load/store unit. For precise traps, the Crusoe uses the method described in Section 7.4 and is based on shadow registers and a gated store buffer.

The memory hierarchy is illustrated in Figure 7.18. The VMM software is held in compressed form in a 512KB boot ROM. At the beginning of the boot process, this software is decompressed into a 2MB region of concealed memory. In the implementation shown, the code cache and various side tables consume 14MB. There are conventional 64KB level-1 instruction and data caches, but, in addition, there are two smaller memories dedicated to the VMM.

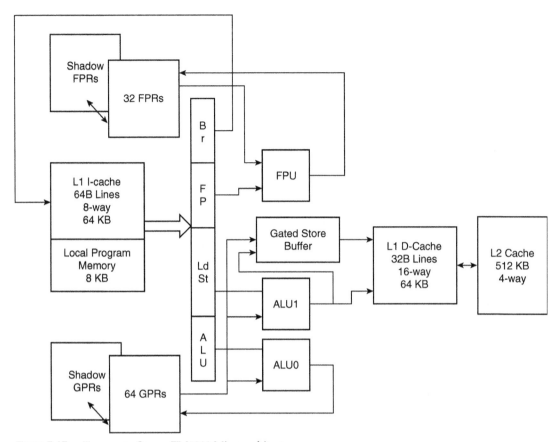

**Figure 7.17**    Transmeta Crusoe TM5800 Microarchitecture.

These are for critical VMM code and data that the designer relies upon for low-latency access.

The big optimization challenges in the Crusoe involve breaking the complex IA-32 instructions into RISC-like micro-ops and then finding parallelism and scheduling them into VLIWs. Because an in-order VLIW microarchitecture is used, code reordering is a key part of the optimization process. To provide support for reordering, the Crusoe designers built some special features into the implementation ISA.

Being able to move load instructions is perhaps the most important type of reordering, because load instructions take longer to execute than most other instructions, especially if there is a cache miss. That is, it is desirable to reorder a load instruction higher up in the instruction stream so that it executes earlier and can therefore eliminate or reduce the wait time of subsequent dependent

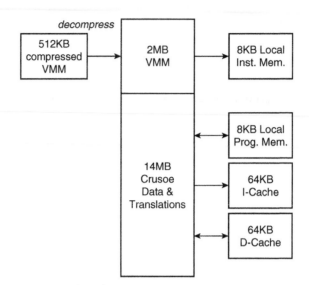

**Figure 7.18**  Transmeta Crusoe Memory Hierarchy.

instructions. For example, consider the code in Figure 7.19a, which contains two loads and two stores with an add instruction that consumes the two loaded values. It would be desirable to move the load instructions higher in the code sequence, as is shown in Figure 7.19b. Then there are other intervening instructions that can overlap with the execution time of the loads. Consequently, the time the add instruction might have to wait for its input operands is reduced, especially if one or both of the load instructions should miss in the data cache. However, moving the load instructions up may be unsafe, because the store

|  Original code  | Rescheduled (unsafe) | Rescheduled (protected) |
|---|---|---|
| st  0(r1),r2 | ld  r3,0(r4) | ldp  r3,0(r4)  x |
| ... | ld  r7,0(r8) | ldp  r7,0(r8)  x  x |
| ld  r3,0(r4) | st  0(r1),r2 | stam 0(r1),r2 |
| ... | ... | ... |
| st  0(r5),r6 | ... | stam 0(r5),r6 |
| ... | st  0(r5),r6 | ... |
| ld  r7,0(r8) | ... | ... |
| add r9,r3,r7 | add r9,r3,r7 | add  r9,r3,r7 |
| (a) | (b) | (c) |

**Figure 7.19**  Safe Reordering of Memory Operations with Load-and-Protect and Store-under-Alias-Mask Instructions. *(a) Original code sequence; (b) unsafe reordering (due to unknown addresses); (c) reordering with protection from ldp and stam instructions.*

instructions may be to the same memory address. For example, if the store to 0(r1) happens to be to the same address as the load from 0(r4), then in the reordered code the load will return the wrong data. Because the register values are often not known until run time and they may change over the course of the program's execution, the binary translator is not able to guarantee that the load and store addresses are never the same, so, to be safe, such a code reordering should be inhibited.

A codesign approach for detecting such memory conflicts is very well suited to this problem (Gallagher et al. 1994), and the Transmeta designers took such an approach by adding a pair of special instructions. The load-and-protect instruction (ldp) performs a load operation and records the address and size of the loaded data in an architected table. The store-under-alias-mask (stam) instruction performs a store and also contains a mask that identifies certain table entries — the ones set by preceding ldp instructions. For each stam instruction, the masked ldp instructions are illustrated in Figure 7.19c with arrows from the stam to the ldp; the table itself is not shown. The second stam in the example identifies only the second load, because the first load was already ordered ahead of it. If a table entry indicated by the mask of a stam instruction detects an overlap between the ldp's memory address and the stam's memory address, then there is a trap to the VMM. At that point, the VMM can handle the situation like it does most other traps: It can go back to the previous checkpoint and begin interpreting the original code in order to get the correct result. If a particular translation block repeatedly traps, then the VMM can reorder the code more conservatively, taking care to leave the overlapping load and store in their original sequence.

The ldp/stam pair is an excellent example that illustrates the interplay between the codesigned hardware and software in a codesigned VM. In this case, where a VLIW is used, the ability to reorder code is very important, and the ldp/stam instructions, in conjunction with the dynamic optimization code, facilitate code reordering.

## 7.8 Case Study: IBM AS/400

The architecture of the IBM AS/400 (derived from the earlier System/38) is perhaps not as widely known as other "textbook" computer architectures, but it is both highly innovative and commercially successful (Soltis 1996). The AS/400 includes a codesigned VM — in fact, the whole system, including system software, was designed from scratch using a fully integrated approach, so one could say the entire system was codesigned from top to bottom. Unlike the other codesigned VMs discussed in this chapter, however, the System/38

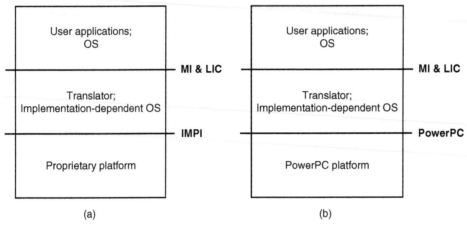

**Figure 7.20**  AS/400 Architectures. *(a) The original System/38 and early-generation AS/400 systems were based on a proprietary ISA (IMPI) and hardware platform. (b) More recent AS/400 systems are based on an extended PowerPC ISA and platform.*

was not designed to support an existing, conventional ISA. Rather, the original System/38 designers invented a new, high-level ISA with the goals of software simplicity and machine (hardware) independence.

The high-level instruction set is referred to as the *technology-independent machine interface,* or just MI for short. Supplementing the MI is a set of standard libraries, the Licensed Internal Code (LIC), which deals with the implementation-dependent aspects of resource management. The MI and LIC together from an ABI layer upon which all implementation-independent software runs.

In the original design, the underlying implementation architecture was based on a proprietary CISC ISA called the *internal microprogrammed interface* (IMPI)[1] (see Figure 7.20a). In developing a high-level ISA that is implementation independent, the objective was to provide for future changes in the underlying implementation, including the lower-level ISA. This feature has been exploited as the AS/400 evolved, first by extending the IMPI in a transparent way and then by a complete shift to an extended PowerPC ISA (Figure 7.20b).

Because the MI is at a higher level than a conventional ISA and was developed with the goal of hardware independence, the AS/400 architecture is

---

**1.** Calling the codesigned software *micro-code* indicates that it was considered to be part of the hardware design, as opposed to being considered conventional software.

similar in philosophy to the HLL VMs described in Chapter 5 and follows the model illustrated in Figure 5.1. That is, the MI compiler is analogous to a conventional compiler frontend, and the MI translator is analogous to a conventional compiler backend. However, like other codesigned VMs, the AS/400 is a system VM. It supports not only language aspects of program execution but also a full system environment. The philosophy of dividing the implementation-independent and implementation-dependent software extends to the OS functions; for example, device drivers and memory management algorithms are in the implementation-dependent part of the OS. These functions are embodied in the licensed internal code, which uses the host ISA (IMPI or PowerPC).

The AS/400 uses an object-based ISA (the MI). So in this way it also follows a similar philosophy to the Java VM and the CLI (Chapter 5). However, in the AS/400, the MI itself is object based, in the sense that there are architected object types and type-specific instructions built into the MI. The programs that run above the MI do not necessarily have to be object based, however. In contrast, with Java and the CLI systems, the V-ISA includes architected primitives that are then capable of supporting the object-oriented programs that run above the V-ISA level; the only architected objects with their own instructions are arrays.

## 7.8.1 Memory Architecture

The MI has a memory architecture composed of objects. The objects are completely isolated from one another and can only be accessed via pointers; see Figure 7.21. There are a number of object types supported and used by MI instructions. The simplest type of object is simply called a *space*, which, as the name suggests, consists of a space for data. Other objects contain object-specific information, i.e., a "functional part" as well as space for constants and other object-related data. An object can be accessed only through a pointer created specifically for that object. To access a location inside a space, a space pointer or data pointer (for typed data) must be used. The functional part of an object is implementation dependent and is manipulated only by MI instructions specific to that type of object; the contents of the functional part are not otherwise visible above the MI. The MI-supported objects can be created, destroyed, and modified by programs.

Actual address values contained in pointers are not made visible to software above the MI level. Pointers can be used only for accessing data, and pointers cannot be modified with ordinary instructions. If an attempt is made to write to a memory location containing a pointer, then its ability to be used as a pointer

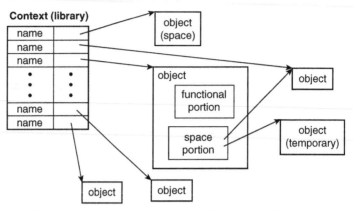

**Figure 7.21**    MI Memory Architecture. *Memory consists of objects, which may be either permanent (persistent) or temporary. A typical object contains a functional portion, accessible only via instructions specific to that type of object, and a space portion that can be modified with conventional instructions. The simplest object consists only of a space.*

is immediately destroyed. The implementation of this feature is described shortly.

Protecting the integrity of pointers is an essential part of any object-based system. It is interesting to contrast this method of pointer protection with the one used in the Java VM, where references are protected by carefully tracking their type so that illegal operations on references simply never occur in a properly verified program.

Although the MI object-based memory architecture is reminiscent of the heap used in Java and MSIL, a fundamental difference is that the AS/400 implements a system VM, so objects must persist over the lifetime of the system rather than just the lifetime of a process. There are no conventional files, from the perspective of the OS and applications. All storage, both in DRAM and disk, is one large object-based memory managed beneath the MI level. All long-term storage is done via permanent objects. Each of these permanent objects has a name that is contained in an MI object called a *context* (or a *library* in the operating system, OS/400). To get a pointer to an object, a program can specify a context and an object name; if the program is authorized to access the object, it is then given the correct pointer. This is similar to opening a file in a conventional system. Permanent objects persist in the system until they are explicitly destroyed.

In addition to permanent objects, a process can create temporary objects for its use as it runs. These temporary objects do not necessarily have a pointer held in a context, and they remain in the system until the system is rebooted. This ensures that there are no active programs that have a pointer to a temporary object at the time it is removed. There is no garbage collection in the AS/400, so this is the mechanism by which temporary space is returned to the system.

The implementation of the object-based memory, including all of memory management, is done entirely below the MI level. Main memory is based on the conventional PowerPC segment/page-mapping structure, as described in Appendix Section A.8.1. The object pointers are encoded in 128 bits, but the upper 64 bits contain type information and in some cases authorization information, and the lower 64 bits are essentially a 64-bit PowerPC virtual address.

The only significant extension to the PowerPC memory architecture is the adding of protection for object pointers, i.e., to prevent a program from over-writing a pointer in memory with an arbitrary value, and then later using it for an unauthorized memory access. This is accomplished by adding special instructions for loading and storing pointers and adding a "65th" bit to each memory doubleword. This 65th bit indicates whether the location contains a pointer (actually half of a 128-bit pointer). A load-pointer instruction checks this pointer bit; if set, it sets a condition flag that can be checked to verify that a valid pointer was loaded. A store-pointer instruction stores a pointer and sets the pointer bit(s). Every conventional (nonpointer) store always clears the pointer bit. Hence, any attempt to overwrite a pointer with a regular store results in what will be recognized as a nonpointer if it is ever accessed via a load-pointer instruction.

### 7.8.2 Instruction Set

The MI instructions are not intended to be executed directly, nor are they intended to be interpreted (although, in theory, they could be). They are essentially in a form that must be further compiled (translated) to the host platform's ISA before they can be directly executed. In the original System/38 this was the IMPI; in the more recent systems, it is an extended PowerPC ISA. The MI ISA performs fairly conventional operations that can operate on normal data types held in a space. It also has instructions that operate on MI-defined objects.

The MI instruction format, shown in Figure 7.22a, consists of an opcode and operand fields. The opcode is two bytes; the opcode extender (described shortly) is also two bytes. There are zero to $n$ operand fields, each three bytes long (in the original System/38, two bytes). For basic arithmetic and logical instructions there is a long format and a short format. The long format is *operand1 ← operand2 op operand3*, where "op" is the operation

| 2 bytes | 2 bytes | 3 bytes | | 3 bytes | 3 bytes | | 3 bytes |
|---------|---------|---------|---|---------|---------|---|---------|
| opcode | opcode extender | operand 1 | . . . | operand n | destination1 | . . . | destination4 |
| | (optional) | (optional) | | (optional) | (optional) | | (optional) |

(a)

| addn & branch | eq 0 | gt 0 | 0 | 0 | sum | addend1 | addend2 | destination1 | destination2 |
|---------------|------|------|---|---|-----|---------|---------|--------------|--------------|

(b)

**Figure 7.22**   AS/400 Instructions. *(a) The general instruction format; (b) an example instruction that performs an addition and a multiway conditional branch.*

being performed. The short form is *operand1* ← *operand1 op operand2*, i.e., the first operand is both a source and a destination.

An interesting feature of the MI is that every instruction can include a four-way conditional branch or can evaluate up to four predicate values (called *indicators* in AS/400). These are implemented via the extended opcodes. If there is an opcode extender, then the instruction also has up to four branch destinations (or addresses for indicator values). The 16-bit extended opcode is divided into four 4-bit fields. Each of the 4-bit fields encodes a condition, such as *greater than zero, equal to zero, less than or equal to zero*, etc. If the opcode extension is for a branch and the result of the instruction matches the first test condition, then there is a branch to the first branch destination; if it matches the second condition, it branches to the second destination, etc. A condition of zero indicates no test (and no destination is given). Similarly, for an indicator-setting instruction, the four destination fields correspond to up to four locations in memory where true/false predicate flags are stored.

For example, the instruction in Figure 7.22b does the following — it performs an addition on *addend1* and *addend2,* and the result is placed in *sum.* Then if the sum is zero, it branches to *destination1*; if the sum is greater than zero, it branches to *destination2*; otherwise, there is no branch, and the next instruction is executed. This instruction takes a total of 19 bytes, but it is important to keep in mind that this is the architected *representation* for the instruction. Before it is actually executed, it is translated to an implementation-dependent form that will be more compact, and it does the work of multiple RISC instructions. This instruction, for example, would likely compile to three PowerPC instructions, an add followed by two conditional branches.

The next matter is the way the operands are specified. The operand fields point into a two-level table that contains descriptors of the operands; this

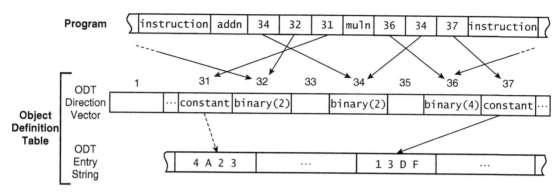

**Figure 7.23** Specifying AS/400 Operands. *AS/400 operands are specified by an object definition table (ODT).*

is called the *object definition table,* or ODT. As used here, the term *object* is being overloaded; these so-called objects are different from the true architected objects to be discussed later. The ODT, along with an instruction referencing it, is illustrated in Figure 7.23. The first-level table is the ODT direction vector (or ODV). This table consists of up to 16 million fixed-length fields that are directly addressed by the 3-byte instruction operand fields. The entries in the ODV contain a description of an operand type along with an optional pointer to the second-level table, the ODT entry string (OES). The OES is used for those operand descriptors that don't fit in the fixed-length ODV entry.

In the example shown in Figure 7.23, two instructions in a program are shown along the top. The first instruction is an addn (add numeric). Its first operand is specified in ODT entry 32 and the other is in ODT entry 31. These operands are 2-byte binary (two's complement) numbers. The second operand is a constant (x4A23), and the pointer in ODT entry 31 points to the OES entry that holds the constant value. The result is also a 2-byte number (as indicated by entry 34). The second instruction takes the result of the first as one operand and a second constant (x13DF) as the second and multiplies them to form a 4-byte binary result. In these arithmetic instructions the opcodes, add numeric and multiply numeric, are generic; the actual type of operation (two's complement, decimal, or floating point) is determined from the types of the operands given in the ODT.

Note that the entries in the ODT indicate the types of operands and the data flow (e.g., that the result of the addn is an input to the muln). The actual storage locations for operands are assigned only after the MI is translated to the implementation instructions. At that time the specified operands may be assigned to registers, to a VMM-managed region of memory, or both.

The constant operands would likely be translated into immediate fields of implementation instructions. This is very much like the register assignment process ordinarily performed in a compiler backend; here, it is deferred to the VMM translator.

As pointed out earlier, all logical memory resides within objects; therefore accessing operands in memory must be done through pointers. Pointers are another operand type that can appear in the ODT. A pointer is returned when an object is created or when a symbolic pointer (e.g., as would be held in a context) is resolved.

As noted earlier, some instructions are object specific. The list of MI-supported objects is given below. Note that because the AS/400 was targeted at commercial applications, it has a number of objects intended to support databases. The operating system can use these objects directly for its purposes (the OS is also object based), or it can use these objects as primitives to build OS-defined objects.

*Access group, Context* — objects used for object management

*Authorization list, User profile* — objects used for supporting security

*Byte string space, Data space, Dump space, Space* — objects whose primary use is to hold data

*Commit block, Cursor, Data space index, Dictionary, Index, Journal port, Journal space* — objects whose primary use is to support database operations

*Class-of-service description, Mode descriptor, Process control space, Queue, User profile* — objects for process management, used by the OS

*Controller description, Logical unit descriptor, Network description* — objects used to support I/O

*Module, Program* — objects that contain translated code

### 7.8.3  Input/Output

Because of the focus on commercial applications, the I/O system in the AS/400 is a very elaborate one, based on I/O processors (IOPs), separate from the central processor. Consistent with the overall AS/400 philosophy, I/O is divided into implementation-independent and implementation-dependent parts, with the MI separating the two. The presence of IOPs simplifies the task of pushing the device-dependent aspects out of the central processor (and well below the MI layer).

At the level of the MI there is no secondary (disk) storage; rather, it is part of the unified memory architecture. In other words, disks are not considered to be part of the I/O system, and they have no presence above the MI level. All disk management software, drivers, etc. exist in the implementation-dependent part of the system. It should be pointed out that taking this approach is simplified in an environment where a single company is designing the entire system, i.e., where there is a high degree of vertical integration. The I/O devices visible above the MI layer are divided into generic types, for example, printers, keyboards, graphics displays. The logical characteristics of each of these general types are characterized by MI-level system objects called *logical unit descriptors*. Similarly, device controllers that may be present in the system can each control multiple devices. Two other MI-level objects, the controller descriptor object and network descriptor object, contain the logical characteristics of device controllers and network interfaces. The operating system interacts with software below the MI level (and, in effect, with the I/O devices) through instructions that operate on the MI-level objects.

### 7.8.4 The Processor Resource

Above the MI level, the operating system establishes overall usage policies, for example, what the priorities the processes should be and what quotas of various resources should be. The actual implementation of the policy is below the MI layer. That is, the implementation-dependent part of the system actually manages the scheduling queues.

Overall, many conventional operating system functions are done below the MI. This again reflects the overall integrated structure of the AS/400 design environment. When both the platform designers and the OS designers work at the same company (and largely at the same company site), it is easier to divide the OS functions in this manner.

### 7.8.5 Code Translation and Concealment

One of the more interesting aspects of the AS/400 is the way that it manages programs while concealing the implementation-dependent details. The process of compiling and translating a program is illustrated in Figure 7.24. First, a high-level language program is compiled, with the resulting MI code and object descriptor table being placed into a space object. Here, it is referred to as a *template* for an object yet to be created. Then a `create program` instruction is executed. One of its source operands is a pointer to the space object holding

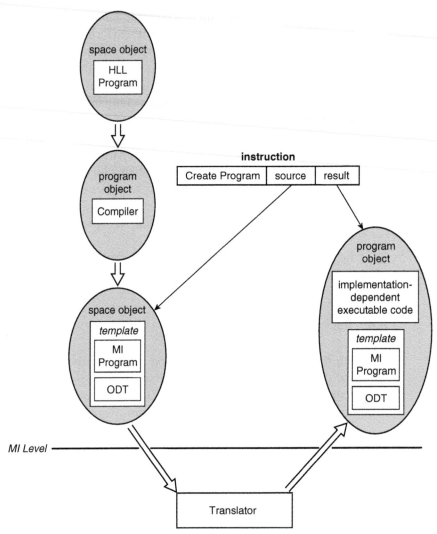

**Figure 7.24** Compiling and Translating a Program on the AS/400. *The steps of compiling an HLL program and translating it into an implementation-dependent form.*

the program template. This instruction is "executed," which in fact results in the complete translation of the template contents into a program object containing the implementation-dependent executable file, e.g., PowerPC code. The `create program` instruction returns a result operand, which is a pointer to the program object containing the translated code. After being created, a program can be executed, and it can be maintained persistently or temporarily, just as any other object.

The contents of the program object cannot be directly observed above the MI level; i.e., the contents are concealed, just as with any other object. However, there are times when it may be desirable to look at the program code, for example, when debugging. To accomplish this, the original program template is also kept as part of the program object. Then the original program can be *materialized*, that is, given back to the user in its original, machine-independent form.

This feature yields another interesting capability. Say that a program has been compiled on a given hardware platform and is stored as a persistent object. Then the hardware platform is changed, as when IBM changed the AS/400 platform to PowerPC. Because the original template is stored in the program object, the platform switch is transparent to the user; in particular, the user does not have to recreate the program object for the new host platform. Rather, when the user attempts to execute the program object on the new platform, the software below the MI layer will recognize that the translated code is for a different platform and use the original program template to produce a translation for the new host platform and place it in the program object.

Finally, it is interesting to compare this overall approach to implementation-dependent concealment with that used by the other codesigned VMs discussed in this chapter. The other codesigned VMs perform both translation and caching of translated code in a concealed manner. This means that each time a program is executed, it must be translated from scratch and then held in a code cache until the program terminates, at which time the code cache contents are discarded. In the AS/400, the fact that programs must be translated is not concealed, yet the actual translated code is concealed (within an object). Because the translation process is not concealed, the system can maintain translated programs in a persistent way, by treating them like any other persistent objects.

## 7.9 Summary

To some extent, modern codesigned VMs, as exemplified by the Transmeta Crusoe, should still be considered a somewhat experimental approach to computer design. This approach is based heavily on dynamic translation to a concealed code cache. Translations do not persist between successive program runs, so translation overhead is a major concern. On the other hand, it takes tens of milliseconds to access the disk when loading a conventional program or when performing other loading and linking tasks, possibly including additional dynamic loading and linking, as the program runs. When viewed from this perspective, the time required for dynamic translation does not appear so great, and, in a sense, it could be considered part of the loading process. Furthermore, the shift to just-in-time compilation for HLL VMs will tend to make this approach appear more conventional as time passes.

The earlier AS/400 object-based approach, although successful and still used in the IBM iSeries machines, has not been copied in other commercial products. It is based on an unconventional separation of hardware and software functionality that probably works best in a completely vertically integrated system development environment. This design environment is much less common today than it was when the AS/400 (System/38) was first developed. A recent research project at the University of Illinois (Adve et al. 2003) advocates a new V-ISA that is in some respects similar to the AS/400 MI; it uses object-based memory architecture and a register-intensive instruction set. A primary goal is passing performance-critical information down to the hardware, where it can be more readily used. In other related work, the DELI project (Desoli 2002), builds on the earlier HP Dynamo project, and provides a callable interface into the emulation layer, thereby allowing application or system software the ability to interact with the emulation process.

Thus far the only real example of a modern codesigned VM is the Transmeta Crusoe, although the IBM Daisy/BOA project was carried far into software development and simulation. Both of these systems use a target ISA based on VLIW, and the suitability of VLIW for general-purpose computing remains a topic for debate. The Transmeta processors are targeted at power efficiency; their performance is not at the same level as the high-end superscalar processors that dynamically reorder instructions. Because most contemporary processors use out-of-order superscalar designs, when evaluating performance it is difficult to separate the codesigned aspect from the VLIW aspect to reach any conclusions regarding the overall suitability of the codesigned VM approach. The bottom line is that the codesigned VM approach remains a very interesting technology whose full potential remains to be fully determined.

Finally, an interesting future application of codesigned VMs is to target multiple source ISAs with the same platform. That is, to develop a single processor capable of executing software from multiple, different ISAs, depending on the emulation software that has been loaded into concealed memory. These *convergence architectures* (Gschwind et al. 2000) would, among other things, allow computers in server farms to be dynamically customized to fit the software they are called upon to execute.

# Chapter Eight
# System Virtual Machines

I t was observed very early that many of the hardware resources in a typical computer system are underutilized. The concept of *time sharing* was developed to improve resource utilization by allowing multiple users to access a single computer system simultaneously, with each user being given the illusion of having access to a full set of system resources. In order to create this illusion, a multiprogramming operating system essentially implements a process virtual machine for each application-level program and switches resources among the programs on a time-shared basis.

System virtual machines take this concept one step further by providing a similar illusion for complete systems. A system VM environment is capable of supporting multiple system images simultaneously, each running its own operating system and associated application programs. Each operating system controls and manages a set of virtualized hardware resources, as illustrated in Figure 8.1. The virtual resources include a processor (or processors), storage resources, and peripheral devices needed to perform input and output (I/O) for the system.

In a system VM environment, real resources of the *host* platform are shared among the *guest* system VMs, with a layer of software, the virtual machine monitor (VMM), managing the allocation of, and access to, the hardware resources of the host platform. The VMM owns the real system resources and makes them available to one or more guest operating systems that alternately execute on the same hardware. Thus, a guest operating system in a virtual machine environment is given the illusion of owning the resources it subsequently allocates to its various user programs.

Each virtual resource may or may not have a corresponding physical resource. When a corresponding physical resource is available, the VMM decides how access will be provided to virtual machines requiring its

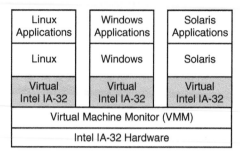

**Figure 8.1** Example System VM Environment. *In this example, the Intel IA-32 platform is capable of simultaneously running the Linux, Windows, and Solaris operating systems, along with their applications.*

use; e.g., the resource may be partitioned or may be time shared. When a virtual resource does not have a matching physical resource, the VMM may emulate the action of the desired resource, typically via a combination of software and other resources that are physically available on the host platform.

System virtual machines have a number of useful applications, some historical, some relevant today, and many that are likely to be important in the future. Some of these applications are described next.

- **Implementing multiprogramming:** Using multiple single-user virtual machines is a simple way of providing multiprogramming and time sharing without requiring a complete multiprogramming OS. Each user in a multiuser environment is given the illusion of having an entire machine, including the CPU, memory, and peripherals. Many of the users of VMs on early mainframe computers, such as the IBM System/370 and its successors, used virtualization as an alternative to a time-sharing system. These users ran a simple, compact, and efficient single-user operating system called the *conversational monitor system* (CMS), instead of the monolithic time-sharing operating systems available at the time.

- **Multiple single-application virtual machines:** This is an extension of the multiple single-user virtual machine concept. Running each application in its own virtual machine increases the robustness of the system. Erratic behavior of one application and its associated OS on a conventional system could bring down the machine. If this happens on a virtual machine, it is less likely to affect the operation of another application running on a different virtual machine. This may be useful in situations where a new application might corrupt the entire system because of either bugs or viruses.

- **Multiple secure environments:** A system VM provides a *sandbox* that isolates one system environment from other environments, thus ensuring a level of security that may not be provided by a single operating system. For example, a user accustomed to running applications on a private machine may be reluctant to transfer the applications to a Web server unless there is some guarantee that the user's resources and activity cannot be accessed or monitored by other users of the same server. In such a situation, a virtual machine can be used to provide an environment that, for all practical purposes, is isolated from the others and through which it is not possible for one user to observe or change another's data and activity.

- **Managed application environments:** In an organization that provides a core set of supported applications to users who also want to install their own applications, VM technology allows the core set of applications to be placed on one virtual machine, protected from other virtual machines on which users install new applications or develop their own programs.

- **Mixed-OS environments:** A single hardware platform can support two different operating systems concurrently. A user may prefer office productivity tools that run on one operating system, for example, but prefer another operating system for application development. The user can do both by installing two virtual machines on a single hardware platform, one for each operating system.

- **Legacy applications:** When a new version of an OS is released, it is not uncommon for OS developers to support seldom-used features with degraded performance while supporting new features that allow most new applications to run with improved performance. In this situation, users who need to run old applications without degraded performance can use one virtual machine to run the "legacy" application under the old OS while using another VM to take advantage of the presumably improved features in the newer version of the OS.

- **Multiplatform application development:** Software developers often need to implement and support software that works on multiple operating systems. Virtual machine technology allows software developers to test their software using multiple virtual machines on the same hardware platform. This is both more convenient and more cost effective than having multiple sets of hardware, one for each OS.

- **New system transition:** A system virtual machine allows a user to migrate to a new operating system in a gradual way. The user can try out a new operating system on one virtual machine even while the old operating system is running applications on a different virtual machine. The old operating system can be removed from the system after it has been ascertained that all relevant applications work correctly on the new operating system.

- **System software development:** In large systems, it is sometimes necessary to develop (or test) new system software while the same system is being used for running important applications. In this situation it could be very costly if a bug in the code under development were to bring down the entire system. This situation can be avoided by encapsulating the development environment on a virtual machine separate from the virtual machine where the production-level applications are running.

- **Operating system training:** It is often necessary to demonstrate techniques and effects of changing parameters or policies when training system management personnel. Such training is better done on a copy of the operating system running on a virtual machine than on the operating system running on the real machine so that other users of the operating system do not suffer from unexpected effects.

- **Help desk support:** Help desk service personnel can bring up a virtual machine that emulates the hardware configuration of a client in order to determine the nature and cause of problems the client may be encountering. It is not necessary to have all possible configurations of hardware physically available — virtual machine technology allows a single hardware platform to be set to any of several different configurations.

- **Operating system instrumentation:** Running the operating system on a virtual machine allows the virtual machine monitor to instrument accesses to hardware resources selectively. Not only can all events of a particular type, e.g., page faults, be counted, they can also be logged with detailed information about their nature, their origin, and how the requests were satisfied. Moreover, the programming for all such instrumentation and measurements can be encapsulated outside the operating system, communicating solely with the virtual machine monitor. Today, it is quite common for operating system researchers to conduct most of their experiments using virtual machines rather than directly on the hardware platform. Keefe (1968) describes early work on IBM mainframes on system evaluation using a virtual machine. The User Mode Linux system (UMLinux 2003) also uses virtual machine technology to test the fault tolerance of a Linux system.

- **Event monitoring:** Some virtual machines provide capabilities that cannot be performed on a native system. For example, virtual machines lend themselves better to providing traces of execution or dumps of the machine state at points of interest. Similarly, the ability of virtual machines to replay a system execution from some saved state is useful for analyzing the behavior of a system to understand unexpected behavior.

■ **System encapsulation:** System virtual machines provide a convenient way of encapsulating the state of the entire machine. This is useful for check-pointing machine state, with a view to resuming execution at a different time or even on a different host machine.

We are nearly ready to describe system VMs in more detail. Before doing so, however, we first point out that this chapter considers a very important class of system VMs but not all system VMs. In particular, as described in the taxonomy given in Section 1.5, this chapter will focus on system VMs where the ISA of the host and guest are the same. Furthermore, most of the attention will be given to uniprocessor systems. Important aspects of VM implementation related to other types of system VMs can be found elsewhere in this book, as summarized shortly.

Multiprocessor virtualization is a simple extension of uniprocessor virtualization. However, there are some special considerations when a multiprocessor is being virtualized. One consideration is that with a single processor, virtualization must be done by time sharing the single processor resource. With multiprocessors, however, virtualization can be achieved by partitioning the multiple hardware processors among the virtual systems. The choice between time-sharing processors and partitioning (or using both) opens up a number of additional design alternatives when multiprocessors are being virtualized.

Another important consideration for shared-memory multiprocessors, particularly when the host and guest ISAs are different, is the memory models supported by the guest and host platforms. The two aspects of memory models that are crucial are memory coherence and memory consistency. Both of these involve the way in which memory operations performed by one processor are observed by other processors in the systems. If the host system does not support the same coherence and/or consistency models as the guest assumes, then the virtualization process may need to take special steps to ensure compatibility. We discuss considerations that are specific to multiprocessor virtualization in Chapter 9.

When the guest and host ISAs are different, software in the VMM can emulate the virtual ISA using the techniques described in Chapters 2–4. Chapter 9 will address some of the system VM issues that arise where the ISA of the guest is different from that of the host.

## 8.1 Key Concepts

In this section we provide an introduction to the various parts of a hardware platform, with a view to understanding how virtualization can be achieved.

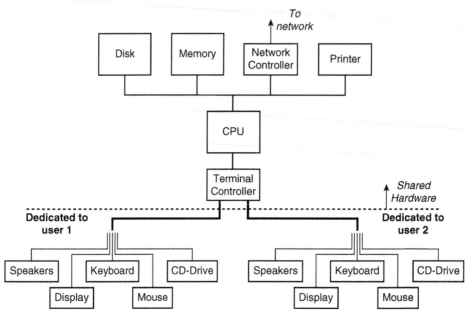

**Figure 8.2** Hardware Replication for a Two-User Virtual Machine System. *The terminal controller collects and tags the requests from multiple users. If such a piece of hardware is not available, the computer backplane must have enough slots to accommodate the adapters for both sets of personal devices.*

### 8.1.1 Outward Appearance

The illusion of multiple machines is an important part of many VM systems. This illusion can be accomplished purely by software means or, in some cases, through a replication of a subset of the hardware resources. For example, there may be cases where the physical resources used directly by individual users — namely, the keyboard, display, and personal peripheral devices, such as a CD ROM drive — are replicated, with one dedicated set for each user, while the rest of the hardware is shared via virtualization software. This situation is shown in Figure 8.2.

Alternatively, when a single user wishes to run two operating systems on the same hardware, there is no need to replicate any of the physical devices. Yet the user can be provided with the illusion of running both operating systems simultaneously. By using a hardware switch or, more typically, by entering a special key sequence on the keyboard, all the personal devices can be switched from one virtual machine to the other.

In some system VM environments, one of the operating systems may be considered more important than the other. The user interface of the first provides a window displaying the full user interface of the second. Interactions with applications running on the second operating system take place within this window. In a hosted virtual machine, for example, if the host operating system were Windows, a graphical window could be established on the desktop interface to interact with a virtual machine on the same platform. This solution is similar to the DOS window that may be brought up within the Windows desktop interface to run legacy DOS applications.

### 8.1.2  State Management

The architected state of a computer is contained in and maintained by the hardware resources of the machine. From a performance point of view, all state-holding hardware resources are not equivalent. There is usually an architected hierarchy of state resources, ranging from registers at the top of the hierarchy to secondary storage (e.g., disks) at the lower end of the hierarchy. In a VM system, each virtual machine has its own architected state information, and there may or may not be adequate resources in a host hardware platform to map each element of a guest's state to its natural level in the host's memory hierarchy. For example, a guest's register state may actually be held in the main memory of the host platform as part of a register context block.

In normal operation, the VMM periodically switches control among the guest VMs. Regardless of where the state is actually held, as operations on the guest's state are performed (e.g., via instruction execution), the state maintained on the host machine should be modified just as it would be on the guest's native platform. This is essentially the VM isomorphism discussed in the book's introduction and illustrated in Figure 1.2. There are two basic ways of managing guest state so that this is accomplished.

One way is to employ a level of indirection, by holding the state for each guest in fixed locations in the host's memory hierarchy with a VMM-managed pointer indicating the guest state that is currently active. As the VMM switches among guest systems, it changes the pointer to match the current guest. This is illustrated in Figure 8.3a, where the pointer actually points to the register context block of the currently active guest virtual machine. This is analogous to the situation in virtual memory systems, where the page table pointer is used by the operating system to point to the address space of the currently active process.

The approach of using indirection can be relatively inefficient if the memory resource that holds state in the guest VM has characteristics that are different from those on the native platform, as in the example of Figure 8.3a, where the register state is actually held in memory. In such a case, in order to

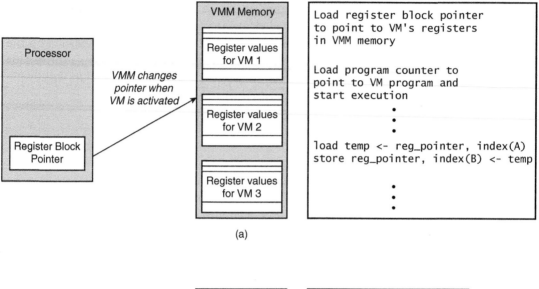

(a)

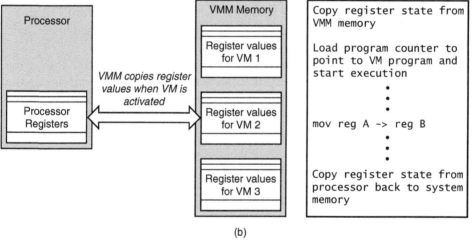

(b)

**Figure 8.3**   Methods of Maintaining Virtual State Illustrated for a Register File. *(a) Using indirection, (b) by copying. The boxes at the right indicate the actions taken when activating a virtual machine and copying a register value. In the first case, the value corresponding to a register is loaded from a table in memory and copied back to another location in the table. In the second case, the registers are used directly to accomplish the move.*

perform a copy operation from register A of virtual machine 2 to register B of the same virtual machine, the VMM would have to perform a memory-to-memory copy by loading the value in the memory location representing register A into some temporary register and then storing the value in the memory location corresponding to register B. Such a copy takes two memory-access instructions and could take more instructions if an address register must be loaded with a pointer to the location of the register file in memory.

To avoid this inefficiency, a second approach for managing guest state is to copy a guest's state information to its natural level in the memory hierarchy whenever it is activated by the VMM and to copy it back when a different guest is activated. For example, in Figure 8.3b, the VMM copies the entire guest register contents into the host's register file at the time virtual machine 2 is activated by the VMM (after saving the registers of the previous guest). With this approach, the operation of moving a value from register A to register B is achieved by directly executing a native register-move instruction. In many system VM implementations, the goal is to execute guest code natively (i.e., without emulation) on the host platform. Thus, in the register example, after the one-time overhead of switching out the old virtual machine registers and switching in the registers of virtual machine 2, execution can proceed at the same rate as on a machine running the guest natively.

The choice between indirection and copying depends on the frequency of use and whether the guest state being managed by the VMM is held in a different type of hardware resource than on a native platform. For frequently used state information, such as the general-purpose registers, it is usually preferable to swap the state of the virtual machine to the corresponding real resource each time the virtual machine is activated.

### 8.1.3 Resource Control

Within a system VM environment, hardware resources, including the processor resource, are assigned to a VM at the time it is created according to configuration specifications. Once resources are given to a guest VM, it is important that there be a way for the VMM to get them back so that they can be assigned to a different VM. Thus, the VMM must maintain overall control of all the hardware resources, even though they are temporarily being used by the guest VM currently running. This section examines ways in which this can be achieved.

First note that a similar issue arises in the case of conventional time-sharing systems — multiple jobs are concurrently being executed on the machine, with each job having full access to its resources at any given instant. However, there are some resources in the machine that are not directly accessible to the user application but accessible only to the operating system. One such resource is the interval timer, which, after being loaded with a value by the operating system, counts down clock ticks and triggers an interrupt when the value it holds becomes zero. Before passing control to a user process, the operating system initializes the timer with the maximum period of time it will allow the user process to run. The timer interrupt will then guarantee that control is transferred back to the operating system within the maximum time interval. Thus, the operating system uses the timer to keep control of the processor by ensuring that no user application can run for an indefinite length of time. And, because the OS has control of the processor, it can then control all the other resources. This control issue is similar to the one discussed in connection with runtime control of emulation frameworks in Chapter 3.

The situation is similar in a system VM environment. Here, the principal issue is that of time sharing resources among the different virtual machines. We will see in Section 8.2.1 that a convenient way to provide the VMM with overall control is for the VMM to intercept all accesses to so-called privileged resources, such as the interval timer. These privileged resources, therefore, are not used directly by the individual virtual machines — rather, the VMM emulates the operation of these resources at all times. Instead of allowing the operating system in a virtual machine to field the timer interrupt, for example, the VMM first handles the interrupt itself. The handler for the timer interrupt includes code that saves the state of the current guest virtual machine, determines the next virtual machine that should be activated, and loads the state for the next virtual machine to be run. It accomplishes this, as mentioned earlier, either by changing pointers, by copying state into hardware resources, or by doing both. Figure 8.4 depicts scheduling actions taken by the VMM.

There may be additional opportunities for the VMM to get control of the system other than through interval timer interrupts. For example, since privileged instructions encountered in the user mode must, as noted earlier,

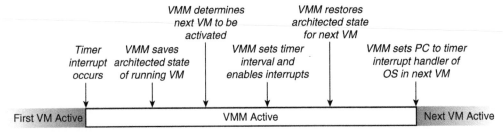

**Figure 8.4**    Actions Taken by the VMM in Retiring One Virtual Machine and Activating the Next Virtual Machine.

be intercepted and emulated by the VMM, the VMM gains control whenever the guest operating system issues privileged instructions (the mechanism for doing so is described in Section 8.2).

A fair scheme for allocating hardware resources to virtual machines is one in which the virtual machines get ownership of the resources in turn for roughly equal amounts of time. The issues here are similar to the issues that arise in multiprogrammed operating systems. If the time allocated to each virtual machine is large, there is the possibility that the resources are not optimally utilized. On the other hand, if the time allocated is small, the overhead incurred in switching between the virtual machines begins to degrade performance.

For a fair scheme to work, the guest operating system on a virtual machine must be denied direct access to the interval timer facility so that it cannot reschedule the next timer interrupt. Furthermore, in order to make operation under a virtual machine completely transparent, the guest operating system should not be allowed to read the real timer value set by the VMM. (This transparency is needed to prevent the operating system from behaving in a different manner when running under a VMM than it would on a real machine.) However, as we will see later in the chapter, the VMM can supply the guest with an emulated *virtual* interval timer.

Strict VMM emulation of a guest's timer interval could potentially lead some user code to run for too long a time, however, starving other virtual machines from using the hardware resources. Hence, the VMM must examine every guest setting of the timer interrupt and override the requested value if it has the potential of being unfair to other virtual machines that may be running on the system. This is an instance where the emulation of privileged resources must be done by the VMM with a view to efficient and fair operation of the entire virtual machine system rather than for the performance of an individual guest.

### 8.1.4  Native and Hosted Virtual Machines

It should be clear by now that the VMM is the key component in any system VM environment. The VMM is responsible for scheduling and managing the allocation of hardware resources to the various guest virtual machines. Hence it is also the point of control for the shared physical resources in the system. Such resources include the registers in the CPU, the real memory in the system, and the various I/O devices attached to the system. For *efficient* operation of the system, therefore, at least some part of the VMM implementation should have privileges higher than the actual privileges of the guest virtual machines it supports. By *actual privilege*, we mean the privilege the code has on the

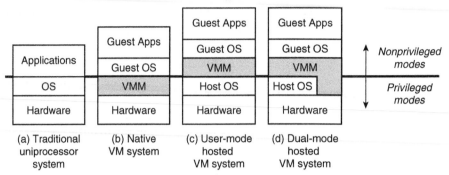

**Figure 8.5** Native and Hosted VM Systems. *(a) The operating system of a traditional uniprocessor executes in the privileged mode. (b) In a native VM system, the VMM operates in the privileged mode. (c–d) A trusted host operating system executes in the privileged mode in a hosted VM system. In both systems, the guest operating system resides in the virtual machine and operates at a less privileged level. The VMM of a hosted system may work entirely in the user mode (c) or in dual mode (d) when parts of the VMM operate in the privileged mode.*

hardware while running in the virtual machine environment. This, as we will see shortly, may be different from the privilege that is *perceived* on the guest.

As pointed out earlier, the relationship between the VMM and virtual machines is analogous to the relationship between an operating system and application programs in a conventional time-shared system. In the latter, the operating system typically works in a privilege level higher than that of the applications, e.g., in *system mode* versus *user mode,* as shown in Figure 8.5a. A virtual machine system in which the VMM operates in a privilege mode higher than the mode of the guest virtual machines is called a *native VM* system. In a native VM, the VMM is the only software that executes in the highest privilege level defined by the system architecture, as depicted in Figure 8.5b. Conceptually, the VMM is first installed on the bare hardware, and the guest operating systems are then installed on top of the VMM. The guest operating systems and other less privileged applications run in levels of privilege lower than that of the VMM. This typically means that the privilege level of the guest OS is emulated by the VMM. Native VM systems have been used and studied extensively and are discussed in detail in upcoming sections.

For user convenience and implementation simplicity, it is often advantageous to install a virtual machine system on a host platform that is already running an existing OS. Such a system is called a *hosted VM* system (in this case the term *host* refers to the underlying OS). In a hosted VM system the VMM utilizes the functions already available on the host OS to control and manage resources desired by each of the virtual machines. Modifying a proprietary commercial operating system is often not possible, either because the source code is unavailable or because of licensing agreements. In these cases, the VMM may be implemented at the user level, a privilege level below that of the host operating system, as shown in Figure 8.5c. Such a system is commonly referred to as a *user-mode* hosted VM system. For efficiency reasons, however, it is desirable to have at least part of the VMM work in the most privileged mode. This can often be achieved by modifying the host operating system through mechanisms commonly provided to extend the functionality of an operating system, such as kernel extensions or device drivers. Such a system that has parts of the VMM operating in a privileged mode and other parts in nonprivileged mode, as depicted in Figure 8.5d, is referred to as a *dual-mode* hosted VM system. We will examine features of such systems further in Section 8.4.3.

### 8.1.5   IBM VM/370

The first virtual machine environment was the IBM System/360 Model 40 VM (circa 1965) (Adair et al. 1966; Creasy 1981). The intention of the developers was to build a time-sharing system that extended the then-novel concept of virtual memory to other parts of the computer system. After debating the alternatives, the design team decided that the most appropriate interface to provide to the user would be the full System/360 architecture interface (the ISA) rather than just the user-level architectural interface enhanced by system library functions (the ABI). The perceived advantage was that this would be the best way to protect users from one another while preserving compatibility as the System/360 architecture evolved. It was not until much later, with a model of the System/370, that VM became mainstream. We will refer to the IBM virtual machine in the rest of the chapter as the IBM VM/370 — many of the principles are still in use today in the z/VM running on the IBM zSeries mainframes. An informative account of the development of VM on the IBM platforms is provided in Varian (1997), while a survey of virtual machine research at that time appears in Goldberg (1974).

The virtual machine monitor of VM/370 was called the *control program* (CP). The CP design team also developed a single-user operating system called the *conversational monitor system* (CMS), mainly to demonstrate the advantages of modularization for system evolution. The CP/CMS design separated the function of resource management from the function of providing services to the user. The success of the project was in large measure due to the design of the System/370 architecture, which allowed an elegantly simple implementation of the virtual machine concept.

Even though CP and CMS are often referred to as a pair, one can exist without the other. In fact, CMS was developed on the bare machine before

CP existed, and CP has hosted many operating systems in its life, including, most recently, Linux. As its importance and popularity grew, special hardware features were added to the System/370, primarily to reduce virtualization overhead. Some of these enhancements will be discussed in Section 8.5.

## 8.2 Resource Virtualization — Processors

The key aspect of virtualizing a processor lies in the execution of the guest instructions, including both system-level and user-level instructions. There are two ways this can be done. The first is through *emulation*. As described in Chapter 2, emulation can be performed through either interpretation or binary translation. Emulation involves examining each guest instruction in turn, either repeatedly when interpreting or once when performing binary translation, and emulating on virtualized resources the exact actions that would have been performed on real resources. Emulation is the only processor virtualization mechanism available when the ISA of the guest is different from the ISA of the host. As we shall see presently, however, an emulation-like process may be necessary at times even when the two ISAs are identical. Such a situation occurs when instructions that interact with hardware resources need to operate differently on a virtualized processor than on a real processor.

The second processor virtualization method uses *direct native execution* on the host machine. This method is possible only if the ISA of the host is identical to the ISA of the guest, and even then only under certain conditions. It is always possible to build a virtual machine by using emulation. However, even with sophisticated techniques such as binary translation, the performance of a program on the virtual machine will rarely be as good as its performance on native hardware. Therefore, a basic design goal for system VMs with identical guest and host ISAs is that a significant fraction of the instructions execute directly on the native hardware. If this is possible, a program will often run on a virtual machine at about the same speed as on native hardware, unless there are memory or I/O resource limitations. The overhead of emulating any remaining instructions depends on several factors, including the actual number of instructions that must be emulated, the complexity of discovering these instructions, and the data structures and algorithms used for emulation.

The following three subsections characterize those instructions in an ISA that must be emulated in order for a VMM to be successfully constructed. The techniques used for emulating the special instructions depend on the characteristics of the ISA. We will see that for a well-behaved, efficiently virtualizable ISA, a trap occurs naturally when an instruction needs to be emulated, the trap handler jumps to an appropriate interpreter routine, interprets the single instruction, and returns control back to the original program. In other, less well-behaved ISAs, the difficulty of isolating the instructions that need to be emulated may force a larger number of other instructions to be emulated. Section 8.2.4 addresses the problem of discovering such instructions. In these cases, emulation performance can be improved by translating a group consisting of several instructions at a time using techniques similar to those described in Chapter 2.

### 8.2.1 Conditions for ISA Virtualizability

In a classic paper (Popek and Goldberg 1974) inspired by Goldberg's doctoral dissertation (Goldberg 1972), Popek and Goldberg formally derived sufficient conditions under which an ISA can efficiently support virtual machines. We summarize in this subsection the valuable insight regarding the construction and understanding of system VMs provided by this work.

In Section 8.1.4 we characterized both native and hosted system VMs. There tends to be an inherent inefficiency in purely hosted VMs because, as we will see in Section 8.4.3, the VMM needs to rely heavily on services of the host operating system. Therefore, we restrict the discussion here to native system VMs. In a native system VM, the VMM runs in system mode, and all other software runs in user mode. Note that this "other" software includes some software originally intended to run in the system mode, a guest operating system being the prime example. The VMM keeps track of the intended (i.e., virtual) mode of operation of a guest virtual machine but sets the actual native hardware mode to *user* mode whenever executing instructions from the guest virtual machine, regardless of whether it is user or system software.

The original analysis by Popek and Goldberg was for "third-generation" machines, such as the IBM System/370, the Honeywell 6000, and the Digital PDP-10, but it still holds for present-day machines (one could argue that from an ISA perspective, we are still in the third generation!). The assumptions made in the analysis are as follows: (a) The hardware consists of a processor and a uniformly addressable memory, (b) the processor can operate in one of two modes, the system mode or the user mode, (c) some subset of the instruction set is available only in the system mode, and (d) memory addressing is done relative to the contents of a relocation register (i.e., a fixed value is added to a virtual address to arrive at a physical memory address). The analysis could be extended to more than two modes and to more complex memory architectures, but the fundamental results remain unchanged. Input/Output is not considered, but the approach and analysis can also be extended to I/O in a straightforward manner.

The machine being virtualized is modeled as a 4-tuple, $S = <E, M, P, R>$, where $E$ refers to the executable storage, $M$ refers to the mode of operation, $P$ is the program counter, and $R$ is the memory relocation bounds register. The memory of the machine is assumed to be located contiguously in physical memory from the location given in the relocation bounds register $R$. The relocation bounds register, as the name suggests, is a pair indicating the physical location and the size of the virtual memory space. The extension to paged or segmented virtual memory systems is straightforward. A *memory trap* occurs if the address accessed by a program falls outside the bounds indicated by $R$. The trap atomically saves the current state of the machine, represented by $M$, $P$, and $R$ in location 0, and copies the contents of location 0 of another process into $M$, $P$, and $R$ — this essentially has the effect of performing a context switch.

A *privileged* instruction is defined as one that traps if the machine is in user mode and does not trap if the machine is in system mode. It is not sufficient for the instruction's behavior to be different in the two modes, and by definition the privileged instruction *must* trap when executed in the user mode. Note that this strict definition is for the purpose of this particular analysis and may differ from definitions used elsewhere when describing specific ISAs. Here are two examples of privileged instructions.

- **Load PSW** (LPSW, IBM System/370): This instruction loads the processor status word (PSW) with a doubleword from a location in memory if the processor is in system mode. If it is not in system mode, the machine traps. The PSW contains bits that determine, among other things, the state of the CPU. One of these bits, the P bit, specifies whether the CPU is in user or system mode. Another part of the PSW is the instruction address (or program counter). If this instruction could be executed in user mode, a malicious user program could put itself in system mode and get control of the system.

- **Set CPU Timer** (SPT, IBM System/370): This instruction replaces the CPU interval timer with the contents of a location in memory if the CPU is in system mode and traps if it is not. Once again, if this instruction could be executed in user mode, it would be possible for a user program to change the amount of time allocated to it before being swapped out.

As noted earlier, in a virtual machine environment, an operating system running on a guest virtual machine should not be allowed to change hardware resources in a way that affects the other virtual machines or the performance of programs outside the realm of its own virtual machine. Hence, even the operating system on a virtual machine must execute in a mode that disallows

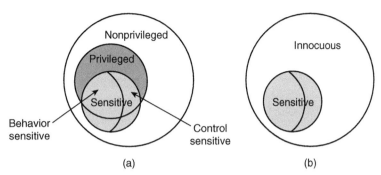

**Figure 8.6**    Types of Instructions. *(a) Sensitive and privileged instructions overlap (although not necessarily completely). (b) Sensitive instructions and innocuous instructions are complements of each other.*

the direct modification of system resources such as the PSW and the CPU interval timer. Consequently, all of the guest operating system software is forced to execute in user mode.

To specify instructions that interact with hardware, two categories of special instructions are defined. *Control-sensitive* instructions are those that attempt to change the configuration of resources in the system, for example, the physical memory assigned to a program or the mode of the system. (If I/O were included in the model, then I/O would also be considered a resource.) *Behavior-sensitive* instructions are those whose behavior or results produced depend on the configuration of resources — in the model, this includes the value in the relocation bounds register or on the mode of operation. If an instruction is neither control sensitive nor behavior sensitive, it is termed *innocuous* (see Figure 8.6).

The LPSW and SPT instructions mentioned earlier are examples of control-sensitive instructions. Their use allows an operating system to change some basic resource of the system, such as the mode of operation or the CPU timer. Examples of behavior-sensitive instructions follow.

- **Load Real Address** (LRA, System/370): This instruction takes a virtual address, translates it, and saves the corresponding real address in a specified general-purpose register. The behavior of this instruction (i.e., the result value stored in the register) depends on the state (mapping) of the real memory resource.

- **Pop Stack into Flags Register** (POPF, Intel IA-32): This instruction pops the flag registers from a stack held in memory. One of the flag registers is the interrupt-enable flag, which can be modified only in privileged mode. In user mode, this instruction overwrites all flags except the interrupt-enable flag. For the interrupt-enable flag, the instruction acts as a no-op when

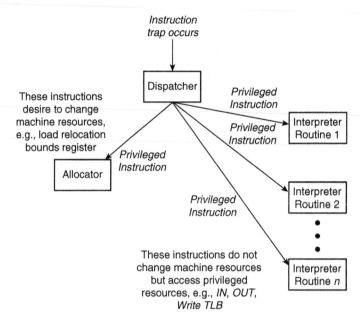

**Figure 8.7**    Components of a Virtual Machine Monitor.

executed in user mode. The behavior of this instruction therefore depends on the mode of operation.

The functions of the VMM can be divided into three parts, a *dispatcher*, an *allocator*, and a set of *interpreter routines*. These components of the VMM are depicted in Figure 8.7. The dispatcher is the top-level control module of the VMM, which decides the next module to be invoked; it is invoked by the interrupt handler when the hardware traps. The allocator decides how system resources are to be allocated, e.g., how to allocate memory resources in a nonconflicting manner. The allocator is invoked by the dispatcher whenever there is a need to change machine resources associated with some virtual machine.

As we shall see, in a well-constructed VMM, any instructions that attempt to change resource assignments or whose behavior is affected by the assignment of resources will trap to the VMM dispatcher. The trapping instructions that attempt to change resource assignments are then directed by the dispatcher to the allocator. The dispatcher directs all remaining traps to the interpreter routines. The interpreter routines, one per privileged instruction, emulate the effects of the instructions when operating on virtual resources. After an interpreter routine finishes, control is passed back to the guest virtual machine at the instruction immediately following the one that caused the trap.

According to Popek and Goldberg, a potential virtual machine monitor must satisfy three properties before qualifying as a true virtual machine monitor: efficiency, resource control, and equivalence. *Efficiency* implies that all instructions that are innocuous must be executed natively on the hardware, with no intervention or emulation by the VMM. *Resource control* implies that it should not be possible for guest software to directly change the configuration of any system resources available to it, e.g., real memory. The allocator must be invoked if the guest software makes any such attempt. *Equivalence* implies that any program executing on a virtual machine must behave in a manner identical to the way it would have behaved when running directly on the native hardware, with only a few exceptions. The allowed exceptions are that (1) performance can be slower due to the emulation (e.g., interpretation) of certain instructions, (2) there may be a limitation on the extent of resources available, e.g., disk space, because of sharing among virtual machines, and (3) there may be differences in performance due to changed timing relationships, e.g., between the I/O and the processor.

Here, the reader should note that this formulation of a VMM is somewhat at odds with the common definition and the definition used elsewhere in this book. It is intuitively clear that the resource control and equivalence properties should hold for a VMM. Furthermore, it should always be possible to construct a VMM with these properties, however inefficient, by employing emulation techniques whenever necessary. In effect, it is these two properties that we (and others) typically assume when defining a VMM. In the Popek and Goldberg formulation, a VMM must also be "efficient" in order to be considered a true VMM. And it is the efficiency condition that most heavily depends on the condition stated shortly ahead in Theorem 1.

An alternative formulation would define a VMM to have only the properties of resource control and equivalence and then to define an *efficient VMM* to be a VMM that also satisfies the efficiency property. With the exception of the Popek and Goldberg theorems, we use these alternative definitions of VMMs and efficient VMMs in this book. Here, then, is the key theorem regarding (efficient) VMMs.

**Theorem 1:** For any conventional third-generation computer, a virtual machine monitor may be constructed if the set of sensitive instructions for that computer is a subset of the set of privileged instructions.

This is a surprisingly simple theorem, yet it has important implications. It says that an efficient virtual machine implementation can be constructed if instructions that could interfere with the correct or efficient functioning of the

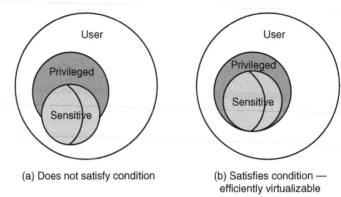

(a) Does not satisfy condition

(b) Satisfies condition —
efficiently virtualizable

**Figure 8.8**    Illustrating Popek and Goldberg's Theorem 1. *In (a), the sensitive instructions are not a subset of the privileged instructions and hence the system may not be efficiently virtualizable. On the other hand, the system in (b) satisfies the condition of Theorem 1.*

VMM (i.e., sensitive instructions) always trap in the user mode. All nonprivileged instructions can be executed natively on the host platform; no emulation is needed. The trapping of sensitive instructions, such as ones that attempt to reallocate system resources or depend on system resource assignments, force control to go back to the VMM. The VMM can then examine the action desired by the virtual machine that issued the sensitive instruction and reformulate the request in the context of the virtual machine system as a whole. Figure 8.8 illustrates the sufficient condition contained in the theorem.

The VMM interprets a sensitive instruction according to the prevailing status of the virtual system resources and the state of the virtual machine. Take, for example, the sensitive instructions LPSW and SPT described earlier in this section. These System/370 instructions are also privileged and hence satisfy the condition indicated in Theorem 1. Let's assume that a particular instance of an LPSW instruction has the net effect of going from one privileged state to another state with the same set of privileges. The LPSW interpreter routine in the VMM determines that this particular transfer is harmless by examining and comparing the contents of the location being loaded with the contents of the virtual copy of the PSW it maintains for that virtual machine. It then transfers control appropriately by modifying the contents of the hardware PSW, using an LPSW of its own. This LPSW does not trap because the VMM operates in system mode. Figure 8.9 illustrates this process.

On the other hand, if the LPSW instruction were executed by a user application running on the virtual machine, the trap handler would generate a virtual trap that is then passed to the virtual machine. The guest operating system

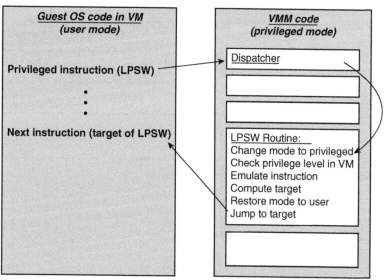

**Figure 8.9** Handling of a Privileged Instruction in a Guest OS. *The privileged instruction causes a trap because the guest OS is operating in user mode. The trap goes to the dispatcher in the VMM, from where it is directed to the special interpreter routine for the specific instruction.*

handles this trap in exactly the same way as a native machine would when an attempt is made to execute a privileged instruction in user mode.

When interpreting the SPT instruction, the VMM examines the contents of the location to be loaded into the CPU timer. It will allow this value to be loaded if the value (say, $t$) is less than the time remaining from the allocated time for the virtual machine itself ($t < T$). Otherwise it will load the timer with the time remaining for the virtual machine ($T$). Meanwhile, it keeps the time difference ($t - T$) in an internal table so that this time can be restored when the guest VM is again activated. In this manner, the VMM ensures that it always remains in control, even in the presence of attempts by some virtual machine to monopolize the system resources. If the guest OS should attempt to read the timer value, the VMM will reconstruct the correct virtual timer value and return it to the guest.

There are several simplifying assumptions made concerning the types of architectures under consideration in developing Theorem 1, and some practical aspects such as I/O and asynchronous interrupts have been ignored. Yet the theorem is useful because it suggests a convenient way of testing an ISA to determine the feasibility of an efficient virtual machine monitor. The theorem also provides clear guidelines for computer architects wishing to ensure that a new ISA lends itself to efficient virtualization.

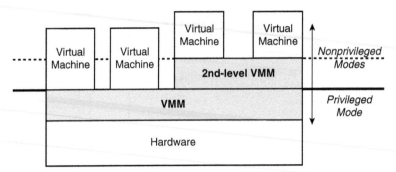

**Figure 8.10** Recursive Virtualization.

### 8.2.2 Recursive Virtualization

It may sometimes be desirable to run a virtual machine system as one of the virtual machines. This implies that the VMM itself would be running in the user mode under the control of a copy of itself running in the privileged mode. The concept of running the virtual machine system on a copy of itself is called *recursive virtualization* (Figure 8.10).

There are two effects that usually restrict the ability to create an efficient recursively virtualizable system. First, if the VMM itself has timing dependences, then its performance could be affected adversely when it runs in user mode within another virtual machine. In fact, the presence of timing dependences in a program could end up violating one of the conditions of Popek and Goldberg — the equivalence property. Thus a strong requirement for a recursively virtualizable system is that a VMM without any timing dependences be constructible for the system.

The second effect comes from the fact that each VMM layer uses up its own resources, particularly system memory resources needed to keep the state of the various virtual machines running on the system. If recursive virtualization is repeatedly performed, then these resources keep shrinking to a point where little is left for allocation to the virtual machines. As a result, the number of programs that run with identical effect on the real and virtual machines shrinks as the number of levels of virtualization increases.

Neither of these is a problem, in practice, however. Seldom does the required number of levels of virtualization go beyond two. At this level of recursion, the overhead is still contained; moreover, the user is usually willing to accept the drop in performance resulting from the recursive virtualization.

Popek and Goldberg formalized the conditions for recursive virtualizability in a second theorem.

**Theorem 2:** A conventional third-generation computer is recursively virtualizable if (a) it is virtualizable and (b) a VMM without any timing dependences can be constructed for it.

### 8.2.3 Handling Problem Instructions

Observe that, as described earlier, the POPF instruction in the Intel IA-32 ISA is sensitive but not privileged — it does not generate a trap in user mode. Hence it violates the virtualizability condition of Theorem 1. The Intel IA-32 has several other instructions that similarly are sensitive but not privileged (Robin and Irvine 2000). In reality, there are very few ISAs that are virtualizable in the sense of the Popek–Goldberg theorem (or efficiently virtualizable in the terminology we use). However, if an ISA is not efficiently virtualizable, all is not lost. It simply means that an additional set of steps must be taken in order to implement a system virtual machine (with possible loss of some efficiency).

The POPF instruction mentioned earlier is a problem instruction because it inhibits the creation of an (efficient) virtual machine monitor in the sense of Theorem 1. For convenience, let us refer to instructions that are sensitive but not privileged as *critical* instructions. It would be possible for a VMM to intercept POPF and other critical instructions if all guest software were interpreted instruction by instruction. The use of interpretation clearly leads to inefficiency (both as formally defined by Popek and Goldberg and in reality). Fortunately, techniques related to those described in Chapters 2 and 3 can be used to reduce the inefficiency considerably. For example, the VMM can scan the guest code stream before execution, as done during binary translation, and in the process discover all critical instructions, replacing them with a trap or a jump to the VMM, as shown in Figure 8.11. This replacement process is known as *patching* (Section 4.7.1). Only the code running on the guest virtual machines needs to be scanned — the VMM code is in privileged state and will work correctly without modification. The problem of scanning and patching critical instructions is discussed in more detail in the next subsection.

In a strictly efficient virtualizable machine, as defined by Popek and Goldberg, all nonprivileged instructions are executed natively. We refer to a virtual machine system in which some of the nonprivileged instructions must be emulated as a *hybrid virtual machine* system. Scanning and patching is a pragmatic attempt by a hybrid virtual machine system to execute *most* nonprivileged instructions natively. Guest VM software containing few critical instructions should not see a significant degradation in performance.

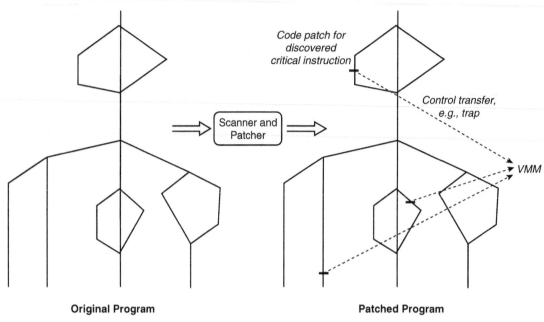

**Figure 8.11**    Scanning and Patching Code in a Hybrid Virtual Machine System.

### 8.2.4  Patching of Critical Instructions

As noted earlier, the problem of discovering critical instructions has a lot in common with the general problem of dynamic binary translation discussed in Chapter 2. The basic idea in both cases is to locate sections of code about to be executed and perform transformations on them. A major difference is that in binary translation, both the target code and the runtime execute in user mode, and hence a switch between them can be done via a jump. In the VM context, there is an actual change of privilege mode, which means that the jumps to the runtime are replaced with system calls (traps) to the VMM.

One way to discover critical instructions is for the VMM to take control at the head of each guest basic block and scan instructions in sequence until the end of the basic block is reached. If a critical instruction is found during this scan, it is replaced with a trap (system call) to the VMM, and the critical instruction at the location is saved in a VMM side table, along with its original address. Another trap back to the VMM is placed at the end of the basic block in order to allow the VMM to regain control when the block completes execution so that it can scan and patch the next basic block to be executed. If the next block has already been patched, the VMM simply jumps to the next block. This method ensures that every basic block to be executed is patched first.

To reduce overhead, the trap at the end of a scanned basic block can be replaced by the original branch or jump instruction after all possible successor basic blocks have been patched; this is analogous to chaining basic blocks in a code cache (Section 2.7.1). For example, if the basic block ends with a conditional branch that has been replaced with a trap, the basic blocks located at both the taken and the fall-through addresses can be scanned the first time the trap is encountered. After patching any critical instructions contained in the successor blocks, the trap is replaced with the original conditional branch. This technique is relatively simple with direct branches, i.e., branches that have a target specified as an offset relative to the address of the branch instruction itself. For indirect jumps and branches where the destination address is located in a register, the trap typically cannot be replaced, because of the difficulty in predicting all possible target addresses.

In order to further reduce overhead, instead of scanning single basic blocks at a time, the VMM can scan through all branches that allow target computation. Thus for a conditional branch, both the fall-through as well as the taken branch paths are followed during the initial scan, and this process is repeated until a control-transfer instruction is encountered for which it is not possible to determine all targets. In order to avoid memory paging caused by scanning possibly unused paths, the scanning should be limited to those code pages already in physical memory.

Observe that a critical instruction appearing in a guest application program (i.e., in the VM's user mode) needs to be patched only if it causes some action to be taken when performed in user mode. For example, if a critical instruction behaves like a no-op in user mode, and if it can be determined that the instruction is to be executed by its VM in user mode, it is not necessary to patch the instruction with a trap. Thus, some of the overhead of trapping can be reduced in the virtual user mode. Unfortunately, as long as the instruction set contains even one critical instruction that, in user mode, performs either a read or a write action on some resource, the instruction must be emulated and the overhead of code scanning and patching must be incurred. Finally, the process of scanning and patching critical instructions is often sensitive to the characteristics of the underlying ISA and is fertile ground for engineering optimizations beyond those described here.

### 8.2.5 Caching Emulation Code

The overhead of VMM interpretation can become a problem when the frequency of sensitive instructions requiring interpretation is relatively high. One way to reduce this overhead is to cache the actions taken during the first

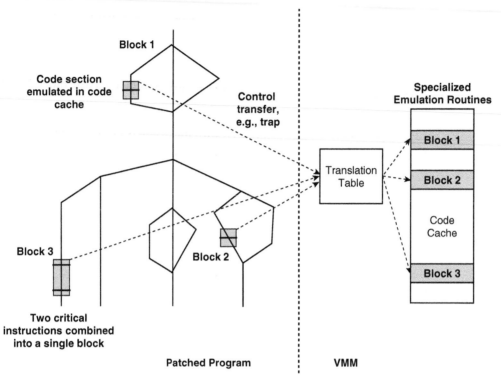

**Figure 8.12**   Code Caching to Improve Performance of Emulating Critical Instructions.

interpretation, with a view to avoiding many of the interpretation steps when the same instruction is encountered in the future. This is similar to code caching as described in connection with process virtual machines in Chapter 3.

Ideally, code caching is done on a block of instructions surrounding the sensitive instruction, since larger blocks lend themselves better to optimization. In contrast to what was shown in Figure 8.11, a system call trap may be inserted at an instruction earlier than the critical instruction. As depicted in Figure 8.12, the trap causes control to be transferred to the VMM, which then locates the cached emulation code via a table lookup using the address of the trapping instruction. This cached code is an emulation of an entire block of the original code, including the critical instruction, and hence is specific to the location of the trapping instruction. When the VMM returns control to the virtual machine, it restores the program counter to the point immediately after the block that was emulated rather than to the instruction following the trap.

Unlike the simple interpretation case, where there is only one copy of the code that emulates all instances of a specific type of instruction, each instance of the critical instruction in the application will be associated with a distinct piece of cached code. The advantage here is that the cached code can be made specific to the instance and hence can be optimized, often in a way that eliminates a significant fraction of the overhead.

In contrast to process virtual machines, the management of this code cache is somewhat simpler, because code in the cache is executed after the trap, when the machine is already in system mode. The user code can never corrupt or read the contents of the code cache, which is therefore always protected from the user application. On the other hand, self-modifying code remains a problem, and mechanisms are needed to intercept modifications of the original code — such modifications may necessitate invalidations of parts of the code cache.

## 8.2.6 Efficient Virtualizability of Common Instruction Sets

The System/370 architecture provides two modes of operation, a *user* mode and a *privileged* mode (what we have been referring to generally as *system mode*). The operating system is expected to run in the privileged mode. Some of the instructions in the instruction set are privileged; they perform the specified action only when the processor is in privileged mode. These privileged instructions typically manage protected resources in the processors. In order to prevent either malicious or accidental modification of these resources, the privileged instructions trap when executed in the user state.

The VMM for System/370 (called the control program, or CP) has to run in the privileged mode in order to be able to allocate resources to different virtual machines at different times. The virtual machine is created in the privileged mode, but it executes in the user mode. This ensures that each virtual machine is isolated from other virtual machines and from the CP itself.

All sensitive instructions on the System/370, in the Popek–Goldberg sense, are also privileged. VM/370 is an example of a virtual machine employing direct native execution.

As noted earlier, an interesting aspect of the System/370 VM project was the development of a single-user operating system that proceeded in parallel with CP development. This operating system, called the Conversational Monitor System (CMS), took advantage of the CP environment by allowing all applications to run in the "pseudo-supervisor," state with the user being allowed to use any instruction, whether privileged or not. This is safe because CMS and applications execute on a virtual machine protected by the CP from wantonly affecting the real resources of the computer. The ability to use privileged instructions in their code allows users to experiment in many ways, e.g., to add input/output devices not allowed by the standard system. Figure 8.13

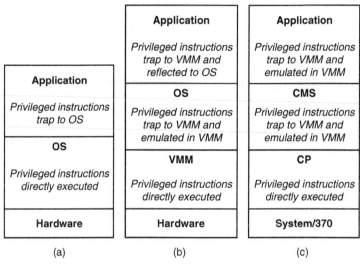

**Figure 8.13**  Comparison of the Execution of Privileged Mode Instructions on a VM/370 with that on a Native System and Other Virtual Machine Systems. *(a) A standard system; (b) a virtual machine system; (c) the CP/CMS system.*

shows a comparison of the handling of privileged instructions at various levels in various schemes. This feature of the CP/CMS system is highlighted in Figure 8.13c.

Despite the fact that most of the concepts in this chapter have been known for at least 30 years, many ISAs developed during those 30 years do not satisfy the sufficient conditions of Theorem 1. For example, the most commonly used ISA today is the Intel IA-32, and the IA-32 contains 17 critical instructions (Robin and Irvine 2000). The likely reason for this is that system VMs have not been considered important because of the tremendous decrease in the cost of computer systems, which makes it easier for each user to have his/her own machine. However, in recent years there has been resurgence of interest in VMs because of the importance of security in a networked environment and the desire to provide cross-platform compatibility of major software packages. Furthermore, large, expensive server systems are shared among many groups of users, and so several of the original VM motivations remain.

## 8.3 Resource Virtualization — Memory

In some respects, a virtual machine can be considered a generalization of the concept of virtual memory that preceded it. Virtual memory makes a distinction between the logical view of memory as seen by an application programmer and the actual hardware memory resource as managed by the operating system. Appendix A presents a discussion of the basic concepts underlying virtual memory. Also included is a discussion of the structures, e.g., page tables, needed to support virtual memory. It turns out that this hardware support is also sufficient for providing each guest virtual machine in a virtual machine system, with the view of having (and managing) its own "real" memory, which, in fact, is an illusion created by the underlying VMM.

### 8.3.1 Virtual Memory Support in a System Virtual Machine Environment

In a system VM environment, each of the guest VMs has its own set of virtual memory tables. Address translation in each of the guest VMs transforms addresses in its *virtual* address space to locations in *real* memory — this real memory would correspond to the *physical* memory on a native platform; in a VM platform, however, this is not the case. Rather, in a system VM environment, a guest's real memory address must undergo a further mapping to determine the address in physical memory of the host hardware. Note that here we are drawing a clear distinction between *real* memory and *physical* memory — terms often used interchangeably in other contexts. Physical memory is the hardware memory. Real memory is a guest VM's illusion of physical memory; an illusion supported by the VMM when it maps a guest's real memory to physical memory. It is this real-to-physical mapping that implements the *virtualization* of memory in a VM system.

The addition of another level in the memory hierarchy necessitates additional mechanisms for memory management. Note that the combined total size of the real memory of all the guests could be (and often is) bigger than the actual physical memory on the system. Hence the VMM maintains a swap space, distinct from the swap spaces of each of the guests. The VMM manages physical memory by swapping guest real pages into and out of its own swap space.

Figure 8.14 shows a set of page table maps belonging to two different guest VMs in a virtual machine system. Each entry in a *page table* maps a location in the virtual memory of an application to a location in the guest VM's real memory. In order to convert a real page address to a physical address, the VMM maintains a *real map table* mapping the real pages to physical pages. In the figure, the physical page frames numbered 500, 1000, and 3000 are assigned to two real pages of VM1 and one real page of VM2. The remaining physical pages may be allocated either to other virtual machines or to the VMM itself.

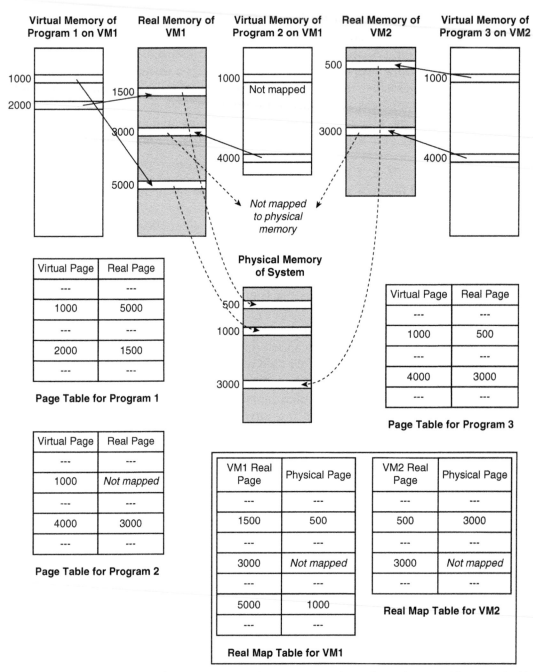

**Figure 8.14** Memory Mapping of Guest VMs. *Virtual pages are mapped to real pages by page tables maintained by each virtual machine. Real pages are mapped to physical pages, using tables maintained by the VMM (at the bottom of the figure). Observe that the real memory of each VM can be larger than the physical memory — the real memory of VM1, for example, is as large as its virtual memory.*

On contemporary platforms, page translation is supported by a combination of a page table and a translation lookaside buffer (TLB); see Appendix Section A3.4. Depending on the ISA, either the page table or the TLB is architected. If the page table is architected, then its structure is defined by the ISA, and the operating system and hardware cooperate in maintaining and using it. In this case, the TLB is maintained and used only by the hardware; it is not visible to the operating system. When there is a TLB miss, the hardware "walks" the architected page table to find the appropriate entry to place in the TLB; if the entry is not mapped to physical memory, there is a page fault and the operating system takes over.

On the other hand, if the TLB is architected, then its structure and special instructions to manipulate it are part of the ISA; the page tables are part of the operating system implementation. Hardware is unaware of the page table structure. With this approach, when a TLB miss occurs, there is immediately a trap to the operating system; the operating system then uses its page table information to perform the appropriate action.

Most of the older ISAs, including the Intel IA-32 and IBM System/370, use architected page tables; some of the more recent RISC ISAs use architected TLBs. Memory resource virtualization in a VM environment is done somewhat differently, depending on whether the page table or the TLB is architected. Because the most common system VMs in use today run on the Intel IA-32 or the IBM zSeries that evolved from System/370, we first consider virtualization with an architected page table. More information about virtual storage concepts in IBM VMs can be found in Parmalee et al. (1972).

### 8.3.2 Virtualizing Architected Page Tables

The OS in each guest VM maintains its own page tables. These tables reflect the virtual-to-real memory mapping that the guest OS manages. As opposed to this virtual-to-real mapping, the virtual-to-physical mapping is kept by the VMM in *shadow page tables*, one for each of the guest VMs. Figure 8.15 illustrates the shadow page tables for the example of Figure 8.14. These tables are the ones actually used by hardware to translate virtual addresses and to keep the TLB up-to-date. The entries in these shadow page tables essentially eliminate one level of indirection in the virtual-to-real-to-physical mapping.

To make this method work, the page table pointer register is virtualized. The VMM manages the real page table pointer and has access to the virtual version of the register associated with each guest VM. At the time the VMM activates a guest VM, it updates the page table pointer so that it indicates the correct shadow version of the guest's current page table. If a guest attempts

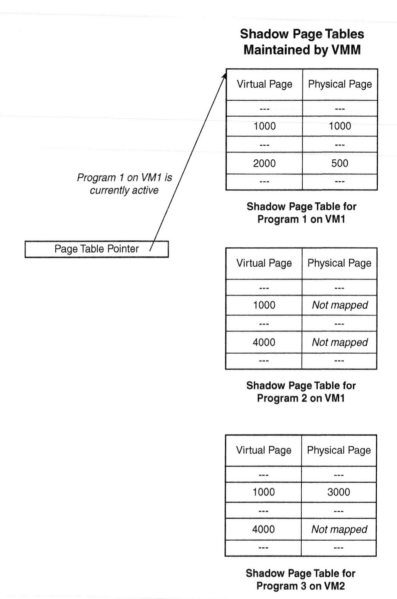

**Shadow Page Tables**
**Maintained by VMM**

*Program 1 on VM1 is*
*currently active*

| Virtual Page | Physical Page |
|---|---|
| --- | --- |
| 1000 | 1000 |
| --- | --- |
| 2000 | 500 |
| --- | --- |

**Shadow Page Table for**
**Program 1 on VM1**

Page Table Pointer

| Virtual Page | Physical Page |
|---|---|
| --- | --- |
| 1000 | *Not mapped* |
| --- | --- |
| 4000 | *Not mapped* |
| --- | --- |

**Shadow Page Table for**
**Program 2 on VM1**

| Virtual Page | Physical Page |
|---|---|
| --- | --- |
| 1000 | 3000 |
| --- | --- |
| 4000 | *Not mapped* |
| --- | --- |

**Shadow Page Table for**
**Program 3 on VM2**

**Figure 8.15**   Shadow Page Tables for Memory Mapping Illustrated in Figure 8.14. *The shadow tables are used by hardware in performing address translation. The VMM manages the shadow tables and is responsible for setting the page table pointer register.*

to access the page table pointer, either to read it or write it, the read or write instruction traps to the VMM. The trap occurs either automatically because these instructions are privileged, or because code patching has replaced them with a trap. If the attempt to access the page table pointer by the guest is a read attempt, the VMM returns the guest's virtual page table pointer; whereas if it is a write attempt, the VMM updates the virtual version and then updates the real page table pointer to point to the corresponding shadow table.

The true mapping of virtual to physical pages may differ from the virtual to real view that the guest operating systems have, and page fault handling must take this into account. First note that the VMM should not have a virtual-to-physical page mapping in a shadow table if the guest OS does not have the same virtual page mapped to real memory in its corresponding virtual table. Otherwise, an access that should page fault from the guest's perspective will not cause a page fault in the VM environment, thereby breaking the equivalence property (compatibility). Therefore, when a page fault does occur, the page may or may not be mapped in the virtual table of the guest OS. If it is mapped, this page fault should be handled entirely by the VMM. This is a case where the VMM has moved the accessed real page to its own swap space. Consequently, the VMM brings the real page back into physical memory and then updates the real map table and the affected shadow table(s) appropriately to reflect the new mapping. The guest OS is not informed of the page fault because such a page fault would not have occurred if the guest OS were running natively.

On the other hand, if the page is not mapped in the guest, the VMM transfers control to the trap handler of the guest, indicating a page fault. The guest OS then issues I/O requests to effect a page-in operation (possibly with a swap out of a dirty page). The guest OS then issues instructions to modify its page table. These requests are intercepted by the VMM, either because they are privileged instructions or because the VMM write-protects the area of memory holding the page table of the guest. At that point the VMM updates the page table and also updates the mapping in the appropriate shadow page table before returning control back to the guest virtual machine.

As we indicated earlier, the real map table contains a mapping of the real pages of each virtual machine to the physical pages of the system. When performing I/O with real addresses (as many systems do, particularly for paging operations), the VMM converts the real addresses presented by a virtual machine to physical addresses using the real map table. Input/output address mapping turns out to be somewhat tricky because contiguous real pages may not be contiguous in physical memory. Thus, the VMM may need to convert an I/O request that spans multiple pages into multiple I/O requests, each referring to a contiguous block of physical memory. It may also be the case that I/O is to a real address that the VMM has swapped out of physical memory into its own swap space. In this case, the VMM must read it back into physical memory before the I/O operation can proceed.

The simultaneous operation of several virtual machines, along with the operation of the VMM itself, can degrade the performance of the system.

In practice, therefore, additional considerations apply in order to enhance the performance of a program running on a virtual machine. An example of this is a policy in the VM/370 CP, which, when ready to activate a new VM, gives priority to the virtual machine likely to have most of its active pages already mapped to physical pages. Another example, used when the same OS is shared by several guest machines, is to employ a common mapping of the OS read-only pages. As VM/370 became popular, hardware features were added that allowed the performance of virtual machines to be comparable to that of native hardware. These will be described in more detail in Section 8.5.

### 8.3.3 Virtualizing an Architected TLB

When an ISA provides a software-managed TLB, then it is the TLB that must be virtualized by the VMM. To virtualize the TLB, the VMM maintains a copy of each guest's TLB contents and also manages the real TLB. Any instructions that modify the architected TLB are sensitive and are intercepted by the VMM so that it can keep the virtual copies up-to-date.

A simple way to manage the real TLB is for the VMM to rewrite the TLB whenever a guest VM is activated. That is, the VMM copies the VM's virtual TLB entries into the physical TLB, after appropriately translating the real addresses in the virtual TLB to physical addresses in the physical TLB. This is essentially the same as the shadow mapping in architected page tables. A problem with this scheme is that all the TLB entries must be rewritten each time control transfers from one guest VM to another (or to the VMM). This TLB rewrite incurs a fairly high overhead, especially for large TLBs.

An alternative method is to leverage the address space identifiers (ASIDs) that are normally included in each entry of an architected, software-managed TLB. These are intended to allow multiple processes to have address space mappings in the TLB simultaneously. There is an architected ASID register, and whenever the TLB is accessed as part of address translation, the current ASID register value must match the ASID value in a TLB entry in order for the TLB entry to be considered valid for the active process.

The ASID mechanism can be virtualized to allow the VMM to manage the TLB in a globally efficient manner. With this approach, each guest VM has a virtual ASID register, and the VMM maintains the real ASID register. At any given time, the VMM maps certain guest ASID values to real ASID values for entries that are present in the real TLB. Hence, some combination of guest address spaces from different guest VMs may be simultaneously present in the real TLB, under control and management of the VMM. If the VMM decides to put an entry in the TLB and a real ASID has not been assigned to the address space used by the entry, then the VMM must assign a real ASID to the new address space. This may involve deassigning the ASID from some other virtual address space and invalidating any TLB entries using the ASID. If a guest writes to its virtual ASID register, the write is a sensitive instruction that is intercepted by the VMM. The VMM can then modify the virtual copy in memory and also change the real ASID with a real ASID value that maps to the virtual ASID.

Figure 8.16 illustrates this method applied to the example given earlier in Figure 8.14. The virtual TLBs are shown at the left. These correspond to the virtual-to-real page mappings for each of the guest VMs. The two programs both have entries in VM1's virtual TLB, distinguished by two different ASIDs. The VMM maintains the same real-to-physical map tables as are shown in Figure 8.14. The real TLB is shown on the right in Figure 8.16. There is one real TLB, and translations from the two VMs are simultaneously present. The ASID map table, maintained by the VMM, maps the virtual ASIDs to real ASIDs present in the real TLB. Note that program 1 in VM1 and program 2 in VM2 have the same virtual ASID (3) in their respective virtual machines.

**Virtual TLBs**

ASID mapping:
prog. 1 – ASID 3
prog. 2 – ASID 7

| ASID | Virtual Page | Real Page |
|------|--------------|-----------|
| --- | --- | --- |
| 3 | 1000 | 5000 |
| --- | --- | --- |
| 3 | 2000 | 1500 |
| --- | --- | --- |
| 7 | 4000 | 3000 |
| --- | --- | --- |

**Virtual TLB of VM1**

**ASID Map Table**

| Virtual ASID | Real ASID |
|--------------|-----------|
| --- | --- |
| VM1:3 | 9 |
| --- | --- |
| VM1:7 | --- |
| --- | --- |
| VM2:3 | 4 |

**Real TLB**

| ASID | Virtual Page | Physical Page |
|------|--------------|---------------|
| --- | --- | --- |
| 9 | 1000 | 1000 |
| 4 | 1000 | 3000 |
| 9 | 2000 | 500 |
| --- | --- | --- |
| --- | --- | --- |
| --- | --- | --- |

ASID mapping:
prog. 1 – ASID 3

| ASID | Virtual Page | Real Page |
|------|--------------|-----------|
| --- | --- | --- |
| 3 | 1000 | 3000 |
| --- | --- | --- |
| --- | --- | --- |
| --- | --- | --- |
| --- | --- | --- |
| --- | --- | --- |

**Virtual TLB of VM2**

**Figure 8.16** Virtualizing TLBs in a System That Implements Architected TLBs. *The system uses the same page mappings as given in Figure 8.14. The VMM maintains the virtual TLBs of the guest VMs (shown at left) and manages the real TLB by remapping virtual to real ASIDs. The ASID map table keeps track of the correspondence between virtual and real ASIDs.*

However, the VMM maps these ASIDs to two different ASIDs (4 and 9) so that they can be distinguished in the real TLB.

## 8.4 Resource Virtualization — Input/Output

Virtualization of the input/output subsystem is one of the more difficult parts of implementing a system virtual machine environment. Each I/O device type has its own characteristics and needs to be controlled in its own special way. The difficulty of virtualizing I/O devices is compounded by the fact that the number of devices of a given type is often very large and continues to grow. Moreover, the number of I/O device types is also increasing. Virtualization of such a large number of devices is a challenge for any new VMM.

On the other hand, techniques to share I/O devices have been developed since the early days of time sharing. The proliferation of I/O devices is also a problem for conventional operating systems, which have developed abstractions to support a wide variety of devices and device types. It is possible to adapt many of these abstraction techniques for use in virtual machine systems.

The virtualization strategy for a given I/O device type consists of constructing a virtual version of the device and then virtualizing the I/O activity directed at the device. A virtual device given to a guest VM is typically (but not necessarily) supported by a similar, underlying physical device. When a guest VM makes a request to use the virtual device, the request is intercepted by the VMM. The VMM converts the request to the equivalent request for the underlying physical device and it is carried out. The next two subsections discuss techniques for virtualizing devices and carrying out virtual I/O activity.

### 8.4.1 Virtualizing Devices

A number of techniques can be used for virtualizing I/O devices, and the specific technique for virtualizing a given device depends on whether it is shared and, if so, the ways in which it can be shared. Following are the common categories of devices.

#### Dedicated Devices

Some I/O devices, by their very nature, must be dedicated to a particular guest VM or at least are switched from one guest to another on a very long time scale. Examples of dedicated I/O devices are the display, keyboard, mouse, and speakers of a virtual machine user, as shown in Figure 8.2. In this case, the device itself does not necessarily have to be virtualized. Requests to and from the device could theoretically bypass the VMM and go directly to the guest operating system. However, in practice, the requests are usually routed through the VMM because the guest OS is running in the nonprivileged user mode. Interrupts from the device are first handled by the VMM, which determines that it came from a device dedicated to a particular guest VM and queues up the interrupt to be handled by the VM when it is activated by the VMM.

### Partitioned Devices

For some devices, such as the disk, it is convenient to partition the available resources among the virtual machines. A very large disk, for example, can be partitioned into several smaller *virtual disks* that are then made available to the virtual machine as dedicated devices. A virtual disk is treated by a virtual machine exactly as a physical disk, except with a smaller capacity.

To emulate an I/O request for the virtual device such as a disk, the VMM must translate the parameters (e.g., the track and sector locations) into corresponding parameters for the underlying physical device(s), using a map maintained for this purpose, and then reissue the request to the physical device (e.g., the disk controller). Similarly, status information coming back from the physical device is used to update status information in the map and is transformed into appropriate parameters for the virtual device before being delivered to the guest VM.

### Shared Devices

Some devices, such as a network adapter, can be shared among a number of guest VMs at a fine time granularity. Each guest may have its own virtual state related to usage of the device, e.g., a virtual network address. This state information is maintained by the VMM for each guest VM. A request by a guest VM to use the device is translated by the VMM to a request for the physical device through a virtual device driver. For a network, the VMM's virtualization routine will translate a request from some virtual machine to a request on a network port using its own physical network address. Similarly, the incoming requests through various ports will be translated into requests for virtual network addresses associated with the different virtual machines.

### Spooled Devices

A spooled device is shared, but at a much higher granularity than a device such as a network adapter. An example of a device that is often spooled is a printer. Conceptually, the printer is solely under the control of the program that is printing until the completion of the printing task. This must be the case even if the program is swapped in and out several times during the printing process. *Spooling* allows this to be accomplished (Madnick and Donovan 1974). In the case of a printer, spooling involves the buffering of the lines to be printed from each program in an area of memory dedicated to that program. A buffer is closed only when the program that owns it sends a special signal to the printer. The operating system schedules the printing of the spool buffers as they close, ensuring that the output of each program is printed completely before the printer is allocated to the next program.

Virtualization of spooled devices can be performed by using a two-level spool table approach, as depicted in Figure 8.17. The first level is within the operating system, with one table for each process active on the system, while

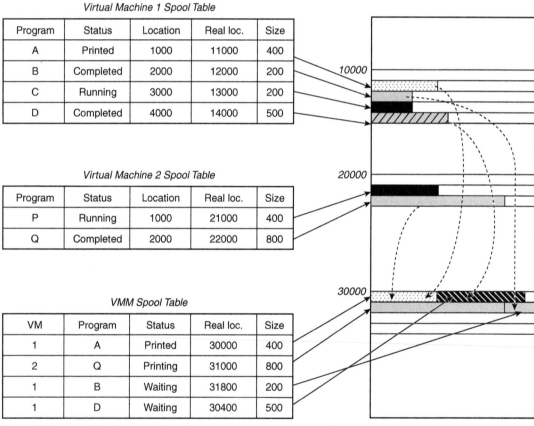

**Figure 8.17** Spooling in a Virtual Machine System. *As programs are "completed," their spool areas are copied over to the VMM spool area. The corresponding entry in the VMM spool table is set to "waiting." At the end of printing, this status is changed in both tables to "printed." The spool area for the printed jobs can be recovered and reused.*

Virtual Machine 1 Spool Table

| Program | Status | Location | Real loc. | Size |
|---------|--------|----------|-----------|------|
| A | Printed | 1000 | 11000 | 400 |
| B | Completed | 2000 | 12000 | 200 |
| C | Running | 3000 | 13000 | 200 |
| D | Completed | 4000 | 14000 | 500 |

Virtual Machine 2 Spool Table

| Program | Status | Location | Real loc. | Size |
|---------|--------|----------|-----------|------|
| P | Running | 1000 | 21000 | 400 |
| Q | Completed | 2000 | 22000 | 800 |

VMM Spool Table

| VM | Program | Status | Real loc. | Size |
|----|---------|--------|-----------|------|
| 1 | A | Printed | 30000 | 400 |
| 2 | Q | Printing | 31000 | 800 |
| 1 | B | Waiting | 31800 | 200 |
| 1 | D | Waiting | 30400 | 500 |

the second level is in the virtual machine monitor, with one table for each guest virtual machine. An operating system's request to print a spool buffer is intercepted by the VMM, which copies the buffer contents into one of its own spool buffers. This allows the VMM to schedule requests from different virtual machines on the same printer.

Various techniques could be employed to optimize the movement of large spool data between the virtual machine and the VMM. For example, the VMM could simply record the location of the spool data and its size, delaying the completion signal to the guest operating system until after the buffer has actually been printed. Another possibility is to have a single physical pool of buffers owned by the VMM, with each virtual machine having a virtual set of spool buffers allocated by the VMM. The practicality of this latter scheme depends on the ability of the VMM to detect such allocation of buffers, and on the ability of the guest operating system(s) to invoke services provided by the VMM.

The virtualization of printers of this kind was more appropriate to the older line printers, which were generally expensive and attached closely to the main computer. Today it is more common to find multiple printers accessible over a network. These printers already have the software to buffer and spool jobs from various nodes in the network. Virtualization of the printer is simple in such an environment as long as the virtual machine is connected to the network and has it own distinct network ID. The printer software in this case is unable to distinguish between requests from real machines and requests from virtual machines.

### Nonexistent Physical Devices

Virtualization makes it possible to provide support for virtual devices "attached" to a virtual machine for which there is no corresponding physical device. For example, each virtual machine could be associated with a network adapter that is used for communicating with other virtual machines on the same platform, without requiring an actual network adapter to be available on the platform. In such a situation the virtual machine monitor can simply intercept the I/O requests coming from the device drivers and emulate the transmission of the network packet, buffering the packet at the device driver of the appropriate destination virtual machine and causing an interrupt to be handled by that virtual machine.

### 8.4.2  Virtualizing I/O Activity

The overall I/O process is illustrated in Figure 8.18. As discussed in Appendix Section A.4.3, an operating system abstracts most of the peculiarities of

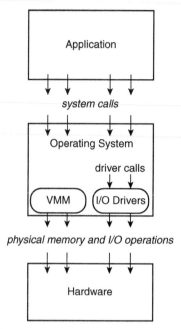

**Figure 8.18** Major Interfaces in Performing an Input/Output Action.

hardware devices and makes these I/O devices accessible through the system call interface and the device driver interface. Then at a level even lower is the actual operation-level interface, where individual instructions interact with the I/O system, typically by placing device-specific addresses and data on an I/O bus. An application program makes device-independent I/O requests such as open() and read() through the system call interface. The operating system converts the device-independent requests into calls to device driver routines. A device driver operates in system mode and takes care of device-specific aspects of performing an I/O transaction. For example, when a file system uses a block device interface to write to a disk, the device driver converts a device-independent request to operations specific to the type of disk controller chip physically attached to the system.

When an I/O action is to be performed, part of the action is carried out by guest software and part by the VMM. In general, the VMM can intercept a guest's I/O action and convert it from a virtual device action to a real device action at any of the three interfaces: the *system call interface,* the *device driver interface,* or the *operation-level interface.* We will discuss all three possibilities, in reverse order, beginning with the operation-level interface. Note that it is the VMM that finally interacts directly with the hardware device. Hence it is the VMM that either invokes the device driver or controls access to the device driver.

### Virtualizing at the I/O Operation Level

Appendix Section A.3.5 contains a discussion of various types of I/O devices differentiated by the way the processor communicates with each device. With memory-mapped I/O, common in many RISC processors, the effect of sending a command to an I/O controller occurs by writing to or reading from special locations in the memory address space. These memory locations are protected by the operating system by making them inaccessible in user mode. On the other hand, processors such as the IBM System/360 and its successors as well as the Intel IA-32 provide special I/O instructions to signal the device controllers. User programs do not utilize these instructions directly; they invoke system routines that use privileged I/O instructions to complete the request.

The privileged (or protected) nature of the I/O operations makes them easy for the VMM to intercept because they trap in user mode. However, once intercepted, it may be difficult for the VMM to determine exactly what I/O action is being requested. A complete I/O action (e.g., a disk read) usually involves the device driver's issuing several I/O instructions or memory-mapped loads and stores of small granularity. These individual I/O operations work in concert — for the VMM to determine the higher-level I/O action to be performed, it must be able to "reverse engineer" the individual operations and deduce the complete I/O action. This could be extremely difficult in practice.

### Virtualizing at the Device Driver Level

In a typical I/O request, as shown in Figure 8.18, a system call such as `read()` is converted by the OS into another call (or calls) to the device driver interface. If the VMM can intercept the call to the virtual device driver, it can convert the virtual device information to the corresponding physical device and redirect the call to a driver program for the physical device. This scheme is straightforward and allows virtualization at a natural point, but it requires that the VMM developer have some knowledge of the guest operating system and its internal device driver interfaces. This would be difficult if the VMM is called on to virtualize an arbitrary OS, with no knowledge of its internals.

In many practical situations, however, the VMM developer may be targeting specific guest operating systems. Today, for example, these might be Windows and Linux. In this case, special virtual device drivers (one per device type) can be developed for each of the guest operating systems. These drivers are part of the overall VMM package distributed to users. Then when a guest OS is installed, the virtualized drivers are installed at the same time.

This approach, when applied to a native VM system (see Figure 8.5), also requires that the VMM have real device drivers for each of the devices attached to the system. This problem can be simplified by "borrowing" the drivers (and the driver interface) from an existing operating system. For example, one could use the Linux drivers. In a hosted VM environment, the drivers in the host OS are used; such an approach is described in the next section.

### Virtualizing at the System Call Level

In theory, the virtualization process could be made more efficient by intercepting the initial I/O request at the OS interface, the ABI. Then the entire I/O action could be done by the VMM. To accomplish this, however, the VMM would need ABI routines that shadow the ABI routines available to the user. These routines would be different for each type of guest OS. Writing the ABI emulation routines would have to be part of the VMM development task and would require much broader knowledge of the guest OS internals than writing drivers (as in the previous subsection). Furthermore, all interactions between the ABI emulation routines and other parts of the guest OS would have to be faithfully emulated. In general, this rather daunting task could be done only if the guest OS is well structured and understood intimately by the VMM developer.

### Example: Network Virtualization

Figure 8.19 presents an example of the overall virtualization process on a system having a host network adapter, with the virtual machines themselves implementing virtual network adapters similar to what was described in Sugerman, Venkitachalam, and Lim (2001). Two cases are shown. In the first case, we assume that the virtual network interface card (NIC) is of the same type as the physical NIC in the host system. A request to send a message to an external computer system typically consists of a number of I/O operations, here assumed to be OUT or OUTS instructions in the IA-32 ISA. Associated with an OUT or OUTS instruction is a port number, say, 0xf0, which is a number in the range of IDs designated for the NIC in the guest system. Also associated with each port is a state bit that indicates whether the system should trap in response to an I/O request for that port.

As part of the state of the virtual machine, the VMM saves the permission map for all ports of the guest machine. The OUTS instruction is a privileged instruction, so when an OUTS instruction is executed, the system traps to the VMM, which examines the permission bitmap of the current guest. If the permission is set, the VMM converts the request to a new OUTS instruction for

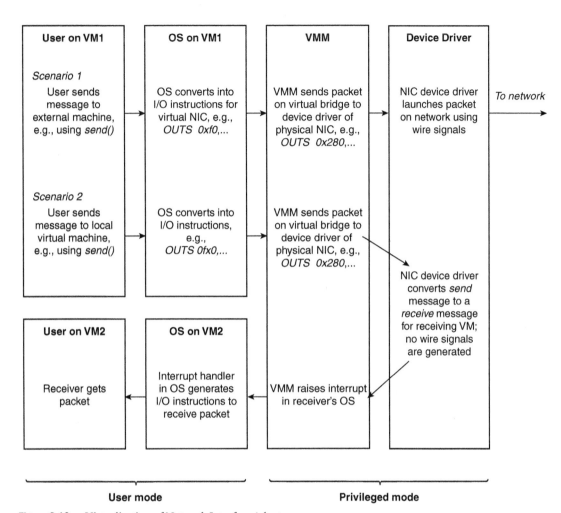

**Figure 8.19**    Virtualization of Network Interface Adapter.

port 0x280, corresponding to the NIC port on the real machine. It also converts the virtual address pointing to the string of data to be moved to a virtual address in the VMM space pointing to the same string of data or a copy. The VMM ensures that port 0x280 is enabled in its own permission map and issues the new OUTS instruction. When executed, now in the VMM's privileged mode, this OUTS instruction traps to the device driver installed on the VMM for the NIC, which then performs the desired transfer.

The second case is where the VMM takes the original request and converts it into a different form, either because the physical NIC available on the system is different from the real NIC or because there is possibly a more efficient means of satisfying the request. When the physical NIC is not of the same type as the virtual NIC, the VMM implements a device driver for the virtual NIC that translates I/O operations directed to it (e.g., OUTS instructions) into other I/O operations directed toward the physical NIC. It is not always possible to perform such translations on the original sequence of I/O operations one at a time. In these cases, it is necessary for the VMM to incorporate a device model of the virtual NIC, which first gathers enough information from a sequence of incoming I/O operations to generate the correct sequence of outgoing I/O instructions for the physical NIC.

In some cases, it is easier to modify the device driver for the physical NIC in order to handle the I/O operations directly. The second half of Figure 8.19 shows a case where the desired communication is between two virtual machines on the same platform. In this case, the host device driver, invoked due to the trap of a translated OUTS instruction as described earlier, determines that the destination address of the message is another virtual machine running on the same platform and does not transmit the message on the physical wires connected to the NIC. Rather, it internally reroutes the message as a received message destined for the receiver's virtual machine and schedules an I/O interrupt for the destination guest.

It would also have been possible to do the rerouting in the kernel of the VMM without involving the device driver; such a solution is more efficient when implementable. This is the case with the minidisk cache (MDC) facility implemented on the z/VM, the current incarnation of the VM/370. The minidisk cache attempts to reduce disk I/O by caching data in processor storage. In many cases, especially those where the data is referenced by several virtual machines, the decrease in disk I/O more than makes up for the possible increase in the paging I/O. The VMM invokes a routine in the MDC layer that determines whether a disk request can be satisfied from the cache. If so, then the call to the physical device driver is completely avoided.

### 8.4.3 Input/Output Virtualization and Hosted Virtual Machines

As described in Section 8.1.4, a hosted virtual machine system is one that works in conjunction with a host operating system running natively on the underlying hardware. In a dual-mode hosted virtual machine system, part of the virtual machine monitor runs natively on the hardware; another part of the VMM operates as a user application on the host operating system in order to invoke resource allocation services provided by the host. An I/O request from a guest virtual machine is converted by the native-mode portion of the VMM into a user application request made to the host. For example, if the driver on a guest virtual machine attempts to fetch sectors from a disk, eventually the user-mode portion of the VMM will issue a `read()` to the host operating system for the corresponding data. The host operating system satisfies the `read()` request by performing its own I/O, but the guest machine and the VMM remain oblivious to the physical details of satisfying the request. Similarly, if an I/O interrupt is received by the VMM, the interrupt gets thrown over to the host operating system and its device drivers before being received by a guest operating system.

An important advantage of a hosted virtual machine is that it is not necessary to provide device drivers in the VMM; the device drivers already present on the host operating system are used indirectly by the virtual machine system. This is particularly convenient in situations where the large number and variety of devices supported make it difficult to provide all device drivers for the VMM. The PC desktop environment is the prime example of such a situation.

In addition to the host OS, there are three additional components that form a dual-mode hosted virtual machine system.

- **VMM-n (native):** This component runs natively on the hardware and has characteristics similar to the VMM on a native virtual machine system. It is the component that intercepts traps due to privileged instructions or patched critical instructions encountered in a virtual machine. It may provide device drivers for a small set of devices that are either performance critical, or that do not have drivers already available in the host operating system.

- **VMM-u (user):** This component runs as a user-mode process on the host operating system. As mentioned earlier, this component makes resource requests to the host OS, in particular, memory and I/O requests, on behalf of the native mode VMM. VMM-u makes these requests using system library functions supplied with the host operating system.

- **VMM-d (driver):** This component provides a means for communication between the other two components. This is done by making the VMM-n appear to the VMM-u as a device attached to the host operating system. The VMM-d is essentially a special device driver installed on the host operating system, and it provides the link from VMM-u to VMM-n. The only user program on the host system allowed to access the VMM-n "device" is the VMM-u component.

As stated earlier, the biggest advantages of a hosted VM are the convenience of installing a virtual machine system on a platform already running a commercially available operating system and the fact that the actual device drivers do not have to be incorporated as part of the VMM.

The dual-mode hosted virtual machine system has some disadvantages also. First, the VMM-n operates in privileged mode alongside the host OS; consequently, the VMM-n and host OS are capable of accidentally (or maliciously) affecting each other. This vulnerability is worsened because the host OS is typically not developed and debugged with the VMM-n in the system. Second, the allocation of resources is completely under the control of the host operating system. The effects of allocation policies in the VMM are less predictable because the VMM has insufficient knowledge and control over the use of resources.

There is also a performance disadvantage compared to a native virtual machine system because of the need to go back and forth between two "worlds," the VMM-n world and the host OS world. When such a "world switch" occurs, sufficient state of one world must be saved before handing control over to the other world. The performance degradation is more significant in an I/O-intensive workload than in a user-mode CPU-intensive workload.

### 8.4.4    Input/Output Virtualization in VM/370

The I/O organization on the System/370 uses an IOP-based model, as shown in Appendix Figure A.5d. The IOP gets commands from the processor, initiates I/O requests on behalf of the processor, controls the transfer of data directly between the I/O device and memory, and informs the processor by means of an interrupt when the I/O is completed. The System/370 IOPs are called *channels*, and communication between the OS and the channels occurs through a program built from special instructions called *channel command words* (CCWs). Each CCW includes an address in memory, the length of data to be transferred, and a command to an I/O device. The process of making a request to the channel involves building in memory a sequence of CCWs and then issuing a privileged start I/O (SIO) command that includes a pointer to the CCW. As far as the processor is concerned, execution of the SIO is completed once the device is detected and the I/O operation is actually started. On completion of the I/O operation, the issuing processor is served with an I/O interrupt.

In a virtual machine, an I/O request to a device takes a similar path, provided the device is physically implemented. The virtual machine sets up the CCW in its virtual address space. The SIO instruction is privileged and hence trapped. The CP (VMM) refers to the shadow page table to map the virtual address of the CCW to a physical address. Based on this CCW it builds a new CCW, translating the device address specified by the virtual machine to the address of the physical device to which it is mapped. The CP also indicates the translated physical storage location for the data to be interchanged with the I/O device and ensures that these pages are physically in memory. The use of paging complicates this translation process, because I/O commands that span more than a page may need to be broken up into multiple CCWs. The CP then sends an SIO command targeting the real I/O device. Since the CP works in privileged mode, this SIO gets transmitted to the channel and does not generate a trap.

Only when the CP returns from its SIO instruction does it unblock the SIO instruction generated by the virtual machine. If there are delays in accepting the command due to, say, an I/O device's being busy, the CP could still schedule other virtual machines to run on the processor. When the I/O operation completes, the IOP generates an I/O interrupt. The CP intercepts this interrupt, reports the relevant information in the status table of the processor that generated the request, and reflects the interrupt to the operating system on the appropriate virtual machine, which then handles the interrupt in the usual manner.

A different scheme is adopted for slower I/O devices, such as printers and card readers. In these cases, the CP emulates these devices and generates software interrupts to the virtual machine while buffering the information on a disk. This spooling technique (discussed in Section 8.4.1) allows more efficient utilization of the resources when several virtual machines attempt to access them simultaneously.

Finally, VM/370 provides for I/O devices for which there are no physical counterparts. The representative device of this type was the *minidisk,* which allowed for virtual disks with far fewer than the 203 cylinders that disks provided in those days. This enabled an economical pooling of what was then an expensive resource among multiple virtual machine users.

## 8.5  Performance Enhancement of System Virtual Machines

Virtual machines can improve the utilization of hardware by sharing resources among multiple users, each provided with the illusion of owning all the resources in the machine. Unfortunately, this also raises the expectations of users, who now want performance on their workload similar to that provided by a complete machine. Performance measurements on early virtual machine systems indicated that even in the absence of other users on the machine, it was difficult to get a performance that was better than 21% of its performance on native hardware on some benchmarks (MacKinnon 1979). In the following sections we examine the sources of performance degradation in virtual machines and examine hardware assists aimed at closing the performance gap.

### 8.5.1 Reasons for Performance Degradation

Performance on a virtual machine differs from that on the native hardware for several reasons.

- **Setup:** Before a virtual machine can be activated, there is overhead involved in initializing the state of the machine. Such initialization includes setting up the timing facilities, the registers, and the program counter.

- **Emulation:** As discussed in previous sections, not all guest instructions can be natively executed. Some guest instructions need to be emulated (usually via interpretation) by the VMM. Often such emulation is not restricted to just the sensitive instruction; it is sometimes convenient to emulate instructions around a sensitive instruction to reduce transitions between executing in emulation mode and in native mode.

- **Interrupt handling:** Interrupts generated by a program running on a virtual machine first have to be handled by the VMM, even though they may eventually be handled by the guest operating system.

- **State saving:** There is overhead involved in saving the state of a virtual machine when control needs to be transferred to the VMM.

- **Bookkeeping:** Often, the VMM has to perform special operations to reflect behavior equivalent to that of a real machine. For example, the accounting of time charged to a user would be different in a virtual machine compared with a real machine, where user-mode activity typically is charged to the user and system-mode activity is charged to the system.

- **Time elongation:** Some instructions require more processing than they would have needed in the native mode. For example, instead of accessing just the page tables, it may be necessary in some situations to access both shadow tables and the local page tables. This has the effect of making the average time taken for some memory references considerably longer than on a real machine.

Hardware extensions may be used to reduce one or more of these effects. *VM assist* is the name given to a piece of hardware that improves the performance of an application when running in the virtual machine mode. One effect of a VM assist is to reduce the number of situations where a user application must enter system mode for some action to be taken by the VMM. Thus not all virtual machine environments benefit from VM assists. In particular, operating systems designed specifically for virtual machine execution, such as the CMS in the VM/370 systems, do not invoke privileged instructions as often as other operating systems. As another example, simple operating systems such as DOS do not access virtual address translation facilities and hence may not benefit from special hardware designed to improve the translation performance.

In the following subsections we discuss various hardware techniques that help improve the performance of virtual machines. Section 8.5.2 discusses techniques to improve instruction emulation performance, while Section 8.5.3 discusses hardware to specifically help the performance of other aspects of the virtual machine monitor. Section 8.5.4 then looks at ways of improving the performance of the system when running in user mode as a guest. Section 8.5.5 examines some specialized techniques to enhance the performance of specific types of guest systems. Finally, in Section 8.5.6 we describe an interesting approach implemented in System/370 that uses hardware essentially to take over a number of VMM functions.

### 8.5.2 Instruction Emulation Assists

This class of assists improves the performance of virtual machine applications in the areas that are the cause of fundamental overheads, namely, those situations that need emulation under VMM control. Recall that in most such situations, the execution of a privileged instruction causes an interrupt that is first handled by the VMM. The VMM emulates the instruction using a routine whose operation depends on whether the virtual machine is supposed to be executing in system mode or in user mode.

An example on the System/370 is the assist for the load PSW (LPSW) instruction. As mentioned in Section 8.2.1, this instruction traps in user mode in order to prevent the manipulation of privileged resources such as the problem state bit by the user. With the assist, the hardware (via microcode) performs the entire action of checking the state of the virtual machine, determining which action to take and performing either the full action if the virtual machine is in system mode or the restricted action if in user mode. The physical resources in the machine are modified by a hardware-assisted instruction if they hold the corresponding virtual machine resource, as in the case of the general-purpose registers. Otherwise, the corresponding location in the state table held in memory is modified. These actions are identical to those that would have been performed by emulation of the instruction in the VMM. Hence the hardware assist depends on knowledge of the implementation of the virtual machine system. In fact, the VM assist implementation provides an additional bit, bit 1 of control register 6, to supply information on whether the guest virtual machine is operating in privileged mode or user mode.

The LPSW still remains a privileged instruction, and because the virtual machine is running in user mode, the overhead due to the trap itself is not eliminated. However, the LPSW hardware assist not only reduces the time taken in emulating the instruction, but also eliminates the overhead due to switching context from the virtual machine to the VMM and back again. Hardware assists of this kind improve the total performance of the system by reducing the number of instructions actually emulated by the VMM.

### 8.5.3 Virtual Machine Monitor Assists

Another way of improving the performance of a virtual machine environment is to use assists for improving performance of the VMM. Here are some of the assists of this nature that have been used on the System/370.

- **Context switch:** Using hardware to save and restore registers and other machine states when switching context from a virtual machine to the VMM and back.

- **Decoding of privileged instructions:** Recall that all privileged instructions trap when running in the virtual machine mode, whereas they trap only in the user mode in a native environment. Since privileged instructions are seldom used in user-mode code, the trapping of these instructions on a native machine is not a significant source of overhead. On the other hand, in a virtual machine mode, even occasional privileged instructions encountered during the execution of the guest operating system could cause a significant overhead in performance. Hardware assists, such as decoding these instructions, normally performed in VMM software, go a long way toward alleviating this overhead. Note that unlike the instruction emulation assists mentioned earlier, this assist only helps with certain critical parts of the emulation, with the rest of the emulation still being carried out in software.

- **Virtual interval timer:** Most operating systems depend on the interval timer to schedule jobs. A guest operating system cannot emulate this function in exactly the same way as in a native mode. The best that can be done is to decrement the virtual counter by some amount estimated by the VMM from the amount that the real timer decrements. More accurate timer functionality needs hardware support. The VM/370 system requires that the virtual timer for each virtual machine be located in location 80 of page 0. Hardware ensures that while the guest VM is running, this location is decremented every time the real timer is decremented. In addition, the hardware assist presents a timer interrupt to the virtual machine when the virtual interval timer turns negative.

■ **Adding to the instruction set:** In order to improve the performance of the VMM, the System/370 also introduced a number of new instructions that are not a part of the ISA of the machine. The nature of operations performed by these new instructions is specific to VM/370, because their inclusion was guided by an analysis of its commonly executed parts. Here are some examples of these instructions.

- ■ Obtain free space from free storage area

- ■ Return space to free storage

- ■ Page lock

- ■ Page unlock

- ■ Translate virtual address and test for shared page

- ■ Invalidate segment/page table

The VMM can detect the presence of these instructions in an implementation by examining the contents of control register 6. Various bits of this register denote which assists are available on the machine. If some specific assist instruction is not present, the machine ignores the instruction and executes the normal software routine it would have executed in the absence of such assists.

### 8.5.4 Improving Performance of the Guest System

The classical concept of *virtualization* postulates that a guest system in the virtual machine environment should not be aware of the fact that it is working in such an environment. It is the job of the VMM to ensure that privileged instructions and interrupts are handled in the same way as in a native environment. This is a requirement if nothing can be changed in software running on a real machine in order to make it operate on a virtual machine.

On the other hand, it is possible to get an improvement in performance if a guest OS knows whether it is currently executing natively or in a virtual machine environment. When there is a choice, an OS executing fewer privileged instructions will observe a smaller degradation in performance when executed on a virtual machine. Alternatively, an OS aware of the presence of a VMM could enjoy a performance benefit by relegating some functions to the VMM or by providing the VMM with additional information to carry out its actions. Such an exchange of information is referred to as *handshaking* (MacKinnon 1979). Handshaking is a programming technique that works in conjunction with hardware assists. A key feature of the System/370 that makes handshaking effective is the ability of the guest operating system to send a message to the VMM. The principal technique to achieve this is by the use of the DIAGNOSE instruction. Different forms of the instruction are defined to send different types of messages between the operating system and the VMM. Variants of the DIAGNOSE instruction are generally nonarchitected — they are implementation-dependent features rather than extensions to the ISA.

Many of the improvements that have resulted from handshaking involve eliminating the duplication of function between the guest operating systems and the VMM. We list a few examples here.

- **Nonpaged mode:** The guest operating system disables dynamic address translation and defines its real address space to be as large as the largest virtual address space it needs. Thus, page frames are mapped to fixed real pages. Translation still occurs from these real pages to the physical pages on the native system. Hence the system as a whole still runs with dynamic address translation turned on. However, improvement in performance results from not having to deal with the bookkeeping of two levels of translation. Further, the guest operating system no longer has to exercise demand paging. The working set of the system as a whole is managed by the VMM, which continues to perform demand paging. Thus, not only is double paging eliminated by this scheme, the effects of potential conflicts in paging decisions by the guest operating system and the VMM are eliminated.

- **Pseudo-page-fault handling:** As discussed earlier in this chapter, a page fault in a virtual machine system can occur not only because of a page fault in some virtual machine but also because of the replacement of a page by the VMM to accommodate a page of a different virtual machine. In a conventional virtual machine system, on the occurrence of the latter type of page fault, the VMM would make the current virtual machine inactive and activate another virtual machine. Control is given back to the original virtual machine when the page fault has been handled. In *pseudo-page-fault handling*, when the page fault is caused by a missing entry in the VMM page table, the VMM attempts to improve fairness by giving control back to the same virtual machine, along with a special page-fault indicator, allowing the virtual machine to schedule an alternative process itself. This is useful in situations where the guest operating system is equipped to handle multiprogramming effectively and has enough threads that it can use to hide the latency of the page fault. The operating system can disable the feature when the level of multiprogramming is low. Pseudo-page-fault handling is enabled by a special Set Pagex CP command.

- **Spool files:** In the absence of any special mechanisms, the guest operating system in the virtual machine closes a spool file and puts it in its spool buffer. It issues I/O commands to dispatch each file in the buffer in turn to the I/O device, e.g., a printer. In order for this to work when multiple virtual machines are using the same I/O device, it is necessary for the VMM to intercept the I/O commands, spool these files in its own buffer along with requests from other virtual machines, and schedule them for printing. Rather than intercept the I/O commands and decipher that the virtual machine is attempting to send a job to the printer, handshaking allows the virtual machine to signal the VMM that a file is ready. In response, the VMM picks up the spool file (or, better still, a pointer to the file) and continues as before to merge this file into its own buffer.

- **Inter-virtual-machine communication:** The objective here is to send data between two virtual machines. Typically, communication between two physical machines involves the processing of message packets through several layers at the sender's side before the message gets physically sent on wires to the receiving machine, once again after being processed through several layers. This process can be streamlined, simplified, and made considerably faster if the two machines are virtual machines on the same host platform. On the System/370, this was achieved by supporting a special virtual machine running a special operating system called the Remote Spooling Communications System (RSCS). The RSCS uses the spool buffer belonging to the VMM either to manage data that may need to be transferred to another virtual machine on the same platform or to stage the data before sending it through network adapters to some remote machine. The RSCS later gave way to more efficient ways of performing inter-virtual-machine communication. In one case a virtual device called a channel-to-channel adapter (CTCA) was used to move data from one virtual machine to another using inexpensive move operations, rather than I/O operations. In another, called Virtual Machine Communications Facility (VMCF), it was possible for data to be communicated from one virtual machine to several virtual machines simultaneously simply by the use of storage-to-storage transfers. The interesting aspect of many of these solutions is that they have the potential not only of reducing the overhead due to virtual machine operation but also of actually improving communication performance between distinct machines.

The notion that the performance of a virtual machine system can be improved by making modifications to the guest operating system has received renewed interest through what is being called *paravirtualization* (Whitaker, Shaw, and Gribble 2002). Paravirtualization presents a virtual machine interface to a system that is similar but not identical to the underlying native hardware. As embodied in the Xen system (Barham et al. 2003), the paravirtualization interface is specifically designed to work around features that make it difficult to virtualize the underlying ISA. Xen specifically targets the IA-32 ISA, which, as we have seen earlier, has critical instructions that make it difficult to design an efficient virtual machine. The Xen system takes an existing operating system, such as Linux or Windows XP, and makes modifications to the machine-dependent parts of the system to eliminate the need to perform complex virtualization tasks such as code detection and patching or the maintenance of shadow page tables. As an example, Xen takes advantage of the fact that popular operating systems today use only rings 0 and 3 of the IA-32 privilege levels by modifying the guest operating system to run in ring 1. Privileged instructions present in the operating system code are paravirtualized by requiring them to be validated and executed within the virtual machine monitor, which runs in ring 0. Xen aims to restrict changes to just the operating system — an application binary works unchanged in Xen. The Xen researchers report that the number of lines of the Linux IA-32 code base that needed to be changed in order to paravirtualize it was less than 3000, or 1.36% of the total. The result is a virtual machine system that performs at a level of 90+% across all benchmarks, compared to a native Linux implementation.

### 8.5.5 Specialized Systems

Further optimization of a virtual machine system is possible if the VMM has some knowledge about, or access to, the internals of the guest operating system. This is the case when the guest operating system is not a proprietary closed box. Following are some examples of this type of performance enhancing hardware (Gum 1983).

■ **Virtual-equals-real (V = R) virtual machine:** In this mode, the host address space representing the guest real memory is mapped one-to-one to the host real memory address space. One advantage of such a mapping is the improvement of performance of channel programs accessing large, data-spanning multiple pages. Normally, contiguous real pages of the virtual machine need not be mapped to contiguous locations in physical memory. Hence such a channel program must be retranslated into multiple channel programs, each accessing a contiguous region of the physical memory.

The V = R mapping eliminates the need to perform such retranslation, thus reducing the overhead experienced by channel programs.

- **Shadow-table bypass assist:** As described in Section 8.3, the shadow page tables for a guest differ from the actual guest page tables only in that the real addresses in the former point to host physical addresses rather than real addresses in the guest machine. The maintenance and update of these tables constitute a fair amount of overhead in a virtual memory system. These shadow page tables can be dispensed with — the guest page tables can point directly to physical addresses if the dynamic address translation hardware is allowed to manipulate the guest page tables. On System/370, however, it is necessary to treat accesses to page 0 in a special way because this page is mapped distinctly for each virtual machine. The shadow-table bypass assist takes this into account in hardware.

- **Preferred-machine assist:** The idea of this assist is to allow a guest operating system to operate in system mode rather than user mode. This eliminates the special treatment required to execute most of the privileged instructions in the guest operating system. Special hardware is needed to support this capability because even though the VMM operates in the same mode as the guest operating system, it has to be protected from unintentional or malicious tampering by a guest operating system. Certain events may still need to be examined to determine whether they are actually meant for the virtual machine currently executing, for the VMM, or for some other guest virtual machine. For example, external I/O interrupts may not be destined for the current guest virtual machine and may need to be handled by the VMM.

- **Segment sharing:** When multiple virtual machines loaded with the same guest operating system are running on a system, it is possible to improve performance by sharing the code segments of the operating system among the virtual machines, provided the operating system code is written in a reentrant manner. In particular, if the code segments contain only read-only information, sharing a single copy can alleviate TLB pressure on the system. While most programs today satisfy the reentrant property, older operating systems often did not — they modified code segments, usually for storing small pieces of data but sometimes to modify code behavior. Sharing in such cases would require the VMM to perform expensive checks to ensure that a virtual machine does not use code modified by another virtual machine. The System/370 provided hardware to perform such segment protection, eliminating the need for software checks.

Hardware assists that enhance the performance of specific guest systems inherently take advantage of knowledge of system details. Often on the System/370, a particular hardware assist may work only for a specific guest operating system; in fact there may be multiple versions of the same assist, depending on characteristics of the virtual machine. Some specialized hardware assists can leave information in guest OS-accessible data structures revealing to the guest OS that it is running in a virtualized mode rather than natively. This, in itself, is usually not a cause for concern, but it does compromise the original principle that any software running on a virtual machine should not know, and hence should not exploit the fact, that it is not running natively.

### 8.5.6 Generalized Support for Virtual Machines

With the success of the virtual machine philosophy, IBM looked into ways to formally include features in the ISA that improved the performance of virtual machine systems in general. This led to the idea of an *interpretive execution facility* (IEF), which provides a way for the processor to directly execute most of the functions of the virtual machine in hardware. Thus, in a sense, interpretive execution is an extreme case of a VM assist, where almost all instructions are assisted. Besides further improving the performance of the virtual machine, interpretive execution benefits virtual machines running all types of guest operating systems and also makes the behavior of virtual machine programs more predictable across a range of architectures and implementations.

An IEF can be viewed as a transparent integration of the various techniques used to assist the performance of virtual machines. The function of the VMM is distributed more cleanly over hardware and software. In fact, the traditional software part of the VMM gives up control to the hardware IEF part through an instruction called *start interpretive execution* (SIE). Before it does so, it takes care of any pending interrupts, determines the virtual machine to be dispatched next, sets a pointer to a table containing the architected state of the virtual machine, and loads some of the resources (such as the general-purpose registers) with corresponding values from the table.

In the IEF mode, most privileged instructions are executed directly in hardware. The notable exceptions are I/O instructions and some of the more complex, though infrequent, instructions. Once the IEF gets control, it starts executing the instruction stream from the virtual machine, directly executing many of the instructions and interpreting others in hardware. As shown in Figure 8.20 there are two ways in which the hardware interpretation of instructions may be suspended and control returned to the software part.

**1.** An interrupt may be generated that is determined by the IEF hardware to be meant for either the VMM or another virtual machine. A return from

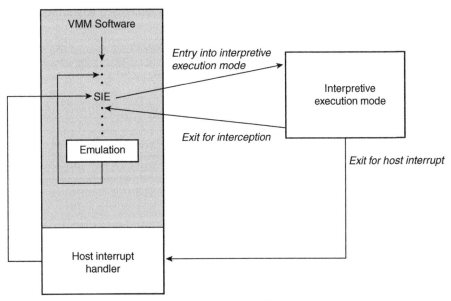

**Figure 8.20**    Interpretive Execution Entry and Exit. *Execution of an SIE instruction causes the processor to enter the interpretive execution mode. Exit from this mode can occur either because an interrupt needs to be handled by the host or due to one of several conditions that require servicing by the VMM. In the former case, the machine returns back to the interpretive execution mode. In the latter it proceeds to the next instruction after the SIE.*

such an interrupt points to the SIE instruction that was executed by the VMM.

**2.** Control can pass to the instruction following the SIE instruction. This is referred to as *interception*. Interception occurs because of the following reasons.

   a.  An instruction is encountered whose interpretation is not supported in hardware.

   b.  An exception occurs during the execution of an interpreted instruction.

   c.  An instruction is encountered in a mode that forces it to be handled in software, as in a traditional virtual machine system.

   d.  An externally set interception condition is detected.

   e.  Some special case is detected; e.g., a guest operating system has entered the wait state.

Before control returns to the software part of the VMM, the IEF hardware must update the table containing the state description of the virtual machine

**Table 8.1** Improvement in Performance of Virtual Machines Resulting from the Introduction of Hardware VM Assists on the IBM System/370 (MacKinnon 1979)

| | | Model 135 | | Model 145 | | Model 158 | |
|---|---|---|---|---|---|---|---|
| | | DOS/VS | VS1 | DOS/VS | VS1 | VS1 | VS2 |
| Elapsed time (seconds) | Native | 2788 | 3035 | 2150 | 1418 | 1386 | 572 |
| | Virtual Machine | 8172 | 11598 | 4520 | 4089 | 3769 | 2696 |
| | Virtual Machine with VM Assist | 4226 | 4063 | 2723 | 2024 | 2004 | 1149 |
| Relative Batch Throughput | without VM Assist | 0.34 | 0.26 | 0.48 | 0.35 | 0.37 | 0.21 |
| | with VM Assist | 0.66 | 0.75 | 0.79 | 0.7 | 0.69 | 0.5 |
| Reduction in supervisor state time through VM Assist | | 74% | 89% | 73% | 86% | 82% | 69% |
| Reduction in elapsed time through VM Assist | | 48% | 65% | 40% | 51% | 47% | 57% |
| Reduction in total number of instructions simulated by VM/370 through VM Assist | | 87% | 95% | 86% | 94% | 91% | 74% |

so that it can resume operation at a later time. It must also store some information about the reason for giving control back to software, including parameters that would be needed for software emulation.

For good performance, the IEF relies on many of the hardware assist features described earlier in this section. By having special hardware assists for the timer and for the time-of-day clock and by using bypass techniques to reduce the overhead of memory address translation, the IEF comes closer to its goal of making the behavior of a program on a virtual machine very similar, only slightly slower, compared to its performance on a native platform. This is evident from Table 8.1 (MacKinnon 1979), which shows the improvement in performance through the use of assists for three different implementations of the System/370 architecture and for three different guest operating systems: DOS/VS, OS/VS1, and OS/VS2 SVS. It can be observed that the difference in performance of a program running natively versus in a virtual machine decreases significantly through the addition of special hardware features that support virtualization.

The interpretive execution facility has evolved considerably since its original introduction. In essence, more and more function was added in hardware to eliminate most of the overhead involved in supporting virtual machines. A comprehensive discussion of the various new features can be found in Osisek, Jackson, and Gum (1991).

## 8.6 Case Study: VMware Virtual Platform

A popular virtual machine infrastructure for IA-32-based PCs and servers is the VMware Virtual Platform (VMware 2000). As mentioned earlier, the VMware system is an example of a hosted virtual machine system. More recently, VMware has included a native virtualization architecture embodied in a product called the VMware ESX Server, which is claimed to provide better resource control, scalability, and performance, but at the expense of full support for all types of hardware. Our discussion here is limited to the hosted system, which has been renamed the VMware GSX Server (VMware 2001). We outline next the various reasons that motivated this development of a hosted system rather than a native system.

In comparison to a native VM infrastructure for a large mainframe, such as the VM/370, the development of a VM infrastructure for a commodity IA-32 environment faces several challenges.

- The IA-32 grew up as an inexpensive microprocessor, never intended to be used in large systems supporting multiple users. Among other things this led to an ISA that includes a number of features difficult to virtualize efficiently. On the other hand, the IBM VM systems have existed almost from the beginning of the System/370 line. The IBM architecture team had close interactions with the team developing the VMM (because they worked at the same company), and therefore they avoided features that could hamper the development of virtual machines on its platforms.

- The other difference between the current commodity IA-32 environment and the IBM System/370 environment is the openness of the system architecture, which has led to a proliferation of different configurations of PCs. Thus, while the VM/370 developers had only to understand the system configurations that IBM shipped to its customers, IA-32 VMM developers must anticipate any of the myriad configurations that a multitude of PC system vendors may ship. The situation is made even more daunting by the proliferation of different I/O devices that are available for users to add to their systems.

- VMware, as a separate company from either a hardware developer, such as Intel, or an operating system company, such as Microsoft, faced an additional challenge. It had to ensure that its VMM software can be easily installed and used. In particular it cannot expect its users to wipe out an existing operating system to install VMware software and then reinstall the old operating system over the VMM. This, in fact, directly influenced the architecture of the VMM developed by VMware.

The VMware Virtual Platform presents a view to the user depicted in Figure 8.21. At this level it looks similar to the VM view presented to an IBM System/370 user. However, as opposed to the native nature of the virtual machine system of VM/370, the Virtual Platform is a hosted system. It depends on the existence of a host operating system, such as Windows or Linux, running on the bare hardware to perform certain critical functions. As we have seen in Section 8.4.3, a principal advantage of a hosted system is that the VMM can avail itself of any I/O device the host operating system supports with relatively little work.

As discussed in Section 8.4.3, a dual-mode hosted virtual machine system must have three components for its VMM: (a) the VMM-n, which is the component working in a privileged native mode, (b) the VMM-u, the component that runs as an application on the host operating system, and (c) the VMM-d, the component that enables communication between the VMM-n and VMM-u. On the VMware system, these three components are respectively named VMMonitor, VMApp, and VMDriver. At any given time, the processor executes either in the host operating system environment or in the VMMonitor environment. Transfer of control between the two worlds is facilitated by the VMDriver and involves saving and restoring all user and system visible state information on the processor. As opposed to the view presented to the user shown in Figure 8.21, the structural view of the VMware system is as shown in Figure 8.22.

Even though the Intel IA-32 architecture features four levels of protection, rings 0 through 3, most operating systems on the IA-32 simply lump the kernel and services, including the device drivers, into ring 0. Thus, for all practical

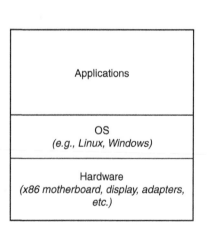
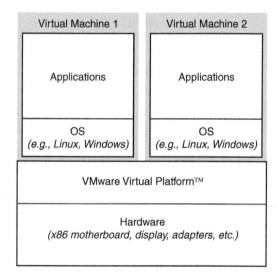

*User view of standard hardware IA-32 system*

*User view of VMWare system*

**Figure 8.21**   User View of the VMware System.

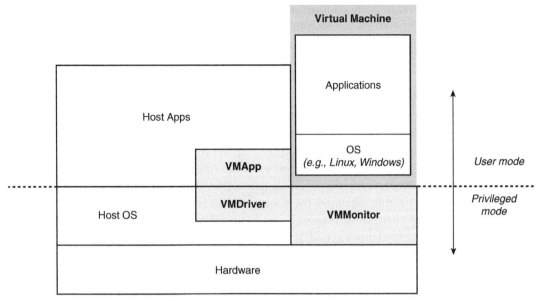

**Figure 8.22** Components of the VMware System. *VMMonitor runs in privileged mode. VMDriver is a device driver installed in the host operating system and hence also has system privileges. VMApp runs as a user-mode application on the host operating system.*

purposes, it is adequate to consider the architecture as having a privileged level, largely consisting of code running in ring 0, and a user level, consisting of code running in ring 3.

VMMonitor operates in privileged mode, but VMApp, which is simply an application that requests services from the host operating system, operates in the user mode. In a sense, VMMonitor can change its personality from being a privileged controller of resources to being just another application on the host operating system. It does this efficiently through VMDriver, a special device driver installed on the host operating system and hence having the same privileges as the host system.

### 8.6.1 Processor Virtualization

The Intel IA-32 architecture is not efficiently virtualizable, i.e., a VMM cannot be constructed in the strict sense of Theorem 1 in Section 8.2.1. Researchers (Robin and Irvine 2000) have identified 17 IA-32 instructions that are critical, i.e., sensitive but not privileged. Hence, a virtual machine system for the IA-32 architecture must be a hybrid virtual machine system. VMware presumably includes mechanisms for discovering these critical instructions and for patching (or caching) them, as described in Sections 8.2.3 and 8.2.4. The 17 critical instructions fall into two broad categories.

- **Protection system references:** These instructions reference the storage protection system, memory system, or address relocation system. The hazard here is the possibility of some virtual machine accessing locations not in its virtual memory. An example of this is the MOVE instruction, which moves a value from a general-purpose register to the CS register, the control register that specifies the current privilege ring number in bits 0 and 1. In order to offer some protection, an instruction such as mov ax,cs executed in the user mode disallows the CS register to be loaded but does not generate a trap. Instead of trapping, the instruction generates a no-op and hence is not efficiently virtualizable.

- **Sensitive register instructions:** These instructions attempt to read or change resource-related registers and memory locations, such as a clock register or interrupt registers. An example is the POPF instruction mentioned in Section 8.2.1. This instruction pops a word from the top of a stack in memory, increments the stack pointer by 2, and stores the value in the lower 16 bits of the EFLAGS register. One of the bits in the EFLAGS register is IF, the interrupt-enable flag, which, in the user mode, is not modified when POPF is executed. To understand why this is a sensitive instruction, consider the case where a guest operating system executes a POPF instruction. The operating system may require that the IF bit be changed; but if it is running in the user mode under the virtual machine, the IF bit is not changed. The guest operating system could later take erroneous actions because the flag bit had not been set as expected. In a hybrid virtual machine implementation, such an instruction would be discovered by the VMM and patched to generate a trap. The trap handler in the VMM would then emulate the instruction and achieve the result expected by a guest operating system.

Let us now examine what happens when a guest operating system in a virtual machine attempts to use a critical instruction. The piece of IA-32 code shown in Figure 8.23 is an example of real code (Rosenblum 2000). In this code, the flags are saved on stack using a pushfd instruction before a small piece of code is executed that could potentially change them. When they are restored, the expectation is that the flags will be exactly the same as before being pushed on the stack. In the privileged mode, the popfd would adequately restore the flags to their original state. However, when the code is executed in user mode, as it

```
pushfd
cli
mov         cax, (0x824)
cmp         cax, 1
jc          5
mov         (0x900), cdx
popfd
add         cdx, cax
```

**Figure 8.23**    Sample Intel IA-32 Code Using the popfd Instruction.

would be on a virtual machine, not all flags will be properly restored, unless the instruction is emulated.

In order to perform this emulation, VMMonitor scans the instruction stream being executed and detects the presence of the popfd instruction in the stream. The monitor then substitutes this instruction with another set of instructions that takes the processor into the privileged state and emulates the action of the original code. The emulation would include a check for the current mode of operation and execute one of two actions for popfd, depending on the mode. Specifically, if the virtual machine itself was supposed to be executing in the system mode, the emulation of the popfd instruction must include the loading of the EFLAGS register or, more accurately, the virtual EFLAGS register belonging to the executing virtual machine. On the other hand, if the virtual machine is not in system mode, the emulation must ensure that certain bits, such as the IF bit, are not modified in the virtual EFLAGS.

The setting of the IF should always be in control of the VMM, so that when a virtual machine is swapped out and another one brought in, the IF is not swapped. For each virtual machine there is a location in memory that corresponds to the EFLAGS register, and the emulation of activity on the EFLAGS register is carried out through instructions operating on the virtual flags in memory, rather than by loading the EFLAGS register and performing the action directly. Emulation of the IF in the EFLAGS register implies that any instruction that reads or modifies this bit must also be emulated. The cli instruction in the example of Figure 8.23, which clears the interrupt flag, therefore, is also emulated by VMMonitor.

## 8.6.2    Input/Output Virtualization

The difficulty of virtualizing I/O in popular IA-32–based platforms was a primary reason that VMware developers chose to implement the monitor in a

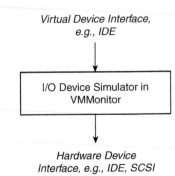

*Virtual Device Interface,*
*e.g., IDE*

I/O Device Simulator in
VMMonitor

*Hardware Device*
*Interface, e.g., IDE, SCSI*

**Figure 8.24**    Mapping a Virtual Device Interface to a Hardware Device Interface in the VMware Virtual Platform.

dual-mode hosted VM style. The PC platform supports many more devices and many more different types of devices than any other platform. This has resulted in a massive number of device drivers written by all segments of the industry, including device hardware vendors, operating system developers, software developers, and even users. VMware takes a multifaceted approach to solving the I/O virtualization problem (Sugerman, Venkitachalam, and Lim 2001).

### Emulation in VMMonitor

The first way to virtualize an I/O device is to emulate the device in the VMMonitor. If the device to be virtualized already has a physical counterpart on the host, the job of emulating it is simply one of converting the parameters in some virtual device interface (VDI) into parameters of the actual hardware device interface (HDI). Thus, the in and out I/O instructions are intercepted by the VMMonitor and converted to appropriate in and out instructions for some actual physical device (Figure 8.24). A situation where such a scheme would be used is that of converting a command to read a block from an IDE drive to one that reads a block from a SCSI drive. Unfortunately, such conversion requires some knowledge of the ports and memory map locations associated not only with the SCSI drive, but also with the IDE drive supported in the guest operating system.

### Using the Services of the Host Operating System

The VMware developers discovered that while some interfaces, such as the IDE interface, appear to be well standardized across the industry, there is a noticeable variation in devices following the SCSI, LAN, or graphics standards.

This called for a different approach to emulating these interfaces. Instead of converting the in and out I/O instructions to new in and out instructions, they are converted into a set of library service requests for the host operating system, which invariably already supports the needed device drivers.

This technique is illustrated in Figure 8.25. The method relies on the dual personalities of the Virtual Platform. The VMMonitor contains device models for each of the virtual devices supported. When a guest I/O instruction is encountered, it traps to the VMMonitor code that alters the state of the device model corresponding to the requested device. If the requested device is not natively supported by VMMonitor but is supported by the host OS, the request is converted into a host OS call. For example, if the host operating system is Windows NT, it is converted into a *win32* system call. The VMMonitor, through VMApp, now acts as a well-behaved application under Windows NT. When the application returns from this system call, the control gets back to the VMMonitor and then into the application running on the virtual machine. VMMonitor uses this approach for virtualizing the floppy disk drive, the CD-ROM drive, the sound card, the serial port, and the parallel port. In measurements taken on a real system, the overhead of switching from one mode to the other was determined to be only tens of microseconds.

The dual personality assumed by the VMMonitor confers advantages beyond reducing the complexity of supporting a large variety of I/O devices.

- As long as the operating system provides a reasonable suite of services to perform I/O, any operating system can be used as the host. All devices supported by that operating system would automatically be available to VMMonitor.

- The VMMonitor need not limit its access of the host operating system to its I/O features. All services available on the host operating system can be taken advantage of because VMMonitor installs on the host operating system just like any other application. In particular, it can use the file system services of the host, say, to emulate disks.

- When making a transition from an old operating system to a newer one, it may be beneficial to use the old operating system as the host, with the new one working in a virtual machine. Performance-critical applications can be run on the host directly during the transition period.

### New Capability for Devices Through Abstraction Layer

VMApp has the ability to insert a layer of abstraction above the physical device. This allows the incorporation of new functionality on the device that may not

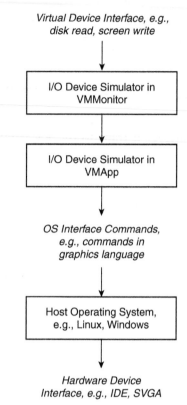

**Figure 8.25**    Use of the Operating System Library Function Interface to Map a Virtual Device Interface to a Hardware Device Interface.

have been possible or convenient with the original device. For example, the disk on a virtual machine in VMware can be treated either as a raw disk or as a file on the host operating system. In the latter case, it then becomes possible to have "undoable" disks, where recent actions taken on the disk can be undone. This also makes it possible to save or discard entire sessions by providing a commit feature that performs explicit commits of disk writes at the end of the session. Such a capability is particularly useful, for example, for a test session or if one needs to discard a session because of an insecure access.

This abstraction layer can also provide a way to reduce performance losses due to virtualization. For example, a virtual Ethernet switch is provided in VMware between a virtual NIC (network interface controller) and a physical NIC to allow multiple virtual machines to share a physical NIC, similar to what was described in connection with Figure 8.19. Different IP addresses can be given to each of the virtual machines. The virtual machines sharing the physical

NIC can communicate with each other through this virtual LAN, exactly in the manner of a more traditional LAN interconnection between physical machines. The latency of communication between these virtual machines can actually be made lower than that encountered in a physical system because the LAN is emulated using special communication paths that are local and more efficient than the standard Ethernet path.

A different type of abstraction is exemplified by the provision in VMware for an alternative user interface. In general, user interface controls such as the video card, the keyboard, and the mouse are physical resources that are virtualized in a manner similar to other physical resources, such as general-purpose registers. A user on a virtual machine takes direct control of these devices just as he/she would on a real machine. Thus the entire screen of the monitor can be under the control of the virtual machine. In addition, VMware also provides the capability to make the user-interface display appear as a window on the user interface of the host operating system, e.g., as one of the windows of a Windows desktop. This capability allows the user to access applications on both platforms in a convenient way. Using special communication paths between VMMonitor and the host operating system, it is even possible to cut and paste between a window on the host and an application on a virtual machine.

### 8.6.3  Memory Virtualization

VMMonitor virtualizes the physical memory of a virtual machine by using the host operating system to allocate or release the real machine's physical memory. The guest operating system does standard demand paging, though physical memory pages for the virtual machine are assigned by the host operating system. Paging requests are not directly intercepted by the VMM. They are converted into disk read/writes by the guest OS exactly as they would be on a real machine. These disk read/writes are translated by VMMonitor to requests on the host operating system through VMApp. The requests are actually made to appear by VMDriver as large DMA requests on the host operating system. The activity of applications on the host determines whether or not such a DMA request is satisfied from the memory of the host or results in paging on the host. The standard replacement policies of the host could end up replacing critical pages, thereby degrading performance of the virtual machine system in the presence of other host applications. In order to alleviate this problem, VMDriver pins some of the critical pages of the virtual memory system in physical memory, especially those pages belonging to the VMMonitor's active working set.

## 8.7 Case Study: The Intel VT-x (Vanderpool) Technology

In describing the VMware Virtual Platform in Section 8.6, we indicated several of the problems in virtualizing the Intel IA-32 architecture. We also saw how the VMware GSX server tackled the virtualizability problem to provide virtual machine capability on this popular platform using a hosted VM system. However, the various techniques used to finally achieve virtualization come at a cost — complexity of code and performance overhead. Some of the overhead, particularly that of scanning and patching the code to get around the presence of critical instructions in the instruction set, will also be present in native virtual machine implementations like the VMware ESX server. This was the motivation behind the current trend towards paravirtualization, where the interface presented by the virtual machine is not identical to that of the architecture of the underlying processor, but rather simplified to eliminate the effect of critical instructions as much as possible.

The performance overhead of handling the sensitive instructions in the VMM still remains, even with paravirtualization. In Section 8.5 we described various ways to speed up virtualization through hardware enhancements of the processor. VM Assists and the Interpretive Execution (IE) capability went a long way in improving the performance of the z/VM system on the IBM zSeries mainframes. Intel recently developed a capability, the VT-x, or Vanderpool, technology for IA-32 processors, that is conceptually similar to the IBM's IE capability, and promises to enhance the performance of IA-32 virtual machine implementations.

The main feature of VT-x is the inclusion of the new VMX mode of operation. When in VMX mode, the processor can be in either VMX root operation or VMX non-root operation. In both cases, all four IA-32 privilege levels (rings) are available for use by software. VT-x, in effect, provides four new less privileged rings of protection for execution of guest software, in addition to the usual four rings for use by the VMM. The behavior of the processor in VMX root operation is largely similar to its function in a normal processor not incorporating the VT-x technology, the main difference being the inclusion of a set of new instructions called the VMX instructions. The behavior of the processor in non-root operation is limited in some respects from its behavior on a normal processor in order to support virtualization. The limitations are such that critical shared resources are kept under the control of a monitor running in VMX root operation. This limitation of control of resources extends also to non-root operation in ring 0, which, in normal processors, is the most privileged level. Thus the intention is for the VMM of a virtual machine system to work in VMX root operation, while the virtual machine itself, including the guest operating system and applications, works in VMX non-root operation. Because VMX non-root operation includes all four IA-32 privilege levels (rings), guest software can run in the rings in which it was originally intended to be run (i.e., the guest operating system kernel can run in ring 0 and guest applications can run in ring 3).

### 8.7.1  Technology Overview

The typical sequence of operations in a virtual machine system is shown in Figure 8.26. A processor which has been turned on in a normal mode can be made to enter VMX root operation by issuing a vmxon instruction. The virtual machine monitor running in root operation sets up the environment for each virtual machine and initiates the virtual machine by issuing a special instruction, vmlaunch. Various situations, especially attempts to reconfigure critical resources shared with other virtual machines or with the VMM, cause the processor to relinquish control to the VMM in root operation. The processor may also exit from the virtual machine explicitly through a vmcall instruction. Re-entering a previously launched virtual machine is accomplished through the lower-cost vmresume instruction, which puts the processor back in non-root operation. Thus, in the steady state, the processor should be working largely in VMX non-root operation with occasional short excursions to the VMM. Finally, when the processor wishes to leave VMX operation, it will bring down each of the virtual machines in turn and return to the normal mode by issuing a vmxoff instruction.

This is a high-level view of how a virtual machine system can be created on a VT-x enabled IA-32 processor. There are many aspects which need to be taken

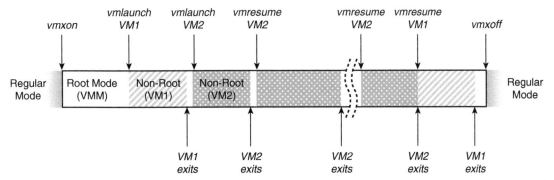

**Figure 8.26**  Transition Between Operation Phases with the Intel VT-x Technology. *White areas represent the operation in root mode of the virtual machine monitor (VMM). The cross-hatched and dotted areas represent the regions in time when the two active virtual machines are executing.*

care of in launching and exiting from a virtual machine; the interested reader is referred to Intel's Preliminary Specification document (Intel 2005) for more details on this topic. We limit our discussion below to the concepts underlying the technology.

### 8.7.2 Capabilities of the Technology

A key aspect of the VT-x technology that allows faster virtual machine systems to be built is the elimination of the need to run all guest code in the user mode, essentially by providing a new mode of operation specifically for hypervisors and VMMs. For code regions that do not contain instructions that affect any critical shared resources, the hardware executes as efficiently as it would have on a normal machine. Since hardware keeps track of the virtual machines that are active, even larger regions can be executed at full speed by temporarily mapping the shared resources to the corresponding resources in the virtual machine. It is only in the few cases where this is not possible that a certain degree of emulation must be performed by the VMM. Thus, once in the virtual machine, the exits back to the monitor are far less frequent in the hardware case than in software virtualization.

The other major source of overhead in a software-based solution is the maintenance of state information. Various tricks in the software, especially mapping the frequently used registers to hardware register elements, reduce the overhead of maintaining and changing state. VT-x technology provides hardware that allows almost all of the state-holding data elements to be mapped directly to their native structures during virtual machine execution. Moreover, the technology provides a formal data structure called the VMCS (virtual machine control structure) that encapsulates all the information needed to capture the state of a virtual machine or to resume a virtual machine. The hardware implementation can take over the tasks of loading and unloading the state from their physical locations, without requiring the VMM to perform expensive load and store operations on large quantities of data.

The VT-x hardware is thus able to reduce the overhead in a classic native VM system considerably. It also eliminates the need for paravirtualization, thereby allowing more standard versions of operating systems to be used in virtual machine systems. The vmcall instruction, which can be used by a VMX non-root guest to communicate with the root mode VMM, can be used as a mechanism to pass hints and data that can help the VMM to perform more intelligent allocation of resources.

VT-x can be adapted also to construct a hosted VM system. Since VMX root operation has been designed to be as close as possible to the normal operation of a processor, it is possible to take a standard implementation of a host OS and make it run in VMX root operation. The VMM, also running in VMX root operation, is then in the same environment as the host OS, and has the same privileges as the host OS, just as in a typical hosted-VM implementation like VMware's.

An important reason for the choice of a hosted system for the VMware GSX server was the need to virtualize the large number of existing devices and device drivers that exist in the IA-32 PC world. This need still remains; the VT-x technology does not address I/O virtualization. It must be noted also that the VMX root operation is not exactly identical to normal operation of the processor. There are restrictions imposed in VMX operation, such as the inability to reset the CR0.PE and CR0.PG bits to 0, which prevent a host OS in VMX operation from running in unpaged protected mode or in real-address mode. Modern applications will not suffer because of this limitation; however, on legacy systems these modes may have to be supported either through emulation in the VMM, or by executing in the normal mode after leaving VMX operation through a vmxoff instruction.

### 8.7.3 Maintenance of State Information

We now turn our attention to the mechanics of state maintenance in the VT-x technology. As mentioned before, the state of a virtual machine is maintained in the VMCS data structure. This structure is fully specified, with the various fields precisely defined. The VMCS can be manipulated only by hardware, or by software running in root operation. The VMCS corresponding to the currently executing VM is identified by a pointer, the VMPTR, which contains the 4KB-aligned physical address of the VMCS. Multiple VMCS structures corresponding to different virtual machines can be active, though only one can be executing at a time on a given logical processor. (There may be more than one "logical" processor in a multithreaded system.) The VMPTR can be modified using the vmptrld instruction in root operation. Similarly, the contents of the VMCS can be accessed only in root operation, and only through vmread and vmwrite instructions. Regular memory load and store operations may not be used to access data in the VMCS because the format used to store the VMCS is not architected, and may change from one implementation to the next.

The different types of information stored in the VMCS are shown in Table 8.2. The state information that is stored for the guest and the host goes beyond the conventional architected state and includes items like the architecturally hidden part of each segment register. This is needed to maintain a behavior of a virtual machine similar to its behavior on a normal machine. The various control fields determine the conditions under which control leaves the virtual machine (VM exit) and returns to the VMM, and define the actions that need to

**Table 8.2** Information Stored in the Virtual Machine Control Structure (VMCS)

| State Area | Guest State | Register State |
|---|---|---|
| | | Interruptibility State |
| | Host State | Register State |
| Control Area | VM Execution Controls | Pin-based Execution Controls |
| | | Processor-based Execution Controls |
| | | Bitmap Fields |
| | | etc. |
| | VM Exit Controls | Control Bitmap |
| | | MSR Controls |
| | VM Entry Controls | Control Bitmap |
| | | MSR Controls |
| | | Controls for Event Injection |
| VM Exit Information | Basic Information | VM-Exit Information |
| | | Vectoring Event Information |
| | Other Exit Information | Due to Event Delivery |
| | | Due to Instruction Execution |

be performed during VM entry and VM exit. For example, since the MSRs on a processor are implementation-dependent, one of the control fields determines how many model-specific registers (MSRs) must be saved on VM exit, and another field determines the physical address where these registers must be saved.

An important part of the VMCS area is the VM-exit information area. This area contains fields that inform the VMM the reason for an exit, as well as other information needed to service the event that caused the exit.

Instructions may cause exits, either unconditionally, e.g., instructions disallowed in non-root mode, or conditionally, e.g., a rdtsc instruction, which causes an exit only if a special control bit "RDTSC Exiting" has been set. There are several such control bits described in the specification document (Intel 2005), that essentially allow the VMM to set up virtual machines with different kinds of behaviors.

### 8.7.4 An Example: The rdtsc Instruction

We conclude this section by demonstrating how the hardware supports a virtual machine executing the "Read Time-Stamp Counter" instruction, rdtsc. According to the IA-32 architecture, the time-stamp counter is maintained in an MSR called the IA32_TIME_STAMP_COUNTER. Execution of the rdtsc instruction causes the 64-bit value in this counter to be transferred to a specified pair of general-purpose registers. However, if the TSD (Time-Stamp

Disable) bit of control register CR4 is set and the privilege level is not 0, a protection-mode exception will result and the counter will not be read.

A flow chart showing the various conditions that arise is shown in Figure 8.27. The first thing the hardware checks is the TSD bit in the

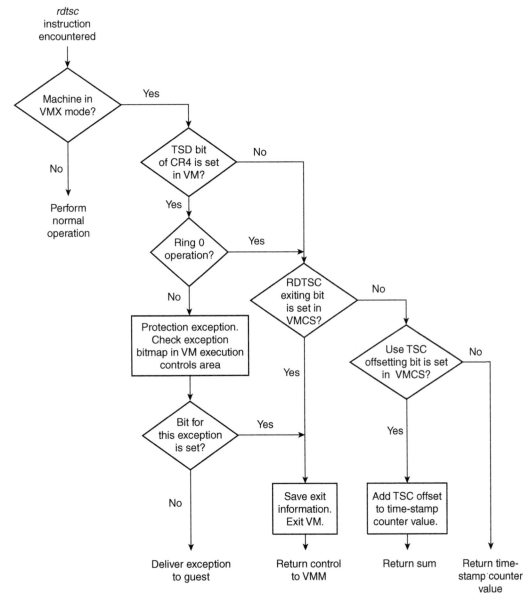

**Figure 8.27**    Actions Taken by Hardware When a Read Time-Stamp Counter (rdtsc) Instruction Is Encountered.

physical CR4 register that is mapped to the CR4 of the currently active VM. If the TSD bit in this register is set and the privilege level is not level 0, the operation must cause a protection-mode exception in the guest. The hardware directly examines a bitmap, called the Exception Bitmap, in the Processor-Based VM-Execution Controls area of the VMCS for the currently executing VM. This bitmap is a 32-bit vector that contains one bit for each IA-32 exception. If the bit corresponding to the mentioned protection-mode exception is set, the hardware forces a VM exit to allow the VMM to take appropriate action. Otherwise, the exception is directly delivered to the guest as in a processor operating in the normal mode. Thus the hardware avoids the need for the VMM to intercept the exception, inspect it, and reflect it back to the guest OS, as typically done in software VM implementations.

If the TSD bit is not set or if the privilege level is 0, the hardware checks the "RDTSC Exiting" bit in another field of the Processor-based VM-Execution Control area of the VMCS. If this bit is set, a VM-exit occurs and control returns to the VMM, which can then emulate the desired behavior of the instruction.

If the "RDTSC exiting" bit is 0, the processor checks another bit, the "Use TSC Offsetting" bit, in the same area of the VMCS. If this bit is 0, the value returned is the actual value contained in the physical IA32_TIME_STAMP_COUNTER. When this bit is 1, it is not directly the physical counter value that is returned, but rather the value obtained by performing a signed addition of this value with a value contained in the "TSC Offset" field of the Processor-based VM-Execution Control area of the VMCS. This mode allows the VMM to approximate different behaviors for a virtual machine. For example, the VMM could use the value in the physical counter at VM-entry and VM-exit to store a TSC offset value such that the processor reports to a virtual machine only the number of cycles elapsed while the virtual machine was active.

This example demonstrates the flexibility provided by the control bits that allows virtual machines with different behavior to be instantiated without incurring a software penalty. And yet, if a more elaborate behavior is needed, a VM-exit can be forced and the desired behavior implemented in the VMM.

## 8.8 Summary

System virtual machines enjoyed a fair amount of popularity in the 1970s and 1980s, but they appeared to go out of favor in the 1990s as single-user computer systems became affordable. Recently there has been a resurgence of interest in system virtual machines, especially in the Web services area, with the need for massive numbers of simple single-thread systems that seldom have to communicate with each other but that share storage resources. For these applications, virtual machines tend to utilize processor resources better than large clusters of uniprocessors. They also reduce administrative costs by making the process of starting up or shutting down a virtual machine trivial, compared to what would be needed to install or remove a real machine.

While the original popularity of virtual machines was due to the ability for multiple users to use a sophisticated system as though it were their own, the future pervasiveness of virtual machines is likely to arise from other factors. As we will see in Chapter 10, there are emerging issues, such as security and system encapsulation, and emerging models, such as the Grid, that are likely to increase the use of virtual machine technology.

# Chapter Nine

# Multiprocessor Virtualization

Many systems today, particularly servers and high-end desktop systems, contain multiple processors. Server systems typically incorporate many processors that share large amounts of memory and I/O devices. Web servers manage huge databases and need to service a multitude of simultaneous requests coming from large numbers of network ports. Computational servers used for large scientific calculations have thousands of processors connected to terabytes of memory and petabytes of disk capacity. Moreover, as levels of integration continue to increase, multiprocessor architectures will soon find their way into laptops and inexpensive desktop systems.

The increasing availability of multiprocessor systems has led to the examination of techniques that can help utilize them more effectively. Often there is a mismatch between the ideal number of processors an application needs and the actual number of physical processors available. With increases in the sizes of multiprocessor systems, it is more often the case that applications cannot exploit more than a fraction of the processors actually available. This may be caused by limitations in the parallelism available in the programs or by limitations in the scalability of applications due to the overhead of communication between processors. This has led to the development of ways in which the multiprocessor system can be *partitioned* so that multiple applications can simultaneously exploit the available resources of the system.

## 9.1 Partitioning of Multiprocessor Systems

In this chapter, we discuss general techniques to virtualize multiprocessor systems. As with other virtualization methods, a virtualized multiprocessor gives

**445**

the appearance of a system that may or may not reflect the exact configuration of the underlying physical system. The term *partitioning* suggests that each virtual multiprocessor system is given a subset of the resources available on the system. The system virtual machine techniques described in Chapter 8 essentially perform partitioning, in time, of the processor resource. Multiprocessor systems provide a new dimension, that of partitioning of processors in space. Moreover, as we will see, the two can be combined so that a virtual system may have even more processors than the physical number of processors available on the system.

Multiprocessor systems can be configured in a variety of ways, as discussed in Appendix Section A.7. One way is as a cluster system, typically consisting of a number of single-processor (or small multiprocessor) systems communicating with each other through high-speed network interfaces. Another way is as a large shared-memory processing (SMP) platform providing a large number of processors that communicate through shared memory. While there may be reasons to virtualize any of the multiprocessor architectures on any of the platforms, our discussion here will be largely restricted to construction of virtual clustered multiprocessor systems on a host SMP platform, with each node in the cluster being an SMP system. Typically the number of processors needed by a guest SMP system node is small. This is important, because many of the partitioning techniques we discuss assume that the number of processors needed in the guest is not more than the number of available processors on the host. Partitioning therefore provides an illusion of several virtual shared-memory systems operating simultaneously on a single shared-memory host system, as shown in Figure 9.1.

### 9.1.1 Motivation

Beyond efficiency, there are a number of reasons for virtualizing multiprocessor systems. Some are extensions of the traditional reasons outlined in Chapter 8. However, with multiprocessors becoming more common, users are finding additional ways to take advantage of the capabilities offered by virtualization. We outline next the expanded benefits typically provided by virtualizing multiprocessor systems.

#### *Workload Consolidation*

The shared-memory multiprocessing paradigm has been used for several years in high-end database servers. This paradigm combines the technological advances made in supporting cache coherence across a large number of

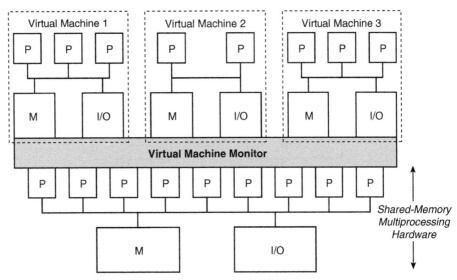

**Figure 9.1**   Large Shared-Memory System Partitioned into Smaller Shared-Memory Systems.

processors with the ease of programming afforded by a single namespace. Today, large database servers almost exclusively use shared-memory multi-processors. The large amounts of memory, the large number of disks, the requirement for high reliability, and the need for special environments driven primarily by cooling and security make these systems very expensive. Yet, for every unit of computation consumed by these large database servers, several more are consumed in other computational layers commonly used in large enterprises. In a three-tier model, for example, there are large numbers of workstations or PCs that feed requests to a first level of servers, commonly referred to as *application servers,* as shown in Figure 9.2. The application servers are responsible for running the business process logic but also make accesses to large database servers.

Administrative costs of computer centers are dependent, to a large extent, on the number of systems that need to be supported. These costs are lowered by reducing the different types of systems in the center. Organizations that already need large servers for their databases find it attractive if there is a way to shift the application server workload to the large servers, as depicted in Figure 9.2.

Another important scenario is the consolidation of multiple workstation users on a large remote server. Users of these small systems may be reluctant to migrate to the large system unless they have assurances regarding the privacy of their data and their environment. Moreover, users differ in their preferred

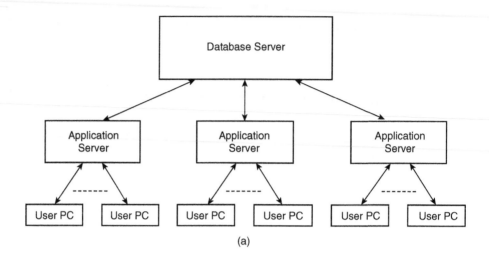

(a)

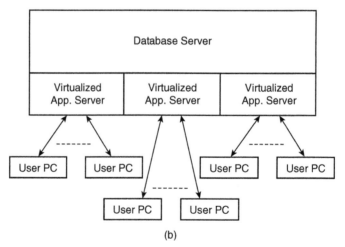

(b)

**Figure 9.2** Consolidation of Database and Application Servers on a Single Platform. *(a) Typical three-tier server model. (b) Consolidation of the application server with the database server.*

operating system and system configuration. Virtualization of large servers through partitioning of physical resources addresses both these concerns — the isolation provided through partitioning satisfies the privacy requirement, while the ability to form variable partitions provides greater freedom to the user compared to a multiprogrammed solution.

### Cluster-Based Programming Model

Large SMP servers provide high performance in many scientific and commercial applications, particularly database applications. On the other hand, there has been a recent proliferation of low-cost cluster platforms, including blade servers. With the rapid increase in programming tools and applications being developed for such platforms, there is increasing pressure to provide the ability to run cluster-based applications on high-end shared-memory systems. Partitioning provides the user of a large shared-memory system with multiple operating system images on multiple smaller virtual multiprocessors that can run such clustered applications. A program written for a cluster using the Message Passing Interface (MPI) (Pacheco 1996), for example, can then work unchanged on such a partitioned system. Moreover, the efficiency of execution may be improved by tuning the message-passing libraries to exploit the shared-memory hardware mechanisms available on such a system.

### System Migration

Rapid improvements in technology have led to the introduction of new systems with new capabilities at a breathtaking pace. To remain competitive, businesses are often forced to use the latest technology for their computation and server needs. Yet the process of migrating to a new system is arduous. New versions of a given application must be thoroughly tested before they can replace older versions. Similarly, new versions of the operating system or middleware can be used in a production mode only when all applications either have a new version that runs on the new system or when these applications are found to run without problems on the new system. The introduction of a new system is therefore a very disruptive process.

A partitioned system goes a long way toward reducing the pain of moving to a new system, by allowing the testing and verification of the various components to proceed in partitions of the system separated from other partitions that execute production processes. The isolation provided by a partition ensures that any problems discovered during testing do not disrupt production applications by crashing the entire system.

### Reduction of System Downtime

Just as with migration to a new system, an upgrade of an existing operating system often involves several installation and configuration steps, which usually can be done only by bringing the system down, i.e., by purging the system of all jobs and users. Having a partitioned system allows system administrators to perform many of the normal downtime activities in a separate partition even when the rest of the system is continuing with production jobs. Thus an upgraded operating system can be completely checked out on a new partition before the rest of the system is brought down and migrated.

### Heterogeneous Systems

It is not uncommon for enterprises wishing to change to a new operating system to be forced to continue running some of their older applications on the old operating system. For example, an organization wishing to switch from, say, a proprietary Unix environment to a Linux environment may still need to keep its old environment to run some critical database applications. A platform that supports virtualization would allow both environments to be run on a single server by partitioning the server and running the two operating systems in different partitions.

### Improving System Utilization

Most systems are designed to meet peak workloads. Yet the average workload on a typical system is only a fraction of the peak for which it is designed. The ability to partition the system and run a variable number of operating system images allows the system to be configured to changing needs. For peak workloads that need the single system image of a large shared-memory system, for example, the system can be configured to run as a single partition. At other times, the system can be configured for multiple partitions and can be used as a cluster of smaller systems running several applications simultaneously, each on a separate operating system. Such a solution both improves the utilization of the large server and reduces the cost for an enterprise, especially compared to the alternative of buying and operating several servers.

Capacity planning, the process of estimating how much compute power is needed by various workloads in an organization, can help in determining whether partitioning is viable for the organization. Flexibility in scheduling of operations can help in keeping the compute requirements closer to the average workload rather than the sum of workload peaks.

Resources such as tape drives, optical storage, and high-performance communications adapters are needed by many applications, but typically only for short time intervals. A system might provide as many of these devices as required by the virtual system running in each partition — in fact, this may be a requirement imposed by the operating system running in the partitions, especially when security is a consideration. However, in a large majority of the cases, it is acceptable for the resources to be available only when they are needed by a system — these resources can be "loaned" to other partitions at other times. Common partitioning techniques allow for the allocation of resources in this manner. Dynamic migration of resources from one partition to another goes a long way toward improving the utilization of resources in a system and hence toward reducing the cost of ownership of the system.

### Multiple Time-Zone Requirements

It is customary for geographically distributed parts of the same international company to run different operating systems for the different geographical regions, each with its own date-and-time setting. The main reason for this is the need to bring down the system for maintenance or upgrade in each region at a convenient local time, for example, at night, when there are few users loading the system. Server consolidation often finds all parts of the company using the same physical server for their computing needs. By running the workload for each region in a partition isolated from that of the other regions, each region can make decisions independent of the other regions about scheduling its batch workload or its downtime.

### Failure Isolation

One of the most important reasons partitioning is becoming popular is its ability to isolate failures. It is not uncommon for today's systems to be vulnerable to either attacks over the network, unintentional software malfunctions of programs, or hardware failures in some part of the system. Thus, a process in a multiuser system can terminate due to a failure, even if the failure does not occur while that process is running or if it occurs in a part of the hardware the application never uses. Operating systems are often able to isolate software failures within applications. However, as operating systems get larger and more complex, there are more situations where the operating system itself is affected by a failure and brings down all applications running on it. Partitioning helps isolate the effects of failures to the partition where the failure occurs. Thus an event that causes a crash in a guest operating system will bring down only that operating system and its applications. To restore the system, only the operating systems running on the affected partitions need to be rebooted. Other operating system images running on the machine continue without being affected by the failure.

Faults may occur in either software or hardware. An example of a software fault is a bug in system software that produces a pointer to an invalid memory region. Most partitioning techniques isolate software faults. Hardware faults, on the other hand, may or may not be local to a partition. If there is a hardware fault that causes an arithmetic unit to produce wrong results, the effect of the fault will depend on the nature of partitioning. In partitioning schemes where the same processor is time multiplexed between several partitions, a failure can affect more than just the partition that manifests the fault. On the other hand, when the system is *physically partitioned,* a processor is assigned to no more than one partition, and hence only that partition will be affected by the failure. Physical partitioning, where each partition uses hardware resources distinct from other partitions, is the closest one can get to isolating hardware faults.

Of course, the reliability of the partitioned system also depends on the reliability of the VMM itself. The VMM typically consists of a program, either in software or in microcode, assisted by special hardware. The reliability of the VMM depends on the reliability of both these parts, though the hardware added is typically small and does not affect reliability in any significant way. The software portion either should be verifiably correct or should be kept small and simple. Contemporary software VMMs are generally quite small, often a couple of orders of magnitude less complex than large operating systems.

### 9.1.2 Mechanisms to Support Partitioning

As shown in Figure 9.1, partitioning needs the help of an additional layer between the physical host hardware and the virtual multiprocessors. We continue to refer to this layer as the *virtual machine monitor* (VMM). The functions to be performed by the VMM determine the complexity of this layer and how it is implemented.

As we observed in Chapter 8, for many ISAs, there can be an appreciable degradation of performance because of the need to execute a guest operating system in nonprivileged mode. Commercial partitioning techniques on large shared-memory systems often provide hardware features to improve the performance of the VMM. In fact, VMMs may be implemented completely in hardware, in microcode supported by hardware, or in software supported by hardware. Performance is traded off for greater flexibility as more of the features of the VMM are implemented in software.

A key difference between techniques that take advantage of hardware modifications and those that do not is the availability of a new privilege mode in which the VMM can operate. This avoids the need to run a guest operating system in user mode and hence the need to take special care of privileged operations executed by a guest OS. One disadvantage of making hardware modifications to support virtualization is the inability to virtualize in a recursive manner — i.e., to run a software VMM on top of the hardware-aided VMM.

### 9.1.3 Types of Partitioning Techniques

As described earlier, the spectrum of possible implementations for a large multiprocessing system with $n$ processors has two extreme points. At one end is a simple cluster of $n$ nodes, each consisting of a single processor. The natural number of system images (operating systems) in such a system is $n$, each operating system running natively on a dedicated processor node. At the other extreme is an $n$-way shared-memory system with $n$ processors, all sharing the same main memory. Here, a single operating system runs across the entire system so that any application on the system can use all the processors while taking advantage of the large shared memory.

Figure 9.3 depicts the various partitioning techniques that have been either implemented or proposed in the literature. As mentioned in the previous section, the implementation of the VMM plays an important role in partitioning, and we have divided the class of partitioning techniques into those that use special hardware for the VMM and those that do not.

On the left-hand side of Figure 9.3 are techniques that take advantage of special hardware to provide efficient virtual machines. These fall under two categories, *physical partitioning* and *logical partitioning*. In physical partitioning, each image uses resources, processors in particular, that are physically distinct from the resources used by the other operating system images. Thus, the number of partitions that can be supported in such a system is limited to the number of processors, though other considerations may limit this to an even lower number.

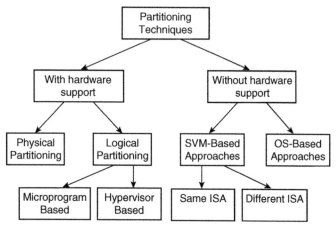

**Figure 9.3** Different Types of Partitioning Techniques.

With logical partitioning, images share some of the physical resources, usually in a time-multiplexed manner. Logical partitioning thus makes it possible to partition an $n$-way system into a system with more than $n$ images if so desired. Logical partitioning is more flexible and needs additional mechanisms to provide the services needed to share resources in a safe and efficient way. Early logical partitioning techniques implemented the VMM in microcode, i.e., in a programming layer higher than the hardware but hidden from general users of the system (Borden, Hennessy, and Rymarczyk 1989). This layer is considered part of the hardware and is sometimes referred to as the *firmware*. Today, the VMM is often implemented as a codesigned firmware-software layer, often referred to as the *hypervisor*. The software component of the hypervisor adds flexibility and provides an interface to system programs that configure the system.

The right-hand side of Figure 9.3 shows partitioning techniques that do not use any special hardware. We have seen in Chapter 8 that the VMM of a system virtual machine provides an elegant way to logically isolate multiple operating systems on a single system. This technology can be used to create multiple virtual shared-memory multiprocessors also. Extensions to VMM methods can achieve many of the major desirable features of partitioning, particularly some degree of physical isolation of operating systems. System VM-based approaches may impose some more overhead, compared to the hardware-supported techniques listed in the left half of Figure 9.3. However, they are very flexible and, as the figure shows, may be the only way to provide a virtual multiprocessing system whose ISA is different from the ISA of the native multiprocessing system.

It may be argued that partitioning of resources is really a function that could be provided by an operating system alone, and indeed there are some operating systems that provide ways of partitioning hardware resources among the processes. While this may help isolate processes from one another, it does not provide a virtual "machine" to the user (or group of users) who may wish to run a different operating system.

This chapter will examine many of the partitioning techniques illustrated in Figure 9.3. Physical partitioning is described in Section 9.2, while two variations of logical partitioning are described in Sections 9.3 and 9.3.3. Section 9.4 describes the system VM-based partitioning, using Stanford University's Cellular Disco system as a case study. Almost all the work done to date on multiprocessor virtualization assumes that the ISA of each processor in the guest system is identical to that of the host system. Section 9.5 attempts to list the issues involved in virtualizing systems with different guest ISAs and, in particular, systems with different memory model characteristics in the guest.

## 9.2 Physical Partitioning

Of all forms of partitioning, the physical partitioning approach is perhaps the simplest to understand and the easiest to implement, and it imposes little overhead on an executing application. Different manufacturers allow their systems to be physically partitioned in different ways. While they often use different terminology, the fundamental feature of these various approaches is that they allow a partition to "own" its resources physically, so there is no danger that another partition will accidentally or maliciously compromise the system security or availability.

Unlike some of the other partitioning techniques, control of the configuration of each partition is mostly in hardware. Physical partitioning does not need sophisticated algorithms for scheduling and management of resources. There is typically a central control unit that receives commands from the console of the system administrator and sends out special commands to the various hardware resources, particularly the system boards, configuring them for use in a partition. This may include, for example, information about how the memory on a board maps to the real address space of the partition.

Once a partition is configured, the operating system is loaded. Loading an operating system into a partition accomplishes the functions generally associated with bootstrapping a system; other partitions on the system are unaffected during this operation. Each partition can run an operating system, which may be different from the operating system running on the other partitions. Figure 9.4 shows a 24-processor system consisting of six physical units (e.g., a board), with four processors on each board, some memory, and I/O logic connected to a set of disks. The six boards are divided into three partitions, with one board dedicated to the first partition, two to the second, and three to the third. The disk units are independently partitioned in a similar way, as shown. The entire system is controlled through a main console (not shown).

As mentioned earlier, several vendors offer large shared-memory systems that can be physically partitioned. Sun Microsystems markets a large SMP server that can be partitioned into several *domains* (Sun 1999). However, each domain must be located in a physical unit that is distinct from that of another domain. A physical unit comprises one system board, consisting of up to four processors, 4GB of memory, and four I/O buses. A partition can span multiple system boards; however, a system board can belong to only one partition — it is not permissible for two partitions to share the resources of a single system board.

Hewlett-Packard also allows physical partitioning in their large server systems (Hewlett-Packard 2000). These partitions are referred to as *nPartitions*.

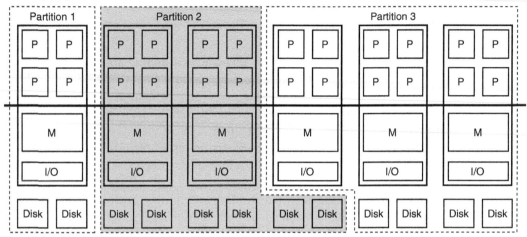

**Figure 9.4**    Physical Partitioning of a 24-Processor System.

Like the Sun systems, each partition is constrained to one or more boards, which are also referred to as *cells*. A cell consists of up to four processors connected as an SMP, sharing up to 16GB of memory, and up to 12 PCI slots. HP imposes further restrictions on its partitions — each cell of a partition must be identical to other cells in the partition in terms of the number of processors and amount of memory.

Fujitsu's PrimePower systems (Fujitsu 2003), with up to 128 processors, can also be physically partitioned. Each of the system boards contains up to eight processors, memory, and I/O, connected through a crossbar switch. Partitions can span one or more boards. However, PrimePower allows partitions to be smaller than one board. Each board of eight processors can contain up to four physical partitions.

Here are the key advantages of physical partitioning over other forms of partitioning.

▪ **Failure isolation:** The robustness of a system to faults of various kinds is of considerable importance in server systems. Physical partitioning attempts to guarantee isolation of a partition from events in other partitions. Physically partitioned systems ensure that in the event of a software failure in a partition, only that part of the physical system that houses the failing partition will be affected. The control unit is designed to be able to reset the partition and reboot the operating system for that partition without the remaining partitions on the system observing any effects of the failure.

This isolation also extends to hardware failures. A physical entity such as a board or a multichip module is associated with only one partition. Hence the system can be designed so that the failure of a processor on a board or module need not bring down any of the other partitions on the system. This does not eliminate single points of failure, however. (A single point of failure in a system is defined as a failure that can bring down the entire system.) In most common systems, there are several single points of failure. The control unit, for example, is a single point of failure. If the control unit fails, the partitions of the system are unable to reset themselves and respond to console commands. However, the probability of a hardware fault in a given unit is roughly proportional to the amount of hardware in the unit; and because the complexity of the central control unit is low and its size small, it is less vulnerable as compared to the rest of the hardware. The crossbar switch connecting different processors or different boards in a system is another single point of failure, and major vendors ensure that this switch is built with intrinsically reliable technology, with robust communication paths, and with sufficient redundancy to ensure very high mean time between failures (MTBF).

■ **Better security isolation:** Each partition is protected from the possibility of intentional or unintentional denial-of-service attacks by other partitions. Even though each partition can run with its own system administrator, a system administrator on one partition cannot take unauthorized action in some other partition.

■ **Better ability to meet system-level objectives:** System-level objectives usually result from contracts between system owners and users of the system. System users pay for specific amounts of computing resources that are guaranteed by the system. Physical partitioning creates partitions more similar to hardware systems than other forms of partitioning. Techniques used to direct resources to applications in stand-alone systems can be applied more readily and predictably in physically partitioned systems as compared to logically partitioned systems.

While physical partitioning has a number of attractive features, it is probably not the ideal solution if system utilization is to be optimized. It is often the case that each of the physical partitions is underutilized, for example, because the system-level objectives force the VMM to allocate resources conservatively. Dynamic workload balancing is also difficult in physical partitioning because of the physical constraints placed by fault isolation requirements. Logical partitioning sacrifices such physical isolation of partitions in exchange for greater flexibility in allocating resources to partitions.

## 9.3 Logical Partitioning

Logical partitioning, like physical partitioning, is a way of providing the illusion of several shared-memory systems on a single large shared-memory system. Unlike physical partitioning, however, the partitioning is "logical," in the sense that a partition has no distinct, time-invariant physical boundaries. In logical partitioning the state of two virtual machines may be completely intertwined, not just in memory, but even in the processors. As we noted at the end of the last section, workload balancing is an important goal of logical partitioning, and this is often best accomplished by sharing resources, especially processors, among the multiple partitions in a time-multiplexed manner.

Logical partitioning was introduced on mainframe computers by Amdahl in 1984, IBM in1988, and Hitachi in 1989. Even though the VM/370 concepts were well established and users had been running several operating systems simultaneously on a single machine, it was felt that an approach was needed that (a) did not require the guest operating system to run in user mode, (b) incurred a lower penalty when running an application on a virtual machine as compared to the native execution, and (c) did not require a complex virtual machine monitor, which, in those days, had almost the same complexity as an operating system. These goals were achieved in Amdahl's multiple domain facility (MDF) (Doran 1988), in IBM's logical partitioning (LPAR) (Borden, Hennessy, and Rymarczyk 1989) using the processor resource/systems manager (PR/SM) feature, and in Hitachi's multiple logical partition feature (MLPF). All three systems used low-level hardware and microcoded firmware to achieve this objective. Firmware provides a level of flexibility that allows extensions to be added to a system even after it has been shipped.

From the point of view of the operating system and the applications that run on it, a logical partition behaves in a way similar to a physical partition. In most cases, the version of the operating system designed to run on the native machine can be loaded unchanged on a partition. The characteristics of the partition determine the characteristics of the machine the operating system sees. However, unlike on a physical partition, the hardware resources available to a logical partition may be shared with other partitions. As with other system-level virtual machines, the logical partition only has the illusion of owning the resources that are allocated for its use.

### 9.3.1 Major Features of Logical Partitioning

Allocations of physical resources are made in logical partitioning during initialization of the partition, as was the case with physical partitioning. The main

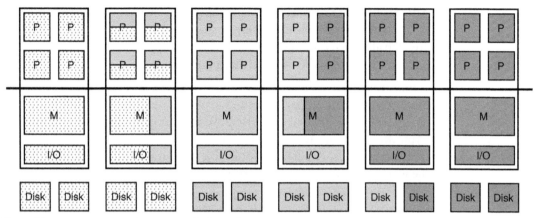

**Figure 9.5** A 24-Processor System Divided into Three Partitions. *Partition 1 (shaded with dots) needs eight processors but only four dedicated processors; partition 2 (shaded light gray) needs ten processors, with six of them dedicated; partition 3 (shaded dark gray) needs ten dedicated processors.*

difference is that allocations must observe certain physical constraints in physical partitioning but not in logical partitioning. This is illustrated in Figure 9.5. It may be observed in the figure that even though the sum of the number of processors needed by the three partitions is 28, the partitions can be accommodated in the 24-processor system because four of the processors are shared between partitions 1 and 2.

Some of the major features of logical partitioning using firmware follow.

- **Allocation of processors:** Either a partition may specify a total amount of processing power it needs and leave the allocation of available processors to workload management software, or it may specify that specific processors in the system be dedicated for its use. A partition can specify that it needs a certain number of processors but that it is willing to share these processors with other partitions. For example, if a total of four processing units is needed by the partition, the partition can specify either that it needs four processors dedicated to itself or that it needs eight processors but only half the available compute power in each of the processors.

- **Allocation of memory:** The total shared-memory is allocated to partitions in chunks of large granularity, e.g., 1MB. Smaller chunks increase the bookkeeping to be performed by the firmware monitor, while larger chunks restrict the flexibility of partitioning. The conversion of real addresses in the address space of a partition to a physical address in the larger memory is done in hardware.

- **Allocation of I/O resources:** A partition gets its own I/O subsystem. An I/O device that has multiple ports may be shared among various partitions that are each allocated a subset of the ports. In the simpler partitioning schemes, ports are allocated when the partition is initialized.

- **Communication between partitions:** In order to allow easy migration of cluster systems to partitioned systems, the modes of communication commonly implemented on clusters are also supported between partitions. Typically such communication uses either shared storage devices or network commands. A partition looks like a separate machine to the rest of the world, including to other partitions.

In the next section we provide a more detailed description of the IBM LPAR system, which implements logical partitioning on mainframe computer systems.

### 9.3.2 Case Study: The IBM System/390 Logical Partitioning Feature

IBM mainframes provide a processor resource/systems manager (PR/SM) that allows an SMP complex to run multiple operating system images using logical partitioning (Borden, Hennessy, and Rymarczyk 1989). The PR/SM consists of special hardware and microcode that can be invoked and controlled directly by the system administrator through the machine console. The machine mode that permits exploitation of the PR/SM feature is termed LPAR (logical partitioning). In this mode, the system can have several partitions — up to six on the ES/3090S systems, where it was first introduced.

Each logical partition is essentially a collection of hardware resources, including processors, memory, and I/O, that are needed to support an operating system. Each logical partition can support an operating system different from those on other partitions. Besides an operating system, a partition can also run the VMM of a conventional system virtual machine. Partitions are logically independent of other partitions — they communicate with each other in ways similar to nodes within a cluster. These methods of communication include shared storage devices, channel-to-channel communication, and network commands.

Some of the hardware resources of the machine are divided between the logical partitions. Each partition sees a portion of the physical memory on the system. The I/O elements, such as the channel paths, subchannels, and logical control units, are also divided among the partitions. On the other hand, any processor in the system can be either dedicated to a partition or shared among multiple partitions. Each partition can use one or more logical (or virtual)

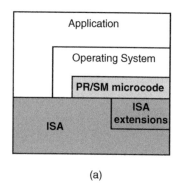

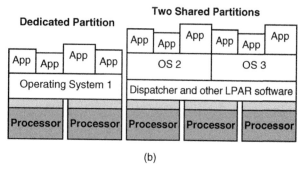

(a)　　　　　　　　　　　　　　　　　　　　(b)

**Figure 9.6**　The LPAR Mechanism. *(a) A snapshot in time of the various active layers on the system. The base hardware has additional instructions and microcode as compared to a standard processor. This hardware enables switching between different partitions. (b) A system view of LPAR. The physical processors may each be either dedicated to a single partition or shared among multiple partitions of potentially different sizes. Allocation of logical processors of a partition to physical processors is done dynamically using dispatchers and job schedulers in the LPAR software.*

processors. Overcommitment of resources is permitted — the total number of processors used by all the partitions together can exceed the actually available number of physical processors.

Contiguous regions of physical main memory are allocated to each partition at 1MB granularity. All references to real memory in a partition are remapped to the appropriate region of physical memory. A check is made to ensure that references are within the range specified for the partition.

Each partition is given its own logical I/O subsystem. A given device is associated with multiple channel paths to allow the device to be shared among different applications. These channel paths are divided among the various partitions and hence provide the desired isolation.

The number of processors used by a single partition cannot exceed the number of physical processors available on the system. The user of a partition can determine whether a partition should be dedicated or shared. A dedicated partition has exclusive use of the physical processors allocated to it and is probably the most appropriate choice for a partition that has a steady demand for the computing resources it uses. Most workloads tend to have demand variations from a peak at certain times to light use at others; in these cases it may be more cost effective to use a shared partition and allow the sharing of processors with other partitions on the system, as illustrated in Figure 9.6. Each processor allocated to a shared partition is associated with a user-defined *weight* that is an indicator of the partition's priority for use of that processor in relation to other partitions that also use the processor.

Partitions on the IBM System/390 are defined by the user, who specifies

- The name of the partition
- The I/O configuration
- The memory configuration
- The processor configuration

Each machine has an operator console used to perform a range of functions, at three different levels of the system hierarchy: to manage either the physical configuration of the entire system, the configuration of the LPAR environment, including the resources within each partition, and the configuration of the operating system running within a partition.

The LPAR functions are largely controlled through the system console. The resources are not dedicated to a partition until the partition is activated and it has been determined that the partition has all the resources it needs for its execution. When all the resources it needs become available, a ready partition is activated. For example, a shared partition is activated only when the number of processors it needs is no more than the total number of physical processors minus the number of dedicated processors allocated to active partitions. Activation is the logical equivalent of the power-on reset performed to boot up a system. The system then goes through the sequence of loading the desired operating system on the partition.

While most of the resources allocated to a partition remain with the partition, there are occasions when it is necessary to move resources between partitions. For example, there may be an I/O device, such as a special recording unit, that is expensive. Only one such device may be supported on the system, but the unit may never be used for long periods of time. In this case, the system administrator can remove the device from one partition and allocate it to another partition that requests it. Reconfiguration of channel paths from one partition to another on the System/390 is also done through the system console.

When a processor is shared between partitions, it is desirable to allocate the processor resource in a fair manner, consistent with the weight of each of the partitions. Scheduling logical processors to run on physical processors is done by a software program called the LPAR workload manager, which runs in a partition of its own. It makes scheduling decisions based on the expected response to I/O operations and on the relative utilization of the available processors. The LPAR dispatcher maintains the state of each of the active partitions and loads the hardware registers with the appropriate contents when it schedules one of the active partitions to run on the processor. Here are some of the considerations for dispatching a waiting partition.

- **The weight assigned to the partition:** The priority of a waiting partition is determined by the weight of a partition relative to the weights of the other waiting partitions.

- **The activity within a partition:** When a logical processor in a partition enters a wait state (i.e., the state in which it is waiting for some external event, such as I/O, to occur, as opposed to waiting to be scheduled), it is usually more productive to unload the partition and load another partition to execute on the processor.

- **High-priority I/O interrupt:** When an I/O interrupt is received for a logical processor that is waiting for the interrupt, the logical processor replaces the logical processor of another partition that is currently executing, provided the priority of the waiting partition is higher than the priority of the current partition.

- **Interval timeout:** The dispatcher allows any partition to execute for a predetermined maximum time. If the logical processor is still active at the end of this dispatcher timer interval, it is swapped out of the system. This is a useful mechanism to prevent either runaway partitions or malicious partitions that could otherwise monopolize the system and prevent forward progress for the other partitions on the system.

- **OS-initiated swap:** It could happen that the logical processor of a partition chosen via the foregoing criteria is in an unproductive mode, e.g., an idle loop. There is a mechanism provided on the System/390 that allows an operating system or a VMM running on a partition to inform the dispatcher that it is in an unproductive mode and so may be swapped out.

IBM's LPAR provides fault containment as expected from a logical partitioning scheme. Any software fault that occurs can cause the failure of only the partition that caused the error. Other partitions cannot be affected by such a fault. Whenever possible, the effect of hardware faults is also limited to the partition that was executing when the fault occurred. A detected fault causes an exception that is transmitted to the partition that was executing. The operating system in this partition then attempts to recover from the fault exactly the way it would have attempted on a native machine. The effect of a hardware fault is localized to a single partition, especially in the case of dedicated partitions. However, unlike physical partitioning, there still are several cases where the failure of a shared component could bring down several partitions or even the whole system.

Today, there are few systems, other than IBM's mainframes, that offer logical partitioning through microcode. With the advent of RISC instruction sets and the resulting move away from firmware implementations, it is more common to find systems that implement the microcode functions in a software layer similar to codesigned virtual machines. This software layer, called the *hypervisor*, is the subject of the next section.

### 9.3.3 Logical Partitioning with Hypervisors

Logical partitioning has been introduced on several systems that do not have microcoded processor implementations. Examples include the current IBM's iSeries servers based on the AS/400 (Boutcher 2001), HP-Compaq's Superdome servers (HP 2002), and IBM's pSeries AIX servers. The complex microcoded instructions that support logical partitioning on the IBM System/390 are replaced by programs that use the basic ISA of the host platform and run in a special mode that is more privileged than all other software on the system. Thus the definition of a new mode of operation is what distinguishes this class of partitioning. This new mode is used by the hardware vendors to provide partitioning capability. If the mode is not exposed in the ISA, then the software that runs in this mode can be viewed essentially as an extension of the hardware itself, very much like the VMM software in a codesigned virtual machine. The common name given to this piece of software is the *hypervisor*.

In order to limit the vulnerability of the system to software failures, an important characteristic of any hypervisor is its small size. Like operating systems in nonpartitioned systems, hypervisors have ultimate control of all resources on a machine. Unlike operating systems though, hypervisors tend to be unobtrusive — their main function is to configure the system and then get out of the way, allowing the hardware that has been allocated to the partition to work directly with the operating system in the partition.

### 9.3.4 Comparison with System Virtual Machines

Hypervisors and conventional system VMMs are similar, in that both run in the highest-privilege mode. However, the principal difference between the two is that hypervisors need hardware support and work in a special mode, while system virtual machines may be implemented on standard unmodified hardware. The guest operating system in a logically partitioned system works in the privileged mode, just as it would on native hardware, whereas in a conventional system VM, the guest operating system works in user mode. Applications running on partitioned systems tend to work more or less at native speed, especially with dedicated partitions, which have exclusive use of the processors allocated to them.

Today's system VMs on the IBM zSeries (System/370 descendents) can support very large numbers of virtual machines, often several times the number of processors on the system. In comparison, because of the high-performance requirements and the fault-tolerance requirements of the markets to which they are targeted, partitioned systems restrict the number of partitions on a system to much smaller numbers. A 64-way HP Superdome system, for example, supports no more than 64 partitions.

Whether logical partitioning is better than a conventional software-based VM is likely to be debated for a long time. There is a certain elegance to the software VM approach that aims to provide a virtual system on unmodified hardware, i.e., on any implementation of the original, untouched architecture. Also, adding special hardware features to allow the coexistence of multiple operating systems on the machine virtually eliminates the possibility of running the virtual machine monitor on a copy of itself. However, at least within IBM, the software only nature of the VM approach had already been compromised soon after its introduction by the incorporation of special performance-enhancing hardware assists for VM. In fact, when IBM designed the PR/SM hardware/microcode feature, it not only included in the design special mechanisms to support logical partitioning, but also leveraged these mechanisms to further improve performance for conventional system VMs.

### 9.3.5 Hardware Support for Logical Partitions

Even if most of the monitor functions can be incorporated into the hypervisor software, there are hardware implementation changes that need to be made to support logical partitioning.

*Hypervisor state registers:* The hypervisor state may have its own set of registers that are not accessible to software in any other mode. For example, as we will see shortly, there are special registers that isolate the real memory of one partition from the real memory of other partitions and also from the real memory used by the hypervisor itself.

*Replicated registers:* Some of the common architected registers may be replicated, depending on how often the hypervisor is invoked. Amdahl's MDF (Doran 1988), for example, replicated the general-purpose registers and all other registers except the floating-point registers, which were not used in the hypervisor mode. Registers that are replicated need not be saved on a mode switch and do not occupy space in memory — this was an important consideration when real memory was much smaller than it is today. Another reason for the replication was the extra level of protection provided by physical separation of the registers, especially against bugs in hypervisor software.

***Hypervisor memory:*** The hypervisor needs to access memory, especially to save information about the various partitions as well as to save the relevant state of each partition on a mode switch. Thus, the physical memory of a system, which in nonpartitioned systems is owned by the operating system, must be under the control of the hypervisor in a logically partitioned system.

One way to do this is to partition the physical memory into disjoint regions. One of these regions is allocated to the hypervisor itself, while each of the other regions is allocated to each of the logical partitions currently active on the system, as shown in Figure 9.7. Corresponding to each partition is a *partition memory base register* (PMBR) and a *partition memory limit register* (PMLR), which determine the bounds of the physical memory accessible only to the partition.

If the hypervisor is allocated an appropriately sized contiguous chunk of the low address space of physical memory, it is possible to bypass translation for memory accesses in the hypervisor mode — the effective address computed in an instruction becomes identical to the physical address. Addresses in a partition, however, must be relocated.

The virtual address generated by a partition is converted to a real address via normal address translation mechanisms (see Section A.3.4). This real address must then be added to the value contained in the PMBR of the current partition to determine the actual physical location of the address. In order to prevent a partition from accessing the physical memory assigned to another partition, the physical address generated must also be checked against the PMLR. An attempt to access a location beyond that indicated in the PMLR corresponds to an attempt by the partition to access a real-memory location beyond the size of the real memory expected by the operating system in the partition and should generate a real-memory violation exception.

The conversion of a partition real address to a physical address could be done in hardware by adding one more stage to the address translation process. However, this penalty can be avoided in a processor with a hardware TLB by simply replacing the real-memory address field in the TLB entry with the physical address. This, of course, assumes that the size of real memory allocated to a partition is an integral number of pages and that it is smaller than the size of the actual physical memory available. In fact the sum of the sizes of real memory of all partitions on the system must be smaller than the size of physical memory, leaving some of the physical address space to the hypervisor. This suggests the reason that typical logically partitioned systems allow only a few logical partitions.

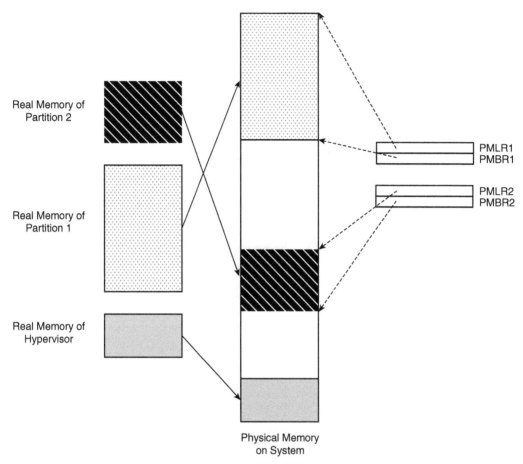

**Figure 9.7**  Mapping of Real Memory of Partitions to Physically Available Memory. *When contiguous chunks of physical memory are allocated to each partition, the mapping table is simple and needs just two pointers as shown.*

Any TLB miss handling depends on whether the system implements a hardware- or software-managed TLB. In a hardware-managed TLB, the miss is handled by the hardware walking the architected page tables to find the page mapping. When the real address corresponding to a virtual address is found by the hardware, one of the TLB entries is replaced and overwritten as usual with the virtual and real addresses of the new entry. But in addition, the PMBR of the partition is used to establish the physical address of the page in the TLB entry.

Efficient and secure mapping to physical addresses requires that the page table, which contains information about physical addresses, be invisible to the operating system in each partition. Thus modifications to the page table

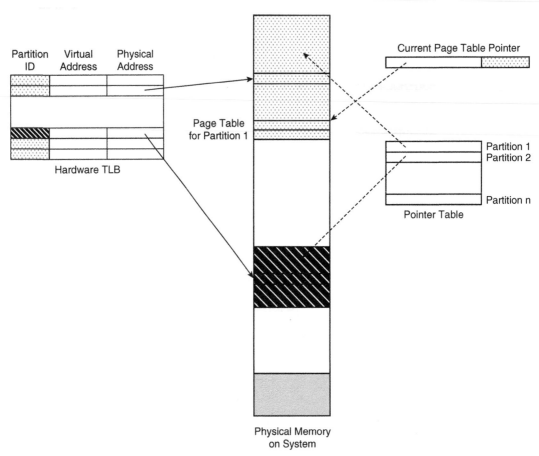

**Figure 9.8**     Adaptation of a Hardware TLB for Logical Partitioning. *The pointer table is typically small and can be maintained in hardware. The current page table pointer is loaded with the entry in the pointer table corresponding to the currently active partition.*

must be done in hypervisor mode. For efficient servicing of page faults, each entry in the TLB is tagged with the identity of the partition to which that entry belongs. As shown in Figure 9.8, the page table pointer is under the control of the hypervisor and must be reloaded with the appropriate pointer whenever one partition is swapped for another.

In the case where the processor implements a software-managed TLB, each partition expects to see a TLB, and hence the TLB for each partition must be virtualized. If the overhead is acceptable, the virtual TLB can be swapped in and out of the physical TLB as active partitions change. Otherwise, the physical TLB can act as a cache for all the virtual TLBs for a processor, with the hypervisor intercepting all actions of a partition that access the TLB and making the appropriate replacement decisions.

### Interrupt Handling

There are three kinds of interrupts meant for the hypervisor. These are generated as a result of actions initiated by the hypervisor itself. One kind is an interrupt from an I/O device responding to a query about its operational status. The second kind involves interrupts from the system management console through which a system administrator instructs the hypervisor, for example, about the requirements of a new partition. The third kind involves interrupts from a partition requesting some service from the hypervisor.

In the case of a machine check interrupt, for example, due to an uncorrectable hardware fault, the hypervisor first attempts to determine whether the machine check affects the hypervisor and its tables. If so, there is not much that the hypervisor can do. It may be able to examine the contents of the tables to determine the partitions affected and reboot these partitions. On the other hand, if the hypervisor itself has not been affected due to the machine check, the hypervisor emulates a machine check for the partition that was running at the time of the interrupt and jumps to a special routine registered by the guest operating system.

This is a general technique that can be used for hardware interrupts meant for a guest operating system. As in the case of the VMM of a system virtual machine, the hypervisor is the first point at which interrupts are handled. The hypervisor determines whether the interrupt is meant for it or for one of the partitions on the system. If the interrupt is for a partition that is not the one currently executing, it may be queued for a later time, e.g., immediately after the partition is reactivated. In special cases, that partition can be reactivated immediately to enable it to handle the interrupt. After an interrupt is handled, control can remain with the partition that handled the interrupt or it can be transferred back to the partition that was executing at the time of the interrupt.

The case of software interrupts (or traps) is considerably easier. The trap can be handled by the guest operating system in privileged mode without the hypervisor's entering the picture.

## 9.3.6 Hypervisor Services Interface

We have assumed thus far that an operating system that works on a native system should work unchanged in a partitioned system. Hardware support for the hypervisor can go a long way in improving the performance of such a system. But it should be clear that the performance can be made even better if a guest operating system is made aware of the fact that it is operating in a hypervisor environment. It may be recalled that, in discussing VM assists in Chapter 8, we also noted that the performance of a virtual machine system can be enhanced by a "handshaking" mechanism between the VMM and the guest operating system.

The communication between the hypervisor and the guest OS is carried out using calls from the OS to the hypervisor. Thus, beyond the ISA of the virtual machine is another interface, called the *hypervisor services interface*. A typical call to this interface involves a request for management of a resource that would normally have been under the control of the OS but that would be managed better if handled by the VMM. An example is the hardware page table management on the IBM PowerPC (Engebretson, Corrigan, and Bergner 2001).

The PowerPC has an architected page table with an inverted page table structure. When a TLB miss occurs, the hardware accesses the inverted page table, also referred to as the *hardware page table* (HPT) of the processor. When running in the native mode, if no entry is found in the HPT, a page fault interrupt is delivered to the operating system, which determines an appropriate page for replacement and then creates a new entry in the HPT. The situation is slightly different in the partitioned case. The guest operating system now has its real addresses mapped to physical addresses, and hence the mapping in the HPT indicates the virtual-to-physical mapping of the pages in memory. For security reasons, this map must not be accessible to the guest operating system. Instead, it is the hypervisor that has sole control of this table. On a page fault, the guest OS does not directly modify the HPT. Rather, it invokes the hypervisor, using calls from the hypervisor systems interface to establish an entry in the table.

Figure 9.9 shows some of the calls in the hypervisor interface related to page table management in the IBM PowerPC.

| Call | Action |
|------|--------|
| find_valid() | Find any valid entry for a given virtual address |
| Invalidate() | Invalidate a specified entry |
| add_validate() | Add a new valid entry |
| modify_pp() | Modify protection status for a specified entry |

**Figure 9.9** Some Calls in the Hypervisor Interface to Support Page Table Management on the IBM PowerPC iSeries.

It is certainly possible to allow the hypervisor to take over the entire page table management, rather than just provide the services to aid the operating system in this function. However, there are advantages if the hypervisor implements just mechanisms rather than both mechanisms and policies. Policies are often best implemented by the operating system, which has a better view of the requirements of the partition and its applications. Further, restricting the hypervisor to the mechanisms makes it compact and less error prone.

As we had indicated in the case of system VMs, the disadvantage of the hypervisor services interface philosophy is that the operating system is no longer portable. Calls made to the hypervisor may need to be changed when the operating system is ported to another platform. This could be a problem, even with a new implementation of the hypervisor on the same platform — new versions should be designed with backward compatibility of operating systems in mind.

### 9.3.7 Dynamic Partitioning

In order to provide versatile operation, partitioning techniques must allow for the possibility of changes in the configuration of a running system. Two types of changes can occur.

1. A partition may complete its task, and a new partition may be ready for installation on the system.

2. A partition may find its own needs changing and therefore desire to change its configuration, for example, the number of processors, the amount of memory, or the devices that are attached.

The first type of change is already accommodated on most logical partitioning systems. In order to shut down a partition, the hypervisor must first recover all the resources owned by the partition that is shutting down. For security purposes, it may need to erase (or otherwise make unreadable) information that may be contained in the memory and on the disks being vacated by the partition. It may also need to perform other tests to ensure that the operation of all freed hardware will be identical to that needed by a system that is being booted up. The freed resources will be placed in a pool of resources from which a new partition gets its allocation.

When the request comes to configure a new partition, the hypervisor examines the resource requirements of the partition and determines whether they can be completely satisfied from the pool of available resources. If the request cannot be satisfied, for example, because of insufficient processors or memory, the hypervisor returns a failed-request message, also possibly indicating the reasons for the failure. If the request can be satisfied, the desired resources are removed from the free pool and a new partition is created. At this point the partition can be loaded with the desired guest operating system.

Note that this technique can be used to migrate a partition from its current form to a new form. The need for such a migration may come in two ways. First, an unrecoverable hardware failure may have occurred in one of its components. In this case, the hypervisor can attempt to configure an identical partition using resources from the free pool and then migrate the state of the partition to the new partition before shutting down the old partition.

The need to migrate partitions can also come from unexpected hardware demands of some partition. If, for example, the paging requirements of a partition have grown to a point where its performance is severely degraded, it may be possible to create a new partition with an identical configuration, except with a larger memory, and migrate the state of the old partition to the new. Of course, such a migration is useful only if the operating system on the partition can also accommodate changes to its memory size in a dynamic manner.

In Section 9.3.2 we saw how reconfiguration of I/O resources of a partition could be accomplished in a dynamic manner on the IBM System/390 LPAR. A similar technique can be used to increase the allocation of processor resources of a partition. However, reallocation of memory poses a problem. The problem is similar to that faced during dynamic memory allocation — the requirement that the real memory of a partition be mapped as a contiguous physical chunk must be relaxed. Thus, support must be provided in the hypervisor to stitch together several pieces of physical memory to create the illusion of a contiguous real memory.

The way segmentation and paging helps with the problem of dynamic memory allocation on a processor is discussed in Appendix Section A.3.4. Similar schemes can be adopted for memory allocation in partitions. In order to take advantage of paging hardware already available in most systems, allocation of memory between partitions should be made at page granularity. This is feasible, except the failure of a memory module can affect a large number of partitions. Moreover, the number of physical pages on typical systems will be so large that the hypervisor may need a lot of space simply for bookkeeping. Whenever a partition is shut down, for example, the hypervisor would need to go through a large number of entries to ensure that every page belonging to the partition is invalidated and then freed. This problem can be alleviated by choosing a granularity of allocation that is much larger than a page though still considerably smaller than the size of typical main memory allocations, for example, 256MB.

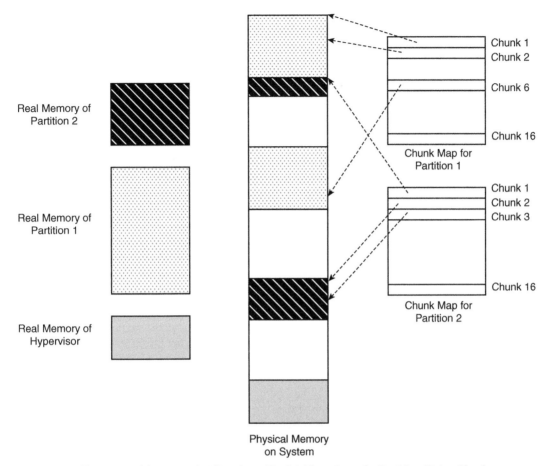

**Figure 9.10**   Illustration of the Dynamic Allocation of Real Address Space for Partitions Using Chunks.

The hardware implication of allowing dynamic expansion, and perhaps even dynamic contraction, of the memory space of a partition is that it is no longer sufficient to have a single PMBR–PMLR pair associated with each partition. Instead, the hypervisor must keep a map between different regions of the real memory and the physical memory for each partition. For example, by allocating 16 pointers for each partition, memory sizes of up to 4GB can be supported, assuming 256MB chunks, as shown in Figure 9.10.

### 9.3.8   Dynamic LPAR

IBM's PowerPC pSeries servers (Jann, Browning, and Burugula 2003) introduced the capability of dynamically migrating resources from one partition to another without requiring a reboot of the affected partitions. This is referred to as *dynamic logical partitioning,* or DLPAR. Resources moved by DLPAR have the same set of capabilities they would have had if they were assigned to the partitions at boot time. Movement of resources currently requires the following steps.

1. A request is made to the guest AIX operating system on a partition, asking it to release a resource and, if necessary, to put it in a quiescent state.

2. The AIX operating system stops the resource and releases it to the hypervisor, which places it in its free pool of resources.

3. A request is made to the hypervisor, again through the system console, to allocate the resource to another specific partition that needs it.

4. When successful, a request is made to the guest AIX operating system on this partition asking it to acquire the resource and configure it for its use.

The AIX operating system kernel was modified to run entirely in the virtual mode in order to accomplish DLPAR. In fact, the granularity of memory allocation in IBM's system is a page. Removal of processors had already been implemented in AIX to support graceful degradation in the event of processor failures. Addition of processors was a feature added to AIX to support DLPAR.

### 9.3.9  Expanding the Role of the Hypervisor

The hypervisor is essentially an extension of the hardware platform provided to the system. The services provided by the hypervisor can therefore include functions that control hardware features of the system.

▪ The hypervisor can monitor power usage in various parts of the system and feed this information back to the partitions. Operating systems running on the partitions can react to high usage of power and take corrective measures by dropping requirements for the particular resource showing high power usage.

▪ The hypervisor can provide similar functions in the event of hardware problems. If an error is detected during computation and if repeated attempts do not lead to the elimination of the error, the hypervisor can take measures to move all partitions using the faulty processor to a spare processor and isolate the failing processor and even to replace it with a good processor without halting the rest of the system.

The traditional tasks of the hypervisor are passive in nature — the hypervisor gets commands from the system administrator and either satisfies the request or informs the administrator it is unable to satisfy the request. This is largely due to the evolution of the hypervisor as an extension of the hardware and hence a desire to make the hypervisor compact, verifiable, and error free. It is conceivable that in the future, the hypervisor will take on the role of a powerful software layer in the hierarchy of layers that make up a system. When this happens, the hypervisor will implement not only the mechanisms but also policies to configure and manage the resources in the system. The hypervisor could then make decisions on its own, based on several different factors, concerning the following.

- Environmental factors, such as the power usage, temperature, or reliability of the hardware

- Business factors, such as the security of the system and the fulfillment of various system-level objectives contracted with users of the system

- Operational factors, such as efficiency of utilization of hardware

- Cost factors, such as the revenue generated by the system as a whole

Figure 9.11 illustrates a time sequence where processors and other resources migrate in a dynamically partitioned system to achieve system load balancing.

Indeed, as the complexity of large computing systems increases, it will be increasingly difficult for system administrators, let alone users, to manage resources of the system efficiently and securely. Increasingly, therefore, systems will provide more automation in the areas of resource allocation and reconfiguration. Systems will monitor their own behavior, learn, and adapt to changing situations without intervention from the operator. It is possible that the hypervisor could end up playing a central role in this "autonomic" system of the future (IBM 2001).

## 9.4  Case Study: Cellular Disco System Virtual Machine–Based Partitioning

Systems such as IBM's 370/VM and VMware's GSX and ESX servers are, in a sense, techniques to partition the system and provide multiple operating system images on a single hardware platform. We discussed such systems extensively in Chapter 8. From the point of view of isolating one operating system from another, these systems are similar to logical partitioning — software failures can mostly be confined to a guest single operating system image; they do not

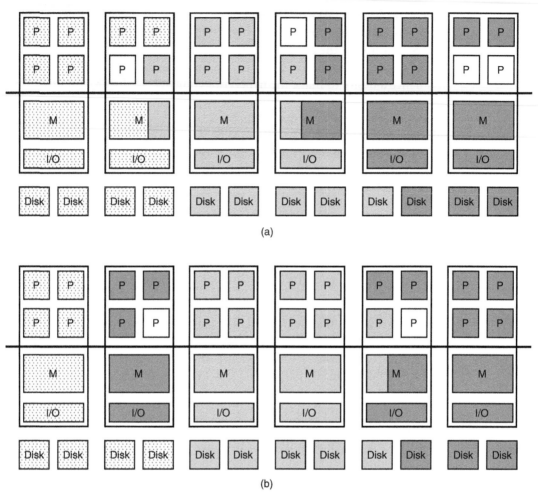

**Figure 9.11**    Illustration of the Effects of Dynamic Partitioning. *The figure shows the use of resources by three partitions at two different points in time. In (a) the usage of resources, for example, just after the system is initialized, it displays some degree of physical locality. However, as time progresses (b) and as the processes get migrated to achieve better load balancing, the physical range of the partitions running these processes start merging with each other.*

bring down other guest operating system images. However the VMM in these systems is a larger body of software, and the chances of an error in the VMM are higher than the chances of an error in the hypervisor of a logically partitioned system. In order for a system VM to provide cluster virtualization capability, it is desirable for it also to emulate the physical fault containment aspects of a cluster or of physical partitioning. This imposes special requirements on the VMM. In particular, each group of physical nodes that emulates a multiprocessing node in the virtual cluster should run its own VMM so that a hardware failure in a node will not cause another virtual node in the cluster to fail.

We illustrate the principles underlying the support of fault-containment features in a traditional system VM by describing the Cellular Disco system (Govil et al. 1999) developed at Stanford University, which was derived from an earlier traditional system VM called Disco (Bugnion et al. 1997).

### 9.4.1 Cellular Disco System Overview

As we saw in Chapter 8, a sufficient condition for efficient virtualization is the ability to intercept all the privileged operations performed by the virtual machine. Cellular Disco, which is designed to run on a MIPS multiprocessor system, achieves this by taking advantage of the fact that the MIPS system provides three levels of privilege — a user mode, a semiprivileged supervisor mode, and a privileged mode — and that most operating systems that run on MIPS systems use only two of these modes, the user and privileged modes. Cellular Disco forces the virtual systems to run in the user and supervisor modes and restricts the use of the privileged mode to the virtual machine monitor. Whenever an operating system on a virtual machine executes a privileged instruction, it traps as shown in Figure 9.12, because execution of such an instruction is not permitted in the supervisor mode. The trap is handled by the VMM, which then interprets the instruction. The MIPS architecture further forces all supervisor and user-mode memory accesses to go through dynamic address translation. All references to real memory made by an operating system therefore can be mapped to a region of physical memory distinct from the regions addressed by operating systems on other virtual machines.

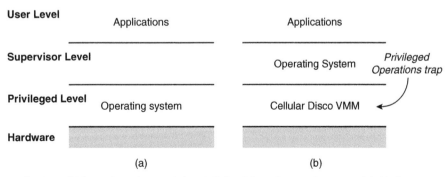

**Figure 9.12**   Modes in Which Various Parts of the Cellular Disco System Operate. *(a) Native system; (b) Cellular Disco.*

The virtual machine monitor also intercepts I/O requests from a guest operating system executing on a virtual machine. After checking for the validity of the request, the VMM either forwards the request to a real I/O device or handles the request itself. An example of the situation where it handles the request itself is virtual paging. In typical virtual machine implementations there are two levels of paging, one by the guest operating system and another by the VMM. It is possible for the operating system to request that a page be written out to its paging disk when the VMM itself has written this page out to its own paging disk. In a simple VMM implementation, such a request would be satisfied by first bringing back the page from the paging disk of the VMM and then writing the page out to the paging device of the guest operating system. Cellular Disco makes this process more efficient by trapping every read and write to the guest operating system's paging disk. It keeps internal data structures that map the status of all pages. Thus when the request to write out a page to the kernel's paging disk is observed, Cellular Disco notices that the page has already been paged out to its own paging disk and simply annotates the internal mapping to indicate the actual location of the page. When the guest operating system subsequently wishes to read from its paging disk, the mapping is consulted to determine the true location from where its contents are to be read.

### 9.4.2 Memory Mapping

The mapping of real memory in a virtual machine to physical memory is performed in Cellular Disco with the help of two maps. The *pmap* data structure is indexed by the real address and returns the corresponding physical address in the system. The *memmap* data structure maps a physical address back to the real address.[1]

Unlike the physical partitioning schemes and some of the logical partitioning schemes where the physical memory is strictly parceled out to the different virtual machines on the system and where every real memory location on a virtual machine is associated with a physical memory location, Cellular Disco operates like a traditional system virtual machine and virtualizes the real memory also. This allows the overcommitment of real memory — the sum of the real memory assumed by all active virtual machines on the system can be more

---

**1.** Note that the Cellular Disco designers refer to the real memory as the physical memory of the virtual machine and to the actually available physical memory of the system as the machine memory.

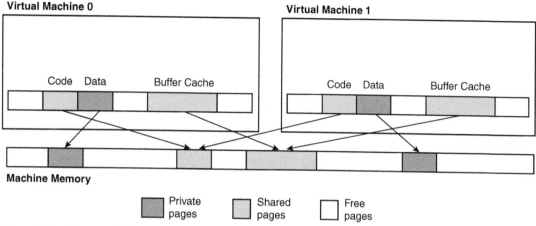

**Figure 9.13**    Memory Sharing in Cellular Disco.

than the available physical memory on the system. Each virtual machine is allocated a resident set size that is dynamically trimmed as the system begins to run low on physical memory. The VMM incorporates a page-replacement policy of its own that takes advantage of information about the usage of pages. If a page contains unneeded data, annotations in the internal data structure allow the VMM to detect this and avoid the overhead of writing the page out to disk. This would be useful, for example, when the page that needs to be swapped out is an unallocated page on a virtual machine.

Cellular Disco provides functions to an application beyond those normally available to the application through the operating system interface. An example is the ability to split large applications into multiple processes working in separate virtual machines that nonetheless share global regions of memory. System calls are provided to allow processes within an application to register such shared regions. The process of registration can bypass the guest operating system because all system calls have to be intercepted by the VMM. Figure 9.13 shows two virtual machines sharing code pages as well as a buffer cache while still keeping their application data regions separate. No additional overhead is incurred in writing to a shared location because the underlying platform is a shared-memory multiprocessor, and cache coherence guarantees that other processors will see the write in the shared region in a timely manner.

This system is a convenient and efficient alternative to the conversion of a large shared-memory application to a cluster application that communicates using messaging and network protocols. The only overhead for the application is the need to relink the application with a different shared-memory library.

Cellular Disco handles the paging of the shared regions to its paging disk, attaching information about all virtual machines sharing the page along with the contents of any page being written out to disk. For efficiency, it places this information in a sector contiguous to the paged-out data, thus avoiding the penalty of an additional seek of a disk sector.

### 9.4.3 Fault Containment

One important aspect that differentiates Cellular Disco from conventional system virtual machines is its support for hardware fault containment. Hardware fault containment is an important characteristic of clustered systems — the effects of a hardware fault in one part of the system are usually contained within the node of the cluster containing the fault. Operating systems and applications running on other nodes usually can continue to operate unaffected. Unfortunately there are a few critical faults that could potentially bring down the entire system. For example the VMM itself, which manages all the resources of the system, is vulnerable to failure of the hardware components it uses. It is important therefore to keep such critical parts to a minimum in order to increase the mean time between failures (MTBF) of the system as a whole.

Cellular Disco treats the hardware as a set of cells, with each cell running its own VMM and managing the physical memory it contains, as shown in Figure 9.14. A failure in a hardware component within a cell does not affect virtual machines on the system that do not use that cell. Cellular Disco increases the MTBF of the system by keeping the monitor code compact (less than 50K lines of code) and by restricting access of the VMM in one cell to only those physical memory locations belonging to that cell. Communication with other cells is achieved through the use of a carefully designed and fast remote procedure call, which serves as an efficient and trusted interprocessor communication primitive.

One way for such a system to manage fault containment is to limit each virtual machine to operate on a fixed set of cells. The main problem with this is that it can lead to underutilization of the system because of the inability of the VMM to move the workload toward idle processors in other cells. Thus, there is a tension between the requirements of load balancing and hardware fault containment. Cellular Disco attempts to get around this problem by associating each processor with a fixed list of virtual CPUs (VCPUs) and by allowing migration, over time, of a virtual CPU from one processor to another, even across cell boundaries. The establishment of a VCPU list for each processor simplifies the scheduling of processors and eliminates a source of contention and lock complexity in conventional systems. The ability to migrate VCPUs,

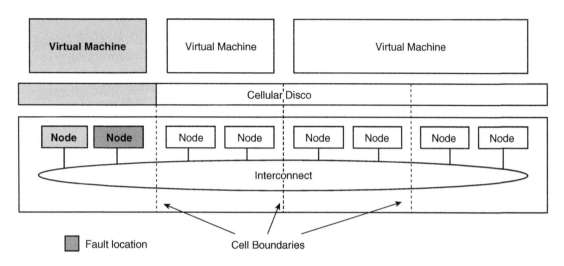

**Figure 9.14** Fault Containment in Cellular Disco. *The impact of a hardware fault is contained in the virtual machines operating on the cells where the fault occurs. Shading indicates affected area due to a fault in the indicated node.*

although at coarser time intervals than conventional systems, permits better load balancing on the system. For fault containment, rather than force the boundaries of a virtual machine to the minimum number of cells that could ideally contain it, Cellular Disco allows local deviations from such a strict policy.

Consider a virtual machine that needs all the CPUs contained in two cells and that has been running well for some time but suddenly finds itself slowing down because of overload on one if its assigned processors, say, due to too many active VCPUs. Cellular Disco will discover such a situation and attempt first to move the particular VCPU of the virtual machine to another, less loaded processor within the same cell. This satisfies the fault-containment requirements of the system. If a lightly loaded processor is not available within the cell but is available in some other cell, Cellular Disco allows the migration of the VCPU to another cell. Thus the virtual machine, which needed the resources of only two cells, becomes vulnerable to faults in three cells rather than the minimum two. Some degree of protection to faults is traded off for better performance on the system as a whole. More components of the virtual machine can migrate to the new cell if the new cell is comparatively lightly loaded. Eventually, if all the VCPUs migrate from one cell to the new cell, Cellular Disco provides a mechanism to eliminate completely all data and control information residing in the old cell, thus reducing the fault vulnerability to two cells rather than three.

### 9.4.4 Memory Borrowing

A second situation where Cellular Disco allows flexibility from a rigid fault-containment policy is in the use of memory. The virtual machine monitor running on each cell manages the memory attached to that cell. This helps in fault containment but can lead to imbalance in the use of memory resources. Thus a cell that is a part of a memory-intensive virtual machine may run out of physical memory and may page in and out of disk frequently, even though other cells in the system may have plenty of free physical memory available. Cellular Disco permits relaxation from the rigid fault-containment policy by allowing a cell to temporarily *borrow* memory from other cells.

Memory borrowing in Cellular Disco is accomplished as follows. Each cell maintains a list of free pages. Initially this list contains only pages that physically belong to the cell. As the pages get used up and the cell begins to run low on physical memory, it considers borrowing memory pages from other cells. The potential candidates from which a cell borrows memory are determined by the following.

- **The list of cells that each virtual machine has designated for this purpose.** Users of a virtual machine can determine the extent to which they wish to protect themselves from faults in the system. The smaller the set the virtual machine designates, the lower is its vulnerability to faults but the higher is the probability of performance loss due to paging.

- **Cells that have already been actively supplying memory pages to virtual machines in this cell.** These cells are kept in a vulnerability list. By ensuring a minimum availability of free pages from cells in the vulnerability list, the policy biases borrowing to favor those cells that have already been supplying pages, and hence prevents an increase in the vulnerability to faults.

- **The availability of pages in the remote cells.** Cells are candidates for borrowing if they have a certain minimum amount of memory available. When the available memory drops below this amount, the cell may refuse a request to borrow pages of its memory.

- **The overall memory requirements of the requesting virtual machine.** In order to keep virtual machines that do not need much memory from having to span multiple cells, Cellular Disco biases its allocation of available local memory in a cell to such virtual machines. Thus a request for memory when the available local memory has fallen below a threshold may actually end up being satisfied locally.

A flowchart indicating the actions taken on a page fault in a cell is shown in Figure 9.15. It is interesting to note that Cellular Disco resorts to paging only when memory borrowing fails. More than one page is borrowed at a time in order to reduce the number of such requests. Once a page is borrowed from another cell, the monitor puts it in its free list, tagged with the identity of the cell that it belongs to. There is no penalty to accessing this memory for routine reads and writes — the only effect of borrowing is the increased vulnerability to faults in the virtual machine that uses a borrowed page.

### 9.4.5  Recovering from a Fault

The flexibility provided to virtual machines for going beyond hard cell boundaries both for CPUs and memory makes the job of recovering from hardware faults more complex. Cellular Disco must ensure that all affected cells and virtual machines are taken care of in the event of a fault. The steps taken by Cellular Disco on a fault can be summarized as follows.

1. The hardware determines the extent of the fault and attempts to recover from it.

2. Through an interrupt the hardware informs all processors in the system of the recovery. This interrupt is handled by Cellular Disco, which then initiates its recovery process.

3. Cells communicate with each other to agree on a set of hardware nodes that are still functioning. The ability to share memory between cells is exploited to expedite this process. The set of nodes determined to be "live" is used to restore the communication mechanism to a state where it is "unjammed" of all messages to and from nodes that are outside the live set.

4. Each VMM on a functioning cell determines all the virtual machines affected by the fault. In doing so, it consults the various internal data structures that contain information about the cells and physical resources that each virtual machine was using.

The entire system needs to participate in order to ensure that all affected virtual machines are properly purged from the system and that all references to the affected virtual machines are eliminated from the data structures kept in each cell. This is a considerably more elaborate process than that needed on a physically partitioned system — and is the cost for improving the utilization of the system under normal operating conditions.

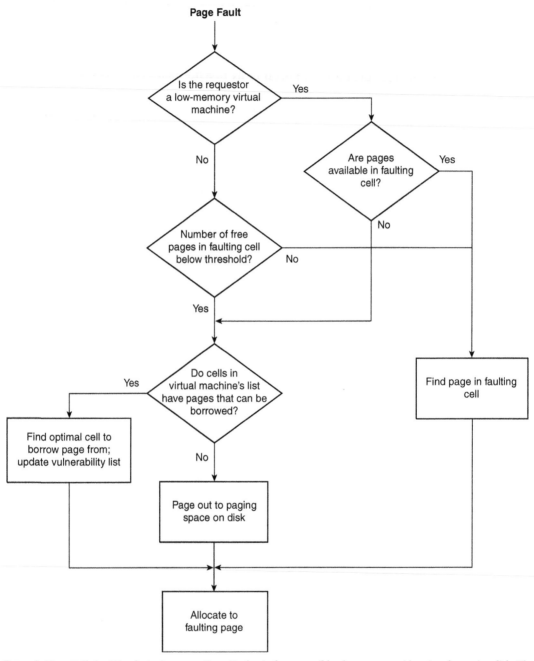

**Figure 9.15** Cellular Disco's Actions on a Page Fault. *As far as possible, the system avoids using the paging disk. The requests of virtual machines with low memory requirements are satisfied locally, if possible. When choosing a cell to borrow from, a cell from the vulnerability list is chosen, if available.*

The Cellular Disco research suggests that it is possible to implement fairly sophisticated virtualization and fault-containment mechanisms in an efficient way. Its general philosophy of using physical boundaries as strong hints for the purposes of fault containment rather than as rigid walls provides a degree of flexibility, especially in situations where an application is willing to trade off some of the fault-containment characteristics for better performance. While the research was conducted in the context of system virtual machines, many of the ideas could eventually find application in hypervisor-based logically partitioned systems.

## 9.5 Virtualization with Different Host and Guest ISAs

All the schemes described thus far have involved situations where the ISA of the virtual system is identical to the ISA of the host system. When the two ISAs are different from each other, added complexities are introduced.

- The instructions of the target ISA must be dynamically emulated by the host system. The translation of instructions from the ISA of the virtual machine to the native ISA is an operation that must not be visible to the virtual machine or the programs running on it, including the operating system. The emulation techniques needed to achieve this are those described in connection with the implementation of process VMs (Chapters 2–4) for most ISA features and codesigned VMs (Chapter 7) with respect to some system ISA features, such as page faults.

- The memory model of the target system, particularly the coherence and memory ordering rules, must be observed on the virtual system. These involve additional actions on the part of the host system. The host could handle this either in hardware, in the firmware, or in emulation software contained in the trusted monitor layer, i.e., either in the virtual machine monitor or in the hypervisor.

As described earlier, there are two different ways in which multiprocessors are generally configured. The processors can be connected in a loosely coupled cluster configuration, where not much other than I/O is shared between the processors. Alternatively, the processors can be configured in a shared-memory configuration, with all processors in the multiprocessor configuration sharing the same memory. Implementing a cluster virtual machine on a native cluster system is fairly straightforward if each target virtual processor is mapped to one real processor. This case is shown in Figure 9.16. Since memory is not shared

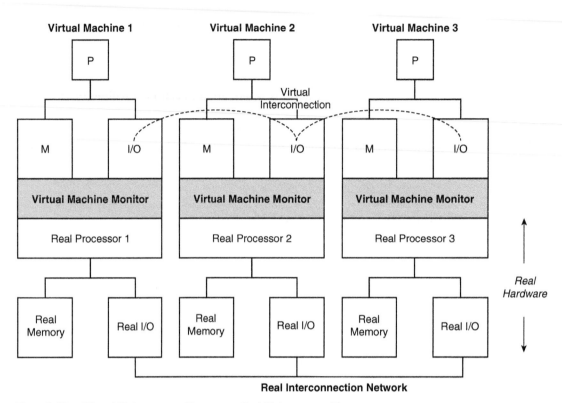

**Figure 9.16** Virtual Uniprocessor Cluster on a Real Uniprocessor Cluster.

between nodes in such a cluster, it is sufficient to virtualize each processor using techniques given earlier in this book. Virtual node communication is through messages that can be translated to similar messages on the host.

When the system to be virtualized is a shared-memory multiprocessor, the situation becomes more complex. Because the memory is shared between the processors, the monitor on each processor must handle shared-memory requests exactly the way they would be handled on a native machine. So, for example, if the guest virtual machine supports coherent shared memory, the monitors running on the separate processors must ensure that information written to any shared-memory location is made visible to all processors that share that location. If the underlying native system is itself a shared-memory system, then the hardware mechanisms that already exist on the system to support coherence can be used to ensure coherence for the virtual system. This is the case, for example, in the FLEX-ES system from Fundamental Software Inc. (FLEX), which provides a virtual SMP for an IBM System/390 system as a user application under Linux on an Intel IA-32 based SMP. The basic IA-32

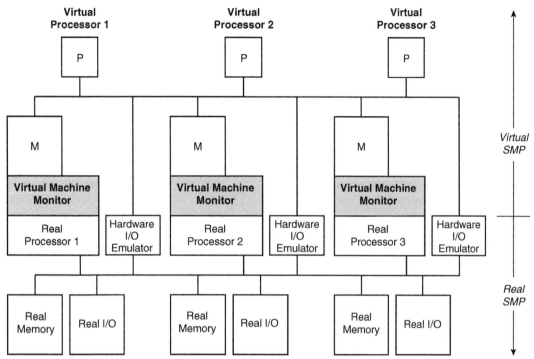

**Figure 9.17**    Virtual Shared-Memory System on a Real Shared-Memory System. *When there is a mismatch between the I/O of the virtual system and the real system, it may be necessary to add hardware, as shown, for efficient I/O emulation.*

SMP is enhanced with special hardware adapters, as shown in Figure 9.17, to emulate the functions of the System/390 communication and channel I/O adapters. Since the underlying Intel IA-32 platform also implements memory coherence, the coherence expected by the virtualized mainframe system is trivially supported. While the memory ordering rules of the Intel IA-32 are not exactly identical to those of the System/390, the differences can be taken care of in the VMM layer without significant degradation of performance.

If the host's model does not match the guest's memory model, then it becomes an additional task of the combination of emulation software running on all processors to communicate with each other and keep track of shared locations. Most solutions to this problem require several instructions and several cycles for each coherence request. Hence, when there is a modest amount of sharing in a system, the emulation performance begins to degrade considerably. The next section examines some ways to handle such cases and discusses the potential degradation of performance. Only a cursory treatment is provided here to this rather complex problem.

### 9.5.1 Memory Model Emulation

As described in Appendix A, the ISA of most processors includes special conventions for the access of shared-memory locations. As with all aspects of an ISA, these conventions represent a contract between the programmer and an implementation of the ISA. A programmer writes a program assuming that accesses to variables shared among processors obey certain rules, while the hardware designer (the processor designer or the system designer) ensures that the rules used by the programmer are indeed guaranteed by the implementation. We note two main aspects of the memory model, the memory coherence and the memory consistency models, that determine how results appear in different shared-memory systems. These are the two aspects that need to be given special consideration when a multiprocessor system is virtualized — the differences in these models between the host and the guest ISAs can produce undesirable results during virtualization, unless special actions are taken by the emulation software.

#### *Memory Coherence Emulation*

Recall that memory coherence is said to be implemented on a multiprocessor system if the order of writes to a given location by one processor is maintained when observed by any other processor in the system. Appendix Section A.7.3 describes the difference in behavior of coherent and noncoherent systems. The nature of actions that emulation software must take to support the coherence model of a guest virtual machine depends on the coherence models of both the guest and the host. We list the various possibilities in Figure 9.18.

1.  **Memory coherence is not required on either the guest or the host:** In this case no action is required because programs have presumably been written in a way that accounts for this absence of coherence. Synchronization in such systems is done through explicit synchronization instructions. The synchronization primitives in the host and the guest may not match, but it is usually not difficult to emulate a synchronization primitive of the guest using synchronization primitives of the host.

2.  **Memory coherence is required by the guest and is available on the host:** In this case, the emulation software ensures that the virtual machine runs with the memory coherence option enabled.

3.  **Memory coherence is not required on the guest but is enabled on the host:** An example of this is a distributed cluster system that needs to be emulated on a shared-memory multiprocessing system. There is typically

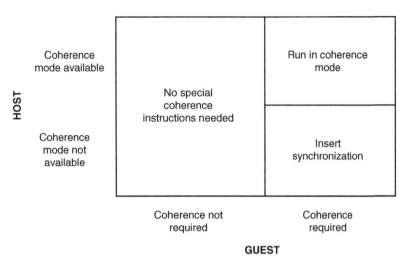

**Figure 9.18**  The Various Actions Needed for Emulating the Coherence Model. *In all cases synchronization primitives of the guest must be emulated on the host.*

no special action that needs to be performed by emulation software. The coherence hardware, which provides a coherent view of memory across the processors, does more than is needed by the coherence model of the guest. If there is a performance disadvantage because of the coherence requirement and there is a faster noncoherent mode available on the machine, this mode can be used, as in case 1 earlier. Synchronization instructions will need to be emulated using the synchronization primitives of the host, even if the host runs in coherent mode.

4. **Memory coherence is required on the guest but is not supported by the host**: An example of this is a shared-memory guest machine running on a distributed-memory host machine. The only option here is to use software to enforce coherence. As we said earlier, even when machines do not provide coherence support, they do provide synchronization primitives so that software can perform explicit synchronization. Unfortunately, the brute-force technique of synchronizing after each memory write by a processor is too slow, because synchronization operations, especially on large multiprocessor systems, are slow. A more practical approach is to use a directory that registers the set of processors sharing various locations, with a coherence operation being triggered on the set of sharing processors when one of the processors in the set changes the contents of the shared location. This operation can get expensive as the size of the directory gets large. The size of the directory can be reduced by increasing the granularity of an

entry in the directory to be a page. Keeping such information at page granularity is also convenient because the available page table structures can be used for storing sharing information and to trigger a coherence action. There have been several techniques of this nature that have been developed in connection with distributed shared-memory (DSM) computing (Hennessy, Heinrich, and Gupta 1999), which also deals with the problem of providing coherence to an application while running on noncoherent hardware.

Fortunately most ISAs today provide coherence support. Hence, coherence emulation is not a source of performance degradation for such virtual machines.

### Memory Consistency Models

Memory consistency deals with the order in which accesses by one processor to different locations in memory are observed by another processor (refer to Appendix Section A.7.3 for a more detailed explanation). This is in contrast to memory coherence, which deals with the order of writes to a single location. Memory consistency deals not only with different locations but with all accesses, whether reads or writes. The important thing to take care of when a program is being run on a virtual machine is that the ordering of reads and writes must be such that it *could have been* produced on a native implementation of the virtual machine. Thus the emulation software should account for differences between the memory consistency models of the host and guest and ensure that the ordering of memory operations is consistent with what the ISA of the guest specifies.

As noted in Appendix Section A.7.3, four hazards have to be considered in a consistency model: the read-read (RR) hazard, the read-write (RW) hazard, the write-read (WR) hazard, and the write-write (WW) hazard. In a strong consistency model, an implementation must ensure that none of these hazards is present. When this requirement is relaxed, we get one of the many relaxed consistency models. Such relaxed models are referred to as being weaker than the strong consistency model.

We could encode the consistency model using four bits, each bit indicating whether ordering is imposed for the corresponding hazard pair. So, for example, a (1111) will indicate strong ordering, while a (1101) will indicate that the WR ordering is relaxed from strong ordering, as in the processor consistency model used on the Intel IA-32 or the IBM System/390. The weakest consistency model (0000) imposes no ordering between any pair of read-write operations. Note that reads and writes to the same location by a processor must be ordered according to program order in all cases (refer to Appendix Section A.7.3).

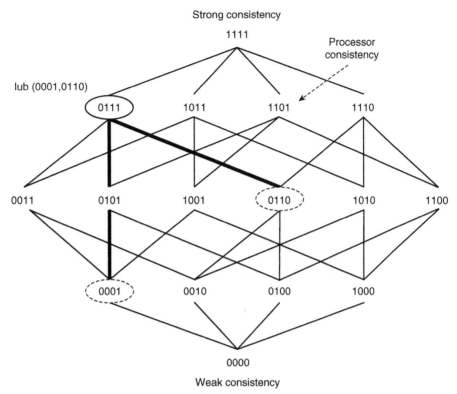

**Figure 9.19**   Lattice of Consistency Models. *Each 4-tuple represents the four hazards RR, RW, WR, and WW. A "1" in a position indicates that the corresponding hazard is not tolerated, while a "0" indicates that the hazard is ignored by the consistency model. The 4-tuple (0000) represents weak consistency, (1111) represents strong consistency, and (1101) represents processor consistency.*

For purposes of comparing two consistency models, it is convenient to draw a lattice, as shown in Figure 9.19, where each node in the lattice corresponds to a consistency model. The least element on the lattice (0000) represents the weakest consistency model, while the greatest element (1111) corresponds to the strongest consistency model. When comparing two consistency models, we determine whether the least upper bound (*lub*) of the pair is itself one of the pair. If it is, then this lub of the pair is defined as being *stronger* than the other. Thus between (1101) and (1001), the lub is (1101), implying that (1101) is stronger than (1001). The model represented by (1111) is stronger than any other consistency model, because it is the greatest element in the set.

As seen from Figure 9.19, the nodes (0001) and (0110) are not comparable. One model is stronger in some respects and the other stronger in other respects. There are two models that are stronger than both these models, (0111) and (1111). The lub of the pair is (0111). Any ordering that satisfies the lub (0111) therefore will also be consistent with the ordering specified by the models in the pair (0001) and (0110).

When emulating a consistency model of a guest using a different consistency model for the host, we can divide the space of possibilities into the following three categories.

1. **The memory consistency model of the guest is the same as that of the host or weaker than that of the host:** In this case there is nothing special that needs to be done by the emulation software as long as the interpretation or translation process does not eliminate or reorder memory accesses to shared locations by a processor. This last restriction ensures that the order of accesses to memory in the virtual machine system belongs to the set of orderings of accesses to memory allowed by the consistency model of the virtual machine. Note that this restriction prevents the elimination of memory accesses — an access to a memory location cannot be safely eliminated just because its contents are available in a general-purpose register, for instance.

2. **The memory consistency model of the guest is stronger than (more restrictive than) the memory consistency model of the host:** In this case, it is important that the additional hazards that must be avoided on the guest must also be avoided on the host. We discuss this case in more detail in the next section.

3. **The memory consistency model of the guest is stronger in some respects and weaker in other respects:** In this case we first find the lub between the two consistency models. The lub consistency model must be stronger than the consistency model of the guest. Hence we would be emulating the guest correctly, though conservatively, if we assumed that the consistency model of the guest is the lub model. Since the lub model is also always stronger than the host model, the problem is now reduced to an example of case 2. So, as a fictitious example, if the memory model of the guest is (0110), which relaxes the RR and WR hazards, and the memory model of the host permits all hazards except the WW hazard (0001), then the lub is (0111). Thus in this example, the ordering satisfied by model (0111) would be consistent with the ordering allowed on the guest. Hence it is sufficient to accurately emulate this lub model.

### Emulating a Stronger Consistency Guest

When a guest virtual machine has a consistency model that is stronger than that of the host, there are certain hazards that may occur in the host that would violate the memory consistency model of the guest ISA. Let us, for example, consider the case of a guest with a processor consistency model and a host with a release consistency model. This is an interesting case because there are several processors that belong to each of these models — a multiprocessor virtual machine implementation of IA-32 running on a PowerPC multiprocessor would be an example in this category. In this case, it is important that any RR, RW, and WW hazards not permitted in the processor consistency model also not be permitted on the virtual machine.

Most ISAs that implement relaxed forms of consistency also provide special *memory barrier* instructions that permit the programmer to specify the points at which ordering needs to be maintained, hence essentially raising the level of granularity at which consistency is implemented. For purposes of illustration, let us define a *membar* instruction, which, when inserted into the code, ensures that there are no hazards between any pair of instructions across the barrier. Obviously then, a trivial solution for any consistency emulation is for the virtual machine emulator to place a *membar* instruction after every access to memory, as shown in Figure 9.20a and b. This ensures that for every pair of memory accesses on any given processor in the host, there is an intervening *membar* instruction that prevents a hazard between the pair. Notice that the same effect could have been obtained by placing a *membar* operation before each memory access.

Unfortunately, the *membar* instruction is an expensive instruction in terms of its execution latency. This can be appreciated better if one understands that the effect of the *membar* instruction is to ensure that all processors in the system have been informed and have acknowledged that some processor wishes to impose such an ordering. Each processor then takes appropriate action to ensure that the request is honored. Since loads and stores form roughly a third of all instructions in an instruction stream, the performance of the virtual machine can be degraded quite significantly because of the insertion of these barrier instructions. It is therefore important for the monitor to restrict the number of *membar* instructions whenever possible.

Notice that the trivial solution just demonstrated works for any consistency model on the guest and, in particular, for the strong model. The first optimization that can be performed is to eliminate those memory barrier instructions where the memory model allows relaxation. In the case of processor consistency, the memory barrier instruction after a write can be eliminated as shown in Figure 9.20c if the subsequent memory access is by a read instruction. The second optimization that can be performed is to eliminate a memory barrier instruction after an instruction if the next sequential memory access is to the same location as the previous memory access — program order requirements take care of these even without barrier instructions. This must, however, be

| Accesses in guest (processor consistency) | Accesses in host (release consistency) | Eliminating membars in host (W-R relaxation) |
|---|---|---|
| ... | ... | ... |
| Read A | Read A | Read A |
| ... | membar | membar |
| Write A | ... | ... |
| ... | Write A | Write A |
| Read B | membar | ... |
| ... | ... | Read B |
| Read C | Read B | membar |
| ... | membar | ... |
| Write C | ... | Read C |
| ... | Read C | ... |
| Write B | membar | Write C |
| | ... | membar |
| | Write C | ... |
| | membar | Write B |
| | ... | membar |
| | Write B | |
| | membar | |
| (a) | (b) | (c) |

**Figure 9.20**  Using *membar* Instructions to Impose Consistency Requirements of the Guest That Are Stricter Than That of the Host. *(a) Original host code. (b) Conservative use of membar instructions after each memory access. (c) Reducing the number of membars to account for W-R relaxation in the guest.*

done with care. In the example of Figure 9.20c the *membar* instruction following Read A cannot be eliminated because the *membar* instruction just after Write A has been removed, thus permitting the following Read B to be done before Write A. However, processor consistency does not permit Read B to be done before Read A, implying that there must be at least one *membar* between these two instructions. Notice that the *membar* that was between the Read C – Write C can be eliminated without danger of the Write B moving ahead. It is important to note that there are other ways of inserting *membars* in the code that achieve the same objective.

This example shows that it is difficult to reduce the overhead of inserting memory barrier instructions when a guest has a stronger consistency model than the host. However, there is another way to reduce the overhead of such emulation. Even in a multiprocessing system there are many occasions when a processor executes a single threaded application or a portion of a multithreaded application that does not share memory with other threads. Since the hazards we are trying to avoid are multiprocessor hazards, there is no need to add barrier instructions if there is some way for the virtual machine monitor to know that a thread does not share memory with an active thread on another processor. The translator in such systems is free to move memory accesses

| Accesses in guest (processor consistency) | Location of membars in host (Location B is not shared) | Location of membars in host (Locations A and B are not shared) |
|---|---|---|
| ... | ... | ... |
| Read A | Read A | Read A |
| ... | ... | ... |
| Write A | Write A | Write A |
| ... | ... | ... |
| Read B | Read B | Read B |
| ... | membar | ... |
| Read C | ... | Read C |
| ... | Read C | ... |
| Write C | ... | Write C |
| ... | Write C | ... |
| Write B | membar | Write B |
| | ... | membar |
| | Write B | |
| | membar | |
| (a) | (b) | (c) |

**Figure 9.21**    Reducing the Number of Memory Barrier Instructions Using Knowledge About Sharing Characteristics of Access Locations. *We leave the last membar in the segment, because at this point we have no knowledge of the sharing pattern of the code that follows the sample segment.*

relative to each other, as long as it provides a way to recover the state of the virtual machine processor whenever it is needed.

A more interesting situation arises when an application is written in such a way that the threads comprising the application are largely independent and only occasionally share memory, perhaps as a form of communication. In these cases, it may be more efficient to restrict the insertion of memory barriers to keep the required ordering of memory access to only the shared locations, as shown in Figure 9.21.

The figure shows that when location B is not shared, we can remove the barriers between Read A and Read B because any reordering of access to location B will not be visible to any other processor. If neither location A nor location B is shared, then the only ordering visible to other processors is the Read C–Write C ordering. No *membar* is needed between this pair because of program order requirements. Hence it is unnecessary to place a *membar* anywhere in the code.

Thus the principal obstacle to good performance is the problem of determining efficiently during translation whether an access is to a shared location or not. This is a difficult problem because, although the history of accesses by an instruction can provide some measure of confidence about whether or not that access is to a shared location, there is a lot of bookkeeping involved in determining whether locations are shared, and extra overhead involved in ensuring that a trap is generated when a previously unshared location becomes shared.

Another problem is that of *false sharing*. False sharing occurs, for example, when the emulation software detects an access to a location by two different virtual processors but does not know that the guest operating system has migrated the thread from one processor to another for load-balancing purposes. False sharing could therefore lead to the elimination of fewer memory barriers than what would be possible.

Real ISAs often allow other relaxations or impose other orderings beyond the ones mentioned here. For example, on the System/390, a distinction is made between instruction reads and data reads. The ISA does not require that instructions be fetched in the order they are eventually executed. It also allows instruction fetches to occur before the reading of operands of previous instructions. Such relaxations, which obviously arise from a desire to make hardware more efficient, also help in reducing the overhead of emulation.

We have seen in this section that creating a virtual machine system with an ISA different from the ISA of the native host is certainly possible, though the efficiency of such virtualization depends a lot on the mismatch between the memory models of the two ISAs. In particular, when the memory model of the host is more relaxed, due either to a weaker coherence model or a weaker consistency model, the potential performance degradation is high, unless the emulation software performs more work in localizing the coherence and synchronization mismatches. As with VM assists mentioned in Chapter 8, hardware could be added to assist the emulation software in this task. An extreme example of this is for the processor to provide a mode in which it supports the stronger memory models required by the guests. There are processor ISAs, such as the PowerPC ISA, that provide both a coherence mode and a mode in which coherence may not be required. There are also processor ISAs, such as Sun's SPARC ISA, that support multiple consistency models.

## 9.6 Summary

Large companies and other organizations are continually grappling with the problem of reducing the number and types of computer systems they must maintain without depriving their important users of the flexibility of maintaining and operating their own system. This has led to an array of systems claimed to enable such consolidation, basically by decoupling the view of the hardware as seen by the operating system from the actual hardware that the system runs on. Virtual platforms on large servers provide users with characteristics similar to those they would have enjoyed on their own private physical systems.

This chapter examined various ways in which large multiprocessor servers can be adapted to provide multiple virtual multiprocessor platforms to various users. We have seen how different forms of virtualization handle the task of isolating virtual machines from each other while still providing the benefits of sharing resources. Some of these solutions, such as physical partitioning, are superior at isolating virtual machines from hardware failures, while others, especially the codesigned hardware–software approaches, excel in the degree of flexibility they provide in the allocation of resources to the virtual machines.

The biggest impediment to the adoption of new instruction set architectures is the existence of large bodies of application programs in binary form for the existing ISAs. Large multiprocessor systems of today are usually homogeneous — they incorporate processors that all execute the same ISA in their native mode. For most organizations, consolidating to a large multiprocessing system with one ISA will still leave a significant number of important applications in platforms of other ISAs that need to be supported, at least until they are ported to the native ISA. Hence virtualization of these other platforms will remain an important subject, at least until a more widespread adoption of platform-independent languages, such as Java, and platform-independent operating systems, such as Linux. We have seen that efficiently emulating applications of one ISA on another, while already difficult for uniprocessor platforms, is quite daunting in the case of multiprocessor systems, especially when there are incompatibilities in the memory consistency model. It is likely that new techniques will be developed, particularly exploiting thread-level parallelism, to improve the performance of emulating one ISA on another.

Same-ISA virtualization, on the other hand, appears to be here to stay. While the advantages of virtualization listed in the introduction to this chapter are compelling for enterprise servers, it is likely that smaller servers, such as those of Internet service providers, will also begin to employ virtualization, particularly as a means of ensuring privacy between users and as a means of protecting users from malicious or accidental failures of the platform employed by other users. Indeed, as more applications use network resources for their execution, the need to protect one application from another, even in a single-user environment, may eventually lead to the adoption of virtualization techniques on personal devices such as laptop computers or even mobile phones.

# Chapter Ten
# Emerging Applications

With ever-expanding computer applications and their associated demands on computer system administration, the role of virtual machines and virtualization are likewise expanding. Virtualization enables the introduction of new system capabilities without adding complexity to already-existing and already-complex hardware and software. These new capabilities will support innovative computing paradigms and will provide critical functions in areas that have assumed major importance in a world grown increasingly dependent on computers.

In an argument reminiscent of those given for the original development of VM systems on mainframes, it has been suggested that operating systems and applications running on real machines today should be relocated to virtual machines. Part of the motivation for this is the desire to allow new services to be developed in a layer between the hardware and the operating system without modifying or trusting either the applications or the operating system. Examples of new services are intrusion-detection systems that help in isolating users from malicious attacks, environment-migration services that help mobile users access their entire computing environment without having to carry their machines everywhere, and enhanced reliability through redundant execution of a program on multiple virtual machines. There have been several efforts that use virtual machine techniques to emulate one ISA on another. Virtual machines are being used to package entire environments and applications to avoid the time-consuming job of installing operating systems and applications on machines. They are also being used to isolate data on a system, thereby allowing the same physical machine to work with confidential and public data without compromising security.

To illustrate the importance of virtual machine technologies to future systems and paradigms, in this chapter we describe three examples of emerging virtual machine applications that can make a fundamental difference in the future of computing. The first of these is the application of virtual machines to computer security, an area receiving increasing attention. Modern computing systems are some of the most complex structures ever created. With the commoditization of both hardware and software and with widespread use of network computing, it has become easier for intruders to cause damage on a large scale by taking advantage of the nearly inevitable loopholes and flaws in such complex, constantly evolving systems. Eventually, systems will mature and become more immune to attack, and it is likely that integrated mechanisms will be developed specifically aimed at thwarting such attacks. The virtual machine intrusion-detection mechanisms described in this chapter promise to be useful tools in the development of such attack-immune systems.

The second application we consider, the migration of complete computing environments, is also motivated by the commoditization and networking of computing systems. A growing number of computer users depend on having their full environment, including all data, programs, and system personalization, readily available at multiple locations (e.g., at work, at home, and while traveling). In order to do this, however, these users must carry their environment with them on a portable machine. It is more desirable, however, both for convenience as well as for security, to allow a user to log in to any computer and immediately reproduce the user's environment on that specific computer. Virtual machine technology, which provides the ability to capture the entire state of a computer system, facilitates migration of a full computing environment. Eventually, users may become accustomed to having their data and computing environment on large, remote computer farms. While such a paradigm may obviate the need for having an entire computer at each location to which the user travels, it will not eliminate the need for migrating entire user environments from one system to another. Load-balancing, system-utilization, and system-latency issues will require means for capturing the state of the user environment and making it portable.

The notion of computing as a service or as a utility is beginning to gain acceptance. The scientific community has been actively promoting this paradigm for some time, and it also appears to be a concept that will be useful for businesses. The concept of a computational *grid* promises a seamless way through which computing resources can be shared by multitudes of users. The grid virtualizes computing resources in a way that is philosophically similar to the virtualization of resources in system virtual machines, though technically it achieves virtualization by redefining the way applications are written. In a sense, the grid concept represents the ultimate evolution of virtual machines.

Just as the Java platform fundamentally embodies virtualization, portability, and safety in its definition, the grid fundamentally embodies these same characteristics at the system and application levels. Virtualization is not optional on the grid — applications running on the grid must accept the notion that the physical characteristics of the real resources they are using are unknown to them. The hardware and operating system of the individual machines have the responsibility for providing this implementation-independent view. Although today this is done by loading extensions on existing systems, it is likely that, as in the case of security features mentioned earlier, support for operation on a grid will be integrated with the design of machine hardware and basic system software. This integration will likely include many of the virtual machine concepts described in this book.

We begin our survey of emerging VM applications in Section 10.1 with a discussion of the role that virtual machines can play in maintaining security in our increasingly vulnerable computer systems. In Section 10.2, we examine the idea of virtual machines as the enabling technology for migrating entire environments from one computer system to another. Finally, in Section 10.3, we take a look at the emergence of the grid computing paradigm, its similarities to other virtualization techniques, and its potential role in making virtual machines ubiquitous.

## 10.1 Security

Users of commercial systems, especially mainframe computers, have long been concerned with system security. These machines, which are used by large institutions, including banks, airlines, and federal agencies, handle sensitive information and are required to be secure against attacks. Security has not been as much of a concern, however, for users of common commodity computers — until relatively recently. Today, with the increase in the number of security attacks as well as the increasing cleverness of the perpetrators, computer security has become a major issue in all types of computing, including low-end desktop machines, portable machines, and even personal digital assistants (PDAs) and cellular phones. Seldom does a month pass when we do not hear about (or, even worse, fall victim to) yet another worm or virus that has invaded many thousands (if not millions) of computers around the world.

The most common way the security of a system is compromised is simply for an attacker to get access to the privileged part of the system, e.g., as a superuser in Unix environments or as an administrator in Windows systems. Interestingly, a large number of attacks are carried out by people who have gained access to such privileges without much effort — for example, through inadequately protected passwords or, more commonly, through repeated attempts to gain access to the system via commonly used passwords. Once the attacker gains access to the system, he or she can tamper with the operating system to gain confidential information or even to destroy data. Often, during the initial entry into a system, an intruder simply modifies the system to ease entry into the system in the future.

Another common type of attack exploits inherent weaknesses in system software. The size and complexity of modern system software, especially the operating system, makes it very difficult to ensure that every security hole is eliminated before the system is shipped to customers. Programs written in languages such as C, which are considered "unsafe," often exhibit bugs (or possess security holes resulting from poor programming practices) that can be exploited to gain access and hence control the system. One common type of security hole involves unchecked accesses to C arrays. When such an array is used as a buffer for user data, the user can fill the buffer with a block of data that is bigger than the array size and cause memory areas adjacent to the buffer to be overwritten. If one of these overwritten areas happens to be an address to which the program jumps, an attacker, through clever calculation, can cause that address to point to a routine, e.g., a shell program, by which the attacker gains control of the system. This is illustrated in Figure 10.1. It is generally not likely for an innocent user inadvertently to do harm to the system in this manner because the probability that arbitrary user data will cause a jump to a sensitive location is low. However, such security holes can be exploited maliciously and cause havoc in systems.

## 10.1.1 Intrusion-Detection Systems

In practice, security holes due to bugs or poor programming, as described in the previous section, eventually get fixed. However, as new code is introduced to a system, new holes appear. Clearly the most effective measure one can take to ensure the safety of a system is to isolate the system from all potential attackers (which is often the same as isolating it from all other systems). This is not a practical solution for most systems — users are dependent on communication with other systems either over local-area networks or over the Internet, and this makes them vulnerable to malicious attacks of the kind mentioned earlier. Using object-oriented programming with built-in type and range checking as is done in Java and MSIL will also provide a high level of security, but only for those programs running within the HLL VM framework. A significant amount of system code and a number of native libraries are likely to remain outside the secure framework for quite some time.

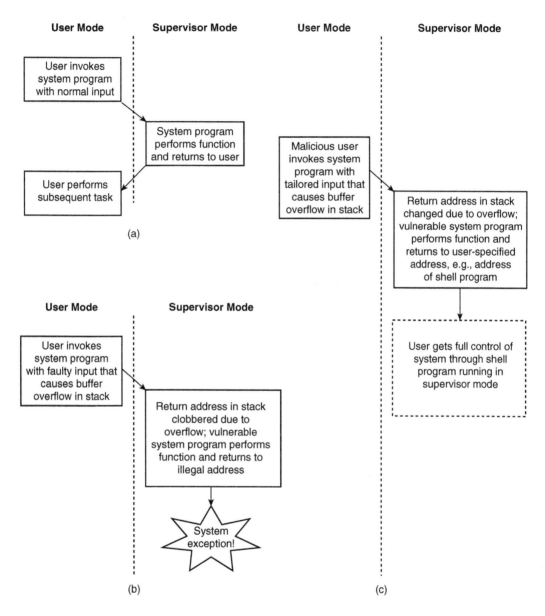

**Figure 10.1** Exploiting Buffer Overflow in a Program Stack. *In the normal course of events (a) the user parameter fits in the buffer. The return address on a stack is that of a location in the user's program. If the user inadvertently causes an overflow of the buffer (b), the return address may be clobbered (overwritten) but typically not with a legal instruction address. In this case, the return causes an exception. A malicious program (c) can manipulate the parameter to be copied into the buffer so that it overwrites the return address with a location that allows the adversary to launch another valid program. This program can be a shell program that, now running in the supervisor mode, allows the user free rein over the system.*

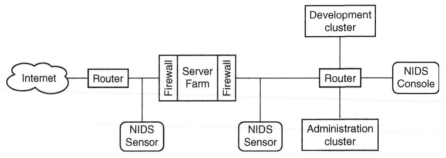

**Figure 10.2** Typical Enterprise Network Intrusion-Detection System (NIDS). *The sensors monitor the network for spurious activity. The console allows the programming of the sensors, logs the activity seen by the sensors, and forms the control point to isolate parts of the system when malicious activity is detected.*

A common way of providing security protection for current systems is through the use of an *intrusion-detection system* (IDS). As the name suggests, these systems attempt to examine a computer either continuously or periodically to check for potential attacks. These systems depend on the general knowledge of how potential attacks may take place. Once the characteristics of an attack are known, an IDS can examine the activity on a computer to determine whether an attack with the given characteristics is occurring and then take action to shut down any malicious processes before they can cause significant harm. Since most attacks are launched from the network to which a system is connected, an intrusion system can be located at some point in the network away from the computer — in this case it is termed a *network-based intrusion-detection system,* or NIDS for short. If, on the other hand, the intrusion system is located within the computer itself, for example, in the operating system, it is referred to as a *host-based intrusion-detection system,* or HIDS.

Network-based intrusion systems (Figure 10.2) work by examining data packets as they move through the network, looking for specific patterns, or *signatures,* of suspicious activities. The traffic can be monitored either at the host or at points more remote from the host, e.g., at firewalls or routers. As soon as suspicious activity is detected, a NIDS can block the activity or reroute the traffic to a quarantine location. Since it is possible for attacks to be disguised, there is no guarantee that malicious activity will always match one of the signatures in the NIDS database. There is also the possibility of innocuous traffic being deemed suspicious because of a similarity in its signature to one in the database (i.e., a *false positive*). Still, the NIDS has proven to be quite effective in many situations, particularly because it is decoupled from the system being protected.

Host-based intrusion-detection systems work by directly examining activity on the host and taking advantage of detailed knowledge of the host's operating system. A HIDS will look, for example, for repeated attempts to login by an intruder, or it will look for attempted accesses to files that should normally not be accessed by a user. Typically, the HIDS is integrated with the operating system and has high visibility over all the actions that take place on the system. Even the HIDS that operates as an application on the host enjoys high visibility by interacting closely with the operating system. In fact, such decoupling of the HIDS from the operating system can provide more protection to the system from intrusions that attempt to attack the HIDS itself.

Thus it is clear that the two types of systems are different in several respects and have their own advantages and disadvantages. A network-based intrusion system has significantly less visibility than a HIDS and has to base its decisions almost entirely on an examination of network traffic. An attacker thus has more flexibility in maneuvering around the detection system, especially by camouflaging itself. On the other hand, the NIDS can continue to monitor activity even after a host system has been successfully attacked — this is invaluable in learning about the nature of the attack and in taking measures to prevent it in the future. A system incorporating a HIDS can become completely disoriented after an attack, perhaps even providing misleading information while giving the intruder enough time to marshal additional resources to gain control of the system.

## 10.1.2 Monitoring and Recovering from Attacks

Attackers are constantly finding new ways to get around the defenses of a system. Thus while it is important for systems to have good intrusion-detection systems, it is equally important to take adequate measures to recover from an attack and to prevent similar attacks in the future. One important part of this effort is to perform *logging*. Logging saves information about critical activity on a system, e.g., login attempts and accesses or changes to certain important files on the system. This type of limited information can help in the analysis of methods used by an intruder and hence help in developing defenses for future attacks. However, in order to be able to recover fully from an attack, it is necessary to save much more information, for example, a checkpoint of the state of the system at some point before an attack occurs.

Many techniques and policies have been proposed for logging of events in a system. Most of these techniques assume that the operating system is functioning correctly, because they use the services of the operating system in order to record various events that occur. In fact many of them even keep the log of activities on the system being monitored. Such systems are doubly compromised. When an attack takes place, not only does the system fall under the control of the attacker, but the log of the system may also be altered in a way that is transparent to the user of the system or in a way that prevents reconstructing the attack for building up new defenses.

There are also difficulties involved with the reconstruction of a system after an attack. The first requirement is determining a known good state of the system before the occurrence of the attack. This implies that a checkpoint of the system must be available for some point in the past. From this state the actions taken by the system can be replayed up to some later point, if complete knowledge were available about all the inputs into the system following the checkpoint. If the times at which these external inputs, such as keyboard activity or network activity were known, the system could be brought back step by step to a point just before the occurrence of the suspicious activity. Unfortunately, not all external input events result in deterministic changes to the system. Asynchronous interrupts occurring because of events outside the core, for example, from an I/O device, may not occur spontaneously or may not occur at exactly the same point when the system is replayed. Such events, must be logged in sufficient detail so that they can be simulated accurately when the system is being replayed.

This completes a brief overview of the typical ways in which systems are attacked and of the approaches used by intrusion-detection systems to detect attacks. We have also outlined the requirements of system logs in order for a system to be able to recover from an attack. In the next section we examine how virtual machine technology facilitates these functions.

### 10.1.3   Role of Virtual Machine Technology

Most of the techniques needed to maintain security in a system have usually been implemented as separate programs on existing systems. It is reasonable to believe there would be significant advantages if the security features were integrated closely with the rest of the system. Yet it is important that techniques used to enforce security and monitor activity on a system be implemented in a way that separates their implementation from that of the system being attacked. This is where virtual machine technology comes in. We will look at three examples of the use of virtual machines in the area of system security.

#### Virtual Machine as a Sandbox

We have seen in Chapters 8 and 9 how virtual machines allow the isolation of complete system environments from one another. Fault containment is

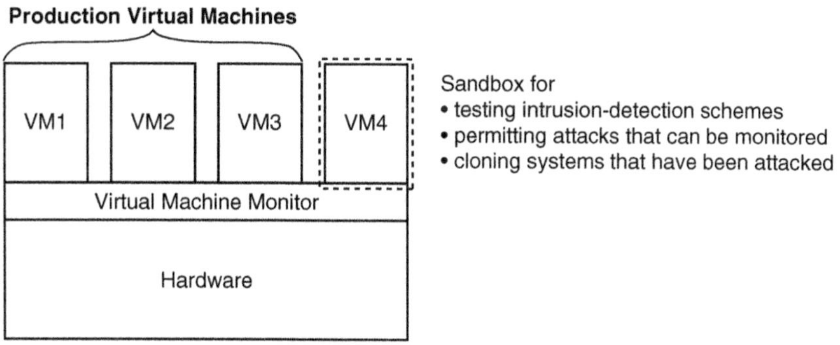

**Production Virtual Machines**

Sandbox for
• testing intrusion-detection schemes
• permitting attacks that can be monitored
• cloning systems that have been attacked

**Figure 10.3**   A System Virtual Machine as a Sandbox.

an important property of virtual machines — a software failure on one virtual machine does not generally propagate to other virtual machines. Typical virtual machine systems are capable of isolating the failed virtual machine, shutting it down, and then restarting a new virtual machine without these actions being noticed by the other virtual machines in the system. This ability to isolate a virtual machine makes it useful as a tool (Figure 10.3) for closely examining the effects of an attack after it has occurred. As noted earlier, such postmortem analysis is useful in designing a defense against future attacks or even toward detecting such attacks before they cause harm.

In a paper describing the advantages of virtual machines, Chen and Noble suggest that the complete state of a virtual machine can be saved, cloned, encrypted, moved, or restored — actions that are not so easy to do with physical machines (P. M. Chen and Noble 2001). They further suggest that the best way to understand the effects of an attack is to replay the attack and gather information about the behavior of the attack by monitoring the system as the attack progresses. While this is risky to do on a real system, one could safely carry this out on a virtual machine by cloning the original machine that was attacked, inspecting the effects of the attack, and throwing away the machine after it has served its purpose. (Cloning of virtual machines can be done using the system encapsulation and restart techniques described in Section 10.2.)

Cloning a system on a virtual machine opens up other interesting possibilities. A potentially suspicious network packet or other suspicious input can be sent to a clone before it is forwarded to the actual system, to see if it has any ill effects. Similarly, during the development of intrusion-detection systems, tests for the effectiveness of the system can be conducted more safely on a cloned system running on a virtual machine than directly on the system that needs to be protected.

### Virtual Machine for Monitoring Low-Level Activity

A system virtual machine forms a barrier between a system and the hardware on which it is running and also between a system and other systems running on the same hardware. This property of the virtual machine can be extended to provide a barrier between a system potentially under attack by intruders and the IDS that monitors the low-level activity of the system. Here are two possible ways to configure an IDS in a virtual machine system to achieve this.

1. The IDS can be written as a separate process in its own virtual machine, or on the host operating system of a hosted virtual machine, with special access to the functions of the VMM through a dedicated interface. This interface must support (a) means to send commands from the IDS to the VMM, for example, to enable certain monitoring functions, (b) a mechanism to efficiently access the physical memory of the system being protected, and (c) means for the VMM to transmit information about activity on the virtual machine back to the IDS.

2. The IDS can be integrated with the VMM. This gives the IDS the privilege and status of the virtual machine monitor and allows it complete access to all hardware activity of the system being protected. The VMM is a critical, central piece of software in a system and should therefore be thoroughly debugged and hardened against attacks and failures. In a scheme where the IDS is integrated with the VMM, it is imperative for the IDS also to be written, debugged, and verified with the same rigor.

Separating the IDS from the VMM makes the functioning of the IDS a bit less efficient because of the need to communicate through an interface, as mentioned earlier. However, it avoids the addition of baggage to the VMM, a component that is central to the operation of the system and hence that must be efficient and verifiable.

The Livewire system (Garfinkel and Rosenblum 2003) is an example of a system that separates the IDS from the VMM. The changes needed to a VMM for supporting the interface required by an external IDS are minimal and need not compromise the robustness and efficiency of the VMM itself. The IDS configures the VMM to gather information about the activity of a virtual machine. To enable this, the system specifies additional events or instructions at which the virtual machine relinquishes control to the VMM so that the required information can be gathered. The VMM is also provided with a list of checks to be made on the gathered information. These checks may be a simple matter of matching the activity against templates of known malicious activity. Thus, once set up, the VMM performs all the needed activity without communicating back and forth with the IDS module. Once the signature of a malicious event is detected, the virtual machine is suspended, and the IDS is signaled and provided with the monitoring data gathered. The IDS examines the data and either responds with a command instructing the VMM to resume operation of the virtual machine or halts the virtual machine if it cannot guarantee that the system has not been compromised.

The system just described is simple because it is conceptually stateless. The decision about whether to halt a virtual machine or to allow it to continue is based only on the information provided by the VMM when suspicious activity is detected. This may be restrictive. Certain security measures require the incorporation of state in the intrusion-detection mechanism. Often, a suspicious event may not be directly identifiable as malicious but may require further examination of specific other events in order to be identified as such. For example, monitoring the system call activity immediately after a series of attempts to log in could give greater confidence in identifying the user logging in as an intruder. To achieve this, the IDS can send a command to the VMM immediately after a series of unsuccessful login attempts, instructing it to monitor all traps and interrupts intended for the virtual machine being protected.

Unlike the VMM, an IDS needs to have information about the type of operating system running on the virtual machine. The characteristics of intrusions often tend to be specific to the operating systems being attacked. As a result, an IDS tends to have several operating system–specific mechanisms. The Livewire system, for example, includes an OS interface library that allows the IDS to perform an analysis on a crash dump generated by a virtual machine, in almost an identical way as it would have been done by an application running on the operating system.

We mentioned earlier that the VMM is provided with a list of checks and templates to be used during the monitoring process. This is the function of the *policy engine*, the part of the IDS that determines how the monitoring should progress and whether the observed behavior matches the signature of malicious activity. The interface to the VMM, along with the mentioned OS interface library, provides a framework on which to build the policy modules of the policy engine. Livewire (see Figure 10.4) used this technique to build several policy modules, each of which was only between 30 and 130 lines of code. More details about the implementation of these for a Linux-based system are presented in Garfinkel and Rosenblum (2003); following are a few examples.

> *Lie detector module:* Attackers often want to mask their activity by lying about the system. They do this by getting control of the system, modifying it, and then masking their activity by providing false responses to system

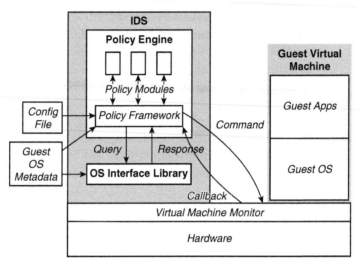

**Figure 10.4**    Livewire Intrusion-Detection System (Garfinkel and Rosenblum 2003). *The IDS may be viewed as another virtual machine built on top of the VMM but with special privileges. The major components of the IDS are (a) the OS interface library, which provides an OS-level view of the monitored virtual machine, obtained by interpreting the metadata returned by the guest OS through the VMM, and (b) the policy engine, which provides a framework to implement common policies as well as a set of policy modules each of which implements an intrusion-detection scheme. The VMM isolates the IDS from the monitored virtual machine.*

queries. A VM-based intrusion-detection system can thwart such attempts by sending an enquiry to the attacked system about the state of the system and comparing the results it provides with the actual state of the hardware of the system, which is completely known to the VMM.

***User program integrity detector module:*** Checking the binary stored on disk is not helpful after an attacker has modified the contents of a long-running program in memory. Livewire uses the VMM to check every code page of a program in memory and generates a signature (e.g., checksum) that is then compared with known good signatures for the same pages saved elsewhere. Any discrepancy is flagged as a potential violation of security.

***Signature detector module:*** Antivirus programs have traditionally relied on the fact that most new viruses and Trojan horse programs simply reuse known techniques — often just copying the basic kernel code of an old virus or Trojan horse. Thus it is often effective to create a signature of these kernels and to check for this signature in files that are likely to be attacked. Virtual machine technology allows such a detection technique to be extended to the entire memory of the system. The VMM has access to the virtual hardware of the virtual machine, and hence an intrusion-detection system can use the interface of the VMM to schedule a periodic scan of the memory for such signatures.

***Memory access enforcer module:*** Traditional operating systems protect code sections and other important parts of memory by rendering them read-only. Integrity check techniques are sometimes employed to ensure that certain critical sections of memory have not been tampered with and are still protected as read-only. But these techniques can detect such attacks only after they have occurred. By running the system inside a virtual machine, it is possible to get better and more immediate protection from such attacks, by rendering the same critical pages as read-only. Any attempt to change the access privilege of these pages is intercepted by the VMM, which can then halt the system.

The implemented policy modules generally fall into two categories: *polling modules* and *event-driven modules.* Polling modules poll the system at regular intervals to look for malicious activity, while event-driven modules report that some undesirable event has occurred on the system. The memory-access enforcer is an example of an event-driven policy module; the others are examples of polling modules.

Virtual machine technology helps eliminate some of the disadvantages that a HIDS has in comparison to the NIDS, with its better isolation characteristics. While it is natural to extend existing virtual machine systems to support intrusion detection, it is also possible that intrusion detection may one day be the reason for deployment of virtual machines.

### Secure and Complete Logging Using Virtual Machines

Logging of activity on a system is an important part in the fight against malicious attacks on a computer system. As mentioned earlier in this chapter, a log of the activity on a system enables analysis of the events associated with an attack, especially if such data is available from the period both immediately prior to the attack and as the attack progresses. Such an analysis could lead to techniques that (a) anticipate an attack and (b) know when an attack has occurred.

A common method of logging is to record all accesses to important and critical parts of the system, e.g., login attempts, network-related events, access to the system registry, and commands invoked at the superuser or system-administrator level. Unfortunately this information is not trustworthy when under attack — an attacker gaining control of the operating system can change the logging information to mask the attack. Moreover, while evidence of the intrusion may be available from the log, there may be insufficient information to determine the exact vulnerability that led to the success of the attack.

Researchers at the University of Michigan (Dunlap et al. 2002) have proposed a virtual machine–based system called ReVirt that attempts to address both these problems, namely, the inability to guarantee the integrity of logging information as well as the incompleteness of traditional logging information. They use the VMM both to separate the logging process from the system being monitored and to collect all information needed to replay instruction-by-instruction system activity for a long period of time — potentially starting from a point before the start of the attack and continuing to well after the attack is under way.

Any computing system may be viewed as a finite-state machine. If the starting state is known, it is sufficient to know only the sequence of inputs to be able to replay its entire execution; the system moves through a set of states that can generally be determined simply by re-executing the program. However, there are situations where the transition between the states of a system is time dependent — reproducing the effects of an earlier execution in such cases requires a simulation of the input at the time recorded during the earlier execution.

A better reference for recording nondeterministic events is the number of instructions that have been completed by the machine rather than the time on the system clock. It has been observed (Bressoud and Schneider 1996) that even when the inputs are completely deterministic, for example, in a program with no I/O, the time at which an instruction is executed varies from run to run, even though the count of instructions executed remains the same. This is due to a number of factors, the most obvious one being the variable latency to cache memory, depending on the interaction with other applications simultaneously running on the system. Modern processors often provide performance-monitoring hardware to count completed instructions, and hence it may be feasible to trigger events at specified instruction execution counts. However, a more efficient and an equally effective measure is the number of branches that have been executed by the machine. The location of an event can be completely characterized by the exact number of branches that have been executed from the program start, along with the value of the instruction program counter when the event occurs.

Counting events, e.g., the number of instructions executed or the number of branches executed, is accomplished through the setting of special performance counters visible at the ISA level. Each time the event occurs, the counter counts down by 1. When the counter reaches a value of zero, an interrupt can be scheduled to inform the application that the desired count has been reached. The designers of ReVirt observed that on IA-32 processors (and possibly on

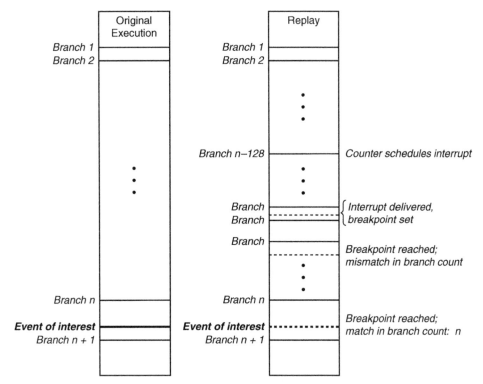

**Figure 10.5**   Two-Phase Method for Delivering a Nondeterministic Event Accurately During Replay.

other processors too), the interrupt generated by the counter does not stop execution immediately and could in fact occur several tens of instructions later. To ensure the delivery of a nondeterministic event at a precise point in the computation, they use a two-phase technique, shown in Figure 10.5. At the start of the replay the precise number of branches to be executed before the occurrence of the event is known. The instruction address of the desired point within the basic block after the last branch is also known. In the first phase, the branch performance counter of the IA-32 processor is set so that 128 branches will still remain to be executed. The interrupt from the counter is received at some point where the number of branches remaining to be executed is less than 128. At this point, the second-phase strategy is invoked. In this phase, a breakpoint is set to the program counter value recorded for the event. Each time the execution arrives at the breakpoint, the number of branches is examined to determine whether the desired number of branches have been executed. The exact point is reached when the desired number of branches have been executed, and execution progresses to the instruction at the desired instruction address.

The number of events to be recorded can grow to an unmanageable size unless one takes care to minimize the logged information. Note that only those events that can affect the execution of the monitored virtual machine need be logged; it is not necessary to log the events that arrive at the VMM but are not delivered to the virtual machine itself. Some of the common events that must be logged are timer and I/O interrupts. There are some cases where, in addition to logging the event itself, it is necessary to log the actual input value, for example, for inputs from the keyboard, mouse, network interface card, real time clock, and CD drive. Input from the hard drive need not be recorded if we ensure that the hard drive will be set to the original state at the start of the replay. Even in the case of a CD drive, the actual input values read from the media need not be recorded if the original CD is available to be replayed; in this case, even these events become deterministic.

It is important to have good knowledge of the characteristics of the specific system to ensure that all nondeterministic events are properly logged. As an example of system-specific aspects that need to be considered, the ReVirt paper (Dunlap et al. 2002) indicates the following three aspects specific to the IA-32.

1. The IA-32 architecture allows a long memory instruction (e.g., a string instruction) to be interruptible, meaning that an asynchronous interrupt could cause a context switch in the middle of execution of the instruction. By saving the value of a register, ecx, as part of the state, an implementation will have the necessary information to resume the instruction where it left off after handling the interrupt. This implies that the register value must also be saved when a nondeterministic event is recorded, in case the interrupted instruction happens to be a string instruction.

2. The read-timestamp-counter (rdtsc) instruction returns nondeterministic values, but this instruction does not trap when in user state unless the control register CR4 is set in a particular way. One way to deal with this instruction is for the VMM to treat it the same way as other sensitive but nonprivileged instructions, as described in Chapter 8, namely, to scan ahead for the instruction, insert a trap, and emulate the instruction. The ReVirt system sets the CR4 so that the instruction traps, replaces the instruction with a library call routine gettimeofday(), which does not use the rdtsc instruction, and scales the value returned to account for the overhead.

3. A similar situation occurs with the read-performance-monitor-counter (rdpmc) instruction. This instruction also exhibits nondeterministic

behavior and usually does not trap in user mode as in the `rdtsc` case. As with the `rdtsc`, the ReVirt system sets the CR4 so that the instruction traps in user mode, but then it simply disallows the instruction in the guest kernel and applications running in the monitored virtual machine.

The ReVirt system was built on a hosted virtual machine system based on Linux (UMlinux 2002). The proper functioning of the system — specifically the ability to detect the occurrence of an external interrupt event as well as to deliver it at the precise point during the computation — was tested using special kernels. The performance overhead due to logging was found to be less than 8% for a wide variety of benchmarks. The growth rate of the log was found to be between 40 and 1400MB per day. This is a reasonable number and, in practice, allows logging for several days, possibly even months.

### 10.1.4  Role of Dynamic Binary Rewriting Technology in Security

In Section 4.7 we described a type of process virtual machine for which both the host and guest ISAs are identical but where the principal aim is the optimization of code for a particular platform. In such a system, a program is executed under the control of runtime software, which interprets the instructions in the program, determines code regions (e.g., superblocks) that are frequently executed, translates such code regions, optimizes them, and saves the optimized binary in a code cache from which the code is executed when encountered next.

The ability to control the execution of a program through the runtime also makes it possible for the runtime to sandbox the execution of a program, both to prevent the program from being attacked by potential intruders and to prevent the program from being the launching point of an attack on the system. This is the principle behind *program shepherding* (Kiriansky, Bruening, and Amarasinghe 2002), a concept that has been implemented on the RIO dynamic optimization infrastructure (Bruening, Duesterwald, and Amarasinghe 2001), which itself is an evolution of the Dynamo binary optimization system (Bala, Duesterwald, and Banerjia 2000) described in Chapter 4.

The fundamental idea behind program shepherding is that a program can be adequately protected by ensuring that every branch or jump is to a legal location and every branch into a code region originates from either another part of the same program or from some other trusted location on the system. This is not done easily at compile time because static analysis fails to resolve addresses of dynamically shared libraries as well as the targets of many indirect jumps. Thus safe execution of a program can be ensured only through runtime checks.

### Restricting Control Transfers

Let us now examine the way in which control transfers can be restricted. One way to do this is to add instrumentation (i.e., instructions) at branch and jump sites to check the validity of the target. However, this could degrade performance of the program quite significantly. Moreover, as long as the program is vulnerable to attack, the attacker could change this instrumentation to circumvent the checks. A more effective way of achieving this is through techniques used in dynamic binary optimization. A section of code is interpreted the first time it is executed. The targets of the conditional and indirect branches are recorded in a safe location. When the same sequence of basic blocks has been executed a predetermined number of times, this sequence of blocks is gathered into a superblock, reoptimized, and placed in a code cache, as described in Chapter 3. The runtime software of such a system performs checks for the validity of branch targets both during the interpretation phase as well as during execution from the code cache. If the superblock represents the typical path of execution, these checks will be performed much less frequently when executing out of the code cache. In order to ensure that the code being executed is not maliciously modified, the code cache itself should be protected by making it writable only when the runtime is in control.

An overview of the RIO system infrastructure is shown in Figure 10.6. The specific characteristic of the system, namely, that the RIO code and the application code both work as part of the same process and share an address

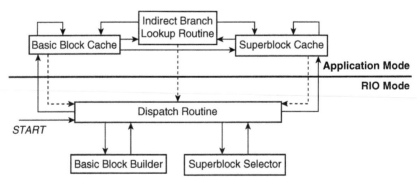

**Figure 10.6**   Flowchart of the RIO System (Kiriansky, Bruening, and Amarasinghe 2002). *Dotted arrows depict performance-critical functions, with the operation switching between application mode and RIO mode.*

space, is an inheritance from the Dynamo system, which was described in Section 4.7.2. Even though they are part of the same process, there are two modes in which the machine operates, the *RIO mode,* in which the infrastructure code operates, and the *application mode,* in which the application work is performed. The system begins by scanning instructions and collecting basic blocks, which are inserted into a *basic block cache,* a region of memory protected from being overwritten. At a branch or jump, a map (hash) table lookup is performed to check whether the next basic block has already been cached. If it has been cached and if a direct address is given, the two basic blocks in the cache are linked through a new direct branch so that the table lookup is avoided the next time. Further performance improvement is obtained by stitching together frequently executed sequences of basic blocks to form a superblock, which is then inserted into the code cache (shown as the *superblock cache* in Figure 10.6). The collection of basic blocks and superblocks is done in RIO mode, but the execution of the code itself is done in application mode. A mode switch into the RIO mode occurs when a control transfer lookup fails to find an entry either in the basic block cache or in the code cache.

Management of control flow transfers is achieved as follows. For each direct branch from one cached basic block to another, security checks are performed at the time the basic blocks are linked. A link is added only if the security policy allows a direct transfer; otherwise control returns to a runtime routine that checks for and handles all potential security violations. Once the link is inserted, it is part of the basic block cache (or superblock code cache), which itself is protected from being tampered with. As long as the program is restricted to such linked branches, there is no overhead in execution. In fact there could even be a performance benefit due to more efficient layout of the code.

Indirect-jump destinations have to be looked up in the map table to determine the mapping of destination addresses to corresponding locations in the basic block cache or the code cache. Only those cache addresses that are validated are placed in the map table; these account for most of the addresses to which jumps are made. Additional checks can be recorded in map table entries. For example, the target of a return from a subroutine can be checked to make sure the program returns to a point immediately after the original call. Such a check would thwart the type of attack that was described in Section 10.1, where the program returns to an inappropriate address because the stack has been clobbered.

In general, the only branch or jump targets that lead to any significant program degradation are indirect jumps targeted outside the code segment being protected. The RIO system checks for the validity of such targets by performing dynamic checks whenever they are encountered.

### Restricting Code Execution

The origin of a piece of code must be authenticated before it is allowed to execute. This authentication must be performed not only at the time the code is loaded from the disk or from the network, but also while it is executing — the code could be changed in memory either by another program on the system or even by itself. Any changes to the code in memory must either conform to the security rules or be disallowed.

Most of the checks in the RIO system of this kind are performed at the time the system copies a sequence of instructions into the basic block cache. The main challenge here is to ensure that the code was not tampered with after being fetched into memory and before being copied into the basic block cache. Modern program binary file formats separate the code sections from the data sections and allow loaders to write-protect code pages as they are brought into memory. Any attempt to change the code results in an exception. However, the system also needs to handle the case of dynamically generated code, permitting the execution of such code when it is legal to do so and preventing it when it is not.

There are two cases of importance. The first is the case of new sections of code that are created and then loaded for execution. In this case, the region of code is usually converted from being writable to being write-protected. The RIO system authenticates the code at this point and allows the conversion only if the request is from trusted code. Similarly, if the program makes a direct jump into writable space, the system verifies the origin of the jump and write-protects the target area before allowing execution to proceed.

The second case occurs when code and data are shared on the same page — this case poses an interesting problem. Since data areas should not be write-protected, it is necessary to have two copies of such pages, one of which is write-protected and is the source of instructions, while the other serves as the target for data reads and writes and is not write-protected. This solution is adequate for most common situations. It does not handle the situation where the code itself is changed by the program, however — the case of self-modifying code. Such writes into the code area must be intercepted by the runtime monitor in order to ensure they are being performed legally. It is necessary for the system to monitor all writes into write-protected regions and to authenticate the source of such writes. If it is a legal self-modifying code situation, the runtime monitor makes the page writable, allows the write to proceed, and then write-protects the code page again, after ensuring that the basic block cache and the code cache are purged of all the affected regions. This is clearly a case that could significantly degrade the performance of the system. Fortunately, it is not a common occurrence in modern programs.

**Table 10.1**    Page Access Privileges in the RIO System

| Page Type | RIO Mode | Application Mode |
|---|---|---|
| Application Code | R | R |
| Application Data | RW | RW |
| RIO Code Cache | RW | R (E) |
| RIO Code | R (E) | R |
| RIO Data | RW | R |

R — read only, RW — read/write, R (E) — executable

### Protecting the Runtime Monitor

The RIO system designers protected the RIO system code itself from attack by using different page protections during the RIO mode of operation and the application mode. The RIO mode has slightly higher page access privileges than the application mode, even though both modes operate within the same address space. An emulated "context switch" occurs when the machine switches modes. Table 10.1 indicates the access privileges to the various types of pages in the RIO mode and in the application mode. For instance, the code cache itself has read and write privileges in the RIO mode, whereas it has only read and execute privileges in the application mode. Tables used by the RIO system, for example, the map tables, have read-only privilege in the application mode whereas they have read and write privileges in the RIO mode.

### 10.1.5    Secure Systems of the Future

Security is an aspect of computing that has not been systematically addressed in the past, and is beginning to gain tremendous importance. Users and organizations are already beginning to think of ways in which they can partition their platforms so that they are able to run open, general-purpose, widely available systems and applications that are insecure alongside other applications and data that have to be protected and kept highly secure. The Terra system (Garfinkel et al. 2003) attempts to achieve this by creating a *trusted virtual machine monitor* that supports virtual machines incorporating the semantics of dedicated, tamper-resistant hardware on the same hardware platform as virtual machines that run normal, open, general-purpose applications.

We have seen in this section the application of various techniques described in earlier chapters of this book to handle the security problem. The process of thinking through the various issues and of coming up with solutions to handle them has motivated and will continue to motivate the search for fundamental ways of avoiding thorny security issues. Thus the world is moving toward new paradigms where security, perhaps even at the expense of some performance, is a fundamental aspect in the design of an environment and its applications. The HLL VMs, as described in Chapters 5 and 6, exemplify this approach. For some time to come, however, the vast legacy of existing environments will continue to call for security solutions of the type discussed in this section.

## 10.2 Migration of Computing Environments

It is not uncommon for individuals to maintain programs and to work on multiple computers at different locations, for example, one at home and one at work. Usually, there is an overlap in the activity conducted in the user's different work locations, and it is clear that the user's data is likely to be needed at multiple locations. To facilitate this multiple work-site environment, it is likely that the same operating system and the same set of applications are installed on different computers. Yet there are often subtle differences between the environments of the various installations that prove frustrating to the user. For example, one location may have a slightly different version of an application program from another, perhaps because an upgrade was applied to the machine at one location and not the other. One might naturally ask whether there is some way in which the user can see an identical environment everywhere he or she works.

Many users get around this problem by working exclusively on portable devices such as laptop computers. While this ensures that the user always sees and works with exactly the same environment, it does have two significant disadvantages. First, the user is required to carry a physical device to transport the environment, and second, this means that the user is responsible for the physical security of the portable device at all times.

In the 1960s, mainframe servers solved this problem (at least within the environs of a large office building) by providing users with simple, "dumb" terminals as the only interface to the system. The operating system, applications, and data of the user resided in a central location and were accessible from the terminal through a network of serial links. The system virtual machine environment described in Chapter 8 extended this concept by allowing each user to perceive the computer being accessed as his or hers exclusively. The virtual machine concept provides flexibility, by allowing each user to customize his or her environment, and security, by isolating a particular user's environment from those of other users of the machine.

The last few decades have seen a dramatic decrease both in the cost and in the size of computing devices. The dumb terminal of the mainframes has now become a sophisticated computer in its own right. Thus, while the concept of the mainframe server still survives, most users today access both mainframes and the Internet through a device capable of performing significantly sophisticated computation. Such processing may include applications such as graphics rendering and game simulation, Web browsing, and the editing of text documents. It is the environment associated with this interface that needs to be replicated when a user moves from place to place.

Replicating such an environment from one computer to another is not trivial, because this implies that a tremendous amount of state information must be transferred. The state of the machine includes not only the state of the resources used by the operating system and the applications running on the machine, but also the code and data belonging to the operating system and applications. Thus, a *capsule* is formed to capture the state of a running machine and hence information about the processes currently active on the system. The notion of a capsule allows a user environment targeted for migration to be treated as an object that can be manipulated.

Even assuming that the actual hardware on multiple sites is identical, replicating the environment requires all this state information to be encapsulated, transmitted across a network, and installed on the other computer before the user can take over operation at a second computer. These operations have to be done efficiently in order for the switch between environments to appear seamless to the user. The following subsections will be devoted to ways to make such environment mobility practical and efficient.

## 10.2.1 Virtual Computers

As we mentioned in the introduction, virtual machine technology provides the ability to capture the entire state of a computer system and thus facilitates migration of a full computing environment. Figure 10.7 shows what is involved in such a migration. Traditionally, in order to migrate from one computer to another, one would close all programs on one computer, shut it down, and either transport the hard drive or copy all information contained on the hard drive of the first computer on to the hard drive of the second.

Often even this seemingly simple scenario runs into complications because of subtle differences in the configurations of the two machines. Virtual machine technology inherently is better at smoothing out such subtle differences. The process of environment encapsulation is simplified if the environment is running on a virtual machine rather than directly on real hardware. The virtual machine monitor must implement data structures that separate the resources belonging to the different virtual machines running on the system.

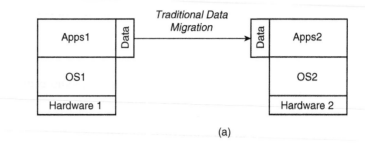

(a)

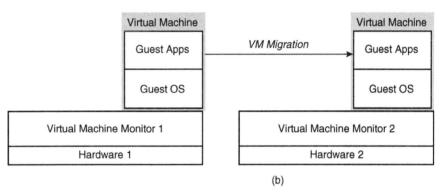

(b)

**Figure 10.7** Environment Migration Using Virtual Machines. *(a) Traditionally, migration involves the movement of data between machines, each with its own hardware, operating system, and complement of applications. (b) A faithful reproduction of the user environment is possible from one machine to another through the use of virtual machine technology. The state of the virtual machine, including the state of the application, and the state of the operating system are packaged and migrated. The data for the application may also be migrated if it is not located on a file system accessible at the destination.*

Thus, the virtual machine itself can serve as a capsule that can be migrated to another system that implements the same virtual machine system, as shown in Figure 10.7b.

The information about a virtual machine that is typically kept for use by the virtual machine monitor is restricted to the configuration of the virtual machine and pointers to tables that link virtual resources such as memory to real resources on the system. A capsule, on the other hand, does not contain any information about the mapping of the virtual resources. A capsule must also capture the state contained in all resources, including the disks and memory. It is conceivable that the information contained in a capsule can be many gigabytes in size and could take several hours to be transmitted on networks commonly used for connecting home computers to the outside world, for example.

Encapsulation of a running machine is similar to checkpointing. It allows the machine to be suspended for an indefinitely long time and resumed exactly from the point where the execution was originally suspended. The capsule is a host-independent checkpoint that can be transported from one machine to another; execution can be suspended on one computer and resumed at exactly the same point on another computer. If the virtual machine architecture is identical to some real machine architecture, the execution can be resumed on a real implementation rather than on another virtual machine system.

It must be remembered that the system virtual machines running on a centralized mainframe such as the IBM z/VM also allow a user to see the same environment when traveling from one location to another. However, in that case, both the data and the processor reside in a remote location and stay there, even during execution. The amount of state information that needs to be transferred to a remote terminal is negligible, and the overhead of updating the environment to make it cognizant of the new terminal is small. The harder problem is the one we have outlined here — that of migrating the environment to work on different data and compute facilities.

There are several issues involved in developing a practical solution for this problem, and we list some of them here.

- The entire state of a computer (which could include tens of gigabytes or more of disk space) can be so large that the time taken to migrate the state may be prohibitive. Note that it is generally not necessary to send the entire state from one computer to another initially. It is usually sufficient to transmit a small part of the state at first, transmitting additional parts of the state as needed. It may also be possible, as we shall see later, to take advantage of information that may already be available on the second computer, e.g., portions of the operating system itself.

- Having decided what portion of the machine state needs to be migrated, there is still the problem of packaging and securely transmitting the information. Compression and encryption techniques have to be employed to reduce the amount of data transmitted and to transmit it securely.

- When the hardware on the two machines is identical and when the virtual machine monitors running on them are identical, the process of transmitting the environment from one machine to another should be seamless. It may be the case that while the processors are identical in the two machines, the memory or I/O configuration on the two machines is different. For example, one machine may be connected to the external network using an Ethernet adapter, the other with a wireless connection. We have already seen in Section 8.4 how such situations are handled, both in native system virtual machines and in hosted virtual machines.

▪ Finally, the ISA of the user's virtual machine and the ISA of each of the host computers determine the extent to which the performance of the system appears identical on the different sites. When the ISA of the guest is different from the ISA of the host, the virtual machine monitor is required to translate from one ISA to the other. We have already discussed various binary translation and optimization techniques that help in doing this.

In the next two subsections we examine the basic functioning of two systems that have implemented the environment-migration concept.

### 10.2.2 Using a Distributed File System: The Internet Suspend/Resume Scheme

Kozuch and Satyanarayanan (2002) proposed the use of virtual machines in migrating the state of a user environment from one computer to another via a technique they called *Internet Suspend/Resume* (ISR). The name attempts to capture the notion that the system essentially allows a user to suspend operation on one machine, travel to another machine, and resume execution on the other machine by migrating the state of the first machine over the Internet (Figure 10.8). The authors use the VMware GSX Server described in Chapter 8 to carry out their experiments. The ISR proposal encapsulates the state of the virtual machine, including the contents of the virtual memory and the disk; the virtual machine monitor keeps this state in a file on a distributed file system accessible also from the destination computer.

One of the longstanding problems with the migration of state from one location to another is the need to change the IP address to access the network and all references to this address in the saved environment. MobileIP technology (Perkins 1998) solves this problem for mobile users of the Internet. The authors of the ISR scheme suggest that migration can be made completely transparent as long as the guest operating system is configured to use only such mobile technology.

The simplest approach for resuming the environment on a new machine is for this machine to access the state saved in the distributed file system and to load it as the state of a new virtual machine. If the system configuration and the virtual machine monitor on the destination machine are the same as those of the originating machine, the loading of the file may simply involve the loading of tables and data structures in the virtual machine monitor of the destination. In order to accommodate the variety of distributed file system definitions, Kozuch and Satyanarayanan suggest that the state file be written to

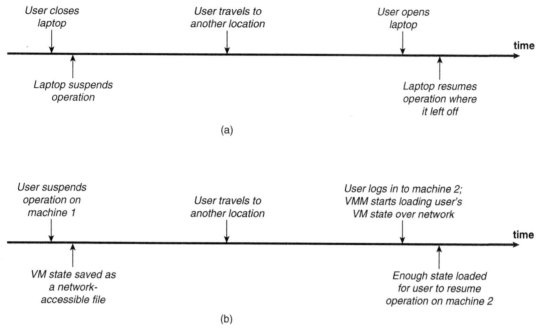

**Figure 10.8** Internet Suspend/Resume. *(a) What happens on a laptop when the user travels from one place to another. (b) How a similar effect is obtained using VM migration. The state of the user's environment is saved on a distributed file system accessible to the machine in the user's destination location.*

an abstract file system interface, with machine-dependent aspects encoded in a small block that resides with the file.

Loading the entire state on the destination machine could take a considerably long time. In order to make the migration experience more responsive to the user, the authors propose the organization of the state information in modules that are loaded incrementally, with the environment resuming on the new virtual machine as soon as the needed elements have been loaded on the destination system, rather than waiting until the entire state has been loaded.

The ISR scheme uses a "pull" model, with the destination computer reading in the environment state file on demand, for example, when the user logs in to the destination machine. This could result in a long latency between the time the user logs in and the time when a sufficient amount of state is available on the destination to allow it to resume the environment. The authors suggest that there may be usage patterns that could be learned by a system in order to hide the latency of the resumption by proactively copying in the state to the local machine even before the user requests it. For example, the system could learn the pattern of travel between work and home for a particular user and bring in a part of the state of the system at the destination before the expected time at which the user arrives at the destination.

The amount of information that is part of the state of a virtual machine is considerably large. Copying the state, compressing it, transmitting it, uncompressing it, and then loading it back on another machine will be time consuming as well as bandwidth consuming. Techniques are needed to limit the amount of information that has to be transmitted in a burst, without compromising the ability to transmit the full state information from one host to another. For example, when a user frequently travels between two sites, the suspension of the environment at a site need not completely eliminate the environment at the site. It may be possible to keep information in some structured way so that when the environment is resumed at the site at a later time, only the changes to the environment need be loaded. Another possibility is to reuse portions of the environment from the environment of other users already on the system. Candidates for such reuse include files associated with the operating system, only a few of which are user specific.

The eventual adoption of such a scheme will depend on the security of information guaranteed by the migration system. Users would not want any information in their virtual machine to be accessible by other users or even by the VMM. Kozuch and Satyanarayanan propose that the state saved in the distributed file system be maintained in an encrypted form. They also suggest that users be validated before being allowed use of a host machine.

### 10.2.3 State Encapsulation in the Stanford Collective

The Stanford Collective project (Sapuntzakis et al. 2002) takes a conceptually similar approach to environment migration. The principal difference from the Internet Suspend/Resume approach is that the capsule that holds the complete state of the user's virtual machine is sent to the destination computer to which the user is headed rather than to a distributed file system accessible by the destination. One advantage of this "push" model is that by appropriately planning the migration activity, the user can have instantaneous access to his or her environment at the destination site.

The virtual machine of the Collective system is an Intel IA-32 platform running on the VMware GSX server (VMware), the basic operation of which was described in Chapter 8. As noted in that chapter, the GSX server is a hosted virtual machine system, with the host operating system being either Linux or Microsoft Windows. On such a virtual machine system, the VMM can take full advantage of the device drivers written for the wide range and types of I/O adapters and devices that already exist for the host operating system.

The Stanford Collective developers noted that there still remain challenges in supporting certain I/O devices, e.g., network adapters, because of the portability requirement. If a virtual machine is using a virtual network card to communicate over the Internet, the encapsulation will include an IP address that may not work on a physical computer different from the physical computer producing the capsule. The Collective system enhances the virtual machine monitor to enable tunneling of network packets travelling to and from the capsule's old network over a virtual private network (VPN).

The Collective system developers performed extensive tuning of their system to be able to suspend a virtual machine and transmit it to a destination machine in about 20 minutes (a period they considered a typical commute time) using standard 384 kbps DSL lines. The system attempts to be oblivious of the details of the guest operating system. Hence many of the techniques they employ are applicable more generally than the ISR scheme described in the last subsection. Some of these are listed next.

### Reducing Memory State Before Migration

Most physical machines today contain hundreds of megabytes of memory, and it is reasonable to expect virtual machines to have main memories that are similarly large. At any given instant, however, the part of main memory that is critical for good performance is relatively small. There is typically a large part of main memory that could be paged out to disk without noticeable difference in the system's response time. Unfortunately it is not possible to determine which pages do or do not belong to the current working set at suspend time without intruding into the guest operating system. The Collective system works around this by starting a *balloon* program on the virtual machine that requests a large number of pages. This program causes pages to be released from the other active processes on the system by the guest operating system — the expectation is that these pages are released from the currently inactive processes that do not need to respond instantaneously on a resume at the destination. The size of the memory state is now reduced by zeroing out the pages requested by the balloon program, thus enabling better compaction of the capsule.

There are several subtle policy issues associated with ballooning. While transmission of the state of the memory is more effective when more of the pages are recovered through the balloon program, the response of the system during the resume operation becomes more sluggish unless the right number and type of pages belonging to the active processes remain mapped in memory. Pages holding cached data or those that are part of dirty buffers are ideally left untouched. On the other hand, active pages that are easily compressible need not be released to the balloon program; there is less benefit in their being zeroed out for compression and possibly greater overhead in their being restored during the resume process.

Note that the balloon program is a process running within the environment of the virtual machine, though it is triggered by the VMM when it receives a suspend request. The fact that this program runs on the guest operating system allows the program to be specialized for the characteristics of the operating system. Operating systems such as Microsoft Windows limit the size of the maximum working set for each process — the balloon program cannot recover more pages than the specified maximum number of pages that may be used by the balloon program itself. On the other hand, Linux does not set a limit to the size of the working set for a process — the Collective system monitors the swap space, while the balloon program keeps allocating and zeroing out new pages, until the free swap space reduces by a preset maximum.

### Reducing the Size of the Transmitted Packet

The balloon-program approach just mentioned goes a long way toward reducing the bandwidth required to transmit the information associated with a capsule. However, with very large disks becoming common, the state represented by the disk is rather formidable. Moreover, disks already hold many types of data, such as pictures and video, as compressed files, and additional compression is seldom effective. On the other hand, typical user migration involves just a few platforms, and the required disk image is usually not a big change from the image that was left on a platform when last visited. The Collective exploits this observation by maintaining differences between capsules rather than the full disk image for each capsule, thus saving a considerable amount of time and resources.

Figure 10.9, taken from Sapuntzakis et al. (2002), shows a sample capsule hierarchy, where each node represents a capsule state. The state of the disk in a node is saved in its entirety only in the capsule corresponding to the root node. Each node in this path inherits a base disk image corresponding to its parent node. Only the incremental difference between the states of the parent and the child is stored in each child node. The state of the disk at any node can be derived from the disk information contained in the nodes along the path from the root down to that node.

Each incremental disk uses the *copy-on-write* concept. The idea here is that whenever a copy of a disk is needed, the entire disk contents are not copied. Rather, the image of the disk is represented by a set of pointers to unique copies of various segments of the disk. Associated with each segment is a reference counter that counts the number of pointers to that segment. When a change

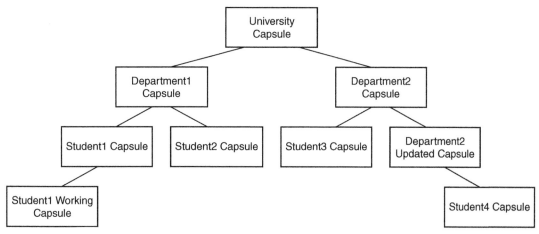

**Figure 10.9**    Example Capsule Hierarchy for a University. *The root capsule contains all the software that will be needed by all students. Each department customizes the capsule to suit its requirements. The department administrator does this by deriving a child capsule from the parent capsule. As mentioned in the text, only changes to the university capsule are saved in each department capsule. Students derive capsules from the department capsule, perhaps having one capsule per course in a department. Alternatively, like Student1 depicted earlier, students may derive their own private capsule. The leaf node, e.g. Student1 Working Capsule, is what migrates when the student moves from place to place.*

needs to be made and a segment must be written into, the reference counter is checked. If the count is 1, then the original copy of the segment can be written into. If not, the segment is copied, the pointer is made to point to the new copy, and its reference counter is decreased by 1. This new copy can now be modified without affecting the earlier versions. Copy-on-write allows many different versions to share a single copy of the actual data; this is particularly effective when these versions are largely the same and differ in only some small aspects.

Before changes are made to the disk image, all nodes in the path from the root to the leaf corresponding to the image have to be transferred. Modifications can be made only to leaf nodes in a hierarchy. For example, in Figure 10.9, if Student4 wishes to make a change to his or her disk on a location that does not already have any of the information corresponding to nodes in the path from the root up to the leaf node, this information is brought over. A new child node is created with Student4 as the parent, and changes are made strictly to the incremental disk at this node. When the student moves to another computer, the currently open incremental disk image is transferred to the new computer. The images corresponding to the other nodes are essentially read-only images and need not be deleted from the computer from which execution was suspended. As students move from computer to computer, various nodes in the hierarchy remain behind, increasing the probability of finding a copy of a desired node and decreasing the incremental traffic that will be incurred when the user moves from place to place.

### Reducing Start-Up Time on a Resume

On a resume operation, a lot of time can be saved if the information in the capsule disks is fetched on demand rather than being prefetched completely, because the working set typically needed by a user in a session is small. On the Collective system this is implemented as follows. All accesses to disks are intercepted by the VMM and forwarded to a disk server. The disk server translates the request to an access in one of the nodes in the hierarchy. If it is a write, the access must be to the leaf node, as mentioned earlier. An access to information residing in one of the intermediate nodes may need a remote access to the node that owns the information. On such an access, local shadow copies of the desired blocks are made from the remote incremental disk image. Thus the desired blocks of the remote disks are incrementally built up on demand on the local system. Note that disk blocks in a node can be shared by all capsules derived from this node. In Figure 10.9, for example, if some blocks of the departmental copy are brought over on demand, they need not be brought over again when another student attempts to access the same blocks.

### Reducing Transmission Time and Bandwidth by Exploiting Redundancy in Disk Blocks

It is not uncommon to find disk blocks that are identical, because the nature of activity on most systems tends to promote similarity among data blocks. Here are some sample situations when a needed block is already available on the system.

- A user moving back and forth between two systems leaves behind a trail of disk blocks that can potentially be reused the next time the site is visited.

- Blocks of program files are often already resident in memory. Most programs do not modify their own code, and hence it is generally possible to copy these disk blocks directly from memory.

- The memory of a machine often contains disk blocks other than program files, for example, blocks that are part of a disk cache.

- Often different users (and hence different capsules) utilize the same programs or data files. If a copy of a block already present in the capsule of a different user could be employed, it eliminates the need to transmit the copy from a remote site.

The Collective makes use of the *hashed copy* scheme. Each block on disk is associated with a hash value that aims to identify uniquely the contents of the block. The hash scheme employed in the Collective is a strong crypto-graphic hash, SHA-1, which has a very low probability of a collision (NIST 2002). Instead of transferring the actual data blocks between computers, the Collective transmits the computed hash values of the data blocks. When a disk block is needed by a computer, it checks to see whether a block with the same hash value is available locally. It then uses this block directly or generates a copy of the block if the block is to be written into (copy-on-write). This avoids the need to transmit the block from a remote location. If the block is not available locally, the computer broadcasts a request for a copy. Other providers on the system receive this request and check against a table of hash values of already-available blocks and satisfy the request. The authors claim that the scheme is reliable because the probability of a collision, i.e., of having the same hash value for different data, is less than the probability that a requestor of a disk block receives a bad block because of an error in a TCP connection or an error in memory. The scheme is also claimed to be secure because SHA-1 makes it practically impossible to manufacture data that produce a given hash value.

Results of experiments (see Figure 10.10) using the Collective system (Sapuntzakis et al. 2002) indicate that these optimizations significantly reduce the traffic and hence the time for migrating a user environment from one machine to another on a typical DSL network. The authors simulated the migration of a user between home and work machines using snapshots based on the Business Winstone 2001 benchmark. The various techniques described earlier appeared to reduce the amount of data transferred to typ-ically around 50MB, which can then be reduced further to less than 22MB through compression using the gzip program. Hashing reduces the trans-ferred amounts even more. Needless to say, there were situations, for example, at the beginning of program execution sessions, where the raw amount of data needed to be transferred was as high as 500MB. However, even in these cases, compression brought down the size by a factor of 2 or more, with hashing providing further reductions. The authors conclude that the experiments indicate that in typical situations of commuting between home and work, the entire environment could be transmitted during the com-mute. This makes it possible for a user to suspend execution at one site and resume execution at the other without noticing any change in the computing environment.

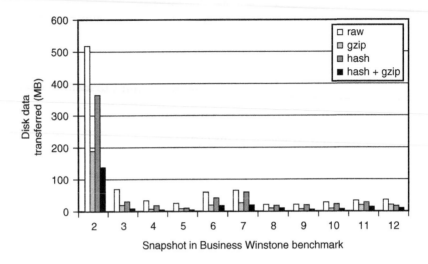

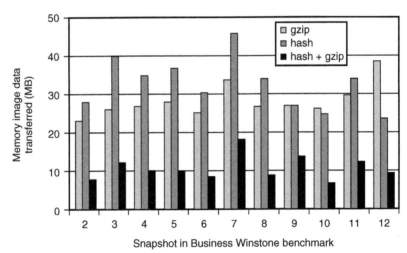

**Figure 10.10**  Performance of Optimization Techniques Used in the Collective (Sapuntzakis et al. 2002). *The raw memory size in the experiments is 256MB. Snapshots were taken while running the Winstone benchmark every minute after the first three minutes. The migration of each snapshot was simulated assuming the destination had all information up to the previous snapshot. The graphs show the effectiveness of the hashing scheme combined with compression using gzip in reducing the traffic from the originating host to the destination host.*

### 10.2.4  Migration of Virtual Machines in VMotion

The Internet Suspend/Resume scheme and the Collective scheme are research projects, and it may be a while before all the issues involving the migration of virtual machines over the Internet are sorted out. Meanwhile, there are aspects of such migration that already exist in VMotion, developed by VMware.

VMotion is part of the VirtualCenter (VirtualCenter) infrastructure management software that manages a cluster of Intel IA-32 virtual machine systems connected in a local-area network, as shown in Figure 10.11. The management functions of VirtualCenter include the deployment and monitoring of virtual machines running on a native virtual machine system called the ESX server. Under certain circumstances VirtualCenter may need to migrate a running virtual machine from one host in the cluster to another. Examples of such circumstances include:

- **Load balancing,** to improve the response time of the system through better utilization of resources
- **Security,** to quarantine a virtual machine that has been attacked
- **Collocation,** to bring communicating virtual machines closer together
- **Fault tolerance,** to move a failing host to another processor
- **Power management,** to move the load away from an overheated processor
- **Maintenance,** to move the load away from some processor while it is upgraded

The migration of a virtual machine from one node to another in Virtual-Center is done using VMotion. This migration involves copying the state of the virtual machine, including the processor state, the memory state, and the state of other virtual hardware resources, such as BIOS, devices, MAC address for Ethernet cards, and chip set states. The issues here are quite similar to the issues we discussed in connection with the ISR and Collective schemes. However, VMotion, being a product, has to grow cautiously — it is currently restricted in its capabilities in several respects.

- The source and destination computers must be in the same server cluster managed by the same VirtualCenter manager.
- The file systems on the source and destination computers must be identical and located on shared disks in a storage-area network (SAN). This avoids the complexities of migrating disks encountered by the Collective.
- The processors running on the two computers must have the same architecture and be provided by the same vendor. This avoids potential incompatibilities that could prevent the state saved on one machine from being directly loaded into the other machine.

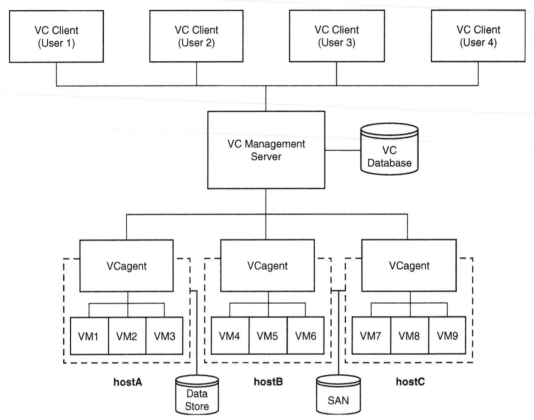

**Figure 10.11** Overview of the VMware VirtualCenter. *VC stands for VirtualCenter. A cluster of three nodes is shown, with the nodes named hostB and hostC sharing a file system on a storage-area network (SAN).*

- The virtual machine supports a Gigabit Ethernet adapter.
- The virtual machines must not be running multiprocessor cluster applications; they should be running only stand-alone applications.

When a request is received to migrate a virtual machine using VMotion, software in the VirtualCenter performs the following actions.

1. It first ensures that the virtual machine is in a stable state on the current host.
2. It then copies the contents of the memory belonging to the virtual machine to the destination host. Data associated with the guest operating system as well as the data of applications running on the virtual machine are copied.

This is referred to as the *baseline copy.* It is not the final copy because the virtual machine on the original host continues to run during this process.

3. The virtual machine on the original host is suspended. VirtualCenter then copies the last changes to memory along with the rest of the state of the virtual machine to the destination host. The information sent to the destination host at this stage is a capsule containing changes to the information sent earlier, similar to the incremental capsule as described in the Collective.

4. It then activates the virtual machine on the new host.

It is almost certain that more migration technology that has been developed in various research projects will continue to find its way into systems such as the VirtualCenter. What we observe is that there are many forms in which the problem of migration of virtual environments presents itself. We have reported here the early work in this area. As research progresses and as vendors get more experience dealing with products that allow migration, many new techniques will be developed. The eventual popularity and success of this paradigm may, in fact, mark the coming of age of virtual machine technology, particularly of system virtual machines.

## 10.3  Grids: Virtual Organizations

In the past couple of decades, the world has seen a rapid increase in the total amount of available computation power. Continual advances in lithographic techniques have allowed silicon feature sizes to shrink to incredibly small dimensions and hence have enabled the incorporation of billions of transistors on a fingernail-size die. This has been accompanied by the development of microprocessors, systems, and applications available at low cost to the common person and by the availability of easy-to-use programs that exploit the Internet. The economics of the computer industry are such that it is more profitable for companies to provide only a few types of microprocessors and a few types of systems rather than to spend the enormous amount of money needed to develop a wide variety of microprocessors, to manufacture them at different locations, and to develop different operating systems for each type of system. The result is the wide availability of fairly high-powered general-purpose computing engines that sit on the desks of millions of people around the world or are being carried by millions of people virtually everywhere they go.

Yet the nature of tasks that most users perform on their computers is such that only a tiny fraction of the available compute power is actually used.

Whether it is browsing the Internet to shop for an appliance or editing a term paper for a history class, the typical user does not exploit anywhere close to the full capabilities of the computer he or she is working on. The immediate impact of this is an environmental one — there is some energy consumed by a system as long as it is turned on — even when it is not performing any useful computation. This impact is being addressed in many ways, especially through the use of automatic power-management techniques. However, as computation and storage keep getting cheaper and as these computers get faster, there is more energy consumed by each of them. Thus, despite the incorporation of sophisticated power-management techniques, there is a sharp increase worldwide in the energy used by computers.

Ironically, there are occasions when users would like even more computation power than what they have available on their own systems. Scientists working with real-time data often do not have the processing capability to manipulate the large volumes of data they gather. They may need such processing capability either simply for visualization or for actually making decisions based on the data in real time. Their ability to perform such computation may be restricted due to the lack of compute capability, but it could also be due to the sophisticated software needed for the computation. Such users may not be willing to spend the large sums of money needed to buy systems that give them the desired response time or to buy the relatively expensive software, because of the infrequent use they make of such systems or software. This scenario has an analog in other areas, such as transportation, where a user generally owns a vehicle that is adequate for most but not all of his or her needs; for the occasional extraordinary need, the user rents an appropriate vehicle, borrows it from an acquaintance, or takes advantage of a service provider such as a public transportation company.

Applying the vehicle rental model to the computer world seems a plausible thing to do. In fact, in the early days of personal computers, computer rentals were not uncommon. However, as the complexity of configuring software increased and as the cost of owning hardware decreased, short-term rental of computers fell out of favor.

With the emergence of ubiquitous connectivity and the Internet, rental is no longer the right model for making more efficient use of compute power. Instead, the public utility is beginning to look like a more appropriate model. Rather than own or lease the physical resources needed to carry out an occasional task, the emerging model for the future is for the user to seek these resources over a communication network and to have the task performed remotely. The computation world is, as suggested in Foster and Kesselman (1998), in a state analogous to the electricity world in 1910, when local generators were the norm. Over time the electrical system evolved toward power grids, where suppliers of electricity pooled their resources for use by a much larger number of consumers. The design of the power utility system allows each user as much or as little power as he or she may need at any given time, with charges based on the amount consumed. The application of this model to the computing world would allow a user as much computation power as he or she may need to get an acceptable response time for a task, without having to own all the required resources.

The utility model for computation is already being driven by the needs of the high-end scientific computation community. The problems in understanding fundamental forces in nature, in the development of new drugs for common diseases, and in the prediction of weather all have one aspect in common — they rely on the ability to conduct large simulations involving massive amounts of computation. The physics community has long exploited large-scale collaboration across the globe ("big science") as an alternative to dividing up the available funding among smaller, less effective projects. This community has been quietly spearheading the adoption of this collaborative model for computing, by championing the utility model under the name of *grid computing*. Just as "big science" converted individual projects and laboratories into one large laboratory aimed at solving one fundamental problem after another, grid computing is bringing together many small and big computers in a heterogeneous "grid," both to make available to others unused computational resources on one person's computer, as well as to allow a bigger group of users to share a variety of specialized, often expensive, computing resources, such as supercomputers, in the manner of a utility.

About a decade ago, the World Wide Web was developed by the scientific computing community as a means for more effective collaboration among scientists to share both data and experimental results. Later, the same model proved to be useful for the commercial world and for the layperson. It is possible that models of grid computing originating with the scientific community will similarly prove to be functional to a much wider set of users in harnessing the enormous amounts of computation power already available and that will become available in the future.

Grid computing is a form of virtualization. It behaves like a system virtual machine by automatically directing a user application to a machine that has available resources and that matches the requirements of the application. Taking the system virtual machine concept to a higher level, grid computing creates a *virtual organization* by allowing a systematic sharing of resources between disparate systems that may be geographically distributed (Figure 10.12). Grid computing thus extends the virtual machine concept from instruction-level dynamic optimizers through process-level and system virtual machines to what we will call *organization-level virtual machines*. Unlike the other types of virtual

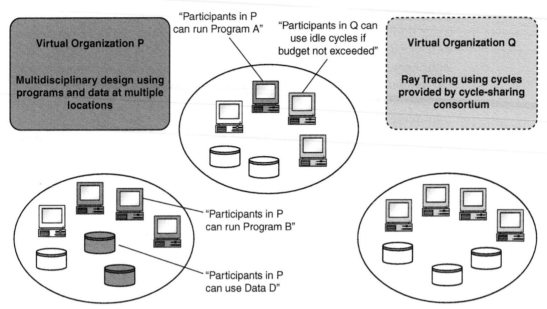

**Figure 10.12**  A Grid as a Set of Organizations, Both Real and Virtual (Foster, Kesselman, and Tuecke 2001). *Pictured are three real organizations (ovals) and two virtual organizations. Virtual Organization P is a collaborative project with distributed resources, as shown by the dark grey shading. Virtual Organization Q is a project that exploits idle cycles in resources on the grid (shown in light grey shading) to perform ray tracing. Sample policies that govern access to resources are shown in quotes.*

machines discussed in this book, the real machine that is virtualized does not have a well-defined, formal architecture. Rather, its architecture is embodied in the procedures and protocols that govern the relationships between the collaborators. Many of these procedures and protocols are often nothing more than a verbal understanding between human beings. The creation of the virtual organization using a federation of computer systems will hopefully provide the impetus to understand and document the interfaces that define these relationships in a formal manner.

The development of such interfaces will facilitate the deployment of new services and allow the grid concept to be exploited by a broader community. Thus, rather than the virtual organization being an attempt to faithfully reproduce the functioning of a real organization, the virtual organization enables the creation of function that did not exist before. The enablement of new function is a property of all virtual machines, as we have seen throughout this book.

### 10.3.1  Characteristics of an Ideal Grid

In this section we attempt to describe the salient characteristics of a grid. These characteristics are a combination of what exists on grids today and a wish list of features necessary for grid computing eventually to become a utility. The discussion here is an adaptation of the discussion of the computational grid described in Foster and Kesselman (1998) and in Foster, Kesselman, and Tuecke (2001). In the former, the authors describe a computational grid as a software and hardware infrastructure that provides dependable, consistent, inexpensive, and pervasive access to high-end computational capabilities. In their subsequent paper, Foster and his colleagues extended this definition, suggesting that a grid is an infrastructure that enables flexible, secure, and coordinated resource sharing among dynamic collections of individuals, institutions, and resources. These latter characteristics led them to refer to the grid as a *virtual organization.* We will now examine each of the characteristics of a grid in more detail.

#### Infrastructure

A computing grid is fundamentally a hardware and software infrastructure that enables sharing of resources. Hardware infrastructure components include computational resources, storage resources, sensors, and instruments. Software infrastructure components include programs to monitor use of resources, programs to schedule resources to requestors, and programs to turn resources on and off.

A computational resource on a grid may be a workstation, a mainframe, a supercomputer, or virtually any other type of computer. A shared storage resource may be a part of a disk on a personal workstation, a portion of a file system, or an entire network-attached storage. One important characteristic of a grid is that the systems comprising a grid need not be homogeneous — there can be a variety of processors and a variety of operating systems running on the grid.

#### Dependability of Service

A desirable characteristic of a grid that follows from its utility nature is that it be dependable. A true grid utility must be designed in such a way that all users of the grid either have equal access to its resources or can be guaranteed a quality of service specified in a contract with the service provider. This is sharply in contrast with most existing grids, which usually comprise a loose collection of resources provided by willing individuals or collaborating groups with a loose understanding of what is provided and what is expected. A grid participant who has volunteered the idle cycles on a workstation may not have any obligation today to provide the cycles that are pledged. As the concept of a grid evolves to that of a service, users will start to depend on the services of the grid for their day-to-day activities, and such informal understanding between participants will inevitably have to be replaced by more formal specifications and contracts. There are already efforts of this nature under way, especially with the establishment of the World Wide Grid Forum and the work being carried out in the Open Grid Services Architecture (OGSA).

Dependability of the grid system also implies fault tolerance — when a computational node in a system fails, the system must be able to recover from the failure and reallocate the resources in a manner transparent to the end user. Dependability also implies guarantee of security — users of the system must be guaranteed that their assets are not accessible to others and that others cannot maliciously prevent their access to resources.

Note that dependability and guarantee of quality of service are important in other forms of virtualization we have already seen. In the system virtual machines of Chapter 8, many VMs access a single complex of hardware, and it is important for the virtual machine monitor to allocate resources in a fair way among the various virtual machines. Similarly, the different forms of partitioning we encountered in Chapter 9 must ensure that resource allocation among the partitions is done both in a fair way and in a way that maximizes the performance of the system.

### Consistency of Service

The behavior of the service provided by a grid must be predictable and consistent. A grid may contain several types of machines and systems, each of which may be able to satisfy the requirements of a particular task. While it would be impossible to ensure that the response time of a task is exactly the same each time it is executed, users will expect consistent results each time a task is executed. They may also expect some reasonable bound on the response time.

### Pervasive Access

An important aspect of any utility is that it be accessible from virtually anywhere. Most current grids, as well as those that are being proposed, use the Internet as their communication medium. Thus, as long as the Internet is accessible from some part of the world, a user in that part of the world should have access to all resources made available by the grid.

### Inexpensive Access

A utility service becomes popular only when the cost of a task to the end user is attractive as compared to the alternative of performing the task on resources owned by the user. Like a utility, a grid should satisfy the needs of both the large organization wishing to perform data-mining tasks on a massive database as well as the individual who would like to have a video rendered.

### Coordinated Resource Sharing

All the attributes of a grid mentioned so far view the grid as a utility. A grid is envisioned to be more than just a utility, however. Users of a utility may not have much in common with each other — they form a community only in the sense that they happen to be using the same service. In its role as a virtual organization, however, the grid is expected to allow diverse groups to pool their resources and work collaboratively toward a common goal. This view of the grid requires the development of conventions for access privileges to various resources, including not only hardware but also content and programs. It also requires the development of protocols for communication between various clusters or even various grids. Coordinated resource sharing requires the precise identification of which resources are shared, who is allowed to share these resources, and in what manner they may be shared. Moreover, the underlying infrastructure must provide the ability to discover appropriate resources that a task may need anywhere on the grid. Development of protocols that address these sharing and communication issues, called *intergrid protocols*, are key to the widespread adoption of the grid model, just as Internet protocols were key to the widespread adoption of the Internet.

### Dynamic Communities

As the grid model evolves, it is likely that a single grid will support not just one community but, rather, several different communities. An example of a community is a group of researchers collaborating to design a new drug. The resources needed by this community may be similar to those needed by another community that is collaborating on a high-energy physics problem. Both these communities should be able to coexist on the same grid. Once again the infrastructure of the grid must ensure that adequate means are provided to identify, monitor, and control the needs of each community and to isolate one community from another.

Communities need not be static. Communities may spring up for the purpose of solving a problem and dissolve soon after this goal is achieved.

A user may enter a community at some point during the lifetime of the community and exit at some later point. A user may even be a member of two different communities at the same time. All these scenarios require that adequate provision be made in the architecture and the interfaces while designing a grid.

Whether or not the grid concept evolves to embrace one unified standard protocol, such as the Internet, remains to be seen. Today there are several different grids, each with its own protocols and each having its own suite of tools and management software. It is quite possible that the model that eventually emerges will be that of multiple grids, one for each community, working on a larger physical grid that pools an appropriate fraction of its resources for each of the community grids. Each community grid, with its own set of protocols, may actually be viewed as a *virtual grid*, much the way virtual machines with different operating systems coexist on a virtual machine system.

### 10.3.2 Evolution of the Grid Computing Model: The Globus Toolkit

A computing grid can take on several different forms, ranging from a simple network of workstations taking advantage of idle cycles on user machines to a complex commercial server that satisfies the requirements of users who may wish to contract out a single application or an entire virtual machine. It is likely that no single paradigm will emerge as the winner. Rather, the grid is likely to evolve ultimately as a service that customizes the solution to the needs of the user.

The number of grid systems being deployed is growing by leaps and bounds. Most of the current efforts are aimed at bringing together researchers in specific communities. Table 10.2 contains different classes of users of the grid ranging from system administrators to the end user. Each of these classes has a purpose distinct from the others and it is important that any toolkit developed to facilitate the use of the grid satisfies the needs of all of these classes of users. The grid developers provide the basic services required to construct the grid. Tool developers construct the programming models and associated tools which are used by the application developers, who construct grid-enabled applications for the end user.

Today there is an active effort to provide basic infrastructure tools to enable users to deploy and manage grids of their own. The Globus project (Globus), for example, is an open-source effort that aims to provide core services, interfaces, and protocols that enable users to create a new class of applications accessing remote resources seamlessly while allowing resources to remain under local control. The Globus project distributes a toolkit that includes software

**Table 10.2**  Classes of Grid Users (Foster and Kesselman 1998)

| Class | Purpose | Makes Use of | Concerns |
|---|---|---|---|
| End users | Solve problems | Applications | Transparency, performance |
| Application developers | Develop applications | Programming models, tools | Ease of use, performance |
| Tool developers | Develop tools, programming models | Grid services | Adaptivity, exposure of performance, security |
| Grid developers | Provide basic grid services | Local system services | Local simplicity, connectivity, security |
| System administrators | Manage grid resources | Management tools | Balancing local and global concerns |

services and libraries to perform discovery, monitoring, and management of resources, to enhance security of transactions on the grid, and to perform more routine functions, such as file management. The expectation is that it will provide a substrate not only for collaboration among the science and engineering communities, but also for businesses and corporations. The effort was originally funded by DARPA but today is sponsored by several federal agencies as well as by corporations.

### 10.3.3  Comparison with Conventional Virtual Machines

In this section we try to highlight the similarities and differences between the concept of a grid and that of other virtual machines we have been describing in this book.

#### Efficient Utilization of Resources

The eventual goal for the first grid systems was the desire to put to use the idle cycles available on the hundreds of millions of computers in the world today. There are many fundamental problems that require a lot of computation power but whose solutions do not need the large, expensive supercomputers commonly employed for such problems. Harnessing the unused resources toward solving such large problems would be an efficient use of the world's computational resources. This is similar to the motivation that led to the development of system virtual machines and to multiprocessor virtual machines, including logical partitioning.

### Sharing of Resources

System virtual machines for both uniprocessors and multiprocessors support sharing of resources. However, unlike grid computing, the sharing in a conventional system VM is usually limited to the physical hardware resources — the VMM in such systems is typically not concerned with the sharing of content, for example.

A central concept in grid computing is the sharing of resources of disparate systems by a community of users working toward a common goal. The discovery of resources needed to solve a problem and the negotiation for use of such resources with their owners play a big role on a grid.

### Distributed Versus Centralized Control

Compared to traditional virtual machines, the grid has a global scope, with resources spread over large areas, perhaps across the world. Control of shared resources therefore cannot be done in any centralized manner. As with the Internet, users of a grid may collaborate with each other to determine appropriate sharing and use of resources. This is quite unlike a conventional virtual machine monitor, which must have a centralized view of resources and must maintain strict control over the use of resources in order not to compromise the privacy and security of users.

### Heterogeneous Nodes

Like operating systems, virtual machine monitors and hypervisors generally do not span nodes of a cluster. A VMM works best when it has the flexibility to reallocate virtual machines among a set of similar real processors. The components in a node may be somewhat dissimilar in terms of their sizes and perhaps in the nature of devices attached to them, but they are similar in terms of the ISA supported by the processors.

On a grid, the expected degree of heterogeneity in the types of components available is much higher. Each cluster could have a processor, memory, and I/O configuration quite different from other clusters on the grid. Moreover, the processors in a cluster could be running a different type of operating system or even a different ISA from those in other clusters. The set of programs that can be run on one cluster may be considerably different from the set that can be run on another. A program that performs a function on one cluster may be completely different from the program that performs the same function on another cluster. Such an environment will breed programs that may not directly specify the instructions needed to solve a problem, but will, rather, specify the function needed to solve the problem. The software infrastructure of the grid will assess the availability of various different types of nodes that could perform the function, choose the best cluster and node on which to run the function, and configure the appropriate program that must be run on that node.

### Adaptation of Applications

One of the requirements imposed on virtual machines in the past was the need to run applications unchanged. The fact that the application was running on a virtual machine, as opposed to a real machine matching an expected configuration, was unknown to the application. In system virtual machines this is true not only at the application level but also at the operating system level.

This level of transparency was not manifested in early examples of the grid. A case in point is the SETI@home project (Anderson et al. 2002), where the solution is tailored especially to the physical characteristics of the grid. In particular, the solution is aware of the latency of communication between nodes on the grid and breaks up the problem in such a way that a given computer can operate on one of the pieces for a sufficiently long time without needing to communicate with other computers on the grid. The solution also accounts for the potential unreliability of nodes on the grid by sending each problem chunk several times to different computers.

The hope is that someday these functions can be taken care of in the infrastructure of the grid so that the solution developer will need to be concerned only with the aspects of the problem at hand rather than the physical characteristics of the platform on which the problem is being solved. There are significant challenges in reaching that point, but efforts are already under way. One example is the development of libraries that will ease the porting of applications meant to run originally on message-passing clusters or on distributed shared-memory systems or even on tightly coupled SMP systems so that they can exploit the computational resources available on a grid (Foster and Karonis 1998).

### Portability of Applications

As noted in the discussion in Chapter 5 on high-level language virtual machines, there is increasing emphasis on enabling applications to be portable so that they can run everywhere. Thus applications are being written with portability in mind. Targeting applications to run on virtual machines, such as the Java virtual machine, rather than on processors with specific ISAs is a step in that direction. Enabling applications for the grid is another step in that direction.

Applications that can exploit not only heterogeneous system configurations but also heterogeneous ISAs are likely to be portable on a variety of platforms, possibly even those that emerge in the future. Further, the potential unreliability of components on the grid as well as the challenges of maintaining security and privacy on such an open structure could lead to the development of infrastructure for creating applications that produce the right results even under adverse circumstances.

### 10.3.4 Coming Full Circle: Implementing the Grid on Classic Virtual Machine Systems

The administration of the grid, as we have noted, involves several pieces of software, often referred to as *middleware*, that perform various operations, including those of allocating the available resources to tasks, scheduling the tasks, and ensuring security and privacy. Middleware supports the process level of abstraction, just as a traditional operating system supports processes. However, the analogy between the grid and an operating system should not be carried too far. For example, like an operating system, the grid has to perform user accounting; unlike the operating system, however, the grid relies on the accounting services provided by multiple administrative domains. Legacy jobs, ordinarily running under the accounting policy of a traditional operating system, may find an inconsistency in the manner they are dealt with because different administrative domains may employ different accounting policies.

An interesting solution to this multipolicy problem, proposed in Figueiredo, Dinda, and Fortes (2003), is to change the level of abstraction of jobs from the user process level to the full machine, which includes the hardware and the operating system. With this approach, the unit of work with which the grid middleware deals becomes a system virtual machine rather than a process. Accounting can now be done conveniently in a hierarchical manner — the operating system running on the virtual machine performs accounting in a traditional manner, while the grid accounts for the resources at the virtual machine level.

Utilizing the conventional system virtual machine as a unit for the grid is suitable from other points of view, too. It automatically addresses the two important aspects of a grid — isolation of jobs from each other and platform independence. Beyond these, it adds the important ingredient of environment flexibility. It is not necessary for the user application to be recast for an OS environment supported at some given node — the unit of work includes the full system environment in which the application executes. Let us examine these aspects in more detail.

- **User isolation:** As we saw in Chapter 8, system VMs were originally designed as an alternative to multiprogramming, with each user isolated from the physical system and from other users by running on a separate virtual machine. This feature of a system VM protects a user sharing resources with other users. This is of particular importance on a grid, where it may not be prudent to trust a provider of physical resources. Moreover, the forced user isolation in the system VM paradigm ensures greater system integrity. Compared to a typical multiprogrammed environment, it is less likely that the actions of a user on a virtual machine will either crash the system or bring down other users. Moreover, as discussed in Section 10.1.3, there is less likelihood that a malicious attack on a single user will compromise the security of the system as a whole.

- **Platform independence:** The platform independence that can be provided by a system VM also helps in its use for grid computing. For example, the user simply has to specify the hardware resources needed — for the most part, it is not necessary for there to be a physical system that matches the exact configuration specified by the user. Through various emulation techniques, such as those described in Chapter 8, the virtual machine monitor can virtualize those devices that do not physically exist. Also, it is not necessary to recompile or relink an application, because the virtual machine monitor ensures compatibility right up to the ISA level.

- **Task management and accounting:** There is a fundamental difference in the way resource control is managed in a virtual machine–based computing grid as compared to a more conventional grid. In process-oriented grid deployments, resource control must be managed for each process, similar to that in traditional multiprogramming systems. In the virtual machine case, the resource control is at a higher level of granularity, namely, at the virtual machine level. This higher granularity can simplify the job of allocating and accounting for resources both for the provider of the resources as well as for the user of resources. Moreover, this model fits better with the prevailing model in mainframe commercial computing, where charges are based on the specified performance of the system where an application runs.

- **Portability:** Portability of applications is a key requirement for a computing grid. A process-based grid and a system VM–based grid both emphasize portability, but they differ in philosophy over how it is implemented. In a process-based grid, the responsibility to ensure portability is left to the application programmer. This may mean, for example, writing the application for an environment supported on a large number of grid nodes. Alternatively, it may mean writing the application in a high-level language, such as Java, which is then supported on multiple nodes, perhaps with different ISAs. The system VM–oriented grid approach, on the other hand, allows an application to run on any platform that has a virtual machine monitor supporting the virtual machine specified by the application. This may even extend to applications on environments with different ISAs, the best performance for an application being given, of course, on a node that matches the ISA desired by the application.

Viewed from the Java computing model, the difference between the process-based grid and the system VM–based grid may be attributed to the nature of virtual machines supported. A node in a process-based grid implements a specific virtual machine environment, such as Java, and expects applications to be written for it. In the system VM–based approach, each node supports a range of virtual machines, especially those expected by the more common applications. Thus the former may have some advantages for new applications currently being written, while the latter is more likely the choice for the deployment of legacy applications on the grid.

In fact, the system VM–based grid could also be the solution to a thorny problem faced when trying to migrate an HLL VM, such as a Java VM, from one platform to another. In a Java VM, for example, it is probably not difficult to encapsulate the pure Java state of the applications and the libraries. But the typical JVM also has its own implementation state in native code and may be running native primitives or even user native code, all of which are difficult to encapsulate at the JVM level. Rather than migrate the JVM, it may be easier to raise the granularity of migration and to migrate the entire system in which the JVM resides. For example, the JVM could be running on a virtual machine with Linux as the host operating system. The encapsulated state of the virtual machine will then include not only the Java state but the rest of the state of the JVM implementation along with the state of the Linux environment. Various techniques outlined in Section 10.2, such as ballooning, could be used to reduce the size of the encapsulated module.

Figueiredo, Dinda, and Fortes (2003) identified three important aspects of a task in an system VM–based grid. The first is the ability to capture the state of a virtual machine, the second is the ability to instantiate a virtual machine either from scratch or from its state description, and the third is the ability to save user data. They point out that these three tasks do not necessarily have to be on the same machine. For example, the state of a virtual machine can be captured at the location where it is currently executing, but it may be resumed at a machine at another location, where the image is transported. This is similar in concept to the ideas embodied in the Collective (Sapuntzakis et al. 2002) and Internet Suspend/Resume (Kozuch and Satyanarayanan 2002), discussed in Section 10.2; many of the optimizations mentioned in connection with those schemes are applicable in this case too. Saving user data in a distributed file system allows the state encapsulation to be small, as already discussed in connection with Internet Suspend/Resume.

One can identify three different types of servers performing these three different functions for a system VM–based grid. The application is run on a virtual machine in a *computation server* (or VM host) whose virtual machine monitor has the capability to encapsulate the state of the machine at some checkpoint and make it accessible from other locations. When the virtual machine needs to be resumed, the image of the state encapsulated earlier is provided by an *image server.* Uniform access to data from any of the computation servers on the grid is facilitated by retaining the data on a *data server.*

The tools needed to manage the grid in such a heterogeneous server system are not much different from those required for the process-based grid, and one could use essentially all the basic infrastructure tools provided for this purpose, for example, by using the Globus toolkit mentioned in Section 10.3.2. Such tools are critical for the success of the system VM–based grid. They facilitate the functions associated with grid management, e.g., the scheduling of virtual machines, the migration of virtual machines, and the enforcement of service-level agreements. More importantly, they also allow users to specify the requirements of their jobs and allow providers to advertise the capabilities of the virtual machines they are willing to support, to bid on user tasks, and to monitor the usage of resources on their systems.

We end this section by reproducing a simple scenario from Figueiredo, Dinda, and Fortes (2003), which takes a fictitious grid (Figure 10.13) and illustrates ways in which many of the functions needed to instantiate a virtual machine on the grid can be performed with tools that already exist today.

1.  User $X$ accesses the grid and publishes his/her requirements using grid middleware on frontend server $F$. An information service is consulted that checks against the list of available physical machines matching $X$'s requirements and that can support a dynamic VM. Alternatively, the user may simply advertise his/her requirements and solicit bids from potential providers for the task.

2.  $X$ also consults the information service to determine an image server that could provide an image with the base operating system installation that meets the needs of the application. Alternatively, $X$ may itself provide a VM image containing a customized version of some operating system.

3.  A new virtual machine is instantiated at physical server $P$, using an image from image server $I$. The image can be transferred from $I$ to $P$ using an explicit command for transferring data, such as GridFTP (Allcock et al.

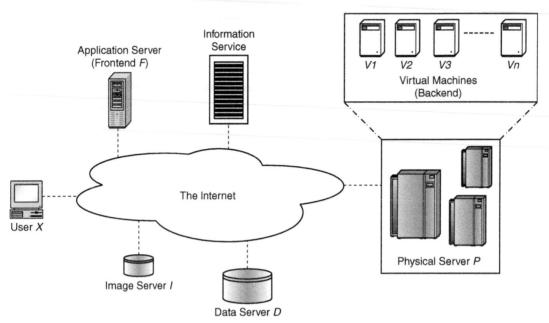

**Figure 10.13**   Example to Demonstrate Some of the Elements of a VM-Based Grid Service (Adapted from Figueiredo, Dinda, and Fortes 2003). *User X avails the services of frontend F and gets allocated a virtual machine Vi on physical server P. The virtual machine gets its image from image server I. The application gets its data from data server D.*

2001), or *P* can access the image through a distributed grid virtual file system.

4. The location of physical server *P* is made known to the user, who then utilizes a secure shell, e.g., OpenSSH (OpenSSH) or Globus GRAM (Czajkowski et al. 1998), to negotiate the start-up of virtual machine *Vi*. This virtual machine may be a new one that is booted up, or it may be an existing virtual machine, which is just being resumed from a saved image. The virtual machine instance *Vi* may also be assigned a dynamic IP address at this time, for example, using DHCP (DHCP). An interesting technique has recently been developed (Sunderaraj and Dinda 2004) that allows a virtual machine to keep its IP address even when it migrates from host to host.

5. Once VM instance *Vi* is running and connected to the network, additional data sessions may be established to connect the guest operating system within *Vi* to application server *A* and to user data server *D*. As before, these sessions can be realized with transfers, such as GridFTP, or implicit transfers through a distributed file system.

6. The application now begins executing under the guest operating system in virtual machine *Vi*. If it is a stand-alone batch application, the application

runs unattended and may inform the user only at completion. If it is an interactive application, the user interacts with the application either through a login session window or through a virtual display, such as VNC (Richardson et al. 1998).

In the foregoing, it was assumed that the user needs to interact only with the application. A more sophisticated user may be presented with a console for the operating system or even for the virtual machine itself. The user, rather than the grid scheduler, can then make decisions about when to shut down, hibernate, restore, or migrate the virtual machine. The mechanisms needed to perform these tasks are similar to those mentioned earlier, namely, file transfer mechanisms for efficient transfer between machines, distributed virtual file systems, and virtual networks.

The virtual machine, like a real machine, may persist even after completion of the application that initiated it. If it remains inactive for a sufficiently long period of time, the grid management system can place it in hibernation, saving its image on the shared file system, or in some other globally accessible space. When its services are required, the virtual machine is reawakened at any one of several possible computation servers, and appropriate changes are made to the handles used to communicate with the image servers and user display sessions that may be open. The virtual machine session ends only when there is no image of the virtual machine present on any of the image servers or in permanent storage anywhere on the system.

The importance of executing legacy applications should not be underestimated. The world is full of such applications, critical for businesses, either because it is difficult to migrate the applications to newer platforms or because the environments on which they run provide a capability not matched by the newer platforms. The high reliability and availability of the original IBM mainframes has been maintained through its evolution into the zSeries, which remains the workhorse of large commercial organizations. The VM-based grid computing system aims to serve a similar role for critical applications being designed today on a variety of platforms. Moreover, the system VM–based model has inherently attractive features, even for the deployment of new applications, as observed earlier. The techniques described in earlier chapters to ensure the correctness and efficiency of virtual machines may eventually find use in such grid implementations.

### 10.3.5 Concluding Remarks

Many of the scenarios mentioned in this section are also relevant for businesses, especially large corporations. Business-specific research and development often involve the use of massive amounts of data, large groups of internal and external collaborators distributed across a geographically wide region, and massive computational resources to perform analysis and mining spread across the globe. There is a feeling in some quarters that just as the Internet developed from a medium for collaboration among scientific researchers to a powerful medium for everyone, particularly for businesses, the grid concept is about to take off and become a vehicle that transcends the scientific community and embraces the business community and the world at large.

## 10.4 Summary

In the earlier chapters of this book we described various types of virtual machines that have been implemented over the years. VLSI process technology progressed so rapidly in the last couple of decades that processing power became relatively inexpensive and this may have caused some of the classic types of virtual machines to temporarily fall out of favor. This chapter suggests that new problems and new organizations for information processing are likely to cause resurgence in interest in such virtual machines. We focused our attention in this chapter on three applications. Security concerns in modern computing systems of all kinds are making headlines almost every day. The potential of virtual machines in protecting systems, both large mainframes and small portable devices, cannot be ignored. We have demonstrated examples of use of virtual machines in combating various types of security problems.

The use of virtual machine technology in the migration of whole computing environments from one hardware platform to another is proving to be of great importance in enterprise computing, where applications often run continuously for large periods of time, and where such migration may be necessitated due to hardware failures, power considerations, load balancing, or system upgrades.

We have also seen how virtualization techniques extend to the emerging concept of grid computing. Indeed, virtualization and virtual machine technology are poised for pervasive deployment in future computing systems of all types.

# Appendix A
# Real Machines

**M**any virtual machines present an interface essentially identical to that of some desired real machine. Furthermore, all virtual machines are implemented on top of some real machine; virtual resources are ultimately realized with real resources. In order to fully understand virtual machines, therefore, it is important to understand the major components of a typical computer system, including their interfaces and the corresponding resources that are managed through the interfaces. This appendix outlines the major computer system components, with emphasis on the ones most relevant to virtual machine implementations.

The discussion will begin with an overview of the three primary computer system hardware components: processors, memory, and I/O. Then we will discuss instruction set architecture (ISA) features and the ways in which the ISA can be used both to perform computation and to manage the hardware resources. Next, the organization of an operating system is described, with emphasis on managing system resources. We follow this with a discussion of the important aspects of multiprocessor systems. Finally, two specific ISAs, the PowerPC ISA and the Intel IA-32 ISA, are summarized; these two ISAs are used in examples throughout the book.

Over the years, many different computer architectures have been defined. As they have evolved, they have tended to take on similar characteristics, although there are still some significant variations among the architectures prevalent today. It is not practical to discuss all these variations here (or to cover them all in the book). We instead consider only typical architecture features that are relevant to our discussion of VMs. It is assumed that the reader has some familiarity with operating systems and the general concept of instruction set architectures (ISAs).

## A.1 Computer System Hardware

Figure A.1 illustrates a computer system typical of what one would find in a desktop system. Multiprocessor server organizations are overviewed in Section A.7. Both types of systems are composed of processor(s), memory, and I/O subsystems containing both high- and low-speed buses. The following subsections describe each of the three major components.

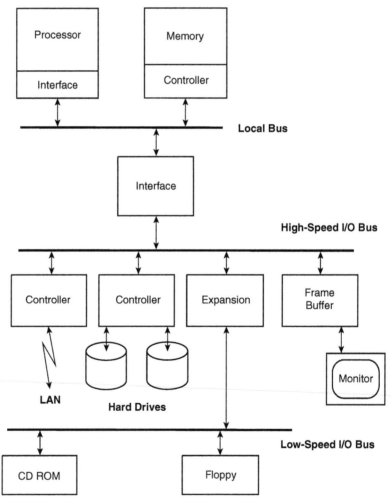

**Figure A.1** System Organization.

### A.1.1  Processors

Processors fetch and execute instructions held in memory. The various types of instructions and their operation are described in Section A.2. In this section, we briefly outline the more important types of processor microarchitectures.

Figure A.2a illustrates a simple in-order pipeline, where instructions pass through a series of stages as they are executed. The pipeline essentially performs its operations in assembly-line fashion. This allows multiple instructions to be in the pipeline at the same time, though at most one instruction is in each pipeline stage at any given time. In Figure A.2a instructions pass through the pipeline in their natural, architected program sequence (i.e., "in order"). They are first fetched and decoded. Then, when the input operands of instructions are ready, they are read either from registers or from memory, and the instructions are executed. Finally, instruction results are written to registers or stored in memory.

Some instructions depend on the results of preceding instructions; if the results are not ready as inputs when an instruction needs them, the pipeline must "stall" the instruction until the preceding instruction produces the result. If an instruction takes several cycles to produce its results, e.g., if it loads data from memory, then a following dependent instruction may suffer a number of stall cycles. It should be apparent that the sequence in which instructions appear and their data dependences influence the number of stalls and, therefore, overall pipeline performance.

Many high-performance processors use a superscalar microarchitecture, as shown in Figure A.2b. In a superscalar processor, more than one instruction can be fetched and decoded in the same clock cycle. Thus, the peak instruction throughput is increased when compared with the simple pipeline. After decoding, instructions are dispatched into an instruction issue buffer. From the issue buffer, instructions can issue and begin execution when their input operands are ready, without regard to the original program sequence; i.e. they can issue "out of order." This avoids many of the aforementioned pipeline stalls when instructions depend on preceding instructions.

A third class of processors, illustrated in Figure A.2c, can execute multiple instructions per cycle but only in the original compiled sequence. It is up to the compiler to arrange and combine multiple parallel (independent) instructions into a very long instruction word (VLIW). All the instructions in one VLIW issue before the next VLIW is considered for issuing. The in-order-VLIW approach simplifies the instruction issue logic, compared to an out-of-order superscalar processor, but it puts the burden of finding and reordering groups of independent instructions on the compiler rather than the hardware as in superscalar out-of-order machines.

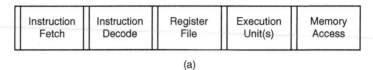

(a)

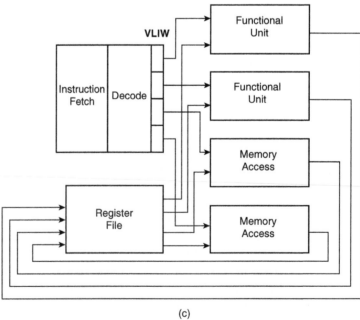

(b)

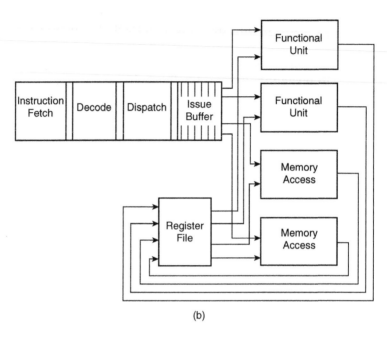

(c)

**Figure A.2** Three Processor Microarchitectures. *(a) Simple pipeline; (b) superscalar processor; (c) VLIW processor.*

### A.1.2  Memory Systems

The memory system of a modern computer consists of a combination of main memory and cache memories. The main memory is explicitly managed by the operating system, while cache memories are generally managed by hardware and hidden from software.

### *Main Memory*

Memory systems are built primarily from random-access memory (RAM) chips, organized so that multiple bits can be accessed in parallel. Usually, at least a word (four bytes) is accessed, but often it is a larger quantity, i.e. a *line* of 32 to 128 bytes. In most modern processors, the smallest quantity of main memory that can be uniquely addressed is the byte, and if there are $n$ real memory address bits, then the $2^n$ bytes form the *real address space*. Processor load and store instructions generate real addresses in a manner to be described in Section A.2.2. However, as seen in Figure A.3, all locations in the real address space do not necessarily correspond to RAM — some of the locations may correspond to addresses in a read-only memory (ROM), and

**Figure A.3**  Real Address Space. *A Real address space is often used for addressing RAM or ROM. Parts of the real address space may also be used for addressing I/O devices, or they may be unused.*

some others may not correspond to memory addresses at all. Of the addresses that do not correspond to memory locations, some may be reserved for I/O devices, as we will see later, and some may be unused, with no memory chips populating that region of the address space.

### Cache Memories

The amount of main memory needed in modern processors is quite large, and, including the delay in the memory controller and buses, accessing a location in such large memories takes many tens or even a few hundreds of processor cycles. In order to reduce the observed latency of accessing main memory, smaller, faster memories, called *cache memories*, are employed for holding both instructions and data likely to be accessed in the near future. Cache memories are designed around the principle of *locality*. This principle states that data or instructions that have been used recently are likely to be used again in the near future (*temporal locality*) or that data or instructions in locations close to locations currently being accessed are likely to be accessed themselves in the near future (*spatial locality*).

A cache memory holds *blocks* (or *lines*) of data and instructions that correspond to recently accessed main memory locations. At any given time, the cache memory holds a small subset of all main memory lines. In order to determine which main memory lines are located in a cache, the cache is designed to be *associatively* accessed — each cache line has an associated tag that indicates the main memory locations (addresses) from which the cache line came. Figure A.4 illustrates a *fully associative* cache, which is one of the easier cache

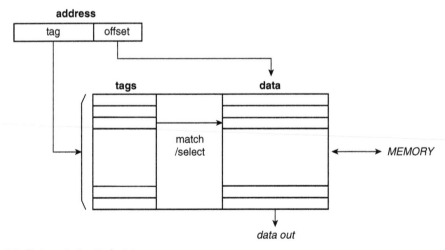

**Figure A.4**    A Fully Associative Cache Memory.

implementations to understand (although not necessarily the easiest to build). In the fully associative cache, a memory address is first compared with all the cache tags to see if the contents of the addressed memory location are present in the cache. If there is a *cache hit*, the data or instructions are read from the cache and are immediately available to the processor. If there is a cache miss, then the contents of the line must be fetched from memory and placed in the cache. To make room for the new line, some other line must be replaced, according to a *replacement algorithm*. Two commonly used replacement policies are least recently used (LRU) and first-in-first-out (FIFO). Temporal locality is exploited by using such a replacement algorithm, while spatial locality is exploited by the fact that a cache line typically holds more data items (e.g., words or bytes) than the one requested; that is, it contains data items that are in a block of contiguous locations adjoining or surrounding the accessed item.

## A.1.3  Input/Output Systems

In Figure A.1, we saw a typical system with its complement of I/O devices along with a variety of interfaces to these devices. This is typical of desktop systems. In comparison, server systems typically have fewer types of devices, although there may be more devices of certain types (e.g., disks), and the devices in such systems are connected using interconnections of much higher bandwidth.

An I/O system consists of a number of buses that connect the processor and memory to the I/O devices. These I/O buses are often standardized, so third-party vendors can manufacture new devices that immediately attach to the system. An example is the PCI bus in desktop systems. Most devices interface to the bus through a *controller*, and typical devices include disks, tapes (which are becoming less common), monitors, keyboards, etc. The bus serves as the conduit through which devices (or their controllers) are addressed and given commands and through which data is transferred between the processor or memory and the I/O devices.

There are four ways in which I/O is organized on a typical system. These are illustrated in Figure A.5. Each organization requires the OS to invoke an I/O operation in a distinct way.

- In *programmed I/O*, shown in Figure A.5a, the OS issues an I/O request over the I/O bus and then polls the device controller until the request is satisfied. In general-purpose systems, this method is not commonly used because it ties up the processor while the I/O operation is being performed.

- The second type of I/O is *interrupt-driven I/O*, shown in Figure A.5b, in which the processor continues with some other task after issuing an I/O

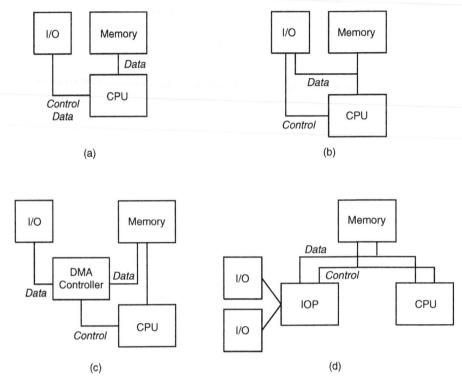

**Figure A.5** Different Types of Input/Output. *(a) Programmed I/O; (b) interrupt-driven I/O; (c) DMA-managed I/O; (d) IOP-based I/O.*

request. An interrupt from the I/O controller informs the OS about the status of the request, e.g., when it is finished. The granularity of control is still quite small: Every unit of data transferred between the controller and memory is controlled by the OS.

- The third type, *DMA-managed I/O*, shown in Figure A.5c, improves on the performance of interrupt-driven I/O by allowing the I/O controller to access memory directly. The controller can use a series of bus transactions to move large blocks of data to or from an I/O device and to interrupt the OS only when it completes the entire task. This I/O method is very commonly used for devices that transfer blocks of data, such as disks.

- The final type of I/O is a more sophisticated DMA-managed I/O method that uses *I/O processors* (IOPs), often referred to as *channels* in mainframe computers (see Figure A.5d). An IOP is a special processor that can execute software on its own and can therefore manage complex I/O transactions.

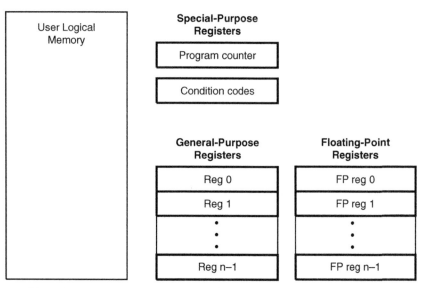

**Figure A.6**   Key Architected User State of a Typical ISA. *This includes a logical (virtual) memory space, a special-purpose register, general-purpose registers, and floating-point registers.*

The IOP gets its instructions from a program in memory set up by the OS. The OS and the IOP communicate through main memory. The IOP can buffer transactions for various devices and bundle them to make the best utilization of the available I/O resources.

## A.2   The User ISA: Computation

The architecture of a processor, in its basic form, typically defines a set of storage resources, e.g., registers and memory, and a set of instructions that transform data held in the registers and memory. The definition of the storage resources and the instructions that manipulate data are documented in the instruction set architecture (ISA) of the processor. In order to ensure software compatibility between various implementations of the ISA, it is necessary that the description of an instruction be detailed enough to specify the exact operations that must occur as a result of executing the instruction. The key elements of the architected storage visible to a user program are illustrated in Figure A.6. The user memory is the bulk of storage, yet it is the registers that are important for performing computation. The register state is more varied, both in format and function, than the memory.

### A.2.1 Register Architecture

In typical applications the registers that are primarily used are the general-purpose registers and a few of the special-purpose registers. The use of other special-purpose registers or specially typed registers, such as the floating-point registers, varies with the nature of the application.

#### General-Purpose Registers

These registers are often referred to as "working" registers. They are commonly used to hold operands for instructions. They are also used as temporary storage for intermediate values of complex operations and for frequently used constants or addresses. General-purpose registers often hold different types of values. For example, the contents of a general-purpose register may be a Boolean variable, a character variable, a string of characters, a halfword, a 32-bit integer, a 64-bit integer, or an address in memory. Occasionally a general-purpose register may have a special function, for example, as a stack pointer.

#### Typed Registers

It is often convenient to provide separate registers for special types of operations. For example, the PowerPC provides separate registers used as operands only for floating-point operations and are hence called floating-point registers. The IA-32 ISA provides a register type for holding pointers to segments of memory. Using multiple register types allows the hardware to be implemented more cleanly, with operands being located close to the functional units that perform the operation. However, in some cases, it can make the compiler writer's job more difficult because it requires keeping track of the register types that hold certain data items, and it may occasionally require movement of a data item to get it into the right register type.

#### Special-Purpose Registers

The most important of these is the program counter (PC). Other special-purpose registers include condition code registers, stack pointers, link registers, and loop count registers. Special-purpose registers often tend to be used implicitly by certain instructions; they may not be explicitly specified as operands in the instructions that manipulate them. This is often the case with link registers used by procedure branches or jumps. As another example, the Intel IA-32 ISA has a single register, EFLAGS, that holds implicitly set condition code bits along with a number of other status bits.

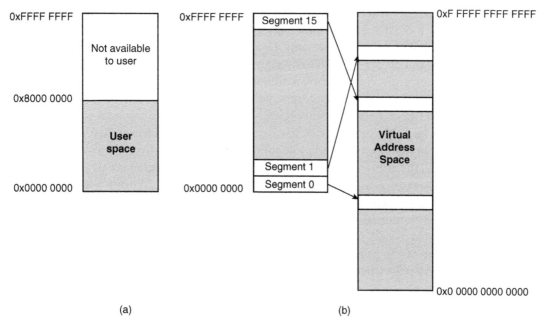

**Figure A.7**   Memory Architecture as Seen by the User. *(a) Linear addressing in MIPS R-series; (b) Segmented addressing in PowerPC.*

### A.2.2   Memory Architecture

From the perspective of application programs, the logical memory architecture is fairly straightforward. In some ISAs, main memory appears as a single linear address space. In other ISAs, main memory appears as a set of segments pointed to by typed segment registers containing their base addresses. The Intel IA-32, for example, is architected as a set of segments, though an OS is able to make it appear as a single linear space by placing identical values in the segment registers (as is done in both Windows and UNIX). The IA-32 memory architecture is summarized in Section A.8.2.

An example of a linear address space is the user-mode address space (*kuseg*), as defined in the MIPS 32-bit ISA and shown in Figure A.7a. The 2GB ($2^{31}$ bytes) user space starts at address zero, 0x0000 0000, and extends to address 0x7FFF FFFF. An address will typically be contained in a 32-bit register. The contents of such a register will be a valid address only if the high-order bit is 0. Any attempt to access memory with any other address causes an Address Error exception.

The PowerPC, on the other hand, divides the user address space into segments that each contain 256MB ($2^{28}$ bytes), as shown in Figure A.7b.

The architecture allows an application to address a large number of segments, even though at any one time only a small number are directly accessible. In the 32-bit addressing mode, only 16 segments are visible to the program. These 16 segments are pointed to by segment registers SR0–SR15. The segments that are currently visible form a contiguous 32-bit *effective* address space, with the high-order 4 bits of an address indicating the segment register associated with the address. Each segment register points to a 256MB segment contained in a very large $2^{52}$-byte address space called the *virtual* address space.

For management and protection, memory can be divided into regions. Typically, the granularity of a management/protection region is a page, containing a power-of-2 number of bytes; 4KB, for example. Within a user's address space, different pages may be marked as having different access privileges, e.g., some combination of read, write, and execute privileges. The application program is usually not concerned about the exact page size, however; it becomes aware of the page size only, for example, when a sequence of accesses crosses from a page where accesses are valid to one that disallows such an access.

### A.2.3 User Instructions

Instructions are the means for transforming data held in registers and memory. Table A.1 gives examples of various types of instructions. Instructions are usually classified according to the resources, specifically the storage elements and functional units, involved in their operation. Thus integer and logical operations generally involve the manipulation of general-purpose registers using integer arithmetic and logical units (ALUs); memory instructions involve main memory; and floating-point instructions involve floating-point registers and floating-point units. Besides these, there is a class of instructions that affect the flow of control of the program rather than the contents of data resources: the branch and jump instructions.

**Table A.1**  Example User Instructions

| Memory Instructions | Integer Instructions | Floating-Point Instructions | Branch Instructions |
|---|---|---|---|
| load byte | add | add single | branch |
| load word | compare logical | multiply double | branch if negative |
| store byte | exclusive-OR | multiply-add double | branch and link |
| store multiple | count leading zeros | convert to integer | jump to subroutine |
| load double | rotate left with carry | compare double | return |
| ..... | ..... | ..... | ..... |
| ..... | ..... | ..... | ..... |

### Memory Load and Memory Store Instructions

These instructions cause the movement of data from a register to memory (a store operation) or from memory to a register (a load operation). The memory location involved is specified in the instruction by means of its address. The address itself is a value derived from adding the contents of one or more registers specified in the instruction. Sometimes an immediate field (constant) in the instruction may be used in addition to register operands. The value thus computed is the address as seen by the user, often referred to as the *virtual address*, the *logical address*, or the *effective address*. An address in a segmented memory may be split into a portion that specifies the desired segment and a portion that specifies the desired offset within that segment.

### Integer Arithmetic, Logical, and Shift Instructions

These instructions perform basic operations on integer or general-purpose registers. In some of the older CISC[1] ISAs, an arithmetic, logical, or shift instruction may use a memory location as one (or more) of its operands. In this case the processor needs to perform an implicit memory load before performing the specified integer operation and/or an implicit memory store afterward. Most modern ISAs, especially RISC[2] ISAs, separate the process of loading an operand from memory from the process of performing the actual arithmetic, logical, or shift operation.

### Floating-Point Instructions

These instructions perform floating-point operations. The operands of the instructions are generally, but not necessarily, held in typed registers called floating-point registers. In the Intel IA-32 instruction set, the floating-point registers are arranged as a stack, and most floating-point instructions refer to the registers only implicitly via the floating-point stack pointer. The principal difference from integer instructions is that the values in the registers are interpreted to be in a specified floating-point format. The standard format is the IEEE floating-point format, which specifies not only the encoding of floating-point data but also the acceptable results of operations performed on floating-point data.

---

**1.** Complex-instruction-set computer.

**2.** Reduced-instruction-set computer.

### Branch and Jump Instructions

While the previous categories of instructions change the contents of the data-holding resources within the processor, branch and jump instructions simply change the flow of control. In stored-program machines, this change is accomplished by changing the PC, thereby changing the memory location from where the next instruction is to be fetched. Conditional branches test values in registers and branch based on the outcome. The register to be checked can be a general-purpose register or a special condition code register set as a side effect of executing other instructions. ISAs also include jump instructions, which are similar to branches, except they transfer control unconditionally[3] and are often used for transferring control to a logically different piece of code from the current one (e.g., to a subroutine or procedure). The targets of jump instructions are sometimes not known at compile time; hence jumps can take place indirectly through the contents of a register. Some jumps have the side effect of saving the location (PC value) of the instruction immediately following the jump in a *link* register. If a procedure is invoked using one of these jump and link instructions, a procedure return can be implemented as an indirect jump to the PC value saved in the link register.

## A.3  The System ISA: Resource Management

While the user portion of the ISA is primarily for getting computational work done, the system part of the ISA is for management of system resources. The operating system receives requests for accessing or altering resources and services them according to its own well-defined resource-management polices. The system ISA contains the actual mechanisms by which the OS communicates with the underlying hardware in order to carry out its requested services and resource-management decisions.

### A.3.1  Privilege Levels

A modern processor can simultaneously support multiple applications or processes, each of which has access to system resources, including real main memory, secondary memory, and other parts of the I/O system. Even though

---

**3.** This distinction between branch and jump instructions is not universal. Some ISAs use only one of the two terms, and others interchange their meanings.

many user programs may be operating on the machine at the same time, the use of resources by any user program should not be seen or affected by the use of the same or other resources by any other program, unless it explicitly grants this permission to the other program. This protection is made possible by the operating system, which also ensures that resources are allocated fairly among all user programs.

To do this, the operating system must enjoy certain privileges not normally extended to a user program. These privileges typically involve the allocation, accessing, and altering of physical resources within the system. Special privileges to system resources are permitted by defining modes of operation in the ISA. Certain resources can be made accessible in one mode and not in the others. Usually an ISA specifies at least two modes of operation, a *system mode*, in which all resources are accessible to software, and a *user mode*, in which only certain restricted resources are accessible. System mode is sometimes referred to as *supervisor mode, kernel mode,* or *privileged mode.*

Many operating systems (including UNIX and its derivatives) rely on only two privilege levels. On the other hand, the Intel IA-32 ISA supports up to four levels, shown in Figure A.8. Both Windows and Linux, when implemented on an IA-32, use only the innermost level, level 0, for the OS and level 3 for user applications.

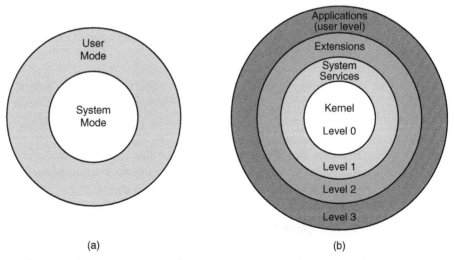

**Figure A.8**    Privilege Rings in a System. *(a) Simple systems have two levels of privilege. (b) Intel's IA-32 allows four rings, with the operating system kernel executing in the innermost level, level 0, and user applications executing in level 3.*

At any point in time the mode of operation is part of the system state, stored in a small special register or as part of a larger special register. When there are only two privilege levels in a system, the encoding of the mode requires just one bit. Modification of the mode bit(s) must be tightly controlled so that a user process cannot arbitrarily change the mode and thereby extend its privileges at will. A controlled change of the privilege level, for example, to perform I/O, is typically effected either explicitly via a system call instruction or implicitly through a trap. A system call instruction transfers control (changes the PC) to a special location specified by the ISA, and the OS is designed so that this location is part of the OS's code region. In addition to the control transfer, the privilege is automatically changed to system mode.

Some ISAs include instructions that behave differently depending on the current privilege level. For example, an instruction that modifies a privileged resource could be designed to perform no operation (act as a *no-op* instruction) if the processor is in the user mode. Thus a prohibited operation cannot be performed by the user. As described in Chapter 8, however, such instructions are problematic from the point of view of implementation of virtual machines; it is preferable for the hardware to transfer control of such illegal instructions to the operating system via a trap so that the OS can then take appropriate action.

In the following sections we briefly describe those parts of the architected state visible only to the more highly privileged operating system and then provide more detailed discussion of the way instructions in the system ISA are used for managing privileged hardware resources.

## A.3.2 System Register Architecture

Most ISAs include special registers to assist with the task of managing hardware resources. These registers are sometimes given only secondary importance because they are not exposed to the application and because the compiler usually does not use them. However, they are very important in system-level virtual machine implementations, because they often are the source of some of the thorniest problems that arise in the implementation of such VMs. Some of the more important registers are shown in Table A.2.

### System Clock Register

This register records the number of clock ticks that have elapsed from the last time the register was reset to zero. A clock tick may be measured either in time (milliseconds) or in processor clock cycles.

**Table A.2**    Typical System Registers

| System Registers | Examples in PowerPC | Examples in IA-32 |
|---|---|---|
| System clock register | Time base register | Model specific; time-stamp counter in newer models; clock in I/O system in older models |
| Trap and interrupt register | Data storage interrupt register Interrupt save/restore register | None, indirect through interrupt table |
| Trap and interrupt mask register | Machine state register | Interrupt enable flag in EFLAGS register |
| Translation table pointers | Storage description register Address space register | Page directory base address (control register 3) |

### Trap and Interrupt Registers

These registers record information about the occurrence of traps and interrupts so that trap or interrupt-handling code can take the appropriate action. Typically, for each trap or interrupt condition, there is a corresponding bit in the register that is set when the trap or interrupt occurs.

### Trap and Interrupt Mask Registers

There are situations when the processor should not be interrupted, for example, when another interrupt is already being handled. Interrupts are typically categorized into ordered classes, an interrupt belonging to a higher class having priority over an interrupt belonging to a lower class. At any given point in an execution the mask register specifies those classes of interrupts that will be ignored. Similarly, software may wish to ignore certain trap conditions, and the trap mask register indicates which should be masked off.

### Translation Table Pointers

The mappings of logical pages and memory segments to real memory are usually kept in memory resident tables, and the locations of these tables are pointed to by page and/or segment table pointer registers. Because the page/segment table pointer registers are used for managing hardware resources, access to them must be controlled. While in all cases the writing of these registers must be limited to the OS, in many cases user-privilege processes must be prevented from reading these registers as well. For example, reading a page table pointer register may reveal properties of other processes, and this can potentially contribute to security leaks. Also, as discussed in Chapter 8, reading resource-related registers in user mode is problematic when constructing system virtual machines.

### A.3.3 ISA Support for Managing the Processor Resource

The processor is perhaps the most important system resource, and, like the other hardware resources, its use is managed by the operating system. The ISA support required for doing this, however, is minimal. First, the operating system must be able to give control to a user process. This is done via a system-return instruction that causes the transfer of control (a jump) to the desired point in the user program and a privilege-mode change to user mode. Second, to make sure that it will eventually get back control from the processor, the operating system can set an interval timer so that when the time interval elapses, there will be an interrupt that returns control to the OS (interrupts are described in more detail in Section A.3.6). The interval timer may be an architected counter, i.e., one of the system registers that can be read or written in system mode. Or it may be built into the I/O system and can be read or written in a manner similar to the way an I/O device would be accessed (Section A.3.5). Control is also given back to the operating system when a user process executes a system-call instruction or when there is a trap or interrupt.

Hence, the only ISA features needed for managing the processor resource are system-call and return instructions and an interrupting interval timer, along with a mechanism for setting it. Other traps and interrupts are not necessary for managing the processor resource; rather, they are mechanisms by which the operating system can be put into a privileged state where it can deal with other resource-management conditions.

### A.3.4 ISA Support for Managing the Memory Resource

By far, the most extensive part of the system ISA is memory related. The memory architecture includes relatively elaborate data structures (page and/or segment tables) for keeping track of the usage of memory, along with mechanisms for manipulating the data structures. The key issue is that there is a limited amount of real memory that must be allocated to a number of programs, each of which has an (often larger) architected amount of logical memory. In general, this means that the real memory must be shared, and most of the time a given process cannot be given as much real memory as the size of its logical address space would allow.

The system ISA also provides a way of protecting the memory in use by one program from the others. That is, the ISA must be able to limit the access of a program to only those parts of memory to which it has been granted permission by the OS, whether to read it, write it, or execute instructions held in it. These mechanisms can also be used to protect a program from itself, in a sense.

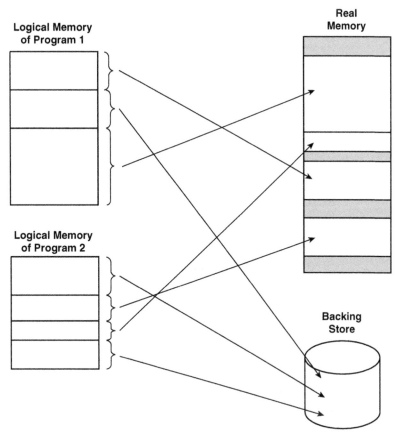

**Figure A.9** Logical-to-Real Memory Mapping. *Some regions of memory are mapped to real memory; others reside on a backing store, usually a disk.*

For example, parts of memory that hold instructions can be protected from being accidentally overwritten by a store instruction due to a program bug.

Figure A.9 illustrates the way real memory resources can be allocated to two programs, each with its own logical memory space. Some portions of each of the programs have real memory allocated to them, and other portions do not. Some of the portions of logical memory that are not assigned real memory have their contents held in a *backing store*, usually a disk. Other portions of the logical memory may be unused. The operating system keeps track of the portions of the logical memory space in main memory and in a backing store. The OS moves memory contents back and forth between real memory and the backing store based on its own internal memory-management policies. Thus, a particular real memory location could represent different logical memory locations at different points in time.

With this approach, program memory has become a *virtualized* resource. The user process can directly address memory resources that are defined by its own logical address space. However, this logical address space represents only a virtual view of memory. The actual real memory resources are assigned in a very different manner. It is for this reason that such a system is called a *virtual memory* system and that logical addresses are often referred to as *virtual addresses.*

For assigning logical memory to real memory, the respective memory address spaces are normally divided into blocks. There are two general approaches for doing this. In one, the blocks are of arbitrary size and are called *segments*. In the other, the blocks are all of fixed size and are called *pages*. Managing the real memory is simplified if the basic elements for management have the same fixed size, so just about all ISAs today use paging. However, as we saw in Figure A.7b, some ISAs add segments on top of paging. When this is done, each segment is composed of some number of pages.

When pages are used, a logical address can be interpreted as having two parts, a page number and an offset within the page. For example, if 32-bit addresses and 4KB pages are used, then the low-order 12 bits identify an offset within a page, and the upper 20 bits form the page number.

### Page Tables

To support logical-to-real memory mapping, a data structure known as the *page table* is used. An example page table that maps logical pages to real pages is shown in Figure A.10, with the page number of the virtual address used as an index into the table. Page table structures can get more complex, but the one shown is adequate for understanding the basic operations. Each entry in the table contains information about the real memory location of an accessed virtual page. When the virtual memory space is larger than the real memory space, as it often is, some of the virtual pages may not be mapped to real memory. Hence there is also a valid bit associated with each page entry to indicate whether or not the page is mapped. Note that the page table can also be used for data that is shared among multiple programs if the same real page is mapped into the virtual address spaces of the sharing programs.

As suggested earlier, in Section A.2.2, it is usually possible to restrict the type of access to a location in memory given to an application program. The granularity at which such access protection is specified is generally the page, and hence each entry in the page table also stores access-protection information. These are the "prot" fields in the page table of Figure A.10. The types of operations that can be performed on a page may be determined by a program's privilege level, e.g., whether it is in supervisor or user mode. The three types

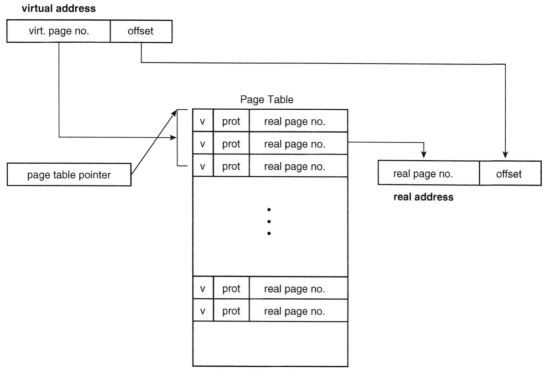

**Figure A.10** Page Table for Mapping a Linear Address Space.

of accesses that are commonly controlled are *read*, *write*, and *execute*. Read and write accesses are checked during execution of load and store instructions, while execute accesses are checked when instructions are fetched for execution. One way of specifying the access protection of a page is to provide three bits, each corresponding to the read, write, execute (R, W, E) privileges. Note that the access protection given to a page is not static. The same real page could have one set of protections when the machine is operating in the user mode and a different set when operating in the system mode.

### Translation Lookaside Buffers

The page table is a relatively large structure and is generally held in main memory. In theory, the page table is consulted for every load, store, or instruction fetch. Actually doing so, however, would be very slow. To make memory accesses much faster, a small associative memory structure called a *translation lookaside buffer* (TLB) is used for caching recent address translations, as

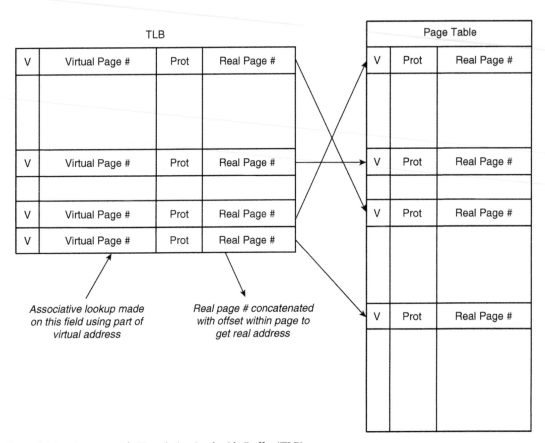

**Figure A.11**    Structure of a Translation Lookaside Buffer (TLB).

depicted in Figure A.11. The TLB is very much like the cache memory described in Section A.1.2 and similarly relies on the principle of locality. When an address needs to be translated, the TLB is accessed by associatively indexing it using the virtual page number of the logical address. On a match, the table returns the real page number for the referenced logical page. As the principle of locality suggests, the number of distinct pages referenced is typically small and changes slowly during the execution of the program. Thus the size of the TLB need not be large, and access to the TLB can be relatively fast. Each entry in the TLB also contains the page-protection bits copied from the page table.

There are three possibilities when a page address is presented to the TLB.

- It matches a TLB entry, and the protection associated with the entry permits the type of access being requested; i.e., there is a *TLB hit*. This is the common case, and the address is correctly translated to a real address. In many microarchitectures, a cache memory access proceeds in parallel with the TLB access, so there is little, if any, performance penalty due to the address translation process.

■  It could match an entry in the TLB, but the protection bits do not allow the requested access type. In this case, an access exception is generated, and there is a trap to the operating system.

■  There may be no entry with a matching virtual page number. This is referred to as a *TLB miss*. There are two reasons a reference can miss in the TLB. The first is that a mapping exists for the address in the page table but not in the TLB. The second reason is that the referenced page is not currently mapped to any page in real memory. In the first case, either the hardware or the operating system copies the mapping from the page table into the TLB, making room, if necessary, by deleting some older TLB entry. In the second case, an addressing exception is generated, and there is a trap to the operating system. The operating system uses a page-replacement algorithm to replace one of the existing real pages in memory with the requested page from the backing store. In doing so, it may have to rewrite the contents of the replaced page to the backing store if the page was modified while it was in real memory.

### Page Table and TLB Interaction

Both the page table and the TLB are important parts of the address-translation process, and their use involves the interaction between hardware and software. The actual architected interface between hardware and software may occur at either the page table or the TLB, depending on the ISA. If the TLB is defined in the ISA, then the actual implementation of the page table is done in software as part of the operating system. If the page table is defined as part of the ISA, then the TLB is part of the hardware implementation and is largely transparent to the software. In the latter case, occasionally the ISA may provide a "purge TLB" instruction that makes the TLB less than completely transparent. The two alternatives are shown in Table A.3.

With an architected page table, the ISA defines a specific method for mapping virtual addresses to real addresses as well as a specific format for each page table entry. The page table itself usually resides in memory, and the page table pointer register indicates the base (first entry) of the page table. If an accessed virtual page is not present in the page table, i.e., if the valid bit is false, a page fault is generated and control is transferred to a special location defined in the ISA that contains the routine to handle the fault (part of the OS). The ISA

**Table A.3**    Architected TLB Versus Architected Page Table

|  | Architected TLB | Architected Page Table |
|---|---|---|
| *TLB entry format* | Defined in ISA | Left to hardware implementation |
| *TLB configuration* | Defined in ISA | Left to hardware implementation |
| *Page table entry format* | Left to OS implementation | Defined in ISA |
| *Page table configuration* | Left to OS implementation | Defined in ISA |
| *Miss in TLB* | Causes TLB fault to OS | Hardware accesses page table |
| *Miss in page table* | Detected by TLB fault-handling software | Causes page fault |
| *New entry in TLB* | Made by OS | Made by hardware |
| *New entry in page table* | Made by OS | Made by OS |

also specifies where the system should save information regarding the accessed page. For example, the address that caused the fault may be placed in a special ISA-defined control register.

With an architected TLB, the ISA defines the specific method format for TLB entries as well as the size and access method. The page table is part of the OS implementation. The hardware implementation is unaware of the page table's presence. There are special instructions in the ISA that allow the operating system to read and write TLB entries. If an address is not in the TLB, then the hardware undertakes an action similar to a page fault; i.e., it saves the faulting address in a special control register and traps to an ISA-defined memory location. The operating system checks its page table, accesses the page from secondary storage if necessary, and, when the page is present in real memory, updates the TLB with relevant information.

For a more detailed description of address translation issues, the interested reader is referred to an article by Jacob and Mudge (1998).

### A.3.5   Managing Input/Output Resources

Typically, the part of an ISA dealing with I/O is relatively small. Because of the wide variety of I/O devices and relatively infrequent I/O management operations, it is more appropriate to deal with the specifics of I/O in software, particularly in the OS software. The ISA needs to provide only a mechanism for addressing I/O devices and to transfer information to and from the devices.

Some ISAs have explicit *I/O instructions*. These instructions usually have a form similar to load and store instructions, but the addresses are completely separate from main memory addresses. The address indicates a specific device (or a register that is part of the device controller). The execution of an I/O instruction causes signals leaving the processor to be activated in a pattern that corresponds to the address and/or data values of the I/O instruction. The system designer is responsible for using these signals to connect I/O devices (e.g., through a bus) and to inform an OS programmer of the I/O signaling conventions. The IBM System/360 and its successors, as well as the Intel IA-32, are examples of computers that provide such I/O instructions in their ISAs.

Many recent processors incorporate another form of I/O, called *memory-mapped I/O*, sometimes in addition to I/O instructions. With memory-mapped I/O, a specific region of the real memory address space is reserved for accessing I/O devices (see Figure A.3). These addresses do not correspond to real memory locations; rather, loads and stores directed to these addresses are interpreted by the memory controller as commands sent to an I/O device. Different memory-mapped locations are used for sending commands to different devices and for different types of requests to the same device.

In order to protect I/O resources in general-purpose computer systems, I/O instructions are usually privileged and can only be invoked by the operating system. Similarly, with memory-mapped I/O, the real memory addresses used for I/O are never mapped to user-accessible pages, so only the OS has access to them. Because I/O operations are only available to the OS, user programs invoke OS calls that first check to make sure the user program should be able to make the requested access and then use I/O instructions to complete the request.

Finally, interrupts are a part of most I/O architectures. They are used by the I/O system to get the attention of the OS by forcing a transfer of control into OS interrupt handler code. The I/O system may interrupt the OS when it is finished with some requested I/O operation or when there is some condition, such as a device error, that requires attention. Interrupts are discussed in more detail in the next subsection.

### A.3.6  Traps and Interrupts

Traps and interrupts are an important mechanism for transferring control to the operating system when events needing special attention occur. Because they often involve changing the privilege mode and crossing protection boundaries, they are an important consideration in virtual machine implementations.

A *trap* is a transfer of control that occurs as a side effect of an instruction's execution. Traps are generally triggered by an *exception* condition, which is typically an unusual condition detected during the execution of an instruction. Examples of exception conditions include arithmetic overflows, page faults, violations of memory-access privileges, and illegal or unimplemented opcodes. The ISA usually specifies the exception conditions associated with each instruction.

*Interrupts* occur due to conditions unrelated to the execution of a specific instruction. Interrupts are caused by events occurring external to the process currently executing. Examples of such external events include I/O interrupts, which occur due to events outside the processor, and timer interrupts, which signal the end of a time interval specified by the operating system.

As described in Section A.3.2, the ISA generally provides a mechanism for disabling certain traps or classes of traps. The usual way to accomplish this is through the use of bits held in a mask register. Not all traps can be disabled, however. For example, it makes little logical sense to disable a page fault, and hence there is usually no mask bit associated with a page fault. Also, some traps may be disabled in user mode. For example, an application may not want any special action to be taken if some arithmetic operation causes an overflow. Other traps, for example, a trap to indicate a memory-access violation, may be masked only in system mode. Often two different mask registers are used, one of which can be written only in supervisor mode and the other which can be written in any mode.

If an exception condition occurs, the corresponding trap bit held in the trap control register is set. If the mask bit corresponding to this trap is set, the trap is disabled and hence no special action is taken. If the mask bit is not set, a sequence of events follows.

**1.** Instruction execution temporarily ceases and the processor places itself in a "precise" state with respect to the trapping instruction:

- All instructions prior to the trapping instruction are completed and make all their specified register and memory modifications.

- Depending on the specification in the ISA, the instruction causing the exception either completes, as in the case of overflow exceptions, or does not cause any change of state, as in the case of page faults.

- None of the instructions following the trapping instructions modify the process state (registers or memory) in any way.

**2.** After a precise state is achieved, the program counter of the executing program is saved in an ISA-specified location, either in a control register or in a special memory location. Some or all of the registers (both general-purpose and control registers) may also be saved by the hardware implementation.

Modern RISC processors leave the job of saving registers to the trap- or interrupt-handling software.

3. The processor is placed in a privileged mode and control is transferred to a memory location that is specified as part of the ISA. Ordinarily, this location is in the operating system, so at this point the OS gains control of the processor.

4. The operating system saves any remaining critical parts of the state of the trapping process that have not already been saved by hardware, e.g., the registers.

5. The OS code at this point may directly handle the trap, or it may analyze the situation further in order to determine the address of the code that specifically handles the trapping condition. This trap-handling code may be OS code, or in some cases, as in arithmetic overflows, it may be user code. In those cases where the user process has defined a trap handler, the OS passes control back to the user trap handler.

6. After trap handling has been completed, the OS (or user trap handler) restores the process's precise state, which had been saved earlier, and jumps back to the location in the user program that caused the exception.

Constructing the precise state of the system at the time of the exception is a way of ensuring deterministic behavior of the program. This requirement, however, introduces significant complexity in most implementations of an ISA, including VM implementations. Some ISAs relax this requirement for certain types of exceptions. For example, the PowerPC does not require precise state to be produced in the case of floating-point exceptions under normal operation. For debugging purposes, however, it does provide a mode in which these exceptions are precisely reported.

ISAs also provide instructions whose principal function is to give control to the operating system via a traplike mechanism. Like branches, such traps may sometimes be conditionally invoked. One important type of explicit trap is invoked by the *system-call* instruction. A system-call instruction is executed when a program needs some service from the operating system, e.g., an I/O operation. The actions taken during a system-call-invoked trap are similar to those described earlier; the main additional feature is that the user may specify arguments and parameters in registers or in a block of memory so that the operating system knows exactly what service is requested. This specification is not part of the ISA but part of the application binary interface (ABI) of the system.

Interrupts are treated in a manner similar to traps. The precise state of the processor must be produced in the case of an interrupt. However, because the interrupt is externally caused, there is some flexibility in an implementation regarding the exact point at which the currently running process is stopped and control returned to the operating system.

Interrupts, like traps, can also be disabled through mask bits held in a special control register. Masking interrupts is useful because there are times when the system software is unable to cleanly handle the interrupt condition. Such a situation arises, for example, when another interrupt has just occurred and software is still in the process of handling it. Masks can also be used to help establish priorities of interrupt conditions; lower-priority interrupts can then be masked off by high-priority interrupts. As in the case of traps, certain interrupts related to the real environment of the processor, such as a "power fail" interrupt or a "high-temperature" interrupt, are not maskable, for they need immediate attention. Most other interrupts related to I/O are maskable.

## A.4 Operating System Organization

Operating systems are complex pieces of software that are responsible for managing system resources and for handling requests from programs for services utilizing the resources. A typical OS is divided into major components that handle processor scheduling, memory management, and I/O. Figure A.12 shows the major blocks of the Linux operating system with its various interfaces, including the system-call interface and the device-driver interface. The following subsections describe the ways an OS manages the major system resources.

### A.4.1 Processor Management

The operating system time-multiplexes a computer system's processor(s) among several processes that may be active in the system. It does this using a scheduling algorithm, often based on priorities, that determines which processes should run and for how long. The scheduler maintains a ready queue that holds information regarding processes that are ready to run. When a processor becomes available, the scheduler selects a process from the ready queue, sets the interval timer according to the amount of time the scheduler decides it should have, and jumps to the process.

If the application process generates an enabled trap condition or performs a system-call instruction, control is given back to the OS. Otherwise, the interval timer will expire, and there will be an interrupt to the OS. In the event of a trap, the OS will invoke the appropriate trap handler (or may terminate the process). If there is a system call or some other condition that requires service from the OS, e.g., an I/O request or a page fault, the OS will set up the needed

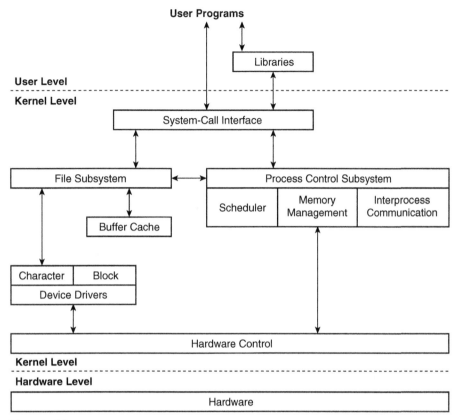

**Figure A.12**   Linux Architecture.

I/O operation and remove the process from the ready queue. When the service completes, e.g., when an I/O device completes its operation, an interrupt is generated, and the OS puts the process back on the ready queue.

### A.4.2  Memory Management

Memory management involves the sharing of real memory among the processes running on the system. The memory manager interacts between the hardware and the user process via the page table and/or TLB, as described earlier, in Section A.3.4. When a process generates a page or TLB fault, the OS takes over and either updates the TLB from the page table if the TLB is architected or handles the fault by scheduling a disk I/O operation to the backing store in order to retrieve the page. In many cases, the OS also prefetches a number of adjacent pages and keeps them in a buffer cache in anticipation of their immediate need.

The OS relies on the locality principle and attempts to give each running process those pages that are actively being used, also referred to as its *working set*. Good page-replacement algorithms, for example variations of the least-recently-used (LRU) algorithm, help to control the number of page faults incurred by a process.

### A.4.3 Input/Output Management

As noted earlier, an operating system abstracts most of the details of hardware devices and makes these I/O devices accessible through well-defined interfaces. As shown in Figure A.13, there are really two major interfaces that come into play when an application invokes an I/O service. The service is invoked using a system call, which transfers control to the operating system. The operating system itself uses an interface to a set of software routines that convert generic hardware requests into specific commands to hardware devices. This layer is referred to as the *device driver layer,* and the interface to this layer is through device driver calls.

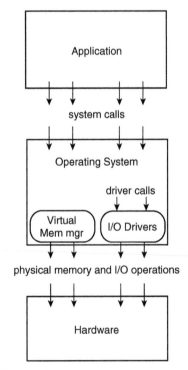

**Figure A.13** Interfaces Are Related to I/O Operation.

The device driver approach is the common technique for conducting inter-actions between the operating system and a hardware device. The device driver takes care of device-specific aspects of performing an I/O transaction. For example, when a file system uses a block-device interface to write to a disk, the device driver converts a device-independent request to appropriate requests specific to the type of disk controller chip that is physically attached to the system. These specific requests are then conveyed to the I/O device via I/O instructions or memory-mapped loads and stores.

There are two types of device drivers in Linux, character device drivers and block device drivers. Character device drivers communicate directly with the user program, with no buffering in between. A terminal is an example of a character device driver; communication between the device driver and the hardware is performed a character at a time. In contrast, the communication between the driver and the hardware is at a much higher granularity in the case of block device drivers, like those for disks. In this case, user programs access information through an area reserved for the transfer of a block of data.

## A.5 The Operating System Interface

We now consider ways in which running processes request service or manage-ment functions from the operating system. To do this, we focus our attention on interfaces 2 and 3 depicted in Figure 1.4. Combined with the user-mode portion of the ISA, these two interfaces form the ABI and the API. The ABI is of most interest because it is the direct interface into the OS. However, the API is also of interest because most user programs access the ABI only through calls to the libraries that make up an API.

Many of the functions specified in an ABI involve the management of hardware resources by the operating system. As discussed earlier, entry into the operating system can occur either through traps and interrupts or through a system-call instruction. The abstraction of traps and interrupts in the ABI is commonly referred to as a *signal*, to be described in Section A.5.4. An example of a system call in the Linux operating system as it is invoked through an API is shown here:

```
# include <syscall.h>
extern int syscall(int, ...);
int file_close(int filedescriptor)
{
    return syscall(SYS_close, filedescriptor);
}
```

The first argument in a system call is a unique identifying number. The Linux kernel uses this number as an index into a table of system-call entry points. Each entry in the table points to the location where the specified system call resides in memory, along with the number of arguments that should be passed to it. The number of arguments supported by a system call in the ABI often depends on the ISA. On Intel's IA-32 architecture, for example, the number of hardware registers available limits the number of arguments to five, in addition to the first argument, which is the system-call number. However, a register can point to data structures in main memory that hold additional argument-related information. Different system calls can be categorized by the nature of the hardware resource they manage. We next describe these categories along with some examples from the Linux operating system.

### A.5.1 Process-Management System Calls

This class of system calls either helps create new processes, terminate processes, or manage various aspects of processes running on the system. A Linux fork() system call, for example, creates a new process, called a *child process*, that is an exact copy of the parent process except for its identifying process ID number. An exec() system call (or one of its several variations) is used to load and execute a program in the current virtual address space. So starting a new process generally involves a fork immediately followed by an exec. A process continues execution until it terminates either voluntarily, through an exit() system call, or involuntarily, by receiving a signal (to be discussed later). The parent process can determine whether a child process has terminated using the wait() system call. Other process-related system calls include sleep(), which can be used by a process to voluntarily relinquish use of the processor for a specified time, or wakeup(), which supplies a signal to wake up a sleeping process. There are other system calls, such as setpriority() and getrusage(), that either set parameters of a process or provide information about the resources being used by the process.

### A.5.2 Memory-Management System Calls

Each process is provided with its own virtual address space, which the OS manages. Even though the virtual address space belongs to the user process, the management of the space is largely controlled through the operating system. The user may request a block of memory, for example, by using the malloc() API routine, which employs sophisticated algorithms to make optimum utilization of the address space. The malloc() call actually invokes a system call, sbrk(), to ensure that the size of the data region, also referred to as the *heap*, is sufficiently large to perform the allocation successfully. The user invokes another library routine, free(), which frees the region pointed to by an argument in the call. The user can also change the protections of a set of pages in its space using the mprotect() system call. For example, an application that wishes to protect itself from writing over a region of data could invoke mprotect() on the page containing the data and designate that page RO (read-only).

Multiple processes that need to communicate with each other often do so by sharing sections of memory. System calls such as shmget() allow a memory segment in the virtual address space of one process to be mapped in the virtual address space of another process. That is, both processes map the same memory regions in their page tables.

### A.5.3  Input/Output System Calls

A program running under the control of an OS does not invoke the routines in the device driver directly; rather, it makes a device-independent request such as open() or read() through a system-call interface. The separation of the responsibilities of the operating system from the device driver, as shown in Figure A.13, enables the addition of new devices to a computer system without changing the operating system.

User programs in Linux communicate with the kernel using generic filesystem commands such as open(), read(), write(), and close(). The open() command associates a file descriptor with a device that has been installed in the system with a file-system name like /dev/abc. A program called the Virtual Filesystem Switch registers the device and enables the mapping of the read() request, for example, with the appropriate routine in the device driver associated with /dev/abc, as shown in Figure A.14.

### A.5.4  Signals: Abstracting Exception Conditions

An ISA supports traps and interrupts, as described earlier. In Linux and other UNIX systems, these are made available to a process via a set of *signals* that are delivered asynchronously to an application through *signal handlers*. Default signal handlers defined by the system take some default action on

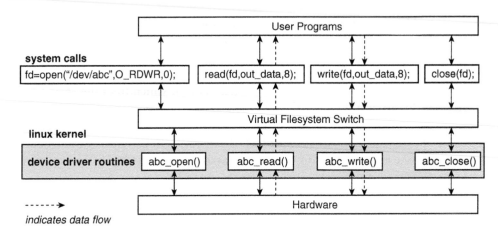

**Figure A.14**   Linux I/O Programming Interface.

receipt of a signal. The default action may stop the process, may terminate the process, perhaps with the generation of a core (memory) dump, or may ignore the signal. However, the application program can override the default action through the use of the sigvec() system call. If the application program decides to take specific action, it invokes a *signal handler*, which specifies the action. Almost any signal can be ignored by the process. The only exceptions are the SIGSTOP and SIGKILL signals — these signals provide a way for the user or the system to stop or terminate a runaway process.

There are two ways in which a signal gets *posted* to a process. It may be due to a hardware trap or interrupt, or it may be generated in software by another process, for example, through the kill() system call. Like hardware interrupts, signals may be masked by a process. If a signal arrives and it is in the masked set, it gets recorded in a list of pending signals, but no action is taken until the signal is unmasked. A signal can be added to the masked list using the sigblock() system call, while the entire set of masks can be set together using the sigsetmask() system call. Normal execution is resumed after a signal has been handled by using the sigreturn() system call.

## A.6  System Initialization

An often-overlooked aspect of an ISA is system initialization, beginning with power-up or system reset to the point at which an application program is ready to run. However, this is an important aspect to be considered in the design of system virtual machines, because these exact operations have to be reproduced whenever a new guest system VM is brought to life by a host.

The term used to describe the process of initializing the system is *bootstrapping* (the system lifts itself up by its bootstraps). Bootstrapping involves a series of actions, each action bringing to life a capability that allows the next action to be performed, until eventually the entire system is brought to life. The process of bootstrapping is a highly privileged operation because it involves the initialization of many important resources in the system. Here is a brief chronology of the actions that take place during a system initialization.

1. A processor "reset" is activated through a pin or a signal that enters the processor.

2. Some of the architected resources are loaded with ISA-defined initial values. For example,

   ▪ The program counter is set to an initial value, e.g., all zeros.

   ▪ Control registers are set to initial values so that initial program execution can proceed; for example, all traps and interrupts will be masked off.

   ▪ Page translation is turned off. (It will be turned on as part of the software initialization process.)

   ▪ Some, possibly all, of the general-purpose registers are set to initial values. Since addresses to memory locations are computed using values in registers, registers have to be loaded in order to gain addressability to memory.

3. Instruction fetch begins at the initial location stored in the program counter. This location usually contains a hardwired set of instructions. Typically these instructions are in a block of read-only memory referred to as the *boot ROM*. The code contained in the boot ROM is small and is just sufficient to initialize a boot device from which more code can be brought in. This device may be a tape reader or a floppy disk or the first track of a hard drive.

4. Initializing code is brought in from the boot device and executed. The execution of this code allows other critical aspects of the system to be initialized. For example, the keyboard and monitor are enabled. This code is also able to access larger storage areas, most importantly, a hard drive (or other device) that contains the operating system.

5. The operating system is loaded, and control is transferred to it.

6. The operating system initializes various internal tables, turns on page mapping, locates other I/O devices by activating the I/O buses, performs a cursory check of the file system, and prompts the user to log in.

7. The system is now ready for running an application program.

Some interesting aspects of the boot process follow.

- It is becoming common to initialize network connectivity early in the process of bootstrapping so that the rest of the initialization proceeds using data and code from a remote system.

- With increases in ROM density, many of the functions that were loaded from floppy disks or CD-ROMs can be accommodated in the boot ROM.

- Many systems also perform a self-test early in the bootstrapping process to ensure that critical hardware elements are functioning properly.

## A.7 Multiprocessor Architecture

Computers are generally capable of handling multiple processes simultaneously. Uniprocessors achieve this through a technique called *multiprogramming*. In multiprogramming, only one process runs on the processor at a specific point in time. The appearance of parallel execution of processes is achieved by running each process for a maximum period of time, typically around 10 msec. At the end of this "time slice," the processor state is saved in memory, and the context of another process is brought into the processor's registers. Thus there is a performance degradation of a process due to this sharing of resources with other processes, though this degradation can be reduced by scheduling the context switch at points in the computation where the process would have to wait for some external event such as I/O. Figure A.15a shows the multiplexing of processes in a conventional uniprocessor multiprogrammed system with a single hardware processor and operating system. The multiple user processes run on the same OS, which time-multiplexes the processor and other hardware resources among these processes.

Multiprocessors, on the other hand, employ multiple processors to achieve parallel execution of processes. The multiplicity of program counters, hardware registers, execution units, caches, and sometimes even memory are used to handle multiple processes. If each process is designed to run on a single processor, there is no degradation of performance of the process as a result of executing other processes on the other processors. However, there are programs that are designed in such a way that the multiple processes running on

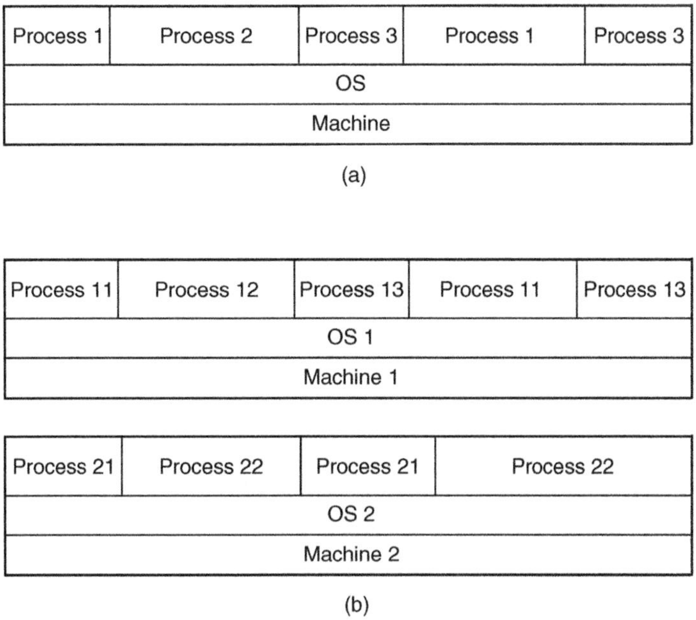

| Process 1 | Process 2 | Process 3 | Process 1 | Process 3 |
|---|---|---|---|---|
| OS | | | | |
| Machine | | | | |

(a)

| Process 11 | Process 12 | Process 13 | Process 11 | Process 13 |
|---|---|---|---|---|
| OS 1 | | | | |
| Machine 1 | | | | |

| Process 21 | Process 22 | Process 21 | Process 22 |
|---|---|---|---|
| OS 2 | | | |
| Machine 2 | | | |

(b)

**Figure A.15**   Comparison of Activity over Time in a Multiprogrammed System and a Clustered Multiprocessing System. *(a) In multiprogramming, several tasks or processes running under a single operating system are multiplexed in time. (b) In multiprocessing, the processes are distributed among multiple processors; however, the number of operating systems cannot exceed the number of processors.*

the different processors need to communicate with each other, for example, to share data values or to signal events. The performance of the program is often determined by the efficiency of implementation of this communication.

Further parallelism in execution can be obtained by implementing multiprogramming on each of the processors of a multiprocessor system, as shown in Figure A.15b. The figure illustrates the case where an operating system and its application processes are dedicated to a specific processor in the multiprocessing system. It is also possible to design the multiprocessor with just one operating system that controls the allocation of processes to processors. In this case, a process may run on one processor at one time and on another at another time.

Historically, many systems have been designed around a single processor, and such uniprocessor systems remain an important system class. Today, however, multiprocessors are in widespread use as servers and are well on their way to becoming commonplace for high-end desktop computing. For server implementations, multiprocessor systems with large main memories, disk systems, and high-bandwidth network facilities provide important economies of scale as well as improved opportunities for balancing resources among a large number of simultaneously active application programs. System software employs systemwide data structures for managing processor, memory, and communication resources. When an application thread is initiated, system software assigns it resources from the pool of available processors, and, as it runs, system software provides it with memory, disk, and communication resources.

### A.7.1 Types of multiprocessing

There are two main paradigms for supporting multiprocessing: *clustered computing* and *shared-memory multiprocessing*. In many server environments, e.g., Web or database servers, the individual application processes are often independent of each other. This type of workload works well on clustered systems, where the hardware associated with each processor, including the memory and sometimes the disks, is separated from the hardware of other processors on the system. System software in this case typically consists of different copies of an operating system running on each processor, as shown in Figure A.15b.

There are other multiprocessor applications where a single program actually consists of a number of closely cooperating parallel processes. Many scientific and engineering applications are multithreaded in this way, as are compute-intensive commercial applications such as data mining. Many other commercial database applications also are structured with multiple processes sharing data, and they are best implemented on a multiprocessor system with a single operating system. The operating system manages the memory in the system as one large structure shared symmetrically among all the processors and hence the name *shared-memory processing*, or SMP. The shared memory acts like a bulletin board and may be used either to pass data values from one process in the system to another or to signal the occurrence of an event to other processors that may be waiting for that event to occur. Reliable management of this communication of data and events needs special synchronization primitives to be supported by the ISA. The two types of multiprocessor systems are illustrated in Figure A.16.

There also are systems that are hybrids of the clustered and shared-memory forms of multiprocessing. For example, *distributed shared memory* (DSM) systems are implemented like clustered systems but are capable of supporting a single operating system image across the multiple processors. It is hard to achieve as low a latency of communication on such a system as on a shared-memory system. A lot of research has been conducted in this area, and several different hardware and software techniques have been proposed to improve or hide the communication latency. But this form of computing did not gain

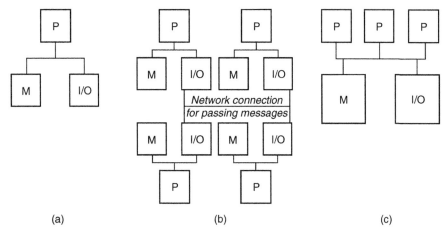

**Figure A.16**  Comparison of Uniprocessor and Two Common Multiprocessor Systems. *(a) Uniprocessor; (b) message-passing multiprocessor system; (c) shared-memory multiprocessor system (P = processor, M = memory).*

popularity, possibly because of the high sensitivity of the performance of applications to the way the algorithms are written and data structures are laid out in memory.

On the other hand, a different type of hybrid appears to be emerging as an important player — *SMP clusters*. Many server systems today are clusters of nodes, where each node itself is a small shared-memory multiprocessor. Communication between processors in a node is through shared memory, while communication between nodes is through messages. Unlike the distributed shared-memory paradigm, there is no effort made in hardware to improve the communication latency between nodes; consequently, operating systems are not expected to span multiple nodes in an SMP cluster.

## A.7.2  Clustered Systems

The most common form of cluster is simply a network of computers. Users access the cluster through *terminals*. Terminals may be simply devices that allow the user to type in requests and receive information to be displayed on a screen. More commonly, terminals are complete workstations or PCs comprising processors, memory, disks, and peripherals. When connected to a network, the terminal can access data located at other nodes in the network. The network itself may be spread over a large area or may be quite compact, with high-speed interconnections. A degree of isolation is achieved on a cluster by the fact that applications generally run on the processor at a local node and cannot easily be affected by applications running on other nodes in the network.

Besides the terminal nodes just described, the network in a cluster typically also has various types of servers attached to it. We have already seen the need for file servers that are repositories of data for users of a cluster. There can also be Web servers, which are nodes that serve as access points to the World Wide Web, mail servers, which are nodes that provide mail services, acting as a repository for new and old mail, and print servers, which service printing jobs from other nodes.

Clustering is also common in very large server systems. Here each node in a cluster may be a large shared-memory multiprocessing system, for example, a 32-way (processor) or 64-way system. Multiple nodes of this type are interconnected by a fast, high-bandwidth, optical network, as shown in Figure A.17. In the largest of such systems, the high-bandwidth interconnection may be a switch rather than a bus. Examples of such clusters are the IBM Parallel Sysplex system for the mainframes (Nick et al. 1997) or the HP Superdome Hyperplex system (Charlu 1999). Originally these systems provided a solution to expand beyond the capabilities of a single box. Their attractive features include a suite of software system management tools that allow workload balancing and

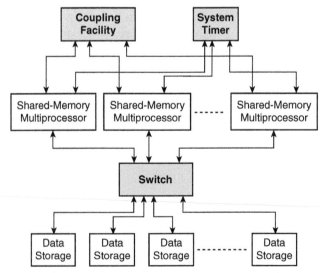

**Figure A.17**  Typical Large Database Cluster. *The coupling facility provides hardware support for synchronization and coherence between nodes of the cluster. The system timer ensures that the clocks on all nodes are synchronized. The data storage, typically on large disks, is shared between nodes and accessed through a high-bandwidth fiber-optic switch.*

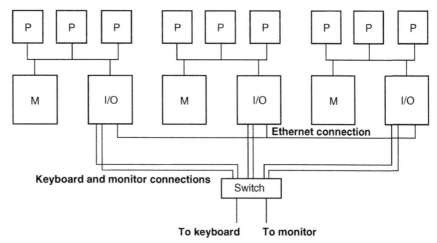

**Figure A.18**   A Cluster of SMP Nodes. *Beowulf clusters are typically built using inexpensive off-the-shelf tower-type desktop computers connected together through Ethernet and sharing a single monitor and keyboard for the use of the system administrator.*

graceful degradation from failures. Additionally, communication routines are provided to enable an application to use resources associated with multiple nodes in a cluster.

The availability of inexpensive commodity uniprocessor systems has led to various architectures that combine commodity components to build inexpensive multiprocessor systems. The nodes in some cluster systems, such as the Beowulf cluster systems (Ridge et al. 1997), are off-the-shelf uniprocessor or small-scale SMP system boxes with off-the-shelf disks, connected together through commodity networks such as 100Mb/sec Ethernet and running an inexpensive (or free) operating system such as Linux (see Figure A.18). A denser form of the Beowulf cluster, called the *blade server*, is rapidly gaining popularity. Blade servers essentially sacrifice I/O expandability, eliminate the monitor, keyboard, case, and power supply of desktop boxes, and put the uniprocessor or SMP subsystem in a thin package called a *blade*. These blades are then slid into standard racks, where a backplane provides the Ethernet connection and other wiring as well as power.

From a programming point of view, the distinction between shared-memory and clustered types of multiprocessor systems arises from the way processes communicate with each other. In shared-memory systems, two processes communicate by writing to or reading from memory locations accessible to both. In clustered systems, processes communicate by sending messages, and hence they are also referred to as *message-passing* multiprocessor systems.

Unlike a shared-memory system, a clustered system presents more of a challenge to an application programmer. In both cases, the programmer is required to organize and partition a program into threads of computation, each to be executed on a different processor. In the cluster case, the programmer is also responsible for the task of synchronizing the computation using messages passed between the threads. Clustered systems would not have gained as much popularity as they have were it not for the software tools and libraries that have been introduced to help develop applications for such systems. Message passing has been recognized as a technique applicable to both closely coupled clusters and more loosely coupled distributed multiprocessor systems. This has led to the development of standard interfaces that allow a programmer to abstract the communication between processors in both types of environments. One of the more widely used interfaces of this type is the message-passing interface (MPI) (Pacheco 1996), which specifies a set of library routines that enable processes to communicate with each other and to exchange data. Portability of applications between systems that implement MPI is one of the biggest strengths of the interface.

### A.7.3 Evolution of Shared-Memory Systems

Many commercial applications benefit from having a shared-memory paradigm rather than a clustered design. The shared-memory paradigm is more convenient to reason with and to write programs for, but the hardware needed to support these systems is more complex and specialized as compared to those for message-passing systems. The complexity in hardware arises from the need to maintain coherence in memory locations, especially in modern memory hierarchies, where memory elements can reside at various levels of cache. Message-passing systems avoid this complexity by shifting this responsibility to the application programmer or to library routines.

The ease of programming shared-memory systems, along with innovative hardware techniques, has led to the development of larger and larger SMP systems over the last decade. Today, we find large shared-memory multiprocessor systems having 128 or more processors.

The ISA of most processors today includes special conventions for the access of shared-memory locations. As with all aspects of an ISA, these conventions represent a contract between the programmer and an implementation of the ISA. A programmer writes a program assuming that accesses to variables shared among processors obey certain rules, while the hardware designer (the processor designer or the system designer) ensures that the rules used by the programmer are indeed guaranteed by the implementation.

### Memory Coherence Models

*Memory coherence* refers to the visibility of a write to a given memory location by all other processors in the system. Ideally, one would like the value written to a memory location to be instantaneously visible to all other processors, meaning that a subsequent read to that location by any other processor should see the new value. This "instantaneous" solution is impractical, however, because of the several layers in the memory hierarchy of most modern systems. So a more practical definition of coherence is adopted — *memory coherence* is said to be implemented on a multiprocessor system if the order of writes to a given location by one processor is maintained when observed by any other processor in the system. Notice that this definition gives flexibility to a hardware designer to delay the observation of changes made by one processor on the other processors. Over the years, there have been several implementation protocols developed to facilitate coherence. These protocols are largely implementation alternatives and are typically not part of an ISA specification.

Consider the example of Figure A.19. Assume that processors 1 and 2 both have write-through caches. When each processor writes to location 50, it does so to a cached version of location 50. As a result, a read following a write will reflect the value in the cached version of location 50. Because the caches are write-through, the value gets written out to memory, though it takes longer for processor 2's write request to reach the memory. In the meantime, the cached value in processor 2 is evicted. When the value of location 50 is requested the next time, both processors get value 1. After a sufficiently long time, when processor 2's write reaches memory and neither processor has a cached copy of location 50, both processors read value 2 from memory. Thus, assuming a starting value of 0, processor 1 sees a transition from 0 to 1 to 2 in location 50, while processor 2 sees the transition from 0 to 2 to 1 to 2 for the same location. This is a violation of the memory coherence rule because it would never be possible for processor 1 to see the 0-2-1-2 order of values observed for processor 2. We note here that such a situation would not have occurred either on a multiprogrammed system or on a multiprocessor system having instantaneous access to memory — models that most programmers are comfortable working with

There are several ways to avoid such memory coherence violations. One way is to ensure that when a value is written to the cache of a processor, copies of that location cached in all other processors are invalidated and, additionally, to ensure that any read request by a processor is satisfied from a cache that has the most recent valid copy, if the memory itself has not yet received the valid copy. The reader is referred to Culler and Singh (1999) for a study of

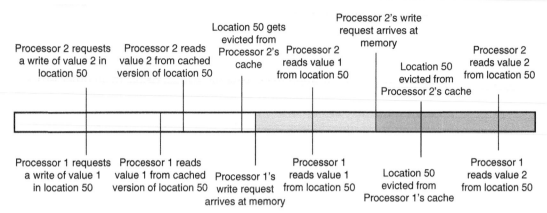

**Figure A.19**   Violation of Memory Coherence. *The bottom part of the figure shows a write followed by three reads of location 50 by processor 1, while the top part shows the same sequence for processor 2. The shaded region indicates the time when the memory contains value 1, while the hatched region indicates the time when it contains value 2. Note that the values read from the caches are different from the values in memory. The sequence of values returned for processor 1 due to reads is 0-1-1-2, while that returned for processor 2 is 0-2-1-2.*

various cache coherence protocols that have been designed to ensure memory coherence.

### Memory Consistency Models

*Memory consistency* characterizes the order in which accesses by one processor to different locations in memory are observed by another processor. This is in contrast to memory coherence, which deals with the order of writes to a single location by a processor. Memory consistency concerns itself not only with accesses to different locations but with both types of accesses, reads, and writes. In general, the more constraining the consistency rules are, the easier it is for a programmer to develop and debug a program but the harder it is for a hardware designer to produce a high-performance implementation of the processor. An implementation that forces all processors to wait until a written value is visible to all processors in the system provides a maximum level of consistency but is uninteresting because of its high overhead. The frequent, and long, waits would negate a lot of the parallelism benefits expected from executing the application on such a multiprocessor system.

The *sequential consistency* model, described first by Leslie Lamport (1979), is an elegant and natural model. A multiprocessor system maintains sequential consistency if the set of observable memory access orderings made by a multithreaded program is a subset of the observable orderings when the program is run on a multiprogrammed uniprocessor system. It is a natural definition, and it is restrictive but still flexible enough to allow the exploitation of most of the benefits from multiprocessing. Even in a multiprogrammed execution of a multithreaded program, the set of observable access orderings is large, with the variation in ordering arising from the variation of points in time that context switches occur and the variation in allocation of waiting threads to the processor. This is illustrated in Figure A.20.

We will simply state here, without proof, that a sufficient condition for sequential consistency in a multiprocessor system is the following: For every pair of accesses to memory by any one processor, the first access in program order is observed by all other processors before the second access is observed. Any implementation that satisfies this condition guarantees sequential consistency in the system.

Processor designers are always looking for ways to improve the single-thread performance in their implementations. Modern superscalar implementations attempt to increase throughput by performing independent operations in the instruction stream in an order that may be different from the original program order. Sequential consistency can get in the way of designing fast uniprocessor implementations. The general philosophy in these implementations is that programmers generally know the exact points in their programs where they would like ordering preserved, and hence it is not necessary to force an implementation to maintain sequential consistency always. Let us now examine some possible relaxations.

When a pair of memory accesses is made by a processor, various conditions in the hardware, specifically the latency of completing these accesses, may cause the second operation to appear to occur before the first. This potential violation of pair order is referred to as a *hazard*. There are four kinds of possible hazards.

- **A read–read (RR) hazard:** This means that if there are two reads that occur in program order, the second read is seen to occur after the first read. One would assume that when there are no intervening writes, such a reordering of reads should not pose any problem. This is indeed the case with single-threaded programs. However, in multithreaded programs on a multiprocessor system, there is the possibility that a processor accessing one of these locations for writing causes the values read to be different from the values read in an alternative implementation that forces a read-to-read ordering.

- **A write–read (WR) hazard:** This refers to a reordering of memory accesses such that a read occurs before a write, even though program order requires

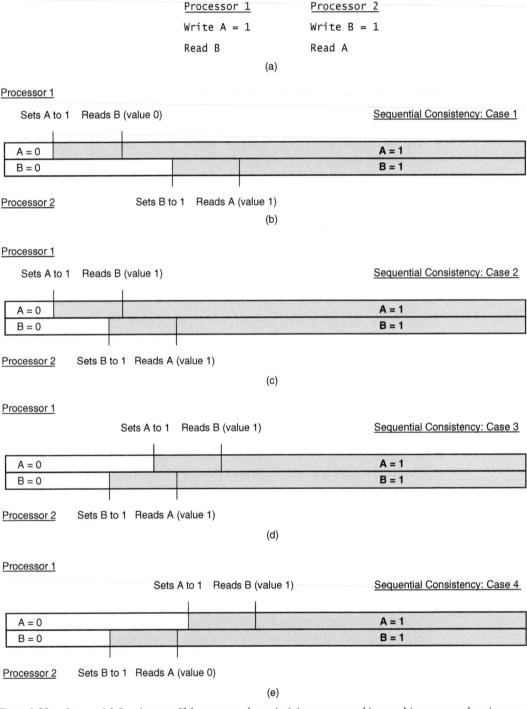

**Figure A.20** Sequential Consistency. *If the program shown in (a) were executed in a multiprogrammed environment, the only possible results are those shown in (b) through (e). Hence any sequentially consistent system must produce one of these results. In particular, it is impossible for the values read to both be 0 at the end of these sequences.*

the read to be after the write. A processor is always designed to avoid such a hazard when the locations addressed by the write and read operations are identical.

- **A read–write (RW) hazard:** This occurs when a write occurs before a read, even though program order requires the write to be after the read.

- **A write–write (WW) hazard:** Such a hazard occurs when two writes are performed in an order opposite to what was required in the program. Once again, correct execution on a single thread ensures that such a hazard cannot take place when the two referenced locations are identical.

An ISA that disallows all four types of hazards in any of its implementations is said to support a strong consistency model. Most processor ISAs specify consistency rules that are weaker than such a strong model. Both the IBM System/390 and the IA-32 processors originally specified one such relaxed ordering rule, referred to today as *processor consistency*. This rule allows the relaxation of the WR ordering; i.e., it permits operands of an instruction to be fetched even before the result of a previous instruction is written all the way to memory. In the absence of such a relaxation, pipelining of operations in a processor would be seriously hampered because instructions would not be allowed to start access of operands even when these operands are independent of the values written by immediately preceding instructions.

Figure A.21 illustrates how a multiprocessor system implementing a processor consistency model can produce results that are not possible if the system followed the sequential consistency model. The program example is taken from Figure A.20. In the example, if both processors perform the reads before the writes, then it is possible for both processors to see old values simultaneously at the end of the program segment. On the other hand, as Figures A.20b through e illustrate, at least one of the processors must see a new value if the system implemented sequential consistency.

With the advent of superscalar processors that decouple memory access from instruction execution, memory models began to specify even weaker consistency rules. For example, *release consistency* (Gharachorloo et al. 1990), which is now supported by many modern architectures, relaxes all memory-ordering requirements except for explicit synchronization operations. The responsibility for correctness in the execution of a multithreaded program is thus shifted completely to the programmer. Special instructions, called *memory barrier instructions,* are provided to allow the programmer or the compiler to impose ordering relationships wherever desired. Examples of memory barrier instructions include the MEMBAR instruction in Sun's SPARC architecture and SYNC in the PowerPC architecture. Both of these ensure that the

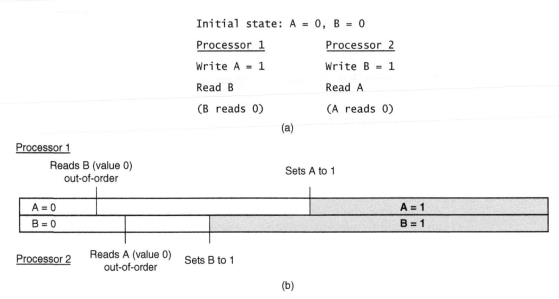

Initial state: A = 0, B = 0

| Processor 1 | Processor 2 |
|---|---|
| Write A = 1 | Write B = 1 |
| Read B | Read A |
| (B reads 0) | (A reads 0) |

(a)

**Figure A.21**    Sample Program to Illustrate Processor Consistency. *In processor consistency, the reads are allowed to go ahead of preceding writes as long as they are not to the same location. If this occurs, the reads result in a value of 0 for both A and B. This combination is not one of the possibilities shown in Figures A.20b through e.*

results of operations after the memory barrier are not seen before the results of operations that occur earlier than the memory barrier have been recorded. Thus, if a strict ordering is desired in the example in Figure A.21a, a memory barrier placed between the writes and the reads would prevent the load instructions from being completed before the results of the store instructions have been recorded.

## A.8   Example Instruction Set Architectures

Most of the examples in this book involve the use of either the PowerPC ISA or the IA-32 ISA. Hence we will describe some of the salient characteristics of these two architectures in the rest of this appendix.

### A.8.1   PowerPC ISA

The PowerPC architecture (IBM 1994) was defined as a joint effort by IBM, Apple, and Motorola in 1993. However, it was very closely derived from the earlier IBM POWER ISA. Currently PowerPC is used by IBM in its pSeries, eSeries, and iSeries lines of computers and by Apple in its Macintosh line.

Versions of the PowerPC architecture are also used in embedded systems developed by IBM and Motorola, in the game machines sold by Nintendo, in the Sony-Toshiba-IBM (STI) Cell processor, and in the IBM BlueGene supercomputer.

The PowerPC ISA is an example of a RISC ISA. The original 32-bit ISA was extended to a 64-bit ISA because of the need to address larger memories and because of the performance advantages of operating on larger units of data. We begin with a description of the state (registers and memory architecture) and then summarize the actual instruction set.

### Registers

The PowerPC register set is illustrated in Figure A.22. There are 32 general-purpose registers and 32 floating-point registers. The floating-point registers

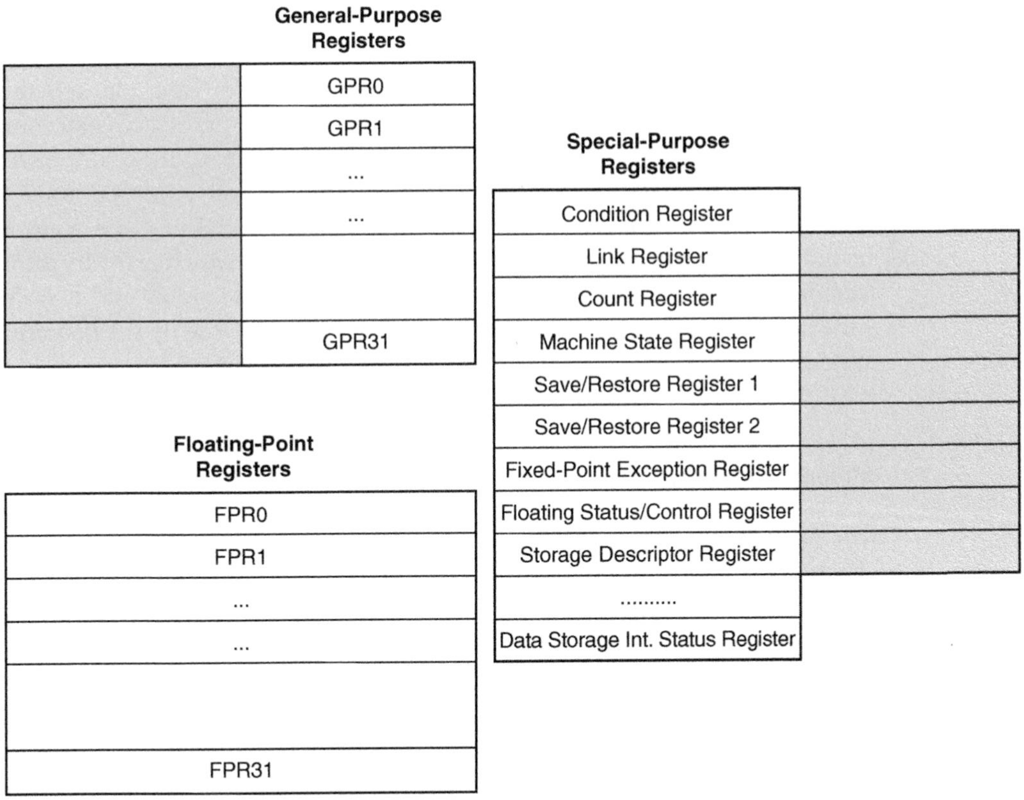

**Figure A.22** PowerPC Register Set. *Shaded areas indicate registers that change size from 32 bits to 64 bits when going to 64-bit mode.*

are 64 bits wide, while the general-purpose registers are 32 bits or 64 bits, depending on the version of the architecture implemented. Both versions can be simultaneously supported in an implementation, in which case the physical registers are 64 bits wide, while only the lower 32 bits will be active when operating in the 32-bit mode.

The main special-purpose registers used by an application are the link register and the count register, each 32 or 64 bits wide, depending on the mode, and the 32-bit condition register, divided into eight independently addressable fields, one of which is set as a side effect of executing certain instructions. The fixed-point exception register contains fields set or used by fixed-point instructions, while the bits in floating-point status and control register allow the monitoring of certain conditions resulting from the execution of floating-point instructions. Both these registers contain "summary" bits that can be set implicitly by the execution of an instruction but must be reset explicitly. These bits provide summary information about whether a certain event occurred since they were last reset.

The remaining registers are generally not used during the compilation of a user program. These include a machine state register, MSR, which provides information about the current state of the machine, for example, whether it is in 32-bit mode or 64-bit mode, whether it is in privileged state, and whether address translation is on. There are two registers, SRR0 and SRR1, the machine state status and restore registers, respectively, that are used to save and restore information on interrupts. Other special-purpose registers include the data storage interrupt status register, DSISR, which provides information about the cause of storage and alignment interrupts, and a set of software-use registers SPGR0–3, specially designated for use by the operating system.

### Memory Architecture

The address used by a PowerPC application is generally called the *effective address*. The term *virtual address* refers to a larger flat address space that includes the effective address spaces of all processes active on the system. Finally, the term *real address* is used in the conventional way to mean locations in real memory.

The PowerPC memory architecture implements segmentation, with segments that contain up to $2^{28}$ bytes (256MB). Pages are $2^{12}$ bytes (4KB) in size. The effective address space is $2^{32}$ bytes in 32-bit mode and $2^{64}$ bytes in 64-bit mode. The real address space is also limited to either $2^{32}$ bytes in 32-bit mode

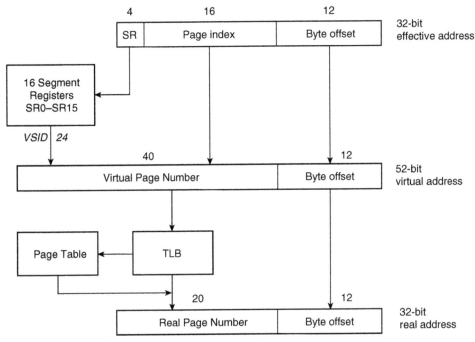

**Figure A.23** Address Translation in the 32-bit PowerPC ISA.

or $2^{64}$ bytes in 64-bit mode. The virtual address space is much larger, up to $2^{52}$ bytes in 32-bit mode or $2^{80}$ bytes in 64-bit mode.

In the 32-bit mode, there are 16 segment registers, SR0–15, that hold the locations in virtual memory of the 16 segments available in the effective address space. The top four bits of a 32-bit effective address point to one of the segment registers, which contains the top 24 bits of the segment address (refer to Figure A.23). This 24-bit virtual segment ID (VSID) along with the 16-bit page index from the effective address forms a 40-bit virtual page number (VPN). The VPN is then converted to a real page number (RPN) by referring to the page table whose location in real memory is determined using the storage descriptor register, SDR1.

The PowerPC has an architected page table; that is, the format of entries in the page table is defined in the ISA. In order to make references to the page table more efficient, the table is accessed associatively via hashing. The VPN is hashed in two different ways to arrive at two pointers, each of which points to an entry group (PTEG) consisting of eight page table entries. A page fault occurs only if the required page cannot be found in either page table group.

The probability of a page fault depends on various factors, including the hashing function used, the number of PTEGs implemented, and reference characteristics of the application.

The PowerPC architecture does not mandate the use of a translation look-aside buffer. However, it does provide instructions to maintain a TLB if one is implemented (as it always will be, practically speaking). For example, the tlbie instruction can be used to invalidate an entry in the page table when an entry is replaced in the hashed page table. All entries in the TLB can be invalidated (flushed) simultaneously using a tlbia instruction.

In 64-bit mode, the effective number of segments supported is $2^{36}$ instead of 16. The mapping of an effective segment ID to a virtual segment ID is done by means of a segment table pointed to by a special register called the *address space register* (ASR). Once again, in order to make accesses to this table more efficient, two hashed pointers are used to access two sets of segment table entry groups (STEGs), each set having eight segment table entries. A miss here causes a segment fault. A segment lookaside buffer (SLB) is used for avoiding a translation on each reference. Instructions (slbie and slbia) are provided to invalidate a single SLB entry or the entire SLB.

### Instruction Set Summary

PowerPC uses a RISC instruction set that has fixed 32-bit-width instructions. All storage operations are conducted through load and store instructions. Thus there are no instructions that perform arithmetic or logical operations on the contents of memory. Any such operation requires that the operand be brought in from memory into one of the registers before being manipulated.

The PowerPC divides the user instruction set into three groups: the branch processor instructions, the fixed-point processor instructions, and the floating-point processor instructions.

The branch processor handles instructions that set or use the condition register, CR, or that change the flow of control modifying the program counter to deviate from the sequential execution of instructions. These latter instructions, the branch instructions, have one of the two following formats.

| | | |
|---|---|---|
| *b* | target | Branch to target address obtained by adding the address of the current instruction with the 24-bit offset specified in the instruction. |
| *bc* | cond, target | Branch conditionally to target obtained by adding the address of the current instruction with the 14-bit offset specified in the instruction. The condition for branching is determined by condition register bit BI and field BO in the instruction. |

A useful variant of the branch instruction is the branch-and-link instruction. When the LK bit in the branch instruction is set, it indicates that a side effect of executing either the b or the bc instruction is to place the address of the immediately following instruction into LR, the link register. This is a useful way of saving the return address while branching to subroutines.

| | | |
|---|---|---|
| *bl* | target | Branch to target and save return address in link register. |
| *bcl* | target | Conditionally branch and link to target. |

The branch processor includes instructions that allow various logical and transfer operations on individual bits or fields of the CR instruction. Another important instruction in the branch processor is the system-call instruction.

| | |
|---|---|
| *sc* | Branch to a special location determined by the contents of the MSR, and save state information in SRR0 and SRR1. The processor enters system mode after executing this instruction. |

The fixed-point processor executes instructions that involve use of the general-purpose registers, GPR0–31. Load and store instructions use the general-purpose registers to specify the address of the memory location involved and hence also involve the fixed-point processor. Here are examples of load and store instructions.

| | | |
|---|---|---|
| *ld* | rt, d(ra) | Load register rt with the contents of memory addressed by (ra) + d. The d field is treated as a signed quantity. |
| *ldx* | rt, ra, rb | Load register rt with the contents of memory addressed by (ra) + (rb). |
| *lwz* | rt, d(ra) | Load lower 32 bits of register rt from contents of memory addressed by (ra) + d; zero out the upper 32 bits of register rt. |
| *lwzx* | rt, ra, rb | Load lower 32 bits of register rt from contents of memory addressed by (ra) + (rb); zero out the upper 32 bits of register rt. |
| *stw* | rt, d(ra) | Store the 32 low-order bits of register rt in the memory location addressed by (ra) + d. The d field is treated as a signed quantity. |
| *stwx* | rt, ra, rb | Store the 32 low-order bits of register rt in the memory location addressed by (ra) + (rb). |

The remaining fixed-point instructions are largely similar to those found in most RISC ISAs. The arithmetic and logical instructions operate on operands, both of which may be in general-purpose registers, or one of which may be a constant defined in the instruction. Instructions are nondestructive — the result register may be different from both operand registers. Examples follow.

| | | |
|---|---|---|
| *add* | rt, ra, rb | Add the contents of ra and rb and put the result in rt. |
| *subf.* | rt, ra, rb | Subtract the contents of ra from rb and put the result in rt. The dot in the mnemonic indicates that as a side effect of the instruction, bits in field 0 (first four bits) of the condition register must be set according to whether the result is negative, zero, or overflowed. This is called a *record-form instruction*, because it sets the record bit in the instruction. |

Because branches are taken conditionally on the contents of the condition register, the compiler must either use a record form instruction or set any of the fields in the CR explicitly using a compare instruction. Here's an example.

| | | |
|---|---|---|
| *cmpl* | 3, ra, rb | Compare the contents of registers ra and rb, treating them as unsigned integers, and set field 3 (bits 12–15) of the condition register according to whether ra is less than rb, rb is less than ra, or both are identical. |

The PowerPC also has a rich set of rotate and shift instructions. These instructions optionally perform a mask operation during the shift process, which allows a wide variety of common operations in compilers and interpreters to be performed in a single instruction. An example is the following instruction.

| | | |
|---|---|---|
| *rlwimi* | ra, rs, sh, mb, me | Rotate the contents of rs left by the amount specified in sh, and merge the masked part into register ra. The part of ra that is changed is determined by a mask of 1's extending from the mb position to the me position. |
| *rlwinm* | ra, rs, sh, mb, me | Rotate the contents of rs left by the amount specified in sh, and use mask to extract a part of the rotated value to be transferred to ra. |

### A.8.2 The Intel IA-32 ISA

The IA-32 ISA (Intel 1999), informally known as the x86, descended from the Intel 8086 through the 286, 386, 486, and Pentium series. The 8086 started as a 16-bit microcontroller chip, primarily for use in embedded systems. An 8086 derivative, the 8088, was selected by IBM for the first PCs in 1981, and soon the x86 ISA evolved to a 32-bit general-purpose architecture. Recently, it has been further extended to 64 bits. Currently the IA-32 is probably the most widely used general-purpose architecture, with applications ranging from laptops to desktops to servers.

The IA-32 ISA is an example of a CISC ISA. The instruction set is more "cluttered" than "complex," there having been several instructions sets that are fundamentally more complex. The clutter comes from its evolutionary history and extensions, coupled with the need to maintain backward compatibility at each step. In this book we feature the 32-bit IA-32 architecture; the earlier 16-bit version of the ISA and the newer 64-bit version are not used in this book. Just as we did with the PowerPC description, we will begin with a description of the state (registers and memory architecture) and then summarize the actual instruction set.

### Registers

The IA-32 register set is illustrated in Figure A.24. There are eight general-purpose registers, six segment registers, and a floating-point stack with eight elements. The general-purpose registers are 32 bits wide, the segment registers are 16 bits wide, and the elements of the floating-point stack are 80 bits wide. For executing 16-bit instructions, the low-order 16 bits of the general-purpose registers are used. Some of the general-purpose registers have the special uses for certain instructions, some of which are listed below.

*eax* — Accumulator for operands and results

*ebx* — Pointer to data held in the DS segment

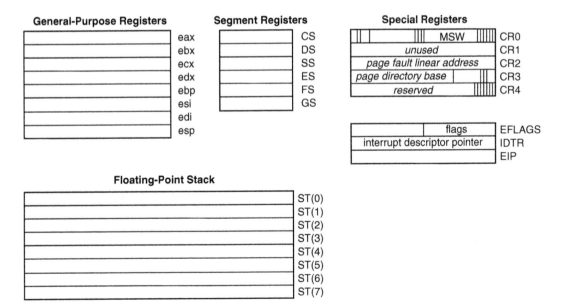

**Figure A.24**    IA-32 Register Set. *Registers shown are for 32-bit protected-mode operation.*

*ecx* — Counter for string operations and loops

*edx* — I/O pointer

*esi* — Pointer to data held in the DS segment; source pointer for string operations

*edi* — Pointer to data held in the ES segment; destination pointer for string operations

*esp* — Stack pointer in the SS segment

*ebp* — Pointer to data held in the stack

The special-purpose registers consist of five control registers, CR0–4, that contain a number of status and enable bits. For example, when a page fault occurs, CR2 is specified to hold the address causing the fault, while CR3 points to the page table. There are three other special-purpose registers, the EFLAGS, EIP, and IDTR registers. The EFLAGS register contains a number of status flags, including condition codes used by conditional branch instructions. The EIP is the program counter (referred to as the *instruction pointer* in Intel terminology). The IDTR, or the interrupt descriptor table register, points to a table in memory that holds interrupt vectors.

### Memory Architecture

The IA-32 memory architecture (Figure A.25) is based on segments, somewhat similar to the PowerPC, but it is often used in a special configuration that presents a flat, linear model to software. The IA-32 ISA supports up to 64K segments, each of which can be up to 4GB. The segments map into a single, contiguous 32-bit linear address space (4GB), though at any given time only six of the segments can be addressed via six segment registers.

Like the PowerPC, a logical load or store address specifies one of the segment registers and an offset of up to 32 bits. Some instruction encodings can only specify one of the first four segments. The logical address points to a location in the linear 4GB address space. When the offset value is computed, typically by adding the contents of a general-purpose register to a displacement value, the segment register is not changed. This is in contrast to PowerPC, where the segment pointer is in the upper bits of the effective address and can be affected by address arithmetic.

When used in its most general form, a segmented memory model can be constructed as shown in Figure A.25a. However, by setting all the segment registers to point to the base of the 32-bit linear address space, a simpler linear

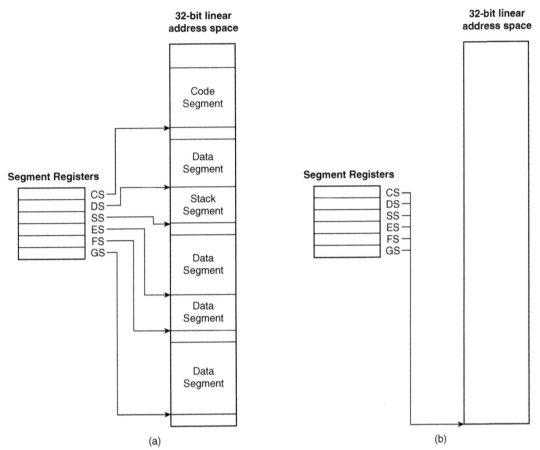

**Figure A.25** Virtual memory Models Supported by IA-32. *(a) Segmented memory model; (b) flat memory model. The IA-32 also supports a real address model which is not shown.*

memory model can be constructed, as in Figure A.25b. It is this model that is used by most UNIX systems.

The linear address space is divided into 4KB pages, irrespective of the segments. The flat linear address space is then mapped onto a real memory that may have up to 4GB. As with the PowerPC, the Intel IA-32 has an architected page table, and hence the format of entries in the page table is defined in the ISA. The page table is similar to the one shown in Figure A.10, but it contains two levels rather than one. The 20-bit page number field of a virtual address is divided into an upper 10-bit directory pointer and a lower 10-bit page pointer. The directory pointer points to an entry in a 1K page directory. Each directory

| Prefixes | Opcode | Opcode | ModR/M | SIB | Displacement | Immediate |
|---|---|---|---|---|---|---|
| 0 to 4 | | optional | optional | optional | 0,1,2,4 bytes | 0,1,2,4 bytes |

**Figure A.26** General Format for IA-32 Instructions.

pointer points to a separate 1K entry page table, which is accessed using the lower 10-bit page pointer. The page directory is located at an address specified in CR3, which acts as the page directory base pointer.

### Instruction Set Summary

The IA-32 ISA has variable-length instructions, from one to fifteen bytes, although most of the commonly used instructions are relatively short. Instruction operands, including instructions that perform common arithmetic, logical, or shift operations, may come from either registers or memory. This is in contrast to RISC instruction sets, where the only instructions that take operands from memory are the load and store instructions.

Figure A.26 illustrates the general form of an IA-32 instruction. It consists of from zero to four prefix bytes. The prefix bytes indicate various special cases, for example, if there is repetition for string instructions and/or if there are overrides for addressing segments, address sizes, and operand sizes. Following the prefix byte(s) (if any) is an opcode byte, which may be followed by a second opcode byte, depending on the value of the first. Next comes an optional addressing-form specifier, ModR/M. It is present only for certain opcodes and generally indicates an addressing mode and register. The SIB byte is present only for certain ModR/M encodings and indicates a base register, an index register, and a scale factor for the indexing. The variable-length displacement field is present only when certain addressing modes are specified. The last field is a variable-length immediate operand, present only if required by the opcode. When needed, a segment register can be specified with some of the opcode bits or by the ModR/M byte.

The IA-32 ISA divides the user instruction set into three major categories: integer instructions, floating-point instructions, and MMX (multimedia instructions). In this brief overview and in examples used in this book, we restrict ourselves primarily to the integer instructions. Within the category of integer instructions are jumps (both conditional and unconditional), load/store instructions, and a wide variety of ALU instructions. However, as we noted earlier, the ALU instructions can specify one or more memory operands, so, in effect, many of them also perform load/store operations.

Jump instructions include all control transfer instructions, regardless of whether they are conditional or unconditional. The conditional jumps test condition code bits that are held in the EFLAGS register. These bits are set as a side effect of many instructions.

| | | |
|---|---|---|
| *jmp* | reg | Jump indirect to the memory location held in reg. |
| *jz* | target | Jump conditionally to target if the zero-condition code bit in the EFLAGS register is set to 1. |
| *jmp* | target | Jump unconditionally to target. |

Procedure calls and returns are performed using instructions that push and pop the return address to/from the stack, pointed to by esp.

| | | |
|---|---|---|
| *call* | target | Push the program counter of the next instruction onto the stack and jump to the target address. |
| *ret* | | Pop the return address from the stack and jump. |

Load and store operations, when not combined with arithmetic or logical operations, are performed by move instructions.

| | | |
|---|---|---|
| *mov* | reg1, disp(reg2) | Load register reg1 with the contents of memory addressed by (reg2) + disp. The disp field is treated as a signed quantity. |
| *mov* | disp(reg1), reg2 | Store register reg2 into memory addressed by (reg1) + disp. The disp field is treated as a signed quantity. |

Most of the ALU operations can take operands from a combination of registers and memory locations. Some representative examples follow.

| | | |
|---|---|---|
| *addl* | reg1, disp(reg2) | Add the contents of reg1 and the memory operand at address reg2 + disp. The result is placed in reg1. Condition codes in the EFLAGS register are set according to the result. |
| *sub* | reg1, immed | Subtract the contents of the immediate value immed from reg1 and place the result in reg1. Condition codes in the EFLAGS register are set according to the result. |
| *xorl* | reg1, reg2 | Exclusive-OR the contents of reg1 and reg2 and place the result in reg1. Condition codes in the EFLAGS register are set according to the result. |

# References

Adair, R., R. U. Bayles, L. W. Comeau, and R. J. Creasy. 1966. A Virtual Machine System for the 360/40, *Cambridge Scientific Center Report No. G320-2007* (May).

Adve, V., C. Lattner, M. Brukman, A. Shukla, and B. Gaeke. 2003. LLVA: A Low-level Virtual Instruction Set Architecture, *Proc. 36th Int. Symp. on Microarchitecture* (December).

Aho, A. V., R. Sethi, and J. D. Ullman. 1986. *Compilers: Principles, Techniques and Tools*, Addison-Wesley, Reading, MA.

Allcock, B., J. Bester, J. Breshanan, A. Chervenak, I. Foster, C. Kesselman, S. Meder, V. Nefedova, D. Quesnel, and S. Tuecke. 2001. Secure, Efficient Data Transport and Replica Management for High-Performance Data-Intensive Computing, *Proc. 18th Symposium on Mass Storage Systems and Technologies* (April).

Altman, E., K. Ebcioglu, M. Gschwind, and S. Sathaye. 2002. Methods and Apparatus for Reordering and Renaming Memory References in a Multiprocessor Computer System, US patent 6,349,361 (February).

Amdahl, G. M., G. A. Blaauw, and F. P. Brooks, Jr. 1964. Architecture of the IBM System 360, *IBM Journal of Research and Development* (April), pp. 87–101.

Anderson, D. P., J. Cobb, E. Korpella, M. Lebofsky, and D. Werthimer. 2002. SETI@home: An Experiment in Public-Resource Computing, *Communications of the ACM* (November), pp. 56–61.

Appel, A. W. 1991. Garbage Collection, *Topics in Advanced Language Implementations*, P. Lee (Ed.), MIT Press, Cambridge, MA, pp. 89–100.

ARM. 2002, ARM 9EJ-S Technical Reference Manual, Ref. DDI0222B.

Arnold, M. and B. G. Ryder. 2001. A Framework for Reducing the Cost of Instrumented Code, *Proc. Conf. ACM SIGPLAN '01 on Programming Language Design and Implementation* (May), pp. 168–179.

Arnold, M., M. Hind, and B. G. Ryder. 2002. Online Feedback-Directed Optimization of Java, *Proc. Conf. on Object Oriented Programming Systems, Languages, and Applications* (November), pp. 111–129.

Arnold, M., S. Fink, D. Grove, M. Hind, and P. F. Sweeney. 2000. Adaptive Optimization in the Jalapeno JVM, *Proc. Conf. on Object Oriented Programming Systems, Languages, and Applications* (October), pp. 47–65.

Arnold, M., S. Fink, D. Grove, M. Hind, and P. F. Sweeney. 2005. A Survey of Adaptive Optimization in Virtual Machines, *Proceedings of the IEEE* (February).

Artigas, P. V., M. Gupta, S. P. Midkiff, and J. E. Moreira. 2000. Automatic Loop Transformations and Parallelization for Java, *Proc. Int. Conf. on Supercomputing* (May), pp. 1–10.

Attanasio, C. R., D. F. Bacon, A. Cocchi, and S. Smith. 2001. A Comparative Evaluation of Parallel Garbage Collector Implementations, *Proc. 14th Workshop on Languages and Compilers for Parallel Computing* (August), pp. 177–192.

Aycock, J. 2003. A Brief History of Just-in-Time, *ACM Comp. Surveys* (June), pp. 97–113.

Ayers, A., R. Schooler, and R. Gottlieb. 1997. Aggressive Inlining, *Proc. ACM SIGPLAN Conf. on Programming Language Design and Implementation* (May), pp. 134–145.

Bala, V., E. Duesterwald, and S. Banerjia. 1999. Transparent Dynamic Optimization: The Design and Implementation of Dynamo, *Hewlett Packard Laboratories Technical Report HPL-1999–78* (June).

Bala, V., E. Duesterwald, and S. Banerjia. 2000. Dynamo: A Transparent Dynamic Optimization System, *Proc. ACM SIGPLAN Conf. Programming Language Design and Implementation* (June), pp. 1–12.

Ball, T. and J. R. Larus. 1994. Optimally Profiling and Tracing Programs, *ACM Transactions on Programming Languages and Systems* (July), pp. 1319–1360.

Ball, T. and J. R. Larus. 1996. Efficient Path Profiling, *Proc. 29th Int. Symp. on Microarchitecture* (November), pp. 46–57.

Ball, T., P. Mataga, and M. Sagiv. 1998. Edge Profiling Versus Path Profiling: The Showdown, *Proc. 25th ACM SIGPLAN-SIGACT Symp. on Principles of Programming Languages* (January), pp. 134–148.

Banerjia, S., W. A. Havanki, and T. M. Conte. 1997. Treegion Scheduling for Highly Parallel Processors, *European Conference on Parallel Processing* (August), pp. 1074–1078.

Banning, J., P. H. Anvin, B. Gribstad, D. Keppel, A. Klaiber, and P. Serris. 2002. Fine Grain Translation Discrimination, US Patent 6,363,336 (March).

Baraz, L, T. Devor, O. Etzion, S. Goldenberg, A. Skaletsky, Y. Wang, and Y. Zemach. 2003. IA-32 Execution Layer: A Two-phase Dynamic Translator Designed to Support IA-32 Applications on Itanium-based Systems, *Proc. 36th Annual IEEE/ACM Int. Symp. on Microarchitecture* (December), pp. 191–204.

Barham, P., B. Dragovic, K. Fraser, S. Hand, T. Harris, A. Ho, R. Neugebauery, I. Pratt, and A. Warfield. 2003. Xen and the Art of Virtualization, *Proc. 19th ACM Symp. on Operating System Principles* (October), pp. 164–177.

Bell, J. R. 1973. Threaded Code, *Communications of the ACM* (June), pp. 370–372.

Berndl, M. and L. Hendren. 2003. Dynamic Profiling and Trace Cache Generation, *Proc. Int. Symp. on Code Generation and Optimization* (March), pp. 276–285.

Bertsis, V. 1980. Security and Protection of Data in the IBM System/38, *Proc. 7th Int. Symp. on Computer Architecture* (June), pp. 245–252.

Boehm, H. and M. Weiser. 1988. Garbage Collection in an Uncooperative Environment, *Software — Practice and Experience*, pp. 807–820.

Borden, T. L., J. P. Hennessy, and J. W. Rymarczyk. 1989. Multiple Operating Systems on One Processor Complex, *IBM Systems Journal* (January), pp. 104–123

Boutcher, D. 2001. The Linux Kernel on iSeries, *Proc. 2001 Ottawa Linux Symposium* (July), http://lwn.net/2001/features/OLS/pdf/pdf/iseries.pdf.

Bovet, D. P. and M. Cesati. 2001. *Understanding the Linux Kernel,* O'Reilly, Sebastopol, CA.

Bowles, K. L. 1980. *Beginner's Guide for the UCSD Pascal System,* McGraw-Hill, New York.

Box, D. 2002. *Essential .NET, Volume 1: The Common Language Runtime,* Addison-Wesley, Reading, MA.

Bressoud, T. C. and F. B. Schneider. 1996. Hypervisor-Based Fault Tolerance, *ACM Transactions on Computer Systems* (February), pp. 80–107.

Bruening, D. 2004. Efficient, Transparent, and Comprehensive Runtime Code Manipulation, Ph.D. dissertation (September), MIT, Cambridge, MA.

Bruening, D., E. Duesterwald, and S. Amarasinghe. 2001. Design and Implementation of a Dynamic Optimization Framework for Windows, *Proc. 4th Workshop on Feedback-Directed and Dynamic Optimization* (December).

Bruening, D., T. Garnett, and S. Amarasinghe. 2003. An Infrastructure for Adaptive Dynamic Optimization, *Proc. Int. Symp. on Code Generation and Optimization* (March), pp. 265–275.

Brunner, R. A. 1991. *VAX Architecture Reference Manual,* 2nd ed., Digital Press, Bedford, MA.

Bugnion, E., S. Devine, K. Govil, and M. Rosenblum. 1997. Disco: Running Commodity Operating Systems on Scalable Multiprocessors, *ACM Transactions on Computing Systems* (November), pp. 412–447.

Carr, S. and K. Kennedy. 1994. Scalar Replacement in the Presence of Conditional Control Flow, *Software — Practice and Experience* (January), pp. 51–77.

Chang, P. P., S. A. Mahlke, and W. W. Hwu. 1991. Using Profile Information to Assist Classic Code Optimizations, *Software — Practice & Experience* (December), table of contents, pp. 1301–1321.

Chang, P.P., S. A. Mahlke, W. Y. Chen, and W.-M. W. Hwu. 1992. Profile-Guided Automatic Inline Expansion for C Programs, *Software — Practice and Experience* (May), pp. 349–369.

Chambers, C. and D. Ungar. 1991. Making Pure Object-Oriented Languages Practical, *Proc. Conf. on Object-Oriented Programming Systems, Languages, and Applications* (October), pp. 1–15.

Charlu, D. 1999. HP Hyperplex Clustering Technology, *1st Int. Workshop on Cluster Computing* (December).

Chen, P. M. and B. D. Noble. 2001. When Virtual Is Better Than Real, *Proc. 8th IEEE Workshop on Hot Topics on Operating Systems* (May), pp. 133–138.

Chen, J. B. and B. D. D. Leupen. 1997. Improving Instruction Locality with Just-In-Time Code Layout, *Proc. the USENIX Windows NT Workshop* (August).

Chen, W.-K., S. Lerner, R. Chaiken, and D. M. Gillies. 2000. Mojo: A Dynamic Optimization System, *Proc. 3rd ACM Workshop on Feedback-Directed and Dynamic Optimization* (December).

Chernoff, A., M. Herdeg, R. Hookway, C. Reeve, N. Rubin, T. Tye, S. B. Yadavalli, and J. Yates. 1998. FX!32: A Profile-Directed Binary Translator, *IEEE Micro* (March), pp. 56–64.

Chien, A., B. Calder, S. Elbert, and K. Bhatia. 2003. Entropia: Architecture and Performance of an Enterprise Desktop Grid System, *Journal of Parallel Distributed Computing* (May), pp. 597–610.

Chilimbi, T. M., B. Davidson, and J. R. Larus. 1999. Cache-Conscious Structure Definition, *Proc. Conf. on Programming Language Design and Implementation* (May), pp. 13–24.

Choi, J.-D., M. Gupta, M. J. Serrano, V. C. Sreedhar, and S. P. Midkiff. 1999. Escape Analysis for Java, *Proc. Conf. on Object-Oriented Programming Systems, Languages, and Applications,* pp. 1–19.

Choi, Y., A. Knies, G. Vedaraman, J. Williamson, and I. Esmer. 2002. Design and Experience: Using the Intel Itanium-2 Processor Performance

Monitoring Unit to Implement Feedback Optimizations, *2nd Workshop on Explicitly Parallel Instruction Computing Architecture and Compilers* (November).

Chou, Y. and J. Shen. 2000. Instruction Path Coprocessors, *Proc. 27th Int. Symp. on Computer Architecture* (June), pp. 270–281.

Cifuentes, C. and M. V. Emmerik. 2000. UQBT: Adaptable Binary Translation at Low Cost, *IEEE Computer* (March), pp. 60–66.

Cifuentes, C., B. Lewis, and D. Ung. 2002. Walkabout — A Retargetable Dynamic Binary Translation Framework, *Proc. Workshop on Binary Translation* (September).

Cmelik, B. and D. Keppel. 1994. Shade: A Fast Instruction-Set Simulator for Execution Profiling, *ACM Sigmetrics* (May), pp. 128–137.

Cmelik, R. F. and D. Keppel. 1996. Shade: A Fast Instruction-Set Simulator for Execution Profiling, *Technical Report UWCSE 93-06-06*, University of Washington, Seattle (June).

Cohen, D. 1981. On Holy Wars and a Plea for Peace, *IEEE Computer* (October), pp. 48–54.

Cohn, R. S., D. W. Goodwin, P. G. Lowney, and N. Rubin. 1997. Spike: An Optimizer for Alpha/NT Executables, *USENIX Windows NT Workshop* (August), pp. 17–23.

Collins, G. E. 1960. A Method for Overlapping and Erasure of Lists, *Communications of the ACM* (December), pp. 655–657.

Comfort, W. T. 1964. Multiword List Items, *Communications of the ACM* (June), pp. 357–362.

Conte, T. M. and S. Sathaye. 1995. Dynamic Rescheduling: A Technique for Object Code Compatibility, *Proc. 28th Int. Symp. on Microarchitecture* (November), pp. 208–217.

Conte, T. M., K. N. Menezes, and M. A. Hirsch. 1996. Accurate and Practical Profile-Driven Compilation Using the Profile Buffer, *Proc. 29th Int. Symp. on Microarchitecture* (November), pp. 36–45.

Conte, T., S. Sathaye, and S. Banerjia. 1996. A Persistent Rescheduled-Page Cache for Low Overhead Object Code Compatibility in VLIW Architectures, *Proc. 29th Int. Symp. on Microarchitecture* (December), pp. 4–13.

Cooper, K. and L. Torczon. 2003. *Engineering a Compiler*, Morgan-Kaufmann, San Francisco.

Creasy, R. J. 1981. The Origin of the VM/370 Time-Sharing System, *IBM Journal of Research and Development* (September), pp. 483–490.

Culler, D. E. and J. P. Singh. 1999. *Parallel Computer Architecture: A Hardware/Software Approach*, Morgan-Kaufmann, San Francisco.

Cytron, R., J. Ferrante, B. K. Rosen, M. N. Wegman, and F. K. Zadeck. 1991. Efficiently Computing Static Single Assignment Form and the Control

Dependence Graph, *ACM Transactions on Programming Languages and Systems* (October), pp. 451–490.

Czajkowski, K., I. Foster, N. Karonis, C. Kesselman, S. Martin, W. Smith, and S. Teucke. 1998. A Resource Management Architecture for Meta-computing Systems, *Proc. 4th Workshop on Job Scheduling Strategies for Parallel Processing* (March).

Dean, J., J. Hicks, C. Waldspurger, W. Weihl, and G. Chrysos. 1997. ProfileMe: Hardware Support for Instruction-Level Profiling on Out-of-Order Processors, *Proc. 30th Int. Symp. on Microarchitecture* (November), pp. 292–302.

Deaver, D., R. Gorton, and N. Rubin. 1999. Wiggins/Redstone: An Online Program Specializer, *Proc. 11th HotChips Symposium* (June).

Debaere, E. H. and J. M. Van Campenhout. 1990. *Interpretation and Instruction Path Coprocessing*, MIT Press, Cambridge, MA.

Dehnert, J. C., B. K. Grant, J. P. Banning, R. Johnson, T. Kistler, A. Klaiber, and J. Mattson. 2003. The Transmeta Code Morphing Software: Using Speculation, Recovery, and Adaptive Retranslation to Address Real-Life Challenges, *Proc. Int. Symp. on Code Generation and Optimization* (March), pp. 15–24.

Desoli, G., N. Mateev, E. Duesterwald, P. Faraboschi, and J. A. Fisher. 2002. DELI: A New Run-Time Control Point, *Proc. 35th Int. Symp. on Microarchitecture* (November), pp. 257–268.

Deutsch, P. and A. M. Schiffman. 1984. Efficient Implementation of the Smalltalk-80 System, *Proc. 11th ACM Symp. on Principles of Programming Languages* (January), pp. 297–302.

Dewar, R. B. K. 1975. Indirect Threaded Code, *Communications of the ACM* (June), pp. 330–331.

DHCP. Dynamic Host Configuration Protocol, http://www.dhcp.org.

Diffie, W. and M. E. Hellman. 1976. New Directions in Cryptography, *IEEE Trans. on Information Theory* (November), pp. 644–654.

Doran, R. W. 1988. Amdahl Multiple Domain Architecture, *IEEE Computer* (October), pp. 20–28.

Dorward, D., R. Pike, D. L. Presotto, D. Ritchie, H. Trickey, and P. Winterbottom. 1997. Inferno, *Proc. IEEE Compcon '97*.

Drayton, P., B. Albahari, and T. Neward. 2002. *C# in a Nutshell*, 1st ed., O'Reilly, Sebastopol, CA.

Duesterwald, E. and V. Bala. 2000. Software Profiling for Hot Path Prediction: Less Is More, *Proc. 9th Int. Conf. on Architectural Support for Programming Languages and Operating Systems* (November), pp. 202–211.

Dunlap, G. W., S. T. King, S. Cinar, M. A. Basrai, and P. M. Chen. 2002. ReVirt: Enabling Intrusion Analysis Through Virtual-Machine Logging and

Replay, *Proc. 5th Symp. on Operating Systems Design and Implementation* (December), pp. 211–224.

Ebcioglu, K., E. R. Altman, M. Gschwind, and S. Sathaye. 2001. Dynamic Binary Translation and Optimization, *IEEE Transactions on Computers* (June), pp. 529–548.

Engebretson, D., M. Corrigan, and P. Bergner. 2001. PowerPC 64-bit Kernel Internals, *Proc. 2001 Ottawa Linux Symposium* (July), http://lwn.net/2001/features/OLS/pdf/pdf/ppc64.pdf.

Ertl, M. A. and D. Gregg. 2001. The Behavior of Efficient Virtual Machine Interpreters on Modern Architectures, *Europar 2001,* pp. 403–412.

Ertl, M. A. and D. Gregg. 2003. Optimizing Indirect Branch Prediction Accuracy in Virtual Machine Interpreters, *Proc. Conf. on Programming Language Design and Implementation* (May) pp. 278–288.

Fahs, B., S. Bose, M. Crum, B. Slechta, F. Spadini, T. Tung, S. J. Patel, and S. S. Lumetta. 2001. Performance Characterization of a Hardware Mechanism for Dynamic Optimization, *Proc. 34th Int. Symp. on Microarchitecture* (December), pp. 16–27.

Figueiredo, R., P. Dinda, and J. Fortes. 2003. A Case for Grid Computing on Virtual Machines, *Proc. 23rd Int. Conf. on Distributed Computing Systems* (May).

Fink, S. J. and F. Qian. 2003. Design, Implementation and Evaluation of Adaptive Recompilation with On-Stack Replacement, *Proc. Int. Symp. on Code Generation and Optimization* (March), pp. 241–252.

Fisher, J. A. 1981. Trace Scheduling: A Technique for Global Microcode Compaction, *IEEE Transactions on Computers* (July), pp. 478–490.

Flanagan, D. 1999. *Java in a Nutshell,* 3rd ed., O'Reilly, Sebastopol, CA.

FLEX. FLEX-ES: The New Mainframe, Fundamental Software Inc., http://www.funsoft.com.

Foster, I. and N. T. Karonis. 1998. A Grid-Enabled MPI: Message Passing in Heterogeneous Distributed Computing Systems, *Proc. Intl. Conf. ACM/IEEE on Supercomputing* (November).

Foster, I. and C. Kesselman (Eds.). 1998. *The Grid: Blueprint for a Future Computing Infrastructure,* Morgan Kaufmann, San Francisco.

Foster, I. and C. Kesselman (Eds.). 2004. *The Grid 2: Blueprint for a Future Computing Infrastructure,* Morgan Kaufmann, San Francisco.

Foster, I., C. Kesselman, and S. Tuecke. 2001. The Anatomy of a Grid: Enabling Virtual Scalable Organizations, *Int. Journal of High Performance Computing Applications,* pp. 200–222.

Fujitsu. 2003. The Next-Generation Engine for Consolidation, http://www.computers.us.fujitsu.com/www/content/aboutus/analysts/data/FujitsuGroup_ConsolidationEngine.pdf.

Gallagher, D., W. Y. Chen, S. A. Mahlke, J. C. Gyllenhaal, and W. W. Hwu. 1994. Dynamic Memory Disambiguation Using the Memory Conflict Buffer, *Proc. 6th Int. Conf. on Architectural Support for Programming Languages and Operating Systems* (October), pp. 183–193.

Garfinkel, T. and M. Rosenblum. 2003. A Virtual Machine Introspection Based Architecture for Intrusion Detection, *Proc. Symp. of the Internet Society's 2003 on Network and Distributed System Security* (February).

Garfinkel, T., B. Pfaff, J. Chow, M. Rosenblum, and D. Boneh. 2003. Terra: A Virtual Machine-Based Platform for Trusted Computing, *Proc. 19th Symp. on Operating System Principles* (October).

Gharachorloo, K., D. Lenoski, J. Laudon, P. Gibbons, A. Gupta, and J. Hennessy. 1990. Memory Consistency and Event Ordering in Scalable Shared-Memory Multiprocessors, *Proc. 17th Int. Symp. on Computer Architecture* (May), pp. 15–26.

Gill, S. 1951. The Diagnosis of Mistakes in Programmes on the EDSAC, *Proc. of the Royal Society Series A, Mathematical and Physical Sciences* (May), pp. 538–554.

Globus. The Globus Alliance, http://www.globus.org.

Goldberg, R. P. 1972. Architectural Principles for Virtual Computer Systems, Ph.D. dissertation, Harvard University, Cambridge, MA.

Goldberg, R. P. 1974. Survey of Virtual Machine Research, *IEEE Computer* (June), pp. 34–45.

Gong, L., G. Ellison, and M. Dageforde. 2003. *Inside Java 2 Platform Security: Architecture, API Design, and Implementation*, 2nd ed., Addison-Wesley, Reading, MA.

Gosling, J., B. Joy, and G. Steele. 1996. *The Java Language Specification*, Addison Wesley, Reading, MA.

Govil, K., D. Teodosiu, Y. Huang, and M. Rosenblum. 1999. Cellular Disco: Resource Management Using Virtual Clusters on Shared-Memory Multiprocessors, *Proc. 17th ACM Symp. on Operating System Principles* (December), NC, pp. 154–169.

Grant, B., M. Philipose, M. Mock, S. J. Eggers, and C. Chambers. 1999. An Evaluation of Run-Time Optimizations, *Proc. Conf. on Programming Language Design and Implementation* (May), pp. 293–304.

Gschwind, M. 1998a. Method and Apparatus for Determining Branch Addresses in Programs Generated by Binary Translation, *IBM Research Disclosures YOR819980334* (July).

Gschwind, M. 1998b. Method and Apparatus for Rapid Return Address Computation in Binary Translation, *IBM Research Disclosures YOR819980410* (September).

Gschwind, M. and E. R. Altman. 2000. Optimization and Precise Exceptions in Dynamic Compilation, *Proc. Workshop on Binary Translation* (October).

Gschwind, M., K. Ebcioglu, E. R. Altman, and S. Sathaye. 2000. Binary Translation and Architecture Convergence Issues for IBM System/390, *Proc. Int. Conf. on Supercomputing* (May), pp. 336–347.

Gum, P. H. 1983. System/370 Extended Architecture: Facilities for Virtual Machines, *IBM Journal of Research and Development* (November), pp. 530–544.

Gupta, M., J.-D. Choi, and M. Hind. 2000. Optimizing Java Programs in the Presence of Exceptions, *14th European Conference on Object-Oriented Programming* (June), pp. 422–446.

Halfhill, T. R. 2000. Transmeta Breaks x86 Low-Power Barrier, *Microprocessor Report* (February 14), pp. 9–18.

Hall, J. S. and P. T. Robinson. 1990. Virtualizing the VAX Architecture, *Proc. USENIX 1990 Summer Conference* (June), pp. 380–389.

Hansen, G. J. 1974. Adaptive Systems for the Dynamic Run-Time Optimization of Programs, Ph.D. dissertation, Carnegie-Mellon University, Pittsburgh, PA.

Hazelwood, K. and J. E. Smith. 2004. Exploring Code Cache Eviction Granularities in Dynamic Optimization Systems, *Proc. Second Annual IEEE/ACM Int. Symp. on Code Generation and Optimization* (March), pp. 89–99.

Heil, T. and J. E. Smith. 2000. Relational Profiling: Enabling Thread-Level Parallelism in Virtual Machines, *Proc. 33rd Int. Symp. on Microarchitecture* (December), pp. 281–290.

Hennessy, J. and D. Patterson. 2002. *Computer Architecture: A Quantitative Approach*, 3rd ed., Morgan Kaufmann, San Francisco.

Hennessy, J., M. Heinrich, and A. Gupta. 1999. Cache-Coherent Distributed Shared Memory: Perspectives on its Development and Future Challenges, *Proceedings of the IEEE* (March), pp. 418–429.

Hewlett-Packard. 2000. HP Partitioning Continuum, *Technical Positioning White Paper* (June), http://h30081.www3.hp.com/products/wlm/docs/HPPartitioningContinuum.pdf.

Hinton, G., D. Sager, M. Upton, D. Boggs, D. Carmean, A. Kyker, and P. Roussel. 2001. The Microarchitecture of the Pentium 4 Processor, *Intel Technology Journal* (Q1).

Hohensee, P., M. Myszewski, and D. Reese. 1996. Wabi CPU Emulation, *Proc. 8th HotChips Symposium* (August), pp. 47–65.

Hölzle, U. and D. Ungar. 1996. Reconciling Responsiveness with Performance in Pure Object-Oriented Languages, *ACM Transactions on Programming Languages and Systems* (July), pp. 355–400.

Hölzle, U., C. Chambers, and D. Ungar. 1991. Optimizing Dynamically Typed Object-Oriented Languages with Polymorphic Inline Caches, *5th European Conference on Object-Oriented Programming* (July), pp. 21–38.

Hölzle, U., C. Chambers, and D. Ungar. 1992. Debugging Optimized Code with Dynamic Deoptimization, *Proc. Conf. on Programming Language Design and Implementation* (July), pp. 32–43.

Hookway, R. J. and M. A. Herdeg. 1997. Digital FX!32: Combining Emulation and Binary Translation, *Digital Technical Journal* (January), pp. 3–17.

Horspool, R. N. and N. Marovac. 1980. An Approach to the Problem of Detranslation of Computer Programs, *Computer Journal* (August), pp. 223–229.

Höxer, H.-J., K. Buchacker, and V. Sieh. 2002. UMLinux — A Tool for Testing a Linux System's Fault Tolerance, *Proc. LinuxTag* (June).

Hsu P.-T. and E. Davidson. 1986. Highly Concurrent Scalar Processing, *Proc. 13th Int. Symp. on Computer Architecture* (June), pp. 386–395.

Hunt, G., and D. Brubacher. 1999. Detours: Binary Interception of Win32 Functions, *Proc. 3rd USENIX Windows NT Symposium* (July), pp. 135–143.

Hwu W. W., S. A. Mahlke, W. Y. Chen, P. P. Chang, N. J. Warter, R. A. Bringmann, R. G. Ouellette, R. E. Hank, T. Kiyohara, G. E. Haab, J. G. Holm, and D. M. Lavery. 1993. The Superblock: An Effective Technique for VLIW and Superscalar Compilation, *Journal of Supercomputing* (May) pp. 229–248.

IBM. 1994. *The PowerPC Architecture,* Morgan Kaufmann, San Francisco.

IBM. 2001. *Autonomic Computing: IBM's Perspective on the State of Information Technology,* Armonk, NY (October).

Intel. 1999. *Intel(R) Architecture Software Developer's Manual, Volume 2: Instruction Set Reference Manual,* http://www.intel.com/design/intarch/manuals/243191.htm.

Intel. 2005. *Intel Vanderpool Technology for IA-32 Processors (VT-x) Preliminary Specification,* Order Number C97063-001, Santa Clara, CA (January).

Jacob, B. and T. Mudge. 1998. Virtual Memory: Issues of Implementation, *IEEE Computer* (June), pp. 33–43.

Jann, J., L. M. Browning, and R. S. Burugula. 2003. Dynamic Reconfiguration: Basic Building Blocks for Autonomic Computing on IBM pSeries Servers, *IBM Systems Journal* (January), pp. 29–37.

Jones, R. 1996. Garbage Collection: Algorithms for Automatic Dynamic Memory Management, Wiley, New York.

Kaeli, D. and P. G. Emma. 1991. Branch History Table Prediction of Moving Target Branches Due to Subroutine Returns, *Proc. 18th Int. Symp. on Computer Architecture* (June), pp. 34–42.

Kane, G. 1996. *PA-RISC Architecture*, Prentice Hall, New York.

Keefe, D. D. 1968. Hierarchical Control Program for System Evaluation, *IBM Systems Journal*, pp. 123–133.

Kelly, E. J., R. F. Cmelik, and M. J. Wing. 1998. Memory Controller for a Microprocessor for Detecting a Failure of Speculation on the Physical Nature of a Component Being Addressed, US patent 5,832,205 (November).

Keltcher, C. N., K. J. McGrath, A. Ahmed, and P. Conway. 2003. The AMD Opteron Processor for Multiprocessor Servers, *IEEE Micro* (March/April), pp. 66–76.

Kim, H.-S. and J. E. Smith. 2003. Dynamic Binary Translation for Accumulator-Oriented Architectures, *Proc. Int. Symp. on Code Generation and Optimization* (March), pp. 25–35.

Kiriansky, V., D. Bruening, and S. Amarasinghe. 2002. Secure Execution via Program Shepherding, *Proc. 11th USENIX Security Symposium* (August).

Kistler, T. and M. Franz. 2000. Automated Data-Member Layout of Heap Objects to Improve Memory-Hierarchy Performance, *ACM Transactions on Programming Languages and Systems* (May), pp. 490–505.

Kistler, T. and M. Franz. 2001. Continuous Program Optimization: Design and Evaluation, *IEEE Transactions on Computers* (June), pp. 549–566.

Klaiber, A. 2000. The Technology Behind Crusoe Processors, *Transmeta Technical Brief.*

Klint, P. 1981. Interpretation Techniques, *Software Practice and Experience* (September), pp. 963–973.

Kogge, P. M. 1982. An Architectural Trail to Threaded-Code Systems, *IEEE Computer* (March), pp. 22–34.

Kozuch M. and M. Satyanarayanan. 2002. Internet Suspend/Resume, *Proc. 4th IEEE Workshop on Mobile Systems and Applications* (June).

Lam, M. 1988. Software Pipelining: An Effective Scheduling Technique for VLIW Machines, *Proc. ACM Conf. on Programming Languages Design and Implementation* (June), pp. 318–328.

Lamport, L. 1979. How to Make a Multiprocessor Computer That Correctly Executes Multiprocess Programs, *IEEE Transactions on Computers* (September), pp. 690–691.

Larus, J. 1991. *SPIM S20: A MIPS R2000 Simulator,* University of Wisconsin — Madison Technical Report, http://www.cs.wisc.edu/~larus/spim.html.

Larus, J. R. and E. Schnarr. 1995. EEL: Machine-Independent Executable Editing, *Proc. ACM SIGPLAN Conf. on Programming Language Design and Implementation* (June), pp. 291–300.

Lawton, K. The Bochs IA-32 Emulator Project, http://bochs.sourceforge.net.

Le, B. C. 1998. An Out-of-Order Execution Technique for Runtime Binary Translators, *Proc. 8th Int. Conf. on Architectural Support for Programming Languages and Operating Systems,* pp. 151–158.

Lidin, S. 2002. *Inside Microsoft .NET IL Assembler,* Microsoft Press, Redmond, WA.

Lindholm, T. and F. Yellin. 1999. *The Java Virtual Machine Specification,* 2nd ed., Addison-Wesley, Reading, MA.

Lowney, P. G., S. M. Freudenberger, T. J. Karzes, W. D. Lichtenstein, R. P. Nix, J. S. O'Donnell, and J. Ruttenberg. 1993. The Multiflow Trace Scheduling Compiler, *Journal of Supercomputing* (May), pp. 51–142.

Lu, J., H. Chen, R. Fu, W.-C. Hsu, B. Othmer, P.-C. Yew, and D.-Y. Chen. 2003. The Performance of Runtime Data Cache Prefetching in a Dynamic Optimization System, *Proc. 36th IEEE/ACM Int. Symp. on Microarchitecture* (December), pp. 180–190.

Lu, J., H. Chen, P.-C. Yew, and W.-C. Hsu. 2004. Design and Implementation of a Lightweight Dynamic Optimization System, *Journal of Instruction-Level Parallelism,* Vol. 6, pp. 1–24.

Lucco, S., O. Sharp, and R. Wahbe. 1995. Omniware: A Universal Substrate for Web Programming, *World Wide Web Journal* (winter), pp. 359–368.

MacKinnon, R. A. 1979. The Changing Virtual Machine Environment: Interfaces to Real Hardware, Virtual Hardware, and Other Virtual Machines, *IBM Systems Journal,* pp. 18–46.

Madnick, S. E. and J. J. Donovan. 1974. *Operating Systems,* McGraw-Hill, New York.

Magnusson, P. and D. Samuelsson. 1994. A Compact Intermediate Format for SIMICS, *Tech. Report R94:17,* Swedish Institute of Computer Science (September).

Mahlke, S. A., D. C. Lin, W. Y. Chen, R. E. Hank, and R. A. Bringmann. 1992. Effective Compiler Support for Predicated Execution Using the Hyperblock, *Proc. 25th Int. Symp. on Microarchitecture* (November), pp. 45–54.

May, C. 1987. Mimic: A Fast System/370 Simulator, *Conf. on Programming Language Design and Implementation,* archive, pp. 1–13.

McGhan, H. and M. O'Connor. 1998. PicoJava: A Direct Execution Engine for Java Bytecode, *IEEE Computer* (October), pp. 22–30.

McGraw, B. and E. W. Felten, 1999. *Securing Java: Getting Down to Business with Mobile Code,* 2nd ed., Wiley, New York.

Meloan, S. 1999. The Java HotSpot Performance Engine: An In-Depth Look (June), http://java.sun.com/developer/technicalArticles/Networking/HotSpot.

Merten, M. C., A. R. Trick, E. M. Nystrom, R. D. Barnes, and W. W. Hwu. 2000. A Hardware Mechanism for Dynamic Extraction and Relayout of

Program Hotspots, *Proc. 27th Int. Symp. on Computer Architecture* (June), pp. 59–70.

Merten, M. C., A. R. Trick, R. D. Barnes, E. M. Nystrom, C. N. George, J. C. Gyllenhaal, and W. W. Hwu. 2001. An Architectural Framework for Run-Time Optimization, *IEEE Transactions on Computers* (June), pp. 567–589.

Meyer, R. A. and L. H. Seawright. 1970. A Virtual Machine Time-Sharing System, *IBM Systems Journal*, pp. 199–218.

Myers, G. J. 1982. *Advances in Computer Architecture*, 2nd ed., Wiley, New York.

Nair, R. and M. E. Hopkins. 1997. Exploiting Instruction Level Parallelism in Processors by Caching Scheduled Groups, *Proc. 24th Int. Symp. on Computer Architecture* (June), pp. 13–25.

Nethercote, N., and J. Seward. 2003. Valgrind: A Program Supervision Framework, *Proc. 3rd Workshop on Runtime Verification* (July).

Nick, J. M., B. B. Moore, J.-Y. Chung, and N. S. Bowen. 1997. S/390 Cluster Technology: Parallel Sysplex, *IBM Systems Journal*, pp. 172–201.

NIST. 2002. FIPS 180-2, Secure Hash Standard (SHS) (August).

Nori, K. V., U. Ammann, K. Jensen, H. H. Nageli, and C. Jacobi. 1975. *The Pascal P-Compiler: Implementation Notes* (rev. ed.), Institut fur Informatik ETH, Zurich, Tech. Rep. 10.

Nystrom, E., R. D. Barnes, M. C. Merten, and W. W. Hwu. 2001. Code Reordering and Speculation Support for Dynamic Optimization Systems, *Proc. Int. Conf. on Parallel Architectures and Compilation Techniques* (September), pp. 163–174.

OGSA. Open Grid Services Architecture Working Group, https://forge.gridforum.org/projects/ogsa-wg.

OpenSSH. OpenSSH, http://www.openssh.com.

Osisek, D. L., K. M. Jackson, and P. H. Gum. 1991. ESA/390 Interpretive Execution Architecture, Foundation for VM/ESA, *IBM Systems Journal*, pp. 34–51.

Pacheco, P. 1996. *Parallel Programming with MPI*, Morgan-Kaufmann, San Francisco.

Paleczny, M., C. Vick, and C. Click. 2001. The Java Hotspot Server Compiler, *USENIX Java Virtual Machine Research and Technology Symp.* (April), pp. 1–12.

Parmalee, R. P., T. I. Peterson, C. C. Tillman, and D. J. Hatfield. 1972. Virtual Storage and Virtual Machine Concepts, *IBM Systems Journal*, pp. 99–219.

Patel, S. J., S. S. Lumetta. 2001. rePLay: A Hardware Framework for Dynamic Optimization, *IEEE Transactions on Computers* (June), pp. 590–608.

Perkins, C. E. 1998. Mobile Networking Through Mobile IP, *IEEE Internet Computing* (January ), pp. 58–69.

Pettis, K. and R. C. Hansen. 1990. Profile Guided Code Positioning, *Proc. ACM SIGPLAN Conf. on Programming Language Design and Implementation* (June), pp. 16–27.

Popek, G. J. and R. P. Goldberg. 1974. Formal Requirements for Virtualizable Third-Generation Architectures, *Communications of the ACM* (July), pp. 412–421.

Richardson T., Q. Stafford-Fraser, K. R. Wood, and A. Hopper. 1998. Virtual Network Computing, *IEEE Internet Computing* (January), pp. 33–38.

Ridge, D., D. Becker, P. Merkey, and T. Sterling. 1997. Beowulf: Harnessing the Power of Parallelism in a Pile-of-PCs, *Proc. IEEE Aerospace Conference* (February), pp. 79–91.

Robin, J. S. and C. E. Irvine. 2000. Analysis of the Intel Pentium's Ability to Support a Secure Virtual Machine Monitor, *Proc. 9th USENIX Security Symposium*, Denver (August).

Romer, T. H., D. Lee, G. M. Voelker, A. Wolman, W. A. Wong, J.-L. Baer, B. N. Bershad, and H. M. Levy. 1996. The Structure and Performance of Interpreters, *Proceedings 7th Int. Conf. on Architectural Support for Programming Languages and Operating Systems* (September), pp. 150–159.

Ronsse, M. and K. De Bosschere. 2000. JiTI: A Robust Just-in-Time Instrumentation Technique, *Proc. Workshop on Binary Translation* (October).

Rosenblum, M. 2000. VMware's Virtual Platform Technology, *Multi-University/Research Laboratory Seminar Series,* http://murl.microsoft.com/LectureDetails.asp?530 (December).

Rotenberg, E., S. Bennett, and J. E. Smith. 1996. Trace Cache: A Low-Latency Approach to High-Bandwidth Instruction Fetching, *Proc. 29th Int. Symp. on Microarchitecture* (December), pp. 24–35.

Sapuntzakis, C. P., R. Chandra, B. Pfaff, J. Chow, M. S. Lam, and M. Rosenblum. 2002. Optimizing the Migration of Virtual Computers, *Proc. 5th Symp. on Operating Systems Design and Implementation* (December).

Sathaye, S., P. Ledak, J. LeBlanc, S. Kosonocky, M. Gschwind, J. Fritts, Z. Filan, A. Bright, D. Appenzeller, E. Altman, and C. Agricola. 1999. BOA: Targeting Multi-Gigahertz with Binary Translation, *Proc. Workshop on Binary Translation* (October).

Scheifler, R. W. 1977. An Analysis of Inline Substitution for a Structured Programming Language, *Communications of the ACM* (September), pp. 647–654.

Scott, K., N. Kumar, S. Velusamy, B. R. Childers, J. W. Davidson, and M. L. Soffa. 2003. Retargetable and Reconfigurable Software Dynamic

Translation, *Proc. Int. Symp. on Code Generation and Optimization* (March), pp. 36–47.

Shannon, B., M. Hapner, V. Matena, E. Pelegri-Llopart, J. Davidson, and L. Cable. 2000. *Java 2 Platform, Enterprise Edition: Platform and Component Specifications,* Addison-Wesley, Reading, MA.

Sites, R. L., A. Chernoff, M. B. Kerk, M. P. Marks, and S. G. Robinson. 1993. Binary Translation, *Communications of the ACM* (February), pp. 69–81.

Smith, M. D., M. S. Lam, and M. A. Horowitz. 1990. Boosting Beyond Static Scheduling in a Superscalar Processor, *Proc. 17th Int. Symp. on Computer Architecture* (June), pp. 344–354.

Soltis, F. G. 1996. *Inside the AS/400,* Duke Press, Loveland, CO.

SPEC. Standard Performance Evaluation Corporation, www.spec.org.

Stichnoth, J., G.-Y. Lueh, and M. Cuerniak. 1999. Support for Garbage Collection at Every Instruction in a Java Compiler, *Proc. Conf. on Programming Language Design and Implementation* (May), pp. 118–127.

Suganuma, T., T. Yasue, and T. Nakatani. 2002. An Empirical Study of Method In-Lining for a Java Just-in-Time Compiler, *Usenix Java Virtual Machine Research and Technology Symp.* (August), pp. 91–104.

Suganuma, T., T. Ogasawara, M. Takeuchi, T. Yasue, M. Kawahito, K. Ishizaki, H. Komatsu, and T. Nakatani. 2000. Overview of the IBM Java Just-in-Time Compiler, *IBM Systems Journal* (February), pp. 175–193.

Suganuma, T., T. Yasue, M. Kawahito, H. Komatsu, and T. Nakatani. 2001. A Dynamic Optimization Framework for a Java Just-in-Time Compiler, *Proc. Conf. on Object Oriented Programming, Systems, Languages and Applications* (November), pp. 180–195.

Sugerman, J., G. Venkitachalam, and B.-H. Lim. 2001. Virtualizing I/O Devices on VMware Workstation's Hosted Virtual Machine Monitor, *Proc. USENIX Annual Technical Conference* (June), pp. 1–14.

Sun Microsystems. 1999. Sun Enterprise 10000 Server: Dynamic Systems Domains, *Technical White Paper* http://www.sun.com/datacenter/docs/domainswp.pdf.

Sunderaraj, A. I. and P. A. Dinda. 2004. Towards Virtual Networks for Virtual Machine Grid Computing, *Proc. 3rd USENIX Virtual Machine Technology Symposium* (May).

Tabatabai, A., M. Cierniak, G.-Y. Lueh, V. M. Parikh, and J. M. Stichnoth. 1998. Fast Effective Code Generation in a Just-In-Time Java Compiler, *Proc. Conf. on Programming Language Design and Implementation* (June), pp. 280–290.

Tamches, A. and B. P. Miller. 1999. Fine-Grained Dynamic Instrumentation of Commodity Operating System Kernels, *Proc. 3rd Symp. on Operating Systems Design and Implementation* (February), pp. 117–130.

Traut, E. 1997. Building the Virtual PC, *Byte* (November), pp. 51–52.

Varian, M. 1997. VM and the VM Community: Past, Present, and Future, *SHARE 89* (August).

Venners, B. 1998. *Inside the Java Virtual Machine,* McGraw-Hill, New York.

VirtualCenter. *VMware VirtualCenter Users Manual, version 1.2,* VMware Inc., Palo Alto, CA, http://www.vmware.com/pdf/VC_Users_Manual_11.pdf.

VMware. 2001. *VMware GSX Server User Manual, version 1.0,* VMware Inc., Palo Alto, CA.

VMware. 2000. VMware Virtual Platform Technical White Paper, http://ftp. hit.edu.cn/linux/Datas/Docs/webmirror/www.vmware.com/ virtualplatform.html.

Wahbe, R., S. Lucco, T. E. Anderson, and S. L. Graham. 1993. Efficient Software-Based Fault Isolation, *ACM SIGOPS Operating Systems Review* (December), pp. 203–216.

Wallach, D. and E. Felten. 1998. Understanding Java Stack Inspection, *Proc. IEEE Symp. on Security and Privacy* (May), pp. 52–63.

Whaley, J. 2001. Partial Method Compilation Using Dynamic Profile Information, *Proc. Conf. on Object-Oriented Programming Systems, Languages, and Applications* (October), pp. 166–179.

Whitaker, A., M. Shaw, and S. D. Gribble. 2002. Denali: Lightweight Virtual Machines for Distributed and Networked Applications, *Technical Report 02-02-01,* University of Washington, Seattle.

Wilson, P. R. 1992. Uniprocessor Garbage Collection Techniques, *Proc. Int. Workshop on Memory Management* (September), pp. 1–42.

Wilson, P. R., M. S. Johnstone, M. Neely, and D. Boles. 1995. Dynamic Storage Allocation: A Survey and Critical Review, *Proc. Int. Workshop on Memory Management.*

Zheng, C. and C. Thompson. 2000. PA-RISC to IA-64: Transparent Execution, No Recompilation, *IEEE Computer* (March), pp. 47–53.

# Index

Printed and bound by CPI Group (UK) Ltd, Croydon, CR0 4YY

03/10/2024

01040339-0007